# UNDAUNTED

Britain and the Commonwealth's War
in the Air 1939–45

## Volume 2

Ben Kite

Helion & Company

**Dedicated to**
**Group Captain Douglas Kite, RAF, 1912–1999**

Helion & Company Limited
Unit 8 Amherst Business Centre
Budbrooke Road
Warwick
CV34 5WE
England
Tel. 01926 499619
Email: info@helion.co.uk
Website: www.helion.co.uk
Twitter: @helionbooks
Visit our blog at http://blog.helion.co.uk/

Published by Helion & Company 2021
Designed and typeset by Mach 3 Solutions Ltd (www.mach3solutions.co.uk)
Cover designed by Paul Hewitt, Battlefield Design (www.battlefield-design.co.uk)

Text © Ben Kite 2021
Images © as individually credited
Maps drawn by George Anderson © Helion & Company 2021

ISBN 978-1-913118-59-4

British Library Cataloguing-in-Publication Data.
A catalogue record for this book is available from the British Library.

For details of other military history titles published by Helion & Company Limited, contact the above address, or visit our website: http://www.helion.co.uk

We always welcome receiving book proposals from prospective authors.

*The gratitude of every home in our Island, in our Empire, and indeed throughout the world, except in the abodes of the guilty, goes out to the British airmen who, undaunted by odds, unwearied in their constant challenge and mortal danger, are turning the tide of the World War by their prowess and by their devotion.*

Winston Churchill

# Contents

# List of Maps

# List of Figures

# List of Annexes

# Acknowledgements

The second volume of this book has benefited from the assistance of several people and organisations – many of whom were also involved with Volume 1. First and foremost is the RAF's Air Historical Branch and in particular its head, Mr Seb Cox, who has been a huge help critiquing the manuscript, offering his wise counsel and providing support in many other ways. Lee Barton has continued to collate and provide a wide variety of compelling images, including many that have never been published before and do great justice to the veteran's own words. They remain an undoubted strength of the book and bring the atmosphere and events of the time to life. Further afield Air Commodore John Meier, Group Captain David Fredericks and the team at the RAAF Air History and Heritage Branch have guided me on Australian and RAAF perspectives. I was also introduced to Flight Sergeant Daryll Fell – who has sourced some amazing images of the RAAF in the South West Pacific including several from the Victoria State Library. I am also hugely grateful to the Chief of the RAAF, Air Marshal Mel Hupfield AO DSC for his foreword. It seems particularly fitting given the book's subject and Australia's inspiring contribution to the war in the air that it should be written by him.

Dr Richard Drucker, a widely acknowledged expert on SOE operations in the Far East also drew my attention to some excellent images in the National Archives and was kind enough to read the chapters on Special Duties. In addition, the volunteers of the Medmenham collection including Timothy Fryer, Mike Mockford and Ruth Pooley have all helped source material on RAF Photographic Reconnaissance and Intelligence for which I am very grateful. Mike Peters, publisher of numerous books on the Second World War, including the brilliant *Glider Pilots at Arnhem,* has kindly critiqued the chapters on Airborne forces and provided some of the map images of DZs.

Three individuals should also be singled out for their patience in reading the earliest drafts of the book, when it was still at a very rudimentary stage. They include my father, Peter Kite, whose aviation background has helped tremendously, Sam Biles a close family friend, whose attention to detail prevented many errors from being baked in and Major Andrew Shepherd, a fellow Army Officer with a very deep understanding of all aspects of the Second World War. I am also grateful for the author Richard Doherty's help in sourcing quotes on the Italian campaign and to Major Rob Feeney for his last minute proof reading.

I judge that Volume 2's greatest strength remains the veteran's own stories. The majority are extracted from autobiographies and I am therefore very grateful for either the author's permission, or those of his family, or publishing house, to reproduce them within this work. I have done my utmost to find the original author, or their descendants, but on the few occasions I have been unsuccessful I ask the copyright holder's forgiveness and hope they will feel I have done the author's work justice. Many of the other quotes in the book come from the sound archives of the Imperial War Museum and Australian Memorial. These are two fantastic resources, which I cannot praise highly enough. They each contain a treasure trove of important historical detail and are a delight to listen too, the two institutions have done a marvellous job in making them available to the public on-line.

Duncan Rogers and his team, particularly Victoria Powell, Rob Griffith and Kim McSweeney, have been brilliant in providing guidance and supporting the book's growth into a two-volume publication. The impact of COVID-19 during the editing stages added a layer of complexity none of us expected. I am especially grateful to George Anderson who has produced brilliant maps and diagrams once more – they play a huge role in helping the reader keep track of what is going on in a complex book. Paul Hewitt and his company at Battlefield Designs also deserve great credit for the front cover design of this book. Paul has now produced the front covers for all three of my books and they consistently draw wide admiration.

In writing this book I have found that military historians are a wonderfully supportive community, with encouragement and assistance routinely offered by many within it. Amongst this group I would single out both Paul Beaver and James Holland. Not just for the quality of their work, which is excellent, but in the generous and amicable way they have guided me on historical details and assisted me in getting my work the necessary exposure novice authors need.

My final and greatest thanks go to Elsa and my two daughters, Jemima and Lucy. They have had to put up with a father and husband who has undoubtedly been over-occupied on this project. Their tolerance, patience and support has meant that this book was completed and not abandoned halfway through. I have now promised to spend more time with my wife at the horse racing, but hope that at some point she will release me to write a further book.

Ben Kite

# Foreword

As the Royal Australian Air Force celebrates its centenary in 2021, there is no better opportunity to reflect upon the history and heritage that has contributed to making the RAAF the modern fifth generation force that it is today. With the introduction of cutting-edge air combat and intelligence, surveillance and reconnaissance platforms like the F-35A Lightning II and P-8A Poseidon – and the selection of MQ-9B Sky Guardian – it is important to pause and consider the evolution of air power to what we have today.

In this regard, I am extremely privileged to be able to provide this foreword to the second and final volume of Ben Kite's exemplary work covering Britain and the Commonwealth's war in the air during the Second World War. Ben's work is not only outstanding in its breadth and depth of historical research but also forms an important basis upon which we are able to look at the operations of British and Commonwealth air forces between 1939 and 1945 through the lens of today's airpower.

The first volume of Ben Kite's work covered the roles of air superiority, strike and the air war at sea in all its manifestations. I was proud to read the many accounts of Australians playing important and courageous parts in Fighter, Bomber and Coastal Commands. In this volume, Ben's work takes us into the roles of intelligence, reconnaissance and special duties; air support to land operations; and airborne and transport operations. As in the first volume, Ben has explored the tactics and technologies used and complemented this with firsthand narratives from the British and Commonwealth airmen who were charged to prosecute these roles, typically at significant personal risk.

I am delighted to see Australians again feature so strongly, fighting alongside their comrades from the Commonwealth and many occupied countries. From the skies over the Western Desert to the steaming jungles of Papua New Guinea, the RAAF's experience in the War reinforces to us that the air forces of today, as with those of World War II, need to not only maintain a technological edge with continuous evolution and innovation in tactics, but also require people of the highest calibre. Our forebears in the British and Commonwealth air forces during the Second World War showed that during a period of extreme adversity, their courage and tenacity came to the fore and their dedication to service and country was paramount. Taken together, it makes me proud of Australia's contribution in the Second World War and the sacrifices our nation was prepared to make to defend both our values and other people's freedoms.

With RAAF personnel currently participating in exercises and operations around the world alongside many Brits, Kiwis, Canadians, Indians, South Africans – and personnel from many other nations – this book reminds us that the air forces of Britain and the Commonwealth have a proud tradition of serving together – of mateship. May this tradition continue into the RAAF's second century.

Air Marshal Mel Hupfeld, AO, DSC
Chief of Air Force, Royal Australian Air Force

# 1

# Introduction

*Undaunted* is the second and final volume in *Britain and the Commonwealth's War in the Air 1939–45*. A book that explains how Britain and the Commonwealth fought the Second World War in the air, what tactics and technology were used and what the experience was like for the aircrew themselves. In the first volume – *Through Adversity* – an explanation was given of how the British Commonwealth's air superiority was challenged, occasionally lost and then regained. Winning air superiority was vital, in that it allowed the Allies to secure the necessary strategic and operational footing from which to launch their own offensives against the Germans, Italians and Japanese. For the first part of the war the major direct British offensive against Germany was in the form of an increasingly powerful series of air attacks executed by Bomber Command. This was largely in accordance with pre-war RAF and British operational concepts, with the notable difference that they were undertaken almost exclusively at night, when the cover of darkness gave the British bombers some protection against German air defences. Bomber Command's strongest supporters had argued that these strikes would be enough to cause a collapse in the German will to fight by themselves. They did not – though the offensive did disrupt German industrial production and prompt Hitler to focus considerable men and material in desperately trying to defend German cities against both the British night offensive and the American day bombers. Though most of Bomber Command was conducting area bombing, small but modest capabilities in precision strike were also being developed by formations such as 2 Group. These skills and techniques would play an important part in supporting the Allied armies when they re-entered Europe.

Volume One also explained how the air war at sea was fought and how the Allied maritime victories, especially in the Battle of the Atlantic, enabled the Allies to apply their strategic resources anywhere in the world. On America's entry into the war, the Allies quickly confirmed that their priority was the defeat of Germany, which included the creation of a major second front in France. Prior to that, it was important that the Allies fought the Germans and Italians in North Africa, both to safeguard Middle Eastern oilfields as well as open the Mediterranean for shipping. The North African campaign also provided an opportunity for the Allied armies to gain experience against the *Wehrmacht* and once Italy was invaded, divert German resources away from the Eastern Front. Indeed, insistent and constant Russian demands for the opening of a second front were a constant theme of the Allied conferences between 1942–44. The British and Americans also understood that any post-war settlement would only be beneficial to the western powers if the Allied armies were fighting the Germans on a major second front. Ironically, the Allied ability to establish such a campaign in France was only made possible thanks to Russian actions on the Eastern Front, for it was primarily the Red Army which decisively engaged and fixed the main body of the *Wehrmacht*, the most potent aspect of Germany's military might. This ultimately made the prospect of an invasion in France directly across the English Channel a feasible proposition.

Volume 1 covered the Japanese offensive in the Far East which by the end of 1942 had reached a a culminating point, from which their military superiority began a gradual decline. In the Burma theatre of operations, the British Army had successfully withdrawn to strong bases in India by the middle of 1942 and was now absorbed in building up its supplies and working out how to launch its own offensive against the Japanese. In Papua New Guinea the Australians and Americans had blunted the Japanese amphibious advances and were now poised to exploit their own air, maritime and land capabilities to drive the Japanese back.

*Undaunted,* the second volume of Britain and the Commonwealth's war in the air, explains how all these land campaigns were supported by the air forces. In Part Six the book explains how the back water of Army Cooperation was turned into a major strand of Allied military power and a decisive factor in all subsequent land campaigns. It shows how both the Army and RAF quickly applied lessons from their disastrous 1940 campaign in France to develop a highly effective air-ground support organisation in the Western Desert. From 1941 onwards this system would be constantly refined and improved in Italy, North-West Europe, the Far East and the Pacific. Part Seven will also show how the Allies copied German innovations in paratrooper and glider capabilities and developed considerable airborne formations of their own. The British used these airborne forces both for raiding purposes, as well as adjuncts to many of the major Allied military operations of the war, including the invasions of Sicily and Normandy, as well as the attempts to cross the river Rhine. Part Seven will also cover how Air Transport was incorporated by the British Army into its campaign in Burma, successfully helping to overcome the appalling lines of communication in that country. This important logistic capability provided extra capacity that would enable the British to manoeuvre against the Japanese in a manner that was unprecedented in warfare.

Even the most cursory study of the Second World War will highlight how inherently dangerous air operations were and the high level of casualties that were often sustained amongst Allied aircrew. Part Eight of this book concludes with a series of studies on the experiences of these casualties, including the burns victims, aircrew shot down in the sea, prisoners of war and those missing aircrew trying to evade capture.

Before getting to these important aspects Volume Two opens with a study on two important functions of air power in the Second World War. Firstly, that of collecting and processing air intelligence, an activity that was necessary not just for enabling air operations, but in the case of air photographic reconnaissance helped determine the strategic direction of the war and was an important supporting function for all land and maritime campaigns. The second function to be studied in Part Five is that of the Special Duties squadrons, who maintained contact with the resistance forces in occupied territory and assisted them in their operations against the Germans, Italians and Japanese. Sometimes these activities are dismissed as providing little more than a local irritant to the occupiers, but as we shall see the scale of these operations was often impressively large and, in some cases, the irregular force's contribution, enabled by air power, presented significant operational challenges to the Axis.

# Part V
# Air Intelligence Photographic Reconnaissance and Special Duties

# 2

# 'Forewarned is Forearmed'[1]
# Air Intelligence

The provision of detailed intelligence on the enemy was an essential element in the Commonwealth air force's ability to function and it needed to be comprehensive enough to cover a wide variety of subjects. These included the opposing enemy air force, its airfields and command and control systems, any enemy capabilities that could strike Allied bases and most importantly any technical developments the enemy might be undertaking that would give them a competitive advantage. For that last reason the RAF was always particularly interested in enemy developments in radar (both ground and airborne) and any new navigation systems for bomber aircraft.

To support wider strategic and operational bombing efforts, air intelligence also had to have foundational intelligence on industrial and infrastructure targets, such as power stations, factories, marshalling yards and bridges. It was not just a question of knowing where these facilities were, the air force also required a detailed understanding of how the enemy's economy, industry and communications worked. What were the critical points in these systems? Where might attacks bring the greatest pressure? Finally, the air force also needed to locate the targets that the other services wished it to strike, these also included industrial and strategic targets, as well as operational or tactical areas such as shipping, docks and submarine pens for the Royal Navy, or gun batteries, armoured concentrations, bridges and large enemy headquarters for the Army.

This intelligence was not easy to collect, or understand, often because the targets were usually far beyond the frontline and deep inside enemy occupied territory. The RAF also found that it was almost impossible to ascertain the capabilities of new enemy equipment from afar and that the technical understanding they required could only be obtained by either deeply penetrative intelligence, or access to the equipment itself.

The requirement to gather all this information meant the RAF had to establish a highly efficient intelligence system. One that was able to direct, collect and exploit all available sources of intelligence, then systematically process this information and disseminate it to either the front-line air force units, or senior commanders. In addition, the RAF also established air photographic reconnaissance and photographic intelligence as one of the most important intelligence collection and analytical capabilities the Allies possessed during the war. Its widespread use in almost every theatre made it one of the key elements of the Allied operational approach on land, sea and in the air.

This growth was in stark contrast to the state of affairs before the war, when Air Intelligence was a tiny branch of the Air Ministry, with just 40 officers split into three Deputy Directorates of Intelligence (DDI). DDI 1 looked after the limited air signals intelligence and air photographic intelligence capabilities and liaised with other agencies including the Security Service (MI5) and the Secret Intelligence Service (SIS, or MI6). DDI 2 and DDI 3 were divided into geographical sub-sections that looked at specific countries, for instance one section dealt with all German matters, including the *Luftwaffe* order of battle, production, tactics and their likely targets for bombing.

---

1    Translation of *Praemonitus Praemunitus* – the motto of the Royal Air Force Intelligence School 1942–1969.

During peacetime the RAF used open-source methods of collecting intelligence, including normal diplomatic exchanges, government announcements, attaché visits and any publicly available literature etc. This was then supplemented with any available clandestine intelligence, including that from MI6 and Allied intelligence services.[2] Interestingly Air Intelligence had no directorate charged with dealing with technical or scientific intelligence – an important omission that needed prompt attention when war began. The RAF's pre-war air intelligence structure lasted until 1940, when the German occupation of most of Europe dramatically altered both the geographical map and intelligence view of the continent.

By the Autumn of 1940 the *Luftwaffe* was spread across most of Europe, increasing the number and spread of potential targets. A number of peacetime intelligence methods were now also redundant, including some friendly intelligence services and diplomatic avenues that had disappeared entirely. On a more positive note signal intercepts were proving more fruitful. This was both because *Luftwaffe* Enigma traffic had begun to be broken by Bletchley Park and there had also been a growth in the overall volume of operational signals being transmitted. Many of these communications were now much easier to intercept as the German military forces were geographically closer to the UK. The British photographic reconnaissance capability also developed rapidly once the war started and the peacetime restrictions in overflying another nation's territory to photograph it were no longer relevant. Finally, enemy Prisoners of War (POW) offered new opportunities to understand the *Luftwaffe*'s operations, and captured equipment gave a chance for the hands-on technical exploitation that helped develop scientific intelligence.

Following the Battle of Britain, the air intelligence community was able to draw breath and re-design its structures, so that by the summer of 1941 air intelligence had been re-designed to work on functional lines. DDI 1 remained focussed on liaison with other intelligence agencies, DDI 2 became responsible for all information on technical subjects, airfields and industries in foreign countries and DDI 3 handled orders of battle, air operations by foreign air forces, target material, reserves and training. A new directorate, DDI 4, was also created and solely devoted to RAF signals intelligence – part of the wider Y service. There were also new assistant directorates set up to deal with photographic and scientific intelligence, and later in the war, an additional assistant directorate was created to deal with POW interrogation. The entire air intelligence organisation was placed under the Assistant Chief of Air Staff (Intelligence) – a new position.

The American entry into the war prompted the addition of AI 12, a section dedicated to liaising with the United States Army Air Forces when they arrived in Europe, other than that there were no other significant changes in the Air Intelligence organisation until the end of hostilities. The American forces in Britain had wisely chosen to integrate their intelligence organisation into the RAF's existing air intelligence structure and this helpfully avoided needless duplication and parallel reporting, as well as allowing the Americans to tap into existing British experience and knowledge of the enemy.

To man this new central air intelligence organisation there was a dramatic increase in personnel and the small pre-war band of 40 officers was expanded to over 700 by the end of the conflict.[3] Even this larger central body was dwarfed by a much wider enterprise which included RAF intelligence officers at all levels of command, right down to squadron level. These individuals, who had all been trained at the RAF Intelligence School at Harrow, played a critical role in briefing missions, collecting information from aircrew in the form of post-sortie debriefs and disseminating any Allied intelligence to the squadrons. This intelligence came from a multitude of sources, all of

---

2    Sebastian Cox, *Air Intelligence Symposium (1996)* (RAF Staff College, Bracknell and Royal Air Force Historical Society, 1997), p. 8.

3    Sebastian Cox, *Air Intelligence Symposium 1996*, p. 10.

which had their own strengths and weaknesses.

Signals intelligence, known as Y until 1943, was intelligence obtained by intercepting the enemy's radio signals. These were generally divided into three categories; Wireless Telegraphy or morse (W/T), Radio Telephony or speech (R/T) and non-communication signals, such as radar or navigational beams, which were colloquially called 'noises'. Each type of signal was monitored and analysed by the RAF signals intelligence service and made an important contribution to the Allied intelligence effort. Eileen Clayton was a WAAF at the time and recalled the early Y service operations:

The unit was under the command of Flight Lieutenant E.J. Alway, and was installed in a signals office tender, which was a sort of caravan located close to the edge of the cliffs. At first our equipment was

Salvage crews dismantle a Junkers Ju 88, brought down during the *Luftwaffe's* attacks on RAF airfields in France, between 10 and 12 May 1940. (Crown Copyright – Air Historical Branch)

meagre, to say the least. We had two civilian receivers, which were the famous Hallicrafters, of the type beloved by pre-war amateur radio enthusiasts, an oscilloscope, and an aerial array. If I remember rightly there was also a sentry in a tent nearby whose duty it was to guard us from undesirable visits by inquisitive strangers. We kept watch throughout the twenty-four hours, working six-hour shifts, earphones clamped to our heads and straining our ears to the unfamiliar task of listening to the often distorted messages passing between *Luftwaffe* pilots, and from German aircraft to their control stations.

At first we listened to short-range (VHF) traffic on the 40-megacycle band, one WAAF operator searching the band until she picked up a likely sounding message. We soon got the hang of this, quickly spotting the words with which the Germans ended their spoken messages, '*Kommen*' or '*Bitte Kommen*': – 'Over to you – Over'. The operator would then enter the message or as much of it as she had heard in her log-book, recording the time of the message, the radio frequency on which it was heard, and the call-signs. In those days we wrote in the log-books on every other line, writing the translation underneath. These details were kept in order to collect as much data as possible for subsequent analysis by the Air Ministry and the cryptographers, for we had not yet sorted out which frequencies and callsigns had been allotted to which '*Geschwader*' (Group) or '*Gruppe*' (Wing). Any messages that were obviously of immediate tactical use were translated straight away and passed on to No. 11 Fighter Group, or to the Navy through the Air Ministry; but the remainder would be dealt with later, whenever there was a lull in the traffic. An experienced RAF Wireless Operator helped us search for stations, and the moment he picked up a German transmission, he would call out 'I've got one' and whichever WAAF was free would start to write down the messages. Our standard of monitoring in those early days was very amateurish and it was tiring work, especially as we were unaccustomed to listening in and searching for traffic. But it was all so fascinating that we just hated to go off watch. Looking back on it now, it is sobering to realise how very little we knew at that time of how the German Air Force operated.[4]

At the outbreak of the war, the RAF Y effort in the UK consisted of one main station at Cheadle, Staffordshire and four small out-stations, this included one at Kingsdown in Kent that played a prominent part in the Battle of Britain. By the time the battle began, the Y service had become increasingly mature with more receivers and linguists available as well as better links to RAF headquarters. The additional receivers often meant that the analysts could listen to the RAF signals as well as the German transmissions and 'read' both sides of the battle. This was an important advantage in improving their overall situational awareness, though there was still room for further developments as Eileen Clayton relates:

> It did not take Fighter Command long to realise that in the Kingsdown Y Service they had a most useful additional source of information. Amongst other things, our intercepts were a means of cross-checking reports of enemy casualties, since in the heat of battle it was not unusual for two pilots to claim to have shot down the same aircraft. There has always been controversy about this; the daily claims made showing that, on both sides, they did not tally with the actual losses... During the Battle of Britain, communications between the signals intelligence units along the south and east coasts and Kingsdown and with the Fighter Groups were so inadequate that the operational value of many of the messages that we picked up was limited, and even wasted. There were occasions when we would intercept a message from a German formation approaching RAF fighters, well above them and out of the sun, and having spotted our aircraft before they themselves were observed. We were then likely to hear: '*Indianer unten funf Uhr, Kirchturm 4, Aufpassen*' (Bandits below at five o'clock, height 4000 metres, look out).
>
> In those days we were unable to get this information through in time for it to be of tactical use and would get hopping mad that we had no means of warning our fighters that they were about to be jumped. Then '*Angreifen!*' (attack) the formation leader would yell, and we would know that the German fighters were diving on their target. I would often hear one of the WAAF operators murmuring: 'Oh God, ... oh God, ... please, ... please look up ...', and I knew how helpless she felt. I could see her willing the RAF leader to notice the approaching enemy. He would already have known from the Controller that the German aircraft were closing in, but that split second of prior knowledge might make all the difference between life and death.[5]

By the end of the summer of 1940, the Air Ministry Intelligence had a detailed picture of the *Luftwaffe's* Order of Battle, particularly in Western Europe. Eileen Clayton explains how this foundational intelligence was exploited:

4    Eileen Clayton, *The Enemy is Listening* (London: Hutchinson, 1980), p. 32.
5    Eileen Clayton, *The Enemy is Listening*, p. 45.

With all this knowledge added to the information that we were amassing at Kingsdown about the callsigns and frequencies used by the various German squadrons to which we were listening, we were able, for instance, to advise No. 11 Group that the enemy raid that was approaching Beachy Head was probably made up of Me 109s of II/JG 51 based at St Omer. This would be most helpful for the Controllers, who would then be able to anticipate the probable return route of the enemy aircraft. Later, when we had direction-finding (D/F) facilities, we could pinpoint the transmissions and thus knew the exact position of the enemy formation whose messages we were hearing. But even in those early days of the summer of 1940, we could almost certainly confirm the height at which the formations were approaching, and we might also be able to give some indication, from what we were hearing, of their intended action.

Obviously a message like 'fly at five thousand metres and rendezvous with bombers over Dover' had useful tactical value, but our ability to interpret fully the traffic we heard did not come all at once. Gradually we were getting to understand the other side, piecing together bits of intelligence from various sources. Regular reports received from the Air Ministry, from the W/T monitoring headquarters at Cheadle in the Midlands, and from the cryptographers at Station X at Bletchley, all helping us to sort out the jigsaw puzzle. Every message we heard was meticulously recorded and later analysed, both by us and by Bletchley, so that the information became of ever-increasing value. Many were the sessions we had late into the night browsing over the day's logs, whilst drinking copious mugs of cocoa. Over and over again we would read some new coded expression heard during the day, puzzling out the probable meaning, working out the grid code. Everyone available would join in, offering their suggestions, arguing and discussing with the fervour of university students. Some of the code-words had been easy to determine – *Moebel-wagen* (furniture van) – was logically bomber aircraft; *'Lucie Anton'* obviously meant *zurueck und landen* (return and land); *Indianer* (Indians) were British fighters. But other code-words were more obscure, and these took time to break. Sometimes we would actually recognise the voice of a pilot, or a callsign, or an expression peculiar to a particular *Gruppe* or *Geschwader* that was in the habit of using it.

'Hey, listen to this,' one of the girls would call out. 'There's old *Taube Drei* [Dove Three: a callsign]. What's he doing on that frequency?'

This might give us a clue that one of the enemy squadrons had moved to another base, and we would watch the frequency carefully to see if our deductions were correct. Conversely, we might have been asked by the Air Ministry to listen for confirmation of the move of a unit to a specific airfield, and this was just the evidence they needed. The Air Ministry's information could have been derived from Ultra sources or it could have been gathered during the interrogation of a prisoner of war, or it could have come from agents. The move of a unit might perhaps, indicate that there had been heavy aircraft losses from some particular base, or in certain squadrons or that reinforcements were being transferred and made ready for a concentrated effort against a particular target. Every scrap of information helped to build up the complete picture of the Luftwaffe's activities and intentions.[6]

Y Service signals interception was also carried out overseas, with a major station at Cairo, and two out-stations at Malta and Aden. The RAF Y organisation was gradually expanded as the war progressed, keeping pace with the growth and variety of *Luftwaffe* signals. The number of fixed stations was increased both at home and abroad, mobile units for field interception were also introduced and Y operators, together with their receivers, were frequently deployed onto Allied shipping and aircraft when required. The Y Service contribution covered almost every aspect of

---

6   Eileen Clayton, *The Enemy is Listening*, p. 34.

the *Luftwaffe,* including order of battle, serviceability, production, targets, bombing results, casualties, airfields, aircraft reporting organisations, training, transport activity, and *Luftwaffe* reaction to Allied raids. In addition, signal intelligence provided the Allied air forces with a great deal of immediate operational information. It was a unique intelligence function developed to an extent never envisaged in the early months of the war.[7] All intelligence disciplines have their strengths and weaknesses, but signals intelligence has three outstanding qualities; the ability to collect intelligence deep behind enemy lines, reliability, and speed – these were all amply demonstrated throughout the war.

After the war the Air Ministry judged that the most successful tactical exploitation of RAF signals intelligence was by the American Eighth Air Force's fighters. During American daylight bomber operations over Europe the controllers of the Eighth Air Force's escorting fighter wings would receive continuous updates from the RAF Y service, including details of German fighter movements. These allowed the controllers to vector fighters on to any German aircraft that were about to intercept a formation of American bombers. RAF signals intelligence often provided unique information, as once the bombers were over the Dutch coast they were out of range of Allied radar, and the American radar operators could not obtain either the bombers' or German fighters' positions. Signals intelligence was therefore the only timely source of information on the position of the German fighters and American bombers.[8] The RAF Y service also helped develop radio counter-measures against *Luftwaffe* bomber raids over Britain. These measures included depriving enemy bombers of their navigational aids, upsetting the German radar reporting organisation and handicapping German night-fighters. Additionally, as the British bomber force began its offensive against Germany the Y service maintained a constant flow of information to 80 Wing, Bomber Command Signals and 100 Group that informed their electronic warfare operations, in some cases the Y service was the actual organisation that delivered the electronic counter measures for bomber operations.

As one example, in early 1941 the *Luftwaffe* commenced night-intruder activity against returning British bombers. The German night-fighter unit being used was identified as *Nachtjagdgeschwader 2 (NJG 2)* based in Gilze-Rijen, the Netherlands, and the RAF Y service were able to identify that *NJG 2* was using the interception of British bomber signals to direct its own efforts. As a result of this intelligence Bomber Command produced a number of counter-measures, including transmitting fake radio signals from Bomber Command stations to simulate operational activity. It was possible for the RAF to determine the success of these efforts when *NJG 2* were directed onto British aerodromes where no activity was taking place, it was assessed at the time that this tactic, which must have frustrated the Germans considerably, was one of the reasons why German intruder activity ceased later that year.[9]

Signals intelligence effectiveness could be disrupted for several reasons, including a lack of enemy transmissions, the adoption by the enemy of efficient security measures, the communication of fake messages and the use of VHF frequencies to restrict the range of interception. These handicaps all occurred at one point or another during the war, but they were never significant enough to prevent the Y Service from making a worthwhile contribution. As an example, by the time they embarked on their 1944 'mini-blitz' the Germans had markedly improved their long-range bombers' signal security measures both procedurally and technically, yet the RAF's Y service continued to be successful. On this occasion they exploited non-communication interception techniques to exploit the *Luftwaffe* bombers' IFF, radio altimeter and rearward-looking air

---

7    Air Historical Branch Papers, *Intelligence in War, Part II* (London: Air Ministry, 1945), p. 59.
8    Air Historical Branch Papers, *Intelligence in War, Part II,* p. 91.
9    Air Historical Branch Papers, *Intelligence in War, Part II,* p. 72.

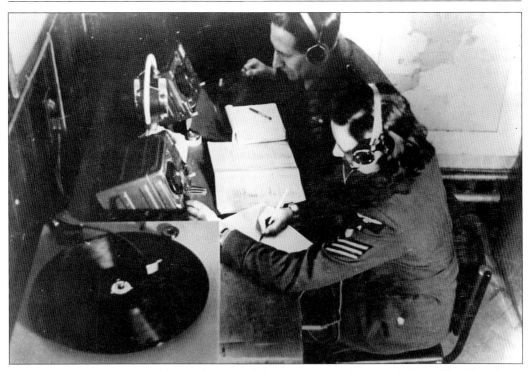

CORONA operating position at the Headquarters of the RAF Y Service, Hollywood Manor, West Kingsdown, Kent. A German-speaking operator is speaking into the ghost voice microphone, while a WAAF flight-sergeant records the exchanges on a German receiver. The gramophone turntable was used for jumbled-voice jamming on *Luftwaffe* radio frequencies. (Crown Copyright – Air Historical Branch)

intercept radar, this produced intelligence that was equal to the frequent W/T messages passed by the German bomber in 1940–41.[10]

It would be incorrect to view air signals intelligence as a purely British endeavour. In April 1942, the Australians formed No. 1 Wireless Unit at Darwin out of just eight personnel who had been trained by the Royal Navy to intercept and read Japanese signals traffic. The unit quickly proved successful in breaking the important *kana* code and was soon giving regular advanced warning of Japanese raids, sometimes as much as two hours before the first bombs dropped. The unit swiftly acquired the reputation as a major source of intelligence on the Japanese and was moved into a specially designed bomb-proof and air-conditioned building at Townsville, in Queensland. There it was much closer to the northern radio Direction Finding stations with whom it worked closely. An advanced post was also established at Port Moresby to support operations on New Guinea. The success of the unit was such that it was sometimes described as General MacArthur's only source of intelligence on the Japanese, and the Australians were encouraged to expand their operations further. By the end of the war the Australian air signals intelligence organisation consisted of six units, employing up to 1,000 RAAF and WAAAF personnel, in stations that stretched from Australia, through New Guinea to Borneo.[11]

British signals intelligence had been able to build upon on an existing peacetime organisation, in contrast the interrogation of prisoners of war during the Second World War was an entirely new

---

10    Air Historical Branch Papers, *Intelligence in War, Part II*, p. 60.
11    Mark Johnston, *Whispering Death* (Sydney: Allen and Unwin, 2011), p. 194.

endeavour. Planning for interrogation operations began in March 1939, when the services jointly agreed that at the outbreak of war a Combined Services Detailed Interrogation Centre (CSDIC) would be established. CSDIC would have an integral RAF unit (Air Intelligence 1K or more simply AI 1K) to interrogate enemy aircrew, though the responsibility for the custody and detention of the prisoners would remain with the Army. AI 1K would also provide a network of field interrogators at various RAF stations, where they could conduct preliminary tactical interrogation of *Luftwaffe* POWs at a point when the initial shock of capture would cause the prisoners to be at their most vulnerable and amenable to questioning. CSDIC was initially located at the Tower of London, though it moved to Cockfosters in December 1939 and then to two camps at Latimer House and Wilton Park near Beaconsfield in July 1942. There CSDIC remained until the end of the war.

Overseas detachments of CSDIC were also established, including one in France with the BEF and another at Ma'adi near Cairo. In due course the Ma'adi detachment became known as CSDIC (Middle East) and was formally subordinated to the UK-based CSDIC. As the war progressed and air transport links improved, the shipment of prioritised prisoners to England for longer term interrogation became routine.[12] AI 1K also established a Security Control Centre at the Royal Patriotic School in Wandsworth, where they interviewed refugees who had fled from Germany and occupied Europe. In some cases, these individuals had useful information on German or occupied countries' air force establishments and industrial concerns, all of which provided the RAF with useful intelligence on potential targets. By 1942 AI 1K had established a school for interrogators and was also de-briefing RAF personnel who had either escaped from POW camps, or evaded capture when their aircraft were shot down. Much of this latter information was used by AI 1K to lecture aircrew on both escape and evasion techniques and the German interrogation system. The branch's constant direct interaction with *Luftwaffe* personnel, meant they were regularly used to advise the BBC and the Political Intelligence Department at the Foreign Office on the production of any propaganda which was designed to influence the *Luftwaffe*.[13]

Levels of field interrogation reached a peak during the Battle of Britain. In most cases the field interrogation officer would be informed through local contacts (mainly the Police or Army) that an aircraft had crashed, or a parachutist had been captured. In the former instance he would make his way to the crash site and inspect the aircraft, usually in conjunction with a member of Air Intelligence's Technical Intelligence branch (AI 2(G)). The interrogator would study any documents found on the prisoners, then conduct a preliminary interrogation to establish the primary facts, such as the unit and base the *Luftwaffe* crew belonged to, the mission they had flown and if possible, any future plans the enemy formation might have. These would all be communicated by telephone on a numbered report to CSDIC and any codes or signals books recovered would also be routinely dispatched to Air Intelligence as a priority. Indeed, all documents were usually sent to CSDIC, including those belonging to dead crew. During busy periods the field interrogator would sometimes only refer to CSDIC those prisoners he judged worthy of attention, transporting them directly to Wilton Park. At later stages in the war the volume of German prisoners was large enough to warrant Prisoner Cages being established at Lingfield and Kempton racecourses, where the sifting and prioritisation of prisoners was an important part of preventing CSDIC from being overwhelmed.

At the start of the war, CSDIC personnel had no established interrogation processes and their techniques evolved as time went on and greater experience was obtained. The CSDIC staff came to conclude that a good interrogator was a practical psychologist with the capacity to rapidly appraise a man's character and an understanding of how to deal with the different prisoners he

---

12   Air Historical Branch Papers, *Intelligence in War, Part II*, p. 100.
13   Air Historical Branch Papers, *Intelligence in War, Part II*, p. 100.

Officers and men of the *Luftwaffe* captured in Norway being landed at a port in Scotland. The Germans are pictured under armed guard shortly after their arrival. (Crown Copyright – Air Historical Branch)

encountered. The interrogator needed to decide whether his approach was to be friendly or strictly official, whether the prisoner could be won over by discussion and argument, or by anger, or even kind treatment including small favours in the form of chocolate, cigarettes or alcohol. A pre-requisite was that the officer should be a reasonably good linguist, though ability to understand German was much more important than the ability to speak it. In fact, it was believed that the *Luftwaffe* prisoners were very suspicious of interrogators who spoke perfect German and were more likely to let their guard down with those who spoke with an accent or made some slips in their delivery.[14]

A successful interrogation depended as much on the prisoner's disposition as it did on the interrogator's skill. Some German POWs had undergone special security training that covered capture and were consequently tough to interrogate, others were political fanatics and would only talk after a lengthy process of de-indoctrination had been delivered. Some Germans were vain, blustering, talkative and with a little prompting could be made to make a show of their knowledge, others would give information away through fear of punishment, or to improve their own treatment. Some prisoners were just careless and would unconsciously give away information, too foolish to realise that even one word may complement some other details previously gathered. A small minority of *Luftwaffe* personnel would deliberately lie and get themselves tied in knots, when this was exposed a few of them would sometimes tell the entire truth through fear of punishment.

*Luftwaffe* prisoners were generally well-educated and discussions on technical or scientific matters, including their own aircraft, could sometimes generate an enthusiastic discussion. An interrogator who displayed a comprehensive knowledge of the German air force, including the nicknames and idiosyncrasies of people within the prisoner's unit, sometimes gave the prisoners such a surprise that they then saw little point in refusing to answer questions on apparently minor matters. The interrogator's rules were clear. They could only use their words to coerce prisoners to talk and the interrogators were instructed to be careful 'to avoid any suggestions of having threatened the prisoner with physical violence, immediate or future. It was advised that his art must therefore consist of innuendo or threat.'[15] The British found that it was more effective to let the prisoner use his own imagination in this regard, for the interrogator could quite easily lose all credibility if he was definite on a threat and his bluff was called.

A kind and sympathetic approach was often very effective in questioning. The RAF interrogator would try to befriend the prisoner, sometimes by pretending to protect them from the Army guards who had been briefed to be hostile and rough in their treatment of the prisoner. Once a prisoner had begun to talk it was important to encourage him to continue to do so and treats, such as trips to London, or a night at the cinema or theatre were sometimes granted. This was also extremely effective in political deconditioning, where the prisoner could see for themselves that contrary to Nazi propaganda London was not lying in ruins, businesses were operating as usual and there were private cars on the streets and goods in the shops.

The periods questioning the prisoner in the interrogation room were complemented by operations using microphones in the prisoner's cell, when inmates thought they were alone and were likely to be off-guard. Use was also made of 'stool pigeons', who would masquerade as prisoners and elicit further information from the captured aircrew. Initially German or Austrian refugees were used as stool pigeons, but genuine POWs also began to volunteer to undertake these roles, either for political reasons or to elicit better treatment. The mental strain on the stool pigeons was acute and better accommodation was provided, as well as dedicated Army officers to look after them. The stool pigeon's success depended largely on his own abilities and he needed the versatility of an actor, as well as the mental fortitude to maintain an air of open transparency despite

---

14   Air Historical Branch Papers, *Intelligence in War, Part II*, p. 104.
15   Air Historical Branch Papers, *Intelligence in War, Part II*, p. 106.

Messerschmitt Me 110E of 8/ZG26, shot down by RAF fighters during the fighting over Tobruk, Libya, in April/May 1941. (Crown Copyright – Air Historical Branch)

the stress he was under. To avoid being tripped up through a lack of specific knowledge the stool pigeons usually pretended to be from another arm of the same service, or from an entirely different theatre of war.

Prisoner of war interrogation yielded a wide range of impressive results, which included uncovering the performance of German day and night fighters as well as the details of various engine and bomb capabilities. As one example the existence of the BM.1000, a bomb which also acted as a mine in water was reported and described by ADI (K) ten days before it was used operationally. Though this was not a large head start, it did allow the Navy to become acquainted with its intricacies and send a signal to the Middle East on the day it was first dropped by German aircraft in the Suez Canal.[16]

The RAF also used MI6 reports for intelligence purposes, this was largely facilitated by the Air Section of MI6 who were able to act as both an intelligence customer and supplier. The MI6 agents' reports were frequently sketchy and important details such as numbers of aircraft were often inflated, and precise locations only achieved once the agent had undergone some form of training. Nevertheless, there were some successes the most notable of which was Jeannie Rousseau, Codenamed Amniarix and part of the 'Druids' network. Rousseau was originally employed as an interpreter for the Germans in Paris and managed to ingratiate herself with those involved in the V-weapon programme, obtaining details of the German experimental site at Peenemunde, the commander of the V1s (*Oberst* Max Wachtel) and the location of the weapon's launch sites from Holland to Brittany. When the British scientific intelligence expert R.V. Jones asked about the remarkable source, he was simply told she 'was one of the most remarkable young women of our generation'.[17] Known as 'The Wachtel Report', Rousseau's intelligence was critical in developing British understanding of the V-weapon programme and ultimately led to the Bomber Command

16   Air Historical Branch Papers, *Intelligence in War, Part II*, p. 115.
17   R V Jones, *Most Secret War* (London: Hamish Hamilton, 1978), p. 351.

Low-level aerial reconnaissance photograph of the 'Freya' radar installations at Auderville, taken
using an F24 side-facing oblique aerial camera. (Crown Copyright – Air Historical Branch)

raid on Peenemunde on 17/18 August 1943. The Germans finally caught up with Rousseau in
1944 and imprisoned her in three successive concentration camps, fortunately she survived the
war and lived until 2017.

In some cases, MI6 sources were German. In November 1939 Hans Ferdinand Mayer, a German
mathematician and physicist disgusted with the Nazi regime, wrote a seven-page report while on a
business trip to Norway. Known as the 'Oslo letter' it detailed the German Ju 88 medium bomber
programme, remote control systems for gliders and rockets, the rockets themselves, the *Luftwaffe's*
test facilities, details of German radar capability, aircraft navigation aids (including *Knickebein*),
torpedoes and a design for proximity fuses. It was described by the Air Ministry as 'probably the
best single report received from any source during the whole war'[18]. Mayer never managed any
subsequent communications as he was arrested for listening to the BBC and criticizing the Nazis.
He too was sent to a series of concentration camps, but also survived the war and his identity, as
the author of the 'Oslo letter', was only revealed after his death in 1989.

Allied intelligence services were also of huge benefit to the British. These included those that had
fled their countries when they were overrun by the Germans and set up shop in Britain instead. In
1944 Polish Intelligence was particularly successful in obtaining details of the German V1 weapon
programme through their network of observers and agents in Poland, particularly around the
SS's Blizna Military Exercise area where much of the German experimentation was taking place.
Colonel Iranek-Osmecki, who commanded the Polish Home Army's Intelligence and Counter
Intelligence Section, recalled this period:

---

18   Air Historical Branch Papers, *Intelligence in War, Part II*, p.162

Finally, in the middle of January, 1944, the mysterious weapon was fired for the first time. We received a report from one of our provincial agents a few days later: an enormous missile had struck a village in his district and destroyed several cottages; a German commission arrived very soon after and scrupulously gathered up every splinter they could find. This place was nearly 200 miles away from the S.S. camp at Blizna and at first the two reports were not considered to be connected. But later, it soon became evident that the new weapon indeed had this unprecedented range.

Some reports stated the bomb often exploded in the air; pieces, parts and splinters of the bomb would then fall within a radius of nearly two miles. In other cases they exploded only on impact. The general direction of the trajectory was fairly stable but the points of impact were dispersed, often 50, 60 or more miles away from each other. Motorised German formations patrolled the line of flight and those nearest the site of the explosion immediately rode there at full speed to collect every fragment of bomb they could find.

The approximate range of the new weapon and the directions in which it was usually fired were soon established. We decided to forestall the Germans in the collection of bomb parts and pieces. Our own patrols operated along the whole line of flight and from that time it was always a race to get to the bombed site first and get the pick of the remnants. In this we were severely handicapped. The Germans could move about from place to place with absolute freedom, they had far more and better cars than we, apart from their telephones and field radio stations; and the Gestapo was very vigilant. The Poles had to operate by stealth and with extreme precaution on an area densely patrolled by a wary and merciless enemy; they had inadequate and often very primitive liaison facilities; they could expect torture and death if caught or even if a breath of suspicion fell on them. When the Germans arrived first, they could take their time and make a thorough job of it; but if the Poles were first, they might only have a few minutes before their rivals appeared. When you think of it, it was sheer impertinence on our part.

In spite of these advantages, the Germans often arrived too late. Every piece or part likely to be of importance was quickly smuggled through to Warsaw where a committee of Polish experts was engaged in unravelling the secrets of the new weapon. Most of the material found was useless: pieces of rudder or fuselage, or parts so fused by the heat of the explosion as to be unidentifiable. But in three cases our men found only slightly damaged turbo-compressor combines, fuel reservoirs, rudder drive-chains and gears, such electrical components as coils, condensers, dry cells etc.

The dispersion of the new weapon later decreased greatly and the bombs fell on an area with a diameter of barely nine or ten miles. This was a great help to the German patrols and made it still more difficult for our men to outstrip the enemy. Logically, they could have given up the unequal struggle, but they carried on and were unexpectedly rewarded. One of the rockets dropped on the sloping bank of the river Bug near the village of Sarnaki, and did not explode. Our boys reached it first and couldn't believe their eyes when they saw the monster intact. I am told they didn't hesitate a moment (except to give one restrained whoop of joy) and rolled it down into the river. They then cleared off and lay low until the Germans gave up the vain search. Salvage operations lasted a long time: they were often interrupted when Germans appeared in the vicinity and in any case they could be conducted only at night. There followed the very delicate operation of 'dissecting' the bomb and extracting the vital parts. Obviously, for this reason (and others) the bomb could not be allowed to explode. It was not ordinary bomb-disposal; any bomb-disposal man will tell you it is relatively safe to disarm a mine or bomb of known construction, but to tinker about with an infernal machine based on absolutely new and unknown principles is somewhat reminiscent of the chances the celluloid cat has in hell.

Thus, after several months of hard work and at the cost of many lives, the secrets of the new weapon were revealed to us, and we also had a mass of observational data on range, trajectory, etc. The Germans were in all probability experimenting with remote radio control of the rocket; they installed special radio stations along the line of flight and some appliances in the rocket indicated remote steering was being tried out. We set up some stations of our own, to see what could be learnt, but the Soviet offensive then started making such rapid progress that the experimental camp was evacuated to the Reich and our task ended.[19]

Colonel Iranek-Osmecki's intelligence team began to send details back by courier and ciphered wireless traffic to the Polish Headquarters in Upper Belgrave Street. The information was so highly valued that on 25 July 1944 a Dakota was flown from Brindisi, Italy to southern Poland, with the sole purpose of bringing back the Polish engineers and some of the recovered V1 parts.

The importance of understanding new weapons like the V1 illustrated the increasingly technological aspects of the RAF's intelligence work that came to be called scientific intelligence. In some ways this new intelligence discipline was about the scientific scrutiny of existing intelligence reports. As an example, Dr R.V. Jones was largely responsible for discovering and understanding *Knickebein*, the German blind-bombing navigational aid. Jones had energetically analysed separate sources of intelligence, including signals intercepts, interrogation reports and captured enemy documents and by applying his scientific expertise was able to prove the existence of *Knickebein* and its operating parameters, as well as help develop counter-measures that bent the navigation beams and reduced the effectiveness of the German night-time blitz. The defeat of *Knickebein* encouraged further investment in scientific intelligence by the RAF and Jones' branch became one of the most productive of the war, pursuing German radar, night fighter defences and the V-weapon programmes with vigour. Jones describes how various intelligence sources might be blended together to help a scientist develop an understanding of an equipment's capabilities:

> One has, in an intelligence attack, various sources – secret agents, cryptography, electronic (in the form of listening to stations etc.) – and the art of intelligence as far as I was concerned was using each source to produce the kind of information that it was best suited to. Photographic intelligence, for example; does not tell you the power of a particular radio transmitter; on the other hand, a photograph of the aerials will enable you to calculate the sharpness of the beams, and what can be done with them. You will have to use electronic intelligence, listening, to get the power. This is of course a very simple example but I always felt that one of the great arts of intelligence was, in the manner of a commander who had tanks, infantry and so forth, is to be able to use each of these resources to the best of its ability in its most effective role.[20]

Nothing is quite as effective in producing scientific intelligence, as getting technical hands on the equipment itself. The Polish operation was an example of how intelligence agencies could sometimes help and combined operations, such as the Bruneval Raid by the 2nd Battalion, the Parachute Regiment to 'steal' a *Wurzburg* radar from a coastal site in occupied France, were also sometimes staged. On rare occasions Air Intelligence simply got lucky, such as the capture of a Fw 190 on 23 June 1942 when a German pilot, disorientated in combat over Devon, followed his reciprocal heading over the Bristol Channel and believing himself to be back over France, mistakenly landed his aircraft at Pembry airfield in South Wales. A technical report, highlighting

---

19   Polish Air Force, *Destiny Can Wait* (London: Heinemann, 1949), pp. 153-4.
20   R V Jones quoted in, *Air Photographic Reconnaissance* (Royal Air Force Historical Society, Journal No.10, 1993), p. 74.

the aircraft's capabilities and vulnerabilities, was subsequently produced by the Royal Aircraft Establishment at Farnborough.[21]

Important though all these Air Intelligence activities were, the RAF's greatest contribution to Allied intelligence in the Second World War was undoubtedly through Air Photographic Reconnaissance (PR) and the Photographic Intelligence (PI) derived from it. It could be argued that this discipline was as significant as Ultra's contribution, as it was often responsible for providing the operational intelligence to help commanders deliver victories in battle, as well as the foundational intelligence that underpinned almost every Allied operation on land, sea and in the air. One would have thought that the development and operation of PR and PI would be more widely known, yet the stately home at RAF Medmenham and what went on there is mostly forgotten, its contribution largely drowned out by commentary on Ultra and Bletchley Park.

---

21   Air Historical Branch Papers, *Intelligence in War, Part II*, p.357.

# 3

# 'I seek'[1]
# Air Photographic Reconnaissance

The development of air Photographic Reconnaissance (PR) and Photographic Intelligence (PI) prior to the Second World War was largely the result of one entrepreneurial individual – Sidney Cotton. Cotton had been an Australian pilot in the First World War and had flown reconnaissance flights with the Royal Naval Air Service and gained some fame as the inventor of the Sidcot flying suit which, for a time, was the standard clothing for all flying crew. Between the wars Cotton embarked on a career that straddled both civil aviation and photography, becoming the Director of Dufaycolor – a camera film company. It was during this period that Cotton was approached by Squadron Leader Fred Winterbotham, an RAF officer working with MI6, who proposed the idea that air photography could be a major peacetime source of intelligence on Germany. This was not an entirely new concept, as PR had been widely used in the First World War, but Cotton and Winterbotham took it to another level. They quickly acquired a Lockheed 12A civilian aircraft, covertly fitting it with cameras hidden by moveable panels, and then flew the aircraft on missions over German and Italian air space. The aircraft typically achieved photographic coverage of an area 11 miles wide when flying at 21,000 feet and produced detailed images of cities, key installations and shipping. The results highlighted the possibilities that PR might have in wartime and attracted the attention of both the RAF and Royal Navy.

While Cotton was operating his Lockheed from Malta against Italian targets, he had a fortuitous encounter with a young Flying Officer, Maurice Longbottom, who was also interested in PR. A series of discussions resulted in Longbottom writing an unsolicited letter to the Air Ministry in 1939. In his letter, entitled *Photographic Reconnaissance of Enemy Territory in War*, Longbottom made a powerful argument that the existing RAF plans to use the Blenheim bomber for strategic reconnaissance were flawed, arguing that: 'This type of reconnaissance must be done in such a manner as to avoid the enemy fighter and aerial defences as much as possible. The best method of doing this appears to be the use of a single small machine relying solely on its speed, climb and ceiling to avoid detection.'[2] This was an important insight by Longbottom, who was effectively advocating that reconnaissance aircraft should not try to fight their way in, but instead use speed, altitude and a little guile to undertake their missions. It took a little time for this to sink in at the Air Ministry, but it would eventually define the British approach to PR in the Second World War.

At the outbreak of war there were many aircraft in the RAF, from bombers to Army cooperation aircraft like the Lysander, that could be fitted with the existing service camera the F24. However, few pilots had been specially trained in PR techniques and results were frequently disappointing.

---

1   Motto of 544 Squadron – a photographic reconnaissance squadron equipped with Spitfires and Mosquitoes. It conducted reconnaissance missions in North West Europe, including on Aarhus, Denmark, five days before the famous air raid on 31 October 1944. It disbanded on 13 August 1945 after hostilities ceased.
2   Flight Lieutenant Longbottom, *Air Photographic Reconnaissance* (Royal Air Force Historical Society, Journal No.10, 1993), p. 7.

Vertical photographic-reconnaissance photograph of the railway station and marshalling yards at Freilassing, north-west of Salzburg. This image was taken prior to bombing attacks undertaken by aircraft of 205 Group and the 15th USAAF, on 25/26 April 1945. (Crown Copyright – Air Historical Branch)

Immediately after the outbreak of war, Cotton was asked to take photos of neutral Eire (where there was a fear that U-boat refuelling bases were being set up), after which he was invited to the Air Ministry on 15 September to discuss the results. There, the Director of Air Operations asked Cotton why RAF aircraft, that had been tasked to obtain photographs of German shipping in Dutch ports, kept returning without pictures – the usual cause being that the cameras had frozen up at medium level. Cotton suggested that it might be condensation rather than freezing that was causing the problem and explained how he had successfully solved this in his Lockheed, by adapting the camera hole on the Lockheed so that the warm air from the aircraft's engines was drawn across the lens. Without waiting for permission, Cotton then immediately flew a sortie to Flushing and Ijmuiden, where he obtained beautifully clear images that he presented to a meeting of startled and indignant RAF officers the next day. Some were clearly impressed, as by 22 September Cotton had been made an acting Wing Commander in the RAF and placed in charge of a new special reconnaissance flight, that was initially called the Heston Flight. The new PR unit was at first placed under Fighter Command's control[3] and the C-in-C of Fighter Command, Air Chief Marshal Sir Hugh Dowding, was unwise enough to ask Cotton what he could do to help. Cotton's immediate reply was to demand two Spitfires. This was a brave request given that Spitfires were like gold dust at that point in the war and the RAF were determined they should only be used as a fighter aircraft. Nonetheless Dowding agreed.

---

3   Roy Conyers Nesbit, *Eyes of the RAF, A History of Photo Reconnaissance* (Godalming: Bramley Publications, 1997), p. 86.

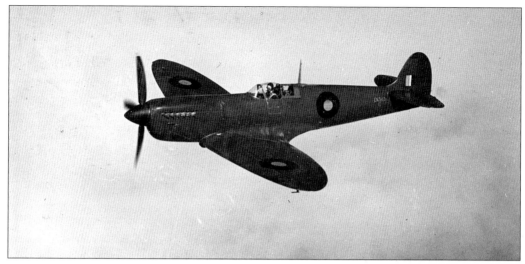

Spitfire PR Mark XI of 542 Squadron RAF based at Benson, Oxfordshire, in flight.
(Crown Copyright – Air Historical Branch)

On 30 October 1940, the first two Spitfires were delivered by Maintenance Command to Heston and the process of what became known as 'Cottonizing' began. Jack Eggleston was one of the airmen photographers on the new reconnaissance flight and describes the transformation:

> The modification of aircraft for wartime photography involved experimenting with different cameras having focal lengths from five to forty-eight inches and various camera fits. This was done in liaison with Mr Harry Stringer together with the aircraft and photographic experts of the Royal Aircraft Establishment at Farnborough… F24 cameras were fitted in vertical positions, as split pairs, forward-facing, and as side obliques. Cameras could be mounted in the wings, housed in small pods, or positioned in the fuselage. They were protected from condensation and the effect of cold by electrically-heated muffs or by air ducted from the engine. Particular attention was paid to obtaining vibration-free mountings for the fixed cameras. All experiments aimed for a camera fit which would be best for the particular conditions air photo recce anticipated… The pilot's cockpit canopy was modified with tear-drop extensions each side for visual navigation, and with marks to aid oblique target sighting.[4]

Cotton believed that the Spitfire, when freed of its service load as a fighter, could carry a considerable amount of extra fuel, oil, oxygen and cameras. His modifications therefore also consisted of stripping the aircraft of all its armament and unwanted weight, including heavy bullet proof windscreens and radios. Gun holes were filled with metal plates and all cracks blocked with plaster of Paris, rivet heads were smoothed over – as were any other protuberance that spoilt the air flow over the aircraft and the surface was highly polished to a sleek gloss. These measures raised the aircraft's speed from 360 to 390 mph. It took a little more experimentation to ensure the aircraft had a suitable colour scheme that was difficult to see at high altitude. Helpfully, Cotton had remembered seeing the Maharajah of Jodhpur depart in his private aircraft from Heston in May 1939, even though there had been clear skies on that day the Maharajah's light blue aircraft quickly merged into the background. Cotton registered the colour commercially as 'Camotint' and it became the

---

4   Roy Conyers Nesbit, *Eyes of the RAF, A History of Photo Reconnaissance*, p. 87.

colour used initially, though by early 1940 a paler sky blue was recognised as a superior colour and by the later stages of the war pink was surprisingly found to be the most effective colour at high altitudes.

If the new PR Spitfire was going to be able to service Air Intelligence's targets, then an increased range was also going to be required. Initially the RAE at Farnborough only authorised an extra thirty-gallon tank to be fitted behind the pilot, but in time they accepted that an additional sixty-five gallons could also be stored in each wing's leading edge, creating one of the first 'wet-wing' aircraft. Christened the PR1D, this new Spitfire had a 215 gallon fuel load and an impressive range of 1750 miles.

An equally important aspect of the PR Spitfire's capability and survivability was its ability to fly at high altitudes. Squadron Leader John Saffrey was a Spitfire reconnaissance pilot and recalls that this was one of the pilot's greatest trials:

> It is the climb through the tropopause[5] into the stratosphere which is like crossing the bar from the shallows into deep water. The climb up has been a matter of constant change. Continually falling temperature, successive layers of cloud, varying winds, the appearance of trails, and turbulence or vertical movements of the air liable to be felt to a greater or lesser degree all the way up.
>
> A point is reached, round about 45,000 feet for the PR Spitfires, where the top speed attainable is only equal to the stalling speed. This is absolute ceiling. At this height troubles assail the pilot. In order to get oxygen into his lungs and to prevent it escaping into the very much reduced atmospheric pressure all round, a gas tight mask and a pressure waistcoat is necessary, or a pressurised cabin. The latter is much the best solution as it increases the pressure all over the pilot's body and so minimises the likelihood of bends. The very painful result when the nitrogen in the blood bubbles out and collects round the joints when the atmospheric pressure is reduced. Bends affect different people at different heights, but can be agonizing and are only relieved by a precipitate dive to lower levels, which is a dangerous proceeding in itself at such heights, as it is liable to lead to compressibility troubles as the airflow over parts of the machine approach the speed of sound.
>
> Flying at or above 40,000 feet in a Spitfire was therefore a fairly delicate matter: the aeroplane was near its ceiling, so a violent or clumsy manoeuvre led to a stall and considerable loss of hard-won height. There was always the fear of passing out with very little warning if anything went wrong with the oxygen system, and to guard against this I used to keep a fairly elaborate log because I reckoned that if I could write legibly, I must be alright. Nevertheless, until the arrival of the pressure cabins we were a bit slow witted from lack of oxygen I think.
>
> There was an extraordinary feeling of muffled remoteness. There was no apparent motion over the very distant ground and one was high above everything else, even the highest clouds. The engine itself, which was practically in one's lap, only made a sort of a ticking noise, like a clockwork mouse. This used to puzzle me, but I think after several hours the hearing becomes insensitive to the roar of the exhaust and one's ears begin to pick out little high-pitched noises.
>
> Before the days of pressure cabins physical effort, even speaking, was quite a strain. One day I held my height until I was crossing the North Sea for the fun of saying 'Angels 41' when calling Benson to notify them that I had crossed out of Europe. I was horrified at the wheezy croak that was all the voice I had. The cold, the low pressure and the immobilizing effect of the elaborate equipment and bulky clothing in the tiny cockpit had the effect of damping

---

5   The interface between the troposphere and stratosphere.

down and subduing all the senses except the sense of sight. One became just an eye, and what one saw was always wonderful.

On a clear day one could see immense distances, whole countries at a time. From over the middle of Holland I have seen the coast from Ostend round beyond Emden, and from the neighbourhood of Hanover seen the smoke pluming up from burning Leipzig. I've seen the Baltic coast from above Berlin and from over Wiesbaden seen the Alps sticking up like rocky islands through the clouds. On such days, which are very rare in Europe, it was more like looking at a map than a view. It used to strike me how precisely like the map the coastlines were, which sounds a bit silly but it was similar to recognizing a man from his picture...

Once I found that my eyes were beginning to smart as I approached my target on a long sortie. I thought I must have hurt them trying to look into the sun so did not worry, but on turning for home they got worse and worse and very soon I was in a bad way as it was very painful to move them at all or even blink. I was over central Germany with nearly two hours flying ahead of me so I climbed to about 41,000 feet for safety as I could not keep any sort of watch and could only just peer at my compass. As soon as I had crossed the enemy coast I got a homing to Manston and they brought me in. Once down I could not bear to open my eyes at all so was taken to the doctor who put something in them and sent me to bed. It was New Year's Eve and I lay in the dark listening to a terrific party.

We found that the trouble had been due to a faulty oxygen gauge. When it indicated 'fully on', the system was in fact delivering oxygen to the mask at the emergency rate so that the gas had been escaping out of the top of the mask straight into my eyes and had been drying them up. They felt like shrivelled up prunes for the next twelve hours.[6]

The Spitfire PR aircraft's ability to fly at high altitudes was one of the greatest advantages it had in avoiding enemy aircraft, but it did not make them invulnerable. Flight Lieutenant Neil Wheeler was a PR pilot during the early part of war and remembered having to keep a careful lookout:

Until the Battle of Britain I have to admit I had never heard of a condensation trail. In PRU [Photographic Reconnaissance Unit] we had removed the fighter bullet-proof windscreen plus the rear-view mirror on the top. We had fashioned teardrops in the side of the canopy, principally to get a better downward view and in them we fitted small rear-view mirrors. The mirrors were less to see approaching fighters than to prevent one producing a condensation trail over enemy territory – signing one's name in the sky was a certain route to disaster! From Heston we carried out a great deal of research work into the formation of condensation trails, aided by Oxford University, before we established that it was the exhaust and not the propeller that produced the tell-tale trail. Normally one endeavoured to keep just below condensation height, but, on rare occasions, one could pass through the layer and fly above with the advantage that one could see fighters climbing up.[7]

By 1940 the RAF judged that the growing size of its new PR capability warranted putting it on a more formal footing. This decision may also have been prompted by Cotton himself, who during operations in France, had begun to irritate and confound his superiors by frequently disobeying orders, going over their heads and generally acting as a law unto himself. On 16 June 1940, as he

6    John Saffrey, *extracts from a paper written by Sqn Ldr John Saffrey DSO*, accessed via the Medmenham Collection.
7    Air Chief Marshal Sir Neil Wheeler quoted in, *Air Photographic Reconnaissance*, (Royal Air Force Historical Society, Journal No.10, 1993), p. 12

A Spitfire PR Mark XI of 541 Squadron RAF based at Benson, Oxfordshire in flight.
(Crown Copyright – Air Historical Branch)

arrived back with his force from France, Cotton was informed by the Air Ministry that he had been removed from command. Later, in March 1941, he was invited to resign his commission. All further attempts by Cotton to contribute to the war effort were rebuffed, arguably poor treatment for such a talented pioneer, though perhaps the usefulness of this unique disruptive character had come to its natural conclusion now the concept had been proven.

In September 1940, the PR unit's base at Heston was bombed and the Photographic Reconnaissance Unit (PRU), now under Coastal Command, was moved to RAF Benson.[8] By 1941 No. 1 PRU. comprised four Spitfire flights, two of which were based at Benson and were responsible for PR over Germany, the Low Countries, most of France and northern Italy. A third flight was at Wick, in the north of Scotland covering Norway and the fourth located at St Eval in Cornwall, looking after Brest and the Atlantic seaboard down to the Franco-Spanish frontier. The number of aircraft in each flight varied to meet requirements, but usually consisted of about six long-range and unarmed sky-blue PR Spitfires fitted with different fuel tank installations. To provide a steady supply of trained PR pilots an Operational Training Unit (OTU) was established at Dyce. Further PR units were also established in Malta, the Middle East and Far East all of which included personnel who had served at Benson – thus ensuring these units all ran along similar lines. By June 1943, 1 PRU was upgraded to No. 106 PR Wing and its four flights

8   Roy Conyers Nesbit, *Eyes of the RAF, A History of Photo Reconnaissance*, p. 87.

expanded into five squadrons (numbered from 540 to 544). In April 1944 it grew once more to become No. 106 (Photographic Reconnaissance) Group.

The specifics of PR flying were very different from other RAF roles and because they invariably flew sorties alone, the pilots often developed a very independent and individualistic frame of mind. There were usually eight or nine pilots in a PR flight and sorties were arranged in a roster, so that when the pilot had completed a mission he would go to the bottom of the ladder and await his turn once more. PR sorties were long, as much as five to six hours in duration, and a pilot was normally expected to fly three or so missions a week – though this could easily rise to six or seven during periods of operational intensity. The day of the sortie started with a brief on the weather at about 7:00 a.m., though the actual mission would not begin until three hours after dawn, when the haze and mist had burnt off and 'photographic first light' had occurred. PR sorties were also normally completed three hours before dusk, for the same photographic-light reasons. The pilot would be briefed on his targets by the Intelligence Officer, together with any possible alternatives adjacent to his track in case the primary targets were covered in cloud, or he had any spare film left over. He was then left to plan his routes and methods as he wished. The PR pilot's route would normally include a number of 'dog legs' to confuse German radar, or any intercepting enemy aircraft. Not all of the sorties were conducted at high-altitudes and the PRU frequently undertook low-level missions too, these were known as 'dicing' and were normally undertaken with an armed PR Spitfire.

Once the pilot had taken-off in his Spitfire, he would climb to altitude and turn on his oxygen. Squadron Leader Alfred Ball recalled these missions:

> The coastal belt was always dangerous for it contained many Luftwaffe bases and one expected to see fighters; however, provided one saw them in good time, one could evade them. The same situation obtained on the return flight and one could not afford to relax when crossing out of enemy territory (we lost some of our best pilots due to this temptation; it was particularly risky coming out of NW Germany with the fighter bases in the Frisian Islands).
>
> The interception threat, of course, continued all through a sortie, but there were high risk areas, such as the coastal belt and over key industrial cities, particularly if they had just been bombed. Furthermore, having to concentrate on map-reading and navigation en-route, made keeping a continuous and effective look-out difficult, but it was essential. One always had to remember that for a sortie to be successful, one had to bring back interpretable photographs of one's targets, not merely to get back in one piece having successfully evaded enemy fighters, although that had its points!
>
> It was, for example, inadvisable to fly in a long straight track to a major target area, such as Hamburg, Stettin or Frankfurt. Irregular feints and doglegs were much more sensible and pragmatic. Although they complicated navigation and used a little extra fuel, they made interceptions far more difficult for the enemy (it was extraordinary how if one did so, one often saw nothing en-route even when, from listening to his radar or from seeing his marker Flak you knew that he was attempting to intercept you). Unplanned doglegs definitely paid off.
>
> Over major targets, such as the Ruhr and Brest, one was almost invariably shot at, sometimes with remarkable accuracy (one of my chaps was hit at 37,000 feet over Hamburg, and another shot down at 30,000 over Brest), but on many occasions it tended to be some distance away and low. A PR pilot was particularly vulnerable during long photographic runs when he was concentrating on accuracy and did not see a fighter or Flak until too late.[9]

---

9   Alfred Ball, quoted in *Air Photographic Reconnaissance*, (Royal Air Force Historical Society, Journal No.10, 1993), p. 22.

Pilots of a photographic-reconnaissance squadron at Benson, Oxfordshire, being briefed by the Intelligence Officer in the Operations Room. (Crown Copyright – Air Historical Branch)

Ray Holmes was originally a Hurricane pilot in the RAF, he had become famous earlier in the war for ramming a Dornier Do 17 that was trying to bomb Buckingham Palace. By early 1945 he had become a Spitfire PR pilot with 541 Squadron at Benson, from where he undertook a sortie to Hamburg – a target that had not been covered by PR for three months. At the briefing Holmes was told by the Meteorological Officer that if he timed it correctly, there would be a short hour-long break of clear sky over Hamburg, offering an opportunity to take good images. He was also briefed that there would be cloud cover all the way there and back, which entailed difficult blind flying but would at least provide Holmes with a covered approach. After climbing to altitude and crossing the coast, Holmes dropped his auxiliary fuel tanks and took several dog legs on route to Hamburg and the nearby docks at Harburg:

> Now the cloud was quite suddenly thinner, becoming even wispy. It was lighter. The rain stopped beating the windscreen. It looked as though those Met wallahs might be right, after all. Sure enough, splashes of blue appeared above. Then all at once I was sitting on a shimmering white eiderdown, the sun blazing down, dazzling my eyes and warming up the cockpit. The quilt exploded, and there, through straggling cloud wisps, was the ground. Not only the ground! By heaven, my navigation, despite the changes of course, had worked like a dream. There was the River Elbe, a shimmering, slimy snake dragging its lazy way over green fields and through dense woodland. Not three minutes flying to the north the fields ended at the docks of Harburg.
>
> Suddenly my heart gave a bound. Above the Spitfire was a contrail, a twin trail, probably an Me 262 jet. He was fast and armed with four 30 mm cannons. The reception committee were in attendance. They were circling, waiting patiently for me. Will you come into my parlour…? My ruse hadn't been so clever after all.

I weaved and looked back to be quite sure we were not making a trail, then headed straight for the target. The jet – I could see only one but he had to have a pal – was still circling and had not yet spotted me 5,000 feet below. Full bore, diving slightly for extra speed, I headed for the four fingers stretching out into the river that were the quaysides where the ships berthed. Even from five miles up I saw immediately that something was missing from the dock scene below. It all appeared bare and white as if under a blanket of snow. Then, as I was starting my cameras, I realised what was lacking. The quays were a mass of dust and rubble. There were no buildings. The ground was pock-marked with bomb craters. This was Bomber Command's revenge for the Luftwaffe's blitzes on Coventry, Liverpool, Birmingham and London. The bombs had flattened the ware-houses, blown away the dock sheds and cranes. Fire had completed the devastation.

I banked vertically to sight my run along the east bank of the river, picked a cumulus cloud to aim at, and levelled out with the Spitfire's nose pointing towards the cloud. I switched on my two vertical cameras to take photographs at two and a half second intervals. A flashing green light confirmed when each exposure was made to produce pictures in stereo pairs.

The Messerschmitt pilot had now spotted me. He was diving angrily from the rear at a tremendous overtaking speed. With no guns to fight back, and no chance of outpacing the German jet, the Spitfire's only chance was evasion. I slammed the throttle closed. The engine backfired as though it had already been shot. The speed dropped to 300, 250, 200 mph. Through the blister hood I could see the Hun now less than 2,000 yards away, and closing the gap. He would open fire at 1,000 yards. With my speed well under 200, I yanked the Spitfire into a vertical right-hand bank then hauled the control column back into my belly until my eyeballs seemed to be rolling down my cheeks.

I blacked out completely with the centrifugal pull and I kicked on hard right rudder. The aircraft went into a fit of convulsions at this ill-treatment. Streamers flew from its wingtips as it spun down vertically off a high-speed stall. The Messerschmitt, at three times the speed of the Spitfire, was firing futilely because he could never turn tightly enough at his speed to get the deflection on the Spitfire. The whirling tracer from the four 30 mm cannons was passing behind me. Surprisingly, I even heard the throaty bark of the guns. Then the Me 262 flashed behind as I eased out of the spin.

The Hun would take ten miles to complete his turn at that speed and would probably even lose me. There was certainly time for another run over Harburg. The cameras were still running (bad show!). But there were 500 exposures in the magazines. A second run was made, this time along the west side of the river. Then I headed for the cloud bank, gaining its welcome cover as a second Messerschmitt, probably answering the call of its leader, was positioning himself for attack.

I sang most of the way home. Crazy songs, made up words, mostly rubbish. I was jubilant. The sound of my own voice came back loud and clear through the radio headset, easing the tension. I did not care that I had to land at my base in the sort of weather that made the birds walk. I started shedding height over the English coast and was down to 2000 feet by what I reckoned to be Oxford. Ops had kept the air clear of all other aircraft.

Control vectored me over Benson at this height. I set the Barometer pressure on my altimeter so that it would read exactly zero on landing. With wheels and flaps down now they sent me on a wide loop to bring me on to the runway bearing, three miles down-wind of the airfield.

By losing height and flying the headings Control gave me, I heard the pips of the outer marker beacon 1,000 yards from the runway at 300 feet. I picked up the pips of the inner marker on the aerodrome boundary at 150 feet. At that instant I came out of cloud, saw the runway ahead with sodium flares along its edges. Muttering a prayer of thanks, I shut the

A Type F8 Mark II (20-inch lens) aerial camera being loaded into the vertical position in a Supermarine Spitfire PR Mark IV at Benson, Oxfordshire. (Crown Copyright – Air Historical Branch)

throttle, held off and was down. The rumble of the wheels along the tarmac was a welcome sound. I insisted on taking my own camera magazines up to the photographic section. I smoked a cigarette as I watched them being clamped on to the developing tank. Then I went up to debriefing. Twenty minutes later, debriefed, I was inspecting rush prints of my photographs of Harburg, all serial-numbered and dated for plotting.[10]

There were usually two cameras (F24s initially and then F36s) in a PR Spitfire and each one carried a magazine holding 500 whole-plate pictures measuring 8½ by 6½ inches. Though the lens on the F36 was only the size of a small saucer its makers had managed to obtain a focal length of 36 inches, an impressive technical achievement that enabled detailed high-resolution images to be taken from great heights.

When photographing targets the cameras would, depending on ground speed and altitude, take an exposure every three seconds, typically expending a full magazine of film on successful sorties. From 32,000 feet the ground covered by each plate would be 1,000 by 800 yards and special filters were often placed over the lens to reduce haze and improve the contrast and detail.[11]

The two cameras would usually produce photographs 'in stereo' which meant that each camera would take a picture of the same subject with a slight overlap. To achieve this the cameras would be set to expose automatically at pre-selected intervals three to six seconds apart. Because each

10    Ray Holmes, *Sky Spy* (Shrewsbury: Airlife Ltd, 1989), pp. 279-281.
11    Ray Holmes, *Sky Spy*, p. 267.

picture overlapped its predecessor by 50 percent every subject was therefore on the second half of the first camera's photo and the first half of the photo taken by the second camera. When these photographs were viewed through a stereoscope, with the left eye focusing on one image and the right eye focusing on the second, they merged into one 3D picture and showed relief in astonishing detail.[12] Good photographic interpretation could not be done on any scale higher than 1:10,000 and photographic runs could sometimes be quite long, as much as 25 miles if the images were to be used for mapping purposes, which was a frequent Army demand.

Mosquito aircraft began to arrive in PRUs in 1943 and undertook 50 percent of the PR sorties in the last two years of the war. Before the arrival of the PR Mosquito, coverage of ports and anchorages north of Trondheim, Norway was dependent on Russian co-operation and use of airfields in the Murmansk area. This meant the Spitfires were able to cover the most northerly targets, but the detachments to Murmansk took time to set up and coverage throughout the year was often not feasible. Using Leuchars, in Fife, as a main base and Wick and Sumburgh for forward refuelling the increased range of the Mosquitoes extended coverage as far north as Narvik. This was a vital port for the PRU to cover, as it was regularly used by the *Kriegsmarine* as a forward base for attacks on the Allied Arctic convoys off the North Cape. The intelligence derived from the Mosquito PR coverage gave the Admiralty very useful early warning on likely enemy intentions. The Mosquito's range also meant it was able to give virtually complete coverage of the Baltic and could stretch as far south as Toulon or Bordeaux with ease.

As well as range, the Mosquito was also able to carry much more than the Spitfire and its bomb bay provided a space for additional cameras and extra radios to be fitted. Ronald Foster describes the PR Mosquito's equipment and operation:

> Usually our Mosquitoes carried two main cameras, 'F/36s' which took side by side photos with an adjustable overlay to obtain stereo effect. On top of each camera a film magazine was clipped each of which held 500 exposures. Another camera was also fitted an 'F/6' that produced a larger print of about nine inches square, and covered a wide and extensive ground area surrounding the actual target. One Mosquito on 544, a fighter mark, had a forward facing camera for use in very low level flights the pilot operated it from a button on the control column. We called this kite, the dicer. At times our usual aircraft were also fitted with an 'oblique' facing camera, an 'F/14' operated by the pilot who sighted along the port wing when flying close to the ground.[13]

The Mosquito's second engine was also an undoubted source of comfort during any long sea crossings, however perhaps the greatest advantage the Mosquito had over the Spitfire was that it could carry an observer who could act as navigator, camera operator and work the Gee navigation system. The observer on a PR Mosquito normally lay flat in the nose facing forward, but he could also turn around and keep a look out to the rear.[14]

The additional, more powerful cameras the Mosquito could carry, together with its extended range, resulted in pressure for all PR aircraft to be Mosquitoes. This was fiercely resisted by the PRU who saw the advantages of a mixed fleet and argued that the Spitfire was less easy to pick up on radar and had a faster rate of climb and greater agility. The PRU's arguments won the day and

12   Ray Holmes, *Sky Spy*, p. 264.

13   Ronald Foster, *Focus on Europe – A Photo-Reconnaissance Mosquito Pilot at War 1943-45* (Ramsbury: Crowood Press Ltd, 2004), p. 93.

14   Frank Dodds quoted in *Air Photographic Reconnaissance*, (Royal Air Force Historical Society, Journal No.10, 1993), p. 27

A Mosquito PR Mark XVI, of No. 544 Squadron RAF based at Benson, Oxfordshire, in flight.
(Crown Copyright – Air Historical Branch)

the PR Spitfire was retained (and upgraded to the new Spitfire PR Mk XI with a top speed of 422 mph).[15]

In Australia the arrival of the PR Mosquito aircraft in May 1944 was particularly welcome. Up to that point important long-range reconnaissance missions (and they were almost all long-range missions in the Pacific) had been flown by Liberators or Catalinas, which were often vulnerable to Japanese interception. In its first month Mosquito PR aircraft flew nine missions from Broome, Western Australia, covering the Kai islands, Timor, Sumba, Celebes, Surabaya and Flores. On one of these early missions in June 1944, a Mosquito suffered an engine loss while over Surabaya, yet Flying Officer Boss-Walker was still able to successfully fly the aircraft the 900-miles back to Broome.[16]

It was not just aircraft and PR techniques that were improving. As photographic reconnaissance grew in scale it was also important that the processing and printing capabilities were able to cope with the increasing demands for air photographs. By 1941 RAF Benson was equipped with a Kodak Continuous Film Processing Machine (CFPM). Similar installations were also fitted to 45ft-Brownhall trailers which were part of the photographic 'trains' that the Mobile Field Photographic Sections (MFPS) used to provide air photographs to frontline Army, Navy and Air Force units in all theatres.

The CFPM was followed by the introduction of the multi-printer developed jointly by Williamsons and the Royal Aeronautical Establishment (RAE), which combined the two operations of printing

15   Frank Dodds quoted in, *Air Photographic Reconnaissance*, p. 28
16   George Odgers, *Air War against Japan* (Canberra: Australian War Memorial, 1957), p. 232.

and processing in one machine. A negative grader designed by the RAE was later fitted to give a better consistency in printing by using a photo-cell to balance the lamp intensity against the density of each negative. This required a skilled operator, though the hardest job might have been the operators at the other end of the machine, whose role was to guillotine prints 'on the run' while sweating over a hot, steaming dryer. Importantly these machines were not just used at static locations but were also sent to the Mobile Field Photographic Sections in the field. As one example in the month of July 1944, 3 Mobile Field Photographic Sections, which supported 285 Wing in Italy, produced a total of 551,338 prints from 54,261 air negatives. Its total for the whole of 1944 was 3,350,000 prints that covered a multitude of subjects from bomb damage assessments, future German lines of defence as well as current coverage of the battle area, including enemy gun positions.[17]

Once an RAF PR aircraft had landed, the magazine of film would be taken from the camera to the processing section and the most suitable negatives identified and selected for rush printing orders. The prints would be brought to the analysts still wet and an immediate interpretation made. This initial report would usually be of a tactical nature and completed on what was known as a 'Form White', before it was sent by teleprinter to all interested parties. The pilot would normally be there to advise and assist and the aim was to have a report dispatched within twenty minutes or so.[18] On 23 January 1942 Flight Lieutenant Alfred Fane Peers Fane (known as 'Fane, Fane') was sent on a sortie to find the *Tirpitz* (often nicknamed the 'old rowboat' by the PR pilots). This was an important sortie because the Admiralty had become worried after losing the whereabouts of the *Tirpitz* in a period of poor weather. Fane and his PR Spitfire made landfall at Stadlandet while flying at 17,000 ft, this was a lower level than normal but had proved necessary because the height at which the revealing contrails were generated by the aircraft had dropped with the weather. Fane continues the story:

> The weather cleared and so I S/C [Set Course] for Trondheim. Photographed Trondheim and aerodromes saw nothing in nearby fiords – so went north keeping good look out. Passing Aas Fiord when I saw something like a ship hidden in the shadow in the far end – No, too big must be a small island – better make sure. By God it's a ship – it's the ship – rolled on to my side to have a good look and remember saying out loud.
>
> 'My God, I believe I've found it.'
>
> Could not believe my eyes or my luck – Did three runs over it and next fiord and turned for home. Took Orlandet aerodrome on the way. Made Statlandet and S/C [Set Course] for home. Flew on and on! Came down through clouds on ETA. Clouds down to 600 ft over sea. Flew on and on! Began to get worried 20 minutes over due. Notice that there seemed to be a hell of a wind from the south so altered course 10 to port. Getting really worried only 20 gallons left!
>
> Land! Turned north and found it was an island – must be the Orkneys – yes there's a block ship – must be Scapa Flow, so turned south. Saw what looked like John O' Groats. (I had not had time to fly up and down local coast before I went on this trip and it was our first day up here). Just when I thought I was near Wick saw an aerodrome with runways – only had 10 gallons left – so did not argue but landed – only to find that it was Skitton – Wick's satellite. Only 4 miles from Wick – didn't know Wick had a satellite – so took off and landed at Wick – to find that they had seen me fly over with my wheels down while making a circuit of the satellite – felt a bloody fool – but with the bloody visibility and not knowing there were two aerodromes here – perhaps I may be forgiven.

17   G Millington, *The Unseen Eye* (London: Anthony and Gibbs, 1961), p. 146.
18   Ursula Powys-Lybbe, *The Eye of Intelligence* (London: William Kimber, 1983), p. 40.

Two low-level oblique photographic-reconnaissance photographs taken of the German battleship *Tirpitz* moored in Aasfjord, Norway, by Flight Lieutenant A F P Fane's Spitfire. (Crown Copyright – Air Historical Branch)

Landed and told Tony I thought I'd found the old 'Rowboat' but could not believe it – Flap!!! Found that they were getting worried by being so late and sea rescue crew had been briefed! Delay was obviously due to the 60mph wind blowing. Hopped about on one foot then the other waiting for photos to be developed. When film was ready tore in to look at negatives. Maybe I'd missed the b- thing. NO! There it was – no doubt now it was the Tirpitz all right. Rushed into the Ops room to report the news. Flap. I adore flaps, they always make me laugh. Group rang up, Coastal Command rang up – the Admiralty rang up. Poor Eve was up all night. Next morning signal of congrats from Butch (the CO). Good old 'C' flight we could not help laughing – a bit meanly – because the Mosquitos had been trying to get there for weeks and we get it in three days. Good old Spitfires! Photos showed stereo pairs of Rowboat – complete cover of Trondheim – so my accuracy is getting much better but still wasting a lot of film. But I suppose it's best to make certain than not get it at all.[19]

The prints and negatives from PR sorties would then be taken to the Central Interpretation Unit at RAF Medmenham. The CIU had initially been set up at Wembley, close to a private company called Aerofilms, who possessed expertise and equipment that was initially useful, but in October 1940 CIU's facilities were struck by German bombs and it was moved to Danesfield House near Medmenham, Marlow where it remained till the end of the war. On arrival the PR photographs were initially handled by the plotters who would study the images and mark the outline of the areas the photos covered on maps. An experienced plotter could plot a 500-frame sortie in about one hour. The photographs would then be analysed by second phase interpreters who worked as part of a shift system, these individuals conducted more detailed analysis of the images and compared them with previous photos taken on earlier sorties. These interpreters had considerable expertise on shipping, aircraft, military installations, infrastructure, industry and communications. The idea was to obtain an overall view of enemy activity in the round which would have been impossible if the images had been sent to specialist sections straight away. On occasions the second phase interpreters were given special topics to examine, such as a study of French chateaux to determine which might be German headquarters, or daily airfield and railway reports to understand how the Germans were using them.

Third Phase interpretation work involved the deep specialists, these individuals looked after particular subjects of strategic interest, such as the German army, navy and air force, as well as the aircraft industry, airfields, bomb damage, industry, W/T and radar, camouflage and decoys.[20] Third Phase sections varied in size, the largest was probably the CROSSBOW team, which tracked the V1 sites in Northern France and the low countries and contained 80 personnel at its peak.[21]

Finally, at Medmenham there were the sections which had specialist skills and functions. This included the Photogrammetry Section which used the Swiss built 'Wild' machine to measure the precise size and shape of objects within the photographs. This was hugely useful for targets such as submarine pens, or viaducts and allowed analysts to ascertain the building's strength and the likelihood of a particular bomb-type being able to destroy that structure. There was also a model-making section, a highly skilled team who were able to construct precise and accurate models of targets, or other areas of interest. These included large scale topographical models of an area, or alternatively more precise ones of a target or installation. The Medmenham models were invaluable as briefing or planning tools and were regularly used for commando and airborne raids

---

19   Ursula Powys-Lybbe, *The Eye of Intelligence*, 1983, p. 110.
20   Ursula Powys-Lybbe, *The Eye of Intelligence*, p. 42.
21   Douglas Kendell quoted in *Air Photographic Reconnaissance* (Royal Air Force Historical Society, Journal No.10, 1993), p. 28

A WAAF flight officer photographic interpreter examines newly-developed prints through a stereoscope with two Canadian PR pilots. (Crown Copyright – Air Historical Branch)

such as those on Dieppe, the Vermork Heavy Water Plant in Norway and Bruneval. They could also be used for Bomber Command missions and good models were provided for the bombing raids on the Mohne and Eder dams, Peenemunde as well as many other industrial targets. The Model Section produced large numbers of models for the beach landing areas during Operation OVERLORD, which helped the Royal Navy and assaulting troops considerably and drew praise from Eisenhower.[22]

RAF Medmenham proved highly successful as a source of intelligence because it was getting very broad and comprehensive photography, not just from the PRU but also from Coastal Command and Bomber Command aircraft. These sorties generated high frequencies of coverage over targets which was very useful for comparison. The understanding Medmenham was able to derive from these photographs was helped by employing individuals who already had some specialist expertise. Recruiting the right PI personnel was done in an imaginative and unorthodox way at Medmenham, drawing on individuals from academia, the City and industry (including the film industry and actor Dirk Bogarde). Those who already understood how a particular industry, factory or refinery worked were very useful, though this previous experience was supplemented by training which included field trips to relevant installations as part of the analyst's continued professional development. Sometimes there were lucky breaks that provided Medmenham with critical intelligence, on one occasion the Ministry of Economic Warfare managed to obtain the entire plans for the Renault factory at Billancourt near Paris. These detailed plans included every factory building, vehicle assembly line, engine shop, foundry and storeroom, which was hugely

---

22    Ursula Powys-Lybbe, *The Eye of Intelligence*, p. 43.

useful for both targeting purposes and in assessing bomb damage. Medmenham had received these documents from Lloyds of London who held the company's insurance policy.[23] Like many other PR pilots Ray Holmes was encouraged to visit Medmenham to gain a better understanding of what was going on there and how the photographs he took were exploited:

> The interpreters were all specialists in finding chinks in the enemy's armour, and a good clear photograph was of untold value to them. Some would specialise in ships, some railways, some airfields and aircraft, and others on oil refineries. The military experts would trace troop movements, and the scientists sought new secret weapons like flying bombs and rockets. Often secret hideaways would be hidden in forests but foot-paths in early morning dew would betray them. It was fascinating to find what these men could learn by careful examination of the photographs through powerful stereo lenses. In one room at Medmenham I found a backroom boy in ecstasy over my photos of a synthetic oil refinery at Merseberg. It was a beautifully designed refinery, almost perfectly rectangular in shape, with all the various sections fitting together with the precision of the works of a wristwatch. He had identified every working part of that refinery as though naming the components of an engine. He knew exactly the use of each building and the output of each machine. By examining bomb-damaged parts he could estimate the drop in output. The same interpreter took me to a board covering one complete wall. Every German oil refinery was on that board like a football league table, with details of maximum output, parts damaged, parts repaired, and present output. He told me Bomber Command never aimed to destroy a refinery completely. 'Much better,' he said, 'to damage it just sufficiently to give them hope of repairing it. PR photos tell how they're getting on with the repairs. Then when they're about ready to go into production again we biff 'em once more. But again only enough to keep 'em busy mending it. With a grim smile he added, 'It breaks their little Hun hearts that way. We like to think of them crying themselves to sleep every night'.[24]

The Photographic Interpreters consisted of many female officers, 150 out of an establishment of 1,700 in total. One of the most famous analysts at Medmenham was Constance Babbington-Smith, who had been a journalist for *Aeroplane* magazine prior to the war. She ended up running the critical German Airforce Interpretation Section and was partly credited with the discovery of the V-1 at Peenemunde. Unlike other WAAF Officers, who also ran sections, she did not have to undergo the frustrating experience of having a non-technically trained man of equal rank placed nominally in charge and in theory supervising her! Like all the interpreters at Medmenham, Babbington-Smith was trained on the Photographic Interpretation course, the fifth one to be run during the war. In later years she recalled learning the fundamentals that helped all interpreters:

> For our first exercise we were given some 'verticals' … and we gradually learnt how to recognise such land marks as railway stations and airfields and distinguish between railways with their invariable gentle curves, and roads, which usually follow the lie of the land. There are always shadows on daytime high-altitude photographs, because the pictures could not have been taken except from a clear sky; and I learnt how much easier it is to look at the prints if you place them with the shadows falling towards you; as though the sun were shining down on the photograph from beyond the table you're working at…

23   Ursula Powys-Lybbe, *The Eye of Intelligence*, p. 155.
24   Ray Holmes, *Sky Spy*, p. 268.

Shipping was of course the first priority, and we practised making accurate counts, listing the vessels by size – large, medium and small. We didn't yet know enough about recognition points to identify many types… The first aerial photograph of an enemy airfield I ever saw was a disappointment and shock. It was a busy fighter base in the Pas-de-Calais, and I had to try and count the aircraft; but even under a magnifying glass the Me 109s were no bigger than pin-heads, in fact rather smaller. My heart sank, and I thought, 'I shall never be able to do this.' A bit later however, we had an aircraft test which was more to my taste: we were given some good clear photographs of a dump of French aircraft which the Germans had written off at Merignac, near Bordeaux, and had to identify as many as we could, with the help of some recognition silhouettes. I thoroughly enjoyed myself, but was rather worried because when I took my list to Kendall [Douglas Kendall – the instructor and highly regarded senior intelligence officer at CIU] there was one aeroplane I hadn't been able to name. Kendall smiled. 'No,' he said. 'Nor can I.'

We started by looking at single prints, but were soon trying to use a stereoscope, that apparently simple optical instrument which presents exaggerated height and depth – if the 'pair' of photographs below it is set in just the right position. There were not enough stereoscopes to go round, and I realised that a 'stereo' was something important and precious. In time I borrowed one. It was an absurdly uncomplicated little gadget, like a pair of spectacles mounted in a single rectangular piece of metal, supported by four metal legs that held it a few inches above the photographs. I stood it above a pair of prints as I had seen some of the others doing. I could see two images, not one, and there really did not seem much point. It was much simpler to work with an ordinary magnifying glass. I edged the two prints backwards and forwards a bit – still two images; and then suddenly the thing happened, the images fused, and the buildings in the photograph shot up towards me so that I almost drew back. It was the same sort of feeling of triumph and wonder that I remember long ago when I first stayed up on a bicycle without someone holding on behind. From then on interpretation was much easier.

Towards the end of the fortnight, Michael Spender came and gave us a talk about the interpretation of shipping. In his hesitant but intimidating voice he spoke of the principles that apply to all interpretation. 'You must know at a glance what is normal, and then you can recognise the abnormal when you see it. When we saw the Dutch shipyards crowded with barges having their bows cut away, we knew the importance of what was happening because we had already been watching the normal life of those yards. And because we knew the normal look of the Channel ports we could recognise the abnormal the moment the barges started appearing there. An interpreter is like a motorist driving through a town, who suddenly sees a rubber ball bouncing across the road from a side street. He can't see any children playing, but he knows in a flash they are there and his brake is on. You must know what is normal, but you must also know the significance of what you see when you see it.'[25]

In late 1941, the Bomber Command Damage Assessment Section and the Night photographic Interpretation Section from No.3 PRU were incorporated into Medmenham. The Americans also integrated their own intelligence personnel into Medmenham when they joined the war and the unit was renamed the Allied Central Interpretation Unit (ACIU). This happy partnership lasted until August 1945 when the Americans departed once more and at the war's end ACIU had 5,000,000 images and 40,000 reports in its library. These covered subjects as varied as the *Luftwaffe* order of battle, the production of German U-boats and the German oil-producing capability. To ensure the smooth running of such a large Allied PR enterprise, a prioritised tasking

25   Constance Babbington-Smyth, *Evidence in Camera* (London: David and Charles, 1957), pp. 81-83.

A flight lieutenant points out details on a model of the port of Kiel, constructed by the RAF Model Making Section at the ACIU, Medmenham, Buckinghamshire. (Crown Copyright – Air Historical Branch)

process had been established and incorporated a Joint Photographic Reconnaissance Committee – which gave strategic direction to the operation, together with a Technical Control Office (TCO) at Medmenham – which enabled day to day tasking of PRU sorties. The latter had sufficient latitude to task sorties on its own authority, which meant the system was both flexible and responsive.[26] The American presence in ACIU also ensured that from July 1943 the TCO had the authority to task the United States Army Air Force's 7th Photographic Reconnaissance Group. Based out of Mount Farm in Oxfordshire, 7th Photographic Reconnaissance Group flew P-51 Mustangs, PR Spitfires and Lightning F-5s (the PR version of the P-38). The unit was commanded by Elliot Roosevelt, son of the American President F. D. Roosevelt.

The contribution of air photographic reconnaissance was not limited to supporting purely strategic or operational intelligence subjects from the UK. Tactical PR aircraft were incorporated into the Fleet Air Arm and camera equipped Hellcats of 888 Naval Air Squadron were operated off carriers within both the East Indies Fleet and the British Pacific Fleet. These aircraft were frequently used in support of strike operations, including the 1945 raids on the Sumatran oil refineries, where they provided useful bomb damage assessment that helped determine the severity of the attack and whether another raid was necessary. Pre-strike reconnaissance was sometimes avoided, for the arrival of these distinctive, naval, short-range aircraft over potential targets might alert the Japanese that there was a British carrier group in the vicinity.[27]

26    Ursula Powys-Lybbe, *The Eye of Intelligence*, p. 39.
27    David Hobbs, *The British Pacific Fleet*, (Barnsley: Seaforth Publishing, 2011), p.64

The British also possessed several RAF fighter reconnaissance squadrons that, though not part of the PRU, still flew tactical photographic reconnaissance missions in support of the Army. These sorties were normally at 6,000 to 8,000 feet, much lower than most PRU sorties, and vulnerable to both flak and enemy fighters at that level. These fighter reconnaissance squadron Spitfires were armed and modified to fly at low level by having the elliptical ends of their wings 'squared off', which gave better aileron control below 10,000 feet. They were also equipped with cropped supercharge blowers that increased engine power at lower levels and were modified to carry both an oblique and a vertical camera. Obliques were hugely useful to Army Commanders and were often used before an assault, or for artillery spotting by Forward Observation Officers (FOOs), Air Observation Posts or Tactical Reconnaissance. Wing Commander G. Millington commanded both a squadron and a wing of fighter reconnaissance aircraft and recalls taking oblique photographs (gridded in this instance) to assist the British Army in the Tunisian campaign in 1942–43:

At this time, the need for oblique cameras became even more pressing because the Army began to call for photographs for artillery reconnaissance against increased shelling from enemy batteries. A static war, when both sides were firmly dug in, and unable to move, always tended to develop into a slogging match between the opposing artillery. Information on enemy guns, relying on flash spotting and sound ranging methods of detection, was coming in, and the 5 Corps Commander, General Allfrey, asked me whether I would be prepared to undertake artillery reconnaissance in order to correct the fire of our guns on to the enemy batteries and destroy them. This was known as Counter Battery. The Artillery Staff at 5 Corps Headquarters were anxious to obtain from us oblique line overlaps of the enemy positions in the valley of the River Medjerda in the area near Medjez-el-Bab, and the prints produced were to be covered by an arbitrary grid system, which was invented by Captain John Merton, a gunner officer then serving at the School of Artillery at Larkhill, on Salisbury Plain. It was the intention to run off sufficient copies of these prints covering the whole frontage in question so that all gunner batteries and pilots would be able to refer to them before and during any particular shoot…

I was very keen to get on with this little project, and planned the Merton Gridded Oblique line over-lap mission, which, in itself, involved flying absolutely straight and level at about 5,000 feet over the front line, covering a frontage of thirteen miles from start to finish.

When planning an oblique line overlap mission, certain important factors had to be taken into account. To start with, the overlap of consecutive prints had to be about 30 percent to avoid distortion, and this figure was achieved by applying the wind speed and direction, at the selected height to fly, to the true air-speed and course of the aircraft in order to arrive at its speed in relation to the ground. Having worked that out, it was then necessary to apply this factor to a simple formula that gave the time interval to be set on the camera control to produce the 30 percent overlap. A further calculation enabled the pilot to determine the number of exposures needed to cover the distance required; this was also indicated by the camera control in the pilot's cockpit.

Having suitably prepared myself for this mission, I decided to take Graham Stewart as my number two, as I wanted a reliable man to watch for the approach of enemy fighters, since all my attention was to be focused on flying accurately, i.e. maintaining the pre-selected height, course and speed, and this meant concentrating on the aircraft instruments, and not on what went on outside.

When all was set, we both took off and set course for Medjez-el-Bab, climbing as we went to make 5,000 feet just north-west of the town to the point where the photographic run was due to commence. Having arrived there, I had a quick look round to see whether the skies were clear, and then turned on to the planned course and switched on the camera control.

A North American Mustang Mark IA of No. 35 (PR) Wing banks over the French countryside during a tactical-reconnaissance mission. (Crown Copyright – Air Historical Branch)

With Graham searching the sky for enemy fighters, I had little to worry about and settled down to fly really accurately. At the end of the run we turned west and headed for base, landed, and waited anxiously for the film to be developed by the Squadron Photographic Section. Later that evening, Major Jimmy Blythe, our Senior A.L.O. rang to say that the mission was an outstanding success and asked to bring the results round to me. I agreed, and sent for Graham Stewart, and we all gazed at the results, which were claimed to be the first Merton photographs taken on operations, and extremely useful they proved to be during later artillery reconnaissance missions, which sealed the fate of several enemy gun positions.[28]

As the Allies re-entered Europe once more, the fighter reconnaissance squadrons were recognised as an important source of intelligence for the 21st Army Group. Montgomery himself had insisted upon a good PR capability, maintaining that 'If the Recce Wing was bad it would be like having one hand tied behind your back.'[29] Low-level oblique shots of the beaches to be assaulted provided some of the most useful images for D-Day planning and were distributed to the landing craft commanders, to aid the run-in to their particular beach zones, as well as the assault troops.

28   G Millington, *The Unseen Eye* (London: Anthony and Gibbs, 1961), pp. 55-57.
29   Monty's handwritten notes for the address at Fighter Command, Friday 28 May 44, Montgomery papers – quoted from Nigel Hamilton, *Monty Master of the Battlefield 1942-44* (Sevenoaks: Hodder & Stoughton, 1983), p. 588.

Once ashore the provision of Photographic Interpreters at levels as low as Division meant that PR images could also be exploited in a timely manner. Major General Richard Gale was the commander of the British 6th Airborne Division which dropped in to Normandy on D-Day and then defended the eastern flank of the bridgehead in the succeeding weeks, often against considerable German counter-attacks. He recalled the use of Photographic Interpreters within his Divisional Headquarters.

> The interpretation of air photographs was done by a small section of experts on my staff known as the Army Photographic Interpretation Staff. They were under the command of one Captain McBride of the Border Regiment. When, in 1934 and 1935, I was Brigade Major of the Ferozepore Brigade in the Punjab, India. I knew McBride well. He was then a very senior subaltern serving with his unit. He was an expert at his job and there were no secrets in these photos we had taken that McBride did not unearth. We found the German mortars, the holes in the hedges where he was wont to run up his self-propelled guns, and his rocket firing mortars. The tracks as well as the tell-tale footpaths and muzzle blast of the guns all showed up on the air photographs. Most nights the Germans came over and gave us a bit of bombing. One July night a bomb, which dropped just outside the office, sent a shower of splinters into the sand-bagged door-way where poor McBride was standing; and thus we lost yet another of the band.[30]

Before the D-Day landings, Allied intelligence had predicted that overwhelming Allied air superiority over Normandy would mean that most German movement would take place during the hours of darkness. The Army therefore requested a night reconnaissance capability to ensure these targets were captured and this was carried out by the Wellington-equipped 69 Squadron based at Northolt. Flight Lieutenant S. Phillips explains how the squadron operated:

> The only night reconnaissance squadron was our own 69. We flew Mk III Wellingtons 'Wimpeys'. The guns of the nose turrets, and other gear, were removed and replaced with clear perspex nose fairings which provided me with a good visual field of view. An open shutter moving film camera and photo flash pistol were provided; plus a flare launch tube for the 54 flares (18 bundles of 3) stowed in the fuselage. The flares were dropped from 3,000 and we were to go down to 800-1,000 feet for visual observation and photos. On a sortie, a particular target might be set for photos: and this would be the priority task. Flares would need to be dropped. Also an area of roads, river crossings or such to cover as visual reconnaissance. If the moonlight were good enough then no need for flares… Many of our trips were for trying to find German troops, vehicles on the move, or bivouacking by night; or under camouflage. We operated from close up for an artillery shoot under our flares or as far-ranging as 60 miles in front of our troops…
>
> The crew was pilot: navigator 1 to get us to and from the target; navigator 2 as target area map reader, pinpoint identification, flare dropper, photo man and the rear gunner.

Flying low level at night is always a hazardous business and required great skill from the pilots of 69 Squadron. Phillips expressed strong admiration for his own pilot, Flight Lieutenant John Stuart, a New Zealander flying with the RAF:

---

30  Richard Gale, *With the 6th Airborne Division in Normandy* (London: Marston & Co Ltd, 1948), p. 113.

In approaching to do photos he couldn't come in too low. There is an ideal field of view of the cameras at 800 to 1000 feet and we were expected to do that. It was always heart stopping for me when I had the photo target lined up, warned Johnny and pressed the camera tit. Now we had six flashes to come, two seconds apart all in a lovely straight line. What a target for the gunners! Yet on more than half the occasions we didn't get any flak. When we did, Johnny just held us straight on, to finish the run. Relaxing a little after climbing out and up, Johnny would go through the routine, asking the crew 'OK Mac? Ok Phil? OK Jackie?' and with our replies came the inevitable 'Good on Yer Phil!'

I was glad when the flare work was done – maybe two targets. Then I could be flare-happy within reason dropping them all over the place... we might see something really special:- an armoured convoy ideally, then the hot potato was mine. I mustn't drop it through my nerve-less fingers. I was supposed to say precisely '3 miles N-West of Senonches, travelling towards Verneuil.' The pilot had authority to break R/T silence there and then if anything really good was seen, so up he climbs gets R/T contact and tells them 'We have 3 melons at Glos-Sur-Risle two miles west of Theirville.'

I had given him my pinpoint. Then it was up to 34 Wing to decide what kind of attack to send in if any.[31]

The provision of night reconnaissance by the RAF highlights the comprehensive nature of the photographic intelligence, provided to both strategic and tactical commanders. Some 36,000,000 reconnaissance prints were judged to have been produced by the end of the war, which underlines the scale and volume this intelligence source achieved. It is that volume of disseminated product which stands in great contrast to Ultra. Although hugely successful in obtaining intelligence on the Germans, the disadvantage with any signals intelligence derived from cryptographic break-throughs is that if the enemy believes you have cracked his codes he can very quickly change his ciphers and communication methods to cut your source of intelligence off completely. For that reason, the guardians of Ultra were fanatical about restricting the dissemination of Enigma-derived material and understandably applied a rigid 'need to know' policy. This meant that Ultra was very rarely disseminated below Army level (e.g the commanders or selected staff of Second British Army, Eighth Army etc were the only ones allowed to see it) and it was unable to be directly used by tactical commanders. In contrast, the occasional downed RAF PR aircraft meant that the Germans were not ignorant of the RAF PR capability, or how the allies might be using air photo-graphic intelligence. Yet there was very little they could do to prevent these fast, high-altitude aircraft from collecting the intelligence the Allies required. This meant that the PR product could be disseminated much more widely and was therefore able to be exploited at much lower levels than Ultra ever was.

It is absurd that the RAF PR/PI achievements have not captured the public's imagination in the same way that the story of Bletchley Park and Ultra has done. One suspects that the limited dissemination and secrecy attached to Ultra has given it an extra cache and mystery that excites the layman. In contrast PI was disseminated widely and used extensively by all branches of the armed forces, perhaps being taken for granted as an assured source of information, its very familiarity may have reduced our appreciation of its massive contribution. It is part of our historical narrative on the Second World War that needs much better balance.

---

31   Imperial War Museum, 12607 03/33/1, Private Papers of S Phillips.

# 4

# 'For Freedom'[1] RAF support to Special Duties Operations

We have already seen that Photographic Reconnaissance was not the only source of intelligence the Allies had on what was going on in occupied territory and that MI6 agents would also report back valuable information. In addition, the Special Operations Executive (SOE) developed a network of saboteurs and resistance organisations that hampered the German military machine and also provided useful intelligence. These clandestine groups and individuals principally kept in touch with London or other Allied headquarters by radio, but they were also supported by the RAF who dropped supplies and reinforcements, as well as extracting personnel when necessary. The operations of these RAF Special Duties flights were a closely-guarded secret during wartime and involved only a select group of pilots and aircrew. Nonetheless they played an essential part in ensuring that the Allied special forces, intelligence organisations and resistance groups that operated behind enemy lines could function and flourish.

The operations by SOE in France and western Europe are perhaps the most well-known of these activities, and the work of many of their agents has been well documented. It was identified early on in the war, that a method of inserting these agents into occupied Europe, and just as importantly picking them up, needed to be established quickly. If the agents were young and fit then parachuting them in was a practical proposition, though selecting good Drop Zones (DZs) on the ground that could also be easily identified from the air often proved problematic. To complement these parachute drops, the RAF set up a specialised air transport service, initially formed from 161 Squadron, that could land on rudimentary landing strips. This squadron was based out of RAF Tempsford in Bedfordshire, but also established a permanent forward presence at RAF Tangmere from which it could also mount sorties.

The main aircraft used by 161 Squadron was the Lysander, often simply referred to as the 'Lizzie'. It had originally been designed by the Westland Aircraft Company for daylight operations as an Army co-operation aircraft and was supposed to be used to direct artillery fire or conduct tactical reconnaissance. Though the Lysander was highly manoeuvrable it was found to be far too slow for front-line flying and was declared obsolete for its original role. It looked destined to spend its war years as little more than an aerial taxi for senior officers. Nonetheless, the Lysander did have some qualities that made it a highly suitable choice for a Special Duties role. It had of course been built for short landings in small fields and its simple fixed undercarriage consisted of an inverted 'V' shaped steel beam, which was immensely strong and able to withstand hard landings on rough ground. Though the pilot's forward view was obscured by the engine, its high wing monoplane design gave him a perfect downwards view on both sides, which was precisely what was needed to pick out a tiny landing ground at night. The Lysander also had a series of slats on each wing, these

---

1   Motto of 161 (Special Duties) Squadron RAF. This squadron was equipped with Lysanders and Lockheed Hudsons and flew missions into occupied Europe from 1940–1945.

A Lysander TT Mark III, T1444 'G-5', of No. 5 Air Observers School based at Jurby, Isle of Man, in flight off the Manx coast. (Crown Copyright – Air Historical Branch)

rose automatically as the flying speed decreased to stalling speed and meant that the aircraft could make very slow and steep descents.

A number of modifications were made to the Lysander, to make it more suitable for its Special Duties role. Firstly, the air gunner's gun-mount and other fittings were removed from behind the pilot and a fixed ladder was bolted to the rear of the cockpit on the port side. This was to let the agents, or 'Joes' to use the collective nickname given to them by the RAF special duties crews, enter and exit the aircraft easily. The Lysander's original 98-gallon petrol tank was also supplemented by the addition of a large 150-gallon torpedo shaped tank slung underneath the aircraft, which gave the Lysander an impressive extended range out to southern France. The Special Duties aircraft were initially painted entirely in matt-black, but it was found that this actually made the aircraft easier to detect by night fighters when it was flying over low cloud, so the paint scheme was modified to have camouflage on its upper surfaces.[2]

One of the most important aspects of the Special Duties Lysander operations in occupied Europe, was that the rough strips for the landings were not selected by a pilot or airmen who understood aviation, but by an agent or other member of the resistance. This entailed a much greater risk for the pilot, though it was partially solved by courses held in England to familiarise the agents with the requirements of a Lysander strip. These included practical exercises in the countryside, where the agents were taught how to judge wind direction without a wind sock and how to site a landing strip into wind. The agents were also taught how to set out and mark a landing strip, using a simple L-shaped flarepath that consisted of just three lamps yet was enough to guide an aircraft's approach to the landing ground. The flarepath's layout consisted of a lamp placed near the agent and the waiting passengers (Lamp A), a second placed 150 metres into wind (Lamp B) and a final one which was 50 metres to the right of that (Lamp C). The agents were instructed that the flare-path needed to start no less than 100 metres from the downwind hedge on to a clear, level and firm strip of ground that should be at least 600 metres long hedge-to-hedge. No trees were allowed in the funnel approaching the strip, from either end, unless their height was below a given angle. The strip should be free of any obstacles (i.e. badly sunken cart tracks, or farm machinery) and the grass should not be too long. Crop stubble was fine, so long as the ground was firm, indeed the hazards of soft mud were typically one of the greatest concerns for the Lysander pilots and this was made very clear to the agents. Those marking the landing ground were also taught to ensure that the torches used were tied to sticks so they pointed downwind and slightly upward.

As the Lysander approached the landing site, the agent at Lamp A would signal the aircraft with an agreed letter in morse and the pilot would acknowledge this by replying with a different pre-arranged letter. Once that was received the ground party would switch Lamps B and C on. When the Lysander had successfully landed, it would taxi up to Lamp A and the passengers would disembark using the ladder. The last passenger passing the luggage out and picking up the bags of those returning to England, before they exited the aircraft themselves. When the new passengers were aboard and the cockpit roof was slid shut, the agent in charge would give a thumbs up and the aircraft would take off and depart. If all went well this entire operation could be completed in under three minutes.[3]

A Lysander Special Duties sortie was flown by just a single pilot, who had a great deal to think about if his mission was to run smoothly. The first notice he would receive of an up-coming operation would be on a completed Air Transport Form, approved by AI 2(c) – a special section of Air Intelligence in the Air Ministry. If it was typed in black, it was from SOE and if it was in mauve, it was from MI6. This form contained the field agent's description of the landing strip, the map reference from the local Michelin map sheet, the dates and times the agent would be waiting and the number of passengers to be flown out and brought back. The pilot would immediately begin to prepare for the mission by selecting and adapting the right maps, cutting sections of 1:500,000 maps so that the flight path, as well as 50 miles on either side, could be followed more easily. He would then fold this map into panels so that he could easily hold the map in one hand, study two panels simultaneously and grip the control column at the same time. For the final stages a 1:250,000 map was used as it provided more detail around the landing strip. All the various maps were folded small, so that they could be stuffed down the side of the pilot's flying boot when they were not needed.

The pilot would then study the briefing folders with care, these included air photographs and positions of any flak defences, which he would spend hours trying to memorise. His final tasks would include preparing his 'gen' card, which contained critical information such as radio beacon codes and the morse letter the agent would signal from the landing ground, as well as the pilot's own response. The pilot would also make sure he had written important navigational data on to the gen card, though he could only confirm these details once the latest meteorological information, including windspeeds, was received shortly before his actual take off.[4]

If the meteorological forecast was satisfactory the operations room at Tempsford would inform the 'firm', usually SOE, but sometimes MI6, that the mission was on. These agencies would then arrange for that evening's BBC French news programme to end with a list of coded 'personal messages', which confirmed to the agent in France that the pick-up or drop-off would take place. Nonetheless, despite positive forecasts the problems of fog or cloud occurring over the target, particularly in winter, meant that in many cases aircraft simply could not see the ground at all,

3   Hugh Verity, *We Landed by Moonlight*, p. 17.
4   Hugh Verity, *We Landed by Moonlight*, p. 22.

let alone an agent flashing an Aldis lamp and the mission would have to be aborted at the last moment. It was frequently a frustrating business for both the pilot and the agents on the ground.

Shortly before the flight began, the agent would be brought to Tangmere or Tempsford by an escorting officer and after a nervous pre-mission supper the 'Joe' would be shown into the back of the Lysander cockpit, where they would sit facing the tail, their luggage stowed under the seat or on the hinged wooden shelf in front of them. They would be fitted into their parachute harness, shown how to clip the observer-type parachute onto their chest and plugged into the intercom. A fuller description of the pilot's duties during a mission is included in Annex A. In the passage below Wing Commander Hugh Verity describes his second operational sortie to Loyettes, east of Lyon. This was a long journey which involved crossing the French coast at Cabourg and trying to avoid the flak concentrations at Le Havre and Caen. Once he was past the French coast Verity reduced height from 8,000 feet to 2,000 feet, which gave him a more detailed view of the surrounding countryside. As his mission progressed Verity ran into cloud over Normandy which began to ice up the leading edges of his wings, so he descended a little into the warmer air, but still above the safe height of any high ground in the vicinity. Verity continues with his account of the mission:

My first fix was near Chateaudun. By the time I approached the River Saone it was quite comfortable below the cloud and there was enough light to see rivers.

I was intending to fix my position North of Lyons and South of Villefranche. When I was sure I was looking at the Saone, but not at all sure which part of it, I kept my head down studying the map for a few seconds too long. I looked up and found I was flying straight at a huge wireless mast one of several in a group. I pulled round to the right in a savage bank and just missed it. The heavy 'g' loading as I pulled the stick back must have increased our apparent weight two or three times – very distressing for my two passengers who could not have been expecting it. I was badly frightened by this near miss and the sudden charge of adrenalin in my blood left me trembling.

I collected myself and figured out the lie of the river below me and found the place on my map. I flew along the river to the point where the track line on my map crossed it and then set off again towards my target. The lights of Lyons showed up very clearly. My field was now easy to find, lying as it did just between the rivers Rhone and Ain. And there was the agent's torch flashing the right letter in steady morse. I flashed my own letter on the signalling key and saw the three other lights switched on. Their inverted 'L' shape looked so familiar – exactly as if I was circling around Somersham on a training course.

I flew parallel with the long leg of the 'L' noting the heading on my direction gyro. I turned through 180 degrees on to the down-wind leg at about 500 feet above the ground, throttled back to reduce speed to 100 mph and wound the tail trim back. I checked that the mixture control was in normal and the pitch control pushed in for fine pitch. I had a good look at the field and its approaches. There were no trees to bother about.

Then about 400 feet above the field, I started a gentle descending turn to port through 180 degrees to straighten out over the hedge at about 70 mph with my slats out, my flaps down and just a little throttle open; then straight down on to the ground after the minimum of flattening out and float, cutting the throttle. I put the brakes on, gently at first, as the Lysander was bumping along a bit. When the second lamp was passing my port wing, about 150 yards from my touch down point, I was trundling along slowly enough to do a sharp U-turn to starboard, inside the third lamp, and taxi back to the reception committee at the first lamp. Meanwhile I did my cockpit drill to be ready for take-off. As I drew up with my port wing tip over the reception committee after another U-turn, I had my right hand on my Luger 9mm automatic in its holster on the port cockpit coaming just behind and above the throttles.

F/o BRIDGER   SIR ARCHIBALD   W/cdr PICARD   W/c BATCHELL
              SINCLAIR        G/cno SIR L.GREG

On 21 April 1943, the Secretary of State for Air, the Rt Hon Sir Archibald Sinclair, paid a visit to the secretive home of the Special Operations Executive, RAF Tempsford. Here, the Air Secretary is pictured with personnel of 161 Squadron – from left to right: Flight Lieutenant Bridger, Sir Archibald Sinclair, Wing Commander P. C. 'Percy' Pickard, Group Captain Sir Lewis Greig and Wing Commander Batchelor. Note the 150 gallon torpedo shaped tank under the Lysander's fuselage. (Crown Copyright – Air Historical Branch)

When I saw the little group clearly I put the safety catch back on, waved to them, shouted my best wishes to the passengers and slid my roof open. The agent in charge jumped on the port undercarriage housing and shook me by the hand with a welcoming smile. His hair was caught by the slip-stream as my propeller continued to turn. He asked me if I was Flying Officer Lockhart [Another pilot in 161 Squadron].

After about four minutes the luggage and the passengers had changed over, the agent shouted 'OK' and with friendly waves I was off. The time was 0014 hours. Really it had been very easy, my first landing in occupied France. The field was good; the flare path and whole reception drill were perfect… I landed at Tangmere after eight hours and twenty minutes flying time since I had left it, tired but very happy. I had broken my personal duck and brought the total of pick-up operations for the war up to about 28. We gave my three passengers breakfast, heard their hair-raising stories, which I cannot now remember, packed them off with their escorting officer and FANY [First Aid Nursing Yeomanry] driver and went to bed.[5]

As the war progressed and the resistance in occupied Europe grew in size, so too did the frequency of RAF Special Duties operations and the scale of the air transport supporting them. This was very apparent in France, where Lockheed Hudson aircraft were occasionally employed.

The Hudson's larger passenger carrying capacity was frequently useful, though it needed a much longer field to land and take off from than the Lysander and the size of the aircraft could also attract undue attention. Late in 1942, SOE officer Peter Churchill found himself amongst a large

---

5    Hugh Verity, *We Landed by Moonlight*, pp. 28-30.

group of people who had travelled, some by car, to see a Hudson land. He records the crowd arriving in the 'usual gay, carefree, noisy style of a charabanc load of football supporters returning after the victory of their side in the cup final.'[6] The British unsurprisingly discouraged such enthusiasm and interest, making it very clear to the agents that their role included ensuring that security and discipline were maintained at the landing ground. This was spelled out in an instruction from SOE to its agents at the time:

> You are in charge of a military operation. Whatever the rank or importance of your passengers they must be under your orders.
>
> There must be no family parties on the field. If the pilot sees a crowd he may not land. Ensure that at the moment of landing you and your passengers and NOBODY ELSE are on the left of light A. and your assistant on the left of Light B. Anybody anywhere else, especially anybody approaching the aircraft from the right, is liable to be shot by the pilot.[7]

As the war progressed the size of the Special Duties air fleet grew to support more and more operations. As late as August 1941, there had been only five Special Duties aircraft based in England, but by November of the following year that number had increased to 27 and by the spring of 1944 at least 37 aircraft were being regularly used.[8] These included the occasional Dakota to support the SAS and Jedburgh[9] operations established in France prior to the D-Day landings. Air drops of supplies to the Resistance, usually by bombers, had been common from the early stages of the war. These were not easy missions as the bomber would have to slow almost to stalling speed in order to drop its supplies. Despite these difficulties the aircraft casualties were normally kept at a low level, mainly because DZs were carefully selected to be far from known flak positions and the German night-fighters were concentrated further north, against the large bomber streams heading across the North Sea to German cities. Navigation was usually the greatest challenge for these supply drops as the official history relates:

> The difficulties of navigation were especially acute for the SD crew, the success of whose work necessitated pin point accuracy on a small, often ill-defined target after hours of flying across enemy country. The navigation, both on the journey and on the approach to the target, must obviously be of a very high order. Reception Committees were instructed to choose sites for their dropping grounds which could easily be seen from the air; but for many reasons this was often not possible for them, and the aircraft, after having found its target area, might have to search for some time before discovering lights half hidden by a wood, or obscured in a valley… the navigator nearly always had to rely on map-reading and Dead Reckoning and in order to enable him to do this, the pilot would take his aircraft across enemy-occupied Europe at a low altitude.[10]

Improvements in communications between the agents on the ground and the aircraft in the air began to help in the coordination of the drops. The S-phone, a micro-wave wireless set, was a great advantage and enabled clear two-way conversations between the agent and aircraft at ranges up

---

6    M.R.D. Foot, *SOE in France* (Abingdon: Frank Cass Publishers, 1966), p. 86.
7    M.R.D. Foot, *SOE in France*, pp. 87-8.
8    M.R.D. Foot, *SOE in France*, p. 72.
9    A Jedburgh team was a special forces unit that typically consisted of three men, (two officers and a wireless operator). Their mission was to contact local resistance forces and conduct sabotage attacks on the Germans.
10   M.R.D. Foot, *SOE in France*, p. 81.

A Handley Page Halifax Mark II of 148 (Special Duties) Squadron RAF dropping parachute canisters of supplies to partisans in Yugoslavia. (Crown Copyright – Air Historical Branch)

to fifty miles. So clear was the transmission that on occasions the security of an agent network, or circuit, could be verified by flying across the relevant MI6/SOE case officer, who could confirm that the voice he heard over the S-phone was that of the actual agent they purported to be. The S-phone transmissions were sometimes connected in to the aircraft's intercom. This occasionally had unexpected results as on the occasion when an aircraft was flying near Bordeaux, hunting for a DZ set up by the 'David' network. One of the aircrew cried out that he had seen the lights and 'bloody awful they were too'. The reply from the previously silent reception party on the ground was swift, 'So would yours be, if the Gestapo were only a mile away from you!'[11]

It is estimated that the Special Duties aircraft made 217 successful landings in France, the majority of which were by Lysanders (180) and Hudsons (36) delivering 443 passengers to France and bringing 635 back.[12] The majority of passengers were agents, though important politicians and occasionally family of resistance members and agents were also extracted. Annexes B and C give further details of personnel and supplies delivered to France including typical container loads and packages dropped.

Resistance activity was a constant irritation to the German forces in France throughout the occupation. In the run up to the invasion of Normandy the sabotage activity conducted by SOE supported forces markedly increased and made a worthwhile contribution to the disruption of German communications and occasionally even troop movements. Noble though these efforts undoubtedly were, they paled into insignificance when compared to the scale and impact the resistance in Yugoslavia presented the Germans.

---

11   M.R.D. Foot, *SOE in France*, p. 80.
12   Hugh Verity, *We Landed by Moonlight*, p. 191.

Yugoslavia was a poor and mountainous country at the beginning of the Second World War, with very limited lines of communication and only a few major cities. On 6 April 1941 the Germans invaded Yugoslavia, quickly defeating its regular army and overrunning the country. Despite this overwhelming Axis victory an internal resistance slowly emerged in Yugoslavia based on two distinct groups. First, the royalist nationalist Serbs (known as *Chetniks*) who operated in Serbia and eastern Yugoslavia under General Draja Mihailovich. Second, the Communist Partisans who were based in central Bosnia and Croatia under Josip Broz – better known as 'Tito'. These two resistance movements began to grow in strength, mainly as a reaction to the increasingly brutal Axis occupation of the country, which included German and Italian soldiers, as well as the *Ustasha* Croatian Fascists under the puppet government of General Nedich.[13]

Initially, there was little the Allies could do to directly support these growing resistance movements, primarily because they did not possess sufficient transport aircraft with the necessary range to reach Yugoslavia. However, in May 1942 four modified Liberator bombers were issued to 108 Squadron in Egypt. Largely crewed by New Zealanders these aircraft began to fly supplies to Yugoslavia, though the cargoes dropped were small and not enough to make an appreciable difference. A further increase to this fleet was made in March 1943, when the RAF established 148 Squadron in Libya and provided it with fourteen Halifax bombers. The modifications needed to turn both types of bomber aircraft into long range Special Duties transports were extensive. The Liberators, for instance, had to have their bomb bays altered and special supply containers built so that up to 18 containers, weighing between 250 to 320 pounds, could be dropped from the internal bomb racks. Both the front turret and ball turret under the aircraft were removed, to provide improved visibility for the bombardier and an additional hatch was created in the airframe, to make it easier to drop bundles and agents. As the Germans were known to operate a small number of night fighters in the skies over Yugoslavia, flame dampers were also fitted to the aircraft, interior lighting reduced and the planes painted a dull black.

The flight profiles of these single aircraft sorties were highly unconventional for large bombers. The missions often required them to fly as slowly as 125 miles an hour, navigating between windy mountain passes to make drops as low as 500 feet. Just as in France, the demands of dead reckoning navigation together with the challenges of identifying DZs, meant that trips were normally only ever made during periods of full moon or immediately either side.[14] This gave sufficient light for the bomb aimer to direct the aircraft in its final run in to the DZ and choose when to drop the supplies, the rear gunner would then observe whether they had been on target or not. In addition to dropping supplies the aircraft would also dispense propaganda leaflets, as part of a wider attempt to persuade the Yugoslavs to join the resistance. Basil Davidson was one of the first British agents to be dropped into Yugoslavia. He had been trained in Egypt by SOE and describes the experience of meeting up with one of the original four Liberators for the long flight to Yugoslavia. Like many of the British agents bound for the Balkans, Davidson had turned up with colleagues on previous occasions only to find the original aircraft pronounced 'U/S' (unserviceable) at the last moment. This was predictably frustrating, though in the vivid account below, Davidson describes the nervous atmosphere when it finally all came together:

> But every now and then all four propellers would turn at once, and W for Willy, or one of his mates, X, Y, and Z, would be pronounced 'on.' And then it was with a different emotion that we stood on the warm sand in the glare of the desert, beneath the enamel sky and a sun

---

13   See Map 1 for details of territory liberated by Partisans in 1943.

14   Monro Macloskey, *Secret Air Missions: Counterinsurgency Operations in Southern Europe* (New York: Richard Rosen Press, Inc, 1966), p. 29.

blazing like incandescent brass, and listened to the terrific roar of Willy's four engines being warmed-up. The man who was going, who had shared the Middle East with us for so long that we had almost forgotten its discomfort, would come out of the dresser's tent—a tiny affair two feet high—in all the fussy paraphernalia of operational jumping, wonderfully trans-formed. The padded strip tease and the windproof Sidcot that were regulation wear against the cold of high altitude flying in an unheated fuselage would be stuffed with his revolver and his bag of gold, his maps and flashlight, compass, odds and ends. He was unbearably hot and very angry about some tedious detail; his Sidcot didn't fit, someone had given him the wrong ammunition, he was absolutely convinced that the essential wireless transmitter hadn't been packed in the load to be dropped with him. God knows what they hadn't done with his stores. In that time and place he filled the whole world and was the centre of the universe.

And there was something right and proper about this; we felt towards him as towards a man who was voyaging to another planet, a man we might perhaps be seeing for the last time, a man whose voice henceforth (if we heard it at all) would be ciphered into code and sent to us in morse. At the back of all our minds was the unanswered question: 'What will it be like?' and we fussed over him and soothed him rather as if we were helping him into the next world. His destination would be anything up to twelve hundred miles away, but for us it might have been a million. We leant against the rushing mighty wind of Willy's engines, and tried to make ourselves heard. The air would be heavy with the sour-sweet smell of aero-petrol. The man who was going would be cheerfully certain that the flight would be a flop, that even if he got there and found the fires—this might be his third or fourth or fifth attempt to find them—and dropped, it would then turn out that all the important things had been forgot-ten in the load, or they would drop him in the wrong place, or they would get there and the signals fail to come up, or anything might happen; but by this time the heat and the clothing and the tension of having to say goodbye had brought him to such a pitch of desperation that he wanted nothing better than to be gone.

Once in the plane and off the ground, with Willy's engines evened down to a level hum of efficiency, his thoughts would clear and he would stop being angry. Hours would pass; and over the sea the night would fall and Willy would be blacked-out, a noise in the sky and nothing more. Then it was that he would begin to feel the nearness of the unseen Continent, its enmity and strangeness as it lay there beyond the night; and this feeling would become a quick thrill of triumph when he sighted the coast of Greece, stark and clearly cut far down below him, the rising moon giving edge to wildly rising mountains and lying milky across the sea. He would lie in the glass nose of the navigator's cockpit and discover how Corfu came out of the sea in combed mountains that were covered with dark silver rocks, a watery gleaming on ragged crumpled cloth. Tiny waves would turn silver in the moonlight like gently moving lips. Willy's four engines would never falter; the pilot in the cockpit seemed made of stone…

Further up the coast, with the mountains still gleaming like watery silver cloth, cut deep here and there with appalling shadows, W for Willy would bank gently inwards, leaving the sea behind. The man who was going would work his way back to the fuselage; the queasy moments before dropping were almost here. The despatcher would fit on parachutes and try to look cheerful; a bottle of rum would go from mouth to mouth; tongues would be drier even than before.

Came the moment to link-up static lines, and the agonizing wait on the edge of the hole while W for Willy circled round and round looking for the signals, and then the moment when the signals were sighted, improbable points of red light flickering and flaring in the darkness below, and then the preliminary run in, and then the run in to drop the Mark 'C' containers that held the stores, and then another run and then another; and then, with the despatcher's voice hoarse in your ear you would watch for the red light and when the red light

British soldiers and Yugoslav partisans transferring parachute containers and bundles of supplies from a lorry to Handley Page Halifax Mark II of 148 (Special Duties) Squadron RAF at Brindisi, Italy. (Crown Copyright – Air Historical Branch)

came on you would watch for the green light, measuring the sickening seconds, and then your heart would leap up into your mouth and you would go pelting downwards into the darkness.

And as you went your whole being and existence would echo one central question: 'What will it be like?'[15]

In 1943, SOE agent Captain Frederick Deakin, together with Captain Stuart Nicholson, were both parachuted into Yugoslavia to form the first British Military Mission to Tito's headquarters. Deakin describes the difficulties in getting into Yugoslavia and the experience of dropping into the country for the first time:

According to plan, our Halifax bomber took off the next evening on our plotted course northwards over the Mediterranean. Weather reports had been favourable. As we crossed high over the frontier between Greece and Yugoslavia we could see, looking down from the bomb bay, the lights of enemy transport columns moving on the roads, but our plane ran into electric storms which tossed us in a swinging violent course away from our flight path, over Salonika to the Aegean.

The members of the mission had no oxygen masks, and as the bomber was forced higher by the weather, each of us lapsed imperceptibly into unconsciousness – unaware that we were being driven to abandon the attempt to reach our rendezvous. At dawn, we recovered

15   Basil Davidson, *Partisan Picture* (Bedford: Bedford Books Ltd, 1946), p. 9.

abruptly. The plane was flying low over the Mediterranean, all guns pointing upwards, speeding away from the German fighter base at Heraklion on Crete, and braced for an enemy air attack which never came. After nine hours in the air, we landed, without further incident, at Derna.

Prisoners of the weather, we spent the next hours in our tents on the rim of the airfield, aware of the tenseness of the watching patrols with the unlit signal fires at the point of our destination.

The air crew received their new briefing. On the early evening of 27 May we again boarded the same aircraft. In the darkness, as the Halifax rose steadily in its northward flight, we sank back among our bundles and equipment into the hum of the engines, which cut us off from the desultory and disconnected small talk which springs up in such moments, into a wordless and noisy isolation. Our second trip through the night hours passed without incident.

We had already adjusted our harness and equipment when a gap through the clouds and the darkness below revealed a cross of fires – the prearranged signal on the ground. Our watches showed that it was just three o'clock in the morning.

The engines of the bomber glided into a quieter note as the pilot turned, throttling back for his run over the fires. He flashed the green light over the exit from the aircraft, and with the sharp downward cut of the dispatcher's hand, we dropped into space.

The whiteness of a parachute was floating level with me, a short distance away. It was Stuart, and we shouted greetings. The night was so thick that we could not distinguish the outline of the ground below. Only bright flashes of gunfire lit the pervading gloom.

There was a strong wind. Our party had dropped out about two thousand feet above the loftiest and wildest part of Montenegro, we were drifting rapidly down, away from the fires which were cut abruptly from our view by the formation of the hills. A wind current in the mountains took me upwards again. Then, falling rapidly, in complete blackness, I shut my eyes, pressed my legs tightly together, and relaxed, waiting. I hit the ground, gave a gasp, and rolled over in astonishment.

It was too dark to see where I was, or where the others had landed. A few moments of whistling brought the whole party together, each of us filled with surprise that no one had received a scratch. We signalled our position with torches and the aircraft overhead turned in a wide sweep to make its second run to drop our stores. Flashing us a friendly signal, the pilot turned away, heading back towards Africa. There was no sign of the fires and no sound.

Leaving the rest of the party grouped round the heaped parachutes, I set off in a direction in which we agreed the fires must lie, marching with a truculent air and holding a revolver in front of me. In a few moments I collided with a soft human object which emitted a sharp cry in Serbian. I replied suitably that I was a British officer. The figure embraced me with energy, and I could dimly see a tall youth in a worn greyish uniform. He was one of the Yugoslav patrols which had moved out from the fires to look for us. As I led him back the short distance to the spot where our party was waiting, he fired his rifle in the air. Within seconds there were sounds of scrambling feet behind me on the grass. My companions had heard the shot and feared the worst.

It was growing light. We found that we had dropped into a narrow upland meadow, less than a hundred yards broad, and bounded on either side by rocks and clusters of fir trees. We were now surrounded by a small group of young men, all shouting at once. Each was equipped and armed in a highly individual manner, some in a greyish uniform, others in worn civilian clothes of every variety. As we gathered our belongings and started to walk off, a burst of dialogues and questions started up simultaneously. Why hadn't we come before? Where had we come from? How old were we? What were our military ranks? All this and more tumbled out of the straggling knot of youths scampering along beside us, eager and excited at this novel form of meeting.[16]

Initially the Allies provided supplies in equal measure to both the *Chetniks* and Communist Partisans. However, in September 1943 Brigadier Fitzroy Maclean and a small liaison team were dropped in to Yugoslavia, Maclean based himself at Tito's headquarters near Drvar and quickly ascertained that it was Tito's Communist Partisans who were providing the most effective resistance to the German forces. Consequently, he recommended to Churchill, to whom he reported directly, that the Allies should focus support on the Partisans at the expense of the Royalist *Chetniks*. MacClean highlighted to the Prime Minister that this decision was not without important long-term consequences, for if he was victorious Tito would inevitably establish Communist rule and probably align his country more closely to the Soviet Union. Churchill was pragmatic and blunt in his reply:

> 'Do you intend,' he asked, 'to make Yugoslavia your home after the war?'
> 'No, sir,' I replied.
> 'Neither do I,' he said. 'And that being so, the less you and I worry about the form of government they set up the better. That's for them to decide. What interests us is, which of them is doing the most harm to the Germans?'[17]

By 1943, the operations to support Yugoslav partisans fitted neatly in to the Allies' strategy of fixing as many German Divisions as possible in the Mediterranean, thereby preventing them from bolstering their defences on the Atlantic Wall. It was especially advantageous that this could be achieved using primarily Yugoslav rather than British or American manpower and the attraction of encouraging and supporting the Communist Partisans grew. The Allied invasion of Italy in September 1943 also meant that providing such support was geographically a much more practical proposition. This was partly because the possession of airfields in southern Italy now meant that air supply could be arranged using shorter range aircraft like the Dakota. Furthermore, daylight supply operations were now also possible as many of the drop zones and landing grounds were within range of Allied single-engine fighter aircraft, who could escort the supply aircraft on their missions. The Allies could also provide air support in the form of ground attack, though this entailed careful planning with the Partisans.

On 3 June 1943, a surprise German attack on Tito's Headquarters on Drvar, necessitated the quick evacuation of both Maclean and Tito to Italy. Tito was installed in a villa at Bari and plans were formulated with Air Marshal Slessor (the Commander-in-Chief RAF Mediterranean and Middle East) on how the Allies could further assist the Partisan campaign. Tito requested three things. First, that German control of the skies above Yugoslavia was countered, second, that the provision of supplies and strike operations in support of the Partisans was stepped up and finally, that arrangements were made for the evacuation of his wounded, who he estimated at 7,000-8,000 personnel.[18] The Allies began to execute this last task immediately, evacuating a total of 11,000 partisans to hospitals in Italy over the next month.

In due course Slessor was able to inform Tito that the Chiefs of Staff had not only agreed to increase Allied support to the Partisans but had also approved the establishment of the Balkan Air Force under Air Vice Marshal William Elliott. This force was composed of many contributing

---

16   F.W.D. Deakin, *Embattled Mountain* (London: Oxford University Press, 1971), p. 3.

17   Fitzroy Maclean, *Eastern Approaches* (London: Jonathan Cape, 1949), pp. 402-3.

18   Hilary St George Saunders, *The Royal Air Force 1939-45, Volume 3* (London: HMSO, 1954), p. 238.

A Bristol Beaufighter TF Mark X of 16 Squadron SAAF, releases its rocket projectiles at an enemy target in the town of Zuzemberk, Yugoslavia. (Crown Copyright – Air Historical Branch)

nations, including elements from British, South African, Italian, Greek, Yugoslav, American and Polish air forces. Even more unusually there was also a Russian Air Group under Elliott, operating twelve Dakotas and twelve Yak fighters. The Balkan Air Force operated ten different aircraft types ranging from fighters, bombers, light aircraft to transport aircraft. Slessor had been adamant that there should be a single coordinating authority for operations in the Balkans, consequently Elliott was not just responsible for the air support to Tito's land campaign, but also coordinated the Allied naval operations, under Flag Officer Taranto and Liaison Italy (FOTALI), and land elements under Land Forces Adriatic. In discharging his responsibilities Elliott maintained the closest contact with Maclean (who also remained Churchill's personal representative), as well as Tito himself, who moved back to the island of Vis in due course.

The Balkan Air Force assisted Tito's operations by conducting significant attacks on German communications, including the Zagreb-Belgrade-Skopje railway line which ran through Yugoslavia to Greece, as well as the subsidiary Brod-Sarajevo-Mostar route. In the first month of these air operations the Balkan Air Force claimed a total of 262 Locomotives destroyed, of which about a third were believed to be transporting troops.[19] The Balkan Air Force expanded throughout 1943 until it comprised four fighter wings, a bomber wing and the Allied 334th Special Operations Wing which moved to Brindisi in January 1944. The 334th Special Operations Wing was also a multi-national air force, including Italian aircraft. Its units and aircraft are shown in Figure 1 below:

| Unit | Aircraft Type |
| --- | --- |
| 148 Squadron | Modified Halifax Bombers |
| 1586 Flight (Polish Air Force) | Modified Halifax and Liberator Bombers |
| 62 Troop Carrier Group USAAF | C-47 Dakotas |
| 1 Sqn Italian Air Force | CZ 1007 |
| 88 Sqn Italian Air Force | SM 82 Cargo aircraft |

Figure 1   334th Special Operations Wing.

Initially the parachute supply drops made by the Allies were executed in a very similar manner to those in France. The agents would select the DZs and signal to the aircraft overhead, usually using torches that flashed the letter of the day in Morse. However, the allies steadily increased the number of their liaison teams operating in the country and many of these teams came equipped with S-phones and the new Mark 1 Electronic homing beacons known as 'Rebecca-Eureka'. The Rebecca-Eureka radio beacon was a particularly useful device for supply dropping and came in two parts. The first part, the Eureka, would be established on the DZ/LZ, where it quietly sat emitting no signal until the approaching aircraft interrogated it with a transmission from the Rebecca set it was carrying. The Eureka responded to this transmission by producing a signal that was converted into a green 'blip' on the Rebecca's screen, which gave the approaching aircraft a precise bearing and distance to the DZ/LZ. If more than one DZ/LZ needed to be used, then several Eurekas could be deployed, each of which could identify itself by a separate letter sent in morse code.

The Eureka sets had a range of 50 miles in open country and 30 miles in mountainous terrain and greatly assisted the Partisans and air forces in improving the accuracy of drops, especially in poor weather or darkness. Nevertheless, the resupply of Partisan forces often remained a frustrating

---

19   Hilary St George Saunders, *The Royal Air Force 1939-45, Volume 3*, p. 238.

experience as Basil Davidson related:

> We stayed in Racha for a month, the whole of February; and the weather was snow and rain and wretchedness. No parachute supplies had reached us for over two months, and there was little prospect of any until the spring. The few planeloads we might have had in February were denied us by the weather; and even when once or twice planes tried to reach us, we with the fires lit upon the ground could only hear the hum of their engines above the overcast, and they in the air could not see our fires. We would stand out in the snow for hours on end around a fire that Steve with inhuman skill had managed to kindle, lighting up at half-past ten and tramping back to bed at two, wet and shivering, angry, disappointed.

Parachute containers are dropped from a Consolidated Liberator of 34 Squadron SAAF, as part of Operation FLOTSAM – the major supply drop to Yugoslav partisans by RAF and SAAF units.
(Crown Copyright – Air Historical Branch)

> In the morning I would wireless: 'Planes heard over our fires zero one-thirty hours. Confirm.'
>
> And base would confirm, trying to be cheerful: 'Sorry, no fires seen.'
>
> Once or twice there were false alarms when we were not expecting aircraft; then we would run out across the mud and snow and shuffle with matches and a little petrol until the fires were going; but the plane would pass over or not be heard again, and Steve would say: 'I guess that's a jerry.' And Stanley would curse it; and I would explain to Slobodan that we had been mistaken. And Slobodan, that grey old man, would pick his teeth and shrug his shoulders, and try not to show his disappointment. Once I mistook Steve's snoring for the hum of aircraft engines, and we were all out in the mud, staring upwards and listening in the silence before I realised the mistake.

This was a poor state of affairs; but it reflected very well the great psychological difficulties of these long-range liaison operations. After much experience in the Balkans it was shown that men should not be allowed to remain inside for more than six months, because after that length of time they were necessarily out of the picture of possibilities at base; and in Italy, later, the period was reduced (as, given the short distances concerned and the relative ease of evacuation through the lines, it could be) to four months. Apart from that, and the obvious reduction of efficiency entailed when men inside were working to a false conception of resources available to support them, it was found that long periods of isolation tended to play upon the nerves and upset the sense of balance that was so essential to the work…

If it was difficult for 'Joes' to understand the lack or complete-absence of supplies, it was quite impossible for the partisans to do so… The weather was an obvious excuse, and often it was genuine; but it was hard to adduce the weather when the B.B.C. could report at the same time that great bomber formations were over some part or other of the Reich. They put it down to political hostility, and reassured themselves that the Russians would be different; and the Russians, luckily for them, were never called upon to show that this belief might be wrong. Slobodan, it was true, was an extreme case; if we had dropped him the moon he would still have looked sour and asked for the sun. The others at least tried to understand.[20]

One great innovation in Yugoslavian operations was the creation of the Balkan Air Terminal Service (BATS). Each BATS team, of which there were five, consisted of an airfield controller, a radio operator and a radio technician. BATS teams were equipped with Rebecca-Eureka homing beacons and established a total of 36 secret landing strips in Yugoslavia during their period of operation. These were critical in delivering supplies more efficiently to partisans and in helping to evacuate the wounded as well. Care of the wounded was always on one of the biggest problems for those conducting guerrilla warfare. Not only is there an obvious benefit to morale in making sure casualties have prompt medical treatment, but any casualties the Partisans sustained had to be protected and transported by soldiers which drastically reduced the amount of combat power available to them and hindered their mobility.

In mid-July 1944 the Germans launched an attack on the II Partisan Corps, who were operating in Montenegro. Despite putting up stiff resistance the Partisans were forced back to a line west of the Pljevla-Niksic Road sustaining 800 wounded in the process, which was increasingly restricting their ability to operate. Fortunately, the II Partisan Corps was accompanied by an Allied Military Mission, which brought in an RAF team on 11 August to begin siting and constructing a landing strip. Disappointingly, this soon came under shell-fire and had to be evacuated, a tough decision to take as it necessitated a four-day march to Brezna, with the 800 wounded Partisans being carried across mountains by their comrades. On arriving at Brezna two fields of corn were selected as the airfield and the crops quickly cleared by the Partisans. At 0900 on 23 August 1944 the first Dakotas of the American 60th Troop Carrier Command arrived to evacuate the casualties. This was followed later by Dakotas from 267 Squadron RAF and the Russian Air Group. In total 1,078 personnel were flown out from this strip including 1,059 partisans, 16 Allied aircrew and three members of the Allied Control Commission. Freed of its casualty burden, the II Partisan Corps was subsequently much better prepared to meet the next German onslaught.[21]

Such life-saving evacuations could not always be taken for granted. During the early years of the Balkans campaign, the Germans were still able to maintain some sort of air superiority over Yugoslavia and were occasionally able to attack and interdict Allied transport aircraft. When Frederick Deakin was due to be flown from Glamoc in Bosnia, he and the accompanying partisans were acutely aware of the German air threat and how vulnerable their aircraft, an old Yugoslavian Air Force Dornier, was while it was on the ground:

20   Basil Davidson, *Partisan Picture*, p. 186
21   Hilary St George Saunders, *The Royal Air Force 1939-45, Volume 3*, p. 239.

Dakota Mark III, FD857 'S', of 267 Squadron RAF based at Bari, Italy, flying along the Balkan coast line.
(Crown Copyright – Air Historical Branch)

The crew were instructed to fly the plane from its camouflaged hideout near Livno up to the air strip just before dawn on Saturday 27 November [1943]. We would travel by lorry an hour earlier and would be waiting for the aircraft to taxi towards us on the air strip, where a small Partisan escort were stationed and scouts posted in the surrounding hills. The pilot was ordered not to cut his engines, and we planned to take off almost immediately after he had touched down.

The group of us gathered, just before daylight, in the centre of the field. I had instructed Walter Wroughton to stand by his radio set in our cottage at Glamoc and to send off a signal as soon as we were airborne. The air strip was a flat path of grass which we had cleared according to specification, but as we had no means of marking adequately its limits, I stood somewhat apart from the others to mark the point of touchdown and to guide in the pilot. He flew in so low that I was obliged to fall flat on my face to avoid being run over, and then ran to join the waiting group which consisted of the party who were to fly to Italy and the other members of both missions. We walked briskly up to the Dornier, whose engines, according to our instructions, were still racing. At the last second, by some instinct, I looked over my shoulder, and saw two objects like small round footballs bouncing a few feet from us and a small German plane diving straight at us. As I flung myself to the ground there was an explosion and fragments flying in all directions. The only risk which we thought we had calculated had befallen us. The attacking Henschel caught us unprotected. We fanned out instinctively across the flat grass, hunted by the plane above us flying in narrowing circles a few feet above our heads and chasing each of us as a personal target while we sought in vain for cover on the vast billiard table of Glamoc field.

The Dornier blew up in a second low bombing run. The ammunition from its machine guns was exploding in aimless directions. One of the British officers was wearing, a sheepskin coat. I had a clear picture in my mind of him running near me as we ran from the burning Dornier seeking some cover from which we might make some kind of defence. There was none. Each man was forced to run in short bursts and fall flat as the Henschel skimmed the field shooting at each of us as an individual target. Exhausting its ammunition, the aircraft flew off over the boundary of the hills.

I found myself in a shallow hollow of ground at the edge of the field with three Yugoslavs. We had remained stuck to the earth as the German plane flew back and forth over our heads attempting to train the trajectory of its guns low enough to hit us. The pilot was only able to wound one of the Yugoslavs. Another, the liaison officer from the Corps Headquarters at Livno, had been lying on his back coolly photographing the scene. As I stood up there was no one in sight and no sound except the engines of the stricken aircraft which were speeding up as the fire reached the controls. For a brief moment there was the macabre spectacle of an empty plane moving slowly and directly towards us. After a few seconds the tail fell off and the debris collapsed in a cloud of smoke and flame.

My first instinct was to find Robin Whetherley, the British officer whom I had seen in my mind running beside me. I called and there was no answer. A search revealed no one except the group with whom I had found frail cover. The rest of our party seemed to have vanished. I walked very slowly and alone towards the aircraft with a sudden thought that I had dropped my brief-case, containing secret documents, at the moment of explosion of the first two bombs. Round the smashed Dornier was a circle of bodies. All had been killed instantaneously. The dead included Robin Whetherley, who had never moved. His running had been a hallucination in my mind. Such happenings were not uncommon in war. I had been standing next to him at the moment of the attack and on the other side of me was Velebit, who like myself was unharmed.[22]

Towards the end of the campaign in Yugoslavia, the risk to RAF aircraft over the skies of Yugoslavia was much diminished and landings in Yugoslavia were becoming almost common place. To have been extracted from the heat of operations in a remote part of Yugoslavia must have been a fantastic feeling. Basil Davidson, together with a number of wounded from another Partisan Brigade operating near Belgrade, was also withdrawn at this time and describes the experience:

The next night completed all our preparations. At about twelve o'clock the two aircraft came, circling high at first and then spiralling down as they recognised our signals.

There were two of them. They came in one after the other and lined up together at one end of our strip, looking huge and improbable although they were only twin-engined Dakotas. There was terrific excitement. The crews were R.A.F., casual in khaki shorts and open shirts, unmoved by the fact that the nearest enemy garrison was four miles away and Belgrade only twenty-five.

'I daresay you've got them taped,' the first pilot said, 'though I must say this doesn't look like my idea of partisan country.' Nothing seemed to worry these crews.

They were on the ground for more than an hour, until in the end I began to get nervous. The wounded were filing slowly into the aircraft, first the stretcher-cases, then those who could sit or lie down without help. At last they were all ready. Fifty-six wounded in both aircraft.

One Dakota got away. I said good-bye to everyone, and Djokay embraced me on behalf of the others. 'I'll be back in a fortnight.'

The door was slammed at last, tight. A few minutes later we were off the ground. It took us two hours to reach southern Italy.[23]

---

22    F.W.D. Deakin, *The Embattled Mountain*, pp. 251-2.
23    Basil Davidson, *Partisan Picture*, p. 317.

A medical team of 31 Mobile Field Hospital back their Ambulance up to the freight doors of a Douglas Dakota Mark III that has recently evacuated casualties from Yugoslavia. (Crown Copyright – Air Historical Branch)

The Balkan Air Force also fulfilled Tito's requests by providing fighters and fighter bombers that not only cleared German aircraft from the skies but could also be used in ground attacks. This had proved its worth from the earliest moments of British involvement in the campaign, when on 24 October 1943 Brigadier Maclean had used a radio on a Royal Navy Motor Launch off the Dalmatian coast to call in a series of air strikes on German troops marching down the Peljesac peninsula. The RAF arranged airstrikes by Kittyhawk fighter bombers over two successive days, which not only broke up the German attacks on land, but also destroyed several German coastal vessels that were trying to conduct an amphibious hook and cut off the Partisans line of retreat. This successful RAF intervention is estimated to have delayed the German advance by two weeks.[24]

The Balkan Air Force strikes against German troops became a regular feature of Allied operations in the Balkans and were increasingly arranged by the British Liaison Officers attached to the Partisan Corps. This trend increased further at the beginning of September 1944, when Rumania and Bulgaria decided to switch from the Axis to the Allied side and declared war on Germany. Additionally, the Russian Army had now reached Yugoslavia's borders with Hungary and Rumania, threatening to cut off the German forces in Greece, Albania and Yugoslavia (known as Army Group E) if they did not begin withdrawing to the north.

The Allies were determined that these German forces should be either prevented or delayed from retreating to Germany and Austria. Tito could have been forgiven if he had been tempted to stand aside and let the occupiers flee from his country as quickly as possible, yet he understood the wider operational picture and cooperated with Operation RATWEEK and its aim to interdict the German's line of retreat (this codename was selected for no other reason than it was the next one on the list – nonetheless it carried connotations of rats leaving sinking ships which obviously appealed to those involved). RATWEEK worked on the basis that the Partisans and the Allied

Military Missions would conduct reconnaissance of the main German withdrawal route. This was primarily the railway line that ran Skopje-Belgrade-Subotica-Zagreb, though other subsidiary lines of communication were also included. The reconnaissance operations identified bridges, railway points, junctions and tunnels – or any other choke point which could be destroyed, blocked or even defended by Partisans. The softer targets would be destroyed by Partisans and the heavier ones by aircraft of the Balkan Air Force, reinforced by heavy bombers from the United States Army Air Force. On occasions the Partisans would also put in place blocking positions along the German withdrawal route, which would need to be attacked and cleared by either Germans, *Chetniks* (who had now switched sides) or the *Ustasha*. When the Germans tried to repair the damage done to railway lines or bridges, the Partisans would radio the working party's location to the Balkan Air Force, who would then strike at those trying to restore the lines of communication. Through these means the evacuation of German Army Group E back to the north was made very difficult indeed.[25]

By October 1944, the Russians had captured Belgrade and joined forces with the Partisans in pursuing the Germans north, the Balkan Air Force continued to harry them on their way. While the lion's share of the credit for the Yugoslav campaign lies with Tito and his partisans, the Balkan Air Force had nevertheless proved to be a massive force multiplier. Throughout the war it had delivered 16,500 tons of supplies to the Partisans, evacuated 19,000 of their personnel[26] and conducted numerous strikes against German forces. This support helped Tito's forces tie down an estimated 600,000 Axis troops in the Balkans, which was a considerable contribution to the Allied war effort and one that came at a decisive point in the conflict. The Allied relationship with Tito was always a tricky one and cooperation noticeably cooled towards the very end of the war, as the tensions between communist and democratic countries became more important. This was an ideological clash that was not altogether without warning. Indeed by 1944, Stalin had already shown how ruthless he could be against any resistance movement that might challenge the hegemony the Soviet Union wished to establish in eastern Europe after the War. This was most evident in his attitude to the pro-democracy resistance movement in Poland, known as the Polish Home Army.

It was as early as 1941 that the Polish Home Army had first asked for equipment to be dropped to them by air. As a response a small number of Polish bomber crews were converted onto the Halifax aircraft and began to fly sorties from Newmarket as part of 138 Special Duties Squadron. The distance from the base in England to the Polish DZs was far – to reach Pomerania was an 800 mile flight and it was 1,000 miles to get to Warsaw. Given that the Halifax, even when fitted with extra fuel tanks, only had a range of 2,175 miles this left little margin for error, or for overcoming any difficulties in finding the DZ. In addition, the extra fuel tanks needed reduced the Halifax's cargo load from 4,200lbs to just 2,400lbs. Unsurprisingly, the casualties to the Polish crews on these missions were comparatively high, partly because of the distances, but also because of the increasingly strong German night fighter defences on this northerly route. By 1943 it was judged that support to Poland might be better achieved by flying from the recently captured bases in Brindisi. Consequently, the Polish detachment of 138 Squadron was deployed to Italy in December 1943 and soon began operations under its new name – 1586 Special Duty Flight. Squadron Leader E Arciuszkiewicz was a navigator on one of the Halifaxes and recalls the special satisfaction many Polish Air Force aircrew felt in supporting their compatriots:

25   Michael McConville, *A Small War in the Balkans*, pp. 270-3.
26   Warren G Harris, *Special Operations: AAF Aid to European Resistance Movements, 1943-1945*, (AAF Historical Office, HQ Army Air Forces, 1947), p. 100.

An oblique aerial photograph showing buildings in the medieval castle at Banja Luka, Yugoslavia, burning from an attack with rocket projectiles by Bristol Beaufighters of 16 and 19 Squadrons SAAF. German troops had established a stronghold in the castle. (Crown Copyright – Air Historical Branch)

Three-inch rocket projectiles heading for railway trucks and tankers during an attack by Bristol Beaufighters of 19 Squadron SAAF on German rail traffic at Banova Jaruga, Yugoslavia. (Crown Copyright – Air Historical Branch)

We cross the Yugoslav coast near Dubrovnik. It is still quite light. The enemy's fighter airfields are not far away, so we are keeping careful watch. No Messerschmitts seen. We are at 10,000 feet. The oxygen is turned on. It is warm and cosy here in the cabin.

The mountains are fantastically grand, even from above: peaks, ridges, precipices and rugged rocky spurs jutting over abysses. We are passing one of the largest groups of peaks; I can see hundreds of twinkling ruddy lights around it – they are the camp fires of Yugoslav resistance forces. Rather lower, on the slopes, are the fires of patrols guarding this mountain stronghold.

It is a bright, moonlit night. Visibility is excellent. We are getting too near Sava – must have drifted a bit off our course. The grey winding ribbon of the Danube can be seen. There is the double bend with its island and just over to starboard, not yet visible, is Vienna's great Fun Fair.

I have now to set course for the Tatras. The old astrologer had nothing on me. A voyage in the third dimension with a sextant! Like travelling in the fourth dimension with an hour glass. No oxygen for me as I squat under the pilot's seat – very uncomfortable and undignified. I was glad to get back to my desk at last. A good swig of oxygen and a well-earned rest: applied 'astrology' is no child's play.

The grey plain ripples up into foothills as it breaks against the Low Tatras, and behind them the snow-clad peaks of the High Tatras rise up against the dark sky.

Our own mountains! And how beautiful they look! We're flying over Cichego Valley. There's Morskie Oko Lake, the lights of Zakopane – they disappear in a blackout. We have dropped to 5,000 feet. Just crossed the Vistula, 2,000 feet. The engines are droning along very quietly. The other boys are probably as deep in their thoughts and memories as I am… How pleasant it would be to knock at that door and be greeted by Polish voices! How surprised they would be! Why can't we fly lower and just glance into a Polish home?

We're approaching the Pilica. A big forest with a clearing in the middle is the reception point, some three miles from the river. The 'committee' have answered our signal and are lighting the five flares of the cross which marks the exact spot and gives the direction of the wind.

We made our first 'dropping' perfectly and then lost sight of the reception point – we had dropped to 200 feet as we circuited and the trees hid it. We picked it up again and dropped the rest of the containers. As we flew away the 'V' sign was flashed up in Morse.

About five or six miles away, two villages suddenly burst into flames. It was no accidental outburst, spreading from a cottage. German reprisals. We had no time to look on and, in any case, could do nothing to help. Yet it seemed wrong to fly back to Italy: not to help the "committee' with the supplies, not to fight with them against a possible German attack, not to help those poor villagers.

We are passing over the Tatras again. We were in Poland – over Poland, 200 feet, say 60 yards away from her soil. So very near. I wonder if anyone I know heard our plane, or saw it. We're getting near Budapest. Searchlights have flashed up, looking for somebody about 15 miles to the east, and the flak is peppering away there for all it is worth.[27]

Supply drops to the Polish Home Army continued throughout 1944, but as the Soviet Army approached the capital the resistance forces in the city revolted against the German occupying forces. The battle which lasted 63 days was probably the largest single military effort undertaken by a resistance force in the Second World War. During the battle, widely known as the Warsaw

---

27   Polish Air Force, *Destiny is Waiting* (London: Heinemann, 1949), p. 219.

A Consolidated Liberator of 205 Group flies between cloud layers, during a supply dropping mission to Partisan forces in Yugoslavia. (Crown Copyright – Air Historical Branch)

Uprising, the Soviet Union paused their operations against the Germans in the area in what was a blatant attempt by Stalin to ensure an independent Polish government was quashed. The Germans used the Soviet pause to slowly crush the revolt, during which it is estimated about 16,000 members of the Polish resistance were killed and between 150,000 and 200,000 Polish civilians died, mostly from mass executions. The only external help that could be given during the Warsaw Uprising was through the air, consequently 306 Allied aircraft flew supply sorties to that city from bases in England and the Mediterranean – the bulk of the effort being delivered by 205 Group from their Italian bases. As in the previous account, the aircraft would take off from Brindisi in the evening and fly over the Adriatic, crossing the Croatian coast as the sun set and reaching the Danube in darkness. They would then climb over the Carpathian Mountains, before approaching Warsaw from the east, over Soviet-held territory. The return leg was spent mostly over Germany and Austria and the last portion of the mission typically involved flying over occupied northern Italy in daylight. These aircraft encountered many hazards during their sorties, including German night fighters (particularly those operating from a base near Cracow) and Soviet anti-aircraft guns, which would frequently open fire on them. The long journey home across the alps was a particularly perilous one for damaged aircraft struggling to maintain height.

The missions to Warsaw were undertaken by Halifaxes and Liberators from three Wings within 205 Group, including one belonging to the South African Air Force. Alan McIntosh recalls the instructions given for the first mission:

> In the forenoon of 13 August, 205 Group air crews were told that a maximum effort was to be flown against an unknown target that night. 2,300 gallons of fuel were to be taken on by each aircraft and we would be topped up for extreme range at Brindisi where the operational briefing would take place. Normally the fuel load for a target in northern Austria used around 1,800 gallons.

The target only became known at Brindisi, when, on entering the briefing room, the aircrews sighted a wall covered with international modified polyconic maps, extending from floor to ceiling. A red line extended from Brindisi at the bottom to Warsaw at the top. A sobering revelation for those about to go out into the night.

The briefing officer was Lieutenant George Z. His briefing was a model; compelling, honest accurate, comprehensive, in a situation in which the aircrews needed to know the political, military and tactical situation of the Polish Home Army in Warsaw; The German Army in Warsaw and the Red Army sitting on its hands across the Vistula at Praga.

For accuracy a low-level drop was essential; height not above 500 feet, speed not above 150 m.p.h. Target maps and photographs were available. Three alignment points (Mokotov in the south, the Old City in the centre, and the Citadel in the north) were given. Take-off time for 178 Squadron was 19:45; estimated time on target 01:30. The twilight was critical for returning aircraft, which would have little chance of survival in daylight over enemy territory extending from Albania to the Baltic sea.

At the start of the operation in support of the Warsaw uprising, RAF aircrews were issued with blood chits. They were silk with a Union Jack on the obverse and something along the lines of 'This chap is a British Officer return him in good shape and in working order and you will be rewarded' – on the reverse side, the same in Russian. Since for the Warsaw operations we were briefed to give nothing other than number, rank, name, if we fell into Russian hands (the same as if captured by the Germans) the blood chits were ominous rather than comforting. After difficult, protracted high-level negotiations, the Russians agreed to allow a free passage route over Russian-held territory; for specifically agreed missions.

Warsaw was burning: not in the manner of fire storms which British and Polish Bomber Command aircrews remember, but as a great city in which a land battle to destruction was going on. Approaching at low altitude in the darkness, it was as if the city was covered in an inverted fish-bowl, inside which the night was a dull red. Individual fires and gun flashes showed up as bright red sparks; flak streamed across the area or burst above the dome amidst the coning searchlight. Inside the red dome, aircraft were seen in silhouette against the fiery city as they made their low-level dropping run.

That night, 13/14 August, over Warsaw, my crew sighted a four-engined aircraft lower than our own, silhouetted against the fires of the city. It was in a nose-down attitude as if coming in to land, very low, and engaged in a gun battle with a German light flak battery and a nearby searchlight. It could only be one of the Halifax aircraft of 1586 (Polish) Special Duties Flight flown from Brindisi five and a half hours earlier. Almost certainly the aircraft had already dropped its load of arms and ammunition and its crew was now joining the land battle while they still had something left to give. Such was the spirit of the Polish aviators who flew in support of the Warsaw uprising.

On my crew's last sortie to Warsaw (night of 10/11 September 1944) we were engaged by Russian AA fire and Russian night fighters along much of the two-and-a-half-hour route. Disenchanted by this, our South African pilots and Australian navigator, at about 12,000 feet and outside gun-range from Lublin, rapidly decided that if we survived the drop on Warsaw and were fated to be shot down on the way home, it would be by the enemy and not by our Russian 'friends'. On climbing away from Warsaw, therefore we followed the direct route through enemy territory, rather than putting our Russian blood chits to the test. Some crews of our force were not so lucky.

With the benefit of hindsight, one wonders what our masters knew (and how much they chose to tell) about our Russian allies.[28]

---

28   Norman Davies, *Rising 44 – The Battle for Warsaw* (London: Viking, 2004), p. 312.

The crew of a Consolidated Liberator B-24 Mark VI of 178 Squadron RAF which took part in the operations to resupply the Polish Home Army during the Warsaw Uprising. (Crown Copyright – Air Historical Branch)

As Alan Mcintosh relates above the 334th Special Operations Wing were also operating in support of the drops. This included the two squadrons of Halifaxes as well as 1586 (Polish) Special Duties Flight which was now equipped with a mixture of Halifaxes and Liberators. The Polish aircrews in this Flight were undoubtedly determined to do the best they could for their fellow countrymen as Flight Lieutenant Chmiel recalls:

> We had been ordered to carry out the sortie regardless of weather conditions. So, though the met. forecast was exceptionally despondent, we took off… Sure enough, right from the Yugoslav coast fog stretched from the ground to 6,000 feet. Fog was hardly the word for it – water vapour or steam would be more appropriate. We had no ground-based navigational aid; I tried map-reading…but we finally flew on solely with star 'fixes'.
>
> We had similar weather all the way until over Poland we saw a Jerry fighter shoot down one of our Halifaxes. (There had been a lot of flak over Yugoslavia and the Danube). We pushed on and got a decent 'fix' by the time we reached the Pilitsa River. After that we flew on guided by the distant glow…
>
> We dropped to some 700 feet, got through a very dense barrage over the Vistula. Fires were blazing in every district of Warsaw. The dark spots were places occupied by the Jerries. Everything was smothered in smoke through which ruddy-orange flames flickered. It was terrible and must have been hell for everybody down there.
>
> The German flak was the hottest I have ever been through, so we got down to just 70 or 100 feet…the flicks [searchlights] in the Praga and Mokotov suburbs kept us constantly lit up – there was nothing we could do about it. We nearly hit the Poniatovski Bridge as we cracked along the Vistula: the pilot hopped over it by the skin of his teeth.
>
> Our reception point was Krashinski Square. So, when we passed the [Kerbeds] iron-girder bridge, we turned sharp to port and made ready for the run in. The whole southern side of

the square was blazing and wind was blowing the smoke south, much to our satisfaction. We dropped the containers and knew we had made a good job.

It was time to clear out. The pilot came down still lower, keeping an eye for steeples and high buildings. The cabin was full of smoke, which got into our eyes and made them smart. We could feel the heat... We ripped along the railway line leading west. Some flak from an anti-aircraft train tried to hit us, so we let go some bursts. We had a breathing space until flicks near Bohnia picked us up again, and the flak got uncomfortably close. We passed over the crashed bomber in the foothills, which was now burning itself out. (Five Halifaxes that had taken off with us never returned). The Home Army people signalled that a supply was received on Krashinski Square at the time we noted in our logbooks. So we knew that at least our flight had not been in vain.[29]

After a heroic and gallant defence, the Polish Home Army finally surrendered on 2 October 1944, a moment which was particularly upsetting for the Polish aircrew of the Special Duties Flight. Flight Lieutenant Glebocki later recalled the reaction of his crew when they were told the city had fallen:

As we were climbing out of our bombers one day after an op, an aircraftman came up and told me. Stanley was just behind me. He's what you'd call a Warsaw cockney with all a cockney's affection for his city. He stopped short and dumped his 'chute on the ground. He just stood there, turning his head from side to side helplessly... He shuffled off without a word.

Later, he came up to me in the Ops Room as I was studying the maps. His eyes were sunken and lifeless. 'Sir, what's the use?' he asked in a hoarse, unfamiliar voice. 'What's the use, sir?' He pressed his face against the [window] and looked out through the panes where the drops of mist were trickling down like tears.[30]

The supplies which the RAF dropped to the Poles were significant. The commander of the Polish Home Army acknowledging receipt of 250 PIAT anti-tank weapons, 1,000 Sten guns, 19,000 grenades and 2 million rounds of ammunition over the course of the battle. The air losses were nevertheless stark and the sacrifices of the Polish Special Duties Flight and the RAF squadrons in supporting the Warsaw Uprising were particularly punishing. An estimated 360 airmen and 41 aircraft were lost out of 306 aircraft dispatched (two American, seventeen Polish, and twenty-two RAF and South African Air Force aircraft in total). To put it another way, the RAF and SAAF effectively lost one aircraft for every ton of supplies delivered[31] and during the Polish Air Force's entire wartime service no other unit sustained casualties at as high a rate as the Polish Special Duties unit that summer. The Polish C-in-C awarded the Polish Special Duties squadron involved the title 'Defenders of Warsaw' and a number of Polish gallantry awards were also bestowed upon both Polish as well as British crews.[32] Perhaps most poignantly, in 1992, following the overthrow of Communism and the final emergence of freedom in Poland, the new Polish government took the step of awarding 67 former members of 31 and 34 Squadrons of the SAAF the 'Polish Warsaw Cross of the Uprising' for their role in these operations.[33] Clearly the Polish had not forgotten the effort that was made.

29    Polish Air Force, *Destiny Can Wait*, p. 222.
30    Polish Air Force, *Destiny Can Wait*, p. 221.
31    Max Hastings, *Armageddon: The Battle for Germany 1944-1945* (London: Pan MacMillan, 2004), pp. 118 and 120.
32    Polish Air Force, *Destiny Can Wait*, p. 226.
33    South African Air Force Museum <https://saafmuseum.org.za/398/> accessed 3 March 2019.

In contrast to Europe, clandestine flying operations in the Far East had a comparatively slow build-up and it was not until late 1944 that a Special Duties squadron (357 Squadron) was formed. This squadron was established to support Force 136 sabotage operations, as well as the intelligence activities of the Indian MI6 equivalent, known as the Inter-Services Liaison Detachment (ISLD). The squadron's operations took them not just to Burma but as far afield as Thailand, Malaya and French Indo-China, consequently a fleet of Liberators and Dakotas were provided to the squadron to cover these long ranges and supplement the dependable Lysander. The size of some of these aircraft, as well as the nature of the terrain and jungle itself, meant that dropping agents or supplies by parachute was the most common type of mission.

A Special Duties pilot's challenges in operating in the Far East were immense. The aircraft would have to fly through the notoriously bad Burmese weather, successfully climb over the Chin Hills and hope that there was no mist over the DZ itself. Arrangements at the DZs were also haphazard. Force 136 had a much looser grip on their teams compared to the SOE in Europe and frequently aircraft would arrive over sites devoid of any sign of fire, or human beings. At other times the lights were so faint (five candle ends in jam tins on one occasion) that the pilots reportedly needed 'the eye sight of an owl'. The squadron also had to tolerate and navigate through the huge bureaucratic squabbles and rivalries that existed between the intelligence agencies and Allies. The ISLD were notoriously prickly about sharing an aircraft with Force 136, or any other agency. Even more dramatically the Americans, for political reasons emanating from Washington DC, were loath to support the French in Indo-China. This American political direction was slavishly followed by the American Commander in China, General Wedemeyer, which was particularly disappointing as it denied the British use of the American bases in China to support French resistance in Indo-China. The American approach damaged their wider reputation and incidents where French wounded were refused evacuation caused much bitterness. On one occasion a downed American air crew were brought to the airfield at Dien Bien Phu. They had been taken there by a French party who, at great risk, had sheltered and protected them from the Japanese. The pilot of the American aircraft that was brought in to evacuate the Americans stubbornly refused to allow any wounded French on board, arguing that he had precise and specific orders not to do so, even ignoring the angry protests of the Americans he had been brought in to evacuate.[34]

The terrain in South East Asia itself made operations difficult. Not least for the parachutist who might drift into the jungle and become snagged in the tree canopy – suspended 60 feet above the ground in their harness. This was a dangerous hazard as many trees in Burma, including the common Teak tree, had long smooth trunks for much of their bottom half and no branches an agent could use to climb down. The agent therefore faced a dilemma of either jumping and almost inevitably breaking a leg, or slowly starving to death. After a while, it became standard practise for agents to carry a 60-foot length of rope, with which they could let themselves down on if they were caught in the tree tops.

The Dakotas and Liberators used for these Special Duty missions complemented each other well. Dakotas were good at getting close to the ground and ideal for dropping supplies or agents into DZs tucked into a narrow valley. The Dakota usually made several passes on such occasions, as the agents always preferred an accurate drop from multiple passes rather than receive a scattered load from a single pass. The Liberator struggled to get into such narrow DZs, but was able to drop compact loads on flat DZs without any nearby hazards, or alternatively drop the agents (unusually through a slide in its belly) in one pass and the containers on a second.[35] Terence O'Brien describes

34   Terence O'Brien, *The Moonlight War* (London: Collins, 1987), p. 312.
35   Terence O'Brien, *The Moonlight War*, pp. 66-7.

MONGOOSE WHITE.
Arrival of Lysander at DZ BOLO-AUK.
Note heavy surrounding country and
bamboo matting to give support surface.

MONGOOSE WHITE.
Arrival of Lysander on BOLU-AUK DZ with
carriers (in undress!.)

Arrival of a Special Duties Lysander at DZ Bolo-Auk in Burma. (The National Archives)

a typical Dakota drop, in this instance the aircraft he was flying had also been fitted with racks to allow it to drop containers:

Without needing to adjust our course we picked out the Mandalay bend that gave a check, then we flew on over the Shan Hills until at last the Salween river gave us the final checkpoint. A few moments later, when we began the descent on course for the site, the T of fires suddenly appeared ahead like five tangerines in precise position down there on the dark slope; they looked like solid fixtures from a distance, like marker buoys on a shipping channel, but as the swirls of smoke indicated they, were in reality raging, twisting bonfires. We slanted down, down and down until the dark mass of the jungle had separated into individual trees, then we levelled out and flew through fleeting wraiths of smoke on the check run over the site. A pleasant scent of burning wood pervaded the aircraft. I gave a flick of the navigation lights. From near the top central fire a torch flashed back at us. LONG….SHORT…LONG. The letter K. We were on target.

The DZ was in a valley. On the test run, when I was lining up the dark yew-green slope of the mountain on the port side to find a checkpoint. I could see the stars go flickering through the palisade of trees lining the ridge. A check on the radio altimeter tallied roughly with both the aneroid ASL reading and visual estimate of 600 feet above the lively fires. I stroked back the trim wheel so that slight forward pressure on the control column was needed to keep us level, then when the fire at the head of the T had passed underneath the wing I eased back the pressure so as to clear the trees on the ridge, and started the 180 degree turn.

By this time the despatcher had taken out the inset door. Only one package was to go out on the first run, a marker, and it would by then be set up near the open doorway, with the despatcher himself clipped on to his safety line. The navigator returned to confirm all was set to go, then switched on the stand-by light at my call. The faint red haze of its reflection appeared in the cockpit window.

I edged the throttles back and the aircraft sank smoothly down into the valley. Shadow gashed hills began to rise up each side of us, the airspeed indicator died away to 90 knots. Down below there were figures waving, witches worshipping amid the sacrificial fires, again that scent of wood smoke. Then just when the centre-top fire was blurred by the port propeller, I called for the drop.

'Green – go,' the navigator repeated.

I saw the movement of his arm, for at that moment I had to glance to the right to pick up a ridge feature as a checkpoint for the next run. There was an easy one – directly over the shimmering prop blade was a tree with a flattened crown that slanted almost parallel with the Milky Way. It was caught in a snapshot, processed and fixed in mind in the time it takes to flick a glance aside, then I flicked another glance down at the ridge ahead.

'Red – stop. Red – stop,' I called.

He repeated the order as his arm jerked. I pushed the throttles forward and again eased pressure on the stick to allow the aircraft to clear the trees, but this time not so smoothly, for at such slow speed she juddered slightly at the beginning of the climb. Once the airspeed had reached 130 knots in steady climb I tightened the turn, and then quickly straightened out, so low over the ridge that you could pick out individual trees, one of them pallid in blossom. We managed to see the landing and collapse of the marker parachute.

Wide to the right, slight overshoot.

After that it was simple. The next run-in adjusted for width, green light switched on just a little before the prop blade reached the tree with the flattened top, and the system worked. All five parachutes landed within the DZ. The containers could have gone out also but I wanted to get the feel of their departure so kept them for a separate run.

Special Duties Dakota dropping rice at an SOE DZ near Shegwyin, Burma. (The National Archives)

That was a satisfying performance. When the navigator flipped the switch you could not only feel a definite jerk-lift of the aircraft, but there was also a dull 'chunk' sound accompanying it. We noted only three parachutes falling, and assumed one had candled; the failure rate for supply parachutes was one in twenty, and most of the contents could be salvaged anyway, so this was mainly a matter for record and not undue distress. So fairly content with our night's work, we climbed away on course westwards across the Burmese plain for India.

We were flying left-wing low – lateral balance must have altered slightly with the departure of the containers – so I leaned down to adjust the aileron trim-wheel until she was flying hands off again. Once that was settled the aircraft moved through the calm night as smoothly as a boat on a flat, smooth lake…

The airfield at Jessore was particularly susceptible to ground mist in the winter. It was a devilish phenomena, for the mist would settle fifteen to twenty feet above the ground, perfectly flat pearly sheets of it, so that you could stand on the balcony of the control tower and see a glittering display of stars, then go downstairs and find yourself in clammy greyness. When a patch of ground mist was directly over the runway, you had to be extremely watchful not to be deceived into accepting it as the concrete surface and stall-land on to it – nearly twenty feet above the ground. The trick was to look over towards the control tower and gauge your height from that, instead of the false surface in front of the aircraft.

There was the mist that night on our return from Hainton. A sheet of it was set above the runway, just about touchdown point, so I was looking left towards the tower as we slanted through it, easing back the control column as I felt towards the stall.

We hit with a thump. She had dropped in the stall instead of levelling out, even though we still had airspeed in hand. The reason for this became apparent in an instant. There was a loud bang, a shimmering flash lit up the mist, and the control column jerked in my hands as if from a nearby shell-burst. A metallic clatter was briefly audible through the popping of the exhaust stubs and I thought at first there had been an explosion in the port engine. But there was no damage visible as we ran clear of the mist between the orange lights of the flare path. It was only when we came to a stop and turned to taxi down the strip that we saw the explanation of the clatter, and of that mysteriously unaltered petrol consumption.

A black container was lying on the moonlit runway amid a tangle of parachute shroud lines and canopy. There had been a hang-up. That explained the wing-dip that had necessitated the unusual adjustment of the lateral trim. It was also the reason for the early stall on landing, the crunching consequence of which had been to jolt the 250-lb container crashing into the concrete runway. It gave off a shower of sparks, bounced heavily and hit the tailplane so that the control column had jerked in my hands, then hurtled forward to finish up wrapped in a confused tangle with the lines and canopy of its parachute.[36]

Whether in Europe or the Far East, the overall scale of all of these Special Duties operations is minute in comparison to the numbers of sorties generated by Bomber, Coastal or Fighter command. Yet they were in their own way very important, for they established a reliable physical link to the irregular forces in occupied countries. In some places, particularly Yugoslavia, these resistance organisations were much more than just a mild irritant to the enemy and served a wider strategic purpose by tying down large numbers of enemy troops on internal security duties far from the Allied front lines. It is hard to imagine how those forces could have developed in the manner they did, had such a two-way air link not been available. Indeed, without the Special Duties flights maintaining contact with them, perhaps the spirit of resistance and freedom would never have survived the long years of occupation in some countries at all.[37]

36   Terence O'Brien, *The Moonlight War*, pp. 40-4.
37   Hugh Verity, *We Landed by Moonlight*, pp. 192.

# Part VI

# Air Support to the Land Campaign

# 5

# 'Swift into Destruction'[1]
# Air Support Matures in the Desert

There is a view in some quarters that the only nation to take air-ground operations seriously during the Second World War was Germany. This perception might be because the blitzkrieg campaigns of 1939–41 integrated *Luftwaffe* support into German Army operations in a way few western militaries were able to match at the time and this unprecedented development left a strong impression on many minds. The myth may also arise because historians typically treat air support to land campaigns in a cursory manner and usually concentrate on the actions undertaken by the soldiers. Furthermore, when the success and impact of Allied air support in the second half of the war is discussed, it is often only to highlight the huge increase in the quantity and quality of aircraft available to the Allies and rarely mentions the important developments made by the British in ground support techniques and tactics.[2]

Prior to the war, the RAF made little progress on air-ground support and any debates, or even initiatives to support Army operations, tended to be marginalised by the RAF doctrinal insistence that the bomber was the decisive weapon of war and would negate the need for costly land campaigns. Nevertheless, there were some modest inter-war air-ground operations conducted in Britain's imperial campaigns of the 1920s and 1930s. In Iraq, Palestine and India's troubled North-West Frontier, important experience of land operations was gained by future Air Marshals such as Coningham, Tedder and Slessor. Of equal importance, future army commanders, including Field Marshals Montgomery, Slim and Auchinleck were also exposed to the potential of air power. It is probably no coincidence that these individuals all significantly contributed to the development of air-ground operations when they held significant commands in the Western Desert, Europe and the Far East. This often included fostering a strong atmosphere of inter-service cooperation.

During the British operations against rebellious Pathan tribesmen on the North-West frontier, the RAF regularly provided direct air support to British and Indian Troops. In 1936 Slessor commanded No.3 (Indian) Wing and pioneered Vickers-Bombs-Lewis (VBL) attacks where RAF biplanes would dive on the enemy positions using Vickers forward machine guns to supress the target, drop their bombs and then use their rear-gunner's Lewis gun to continue engaging the Pathans with fire as they flew off. The RAF and Army not only concluded that these were highly effective tactics, but also noticed that VBL attacks worked best when there was the closest coordination between the two services, so that targets, orders and the location of friendly troops could be quickly shared.

These early operations also reinforced the concept that the air commander must remain independent of the Army, retaining centralised control of his air forces and concentrating their

---

1   Motto of 112 Squadron, this squadron flew Tomahawks and Kittyhawks as part of the Desert Air Force and pioneered fighter bomber support to land forces.

2   Brad William Gladman, *Intelligence and Anglo-American Air Support in World War Two* (New York: Palgrave Macmillan, 2009), p. 2.

efforts at the most decisive areas and moments of the battle.[3] Slessor, together with his imme-diate Army counterpart, captured some of the main lessons learnt in a report to both Army and Air Headquarters. The report included several conclusions that Slessor believed offered a strong pointer to subsequent developments in the war:

> We said for instance that the Air Force Commander cannot possibly influence effectively the action of his aircraft on the battlefield if he is fifty miles away at the end of a bad and congested road, which is closed to traffic in the hours of darkness… The Air Force commander should use foresight, think quickly and ahead, should be up forward where he can see for himself what is happening and make decisions quickly, and should always be prepared to act on his own initiative and without specific orders… To the popular claim that military command-ers were so highly trained that they could be trusted to use their aircraft properly without assistance we replied 'we think that when column commanders are prepared to dispense with an artillery commander and to make all their fire plans without an artillery adviser, it will be time to take that argument seriously.'
>
> We emphasised the overriding importance of adequate signal communications, both between air and ground and between Column Headquarters and the airfield; had some caustic things to say about the grossly uneconomical inefficiency of the then existing signals equipment…and strongly recommended the early provision of reliable, up-to-date W/T and R/T sets. We recommended the standardisation of a system whereby reconnaissance areas should be sub-divided into lettered zones bounded by easily identifiable features such as deep nullahs, and said that if aircraft were able to intervene immediately in an emergency they must be already in the air, capable of being called down by signal when required – a foretaste of the 'cab-rank' system of later years. We said we thought authority to call for close support should be vested in the force commander and very rarely delegated to his subordinates; and made various recommendations about the identification of the enemy's positions by coloured smoke shell and of our own troops by orange strips, on much the same lines as those which became commonplace in Hitler's war.[4]

Despite these admirable local initiatives on the fringes of the empire, the prevailing RAF concep-tual view remained that the main role of the RAF was strategic bombing and support to land campaigns was of secondary importance. Against a conventional European enemy, there was an absence of plans for the sort of cooperation evident on the North West Frontier and pre-war concepts of air-ground cooperation were limited. Even the resources devoted to the task were pitifully small – each Army division was allocated just one Army cooperation squadron with a further one held at corps level.[5] The roles of these cooperation squadrons were also limited to reconnaissance, transportation and communication duties and any idea of ground attack by these aircraft was actively discouraged, not least because the available aircraft, the slow and under-armed Lysander, was manifestly unsuited for such a task.

On his return to the UK Slessor challenged this orthodoxy on his return to the UK, writing a medal winning essay for the Royal United Services Institute in 1937 entitled *Air Power and Armies*. This was followed up by a book on the same subject, in which he articulated a future where the army and air force worked in a mutually supporting manner. In this scenario the role of the Army was to engage its opponent offensively, creating a situation where the enemy required an intensive

---

3    Brad William Gladman, *Intelligence and Anglo-American Air Support in World War Two*, p. 27 and pp. 37-8.
4    John Slessor, *The Central Blue* (London: Cassel, 1956), pp. 128-9.
5    See Annex D for further details of the RAF Command Organisation.

Three Fairey Battle Mark Is of 218 Squadron RAF, based at Auberives-sur-Suippes, in flight over northern France. (Crown Copyright – Air Historical Branch)

flow of reinforcements and supply. The air force in turn would provide defence against the opposing enemy air operations and 'attack the communications serving the adversary's army, to disorganise and delay the reserves coming in to support his forward troops, and to prevent traffic bringing up food, ammunition and the mass of other material essential to their continued resistance.'[6] Slessor's work was prescient, but academic essays are no substitute for properly resourced operational plans.

Between the wars, the British had been very wary of making any promises to send a large army to continental Europe, but the loss of Czechoslovakia (and its 35 divisions) led to staff talks with the French and the eventual British commitment on 21 April 1939 to provide an army of six regular and 26 Territorial divisions. Such a large force not only necessitated peacetime conscription for the first time in Britain's history, it also meant that the RAF would have to dramatically increase their Army cooperation capability. This was sadly too little, too late and RAF/Army cooperation was found to be hopelessly deficient once the war started.

The disastrous 1940 campaign in France hammered home three compelling points on air-ground support to the British. First, that the most important task of any air-land campaign was for the air force to achieve some measure of air superiority. Having forfeited this early in the campaign the RAF and French Air forces found they could not protect the Allied ground forces and the *Luftwaffe* was free to strike the retreating troops at will. Second, that the light bomber aircraft used by the British were not suited to tactical ground support operations. The Fairey Battle was simply too slow and easily shot out of the sky by either enemy aircraft or AA fire and even the supposedly modern Bristol Blenheim was sluggish, clumsy and unable to evade German fighters. Finally, it was evident that the Army/RAF command and control system was not fit for fast moving joint operations. If RAF strikes in support of a mobile land campaign were to be effective, then the frontline air commanders needed both timely intelligence on fleeting enemy targets, as well as accurate situational awareness on Allied ground force activity. Both the Army's and the

6    Brad William Gladman, *Intelligence and Anglo-American Air Support in World War Two*, p. 33.

RAF's command and control systems were simply too slow for this and did not provide an effective channel of communication between the services, the results were that opportunities were regularly and repeatedly missed.

This last command and control weakness stemmed partly from the RAF force in France being split into two separate parts. The first element consisted of a small number of squadrons allocated as an 'Air Component' to the British Expeditionary Force (BEF) and tasked to provide fighter and bomber support for them. The second formation was an 'Advanced Air Striking Force' that was formed to strike targets further removed from the battlefield. Both came under the command of the RAF, which theoretically allowed centralised control of air resources, but any request for air support had to be reviewed through a hierarchical chain of Army and RAF headquarters before any squadron was tasked. Given the poor state of Army and RAF signals equipment this was cumbersome at the best of times. Worse still, the system catastrophically broke down once the campaign began and the British Army became mobile, to the extent that RAF aircraft were simply unable to strike fleeting targets in sufficient time.

By 21 May 1940, only eleven days after the invasion, the RAF force in France had become even more fragmented, with some squadrons having withdrawn to English bases and a second element, which included the RAF's own headquarters, retreating further south into France. At this point the RAF headquarters was no longer in direct communications with the BEF and any army requests for air support in France had to be sent via the Air Ministry in London. The delay this had on requests was simply too long. As one example, on 20 May German armoured columns were reported to be approaching Arras at 1400 hours, but RAF Blenheim bombers failed to appear over the scene until four and a half hours later at 1830, by which time the Germans had advanced considerably. As there was no way for the Army to directly communicate with the bombers over-head and re-task them, the mission proved fruitless.[7] These were frustrating and disappointing times for both the Army and RAF and sour inter-service sentiments, exacerbated by the high levels of *Luftwaffe* attacks on British troops, increased. These discordant views inevitably coloured subsequent debates, but the debacle in France did at least force the RAF and Army to consider air support arrangements with energy and a fresh pair of eyes.

This situation prompted experiments in late 1940 (led by Group Captain Wann and Lieutenant Colonel Woodall) which produced two important innovations, that were subsequently endorsed by both the RAF and the Army. Firstly, the concept of a Tactical Air Force trained to support ground forces by achieving air superiority and striking ground targets on the battlefield, this Tactical Air Force would be specially equipped with aircraft designed for those roles. It was also recognised that a Tactical Air Force would have to possess the mobility needed to operate in the field alongside a manoeuvring Army and be prepared to advance and retreat as circumstances allowed. The Western Desert Air Force (October 1941) was the first of these Tactical Air Forces to be established, changing its name to the Desert Air Force on the invasion of Sicily in July 1943. It was followed by 2nd Tactical Air Force (June 1943) for the North West European Campaign, the 3rd Tactical Air Force (December 1943) for the Burma campaign and the Australian 1st Tactical Air Force (October 1944) for the South-West Pacific theatre. As the war progressed these forces were all increasingly equipped with larger numbers of high-quality aircraft, specially designed or modified for ground support.

The second key innovation was the establishment of a vastly improved communication system, which included light, mobile communication detachments able to operate with the Army's forward units. These detachments were known as 'Tentacles' and relayed tasks for air support via a direct communication channel, to a joint control centre known as the Army Air Support Centre

---

7    Ian Gooderson, *Air Power at the Battlefront* (London: Frank Cass, 1998), p. 203.

A low level attack by Fairey Battle aircraft on a German horse-drawn transport column, May– June 1940.
(Crown Copyright – Air Historical Branch)

(AASC). At this location RAF and Army officers could track requests, monitor the bomb-line and task squadrons against nominated targets. The squadrons would then receive the target details at their airfields or landing grounds through briefs by dedicated Army Liaison Officers, who would also update them on the wider context of the land battle and any supporting details for their missions.[8] This new system was continually developed and improved upon during the war, but its basic principles and architecture remained the core element of the RAF and Army's air support system and was copied by American forces upon their entry into the conflict. Though the Army and RAF had agreed on a system of air support for land campaigns, that did not imply there was unanimity on the way air support was provided. Agreeing the relative priorities and aims of the different types of air support available took further debate and it was some time before the two services were in full agreement.

Air forces deliver several different types of air support to a ground force. The principal one is to provide air superiority over the battlefield, as this allows the Army to manoeuvre and operate free from enemy air interference. As we have recorded in the first volume of this book achieving air superiority requires a combination of combatting the aircraft in the skies, as well as attacks on his airfields, early warning, and command and control systems. Unsurprisingly much of this activity is not observed by either ground commanders or their troops. At Dunkirk for instance, RAF fighters frequently engaged attacking *Luftwaffe* aircraft successfully, but this was rarely in sight of the Army and it went largely un-appreciated. Army commanders often attached disproportionate importance to RAF activity they could see over the battlefield and placed less weight on operations further removed, even though these might have a greater impact on the enemy ground and air forces. These instinctive Army preferences for direct, overhead cover, or 'air umbrellas', as

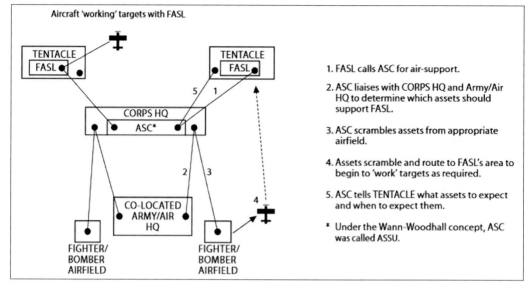

Figure 2  Tactical Air Control procedures developed by Group Captain Wann and Lieutenant Colonel Woodhall.

a means of providing air superiority were not unique to the British and plagued both the German and American forces too.

Not only was the method of achieving battlefield air superiority sometimes challenged by a ground force commander, but its overall primacy when compared to other forms of air operations was also subjected to debate. Intelligent commanders, such as Montgomery, quickly grasped the pre-eminence of achieving battlefield air superiority and educated their Army subordinates that: 'The winning of the air battle, and with it the achievement of a favourable air situation, is at one and the same time the primary task of the air forces, and the greatest contribution they can make to the land battle. It is in fact a pre-requisite to military success.'[9] It was probably in North Africa[10] that the correct prioritisation first began to be universally accepted, with all three service C-in-Cs in the Middle East stating that:

> The Italian (possibly supplemented by German) air forces are likely to constitute the greatest threat not only to Egypt itself but also the Naval base at Alexandria and in certain circumstances to the military forces, and, therefore their neutralization is to be regarded in principle of primary importance. On the other hand, direct support for the land and naval forces may from time to time and for limited periods have prior claim to our efforts.[11]

This may seem obvious in retrospect, but the Germans in the same campaign never sought to achieve or maintain air superiority with a similar level of determination. Had Rommel given such clear orders to his *Luftwaffe* commanders, then the campaign might well have tipped in his favour. For all his strengths as a ground commander, Rommel often ignored his *Luftwaffe* commanders,

---

9    B.L. Montgomery, *'Some notes on the use of air power in support of Land Operations'*, HQ British Army of the Rhine, October 1945. Accessed at Defence Concepts and Doctrine Centre Shrivenham.

10   See Annex E for the RAF's order of Battle in the Middle East.

11   The National Archives (TNA) WO 201/335, HQ RAF Middle East *'Royal Air Force Middle East Operational Plan'*, 14 Sep 1940.

failed to appreciate both the central importance of air power and air superiority during the North African campaign and was frequently culpable in dissipating his significant air strength, or simply taking it for granted. Once the British had begun to establish enduring air superiority in 1942, the consequences for Rommel's *Afrika Korps* were severe and the implications of what he had lost suddenly dawned on him. They would colour his judgements for the rest of the war:

> British Air Superiority threw to the winds all the tactical rules which…had hitherto applied with such success. There was no real answer to the enemy's air superiority, except a powerful air force of our own. In every battle to come, the strength of the Anglo-American Air Force was to be the deciding factor.[12]

Pilots and ground crew with P40 MkIIb Tomahawk of 3 Squadron.
(State Library of Victoria, Melbourne, Victoria, Australia)

The Germans lost air superiority in the desert not because of the quality of their aircraft many of which, such as the Me 109 G and F, surpassed that of the British, but through the inefficient way they employed them. This included standing patrols over *Afrika Korps* ground units, whose commanders suffered from the same tendency to prioritise and demand air cover they could see. In contrast, by late 1941 the British had developed a much more sophisticated understanding of how the British Army should be able to largely defend itself from air attack and free the RAF to achieve air superiority through offensive actions. Churchill's guidance to Tedder prior to Operation CRUSADER (December 1941) captures this well:

> Nevermore must the ground troops expect, as a matter of course, to be protected against the enemy air by aircraft. If this can be done it must only be as a happy makeweight and a piece of good luck. Above all, the idea of keeping standing patrols of aircraft over moving columns should be abandoned. It is unsound to distribute aircraft in this way, and no air superiority will stand any large application of such mischievous practice. Upon the military Commander-in-Chief in the Middle East announcing that a battle is in prospect, the Air Officer Commanding-in-Chief will give him all possible aid irrespective of other targets, however attractive. Victory in the battle makes amends for all, and creates new favourable

---

12   Rommel and Bayerlein, *Rommel Papers* (London: Collins, 1953), p. 284.

situations of a decisive character. As the interests of the two Cs-in-C are identical it is not thought any difficulty should arise. The AOCinC would naturally lay aside all routine programmes and concentrate on bombing the rearward services of the enemy in the preparatory period. This he would do not only by night, but by day attacks with fighter protection. In this process he will bring about a trial of strength with enemy fighters, and has the best chance of obtaining local command of the air. What is true of the preparatory period applies with even greater force during the battle.[13]

By the second half of the war Allied battlefield air superiority would become a largely persistent state of affairs. It permitted the Army not only to conduct tactical manoeuvres free of enemy air interference, but also allowed them to undertake important logistical and administrative actions in preparation for major ground offensives. The tactics and techniques for achieving air superiority over the battlefield are broadly like those already covered earlier in this book, though there are one or two extra considerations. These include the requirement for ground commanders to support the air force by capturing ground upon which airfields either exist or can be constructed. Without these arrangements the air force would not be able to deliver its functions across the battlefield and into the depth of enemy territory. Therefore, part of the ground commander's plan must include measures to ensure that the airfields are cleared and constructed, which often requires considerable Royal Engineer effort. Additionally, once constructed the airfield must be secured and defended by the Army from enemy ground interference. This is not just defence against swift advances by conventional forces, it also needs to consider raiding parties. The British Special Air Service administered a punishing lesson to the *Luftwaffe* on this latter point, when it destroyed 350 German aircraft on the ground between November 1941 and October 1942. It was not just machines that were wrecked, the SAS also inflicted casualties on many skilled *Luftwaffe* personnel, including pilots, and important equipment and stocks of fuel were frequently destroyed.[14] These British raids were executed at a decisive moment in the campaign and given the additional pressures on the *Luftwaffe's* supply and reinforcement situation, probably played an important part in helping air superiority pass from the Germans to the British.

The achievement of battlefield air superiority not only allowed the Army to operate with greater freedom, it also meant that the air force was better able to support land operations through attacks on enemy forces and other ground targets. Initially the RAF described ground support to the Army as being in either 'direct' or 'in-direct' support, but terminology developed throughout the war and eventually settled on three basic types of ground attack delivered in support of a land campaign. This included firstly 'close air support', which was against targets that were engaging or being engaged by forward British troops with the aim of improving the immediate tactical situation. Close air support needed to be as rapid as possible and was always at the Army's specific request. Secondly, 'general air support', these were operations against targets that were located immediately behind the battlefront. These attacks could be against mobile targets, such as transport supplying the front line, or static targets such as bridges, supply dumps or enemy headquarters.[15] 'Interdiction' was the third type of air support and usually took place some distance from the battlefield, it targeted communications, reinforcing enemy forces, supplies and transportation links. There is clearly a considerable grey area between general air support and interdiction, but the former is generally more tactical in nature and geographically closer to the battlefront.

---

13   TNA AIR 23/1395, Churchill quoted in letter Charles Portal to Arthur Tedder, 5 September 1941.
14   Robert Ehler, *The Mediterranean Air War* (Kansas: University Press of Kansas, 2015), p. 209.
15   TNA AIR 23/1826, Desert Air Force Paper, *The Employment of Fighter Bombers – Policy*, p. 5.

Enemy motor vehicles being abandoned by their drivers during an attack by Bristol Beaufighters of 252 Squadron RAF in the Western Desert. The picture is taken from the nose camera of one of the attacking aircraft. (Crown Copyright – Air Historical Branch)

Three Bristol Beaufighter Mark ICs of 272 Squadron RAF based at Idku, Egypt, flying in line abreast formation. (Crown Copyright – Air Historical Branch)

Close air support was in many ways the most challenging form of air support for the RAF to provide and certainly took the most coordination. To be effective close air support required a system that enabled troops to request strikes and for these to be processed and prioritised before being forwarded to the airfields, where aircraft could then be tasked and directed to the battlefront. Once the aircraft was over the battlefield the target had to be precisely identified for the pilot and the subsequent air strike properly integrated with the fire and movement of British forces. This entire process had to be conducted as quickly as possible if the strike was to have the best chance of being successful.

Close air support was also the most controversial element of air support the RAF gave to the Army. Even strong advocates of air-ground operations, like Slessor, felt that the business of destroying front line positions was both the preserve of the Army and a misuse of air power, which could be much better employed on either interdiction or general air support tasks.[16] These beliefs often rested on views developed in the First World War, where aerial weapons were often found to be ineffective against the strongly fortified German trenches. There was an additional belief that it was more appropriate and economical for the Army's own artillery to take on forward enemy targets. Furthermore, the experience of 2 Group's Blenheim and Battle light bombers in France, in 1940, had highlighted the high casualty rate enemy frontline AA artillery could inflict. On some occasions the losses in British aircraft was out of all proportion to any damage inflicted upon the enemy, though this latter factor could be reduced if the right type of aircraft and tactics were employed.[17] The campaign in the Western Desert proved a particularly useful testing ground for evolving such ideas, primarily because it was the only place where the British Army was consistently engaged in direct combat with its Axis counterparts. Many have commented more widely that it was in the Western Desert that the British Army learnt how to beat the Germans. An essential ingredient in that success was the integration of RAF support.[18]

For those RAF personnel who arrived in Egypt, after a journey that usually took them around the Cape, the Middle East must have made a profound initial impression. After disembarking at Port Suez and undergoing some form of administration in the Canal Zone, those joining the Desert Air Force would leave the startlingly green Nile valley and the fleshpots of Cairo, to begin a westwards journey into a vast desert, largely uninhabited except for a small number of Bedouin Arabs. Their transit to the battlefront would have been along the only metalled road in the Western Desert, which hugged the coast for its entire length from Alexandria to Tripoli (1,177 miles). Distances were vast in the Western Desert – even the journey to the small port of Tobruk was 410 miles. In this theatre of operations there was very little fertile country, just a few Italian colonial community farms mainly concentrated in the large hump of land to the east of the major port of Benghazi – known as the *Jebel Akdar*. The absence of any significant population, major city or industrial base meant that there were no major strategic targets for the RAF bombers. This avoided controversial arguments and meant the ports of Tobruk, Benghazi and Tripoli became major 'interdiction' targets almost by default and together with the German airfields these towns were the main operational focus for the RAF medium and heavy bomber efforts.

The Desert Air Force lived a nomadic life in the desert, there were no permanent stations, no tarmac runways, hangars, barracks or control towers. The desert landing grounds were simply flat stretches of the desert over which a grader might have been passed to flatten the camel thorn bushes. The aircraft themselves were normally dispersed around the edges of the landing grounds,

---

16   TNA AIR 20/2970, *Use of Bombers in Close Support of the Army* Memorandum by Air Vice Marshal Slessor 6 May 1941.

17   TNA AIR 20/2970, *Use of Bombers in Close Support of the Army* Memorandum by Group Captain Embry, A.V.M. Slessor 17 May 1941.

18   See Maps 2 and 3 for details of the Eastern Mediterranean and Western Desert including major airfields and fighter and bomber ranges.

Armourers of 89 Squadron RAF servicing the 20mm Hispano cannons of a Bristol Beaufighter Mark VIF at Castel Benito, Libya. (Crown Copyright – Air Historical Branch)

with a few protective RAF armoured cars to defend them. The operations rooms, messes and other administrative elements, were all housed in tents, with a handy V-shaped slit trench dug alongside each one as an air raid shelter. Everything else was kept mobile and on wheels, including signals trucks, the commanding officer's trailer and the mobile cookhouse.

The Desert Air Force made themselves as comfortable as they could in this unfamiliar environment, they typically wore a uniform of khaki shorts and shirts in summer and battledress in winter, the latter augmented by pullovers and jerseys as the desert nights were frequently cold. Torrential rains sometimes fell in winter and could frequently bog in an aircraft, or turn tracks into a morass of mud through which vehicles would slide and flounder. Despite the difficulties these rains presented, many airmen would probably agree that their chief torment was the *Khamsim*, a hot wind which frequently blew during the spring and usually with enough force to collapse tents and reduce visibility to that of a traditional London smog. In this half-darkness a driver would not be able to see the bonnet of his car and life quickly de-generated into a hot and gritty misery. Even when the *Khamsin* was not blowing, the dust and sand got everywhere and machines and engines obviously suffered, prompting mechanics to resort to measures such as stuffing socks down exhaust pipes or fitting pillowcases over the air inlets to try and reduce the damage to the aircraft. Australian Ian Rawlinson was a P-40 fighter pilot with 3 Squadron RAAF and describes his own personal experience of the Western Desert:

The coastal strip of the Western Desert, where all of the many campaigns were fought, was mainly firm, but with sandy patches in parts. The large sand dune areas were further to the south, away from the coast. The hard surfaces were dotted with low woody bush called camel thorn. The blowing sand gathers around these small bushes and gives them a lumpy character in the event of a forced landing. Airfields were easily established by just grading it. The summers were very hot and dry and the winters cold and dry. Winter rainfall resulted from cooler unstable sea air, but there was not a lot of it.

Drinking water was always short and heavily chlorinated. Ancient wells were salt impregnated and fouled by both sides as the desert battles ebbed and flowed over hundreds of miles. Hard rations were routine – bully beef, M&V (Meat and Veg), beans, bacon and tinned milk. Powdered eggs and the ubiquitous hard army biscuits. On rare occasions we had fresh meat. More strictly raw meat, not very fresh and of doubtful origin. I recall seeing fresh fruit twice...

During stationary periods our Messes were sometimes made of wood, but usually they were canvas marquees called E.P.I.P.s (English Patent Indian Pattern). Sometimes there was a concrete floor. We used trestle tables, folding chairs, camp stretchers and sleeping bags, enamel mugs and plates. For sleeping we had ridge poled tents, 2 or 3 per tent. Issue blankets – we bought the odd sheet. A small canvas basin on folding legs for washing, a larger one resting on the ground as a bath – if ever there was enough water or time. Salt water soap sometimes worked best.

A cup of water in the morning did for teeth, rudimentary face wash and cold shave... Once a week, fortnight, or possibly a month, depending on the water supply, a stand-up wash in the open with about a quart of water. Latrines were two or four holers or squat slits when on the move (or a shovel!). Fine powdered dust caked into one's clothes and head, as the flying environment was always hot and sweaty. A breeze raised dust. Aircraft operations or engine tests made things unpleasant. *Khamseens* or *Sirrocos* occurred now and then.

After a dust storm the aircraft flying controls were jammed solid. Pressure washing (pneumatic) was needed to clear them. Sometimes the aircraft were flown and turned upside down to shake out the dust. It was disconcerting to get a face full of dust in the middle of a dogfight.

Aircraft servicing, particularly guns, was a very difficult task for our groundcrew. They achieved wonders in those appalling conditions, and we were rarely let down.

Particularly on the move there were no lights after dark. We then ate from one kitchen, with rarely any tables or chairs. Sleeping bags on the ground, about 7 or 8 to a tent. We dug the tents in to about 18 inches as bombers were always roaming about dropping odd ones here or there to keep us awake. Being dug in we ignored them. A direct hit is rare in those conditions. We slept in clothes for days – and weeks on the move. In winter with flying suits (Sidcot), and flying boots as well, on occasions sleeping under the aircraft. Caked in dust and sweat for days, but strangely very lean and fit. When the dust was dry it was like a sort of talcum powder, well sort of.

As a newcomer to the desert sand-fly bites turned septic. Lots of small spots with yellow heads. From then on immunity prevailed. Dysentery was rare – diarrhoea less so.

Flying conditions were good with odd exceptions like dust storms – or showers which produced slushy surfaces. It was a routine procedure from 1940 for Airfield operations to send HQ Desert Air Force, a dust rising signal when appropriate. Being an area where the weather was generally flyable – VFR [Visual Flying Rules] – the prospect of dust storms was important information, also their extent and direction of movement. Aircraft operations and large ground movements encouraged the development of dust storms. They could persist for 24 hours.

The fine powder penetrated any man-made structure. The issue anti-gas goggles were helpful on the ground. Cockpit hoods were permanently scratched. In the sunny conditions they spangled hopelessly, and we flew with them open to achieve a clear view. Goggles were the same and we wore them 'up' more to have them there in case of fire. Hoods could jam with dust, another preference for leaving them open.[19]

19   Russel Brown, *Desert Warriors – Australian P-40 pilots at war in the Middle East and North Africa 1941-43* (Maryborough: Banner Books, 2000), pp. 2-3.

A Curtiss P-40 Tomahawk Mark IIB of 250 Squadron RAF raises the dust at LG 13/Sidi Heneish South, before taking off on a patrol. (Crown Copyright – Air Historical Branch)

Phil Darby was a Wellington bomber pilot during the campaign and he also remembers the austere environment the desert presented:

> Even at a main base like Kabrit the Wellingtons were permanently stationed outside with very little protection. When there was a sandstorm, which was more often than not, heavy drifts built up around the aircraft and these had to be cleared before any kind of work could be carried out prior to an operation. In addition, the high temperatures made the take-off procedure much more lengthy than usual and the surface of the desert was much more demanding than the concrete surface of a normal runway; during both take-off and landing procedures the aircraft was subjected to far more stress than in the European theatre.
>
> Tyres had a very short life and the sand whipped up by the propellers was sucked down the carburettor air intake and had a disastrous effect on the precision engineering of the engines. Consequently large air filters were fitted which reduced the sand intake — but created a major operational defect. When trying to evade a searchlight beam it was usual to cut power and dive down the beam, while the front gunner 'opened up' to keep enemy heads down. Then, with a heave, the dive would be terminated, and the engines opened up to full power. This sudden surge of power caused a backfire which unseated the filters and allowed them to be sucked up the carburettor air intakes, instantly reducing the power of the engines by about fifty percent.
>
> In spite of the filters, the engines still had a very short operational life, and to compensate for this, additional oil tanks were fitted within the fuselage and every two or three hours one or other of the crew had to pump oil out of these tanks into the nacelle tanks of each of the engines. At low level this was a chore, at high level, when the oil had virtually solidified, this was extremely hard work.

There was also the additional problem of sand being driven into the flying controls when the aircraft were standing out in the desert, and we adopted an extra pre-flight procedure of sweeping out the sand that had accumulated in the bearings of the control surfaces. If one omitted to do this, there was very little movement in either the control column or the flying controls generally. The rather primitive resolution to this problem was achieved by making a besom out of the scrub which grew in the desert and then walking along the wings brushing out the apertures between the moving and fixed surfaces. Normally during this operation the skipper sat in the aircraft wiggling the controls and when he deemed there was sufficient movement to enable the aircraft to take-off, the exercise was terminated.

The rest of the de-sanding operation could take place when the aircraft was airborne. Various crews had their own techniques. Ours was simple but quite effective. As soon as we were airborne we opened the bulkhead doors behind both the front and rear turrets. Normally when the gunners got into the turrets these doors were closed behind them to prevent the slipstream coming through the aircraft; by opening both these doors we had a one-hundred-and-fifty-mile-per-hour gale through the aircraft which would blow away the sand and take anything moveable overboard. So as a preliminary to this exercise, everything had to be sat on, pushed into a corner or otherwise secured.[20]

The Middle East serviceability and maintenance procedures were often outrageously spartan when compared to the standards in the United Kingdom. The difficulties of operational flying were also exacerbated by the hot climatic conditions as Phil Darby continues:

At the best of times the heat produced 'thin air'. No one really explained to me what this was or how to overcome it, but when nearing the ground on a landing approach there was a tendency for the aircraft to fall out of the sky for no discernible reason, and so damage the skipper's reputation.

On take-off, the reverse problem occurred, the Wellingtons did not really want to leave the desert, particularly when we had a heavy bomb load on board. It was usual to select fifteen degrees of flap down, and then hurtle across the desert hoping the thing would get airborne. Usually by the time it did the engines were virtually glowing with heat. Once airborne, the problem of getting rid of the flaps was paramount. It was difficult to climb with them down and we could not get rid of them until we had reached about five hundred feet as every time we took off a few degrees the aircraft would sink a hundred feet or so. It was a dodgy exercise and I was always relieved when the end was achieved.

In short, this was your take-off procedure. You opened up and got into the air as soon as possible. As soon as you were in the air you got rid of the flaps, then opened the bulkhead doors and got rid of the sand. When these functions were complete it was a case of finding out where you were. Normally this meant going back to the flare path and then setting course for the target.

At this period, when we were operating from a back base, it was necessary to leave in the afternoon, fly to an advanced landing ground, such as LG60 or LG108 or LG104, arrive two or three hours later, refuel, rest for two or three hours and then take-off in the early part of the evening for the target, bomb it, return to the advanced landing ground early in the morning, refuel and then get back to the main base sometime in the late morning. In other words, practically every operation was twenty to twenty-four hours long. This effectively meant that

---

20   Phil Darby, *Press on Regardless* (Privately Published by the author, 1997) pp. 67-72.

Armourers with 250lb GP bombs prepare to load Vickers Wellington B.IIs of 104 Squadron at LG224/Cairo West in November 1942. The sortie to be flown was against enemy columns retreating after the Battle of El Alamein. (Crown Copyright – Air Historical Branch)

the squadron could operate only every other night and this was a patently inefficient use of a fighting unit.

Apart from these basic logistical problems, there were those associated with the mainte-nance of the aircraft and their preparation for an operation. The ground crews were very constrained in the way they could work. If there was a sandstorm, then any work on the aircraft was quite impossible, so it was usually a case of all maintenance checks being carried out first thing in the morning. The pilot would then carry out an air test to confirm that the aircraft was fit for operations. Having declared it operational, he would hand the aircraft over to the armourers who would bomb up and arm the gun turrets. If they were lucky they would manage this before the sandstorm developed. If not they would have to complete the work after it had subsided, usually just before take-off.[21]

The ability of the Air Force to support the Army in the Western Desert was largely dependent on the type of aircraft with which they were equipped, it is worth therefore considering how these were developed. The experience in the early years of the war had initially led the British Army to believe that a bespoke dive bomber aircraft, such as the German Ju 87 Stuka, would be the best aircraft with which to conduct close air support. The Army had been so impressed with the

---

21    Phil Darby, *Press on Regardless*, pp. 67-72.

Stuka attacks inflicted upon them in France, that they lobbied the RAF to bring into service a special-purpose dive bomber. However, the Stuka's capability was overstated and their subsequent poor performance in the Battle of Britain revealed the fatal weakness of the aircraft when caught by high performance fighters. An early indication of such vulnerability had also been apparent in France, when a patrol of five French fighters was able to destroy an entire formation of twelve Ju 87s without any loss to themselves.[22] The Stuka's poor performance in the Western Desert prompted a further deterioration in its reputation. Air Chief Marshal Sir Arthur Tedder, the RAF C-in-C in the Middle East, asked troops who had fought at El Agheila in the Libyan desert in January 1942 what they thought about the Stuka. They described it as an 'expensive and harmless amusement' and claimed they had shot down twenty-seven Ju 87s in a two-week period, for the loss of only three vehicles. This statement may have been frontline exaggerations, but what was equally interesting was these soldiers' view of the low-flying Me 109 which was increasingly being used in the ground attack role at the same time. When equipped with bombs, as well as its own machine-guns and cannon, it was proving to be a huge menace, killing and wounding personnel as well as destroying numerous vehicles. 'We hated them' one soldier told Tedder.[23] Fortunately the British had also been converting its own fighters for ground attack roles and was able to take full advantage of one of the most important innovations of the Second World War – the fighter bomber.

One of the first British fighters to be converted into a fighter bomber was the Hurricane IIA, which was fitted with underwing attachments for external fuel tanks, that could also carry 250lb General Purpose (GP) bombs. These Hurricane conversions had originally been designed for attacking ground targets during Rhubarbs[24] in France, but they also showed clear potential for future support to ground forces. In addition, newer models of the aircraft, such as the Hurricane IIC were equipped with four 20 mm cannon. This aircraft's potency against lorries and guns was demonstrated to General Sir Alan Brooke, Chief of the Imperial General Staff, in November 1941 and he perceptively wrote in his diary that 'these converted fighter bombers were destined to play an important ground attack role'.[25] The Hurricane proved to be an ideal ground attack aircraft, it was a very steady and stable gun platform and the pilot had a fine view of ground targets from the aircraft's high cockpit. Its wide undercarriage also meant it could happily operate from rough and ready airfields and the Hurricane's fabric and tubular airframe could not only absorb more punishment than stressed metal-skinned aircraft but was also much easier to repair if damaged.[26]

However, the Hurricane had one major drawback. Like many of the fighter bombers used by the allies in the war the Hurricane had an in-line engine cooled by glycol, it therefore only took minor damage on radiators and engines for glycol to flood out and the engine to quickly overheat and seize up. Radial engines, such as those that existed on the Republic P-47 Thunderbolt aircraft or the twin-engined Beaufighter, could take much more damage and even the loss of a few cylinders was not necessarily catastrophic. These were important advantages for aircraft that would have to routinely fly at low levels through enemy AA or small arms fire.

The Hurricane fighter bombers were first used in ground support roles in the Western Desert as part of Operation CRUSADER (18 November to 30 December 1941). Though a success in that battle the Hurricane's performance as an air superiority fighter was quickly becoming eclipsed and

22   Richard Hallion, *Strike from the Sky* (Shrewsbury: Airlife Publishing Ltd, 1989), p. 146.
23   Robert Ehler, *Air War in the Mediterranean*, p. 106.
24   See Chapter 5 of Volume 1.
25   Ian Gooderson, *Air Power at the Battlefront*, p. 58.
26   See Annexes J M for details of British, Allied and enemy aircraft.

Hawker Hurricane Mark IIb, of 213 Squadron, taxying at El Adem, Libya, before taking off to escort Lockheed Hudsons of 216 Group to a forward landing ground in December 1942. To the right, Hudson VI, EW947/ LD-N, of 117 Squadron turns into the wind for take-off. Note the long-range fuel tanks under the Hurricane's wings. (Crown Copyright – Air Historical Branch)

though it lingered in the Desert Air Force's inventory for at least another year, it was becoming increasingly time-expired in that theatre – even as a fighter bomber.

This was an important factor because where the fighter bomber showed greatest flexibility was when it could be employed as both an air superiority fighter and as a fighter bomber. The increasing arrival of the Curtis P-40D Kittyhawk, in the Middle East, the replacement to the P-40 B and C Tomahawks, allowed RAF commanders to employ these new aircraft in a highly versatile and flexible manner as both an air superiority fighter and as a fighter bomber. The Kittyhawks that deployed to the desert had a top speed of 350-370 mph (depending on the variant) and were equipped with a battery of six 0.5inch machine guns. Robert 'Bobby' Gibbes was an Australian pilot with 3 Squadron RAAF and recalls that though an undoubted improvement on the Hurricane, the Kittyhawk's relative performance against German aircraft still left a lot to be desired:

> Against the Italians we had a superior aeroplane but when the Germans brought the 109s in they were in almost every way a better aeroplane, they could outclimb us, they were faster, they had a much better ceiling, they could get much higher and they looked down on us we could never look down on them. The only thing was that we were able to do was out-turn a Messerschmitt and because we were a very heavy aeroplane out dive them. But when the Germans woke up to the fact that we could out turn them they very rarely stayed to dog fight and would simply dive and do what they called 'pick and zoom'. They would dive, pick off a straggler and then climb up again and you would only get a very fleeting shot at them because they would be travelling at very high speed. Or they would dive straight past their target aircraft and keep on going down and with an initial speed there was no way you could catch them.

We were a little disappointed with the Kitty as we thought it would be way ahead of the Tomahawk, but in actual fact it was only a little bit better, one thing I didn't like about it was that the Tomahawk had fairly high sides and you would be sitting behind thin sheets of metal but you felt better. The Kittyhawk had great big Perspex sides and when you were sitting up there you felt very vulnerable as you could see out so much… We used to have a terrific amount of gun trouble, sand used to get in the mechanism and there were times when you would find you had no guns firing and in the middle of combat that wasn't much fun, also it was very frustrating if you had the opportunity of shooting some chap down and your guns would pack up one after another until you had nothing to shoot with.[27]

Following Operation CRUSADER, the Western Desert Air Force experimented with fitting the Kittyhawks with a single 250lb bomb, this may seem a tame load given the heavier bombloads fighters would eventually carry, but at the time fighter bombers were still a relatively novel idea. The Kittyhawk pilots were initially highly dubious of this innovation and their leaders were adamant that they would also need to be properly trained on ground attack techniques if their aircraft were to be converted. No. 112 Squadron (who habitually painted shark's teeth on their aircraft) started training first on 16 May 1942 and 3 Squadron RAAF followed later.[28] Bert Horden of 112 Squadron relates how the bomb loads on the Kittyhawk progressively increased through the desert war to the Italian campaign:

In North Africa, Warrant Officer Smith, our engineer, had invented and designed a special bomb rack for the Kitty to carry two 250lb (113kg) bombs under the fuselage… These 250-pounders were useful for anti-personnel and anti-MT work. When we were to attack these targets our armourers would fit the bomb nose-caps with 12 inch or 18 inch (30 or 45 cm) rods to lift the explosion level and cause maximum damage.

In North Africa the weather was so good we didn't need our artificial horizons on the instrument panel. When it was decided to uplift the bomb-load to two 500-pounders under the wings the authorities decided to remove the artificial horizon and other equipment to compensate for the additional bomb load. Among other measures, they fitted a very small electric battery instead of the large capacity one in the fuselage. The heavy steel wheels were replaced by aluminium ones.

Now we carried a 500lb (226 kg) bomb under the fuselage and two more 500-pounders under the wings. This total of 1,500 lbs (680 kg) caused us to take off with some flap and to stand on the brakes until the revs had mounted up before moving forward.

Now in Italy, with winter drawing near, the weather was different and suddenly we needed that artificial horizon again! Also we had continuous trouble from the battery behind the seat, too small to cope with all the 'electrics'. So the instruments were put back in and the full size battery re-instated. The aluminium wheels occasionally cracked under the additional weight of bombs, so we went back to steel wheels. Then, would you believe, we were persuaded to try a 1,000lb (453 kg) bomb under the fuselage. So now we carried, on special occasions, 2,000lbs (907 kg) of bombs. This was nearly as much as the B-25 Mitchells that we escorted.[29]

The 250lb General Purpose bomb could be fitted with a wide range of fuses and used effectively against a variety of different targets, as a result the Desert Air Force ensured considerable stocks

27    Australian War Memorial Sound Archives SOO938: Interview with Squadron Leader Robert Gibbes.
28    Roderic Owen, *The Desert Air Force* (London: Hutchinson, 1958), p. 89.
29    Bert Horden, *Shark Squadron Pilot* (Bromley: Independent Books, 2002), p. 126.

An RAF Wing Commander inspects a 1,000-lb GP bomb slung beneath the fuselage of a Curtiss P-40D Kittyhawk Mark IV of 450 Squadron RAAF. (Crown Copyright – Air Historical Branch)

A Curtiss P-40D Kittyhawk Mark IV of 450 Squadron RAAF with a 1,000-lb GP bomb slung underneath the fuselage, and two 500-lb GP bombs slung from the wing loading points. (Crown Copyright – Air Historical Branch)

of this ammunition were built up at forward dumps in the desert. It was originally thought that as the fighter bombers were based further forward, their strikes would be quicker to arrange and save time and that their new strafing and low-level bombing role would complement, rather than supplant, the light and medium bomber operations based further back. However, as the fighter bombers conducted more and more operations and the bombloads on the Kittyhawk steadily increased, the comparatively effective nature of these aircraft attracted attention. Particularly when the fighter bombers were compared to the light or medium bombers then in service in the Western Desert, such as the Martin Baltimore, Douglas Boston or, Mitchell or B-26 Marauder. One study highlighted that a squadron of Kittyhawk fighter bombers could fly three missions a day and carry 54,000 lbs of bombs to the target over that period, the ground and air crew required to accomplish this amounted to 243 personnel. In contrast the greater demands of maintenance, armaments, dispersal and re-fuelling meant that a medium bomber squadron could only fly two missions per day, during which they carried a smaller total of 36,000 pounds of bombs to the target. Yet these medium bomber squadrons needed 349 ground and air crew personnel to achieve this.[30]

Fighter bombers such as the Kittyhawk were also much more flexible than their medium bomber counterparts and could switch in the air from close air support to interdiction, or even jettison their bombs and revert to an air superiority fighter-role (albeit one that still struggled against Me 109s). Medium bombers typically needed escorts for daylight missions, whilst the Kittyhawk fighter bomber could generally look after itself when flying ground support operations, though a formation of Kittyhawks in the pure fighter role would usually provide top cover as a precaution. Finally, fighter bombers, particularly those as rugged as the Hurricane and Kittyhawk, could be used from rough and ready frontline airstrips, whereas medium bombers often needed more established facilities.[31] Not surprisingly the Kittyhawk fighter bomber was increasingly viewed with favour as a valued and welcome addition to the Desert Air Force.

It was also during 1941–1942 that the concept of Army/RAF joint planning underpinned by timely command, control, coordination and communication really matured. If there was one individual who deserves the credit for this transformation it must be the New Zealander, Air Vice-Marshal Arthur Coningham, known to all as 'Mary' (a corruption of 'Maori') and widely regarded as a popular and highly effective commander. Stanley Lee a fellow RAF officer recalled Coningham taking over the Desert Air Force, describing him as 'Big, masculine, confident…he had an easy, attractive personality, a ready and colourful flow of talk and a gift for decentralising the detail of his work and so leaving him free to deal with broader issues.' Coningham observed from the outset that a combined Army/Air Headquarters made sense and when the Eighth Army was formed from the Western Desert Force in September 1941, he suggested they co-locate. The Army responded to Coningham's initiative and the two headquarters jointly occupied a site at Ma'aten Bagush.[32]

By the beginning of CRUSADER, the RAF concept of support for the ground battle had matured into three distinct roles. These included first achieving and maintaining battlefield air superiority, second isolating the battlefield from enemy supplies and reinforcements through interdiction and thirdly attacks against targets on the battlefield itself (i.e close air support and general air support). CRUSADER witnessed the first use of the newly established Army Air Support Centres (AASCs) which would select targets on the battlefield. They would be assisted by the RAF's Air Support Controls (ASCs) which were located with each Corps and Armoured Division headquarters, as well

30   Roderic Owen, *The Desert Air Force*, p. 89.
31   Brad William Gladman, *Intelligence and Anglo-American Air Support in World War Two*, p. 87.
32   Vincent Orange, *Coningham* (Washington DC: Center for Airpower Studies, 1992) p. 78.

as the 'Tentacles'[33] that would move forward with each Brigade communicating requests for air strikes and passing on information about the battle. An RAF Forward Air Support Link (FASL) was also deployed with each Brigade and importantly possessed radios for communicating with RAF aircraft directly overhead. A final important element in this increasingly networked system was the Rear Air Support Link, which connected the AASC to the airfields themselves, it was through this channel that RAF and Army commanders could listen in on RAF tactical air reconnaissance reports. All these new measures helped improve situational awareness and speed up response.[34]

Coordination methods had also been improved and clarified. Aircraft now received directions to the target from pre-planned coordinates and were often led in by reconnaissance aircraft. Bomb-lines, the line short of which no aircraft could bomb without the Army's express permission, were now not only more up to date thanks to reliable communications but were also sensibly sited on distinct geographical features that could be more easily identified from the air. This was a sensible innovation, though Kittyhawk pilot Bobby Gibbes remarked that it was often easy to tell where the bomb-line was in the desert based on the tracks made by friendly tanks and vehicles and the enemy beginning to fire as soon as their aircraft crossed the frontline.[35] Coloured smoke, Very lights and vehicle markings were also becoming more routinely used to mark both targets and friendly forward troops. In addition, all Army formations were prepared to put out artificial landmarks by day and night to help pilots pinpoint themselves in the desert, these were selected by the Army and the map references made known to the Royal Air Force through the Army Air Support Control. In daylight hours these landmarks took the form of letters 20 yards in length, and by night a 'V' sign 100 yards long constructed of burning petrol tins 25 yards apart. These were a huge help and enabled air support to be given with a much greater degree of accuracy.

Vehicle identification was also improved, initially the white cross of St Andrew on a black background had been painted on all vehicles, but this had not proved satisfactory. By the spring of 1942 the RAF Roundel was being used instead, as it was a marking 'for which all fighter aircraft are on continual watch in the air', however a shortage of materials meant it was still some time before it came into general use.[36] These identification devices would be continually refined throughout the war, until by mid-1944 the fluorescent panel was being issued and this, in combination with other methods, improved the air-to-ground recognition of AFVs greatly, though the problem was never solved entirely.[37]

The speed of air response was further improved by having a formation of six aircraft within each squadron at 'instant readiness', the remaining aircraft being held at two-hours notice. The system was further improved following CRUSADER, when more VHF radio sets were made available and the system became dynamic enough to re-task fighter bombers whilst in flight. Intelligence to focus air strikes was also improving and now involved POW interrogation, Y service radio intercepts and better photographic air reconnaissance, all of which assisted both accurate targeting as well as the correct assessments of the damage being inflicted upon the enemy.

Not only was inter-service cooperation and the ability to conduct strikes steadily improving, the Desert Air Force was also organising itself properly into a Tactical Air Force that was highly mobile, had a tight control over its units and was able to protect itself. Much of the credit for this belongs to Air Commodore Tommy Elmhirst, the Desert Air Force's Chief Administrative Officer

33  A Tentacle normally consisted of an armoured half-track, driver-mechanic and 3 wireless operators.
34  Robert Ehler, *Mediterranean Air War*, pp. 121-2.
35  AWM Sound Archives S00938: Interview with Squadron Leader Robert Gibbes.
36  Air Publication 3235, *Air Support, The Second World War 1939-45*, (Air Historical Branch, Air Ministry, 1955), p. 65.
37  Air Publication 3235, *Air Support, The Second World War 1939-45*, p. 98.

A Douglas Boston Mark III of 12 Squadron SAAF raises the dust while opening up its engines for take-off at Bir el Beheira, Libya. (Crown Copyright – Air Historical Branch)

who would also go on to establish Tactical Air Forces in Tunisia, Italy and Normandy. Elmhirst was in the words of one of the Desert Air Force's fighter leaders, a man who 'created order where there had been disorder, supply, where there had been shortage, confidence where there had been doubt and, above all, a belief amongst those doing the fighting that here was a man who understood what they needed.'[38] The pressing requirement to improve the Desert Air Force's administration and organisation was brought home to Elmhirst on the second day of his new post, when he encountered a sergeant in charge of a Mobile Bath Unit that had been sent from Cairo, 300 miles away, to provide baths for the airmen:

> A very good idea, but of course there was hardly sufficient water in wells to make cups of tea or fill radiators. I asked the Sergeant who he was under. He didn't know. Were his troops getting pay? No. Were they on anyone's strength so that they could draw rations or get their letters from home? No. It was an unhappy unit, with no chain of command to someone above who might help and direct it. It had no establishment, so no promotion or preferment for the men was possible.[39]

It was a symptom of a dangerous lack of organisation and control within the Desert Air Force. Elmhirst got to work immediately and within one week he had produced an establishment for the Desert Air Force that catalogued every officer and airman within it, as well as the equipment that the various elements within the formation required. The order of battle importantly included a new wing structure within the Desert Air Force, where maintenance, servicing and other support elements were all centralised.

To make this new structure work, Elmhirst and his staff tried to make sure that the squadrons in each Desert Air Force wing were usually based at the same airfield and could therefore take advantage of the wing's centralised support. Although some squadron commanders resented

38   Vincent Orange, *Coningham*, p. 89.
39   Vincent Orange, *Coningham*, p. 91.

Vickers Wellington Mark IC running up its engines at Bir el Beheira, Libya, prior to taxying for take-off.
(Crown Copyright – Air Historical Branch)

having their maintenance and administration services taken from them, the change was beneficial as it freed the leadership at squadron level from non-operational burdens and allowed them to concentrate on fighting and leading their squadrons in the air. Furthermore, a system of central-ised administration and servicing was found to be both more effective and efficient. Elmhirst also made sure that the new wings were mobile and were able to operate, fight, advance or withdraw with sufficient fuel, ammunition, bombs, reserve parts, stores and other equipment either on the airfields, or within easy reach. Additionally, two mobile operations rooms for control of fighters were established, a forward one at Gazala and a main one at El Adem. These had identical equip-ment and staff so that they could leap-frog each other in advance or withdrawal. The changes made by Elmhirst helped simplify the Desert Air Force's internal communications to one with less individual points and no 'orphaned' units. In Tommy Elmhirst's words these measures collectively ensured that 'No-one was left out or forgotten and consequently in retreats and advances, no-one failed to receive orders'.[40] This organisational design was to prove critical in the coming months.

By the time of the Gazala battle in May 1942, the Desert Air Force was an increasingly large and potent force that included twelve squadrons of fighters in the newly formed 211 Group (a mixture of Hurricanes, Spitfire VBs, Kittyhawks and Tomahawks). A light bomber force of three squad-rons of Bostons and Baltimores in 3 South African Air Force Wing, which were ideal for general support as well as interdiction tasks, and finally a host of miscellaneous units including tactical and photo reconnaissance aircraft, air ambulances and communications flights. Although not directly under its command, the Desert Air Force could also regularly call on the seven squadrons of Wellington bombers that formed part of 205 Group and were based further east. These had the range to bomb Rommel's principal port of Benghazi and help isolate the battlefield, there was also a torpedo carrying Wellington squadron for long range shipping attacks. Finally, 205 Group possessed two newly arrived long range Bristol Beaufighter squadrons (252 and 272 Squadrons) which would prove ideal for interdiction and helping to seal off the battlefield.

---

40   Vincent Orange, *Coningham*, p. 91

# 6

# 'Harass'[1]
# Air Support Tips the Balance in the Desert

The first half of 1942 was not a good period for the Eighth Army. Although the British CRUSADER operation had concluded successfully in late December 1941, it had not provided a decisive victory over Rommel and by 4 February 1942 the British were withdrawing to the Gazala line, a defensive position located a few miles west of Tobruk between Gazala and Timimi. Both sides quickly began building up supplies for their next offensive, that Rommel was able to do so owed much to the ferocious *Luftwaffe* campaign that was temporarily neutralising Malta. Conversely the British lines of communication stretched right the way back to the Canal Zone. Rommel managed to beat the British to the punch with an assault on the Gazala line in late May. After bitter fighting he defeated an ill-equipped and poorly led force, smashing through Eighth Army positions that lacked mutual support and capturing Tobruk. It is often regarded as Rommel's finest victory, conversely British operations lacked skill and grip. During these dark moments the only significantly bright spot in the British performance was that of the Desert Air Force.

During the Gazala battle, the RAF had played a prominent part in assisting the 1st Free French Brigade holding the southern defended box of Bir Hakim. Here both Kittyhawk fighter bombers and formations of Boston medium bombers provided close and general air support to the beleaguered French. The Desert Air Force performance was such that the Free French commander at Bir Hakeim, General Koenig, signalled to Coningham 'Bravo, merci pour la RAF' to which Coningham replied 'Bravo a vous. Merci pour le sport'.[2] Despite determined resistance in places, the Eighth Army line was broken, forcing the British to embark on a long retreat to the El Alamein line. This was the moment the *Luftwaffe* could have struck, as from 4 June onwards the road east of Gazala was packed with a slowly moving concentration of British men and transport for three consecutive days, offering precisely the sort of target the *Luftwaffe* had exploited so well in earlier campaigns. Yet the Desert Air Force kept the Axis air forces largely at bay.[3] The New Zealand commander, General Freyberg, who had commanded the British garrison at Crete in 1941 and been a strong critic of the RAF performance over Greece and Crete commented: 'Thank God you didn't let the Hun Stuka us, because we were an appalling target.'[4]

---

1    Motto of 450 Squadron RAAF, this squadron arrived in the Middle East on 9 April 1941 and flew Tomahawks and Kittyhawks, operating in Syria, Egypt, Libya and Tunisia as fighters, before converting to the fighter bomber role. No. 450 Squadron also took part in the Italian campaign, continuing to fly Kittyhawks and becoming an almost entirely ground-attack unit.
2    Roderic Owen, *The Desert Air Force*, p. 95.
3    RAF Middle East, *The Official Story of Air Operations Feb. 1942 – Jan. 1943* (London: HMSO, 1945), p. 48.
4    Roderic Owen *The Desert Air Force*, p. 97.

The RAF's air support to the Army was maintained throughout their retreat to the Alamein Line, where the British Army eventually stopped and held the Germans. The benefit of ensuring that the Desert Air Force was tactically mobile paid off and squadrons were able to leapfrog neatly from one airfield to another. The squadron support elements had by this stage been split into A and B parties. If a move was required the A party would go by road, whilst the squadron would continue to operate supported by the B party. When the A party had reached the new landing ground, they would signal that they were ready to support aircraft operations and the squadron would then fly to the new airfield. At this point the B party would pack up and follow up by road. These moves called for some courageous decisions in keeping airfields open to the last safe moment, at Gambut for instance enemy tanks were on the airfield within an hour of the aircraft evacuating.[5] Such risks had been partly mitigated by the use of the RAF's own armoured cars, which acted as a reconnaissance screen and provided warning to the airfield commanders. Reliance on the Army for notification was important too, but Desert Air Force commanders remembered the occasion at Antelat on 23 January 1942 when the first warning that the Army gave 258 Wing that the Germans were near was the message 'Move back at once, enemy coming.' On that occasion the airfield was being shelled as the last aircraft was taking off.[6] At other times, the fighting was so fluid and confused that there had been no warning from the Army at all. As the withdrawal from the Gazala line back to El Alamein took place Coningham, signalled to Tedder on its progress:

> Having thinned out all units, the guiding principle being that all wings must be able to work full pressure. We are all at one hour's notice to move and owing to proved value of force Army has given one brigade for close defence which helps my judgement of night security. I have prepared landing grounds all the way back to the frontier [the Libyan/Egyptian border] and plan is steady withdrawal of squadrons keeping about 20 miles away from enemy. See our own bombs bursting is rough deadline. As units move the R.S.U. [Rear Servicing Unit] Squadrons are fearful of being too far away from enemy as they like present form of warfare. Squadron commanders explain situation to voluntary parade of men daily and point of honour there are no flaps and nothing left for enemy. Am content that whole machinery working very smoothly. Work of both bombers and fighters has been brilliant.[7]

George James was an Australian armourer with 450 Squadron and withdrew with his unit, on the night of 28 June 1942, from Matruh to LG 91 near Amiriya, some sixty miles east of El Alamein. By this point in the battle the *Luftwaffe* had recovered and begun to attack some of the withdrawing ground columns:

> The retreating vehicles, of course, were more or less nose to tail on the one and only road. They were a mixed bag, as trucks of different units were joining in wherever a gap was created, and there were many deserted trucks along the side of the road. Some may have broken down or been damaged possibly by enemy strafing. Most of this road was through soft, stony sand where it was not possible to drive off the road. My mates and I cruised along with all the others, taking it in turns to watch front and rear for enemy kites.
>
> At one point I was in the truck and had just removed my boots and socks (for whatever reason I don't remember) when the truck stopped and someone shouted 'Run!' Along with the others I went over the back and on to the surrounding desert for a hundred yards or so before

5    Arthur Tedder, *With Prejudice* (London: Cassell, 1966), p. 290.
6    Vincent Orange, *Coningham*, p. 88.
7    Arthur Tedder, *With Prejudice* (London: Cassell, 1966), p. 290.

Pilots of No. 112 Squadron RAF grouped round the nose of one of their Curtiss Tomahawks at LG 122, Egypt.
(Crown Copyright – Air Historical Branch)

stopping. Three 109s were strafing the vehicles on the road but luckily our vehicle wasn't hit. It was then I discovered I was barefoot and couldn't walk back across the stony desert to the truck! One of the boys had to get my boots for me. Fortunately for me, the convoy couldn't move as some trucks ahead had been immobilised and had to be pushed off the road. I put my boots on and while walking back to the truck I wondered how the hell I had got so far over such stony terrain without touching down![8]

The twenty-three days of battle on the Gazala line, (26 May to 17 June 1942) had been followed by thirteen days of retreat to the Alamein line (18–30 June 1942) and then a period where the new defensive position was assailed, tested and held (1–6 July 1942). Throughout this time the RAF had successfully maintained air superiority, interdicted enemy forces both at sea, as well as on the

---

8    Russel Brown, *Desert Warriors – Australian P-40 pilots at war in the Middle East and North Africa 1941-43*, p. 134.

long road to the front line and provided close and general air support over the battlefield itself. The newly arrived American Air Force General Lewis Brereton put the British ability to hold the line at Alamein down to two factors saying 'No account of the British stand which stopped Rommel can fail to record the fine part played by the RAF and the New Zealand Division under General Freyberg. These two undoubtedly saved the Eighth Army from complete defeat.'[9] General Auchinleck, who took over command from General Ritchie on 25 June, also appreciated that the RAF were probably decisive in preventing the Eighth Army retreat descending into a rout. Though the RAF contribution was well-understood by commanders on the ground, it did not prevent those at home, including the media, blaming the Army's reverse on lack of RAF support. It prompted Auchinleck to signal the Prime Minister personally about this harmful press campaign:

> So far as the Army is concerned NOTHING could be further from the truth. So far as my knowledge goes, air support throughout has been continuous and most effective, great damage having been caused to enemy. This lying campaign, if allowed to continue, can NOT fail to prejudice efficiency of both Army and Air Force at this very critical juncture. We are NOT strong enough to fight our own people as well as the enemy, and I beg your personal intervention to put matters right.[10]

During this period the Desert Air Force's new fighter bombers were arguably the most effective aircraft for ground support. Using a combination of strafing and bombing they were able to inflict punishing attacks on Axis troops and transport at the front and proved effective against concentrations of soft-skinned vehicles, especially when these were caught in defiles from which dispersal or escape was difficult. The fighter bomber was very adept at stopping convoys as a preliminary to machine-gunning, but once halted the targets often became more difficult because of the increased anti-aircraft fire that was immediately encountered.

Kittyhawk attacks were conducted by either dive-bombing or low-level bombing attacks. As the aircraft did not have air brakes to control their descent, the fighter-bombers had to conduct dive-bombing attacks at angles of between 45 and 60 degrees. Even so they would quickly begin to reach high speeds in their dives and normally released their bombs between 2–3,000 feet, which gave them enough time to pull up. A limitation of single engine fighters was that the pilot could not see over his nose straight down to the ground. This meant that his No. 2 had to fly a little distance away, so that the leader could tip his wing when over the target and judge the right moment to roll over for the dive.[11] Kittyhawk pilot Bert Horden describes the process:

> I learnt that the formation to be flown was twelve 'Kittys' in two boxes of six with the second box flying a hundred feet above, behind and slightly to one side of the first six, preferably between them and the sun. Dive bombing was from about 6,000–8,000 ft down to 1,000 ft. The target was approached until it disappeared under the centre of the port wing, count to three and then go into a dive down to the left until the target was in front of the aircraft nose. At about 2,000 ft pull up, count one, two and then release the bomb or bombs. Then we were to reform at about 5,000 ft in the same formation. The dive was about sixty degrees but felt like ninety![12]

9    Vincent Orange, *Coningham*, p. 103.
10   Arthur Tedder, *With Prejudice*, p. 292.
11   Ian Gooderson, *Airpower at the Battlefront*, p. 71.
12   Bert Horden, *Shark Squadron Pilot*, p. 52.

The physiological effect of such dive-bombing was significant as Horden relates further:

> Dive bombing caused some physical problems for the pilot. Starting perhaps at 6,000–8,000
> ft and only starting to pull out at about 2,000 ft, meant a great force of gravity known simply
> as 'G' pushing us down into our seats and causing a blackout for a second or two as we came
> out of it. Also it was painful for the eardrums. Our squadron MO often told us, with a 'tut-
> tut', that we would suffer for it in later life. He was right of course. There was also the danger
> of not pulling out in time especially if there were hills in the area. We were usually about
> 1,000 ft from the ground at the lowest point. We had to be that low to attain some degree of
> accuracy for our bombs. In a dive the altimeter was spinning around too fast to read how high
> we were, so it was purely a visual judgement that was required to avoid hitting the ground. All
> this was in addition to the chances of being hit by ground fire at any stage.[13]

On occasions low level bombing attacks were also conducted, usually at heights of 800 feet with
the aircraft in a 30-degree dive. Having discharged its bombs, the fighter bomber would often
come back to strafe the target at low level where the high speed and manoeuvrability of the
fighter increased its chances of surprise and survivability.[14] Indeed, the wide-open spaces of the
desert seemed particularly suitable to these types of attacks. It was also recommended that fighter
bombers should normally approach targets from the direction of the enemy bases, as this not only
gave them a quick getaway in the direction of Allied territory, but sometimes convinced Axis
forces that the aircraft were friendly. Usually the attacking fighter bomber formation would split in
two, one acting as a decoy and top cover and remaining at altitude, whilst the other descended to
ground level for the attack. The formation in the final approach to the target would depend on the
ground, line abreast was preferred as it was believed it alarmed enemy ground troops the most. If
this was not possible, a line astern formation was used, though there was a danger that the enemy
troops would focus their fire at a point in the lead aircraft's path and hope that one or more of the
following planes would also fly in to this concentrated cone of fire.[15]

   A further target for ground-strafing fighter bombers were the Axis airfields. It was found that
fighter sweeps over these targets were a much more effective way of achieving air superiority than
simply area cover over the British forces. One fighter-bomber squadron commander related a
successful attack:

> It started as we came in over the coast, where a group of 10 men probably the crew of a coastal
> battery, were staring at us with open mouths. I was only 150 yards away when I opened fire. I
> saw my ammunition strike their bodies and they must all have been killed. Over the landing
> ground itself there were dozens of our fighters all close to the deck dodging amongst the tents
> and trucks, their guns firing streaks in every direction. Several of us came across aircraft
> parked in dispersals and shot them up thoroughly. The confusion amongst the Jerry troops
> must have been awful. They were rushing out of tents and dashing over to slit trenches, which
> quite a lot of them never reached.[16]

When attacking mobile motor transport, the fighter bombers would approach perpendicular to
the vehicle convoy in line abreast, with each pilot picking out a vehicle to attack. As the aircraft

---

13   Bert Horden, *Shark Squadron Pilot*, p. 88.
14   Ian Gooderson, *Airpower at the Battlefront*, p. 72.
15   Brad William Gladman, *Intelligence and Anglo American Air Support in World War Two*, pp. 85-6.
16   RAF Middle East, *The Official Story of Air Operations. Feb. 1942 – Jan. 1943*, p. 98.

Bristol Beaufighter Mark IC, T3314 'O', of 272 Squadron RAF, at Idku, Egypt.
(Crown Copyright – Air Historical Branch)

neared the convoy it would gain just enough altitude for it to make a shallow diving attack, the aiming point for the pilot being just behind the driver's cab to maximise the chances of both killing the driver and destroying the cargo. Dispersed vehicles were a much harder proposition, not only because they provided a scattered target but also because the AA fire was likely to be heavier.

The long-range Beaufighters adopted a slightly different approach to the single-engined fighter bombers, as their ability to penetrate deeper into enemy territory gave them a chance to surprise the enemy and enjoy greater freedom once there. Squadron Leader C. V. Ogden was a member of 272 Squadron and commanded a Beaufighter flight from February 1942. He recalled the work undertaken during this period:

> I personally think the Beaufighter did its best work on ground-strafing missions. Various types of targets were attacked, but I always felt that the best results were obtained on road-strafes. Our usual technique was to send out two sections, fly about 15 miles out to sea, then turn west parallel to the coast until opposite the target area and then turn in. Having approached well below any radar cover, we preserved an element of surprise. As we approached the road one section would turn right the other went left. With No 2 about a mile behind the leader, we would then fly down the road at zero feet and fly straight at any vehicle on the road. A quick burst at 100 to 50 yards, pull up over the roof of it and down on the road again, ready for the next. Any vehicle missed by the leader would be finished off by his No.2 and if we ran into a convoy there were plenty of pickings for a No 2. Only on two occasions did aircraft scrape the road with their airscrew tips, but in each case the Beau returned safely.[17]

---

17    Chaz Bowyer, *Beaufighter* (London: William Kimber, 1987), pp.107-8.

A petrol tanker and trailer on fire on the road between Homs and Misurata, Libya, after an attack by Bristol Blenheims interdicting enemy fuel supplies in support of Operation CRUSADER.
(Crown Copyright – Air Historical Branch)

Being the rear-most Beaufighter on such ventures was no fun as Sergeant 'Dinger' Bell of 272 Squadron recounts:

My time on Beaus was pretty short – just seven ops – then I was hospitalised after a crash landing and never returned to the same unit. The crash came after my seventh sortie which proved rather memorable for me personally. Five Beaus set out that morning for a general sweep of the coast road looking for enemy transport mainly, but briefed to fire at any concentration of troops or vehicles – so called 'opportunity targets'. By then I was beginning to feel fairly experienced at this deck-level stuff, so had no real worries about the sortie. One Beau aborted after about half an hour – presumably engine troubles – but the other three and myself pressed on.

We finally came upon a line of three-ton trucks, about seven in all, belting along the coast road, and went down to a height virtually level with the truck's roofs, flying in a line astern single file so that each man could fire at anything the Beau in front of him missed. I was No 4 in this file, the tail ender, and therefore had slightly more time in hand before choosing my targets. It also meant I would be flying through anything thrown up from the convoy incidentally! The leader and his No 2 must have hit something because a cloud of smoke and dust erupted ahead, then No 3 put his shells right inside the back of one truck which exploded right in front of me. Startled by this I failed to fire, but felt chunks of something hard hitting our Beau – then a body of a man rose directly ahead and disappeared overhead! The sight of that poor devil shocked me badly and I began shuddering – nervous reaction.

Clearing the convoy – still without firing a shot – I regained control of my nerves and gradually calmed down. Checking with Reg, my nav, as always, he reported that he was OK but was sure we'd been hit somewhere 'underneath' because there was a bloody great hole in the floor'. He then made some facetious remark about 'having to walk home'. I checked all my instruments but all seemed well, so I began the return trip.

On reaching base I let down for a normal landing, but as the wheels touched the whole undercart folded up and I crashed in a belly-landing which threw me forward bashing my head. Once the noise and dust settled down, Reg helped me out and got me well away from the Beau in case it fired. Apart from some dizziness I felt OK so didn't bother to see the medic and debriefed as usual – having my leg well pulled about 'conserving ammunition'… I was off ops next day, but the following morning when I was due for my eighth trip I woke up with a splitting headache and felt generally ropey. Since I was obviously unfit to fly I saw the squadron quack who examined me pretty thoroughly then told me he was sending me back to the nearest proper hospital with a suspected skull fracture![18]

In the battles between the Eighth Army and the *Afrika Korps,* armoured mobility was at a premium and tanks and other Armoured Fighting Vehicles (AFV) were one of the most valuable targets on the battlefield. In June 1942, the RAF equipped two Desert Air Force squadrons (6 Squadron RAF and 7 Squadron SAAF) with the Hurricane IID, which was armed with two 40 mm Vickers 'S' cannons. The effectiveness of this new aircraft's weapons was conveyed by German tank crews at the time of the Gazala battles, one German soldier claiming that six out of twelve tanks in his unit had been knocked out by Hurricane IID cannon hits on engines, ammunition or fuel tanks. Another member of a German tank crew commented that the new aircraft caused 'panic whenever they appeared.'[19]

Engaging targets in a Hurricane IID was not easy. This was partly because the flying attitude of an aircraft changes with its speed and the Hurricane IID flew with its nose slightly up at slow speeds and slightly down at high speeds. The Hurricane's sights were therefore set at 500 yards and the cannons harmonised so that if the pilot flew his aircraft at 240 mph they would hit the target. If the aircraft flew any faster, then the shells would land in front of the point of aim, if it flew any slower, then they would go too high. If the pilot opened fired before 500 yards the shells would briefly converge in front of their target, before splitting up and missing it altogether. The recoil of the cannons on the Hurricane IID was so great that it momentarily slowed the aircraft down by 40 mph and if one cannon was jammed, or failed to fire, the aircraft would slew to the left or right and miss the target altogether.[20] The Hurricane IID fired its 40mm armour piercing cannon shells at the rate of one pair per second and the size and weight of the shells meant that it could only carry fifteen in each of its two magazines, with one loaded in the breech. The .303 machine guns on the aircraft were loaded with tracer rounds for psychological effect and to cause any spilt fuel to burst into flames. Unsurprisingly, the weight of the 40mm cannon reduced the Hurricane's speed dramatically and consequently armour was sacrificed on the aircraft to improve performance. This made the Hurricane IID highly vulnerable to ground fire and it was temporarily withdrawn after the battle of El Alamein following concerns about high casualties, though the aircraft was subsequently re-introduced in to front line service in Tunisia and Burma. A report by 6 Squadron (whose nickname became the 'flying can-openers') was produced in November 1942 and gives some indication of the way this remarkable aircraft operated:

During the early stages of operations the Hurricane IID's operated in flights of three aircraft flying in line astern, with one squadron of Kittybombers, one aircraft leading and the remainder on either side, as close cover, and one squadron of Kittybombers as top cover. This was adopted as the Kittybombers were very familiar with that part of the country. The formation went out at about 5 to 6,000 feet until over the target, The Kittybombers dived down and released their bombs at the same time the Flight or Flights of Hurricane IIDs broke away and

---

18    Chaz Bowyer, *Beaufighter*, pp. 119-20.
19    Ian Gooderson, *Air Power at the Battlefront*, p. 105.
20    Andrew Millar, *The Flying Hours* (Hitchin: Fighting High Ltd, 2015), p. 93.

dived down to about 1,000 yards from the target, where they flattened out at about 15 feet from the ground and made their attack.

Very heavy A/A was encountered in these attacks. Great difficulty was experienced in picking out tanks from the various M.T on the dive down and attack, and it was quite impossible on the approach to the target area, at the height the Kittybombers used to fly in order to avoid the A/A fire. In a number of cases tanks which were thought to be there were not found, The Hurricane IIDs had to fly at +1lb. per. sq. inch boost in order to keep up with the Kittybombers. It took the Army Co-operation trained pilots a very short time before they knew the country as well as the fighter pilots, also their own pin-pointing was much more accurate. From that time onwards the Hurricane IIDs led all formations, going out at 180 mph indicated 2400 RPM 0 boost, with one squadron of Kittyhawks weaving as close cover and one squadron as top cover. This put the range of the IID up from about 75 miles to 95 miles radius of action allowing enough petrol for three attacks and about 15 minutes searching over the target area.

Later, it was decided that a good target for Anti-tank Squadrons was not a good target for the Fighter Bombers, so two squadrons of cover were provided, without the bomber diversion as used at first. During this period, the withdrawal from Bir Hakeim to Alamein, there were numbers of excellent targets and a large number of Anti-tank aircraft could have been used to great advantage.

A number of successful anti-tank sweeps were carried out by No.6 Squadron, with medium and high cover, in the southern sector of the Alamein line. The country was fairly open desert with the normal small wadis and sand dunes etc., here and there were quite a lot of armoured patrols operating, which could be attacked without large numbers of M.T in the vicinity. The latter were always avoided where possible, as the German M.T. appears to carry a very large amount of very effective light A/A. On these sweeps the Hurricane IID used to search an area for 15 minutes, attacking any armour that they saw...

The most usual number of IIDs employed has been either 3 or 6 aircraft according to the target. These are escorted out and home by a squadron of medium and high cover. This escort is essential, since in no way can the IID be considered a normal fighter, the extra weight carried and the harmonisation of the guns alone precluding this. In order to keep changing the formations, 4 or 6 aircraft sometimes work in pairs which look like an ordinary fighter formation giving cover.[21]

It was considered that the best time to attack tanks was when they were about to attack or were being attacked themselves. At that point the vehicles would be 'closed down' (i.e hatches and cupolas shut and their visibility impaired). The engines on the tanks would also be noisy enough to drown the sound of an attacking aircraft and any accompanying light AA, which was normally transported in soft-skinned vehicles, would have been moved to the rear. The RAF and Army chain of command would have to be very quick to spot and report such fleeting opportunities. On many occasions it would be the Army's armoured cars who would identify an enemy armoured concentration, they would communicate to their regimental headquarters who would pass the sighting on to brigade headquarters where the Air Support Control Tentacle was located. The Tentacle would then pass the information to the Army Air Support Control which was often situated at the combined Army/Air Headquarters. There the Air Operations Cell would filter out messages that identified particularly suitable targets for Hurricane IIDs. When approval was given a message

21   No. 6 Squadron, *Hurricane IID Aircraft (Anti-Tank Role), Report on Operations of No. 6 Squadron RAF (Middle East) June/November 1942,* Reproduced and circulated by Air Ministry, March 1943.

A Hawker Hurricane Mark IID of 6 Squadron RAF gives a demonstration of the firepower of its Vickers 40mm Type S anti-tank guns against derelict German tanks in the North African desert. (Crown Copyright – Air Historical Branch)

would be transmitted on the rear link directly to the airfield and the Hurricane's scrambled – they would maintain radio silence at least until the homeward journey. The 6 Squadron post operation report continues with a description of the actions undertaken when enemy armour was identified:

> On sighting the target the formation goes down to a height of 15/20 feet and approximately 1,000 yards away. On the leader turning into the target, the formation turns inside him and goes into the attack in a rough echelon, each member of this formation selecting his own target. The approach is made at a speed of 240 m.p.h., since the datum line is then 2 degrees down, sights being set parallel. Variations of more than 30 m.p.h. will affect the accuracy of the shooting. Fire is opened at 700 yards closing to 200 yards, and both Brownings and 'S' guns are used. The Brownings and 'S' guns are harmonised at 500 yards. After each burst of one shell per gun the sights are realigned on the target. Normally about 5 bursts can be got in on each attack. The breakaway is made before reaching the target if possible, to avoid being hit by splinters and the area is cleared by low flying weaving.
>
> If the tanks are isolated, up to three attacks can be made. This is left to the Flight Commander, and depends on A/A Fire encountered. Breakaways were always made towards our own line – this may have been the cause of only one pilot missing during operations.
>
> During this time, the escort remains above ready to escort the IIDs home. If, however, they lose sight of the IIDs, they should remain in the area sufficiently long to draw any possible opposition away from them. The IIDs, when away from the danger area, climb up to meet their cover at a point previously fixed as a rendezvous, but in the event of being separated, they fly home at nought feet. The escort is told before take-off how long the IIDs will remain in the target area.[22]

Though Auchinleck was able to stem the German advance at El Alamein, his time as the Army Commander in the Western Desert was curtailed and he was replaced by General Harold Alexander as the overall Middle Eastern Commander and General Bernard Montgomery as Commander of

---

22   No. 6 Squadron, *Hurricane IID Aircraft (Anti-Tank Role), Report on Operations of No. 6 Squadron RAF (Middle East) June/November 1942,* Reproduced and circulated by Air Ministry March 1943.

Hurricane Mark IID, BP188 'JV-Z', of 'B' Flight, 6 Squadron RAF, based at Shandur, Egypt. The two 40mm Vickers anti-tank cannon can just be seen under each wing. (Crown Copyright – Air Historical Branch)

the Eighth Army. Montgomery's arrival brought many changes, not least in his approach to cooperation with the RAF and Coningham was delighted that his Army opposite number recognised the primary importance of air power, the RAF's unified control of air units and the value of a strong joint command and control system.[23] Montgomery put his money where his mouth was and ensured that his headquarters would once more be co-located with Air HQ, the previous practise of co-location having been abandoned by his predecessor. Montgomery describes his initial actions in his diary as follows:

> When I took over command, Army HQ was right forward, and Air HQ Western Desert was right back near the landing grounds. The Army was fighting its battle and the RAF fighting its battle. There was no combined HQ, with the two Commanders and the two staffs completely in each other's pockets. I gather there had been very close touch in the past. But the arrival of AUCHINLECK and DORMAN-SMITH at Army HQ seems to have altered that; the RAF had no use for either of these two, and Army HQ and the two staffs seem gradually to have drifted apart.
>
> I decided to remedy this at once and moved Army HQ back to Air HQ, and brought the AOC and his senior staff officers into my mess. This was a good move, and from that moment we never looked back.[24]

Though Montgomery's well-known hostility and contempt for Auchinleck clearly colours the above account, both he and Coningham still deserve considerable credit for the admirable level of inter-operability the co-located headquarters achieved. Not only did the respective RAF and Army commanders share the same mess, but so too did their principal logistics and operations staff officers. The Army and Air operations cells were also helpfully sited adjacent to one another and Army liaison officers were attached to operations cells at Air HQ as well as at all RAF groups and wings. These were reciprocated by placing RAF officers at Army Divisional HQs. The two services were also logistically tied together, RAF stores and equipment would be loaded by the RAF in the rear and shipped to a port and railhead to be moved to forward dumps on Army transport. The

23   Robert Ehler, *The Mediterranean Air War*, p. 233.
24   Nigel Hamilton, *Monty – The Making of a General* (New York: McGrawhill Book Company, 1981), p. 638.

RAF's own motor transport would then carry the supplies on the final leg to their own landing grounds. The Rear Administrative Headquarters for both the Army and RAF kept each other well informed of their numbers of men and vehicles as well as future demands. The siting of Army HQ was even adapted to suit the mutual interests of their Air Force counterparts: Air HQ needed to be relatively close to their forward aerodromes and near a landing ground, this was usually some forty or sixty miles behind the front line which normally suited the Army HQ.[25] This close relationship meant that the Army and Air Force would, for the first time, have the opportunity of producing a joint plan. As Montgomery said on one his many trips to talk to his Army over the coming months:

> I have brought you together to tell you that I have made a plan – and when I say I've made a plan it's not quite right because I've made a plan in conjunction with the Air Force. Every plan has to have an intention – mine is to go to Tripoli, and it's the intention of the Air Force too to go to Tripoli. In fact we're all going to Tripoli together.[26]

Montgomery was fortunate in turning up when the British air-ground machinery had at last become highly effective, and Malta, reinforced by Spitfires ferried from the aircraft carriers, was now meting out punishment to the Axis convoys crossing the Mediterranean. Rommel had taken a gamble in pursuing the British to the El Alamein line, probably because he had fortuitously captured 4,000 tons of petrol at Tobruk. This meant that he and his superiors had felt that they could temporarily ignore Malta and capture it later, after the British had been finished off in Egypt. That was a fatal mistake, the island became resurgent once more and soon began sinking Rommel's shipping crossing the Mediterranean. Additionally, the Allies had built up a heavy bomber force in Palestine over the summer period and that began to hammer Benghazi with long range Liberator and Halifax bombers. This force included the newly arrived American 376th Bombardment Group and 98th Bomb Group under General Brereton. As the British frontline had withdrawn to El Alamein the Wellington bomber squadrons in 205 Group now struggled to reach Benghazi, so they turned instead to bombing Tobruk harbour, often called the front door of Rommel's re-supply system, with Benghazi described as the back door.[27]

The deteriorating German supply situation meant that Rommel now had just one last throw of the dice to break through to Alexandria, only 60 miles up the coast from his front-line positions. The British defensive battle of Alam Halfa (30 August–5 September 1942) which blocked the German attack, was Montgomery's first victory in the desert. The plan was jointly created with Coningham and forced Rommel to fight on ground dominated by the ridge at Alam Halfa, where British armour would stand and fight, supported by large concentrations of air and artillery firepower. The Desert Air Force was well prepared for the encounter with landing grounds fully-stocked and the ASCs well-sited and connected to a full array of Tentacles covering the battle area. Coningham continued his efforts to maintain air superiority by attacking airfields and conducted raids on the enemy's supply lines to isolate the battlefield. He also launched many strikes on the enemy's ground forces, including *Afrika Korps* vehicle concentrations, which were a primary target for the medium bombers to carpet or pattern bomb. Pattern bombing experiments had already shown that on typical desert terrain, of about six inches sand with limestone underneath, soft skinned vehicles were set on fire at distances up to 40 yards from the nearest bomb and that adequate fragmentation was produced at 60 yards to render almost all vehicles temporarily

25    Roderic Owen, *Desert Air Force*, p. 110.
26    Robert Ehler, *The Mediterranean Air War*, p. 233.
27    RAF Middle East, *The Official Story of Air Operations Feb. 1942 – Jan. 1943*, p. 114.

The crew of Douglas Boston Mark III, W8376 'C', of 24 Squadron, SAAF, walking away from their aircraft on an airfield in Libya after a sortie. (Crown Copyright – Air Historical Branch)

immobile. As a result, when bomber units were attacking vehicles in leaguer, they would attempt a bomb spacing of about 100 yards in line and width.[28]

Jack 'Cobber' Weinronk was a Boston bomber pilot with 24 Squadron SAAF at the time of Alam Halfa and recalls the punishing daylight attacks by the close formations of Boston aircraft:

> The pace has hotted up considerably. Jerry had made a bulge in the Alamein Line and pushed in about 5 miles between the New Zealand Division and the Quattara Depression. There was really a flap going on for, if he did break through, we'd have been in trouble as the Alamein Line was our last natural defence before Cairo and Palestine. Jerry was really gunning for the oil wells of the Middle East.

> **Wednesday, 2nd** Had a very busy day today and feel damn tired at the moment. I flew on four raids. Was up at 05.30 and did the first at 07.00. The second at 10.00. The third at 13.00 and the fourth at 16.00. On the first three raids the ack-ack was particularly heavy, but the fourth was a 'bit of a milk-run' (very light flak). The target was armoured vehicles near Deir el Agram and there was so much of it that one could not miss. The only problem was that it was very near our own troops and our leading observers had their job cut out not to hit our own troops. My flying log-book states: 'September 2nd Boston Q687, bombed enemy transport, ack-ack extremely heavy. September 2nd Boston Q687, bombed MT Deir el Ragii,

28   Air Publication 3235, *Air Support, The Second World War 1939-45*, pp. 61-62.

Boston Mark III, Z2183 'E', of 24 Squadron SAAF in flight, shortly after the Squadron re-equipped with the type at Shandur, Egypt. (Crown Copyright – Air Historical Branch)

ack-ack very heavy. September 2nd Q687, bombed tanks and MT, ack-ack slight. September 2nd Q687, bombed Southern Alamein Sector, ack-ack slight.' We felt Jerry had taken such a pounding that his anti-aircraft gunners were keeping their heads down.

**Thursday, 3rd** Boston L2300, bombed Deir el Risw. Ack-ack fairly heavy. Boston S-AL785, bombed MT, Southern Alamein Sector. Got holed in flaps, fuselage and bomb-bay.

**Friday, 4th** Boston AL706, bombed troops Munassib Area. Visibility fair. Ack-ack light. Landed in a dust-storm. At this point the Germans had had enough and returned to the positions they had occupied before the latest push... The dust-storm was very thick when we returned from this raid. The Colonel led the formation to a drome where the dust was not so intense. My Vic Leader broke from the formation and landed, and so did Neville and I. We all took a bit of a chance as visibility was shocking. Just heard that a friend of mine, Maurice Rabie from Oudtshoorn, was wounded in the leg on this raid.[29]

The daylight raids on the *Afrika Korps* by the Bostons were complemented by night raids from Wellingtons to achieve what came to be known as 'round the clock bombing'. The Wellington raids were guided by flares dropped from the Fleet Air Arm Fairey Albacore aircraft of 821 and 826 Naval Air Squadrons,[30] who took justifiable pride in considering themselves to be the first Pathfinders. The Albacore's would typically fly in at 5,000 to 6,000 feet, fifteen minutes ahead of the bomber force and begin dropping magnesium flares to illuminate the target. Coloured flares would also be dropped to mark high value targets. The Albacore's slow speed and ability to carry many flares made it ideal for this task and allowed the RAF to keep up the bombing attacks and maintain the pressure on the *Afrika Korps*. This not only caused much material damage but also left German units exhausted and demoralised.[31] Commander F. A. Swanton flew Albacores with

29   Jack Weinronk, *The Vaulted Sky* (Braunton: Devon, Merlin Books Ltd, 1993), p. 55.
30   Vincent Orange, *Coningham*, p. 107.
31   Robert Ehler, *The Mediterranean Air War*, p. 236.

821 Naval Air Squadron during this period and recalled the combined RAF and Fleet Air Arm operations:

> As the Axis forces pushed steadily Eastwards, we were to take on a more offensive role. By flying up to one of the forward L. G. during the day, we were then able to bomb enemy targets at night. But of course the bombload we carried was nothing compared with that of a Wellington bomber. On the other hand it was extremely difficult for the R.A.F. pilots to locate and make a bombing run on a target they probably could not see in a featureless desert at night. So we made it a joint operation and instead of bombs we carried parachute flares. These helped us to pinpoint a worthwhile target and having found it we could bring in the bombers with green Verey lights. They, of course, were flying at a greater height than our Albacores and if they were to drop their bombs accurately, it was essential that we laid a line of flares slightly upwind of the target. These would float down on their parachutes and after a few minutes a further line would have to be dropped in order to maintain the illumination. It was a strange feeling to watch the bombs exploding on the ground below us when we knew full well that they had been released from above our heads only seconds before. However, I suppose the chances of being hit in mid-air by a bomb released from another aircraft, must be fairly remote.
>
> We did lose an aircrew from time to time, of course, but our casualties as a result of enemy action were gratifyingly few. On one occasion a flare dropping crew failed to return and some-time later we learned that they had been involved in a mid-air collision with a Wellington bomber. I don't know if there were any R.A.F. survivors, but I do know that the Albacore pilot survived – I met him years later at an 'air day' at R.N.A.S. Yeovilton.[32]

Major H Woods was a member of the Kings Royal Rifle Corps in 7th Armoured Division and during the Alam Halfa battle his rifle company was holding the extreme left of the British position on Himeimat Hill. He recalled that the British bombers had not been able to operate effectively during the day because of a dust storm, but by the night of 1 September they were able to strike the German formations attacking his position:

> At 12:30 am our bombers, returning from Tobruk, found his whole strength had moved east-wards and located him with flares in the valley below us. It was one of the most awe-inspiring sights I shall ever see, I think – there were seldom less than twenty flares in the air at any one time and the whole valley was lit up like a huge orange fairyland. All the time, red-orange, white-green tracer was darting hither and thither like little 100 mile-an-hour coloured fairies. The huge flash of the bombs, which included two of 4,000 lbs., also inspired the whole thor-oughly warlike scene, with little figures silhouetted against their vehicles as they tried to find cover from our bombs. The bombers were so accurate that they bombed right up to the mine-field beyond which, 2,000 yards away, was another of our companies.[33]

Rommel's forces were unable to break through at Alam Halfa and instead retreated to their Alamein positions. The *Afrika Korps* were now at the end of a long line of communication, facing an enemy with growing numerical and material strength, assured air superiority and close, secure

---

32   IWM 2077 Private Papers Commander F. A. Swanton, p. 12.
33   G.L. Verney, *The Desert Rats – The History of the 7th Armoured Division 1938-45* (London: Hutchinson, 1954), p. 131.

access to his supply base. In contrast it was a decisive defensive victory for the British and a moment for Coningham to reflect on the key lessons for fighting the *Luftwaffe*:

1.  Fighter governs the front.
2.  Air Commander must have control of all air forces in forward areas.
3.  Bombing by day in battle area involves permanent fighter escort.
4.  Within range of shore-based fighters the Stuka is dead.
5.  Necessity for continuous bombing by day and night.
6.  Germans very susceptible to attacks with delay-action bombs on their landing grounds.
7.  Use of fast fused bombs [instantaneous fuses] at night means that Germans have to check aircraft for blast and splinters before they can fly next day.
8.  Need for communication aeroplane which can land and take off from smallest possible space.
9.  Fighters need speed and performance below 15,000 feet.
10. Over specialisation of fighters to be discouraged.
11. Need for larger proportion of fighters to bombers: say 4 to 6 fighters for one bomber.
12. In combined operations Army and Air commanders must live together and see each other daily.
13. Need for forward planning on a pessimistic basis.[34]

While Rommel was battling to supply and reinforce his army, the Desert Air Force was in contrast benefitting from a well-ordered and efficient logistic system that maximised the serviceability and availability of aircraft. At the front line this consisted of the salvage operations undertaken by the Repair and Salvage Units (RSU). Sections of this unit were normally commanded by an NCO and consisted of a mobile crane and an articulated truck to pick up and recover the damaged aircraft. The units were mobile, largely self-sufficient and could be tasked to retrieve an aircraft from even the most unlikely sites. On one occasion this necessitated a combined operation with Eighth Army infantry and sappers to breach a minefield, mark a safe lane with white mine-tape and recover a downed Hurricane through the gap and to safety.[35] During one seventeen-week period 800 out of 1,000 damaged aircraft, scattered over 100,000 square miles of desert were successfully recovered by the RSUs, brought back for base repair and then subsequently returned to service in the frontline.[36] During the retreat from the Gazala line the RAF left just five aircraft behind, all of which were considered damaged beyond repair. In contrast when the Germans had withdrawn the previous year, they had left 200 repairable aircraft behind.[37]

Another advantage the British possessed was the sizable administrative area in the Canal Zone which had been established prior to the War. This logistics base was now much larger and included many more maintenance units, some of which were securely sited in the spacious caves of the Mokkatam hills, from which the stones for the pyramids had been excavated. These caves were re-furbished and turned into stores, depots and workshops. Perhaps even more remarkably the British created an entire network of machine shops in the back streets of Cairo. Here they were able to utilise local labour to undertake highly technical repairs: gun turrets were refurbished, as were worn out engines, which sometimes included complicated processes such as chromium plating.

34  TNA AIR 23/1292 Fourth Conference of Air Officers Command, HQ RAF Middle East, 18 September 1942.
35  RAF Middle East, *The Official Story of Air Operations Feb. 1942 – Jan. 1943*, p. 34.
36  RAF Middle East, *The Official Story of Air Operations Feb. 1942 – Jan. 1943*, p. 34.
37  RAF Middle East, *The Official Story of Air Operations Feb. 1942 – Jan. 1943*, p. 64.

Personnel of 53 Repair and Salvage Unit brew tea and stretch their legs in the Western Desert while transporting salvaged Hawker Hurricane fuselages to Helwan, Egypt. (Crown Copyright – Air Historical Branch)

Perhaps most impressively propeller blades that had been bent on crashing could be re-shaped, this was a very technically demanding process that necessitated the blades being cleaned and stripped and then made pliable in a solution of molten salt. The blades were then bent and twisted back through a series of locally procured presses before being immersed in the salt solution once more, followed by a plunge into cold water and final polishing, painting and balancing.[38] The British had to adopt such unorthodox measures primarily because they were at the very end of the supply line and it was more economic to refurbish equipment than scrap it.

Salvaging and repairing equipment was one thing, but the British still required a steady stream of new machines to maintain and increase the Desert Air Force's fleet of aircraft. The essential supply of replacement aircraft came to the Middle East via two main routes, one, for longer range aircraft, such as Wellington bombers, was via Gibraltar and Malta. The second, for shorter range aircraft, was the Takoradi route, which was based on an old British Overseas Airways Corporation (BOAC) course from West Africa to Sudan. The British would assemble Hurricanes, Kittyhawks or other short-range aircraft from crates at Takoradi, in the Gold Coast and then, usually guided by a Blenheim or Hudson, the formation would fly via several staging posts across Africa to Sudan and then finally to Egypt. The route meant there was always a steady trickle of new aircraft reaching RAF Middle East.[39]

---

38   RAF Middle East, *The Official Story of Air Operations Feb. 1942 – Jan. 1943*, p. 39.
39   RAF Middle East, *The Official Story of Air Operations Feb. 1942 – Jan. 1943*, p. 32.

The entrance of one of the caves in the Mokattam hills, south of Cairo, used as storage and maintenance workshops by 111 Maintenance Unit. (Crown Copyright – Air Historical Branch)

Hawker Hurricanes being assembled for despatch to the North African and Mediterranean theatres, at Takoradi, Gold Coast. In the foreground Hawker Hurricane fuselages are pulled by labourers from their packing crates for assembly. (Crown Copyright – Air Historical Branch)

Having won the decisive battle of Alam Halfa, the British began planning their own offensive operation to drive Rommel out of North Africa. This new plan still rested upon using air power in a comprehensive and flexible manner and included first, maintaining battlefield air superiority through offensive action on enemy airfields. Second, the interdiction of Axis supplies and lines of communication, through a combination of shipping strikes from Malta, bombing of ports (Benghazi and Tobruk initially, and then Tripoli and Tunis as the Eighth Army advanced). Third, attacks on his road and rail communications to isolate the battlefield and finally providing close and general support to the Eighth Army as they attacked the *Afrika Korps*. These operations were coordinated with the Eighth Army's ground offensive at El Alamein, which started on 23 October 1942 and finally turned the tide in the British favour. Once the advance began to get underway the Desert Air Force's ability to move and occupy airfields quickly, on some occasion ahead of the advancing British column, began to pay off. The longer range Beaufighters were also able to help maintain air superiority, by harassing German aircraft at their own airfields. As Sergeant Bell describes:

> As a relative newcomer to the business of Beaufighter ground attacks in late 1942, I found such operations both thrilling and terrifying. At OTU I'd been firmly warned against all forms of low flying, and therefore had no real experience as such before joining my Beau squadron for ops. My first sortie, only two days after joining was a strafe of an enemy landing ground known to be in use by the Luftwaffe. There were four of us detailed, led by my Flight commander, and we set out just about sunrise to gain surprise. We flew slightly out to sea off the African coastline for most of the outward leg, keeping right down over the water to stay below enemy radar, then at a wing-waggle from the leader – we had maintained R/T silence all the way out – we wheeled to port and crossed inland, turned again, and flew along the long, black single coast road with eyes wide open in case any road convoys were about. My nav soon reported, 'Target due in two minutes, Dinger' and I prepared myself for the actual strafe, my right thumb poised over the cannon firing tit on the control spectacle. My next sight was smoke and empty shell cases streaming back from the leader's Beau – we'd arrived!
>
> Ahead of me were several German aircraft on a bare piece of desert with the usual scattering of pup tents etc. further on. I automatically lined my sight on the nearest couple of kites and fired, even though I must have been about 6-700 yards range at first. A line of sand bursts began running ahead of me as my shells tracked towards my own targets, then hit the nearest aircraft which immediately exploded violently.
>
> Seconds later I was flying through the muck and smoke of that explosion which reached way over my cockpit, and I actually ducked in fright! Scared or not I kept my thumb down on the gun button and saw my shells plough through several small tents and a lorry parked nearby, and suddenly I was across the airfield and out over bare desert again. It all happened so damned quick that it felt unreal.
>
> Coming to my senses I looked around for the other Beaus and was relieved to find all three not too far away, beginning to close up again on the leader. My nav reported that we'd definitely set fire to at least four aircraft apart from any other items. I asked him if he was OK to which he replied yes, but he felt he needed a change of underwear – I knew how he felt! We both checked around as far as possible for any damage to the Beau, but found none. According to my nav there'd been no flak defence fire so we must have achieved total surprise.[40]

40   Chaz Bowyer, *Beaufighter*, pp. 119-20.

The Allied situation in North Africa and the Mediterranean improved dramatically after the victory at El Alamein, the capture of airfields around Benghazi was particularly important and meant that the convoys to Malta could be better protected.[41] Furthermore, the Anglo-American landings in Morocco and Algeria between 8–10 November 1942 (Operation TORCH) now threatened the Axis position in North Africa from both the East and West. The hopes for speedy success on this new front were sadly short-lived and after overcoming the patchy French resistance the advance to Tunis ground to a halt in the face of German reinforcements, including air units. The Tunisian campaign turned into another frustrating period for the Allies and it was evident that both the newly arrived Americans, as well as the First British Army, lacked the skills and experience of air-ground integration that their desert counterparts had obtained. There was also a strong degree of cultural and institutional prejudice to overcome, for instance many American Army officers viewed their Air Force as simply aerial artillery and believed that the Army commanders should own and command every asset operating in 'their' area of the battlefield. As the Germans began to assert a degree of air superiority over Tunisia, familiar cries arose from commanders such as General Patton, the commander of the US II Corps, for permanent defensive air umbrellas over ground troops. There was no recognition that in prosecuting a successful campaign the air force commander was a partner, not a subordinate, to the army commander. Or even that the priority for a joint campaign was the requirement to achieve air superiority, which must include offensive actions against the adversary's airfields. Finally, there was little acceptance from Army commanders in Tunisia, that the air force could make a large contribution to the campaign's success through interdiction missions against the enemy's ports or lines of communication.

While the Anglo-American Army struggled in Tunisia, the British Eighth Army and Desert Air Force was liberating Libya and approaching the south-eastern border of Tunisia. By this stage the Desert Air Force's close relationship with the Eighth Army had become almost second nature. Coningham's pride in this association was so great that he personally sought permission from the Air Staff to have an '8' emblazoned on his North African medal ribbon, like every soldier in the Eighth Army. He was refused. Eisenhower, the overall commander of the forces in TORCH, noted the strong partnership between the Eighth Army and the Desert Air Force and contrasted it to that of his own forces. As a result, he instituted a shake-up of the TORCH command structures and brought in experienced leaders, such as Alexander, as well as Coningham who was given command of the newly created North African Tactical Air Force, which consisted of both American and British air components. Coningham quickly unified his new command and concentrated on achieving air superiority, carrying out longer range interdiction tasks and then providing ground support to the Army. Air Vice Marshal Harry Broadhurst took over the Desert Air Force from Coningham and emulated the practices of his predecessor, including maintaining a deep partnership with the Army.

One of the hardest tasks for any Tactical Air Force is to provide close air support to the Army during a mobile offensive operation. The Desert Air Force operations to support the outflanking of the Mareth line by 2nd New Zealand Division and 8th Armoured Brigade was just such a challenge and allowed Broadhurst to set a new benchmark in air-ground coordination. In this operation the New Zealanders followed an obscure 90 km route through the Matmata Hills, before launching an attack on the Tebaga Gap on 21 March 1943.[42] Day pattern bombing from the Desert Air Force's three light bomber wings would precede the attack, which would be followed by ground attack missions from the three fighter wings and a Hurricane tank destroyer squadron. The air support operation was not only large, it also included the first use of Forward Air Controllers

41   See Map 4 for Advance from El Alamein.
42   See Map 5 for details of Battle of Tebaga.

Vickers Wellington B Mark IIIs of 150 Squadron RAF under maintenance prior to receiving their bomb loads at Blida, Algeria. (Crown Copyright – Air Historical Branch)

with armoured formations, as well as Forward Bomber Controllers for the light bomber wings. The use of these controllers would subsequently become standard practice in both Italy and North West Europe. Eighth Army's highly respected Chief of Staff, Freddie de Guingand, described how the operation was set up:

> On my return to Main Headquarters I had a long discussion with Broadhurst, A.O.C. of the Desert Force. I explained the situation to him. We in the Army had always wanted to try out what is generally called a 'Blitz' attack. The Germans employed it on frequent occasions, and used their dive bombers for that very close and intimate air support which we felt would prove very effective. Hitherto the close support given to the attack had always been by bomb from the light bomber, and the fighter bomber. The R.A.F. had for very good reasons been against the dive bomber, but we felt the cannons from the fighters might prove more deadly and disrupting to the enemy than the fighter bomber with their bombs dropped from comparatively high altitudes. In view of the importance of the attack, and the narrow frontage to which we were confined, this did look to be the right occasion for trying out this type of attack.
>
> Using the fighter in this low-flying role over the immediate battle area was a considerable risk, and it was possible that the casualties would prove very severe. On the other hand we felt that, from our own experiences from low-flying attacks, the defence took some time to recover equilibrium, and that some sort of temporary paralysis often set in.
>
> Broadhurst listened to the arguments, and after a long discussion said, 'I will do it. You will have the whole boiling match—bombs and cannon. It will be a real low-flying blitz, and I will talk to all the pilots myself.'
>
> The 24th and 25th were spent in a maze of planning. There was a tremendous lot to be done between the Air and ourselves. We wanted to let every pilot know what to go for and what to expect, so we prepared detailed maps showing the exact locations of the enemy guns,

transport and defences.[43] These were reproduced from air photos and other intelligence. The squadron leaders were sent to fly over the battle area and so get to know their way about. An experienced squadron leader was to direct the Kittybombers by wireless. An R.A.F. officer was also detailed with a wireless set in an armoured car to be positioned far forward from where he could warn our aircraft if they were shooting up our own troops. Then there was all the detail in connection with landmarks, timings and coloured smoke signals. Later on all these ideas became a matter of routine, but then they were in their experimental stage.

The final air plan catered for a 'crump' by forty light bombers on the narrow frontage of attack, to take place just before it commenced. Then, with five Spitfire squadrons as top cover, sixteen Kittybomber squadrons would operate over the battlefield for two and a half hours, at an average density of two squadrons at any one time. These using bomb and cannon would shoot up everything they saw. In addition a specially trained squadron of 'tank busters' [Hurricane IIDs with 40mm cannon] were to go for the enemy armour when located. In order to cause disorganization to the enemy's rear areas, it was agreed to carry out night bombing raids during the previous two nights. The pilots were brought up to a great state of enthusiasm, and as will be seen the whole operation was an unqualified success. Montgomery agreed to the final plan that Freyburg and Horrocks hatched out between them. It was simple in the extreme. The attack was on a narrow front, preceded by a heavy creeping barrage, and with artillery concentrations and smoke dealing with the enemy on either side of the valley. Behind this barrage the tanks would move forward, and behind them the infantry. It was hoped that all dangerous minefields had been dealt with, but in case of unexpected trouble sapper parties were available. Then, of course, super-imposed on this were the aircraft, the pilots being able to see exactly how the attack was going by the barrage. They therefore knew what to go for; the barrage gave them the bomb-line [provided that the infantry kept up with it]. The New Zealanders were to make the hole and the 1st Armoured Division was to be positioned behind ready to push through the gap so made towards El Hamma. They were to go by night or day—preferably by night as a good moon would be shining. The attack was to take place at 16.00 hours, as this would give us the sun behind, shining into the defenders' eyes.[44]

Brigadier Kippenberger was the commander of 5th Infantry Brigade, part of 2nd New Zealand Division and described how his troops began the operation:

[The assaulting New Zealand troops] moved forward to their start-line, dug in, and camouflaged themselves as well as they could. The tape marking was taken up before daylight and they stayed in their pits with an absolute prohibition against anyone moving until zero hour. Signals were all linked up and at daylight the whole area looked empty. The morning and early afternoon passed slowly, very little movement visible anywhere and, except that the Twenty-First on Hill 184 were steadily hammered by mortars, there was very little fire. The infantry forward lay very still and were apparently unobserved. I played chess with Blundell, read, and wrote letters.

---

43   Major General Tuker, GOC 4th Indian Division, which flanked the New Zealanders made the point that had these accurate maps and photographs been in the hands of the artillery, the wasteful creeping barrage mentioned later would not have been needed. Each enemy post could have had the concentrated treatment from all guns. It seems that the mapping of enemy defences for the whole Mareth fighting, compiled from highly detailed photographic reconnaissance, could have been better disseminated. (Francis Tuker, *Approach To Battle* (London: Cassell, 1963) p. 302.

44   Freddie De Guingand, *Operation Victory* (London: Hodder and Stoughton, 1947), p. 256.

Punctually at 3.30 p.m. the fighter-bombers appeared, squadron after squadron: all along the line of the forward infantry little columns of orange smoke appeared indicating their positions, and this smoke steadily grew and spread. The bombers made no mistake and nothing was dropped on us, but for half an hour they turned the enemy position into a pandemonium. Very soon there were several columns of black smoke from burning trucks or tanks. The whole narrow area between the hills looked like a cauldron. I noted with concern that Hill 209, the Maori objective on our right flank, was scarcely being attacked. Otherwise the 'blitz' seemed likely to be an effective preparation.

Under cover of the noise and smoke of this bombardment, in clouds of dust, the Sherman tanks of the Notts. [Nottinghamshire] Yeomanry and Staffordshire Yeomanry rumbled up, passed on either side of Hill 201 and deployed along the infantry start-line. They were moving into position when the guns opened, firing for twenty-three minutes on the enemy positions, and at 4.15 p.m. the tanks moved majestically forward, followed closely by our little carriers. The infantry climbed out of their pits—where there had been nothing visible there were now hundreds of men, who shook out into long lines and followed on 500 yards behind the tanks. At 4.23 p.m. the barrage lifted a hundred yards—an extraordinarily level line of bursting shells—tanks and infantry closed to it and the assault was on.[45]

In addition to the control measures outlined by De Guingand and Kippenberger above, three large letters, A, B and C had been marked on three prominent hills short of the frontline. These locations were briefed to pilots who were instructed to orbit them, not only to pin point their location, but to also give warning to ground troops that their attack was about to commence.[46]

Kittyhawk pilot Bert Horden was on the Tebaga operation and describes the mission:

Before going we were to attend a Wing pep talk by Group Captain Harry Broadhurst [He was actually an Air Vice-Marshal at the time] from Group Headquarters. There must have been nearly eighty pilots gathered round the Group Captain as he stood in the back of a 3-ton truck to deliver his oration. Shades of Agincourt! He was most depressing. He told us we were an important factor in this great battle just beginning. He said that some of us would have to walk back, some would be prisoners of war and some of us would not get back at all! But, of course, he knew he could count on us all to do our duty, etc, etc. I was not motivated just plain shit scared.

Back at the Squadron I learnt that I was to fly No 2 to the CO again. I felt better about this because he inspired confidence. He told me to stick as close to him as possible all the way from a formation take off to hopefully, a formation landing on our return. So the Squadron took off, CO first followed by myself, tucked in as tight as I dare, then the other ten Kittys…

It was not many minutes to our flying area. On the way we could see other Kittyhawk squadrons moving towards the same area. It was all very well having a clear bomb-line on a map in the IO's truck but there was little on the ground to indicate where our lot ended and the Jerries began. This time, however, along the main road to El Hamma we could see tanks and trucks moving up while beyond, in enemy held territory there was little to see.

Geoff Garton soon identified some German 88 mm gun emplacements for us to bomb. There was no ack-ack aimed at us at this stage as no doubt the German gunners were pointing their guns up the road at the New Zealanders' tanks instead of at us. The CO went down. Then it was my turn. I clearly saw the emplacements disappear under my port wing before

---

Kairouan, Tunisia. c. April 1943. Two armourers of 450 Squadron RAAF, a fighter bomber squadron, at work bombing up. (Australian War Memorial)

RAAF crews running for their P-40 aircraft. (State Library of Victoria, Melbourne, Victoria, Australia)

going down to the left. The dive felt like 90 degrees but was only about 60. I saw the CO's bombs burst on target just as I released mine. Others that followed also found the target so it was accurate bombing. It wasn't always.

Now we were to strafe any enemy targets that we could find. I saw some other guns at the side of the road and set about strafing. The six .5 inch guns all firing could be felt as a braking sensation on the flight of the Kitty and the destructive power at the receiving end was enormous. Most were explosive bullets mixed with a few tracers. As I went in to strafe, I noticed some objects going past the cockpit hood. At first I thought we were being attacked by enemy fighters but they were large objects. Then realised they were artillery shells the New Zealanders were lobbing at the enemy – or vice versa – I didn't stop to find out which.

I continued strafing for a short time with tracers going into the enemy positions. Some small arms fire came up at me. Then I pulled up to orientate myself, only to find I was completely on my own again; not an aircraft in sight. I spotted some German trucks scurrying at high speed down the road – a rare sight – so set about them. I caught the rear truck, which burst into flames. I saw my bullets spraying the other two which crashed off the road into the scrub but didn't flame. I couldn't see any more targets and thought I may be nearly out of ammunition so pulled up and set off towards base. I wondered what my CO would say when we got back. I was half way when I spotted a lone aircraft at about 5,000 ft. I gradually caught up with it, made sure it was one of ours and to my amazement, it was the CO. What luck! He waved to me. I think he was as amazed as I was, so I tucked in behind him to guard his tail and shortly arrived over base. I did a very close formation landing in the hopes of impressing him. At the de-briefing he nodded his thanks for staying with him.[47]

The close air support operation at Tebaga was a huge success and played an important part in allowing the Eighth Army to break through. The British press quite rightly observed the unique nature of this close air support and made a big business of it. However back home, the Air Ministry was keen to play down the significance of the 'Tebaga Gap Blitz', perhaps fearing that the Army would come to expect such support as routine, which would pose a heavy drain on the RAF's fighter strength that would distract them from their other roles. De Guingand felt that this attitude inferred great stupidity and ignorance on the Army who understood the exceptional nature of such support. He also observed that downplaying the attack was grossly unfair on Broadhurst and his pilots, who he felt had fought magnificently. Fortunately, the casualty bill for the Tebaga Gap operation was not as severe as had been feared and only eight pilots were killed or missing as a result of the operation.[48]

The fighting in North Africa concluded on 12 May 1943. The final stages of the campaign included Operation FLAX, the Allied interdiction of German reinforcements from Italy, which towards the end were usually transported in Ju 52 and Me 323 Gigant transport aircraft. The slaughter of a large fleet of Ju 52s, during what became known as the *Palmsonntag Massaker* (Palm Sunday Massacre), was a particularly noteworthy affair. Operation FLAX, together with the decimation of German transport attempting to re-supply Stalingrad, effectively destroyed what had been one of the most impressive air transport fleets in the world. The *Luftwaffe* would never recover from it.

47   Bert Horden, *Shark Squadron*, p. 66.
48   Freddie De Guingand, *Operation Victory*, p. 264.

# 7

# 'Swift and Strong'[1]
# Air Support reaches maturity in the Italian Campaign

As the campaign in North Africa concluded, Coningham decided that his time spent roughing it in the Western Desert justified a bit of luxury. With a requisition order from Alexander he obtained arguably the best accommodation in Tunisia, the Sebastian Villa in Hammamet, and moved in to this beautiful old Moorish building with a pool and gardens that sloped down to the beach.[2] Whilst luxuriating in his new dwellings, Coningham could feel a sense of satisfaction at the operational framework he had helped create in the Western Desert and the role it had played in the prosecution of the campaign. The combination of aerial superiority, interdiction and ground support roles performed by the Desert Air Force had worked well.

Coningham and his Desert Air Force had been fortunate in that understanding how to interdict Axis convoys and transport in Egypt and Libya had been comparatively simple, there were only a few ports, a single major metalled road along the coast and a solitary railway line from Tripoli to Alexandria. Even Tunisia had lacked a particularly sophisticated communications infrastructure. The next operational theatre the Allies intended to campaign in, Sicily and the Italian mainland, were more developed and posed a much more complex targeting challenge, namely what could fighter bombers and bombers achieve against these enemy lines of communication? Which targets should they concentrate upon? Road and rail bridges to act as blocks and gaps in the arteries? Or railway marshalling yards and rolling stock? The former were less well defended and took a long time to repair, but they could also be circumvented, the latter were usually heavily defended by concentrations of flak, but the rolling stock might be harder to replace.[3]

Though the answers to these questions were not immediately apparent, a remarkable scientist had spent the early part of the war studying the effects of aerial bombing and had produced a growing body of evidence that assisted in the planning of air interdiction operations in the Italian campaign, as well as in North West Europe.

Professor Solly Zuckerman was a South African zoologist whose first venture into operational analysis had been to study *Luftwaffe* bombing of British cities. He had then been posted to the Middle East as an Operational Research scientist and had studied the effects of Allied bombing

---

1    Motto of 260 Squadron Royal Air Force. The squadron reformed on 22 November 1940 at RAF Castletown, Scotland and operated Hawker Hurricanes. It then moved to Egypt in 1941 and operated Kittyhawk fighter bombers over the western desert and advanced with the Eighth Army into Tunisia. It moved to Sicily as part of Operation HUSKY and as the Allied forces advanced into Italy it converted to the North American P-51 Mustang. The Squadron disbanded at Lavariano on 19 August 1945.

2    Vincent Orange, *Coningham*, p. 156.

3    See Map 6 for Italian lines of communication targeted during Operation STRANGLE as well as major German defensive lines and the dates major towns were liberated by the Allies.

Armourers load a Curtiss P-40D Kittyhawk Mark III of 239 Wing RAF at Agnone, Sicily. The aircraft was being prepared for a sortie against enemy positions in the foothills of Mount Etna.
(Crown Copyright – Air Historical Branch)

Pilots of 3 Squadron RAAF assembled in their Operations Room in a barn on the edge of the airfield at Agnone, Sicily. (Crown Copyright – Air Historical Branch)

on Tripoli. He was an advisor during the invasion of Pantelleria and also predicted the impact bombing might have on Palermo and the Sicilian railway system. By the time of the invasion, he had concluded that it was better for aircraft to strike the marshalling yards across the country; principally in the six railway centres of Naples, Foggia, San Giovanni (near Rome), Reggio, Messina and Palermo. His judgement was that this would destroy both rolling stock and repair facilities, thus paralysing the Sicilian and southern Italian railway systems. As Zuckerman later commented in a report in December 1943, 'The efficiency of a railway system appears to fall very rapidly when bombing simultaneously leads to an increase in the calls upon, and a decrease in the capacity of the repair facilities'.[4]

As the campaign in Italy developed the idea that the RAF[5] could best support the Army through attacking the Axis lines of supply would become an increasing focus of the air effort. By early 1944 Operation STRANGLE had developed into a critical part of the Allies plan to break the Gustav line and involved 65,003 sorties delivering 33,104 tons of bombs in preparation for the major Allied ground offensive, known as Operation DIADEM. Once the Allied armies' attack commenced a further 72,946 sorties were launched, which dropped another 51,000 tons of bombs by 22 June. These attacks not only destroyed marshalling yards and rolling stock, they also cut every railway line, destroyed 6,577 vehicles and sank most of the enemy's small coastal vessels.[6] This was an impressive level of destruction, yet the Allies learnt one valuable lesson, namely that an air offensive by itself would never force the Germans to abandon its prepared defensive positions. This could only come through a combination of an air offensive _and_ a land attack. Slessor, who was now C-in-C RAF Mediterranean and Middle East, captured this tension well:

> We are not forcing him to expend fuel and or ammunition. I know it is necessary for the Army to rest, refit, regroup and train divisions for a major offensive, and that it is very difficult if not impossible with our present strength to maintain constant offensive pressure at the same time. But we must face the fact that by these long periods of inactivity the Army is automatically making its own task more difficult when it does not resume the offensive, by making it more difficult for us now to reduce the enemy's capacity for resistance. As Joe Cannon said at Alexander's conference a fortnight ago, in this phase it is not a question of the Air supporting the Army – the Army must support the Air by making the Hun expend fuel and ammunition while we prevent him replenishing his supplies.[7]

Slessor was right, as the land offensive began it became apparent that the German Army could not maintain their forward positions whilst the marshalling yards as well as roads, rail bridges and other chokepoints were being persistently attacked. The German requirement to replenish the frontline with ammunition and other supplies, as well as bring forward reinforcements and tactically move troops around was simply too much for the German Army. Consequently, the eventual collapse of the Gustav Line had much to do with Operation STRANGLE, but only when land operations were launched. These lessons were studied carefully by the planners for Operation OVERLORD and formed the basis of the 'Transport Plan' carefully put together by Zuckerman prior to the invasion.

The Italian campaign also generated several important tactical lessons in air-ground cooperation, many of which would also be relevant in other theatres. These included firstly the provision

---

4   Solly Zuckerman, *From Apes to Warlords* (London: Hamish Hamilton, 1978), p. 210.
5   See Annex F for the Order of Battle Mediterranean Air Command in July 1943.
6   Robert Ehler, *Mediterranean Air War*, p. 332
7   Robert Ehler, *Mediterranean Air War*, p. 333.

of air cover during amphibious operations, this was always a major planning factor and hard to deliver in practise. At Salerno (Operation BAYTOWN – 9 September 1943) the amphibious forces were successfully protected through a combination of long-range fighters and carrier-borne aircraft. Elsewhere in the Eastern Mediterranean a painful reminder of the consequences of not achieving air superiority at the outset of a maritime campaign was being administered to the British.

The Battle for Leros and the British attempt to seize the Dodecanese islands is not a widely known event in the Second World War.[8] In some ways it shows the British at their most audacious, seeking to capitalise upon the Italian capitulation on 2 September 1943, by grabbing the Italian-garrisoned Dodecanese islands including Rhodes, Kos and Leros. The British hoped that by doing so they could open a new front in the Balkans, potentially persuade Turkey to join the war, prompt the capitulation of Bulgaria and Romania and bring the Ploesti oilfields under Allied control. Key to such ambitions was a lack of German opposition and enough air cover to allow the Royal Navy and Army to occupy these islands. The British understood that the island of Rhodes was vital to the region and possessing its landing grounds would give the British an undoubted advantage. Yet the British fell into the trap of both overestimating the Italian readiness to switch sides and fight the Germans and underestimating German ruthlessness. By 11 September, the 7,500 strong German division on Rhodes had easily crushed the Italian garrison of 35,000–40,000 on the island, dashing British hopes of achieving this important first objective.[9] This might have been the moment to call it a day, but the British, perhaps emboldened by Churchill's guidance that 'This is a time to play high. Improvise and dare'[10] adapted their plan. RAF Dakota air transport was used to quickly seize Kos, with a parachute drop from a company of the 11th Parachute Battalion, followed by the air-landing of elements of the 1st Battalion of the Durham Light Infantry on the island's airfield at Antimachia. These were then reinforced by support troops and two squadrons of Spitfires (7 Squadron SAAF and 74 Squadron) from 243 Wing. Elsewhere in the Dodecanese British Special Forces, in the guise of the Special Boat Service and the Long Range Desert Group, were spearheading 234 Infantry Brigade as they occupied other islands including Leros and Samos.

The Germans did not remain idle and reinforced the *Luftwaffe* units in the region to bring them up to a strength of 326 aircraft. These aircraft, based at airfields on Rhodes, Crete and the Greek mainland, swiftly began to neutralise the small number of British fighters on Kos and painfully reminded the British that it is impossible to sustain small and isolated forces of aircraft in the face of much heavier opposition. Having swept the Kos-based Spitfires from the sky, the Germans then began to neutralise the British and Italian soldiers on Kos with light and medium bombers. The level of air superiority the Germans achieved was enough for even the Ju 87 to reappear and dive-bomb the British soldiers in a manner more reminiscent of 1940 than 1943. The Germans bombed Antimachia heavily and this together with the lack of dispersal pens and the difficulty in digging in the rocky ground, led to high casualties in both men and machines. The Germans invaded Kos on 3 October and after a brief battle Allied resistance had ceased by 4 October.

The position of the remainder of 234 Infantry Brigade on Leros and Samos became increasingly precarious and the task of the Royal Navy in sustaining and even reinforcing these islands more difficult. The Royal Navy losses in ships included four cruisers damaged, two submarines destroyed, as well as six destroyers and ten other smaller coastal vessels and minesweepers also sunk.[11] On 26 September the captain of HMS *Intrepid*, Commander Arthur Kitcat, was carrying elements of the Royal Irish Fusiliers to Leros to reinforce the garrison. He describes how *Intrepid*

---

8    See Map 2 for locations of Dodecanese Islands in Eastern Mediterranean.
9    Anthony Rogers, *Churchill's Folly – Leros and the Aegean* (London: Cassel, 2003), p. 35.
10   TNA AIR 41/53 Operations in the Dodecanese Islands September-November 1943 p.7
11   Spencer Tucker, *World War II at sea: An Encyclopaedia* (ABC-CLIO, 2011), p. 241.

and a Greek destroyer the *Queen Olga* were attacked at their moorings in the island's port of Lakki that day:

> At about 0915 I set out for shore by motor boat… When approaching the jetty I heard the sound of aeroplane motors overhead, and looking up saw a large formation of Ju 88s at about 5,000 feet. As I watched they commenced to dive, directing their attacks on the two destroyers. I at once returned to the ship, but before reaching it HMS *Intrepid* had received a hit on the bulkhead between No. 3 Boiler room and the Engine room port side and within half a minute HHMS *Queen Olga* received a hit in the after magazine. No warning whatever of attack was received; no Italian guns opened fire. Anti-aircraft armament of HMS *Intrepid* was at five minutes notice but was in full operation before the first bomb had dropped. I saw pieces fly from one machine, obviously hit by her fire, and am informed that this machine crashed on the island. HHMS *Queen Olga* rapidly filled, heeled over and sank. It is regretted that loss of life was considerable. Her Captain, Commander Blessas, was wounded when the bomb struck and was subsequently killed by cannon shell from an aircraft…[12]

Naval Lieutenant G. W. Searle was on board his vessel, the motor launch ML 355, on the south side of the harbour and also recalled the attack:

> With a shattering explosion the stem of the *Queen Olga* blew off. She had a direct hit in the after-magazine. One destroyer sunk, the other was badly damaged. The repair shops, the barracks and the southern jetties were hit with considerable destruction. The German pilots could be proud of their precision but the defences should have done better. MLs 351 and 355 both claimed hits on the planes but could not claim that any were brought down … The *Queen Olga* had gone down with great loss of life. First there was the explosion itself; then as oil from the ship spread over the water, it ignited and the place where she had been lying at a buoy became a patch of blazing oil around which MLs 836, 356 and 354 circled as they tried to pick up survivors. MLs 356 and 354 had actually been alongside *Queen Olga* when the raid started and had only just cast off in time to avoid destruction themselves. Astern of us, only some fifty yards away, were the smashed remains of two Italian MS boats which had suffered direct hits by bombs. Ashore, the workshops and barracks were on fire and bodies were being carried out.[13]

The Royal Navy were naturally seething that they were carrying out such operations in the fourth year of the war, by which period the hazards of operating ships in daylight in areas where an enemy had air supremacy should have been well understood.

The events at Leros followed the same script as at Kos. The Germans neutralising the British and Italian defenders with air strikes, before subjecting them to a combined amphibious and airborne assault on 12 November. Many mistakenly believe that Germany never launched an airborne assault after Crete, this is untrue as at Leros they dropped approximately 600 paratroopers from Ju 52s on the afternoon of 12 November. The larger garrison at Leros took longer to subjugate, but German airpower often made a substantial difference. Corporal Vic 'Taffy' Kenchington was a stretcher bearer with the Royal Irish Fusiliers and recalls the difficulties his company faced while trying to counter-attack the German positions, who were able to bring down defensive close air support upon the advancing British:

---

12    TNA ADM 199/1040, Commander C.A. de W Kitcat, Report of Proceedings, dated 5 October 1943.
13    G W Searle, *At Sea Level* (Sussex: Book Guild Publishing Ltd, 2005), pp. 128-9.

I was feeling very nervous and shaky and wished I was somewhere else, as suspense and fear of the unexpected took hold. The troops in front of us went forward at a steady trot, with weapons at the high port. We could hear the 'swish-swish' of the German mortars and the buzzing of spandau bullets coming our way. Red Verey lights from the German positions signalled the Stukas to come in with 50-kilogram bombs and MGs. A bomb landed about three yards from me – we had taken cover behind a small wall – and I felt a bang on my back and I really thought that I had been hit, but the bomb fin had hit the wall above me and then landed on my back so I just got a singed shirt and bruising. The Stukas were lined up just like a 'taxi-rank', awaiting the Verey lights and down they would come. Soon, we got the call: 'Stretcher bearers!' We ran forward to our first wounded, passing men in statuesque postures who we knew would never get up again. They had that greyish white, or pale blue-green tinge with blood seeping from nose or ears, although we could see no real wound. They had been killed by blast. We reached our first wounded man. He was from the Buffs and had a very bad scalp wound. It took a shell dressing to cover it. I gave him a shot of morphine as he was babbling a lot of gibberish and was relieved to get him back to the RAP [Regimental Aid Post].[14]

By 16 November the isolated British brigade's resistance had ceased, and the island was captured by the Germans with 4,300 British soldiers surrendering. A lack of coordination between all three services and an unexpectedly aggressive response by the Germans were undoubtedly factors in this defeat, but the lack of air superiority was probably most decisive in what was one of the last large British defeats in the war and arguably the last outright German victory. It is easy to become glib about allied air superiority in the second half of the Second World War and complacent about the security it bestowed upon Allied offensive activity. The Leros campaign is a sharp reminder that such conditions should not be easily assumed and the Germans were often quick to punish recklessness.

In Italy Allied air superiority was no longer such an issue. There were plenty of airfields available, including many new ones constructed by the Royal Engineer and RAF Airfield Construction Groups who, though facing a much harder task than in the desert, were still able to provide enough landing grounds for the growing armada of Allied aircraft. By the beginning of 1944 the size of the Allied air forces also meant that there were enough medium and heavy bombers to be used for close air support as well as interdiction and general support. Nowhere was the use of heavy bombers in this close air support role more controversial than at Monte Cassino, where the disadvantages of mass bombing of built up areas first became apparent.

The Cassino Benedictine Monastery, which dominated the Liri Valley and the southern approach to Rome, was bombed at the request of the commander of 4th Indian Division on 15 February 1944. The monastery was pounded into rubble by 450 tons of explosive and the Germans, who up to that point had not fortified the monastery, moved in to occupy the wreckage and turn it into a series of strong defensive positions. A second larger air attack was also made on the town of Cassino itself, which nestled on the floor of the valley. This air bombardment was to be complemented by the Army's artillery and swiftly followed up by an advance from 2nd New Zealand Division. Safety concerns meant that the New Zealanders had to withdraw 1,000 yards before the attack began. The main object of the attack was the complete reduction of Cassino town and to that end no bombs smaller than 1,000 lbs were dropped and there was no attempt to use fuses with long delays. Eleven heavy bomber groups were employed in a period that lasted from 0830 to 1200 hours with no bomber operating any time after 1205 hours. Heavy bombers released their

---

14   Anthony Rogers, *Churchill's Folly – Leros and the Aegean*, p. 164.

A ground crewman helps a pilot of 601 Squadron RAF into the cockpit of his Supermarine Spitfire Mark IX at Venafro, Italy. The aircraft is about to undertake an offensive sweep in support of Operation DIADEM.
(Crown Copyright – Air Historical Branch)

munitions from 15,000 to 16,000 feet and medium bombers from 7,000 to 9,000 feet. There were no specific aiming points at Cassino, the target area was simply divided in half and the bombing alternated every 15 minutes to allow for the aircraft to manoeuvre into position and the smoke and dust to settle.

The mission was not executed well. One bomber group failed to find the target, thirteen Liberators dropped 40 bombs in friendly territory causing 105 military and 60 civilian casualties and only 300 out of 988 tons fell in the target area. The few shattered buildings left in Cassino were comprehensively flattened, but the German resistance remained strong. Additionally, all the routes through the town were choked with rubble and during the night the craters filled with rain, preventing both Allied armour and Royal Engineer bulldozers from being able to operate. The New Zealander's subsequent attack slowly ground to a halt, until it was finally abandoned on 23 March. Cassino would eventually fall two months later when it was bypassed and isolated by advancing Allied troops. The bombing of Cassino town was the first occasion when the Army requested heavy bomber support to break an operational deadlock. Whilst the tactical employment and coordination of heavy bombers would improve, the often counter-productive results of bombing built up areas about to be assaulted was a lesson that would have to be re-learnt more than once.[15]

On a more positive note, the Italian campaign saw progressive developments in the direction of artillery fire by Air Observation Posts. This was one of the more novel techniques generated by the British during the air war and though introduced by the First British Army in Tunisia, it was more widely employed in Italy where allied air superiority was much more favourable. Up until the Boer war artillery was typically used in a direct fire role, where gunners had a clear line-of-sight from their guns to the targets they were shooting at. From the First World War it was more common for artillery to be sited behind a ridge, or piece of high ground, that gave cover from the enemy's direct fire weapons. This meant that the artillery had to have an observer positioned so that they

---

15    Air Publication 3235, *Air Support, The Second World War 1939-45*, pp. 110-1.

could see the target and direct the fall of shot to the guns located in the rear. Initially observers were allocated to a single battery of guns and used a land line to communicate instructions, but the improvements in wireless technology after the First World War meant that it was possible for an observer to direct the fire of many batteries of guns. There were nevertheless still difficulties with observing fire from a ground position, not only was the range of view limited, particularly in flat areas, but it was often hard for the observer to judge the precise distance the artillery had missed the target by. This meant that the bracketing of targets until the artillery was accurately hitting it could be a long process, by which time the enemy had usually taken cover, or moved off entirely. If the observer was able to view the target from even a modest height, such as in an aircraft, then their ability to spot targets and direct the artillery increased dramatically.

Initially Army Cooperation aircraft, like the Lysander, were thought to be suitable for this airborne artillery spotting task. However, the Lysander's speed was too quick to be able to loiter for long periods in one area, nor was it nimble enough to take avoiding action from enemy fighters. Aware of the Lysander's limitations a group of Royal Artillery officers began to advocate for a low and slow aircraft that could be dedicated to directing artillery fire. They argued that it should be piloted by trained artillery observers, rather than RAF pilots, and must be able to communicate directly to the batteries by wireless. They also added that whichever aircraft was selected should be agile enough to land on a small field close to the guns and that its survivability must rest on being hard to detect and able to take sprightly avoiding action if confronted by fast moving enemy fighters. The RAF was initially lukewarm to this idea, continuing to argue that Army Cooperation squadrons were suitable for the task of directing guns and that there was therefore no requirement for Royal Artillery Air Observation Posts (Air OPs). The campaign in France in 1940 changed the RAF's opinion as the Lysander aircraft were shot out of the sky whenever they approached the front line and the Royal Artillery idea was given momentum. Interestingly, the lessons the Germans drew from the same campaign led them to negate their artillery arm and instead put further faith in the Ju 87 dive bomber to provide battlefield firepower. This was not a bad proposition when the *Luftwaffe* had air superiority, but once this was lost the Stuka was found to be very vulnerable and the Germans were to subsequently regret diminishing their artillery capability.

The Royal Artillery had initially favoured the American Stinson Vigilant for the role, this was a very specialised aircraft that resembled the famous German Fiesler Storch aircraft in capability. A number were duly ordered but the crates in which they were packed on the ship were placed under a large cargo of cheese and the aircraft arrived in the UK badly damaged. It may have been for the best, as it forced the Royal Artillery to re-visit the Auster aircraft, an American design built under license by Taylorcraft in the UK. The Auster consisted of a strong tubular frame made from hollow steel and welded together to make a single entity. The wings were wooden-framed and like the fuselage covered with fabric. The high wing design allowed the pilot to get a good downwards and sideways view of the target and this view was improved even further on the Auster Mark III and IV, where more of the fuselage surrounding the cockpit was covered with Perspex rather than canvas. A strong set of wheels on fixed sturdy undercarriage meant the aircraft could land in very small areas, though the absence of any flaps on the Mk I Auster made landings a little difficult. Flaps were subsequently fitted onto the Mk III and Mk IV Auster which substantially improved matters. A wireless was placed right beside the pilot, close to hand so he could tune it if required, a pressel switch was attached on to the control column, which the pilot pressed to transmit his fire control orders to the artillery when necessary.

The crew of the Auster normally consisted of just a pilot and the stability of the aircraft was very important when operating as an Air OP and directing gun fire. Fortunately, the Mark III and IV Auster aircraft were so balanced and well-mannered that the pilot could afford to pick up his binoculars, detect, identify and locate the enemy targets, transmit the details to the guns without being overly distracted by flying the aircraft. Of course, he would still have to keep a careful look

A Taylorcraft Auster AOP Mark I of 651 (AOP) Squadron, being cleared of its camouflage netting at Souk el Arba landing ground, Tunisia, in readiness for an artillery-spotting sortie while attached to 12th Royal Horse Artillery, 6th Armoured Division, on the Bou Arada front. (Crown Copyright – Air Historical Branch)

out for enemy aircraft, but sometimes the gun battery themselves would often assist and give him warning of aircraft they may have seen in the area. The Auster was not very big, having a wingspan of 35 feet and length of just 22 feet 10 inches. This was a distinct advantage in landing in small fields, or on short stretches of roads, it also meant that it could be easily dismantled and carried in a three-ton lorry, a landing craft or even in a Dakota.

The first time the Auster was used was with First British Army in the Tunisian Campaign, when three flights of 651 Squadron were deployed to support 78th Infantry Division, 6th Armoured Division and 46th Division. Despite a challenging German air superiority threat the Air OPs were able to prove they could both survive and operate successfully in such conditions and it was clear that this was a capability that would be welcome during the Italian Campaign. Although the pilots were Royal Artillery officers the ground crew for all Air OP squadrons were drawn from the RAF. Initially these airmen were sceptical of their squadron's contribution, but they soon took pride in often being the RAF personnel deployed furthest forward and recognised that the improvement the Air OPs made in directing artillery fire was an important role. The RAF's initial frostiness also thawed and they too recognised that the Air OP's role improved the artillery's ability to effectively engage targets near the frontline, which freed their own air support aircraft to strike a greater number of targets in the enemy's depth.[16]

The Italian campaign witnessed continuous improvements amongst the Air OPs operational techniques and provided further evidence of their wider value. The Air OPs had been instrumental during the early stages of the Salerno and Anzio amphibious operations. At Salerno they were

---

16    H.J. Parham and E.M.G. Belfield, *Unarmed Into Battle* (Chippenham: Picton Publishing Ltd, 1956), p. 42.

brought ashore in trucks and at Anzio they flew into the rudimentary landing strip established in the beachhead at an early point in the campaign. The Air OPs' utility during these operations was particularly evident in their ability to direct naval gun fire support, which provided a significant element of the Allied firepower during the early stages of the landings, before either proper airfields were constructed, or large numbers of artillery and ammunition had been unloaded into the beachhead.[17] The Air OPs made a huge contribution during the early period of the Salerno landings as the toehold the Allies had secured came under sustained German attack. For the landing 654 Squadron was operating under the command of British X Corps, part of the American Fifth Army which was leading the operation. On the first day of the assault the CO, three flight-commanders and A Flight complete, landed at Salerno and four aircraft were unloaded from three-ton lorries and assembled on a landing ground 150 yards from the beach. By 0900 hours on D + 1 they were ready for operations and by D + 7 the whole squadron was deployed, with A Flight in support of 46th Division, C Flight in support of 56th Division, and B Flight in support of the 7th Armoured Division – which was held in reserve. Two pilots were allotted to observe naval fire one of whom outlined the work in a letter home:

> At one point things were not going too well, particularly at the juncture of Brit. 10 Corps and U.S. 11 Corps. The Germans moving out from Battipagelia were trying to drive a wedge between the two allied forces; their armour was reported to be massing in the area of the factory about one-and-a-half miles from this town. Peter Newman operating in support of an American Ranger Group (there were no U.S. Air O.P. in the bridgehead at the time) took on this factory with the guns of the U.S. Cruiser *Philadelphia*. The guns were magnificent and after ranging on the target area 'hotted up' with some 8–10 salvoes. The factory was hit several times, the roof caved in and fire broke out. The German attack did not materialise, and our patrols that night penetrated to the factory itself, and reported that there were 'mountains of dead'; the Germans had been caught when the factory was hit. Newman himself when flying at 500 feet over the place later found that even at that height the odour confirmed the report. Peter was killed later when his aircraft hit a tree, crashing in flames, just after he had given orders for fire for effect.[18]

The flexibility of the Air OPs meant that they increasingly carried out many other roles. These included spotting German AA positions during RAF close support missions and engaging them with artillery; the reconnaissance of artillery regimental gun areas, roads and tracks; taking infantry and other commanders in the air so that they could observe the ground they had to fight over; sorties to confirm the positions of enemy and friendly troops; supplying information about landing grounds to the RAF; communication flights; couriering important written orders and maps; the transmission of a 'running commentary' by R/T direct to Corps HQ on the progress of an operation; taking air photographs; night observation of fire and finally observing the effectiveness of smoke screens – including advising on its density and position.[19] It was frequently very hard work and quite often the challenges of flying and directing guns would be too much for the tired and overloaded Air OP pilot. One officer in 651 Squadron made the mistake of not rubbing the Chinagraph pencil marks from a previous sortie off his map. When in the air he managed to confuse himself as to which target should be engaged, fortunately the Polish artillery regiment he was spotting for saw the funny side of his error:

17   H.J. Parham and E.M.G. Belfield, *Unarmed Into Battle*, p. 47.
18   H.J. Parham and E.M.G. Belfield, *Unarmed Into Battle*, p. 47.
19   H.J. Parham and E.M.G. Belfield, *Unarmed Into Battle*, p. 49.

An Air OP Auster Mk IV undergoes repair after being damaged by anti-aircraft fire while flying over the Eighth Army front in Italy (Crown Copyright – Air Historical Branch). (Boscombe Down Aviation Collection)

Pilot: 'Hullo 6, Target 123456 Over'
Polish Artillery Regiment: 'Hullo 6, You say Target 123456, Over'
Pilot: 'OK Over'
Polish Artillery Regiment: 'Hullo 6, please you check map reference over.'
Pilot: 'Target 123456, Over'
Polish Artillery Regiment: 'Hullo 6, my officer, he says you to wait while he points guns the
    other way.'[20]

The Air OPs increasingly benefitted from the assured air superiority the allies had achieved over Italy. This meant that they could loiter around areas for longer and potentially fly over the front-line, or even climb to altitude for a broader and better view. German soldiers became very familiar with the little Auster aircraft nicknaming them the 'flying flea', the 'sewing machine' or the 'orderly officer', the latter was a joke based on the regularity with which it visited their positions. The Germans were often unsure what to do when an Air OP was overhead, opening fire usually invited a hostile barrage of gunfire and small arms fire rarely seemed to have any effect, often they therefore just ignored the Air OP which meant that the Austers could obtain an impressively precise situational awareness. Captain Simms of 657 Squadron recalled how he was able to intervene during a Canadian assault in July 1944:

I had been briefed to report on the progress of a tank attack being directed against a piece of gently rising ground which was dotted here and there with small clumps of trees. My wireless

20    H.J. Parham and E.M.G. Belfield, *Unarmed Into Battle*, p. 61.

was netted to the Flight Commander's set at Division. Cloud base was such that a ground level run was indicated, and this I did. It was only a short distance to the front, and almost immediately I spotted some six Canadian tanks formed up on the rear slope of a small fold in the ground, ready to move up and exploit such success as their forward elements might have. I passed these tanks, flying as low as possible, and was among the forward elements before I realised it. In the short time taken to fly about 100 yards I saw three of our tanks stationary near two trees and immediately in front of me. The right-hand one was on fire and the left-hand one firing. I was within thirty yards of the centre one when it fired and I remember the blue smoke ring that came from the muzzle of the gun barrel. Simultaneously with that smoke ring there came a myriad of sparks from all round the base of the turret and it blew up. I turned sharply away and then came in for one more run. I saw two more tanks some fifty yards or less to the right front of the other three and these were both on fire. I stayed for another two or three minutes to check map references and also pulled up to have a quick look at the ground ahead before returning to the landing ground. I tried to put a message through on my set but interference made it impossible so I landed and pushed my report in over the telephone.

Though I had no actual evidence, I suggested that the enemy fire was coming from a piece of fairly high ground with numerous trees dotted about (this subsequently proved to be the case.) Artillery fire was brought down on it and dive bombers requested, and together these two measures effectively dealt with the situation.[21]

One other highly positive tactical development in Italy included improvements in the system of Forward Air Controllers. These had first been used at Tebaga on an ad-hoc basis, but by the time the Eighth Army was crossing the River Sangro (December 1943) the system had become more formalised and included Forward Control Points, known as 'Rovers'. The Rovers began in Italy as a normal armoured Tentacle that carried a Royal Air Force controller, an Army Liaison Officer (ALO) and a VHF radio for communicating with the aircraft overhead. The difference between a Rover and a Tentacle was that the latter would only pass requests and messages, whereas the Rover would control and direct the aircraft. The Rover was usually sited on a piece of high ground overlooking the battlefield and by visual observation and a knowledge of forward troops provided by the ALO, the RAF controller was able to contact aircraft and direct them onto often fleeting targets. A shared 1/30,000 gridded photo-mosaic of the area was often helpful in coordinating the actions of both the attacking aircraft and controller.

Another important element in this improvement of close air support was the provision of a constant 'cab-rank' of aircraft timed to arrive in the area at thirty-minute intervals. These aircraft had been briefed to attack specific targets, but for a twenty-minute period they would orbit overhead in case the Rover had any targets that were of greater priority for them. If no call was received from Rover, then the aircraft would attack its original planned target and return to base. The Rover controller also had communications with the artillery and he could call on smoke to indicate a target. He would also ensure that any special characteristics of the terrain, target, its nature and AA defences were all briefed to the pilot, as well as ensuring that the pilot had positively identified the target where possible. On occasions Royal Artillery Forward Observation Officers (FOO) were co-located with Rover, this meant additional fire support could be provided as the FOO could direct the artillery guns to take on targets which the Rover turned down, either because they were too close to Allied troops, or were in some other way unsuited for air attack. The artillery could also help supress AA fire and would sometimes shell a target a few minutes after a bombing attack had ceased, just as the enemy was emerging from his slit trenches. When all worked satisfactorily

21   H.J. Parham and E.M.G. Belfield, *Unarmed Into Battle*, p. 61.

calls for air support from frontline troops could be answered in as little as seven minutes. As the campaign developed it became less important for the Rover to occupy a position overlooking the battlefield, and the Rovers were sited at more convenient locations near the front.

The first Rover was christened 'Rover David', after its inventor's Christian name (Wing Commander David Heynsham) and consisted of armoured cars with VHF radios, as well as a jeep and truck. A description of how Rover worked in Italy is captured by Roderic Owen who flew with the Desert Air Force and chronicled their achievements:

> The workings of Rover are best illustrated by a reconstruction. The time is six o'clock; the place is Air Commodore Pike's caravan at D.A.F. Headquarters. The conference – though that is perhaps too formal a word to describe a friendly meeting – is due to begin. The RAF are represented by the Senior Air Staff Officer, the Group Captain Operations, the Wing Commander Operations, and the Wing Commander Intelligence. On the Army side sit the Brigadier General Staff, G.1.[22] Intelligence, G.1. Operations, and the G.1. Air.
>
> The army outline what they have done during the day. The RAF then give a resume of their work. The army say what they propose to do the next day. The RAF then consult amongst themselves and say what they can do to help. For instance, the army might say, 'Can we have Rover Control from ten to twelve o' clock in the XY area?' The RAF would answer: 'Yes. What sort of targets?'… 'Various buildings we have our eye on.'
>
> After the conference the directive for the next day's operations will be sent to M.O.R.U[23] which will then normally allot Wings. At Wing, one of the squadron Intelligence Officers will be warned of what is in store for tomorrow. Briefing will be simple, since the aircraft are to fly to some easily distinguishable landmark and orbit overhead for twenty minutes, or until given instructions from the ground.
>
> From nine o'clock next day all sorts of requests will be sent to the Rover control post; and if telephone communication is good the army representative can check the priority of the targets by direct consultation. If, for some reason, this cannot be done, then he will have to draw upon his military experience to decide which to accept. The Rover staff, all of them officers, were capable of assuming complete responsibility whenever necessary without further sanction from Higher Authority.
>
> Imagine, then, a battered hut with peeling walls set on a slight eminence – possibly, though not necessarily within sight of the battle area. Imagine, if you wish, the noise of gunfire, the crackle of radio, the difficulties with the telephone, the coarse jokes, in short the undramatic setting and undramatic behaviour of men who find themselves doing a particular job in circumstances sometimes dangerous, but whose conversation is neither high-flown nor terse, nor preoccupied with anything other than everyday matters. Hysteria and the crusading spirit alike, both are at a discount here.
>
> As though to insist on individuality, dress is anything but uniform. One has a sheepskin coat; another has corduroy trousers – in fact they are typical, in their diversity of appearance, of all men of Desert Air Force.
>
> The moment for which they were waiting has arrived; the Kittybombers will soon be overhead. By the time that the aircraft are in the cab-rank the RAF controller will have marked the first target on his map and discovered the grid reference…

---

22  General Staff Office Number One.

23  Mobile Operations Reporting Unit: the headquarters that commanded the wings within the Desert Air Force, it performed much the same role as a sector operations room at Fighter Command, but as its name implies it was mobile.

'Hello Rover David: Shabby Leader calling'

'Hello Shabby Leader: Rover David'

'Have you a map of the Sangro North'

Call-signs will be repeated each time; as also any instructions given. The conversation continues:

'Look at Square B15…have you got it?'

'At the top right-hand corner you will see a bend in the river turning sharply to the west… just in the north of the bend there are two houses side by side…take the left hand one, the west one, that is your target.'

Shabby leader then repeats the instructions and checks with each of his aircraft in turn to make sure that all have seen it. The final words may be:

'O.K. One more circuit and down we go!'

When the formation leader repeats the target instructions he may add one or two more details as to the colour or type of country – ploughed field, line of green trees, etc. For he can see his target clearly, whereas Rover David might well be sited out of view. Rover briefing could be carried out at some distance from the battle, even from behind a hill; for the object of Rover was not to see the target he was describing but to act as an agent for immediate air support.

Theoretically a target could be attacked very shortly after request, the only time-lag being the actual passing of close-support calls from Brigade via Rover to the aircraft overhead. The system was particularly effective against enemy guns liable to change sites overnight. The latest analysis of the Army Counter-battery Officer could be flashed via Rover to the waiting squadron. There was less chance of wasting bombs on vanished foes.[24]

The Rover system was popular with the Army, who appreciated its dynamic response, the RAF pilots also liked them because they felt that the missions were better focussed and well controlled. Bert Horden describes it from an aircrew's perspective:

It was about this time [January 1944] that we began to develop the 'Cab-Rank' system of close army support. The idea was that soldiers on the ground could contact Kittyhawks flying above to direct and strafe exactly where needed… The Kitty's took off in sixes at twenty-minute intervals having been allocated the target area of Rover David and a secondary target if he did not call for support during that particular twenty minutes. Each pilot had a copy of the gridded map. The leader would patrol the primary area for twenty minutes calling up Rover David to ask if he had a target. If he had, then it was not only identified on the gridded map but sighted on the ground by the leader. He and his No.2 would then dive bomb the particular target, which would be say a wood, or a farmhouse.

Everyone watched the target to see how near the bombs fell. For the next two to go down Rover David could correct the initial bombing by an instruction such as 'place your bombs 100 yards (91m) to the north-east of the first bomb bursts' and so on. Then the Kittys could be requested to strafe a particular area. In this way the Army could be said to be using our Kittys as 'Air Artillery', with the service always available as we queued up to cover the area in twenty-minute slots. Hence the name 'Cab-Rank'.

If Rover David had no target in that particular twenty minutes, then our Kittys could proceed to the secondary target and bomb and strafe without further reference to him. It could be very motivating to be told by David that we had been exactly right – much jubilation.

24   Roderic Owen, *The Desert Air Force*, pp. 200-1.

Curtiss P-40D Kittyhawk Mark IV of 450 Squadron RAAF, taxying to the runway at Cervia, Italy, loaded with three 250-lb GP bombs for a sortie in support of the Eighth Army's spring 1945 offensive in the Po Valley. (Crown Copyright – Air Historical Branch)

North American Mustangs of 112 Squadron RAF, loaded with 500-lb GP bombs. These aircraft are also flying from Cervia, Italy in support of the Eighth Army's spring 1945 offensive in the Po valley. (Crown Copyright – Air Historical Branch)

If our bombs were not right or even too near David himself, then his comments could be unprintable! The truth was that our dive-bombing had an element of luck and was therefore not always accurate… Our Army would help us as much as possible by firing at the enemy as we came down to bomb, with the effect of concentrating the enemy mind on ground attack rather than firing their guns up at us. A very rewarding spirit grew between the two services, each with a great respect for each other's efforts.[25]

---

25   Bert Horden, *Shark Squadron*, p. 132.

Variations of Rover David arose. Rover Frank was specifically developed to support the Army's counter battery efforts, enemy artillery would usually move at night therefore the 'cab-rank' aircraft would call up Rover Frank as they neared the front line and he would update them on the very latest active batteries. The enemy guns were not ideal targets for bombs of 500lb or over and it was not always possible to use the more effective anti-personnel bombs. Nevertheless, even the presence of hostile aircraft was occasionally enough to quieten the German artillery sufficiently for the infantry to successfully attack. Rovers were sometimes placed in armoured cars known as Contact Cars where they could act as a Visual Control Post and keep up with armoured formations in a mobile battle. On occasions they were placed in light aircraft and known as 'Horsefly'. Though visual observation was much improved in these instances, it was hard for the controller to brief the 'cab-rank' pilots and there was little space for consultation and study with the ALO. Additionally, the controller on the ground could call for an Air Observation Post aircraft at any time and the information or targets the Air OP could see could always be passed to the fighter bomber if desired.[26] Major Neathercote was a Royal Artillery Air OP pilot in the Italian campaign, he recalled working with RAF close air support in April 1945:

> I saw a German Tiger tank going slowly down a road, and although he was not at the time engaged in any hostile action, he obviously had been or intended to be. So I decided to follow his every move until he stopped. This I did for nearly thirty minutes. He covered about five miles across our front at about 4,000 yards back from the German front line. Eventually I saw him turn off the road into a small Italian farmhouse which had a barn attached to the house. He drove right into the barn and right under cover. From the outside the very slightest track mark was the sole evidence of his whereabouts. I then called up Rover David (code name for R.A.F. ground control officer) and was allotted two Mustangs, each carrying two 500 lb. bombs. I explained exactly where this tank was, since I knew that the bombing aircraft would not be able to see it. They had to bomb the right barn which they did. The first aircraft bombed about fifty yards plus of the house and barn; the other one hit the house. The barn was a mass of rubble as was the house. Before going home I waited for a short time to see if the tank was moving out from underneath. I went to this farm soon afterwards and talked with a neighbouring farmer who told me that the tank had got away later from the midst of the rubble, but of the crew only the driver had survived the attack.[27]

The final evolution of Rover was the 'Rover Timothy' method of air support. This was first used during Operation TIMOTHY in November 1944, when the 12th Brigade of 4th Division were launching an attack on German positions in the area of the River Montone. The commander of the division requested three 'blitzes', 1,000 yards parallel to and on either side of the brigade's axis of advance. The blitzes were to be undertaken by twelve aircraft arriving every ten minutes and timed to commence alongside the infantry assaults. The method was very similar to the Tebaga Gap 'blitz', though the use of artillery smoke called in by the Rover as a visual bomb line was a new technique. The Army were delighted with the air support taking their objectives and 106 prisoners for the cost of only 13 casualties. 'Timothy' was to become a standard term to be used for these type of attacks in the future, a variation being 'Pig' which was used when the fighters only strafed with machine guns and did not drop bombs. 'Pig' had been first used by 1st Canadian Division in December 1944 when weather conditions did not permit bombing.[28]

26   Air Publication 3235, *Air Support, The Second World War 1939-45*, p. 113.
27   H J Parham and E M G Belfield, *Unarmed into Battle*, p. 69.
28   Air Publication 3235, *Air Support, The Second World War 1939-45*, p. 120.

At the conclusion of the war in Europe, the Eighth Army and the Desert Air Force could reflect with great pride that they had established and pioneered many different aspects of air-support to land campaigns. They had also formed a trusted and mutually supporting partnership that endured throughout a difficult and arguably under-resourced campaign. Not for nothing did General Richard McCreery, Eighth Army's last wartime commander, describe the Desert Air Force as 'the finest Tactical Air Force in the World – with years of experience behind it.'[29] Many of the Desert Air Force's techniques would find their way across to Normandy and the campaign in North West Europe, but there were nonetheless subtle differences between the two theatres. In particular, the disappointing relationship that emerged between very senior air and ground commanders in Normandy stood in stark contrast to the cooperative spirit that had been established in the Western Desert.

---

29   Richard McCreery, *The Final Offensive in Italy,* (RUSI Journal, Vol. XCII, No.565, February 1947), p. 7.

# 8

# 'We Cleave the Sky'[1]
# Air Support in North-West Europe

By the time the British and their Allies began to turn their minds to invading Normandy, they should have been confident that they had ironed out the methods, systems and processes required to deliver effective air support for land forces. However, the machinery of air-ground cooperation in the UK was not as well-oiled as it could have been. Furthermore, military commanders may have struggled to recall the desperate days of 1941 and 1942 and the imperative for air and land commanders to work closely together. In some cases, a degree of arrogance and complacency had crept into some individual's approach to relationships with the other service. Proximity to the Air and War Ministries may have meant that inter-service agendas were a little more acute, this included exposure to some of the Bomber Command advocates who argued that they had the ability to unilaterally win the war without the need for an invasion at all. Finally, though some veteran Army formations and their commanders were brought back from the Mediterranean theatre for the invasion of Normandy, much of the UK based Army had little experience of war or had last seen action in 1940. Joint training might have helped, though Second Tactical Air Force (2nd TAF), the RAF element that would support the British 21st Army Group, was often unable to participate because it was occupied conducting air operations over the continent.[2] These operations were essential in creating conditions for an Allied entry onto the continent and 2nd TAF therefore had little time for the joint exercises that might have ironed out inter-service issues, or reinforced the essential trust and confidence between the RAF and Army.

Strong leadership amongst senior commanders and a sensible supporting command and control structure should have mitigated this unhelpful situation, but sadly the Allied victories in the Mediterranean had accentuated both the egos and the petty jealousies amongst senior air and land commanders. Tedder and Coningham had developed an intense aversion to Montgomery, strongly resenting his failure to sufficiently credit the Desert Air Force with the Allied victory at Alamein and viewing him as a self-serving publicist. Tedder served as deputy commander to Eisenhower, the Supreme Allied Commander, and as the Normandy campaign unfolded, he conducted an unseemly whispering campaign against Montgomery. Coningham was given a senior appointment as the commander of 2nd TAF but struggled to repeat the close partnership with Montgomery that had worked so well in the Western Desert. Like many others in the RAF, Tedder and Coningham, also bore a grudge with Leigh-Mallory, the overall Allied Expeditionary Air Force Commander. Despite his grand sounding title, Leigh-Mallory struggled to find a role, or establish any authority with either subordinates like Coningham, or strong-willed peers and superiors such as Harris and

---

1    Motto of 197 Squadron – a Typhoon equipped squadron that was part of Second Tactical Air Force and provided air support to the British Army during the Normandy landings, re-locating to France and following the Army in its subsequent advance across North-West Europe.

2    See Annex G for the Order of Battle for the Allied Expeditionary Air Force 6 June 1944 – including Second Tactical Air Force.

Tedder. The only RAF individuals who come out with any credit during this fractious period were the Group commanders within 2nd TAF including Broadhurst, who commanded 83 Group which supported Second British Army and Brown who commanded 84 Group which served First Canadian Army. It is interesting to note that both were censured by Tedder and Coningham during the campaign for getting too close to the Army. Brown in particular was close to being sacked by Coningham in the summer of 1944, for apparently being too subservient to Army requirements.[3] Despite this hostile atmosphere at the higher levels of command, Montgomery was still making the right noises about close RAF/Army cooperation, taking the time to write to his commanders just one month before D-Day on the importance of good Army/Air relations:

> I feel very strongly on the whole matter, and that we can achieve no real success unless each Army and its accompanying Air Force can weld itself into one entity... The two HQ have got to set themselves down side by side, and work together as one team; that is the only way.[4]

Yet Montgomery failed to follow his own advice, delegating nearly all the detailed planning and negotiations with airmen to his Chief of Staff, Major General Freddie de Guingand. In Montgomery's defence, this was partly so he could tour his Army and give them the necessary confidence for the forthcoming operation – an important command responsibility often under-rated by historians. Geography did not help foster close relations either and the commanders were frequently distant from one another at important periods. Montgomery was located at Southwick, near Portsmouth, Coningham was at Uxbridge and Leigh Mallory was at Stanmore – gone were the days of shared messes and headquarters. The situation would deteriorate further when Montgomery crossed the Channel with his tactical headquarters, this early move to Normandy was a perfectly sensible decision that would give him a good feel for the land battle, unfortunately it also further removed him from the air commanders he needed to work with.

Prior to D-Day the Allied air forces executed a finely tuned air campaign that softened-up Normandy for the invasion, including isolating it from German formations who might reinforce it. In order to preserve the security of the point of invasion, many of these operations were conducted far away from Normandy to support the overall Allied deception plan (Operation BODYGUARD) which convinced the Germans that the invasion would take place in the Pas de Calais area.

Tedder and Leigh-Mallory proposed that an important element of this preliminary air campaign was the 'Transport Plan', which targeted marshalling yards across France and Belgium, including railway stock and repair facilities. Air Marshal Harris was initially opposed to the use of heavy bombers on such a task, complaining that his crews were not trained or capable of such operations and he continued to advocate that nothing should be allowed to interfere with the area bombing of Germany which could win the war unilaterally. Nevertheless, Bomber Command conducted trial raids in March 1944 against nine railway targets, the most notable being that against the large railway centre at Trappes, south-west of Paris on 6 March. This raid was a conspicuous success, all the targets were struck accurately and none of the 263 aircraft employed in the raid were lost, it demonstrated that RAF heavy bombers could be employed against precise targets within the Transport Plan. General Spaatz, the commander of the American heavy bombers in the US Eighth Air Force, also opposed the strikes on railway targets as a preliminary operation for OVERLORD. He proposed that there should be strikes on the German synthetic oil plants and refineries instead and identified twenty-seven targets which he claimed accounted for eighty percent of German oil production. However, Spaatz's plans would 'only expedite the success of OVERLORD in the

3    Ian Gooderson, *Air Power at the Battlefront*, p. 55.
4    John Terraine, *Right of the Line* (London: Hodder and Stoughton, 1985), p. 612.

North American Mitchell Mark II of 180 Squadron RAF, being refuelled and bombed up at Dunsford, Surrey, between cross-Channel sorties in support of Operation STARKEY (a cross-channel raid launched to deceive the Germans in 1943). (Crown Copyright – Air Historical Branch)

period subsequent to D-Day'[5] and Eisenhower, was more interested in the assault landings and the opening fight which the Oil Plan would not be able to assist. As the Supreme Allied Commander for the invasion, the decision was Eisenhower's to make and with the backing of Portal, who represented the Combined Chiefs of Staff, he selected Tedder and Leigh-Mallory's proposed Transport Plan and a directive to that end was issued on 17 April 1944.

Controversy did not end there, Churchill became agitated about the potential loss of French civilian lives the bombing of French railway targets would entail. His concerns prompted a temporary halt to the bombing of some of the targets on 29 April 1944 and Churchill raised his concerns by telegram with Roosevelt. The President's answer was swift and unequivocal replying 'However regrettable the attendant loss of civilian life is, I am not prepared to impose from this distance any restriction on military action by responsible Commanders that in their opinion might militate against the success of Overlord or cause additional loss of life to our Allied forces of invasion.'[6] As the responsible commanders referred to by Roosevelt included Britain's own Chiefs of Staff, Churchill backed down and the bombing against the suspended targets was resumed on 5 May.

Of the 80 primary targets in the Transport Plan, thirty-nine were struck by Bomber Command, twenty-three by the US Eighth Air Force and eighteen by the Allied Expeditionary Air Force. By 6 June, 51 out of the 80 targets selected were destroyed, with a further 25 judged to be severely

5    L.F. Ellis, *Victory in the West, Volume 1* (London: HMSO, 1962), p. 99.
6    L.F. Ellis, *Victory in the West, Volume 1*, p. 101.

damaged. By 19 May 1944, the methods of air attack had broadened from the heavy bomber attacks to include fighter bomber strikes which began to destroy locomotives by strafing attacks. A total of 3,932 of these latter sorties were undertaken prior to D-Day. From 21 April 1944, the road and rail bridges across the River Seine were also regularly and repeatedly attacked by both medium bombers and fighter bombers. The most successful method in collapsing bridges apparently being those executed by the American P-47 Thunderbolts dropping a 1,000lb bomb. By D-Day twelve of the rail and road bridges across the Seine had been dropped, with many more bridges over other rivers in northern France also destroyed. These interdiction attacks would continue after D-Day itself and meant that the German ability to reinforce and resupply the invasion area was greatly diminished.[7] Such was the level of destruction inflicted upon the French transport system that many German vehicles had to be off-loaded from railway flat-beds in eastern France and undertake a long drive, mainly at night, to the battlefield area. This took precious time and fuel, as well as incurring excessive wear on the German tracked vehicles.[8]

Spaatz's oil targets were struck by the Allies later that year and as he predicted they eventually crippled the German Army. They were particularly effective at this stage of the war because German oil reserves relied heavily on imports from the Ploesti oilfield in Rumania which was overrun by the Soviets in August 1944. The results of these concerted bomber attacks on German oil production and refinery installations were severe for all branches of the German military.

While the lessons from the Mediterranean on using bombers to interdict the enemy's forces were incorporated into the OVERLORD plans and clearly had a telling effect as the campaign progressed, so too were many of the techniques on providing close and general air support to the Army. What was noticeably different however were the aircraft involved in these missions, some of which had not seen service in the Mediterranean.

The Hawker Typhoon is arguably one of the most famous ground attack aircraft of the Second World War. That it was so successful is somewhat surprising, as few aircraft have had such an appalling introduction into service as the Typhoon, many wondering if it had any future as an operational aircraft at all. David Ince transferred from Mustangs to Typhoons and remembered both the early problems with the aircraft, as well as the way they were successfully cured:

> Much had happened since I had sat in that early Typhoon at Snailwell beside Cocky Dundas and, in my enthusiasm had told him that it was the aircraft for me. I well remembered how he had looked at me through the open cockpit door more in sorrow than anger: 'We've lots of problems,' he said 'and you're an idiot!' Since that conversation Cocky had fought in Malta and been given a Spitfire Wing in Italy. He had risen to be the youngest Group Captain in the Royal Air Force. In those same years the Typhoon problems had largely been sorted out.
>
> The most visible changes surrounded me now. A glazed rear fairing had appeared almost immediately. This despite Sydney Camm's insistence that his new 400 mph plus aircraft was so fast that its pilots did not need to see backwards. The unloved main hood assembly with its car type doors – the so called coffin job – took much longer to replace. But the final teardrop sliding canopy, which set a new standard in all round visibility, was fitted to all squadron aircraft before D-Day. The bomb racks and rocket rails were a squadron fit not normally seen on GSU aircraft.
>
> Other changes were less visible but pretty fundamental. The concern about carbon monoxide poisoning, as the cause of some early fatal accidents had led to the mandatory use of

---

7    Air Publication 3235, *Air Support, The Second World War 1939-45*, p. 120.
8    See Map 7 for details of pre-OVERLORD targets including Railroads and Bridges.

oxygen from start up to shut down on every flight. It was on my list of vital actions for the morrow.

The vibration was said to be so bad that you would become infertile if you flew Typhoons for too long. Probably quite untrue for there was no sense of emasculation at the time. Nor later when many of the survivors got married and produced offspring! In reality the pilot's seat was very close to the engine bearers with little intervening structure to act as a damper. Spring seats helped considerably. But they bottomed when you pulled G. Fortunately the last major modification – a four-bladed propeller which needed the larger Tempest tailplane for longitudinal stability reasons alone – reduced the vibration considerably.

Worst of all had been the fatal accidents arising from rear fuselage failure at the transport joint. This had been reinforced by a strap, then by fishplates, but the accidents continued.

Eventually two things happened. An elevator mass balance bracket broke before take-off and a pilot diving at high altitude was thrown out – and survived – as his aircraft pitched nose down and broke up. Fatigue failure of the offending item had been diagnosed in each case. When the bracket was modified there were few subsequent accidents and all was thought to be well. But, as Hawkers later, and privately, admitted there was never an absolute cure.

There were many sleeve-valve failures on the early Sabre engines. Air Commodore Rod Banks, widely respected for his pre-war work on Schneider Trophy fuels and wartime Director General of Engine Development, was a man of some determination. This was a crisis. He insisted that Bristol engines, with their successful range of sleeve-valve radials, should work flat out to help Napiers.

The problem was speedily solved. Even better, there was a suitably sized forging in production for the Bristol Taurus [engine]. Enough were machined to make sleeves for a trial installation and a modified engine for type test. Six months later the Sabre had become one of the most reliable engines in service.[9]

Weighing a mighty seven tonnes and equipped with its 24-cylinder Napier Sabre engine capable of producing 2,200hp – one of the largest and most powerful piston engines ever fitted to a British fighter, the Typhoon looked large and intimidating. Some of this impression was generated by the size of its wings, which were much thicker than the Spitfire (which was half its weight) and from which its four 20mm cannon jutted out aggressively. Even the twelve exhaust stubs that flanked the engine gave an impression of power and menace as the aircraft sat on its wide undercarriage. When the Typhoon's visual impression was combined with its doubtful history and reputation for brutish handling it created a machine that was certainly not for the feint hearted. New Zealander Desmond Scott would go on to command a wing of Typhoons in the North-West European campaign and recalled the aircraft:

Whereas the Spitfire always behaved like a well-mannered thorough-bred, on first acquaintance the Typhoon reminded me of a half-draught; a low-bred cart horse, whose pedigree had received a sharp infusion of hot-headed sprinter's blood. It lacked finesse, and was a tiger to argue. Mastering it was akin to subduing the bully in a bar-room brawl. Once captured, you held a firm rein, for getting airborne was like riding the wild wind. One casual crack of the whip, and the jockey was almost left behind. But like the human race, the Typhoon had its good points too. In sharing the dangerous skies above Hitler's Europe I had good reason to respect its stout-hearted qualities. It gave no quarter; expected none. It carried me into the

9   David Ince, *Brotherhood of the Skies* (London: Grub Street, 2010), pp. 63-5.

A section of Hawker Typhoon Mark IBs of 175 Squadron RAF take off from B5/Le Fresne Camilly, Normandy, watched by armourers at work on another Typhoon of 245 Squadron RAF. (Crown Copyright – Air Historical Branch)

A Hawker Typhoon Mark IBs of 198 Squadron RAF, taxy through clouds of dust on the perimeter track at B10 Plumetot, Normandy. (Crown Copyright – Air Historical Branch)

heart of the holocaust – and even when gravely wounded delivered me from its flames. As a young pilot I grew not only to respect the Typhoon, but also to trust – even to love – it.[10]

Frenchman Pierre Clostermann also flew Typhoons and even though he was a highly experienced pilot with an operational tour on Spitfires already under his belt, he remembered his cautious approach to this new aircraft. Clostermann's description of starting up and taking off in the Typhoon highlights both the performance, as well as the unforgiving nature of this machine:

With my parachute on my back it took three people to help me up the Typhoon's cockpit, which is nine feet off the ground. As the plane is very streamlined there is nothing to hang on to. You have to get your fingers in hollows which are covered by metal plates on spring hinges. They close up again when you remove your hand or foot, just like a rat trap. In the end they hoisted me up, settled me in, slapped me on the back, shouted 'good luck', and I found myself all alone inside the bowels of the monster…

I switched on the instrument panel light. I regulated the throttle lever – open five-eighths of an inch (not one fraction more, otherwise the carburettor would flood and there might be a blow-back). I pushed the pitch control lever right forward, and then back an inch or so, to avoid run-away in the constant speed unit.

I verified that my tanks were full and selected the centre fuselage tanks for the take-off (gravity feed in case the pump packed up). I unscrewed the wobble pumps; one sent a mixture of alcohol and ether into the carburettor, the other a mixture of petrol and oil to the cylinders.

I inserted a cartridge into the starter. (The Koffman system, which uses violent expansion of explosive gases to get the engine turning. If the engine doesn't start first time it will almost certainly catch fire, being bung-full of juice.) With one finger on the coil booster and another on the starter button, I fired the cartridge. The mechanic hanging on to the wing, helped to 'catch' the engine and it started with a deafening roar. The amount of noise is about five times as great as in a Spitfire. After missing a few times, the engine settled down to a reasonably steady rhythm, though not without exuding oil at every pore. The sound of the engine and the way it vibrated struck me as suspicious. My nerves were very much on edge and I didn't feel at all easy in my mind… I began to taxi – a bit too fast. I must be careful not to overwork the brakes. They over-heated very quickly, and hot brakes don't function.

That engine! You moved forward quite blindly, picking out the way like a crab, with a bit of rudder now left, now right, so as to be able to see in front. Once I was on the edge of the runway, before venturing further I cleared the plugs, as per instructions, by opening up to 3,000 revs, and a film of oil immediately spread over my windshield…

The controller replied by at last giving me a green light. Here goes! I tightened my straps, released the brakes, carefully aligned myself on the white line down the middle of the concrete and slowly opened the throttle, with my left foot hard down on the rudder bar. I had been warned that Typhoons swung, but surely not as much as this! And that brute gathered speed like a rocket! I corrected as much as I could with the brakes, but even then I found myself drifting dangerously to the right.

Half-way down the runway my right wheel was practically on the grass. If I came off the concrete I would gracefully flip on my back! To hell with it! I tore her off the ground. This plane just had no lateral stability at all. I still went on drifting to starboard and, with those miserable ailerons that only 'bit' at speeds higher than 100 m.p.h. I daren't lower the port wing too much. Luckily they had hauled F hangar down, after a series of accidents all due to

10   Scott, Desmond, *Typhoon Pilot* (London: Arrow Books, 1988), p. xi.

the same cause, but even then I passed uncomfortably close to E hangar. I retracted my under-cart but forgot to put the brakes on. A terrific vibration which shook the whole plane from stem to stern reminded me that my wheels had gone into the cavities in the wing still revolving at full speed… In the end I got my hand in a bit and felt better. There was a tendency to skid in the turns, but it wasn't too bad.

Just a wee dive to see what happened. Phew! With its seven tons, the things acceleration downhill was simply fantastic. I realised with satisfaction that as far as speed was concerned this was much better than a Spitfire.[11]

Desmond Scott, too enjoyed the handling of the Typhoon once it was in the air:

My Typhoon and I began our airborne association by climbing up to 15,000 ft, where I pulled her up straight on to her tail. After reaching her zenith she spun off quickly, and I was agreeably surprised when she recovered almost as soon as I applied corrective action. To make sure she was not fooling me I again put her into a spin and she recovered beautifully. We then headed earthwards in a vertical power drive. As the speedo needle was winding up to the 450 mph mark, I pulled her up into a loop and rolled off the top. We did ever-increasing tight turns until she blacked me out. We slow-rolled and barrel rolled as I thrashed her about the sky for a full half-hour.

She roared, screamed, groaned and whined, but apart from being rather heavy on the controls at high speeds she came through her tests with flying colours. She rocked a bit as the landing wheels were forced down into their locked positions, and she also gave a final high-pitched whine as I moved her propeller into fine pitch. Applying a few degrees of flap we swung on down into the airfield approach, levelled out above the runway, and softly eased down on to her two wheels, leaving her tail up until she dropped it of her own accord.

We were soon back in her bay by the dispersal hut, where I turned off the petrol supply cock. After a few moments she ran herself out, and with a spit, sob and weary sigh, her great three bladed propeller came to a stop. So that was it: I was drenched in perspiration and tired out. Clambering out of the hothouse, I slid down the wing and on to the ground, thanked my fitter and rigger and drove straight to the officers' mess.[12]

The Typhoon had not been originally designed as a ground-attack aircraft and was supposed to operate as an air superiority fighter. However, though the aircraft was very fast from ground level to 10,000 feet it lost much of its power above that altitude, which by 1942 was where most air combat was taking place. This might have meant that the Typhoon was scrapped altogether, but the *Luftwaffe*'s low-level fighter bomber raids on towns along the south coast in 1943 gave it a reprieve, for here the Typhoon's speed of 410 mph and powerful 20mm cannons meant it was a fast and dangerous opponent, one that could catch up and administer severe punishment on the raiding German aircraft. The RAF also came to appreciate the aircraft's performance in low-level fighter sweeps over France and it was a natural evolution to begin to attach bombs to the Typhoon, by which it became known as the 'Bombphoon'. This was then followed by fitting eight 3-inch rockets underneath its wings, which cemented the Typhoon's role as the primary ground attack aircraft to support the British Army's re-entry onto the continent in 1944. The conversion to a ground attack role was not an altogether popular decision for RAF aircrew, many of whom were proud of their status as pure fighter pilots. Dennis Sweeting recalls the discontent at the time:

---

11   Pierre Closterman, *The Big Show* (London: Chattos and Windus, 1953), p. 149.
12   Desmond Scott, *Typhoon Pilot*, pp. 17-18.

Pilots of 245 Squadron RAF walk past their Hawker Typhoon Mark IBs to their dispersal hut at Westhampnett, Sussex. They have just completed a sortie over northern France. (Crown Copyright – Air Historical Branch)

The next day we had the bad news that Johnny was posted to 11 Group on rest. We felt that we were losing a leader who could never be adequately replaced. The squadron had now left 11 Group, in which we had served at Manston, and was in 84 Group, part of the Second Tactical Air Force. We lived in tents to condition us for life in France when the invasion took place. There were now four Typhoon squadrons at Tangmere under the command of Gp Capt D E Gillam, DSO, DFC, AFC, privately called 'Kill 'em Gillam' because in his long and distinguished operational career he was reputed to have lost thirteen pilots as his No.2; no doubt due to his habit of pressing home attacks regardless of the fierceness of opposition. His unfortunate No 2's, flying close to him, were the ones that got hit.

We had been the top scoring fighter squadron and now we learned that only Spitfires would be fighters, the Typhoon being strictly for ground attack. There was a lot of dissension in our squadron because we were converting to dive bombing and coupled with the posting of the CO the atmosphere was near to mutiny. This all got to the Group Captain and he called an emergency meeting of the pilots of the four squadrons. We crowded into the operations marquee that evening, when he addressed us in no uncertain manner and with a considerable amount of unfriendliness, suggesting that those pilots who did not wish to carry out dive bombing were 'lacking in moral fibre' (the well known category of LMF) and that he would be pleased to see them in his office after the meeting to arrange for them to be posted to other squadrons. It was not specified to where they would be posted, but it did not appear likely to be a Spitfire squadron. A sullen muttering crowd left the tent, but no one went to his office.[13]

The immediate task facing the Typhoons prior to D-Day was to prepare the ground for an invasion, this included tasks within the Transport Plan, as well as other missions such as suppressing enemy airfields and knocking out radars to reduce the chance of the Germans receiving any early warning of the Allied assault. Squadron Leader C. D. North-Lewis, OC 181 Squadron recalls this period:

---

13   Dennis Sweeting, *Wings of Chance* (Singapore: Asian Business Press, 1990), p. 68.

We did an R/P [Rocket Projectile] attack on a radar station at Auderville, and a cannon attack on the site at Vaudicourt, both on the 22nd May. A cannon attack on the radar at Maupertus on the 23rd, a cannon attack on the station at St Peter Port, Guernsey on the 27th an R/P attack on the radar station at Fort St George, Guernsey, on 2nd June and another R/P attack on the site at Caen on the 3rd. We suffered pretty heavy casualties all the time from flak, but virtually didn't lose anything from German aircraft. In fact I personally – and I did quite a lot of sorties – don't remember ever being engaged by a German aircraft.

I remember Guernsey – it was very exciting – because it was fine sunny weather then and we attacked the radar site just by St Peter Port and then went out low level through the harbour. The Germans had flak positions on all the little outlying islands round there and everyone was blasting away full bore. [14]

Desmond Scott also recalls the danger of these radar raids:

These radar installations were without doubt the most formidable targets and getting at them was like fighting your way into a hornet's nest. Most were near the coast and all held a commanding view; no matter from which direction you approached you could never surprise them, and the amount of light flak surrounding them was a true indication of their value. But with the approach of D-Day they had to be destroyed. While they remained intact it was impossible for aircraft or shipping to approach the Continent without being detected. As our squadrons weaved their way into the strongest parts of the Atlantic wall, the radar site defences fought back like demented tigers. In attacking heavily defended ground targets there was no rule of thumb, no advice to give. The experienced pilots shared the same deadly flight path as the inexperienced, and as the casualty rate mounted with the number of attacks, it became clear that our squadrons were being stripped of their backbones, those at Thorney Island losing six commanding officers in three weeks.

A classic and heroic example of one such attack was by four of our aircraft on the radar station at Cap de la Hague/Joburg on 24 May. This mission was led by Squadron Leader Niblett of 198 Squadron, who was killed a week later when attacking a similar target at Dieppe. His report read: '32 x 60lb rockets and cannons were fired. One missing aircraft seen to crash at base of installation. Flight Sergeant Vallely crashed on target.'

A German soldier who saw the attack and was captured some months later, was so impressed that he insisted on recounting it to his interrogators:

These Typhoons came in from the valley, flying very low. The second aircraft received a direct hit from 37mm flak which practically shot off the tail. The pilot, however, managed to keep some sort of control and continued on straight at the target. He dived below the level of the radar structure, fired his rockets into it and then tried at the last moment to clear it. The third aircraft, in trying to avoid the damaged Typhoon, touched the latter's fuselage, and both crashed into the installation. This radar site was never again serviceable. Of the cables leading up to the target, 23 out of the 28 major leads were severed. [15]

The casualties suffered by the RAF in preparing for the invasion highlight the effort and sacrifice being made in support of OVERLORD well before 6 June 1944. It is arguably a contribution that is not given enough emphasis in popular studies of the Normandy invasion. The RAF also had to consider how it would provide the necessary air support to the Army once it had secured

---

14   Norman Franks, *Typhoon Attack* (London: William Kimber, 1984), p. 103.
15   Desmond Scott, *Typhoon Pilot*, p. 101.

Pilots join ground crews in moving a Hawker Typhoon Mark IB of 182 Squadron RAF which had become bogged down at B6 Coulombs, Normandy. (Crown Copyright – Air Historical Branch)

its lodgement in Normandy. The invasion location had been selected as Normandy for a variety of reasons: it not only had wide open beaches and was less obvious than the Pas de Calais, but it was also still within range of single-engine fighter aircraft who could provide the necessary air superiority. However, the distance across the channel meant that until landing grounds were established in Normandy those aircraft would have limited patrol times over the bridgehead. Consequently, the Army recognised it had to provide the RAF with airfields as soon as possible after the assault. The Army's Royal Engineers had become increasingly adept at building airfields and for the campaign in North-West Europe five Airfield Construction Groups had been created, all of whom would land at Normandy between D-Day and D+3. The Royal Engineers constructed three types of landing ground in France. The first of which were Emergency Landing Strips (ELS), which usually consisted of little more than a simply graded, flat piece of ground with a minimum length of 1,800 ft. As their name suggests these strips could be used if a pilot had a mechanical or other emergency. Second, Refuelling and Rearming Strips (RRS) were constructed, these were 3,600 ft in minimum length and had marshalling areas at each end where aircraft could be replenished with ammunition and topped up with fuel. Aircraft were not based at the RRS, but these strips helped generate extra sorties over the bridgehead during the very early stages of the invasion. Finally, the Royal Engineers built the Advanced Landing Grounds (ALGs) themselves, which were at least 3,600 feet in length for fighters, or 5,000 feet for fighter bombers, and usually had enough dispersal facilities for 54 aircraft. The Allied ambition was that by D+25 there would be fifteen airfields in the British sector and twelve in the American. British ALGs all had the prefix 'B' (e.g B6 Coulombs) and the American airfields used the letter 'A' (e.g A11 Saint Lambert). At these Advanced Landing Grounds refuelling and re-arming would take place, as well as servicing, maintenance and operational planning, the ALGs effectively became the temporary homes of the RAF squadrons or wings, until the front moved on and they leap-frogged forward.[16]

---

16    See Maps 8 and 9 for details of Air Landing Grounds used by Second Tactical Air Force in France and the

No. 25 Airfield Construction Group offers one example of the Royal Engineer's work in estab-lishing these ALGs. The group was supposed to land on the first tide of D+2 and to construct an ALG for a Spitfire fighter wing at Villons-Les-Buissons, or if that was impossible at Beny-Sur-Mer. On arrival in France they were briefed that Villons-Les-Buissons was not yet clear of the enemy, so adjusted their plan. Lt Col G.C. Clark describes the operation:

D plus 4 to D plus 8
Work was well in hand on the ALG B4 Beny Sur Mer on D Plus 4. The site presented no great constructional difficulties, being on fairly level corn land. A considerable amount of work was involved in the construction of separate disparate standings for each individual aircraft, with the consequent increased length of taxi track. As a result of the inactivity of the Luftwaffe such dispersal was soon abandoned and most of the later fields were built with more congested standings.

The site was somewhat restricted by the fact that the woods to the East of the field were occupied by troops engaging the enemy strong point near DOUVRES LA DELIVERANDE.

The first aircraft to use the field was a damaged Spitfire which crash landed on the evening of D plus 6, being unable to get back to its field in ENGLAND. The young Rhodesian pilot celebrated his landing by finishing most of the CRE's [Commander Royal Engineers] bottle of whisky – which, it was felt, was a most suitable way of christening the field.

The field was ready for use, although not complete in minor details, by last light D plus 8 and the RAF flew in next morning.

During this time the area was under occasional shell fire from an unpleasantly eccentric HV [High Velocity] gun. There was, however, remarkably little result, only two men being wounded and one vehicle slightly damaged. No casualties resulted from the enemy's aerial night activity, but one sapper was unfortunately killed by a damaged aircraft which landed out of control.

As it was impossible to do any work on the site at VILLONS LES BUISSONS, a part of the Group was available for work elsewhere…

Orders had now been issued by 1 Corps for the reconnaissance, and, if possible, construc-tion of a second ALG near PLUMETOT. Once more the site lay on magnificent cornland and presented few difficulties from a constructional point of view. The main difficulty was to obtain an area clear of troops, not only for the men working on the strip but even the actual field itself.

In the congestion which existed at the time in that part of the beach head it appeared difficult to convince other people that an airfield really did require the space it does. AGRAs [Army Groups Royal Artillery], supply points and medical units littered the ground and it was only after much argument, some of it regrettably acrimonious, that we were able to get on with the job…

The plan for ALG B10 (PLUMETOT) was to construct, as early as possible, one earth strip (1200 yards) for one wing of fighters and then to construct an additional all-weather strip, surfaced with PSP, parallel to the earth strip. Unfortunately the weather started being unkind and caused delay in the work which was not completed until after D plus 15.

B10 (PLUMETOT) was a particularly exposed airfield being under observation from the high ground East of R ORNE and from the factory at COLOMBELLES. A certain amount of intermittent shelling occurred and some casualties were caused. However on several occa-sions we were amply recompensed by being able to see our own Typhoons take off from the

Low Countries.

field and actually watch them deliver their strike on enemy AFVs – the cycle of take off, attack and return to land occupying little more than ten minutes.

One never ceased wondering why the enemy did not shell the field more vigorously. With a whole wing of fighters operating from it in full view of his OPs he should have had a wonderful shoot. As it was the only type of aircraft which really seemed to sting him into action was a Dakota. If one of these landed there was a fair chance of unpleasantness, and once when about ten of them arrived to evacuate wounded, there was quite an outburst…

One's main memory of this period is one of congestion. One seemed to fall into slit trenches wherever one went. Perhaps it was this reason, or it may have been sheer idleness, that caused one officer to instruct his batman to make him an essential article of bedroom ware from a petrol tin. In the small hours of the night a sleepy officer groped for and found his new treasure. The night was cold and he was disinclined to leave the warmth of his blankets. The article could be taken into bed with him. It was only when the operation was almost over that he sensed that all was not well, and to his horror he found that his batman had rejected the bottom half of the tin and used the top half from which, of course, the cap had been removed! The batman, wisely, made himself scarce for the next twenty-four hours, and a delighted company watched the officer hanging his blankets up to dry.[17]

The ALG's runway was normally constructed from Square Mesh Track (SMT) – squares of thin steel rods, like that seen on building sites to produce reinforced concrete – this was cheap, easy to transport across the channel and only required picketing on to the ground. It was best laid straight over the crops as that helped keep the dust down, at least initially. With prolonged use the track might begin to billow in some areas, but this was easily rectified by tension equipment. Pierced Steel Planks (PSP) could also be used as a runway surface, but as it was expensive and heavy to transport it was usually just reserved for dispersal areas and taxiways.

The initial stages of these air operations required the use of RAF Servicing Commandos. These were RAF servicemen who deployed forward to provide essential refuelling and re-arming services for the fighter and fighter bomber aircraft, until the squadron's ground crew were brought over. The Servicing Commandos were not intended to fight, or even capture their own airfields, but they had received additional military training and were expected to protect themselves and their airfields more than other RAF ground crew might be able to do.[18] Joe Grainger was a member of No. 3205 Servicing Commando and recalls the work on the Normandy ALGs:

From the Beach we made our way to the rendezvous point, the small village Ver-Sur-Mer. There between the villages of Ver-Sur-Mer and St Croix-Sur-Mer, we found that the Army Construction lads had started forming an airstrip on wheatfields. We started offloading and digging in, and by 10:30am the Unit was reassembled. Some of us assisted the Army lads, and others went off in trucks to start the endless task of collecting fuel, all in Jerry cans, ammunition and food stocks from supply craft at the beach. The rest dug slit trenches. It was a case of organised chaos. The biggest job was offloading hundreds of Jerry cans, each containing four and a half gallons of 100 Octane aircraft fuel, and weighing about fifty pounds, from the trucks and forming a number of dumps around what would be the main aircraft dispersal area. Similarly ammunition had to be manhandled and stockpiled – all sorts, from .303

17   Chief Engineer BAOR, *Royal Engineers Battlefield Tour, Normandy to the Seine* (Germany: HQ BAOR, 1946), p. 120.

18   Tom Atkinson, *Spectacles, Testicles, Fags and Matches – The Untold Story of the RAF Servicing Commandos* (Edinburgh: Luath Press Limited, 2004), p. 23.

Square mesh type tracking is laid by Royal Engineers during the construction of the first airfield in Normandy to be built by the RAF at B19 Lingevres (B19). (Crown Copyright – Air Historical Branch)

machine gun, through .50 and 22 mm, on to sixty pound rocket heads and bodies and 250lb, 500lb and 1,000lb bombs. This was made all the more exciting by the irregular and haphazard shelling…

By the evening of the 9th June, D plus three, we had finished our preparations, and the airstrip was designated 'B3' and became operational next morning at first light. The 'buzz' was that the first aircraft to land would be the personal Spitfire of Air Vice Marshal Sir Harry Broadhurst… and we all looked forward to seeing this very popular Commander 'christen' our airstrip. It was not to be. Almost before first light a lone Typhoon, flown by a Canadian of 245 RCAF Squadron, circled, signalled engine trouble, and of course was immediately called in. On inspection we could find nothing wrong, and when the pilot learned of the impending arrival of the AOC he suddenly decided he had been wrong, and took off without more ado. Minutes later the AOC came in, with his personal Spitfire HB. He was greeted formally by the CO, who had warned us that no mention was to be made about the queue jumping Canadian…

Now our real work began, and throughout this and succeeding days the pattern was unchanged. Aircraft came in, usually Squadrons, taxied to Dispersals, stopped, and refuelling and rearming began immediately. As the days went by, the volume of work increased, and on one day 3205 SC recorded over 1,000 sorties. Every one involved refuelling and rearming and Between Flight Inspections. Every drop of fuel involved carrying Jerrycans from the nearest dump to the aircraft. There two or three men stood up on the wing, opened the fuel tank and placed a large steel funnel, lined with chamois leather, in the filler neck. The cans were then lifted six or eight feet up to the men who opened them and poured the fuel in, returning the empty cans back down. They could not be handled roughly for fear of a spark or a bad spillage.

During the day as opportunity arose, or at evening and well into the night, the empty cans had to be taken back to the beach dumps and replacement full cans brought to the

A group of RAF Servicing Commandos rest in their workshop area in a cornfield at B2 Bazenville.
(Crown Copyright – Air Historical Branch)

airstrip. This was always a hazardous and even dangerous task. It was only in darkness that the German Air Force could get over the beachhead, so no lights dare be shown and all travelling, loading and unloading was in pitch darkness, at least until Jerry did fly over, and then the hundreds of AA and other guns firing continuously, with tracer and incendiary ammunition, lit the whole sky sufficiently for all purposes. The trouble was that Jerry strafing and bombing, in addition to the usual shelling, which was mainly haphazard, made the job of carrying hundreds of Jerry cans of 100 Octane fuel and boxes of ammunition in our open three ton trucks most exciting, being very good for the digestion and soul.[19]

Dennis Sweeting was a member of 198 Squadron and recalls landing his Typhoon at one of the new Refuelling and Rearming Strips shortly after D-Day:

A British offensive called 'Epsom' was now underway over the River Odon to the west of Caen and Carpiquet. Due to the weather little air support had been possible and German armour held up British progress. Only when the weather cleared were we able to fly over and give our support to the Army. We also carried out an attack on the railway yards at Conches. For this we dispensed with long range tanks, allowing us to take the full eight rockets. On the way back we were low on fuel, so Paul Ezanno decided we would land in Normandy to refuel. To relieve the load on the Servicing Commandos, four Typhoons landed at B-5 (Le Fresne Cammily) and the other four, which included me, at B-2 (Bazenville Crepon). This, the squadron's first landing in France, we looked forward to with some excitement.

---

19    Tom Atkinson, *Spectacles, Testicles, Fags and Matches – The Untold Story of the RAF Servicing Commandos*, pp. 135-6.

The airstrip, bulldozed out of farmland, was covered in wire mesh tracking. We landed making clouds of dust and taxied rapidly to sandbagged bays at dispersal points off the strip. RAF Servicing Commandos appeared from their slit trenches and rapidly started refuelling our aircraft from jerricans passed from hand to hand. The Germans alerted by the rising dust, started shelling, so we got out of our cockpits, had a quick look around the aircraft, and at the suggestion of the Commandos, went into their slit trenches. It was rather exciting to walk on French soil and hear the artillery fire, although also a bit frightening. We were pleased when the ground crew told us they had put in enough fuel to get us back to England. We leapt out of our trenches, into our aircraft and taxied as fast as we could to the take-off end of the runway. The dust clouds came up again as we took off and the shelling increased. As we climbed away exploding 88mm shells made little black clouds appear around us. Once we left the area, the shelling ceased and the ground crew could drink their mugs in peace. Our enthusiasm to move to France to get more directly involved in the battle was somewhat dampened by this experience.[20]

It was only a few days later that Denis Sweeting's squadron, along with others in 123 Wing, were permanently moved to France. The wing was originally to be based at B10 Plumetot, but because this ALG's runway was out of action the plan was altered to base them at B5 Le Fresne Camilly, though the pilots 'accommodation' would remain at B10. Sweeting continues his story:

We flew across the Channel, still full of ships travelling to and from France, over the beaches near Arromanches, where we could see the Mulberry Harbour being extended; then about six miles inland we came to B-5. We formed in line astern for landing, keeping close to the airfield so that we did not go over the German flak guns and keeping an eye open for FW 190s that might try and pick us off as we came in. After landing we taxied at speed towards waving ground crews. I parked MN 813 under some trees and switched off the engine. It was then that I heard the continuous roar of a heavy artillery barrage, 'Good God' I shouted to the airman on the wing, 'Is it like this all the time?' 'There is a battery of 5.5 inch guns just behind those trees and they have just started shelling Caen.' He shouted back.

I hopped out of the cockpit; while my aircraft was being refuelled I walked over to the trees. Eight guns were in position with the crews loading and firing as fast as they could. The noise was shattering but I found it fascinating to stand behind one of the guns and actually see the shells leave the barrel to go hurtling into the sky on their lethal journey to Caen.

I felt it was a culmination of all our efforts during the last four years that I should be walking on French soil and operating close to the Army. It really was a good feeling. I looked around with interest at the orchards, green fields and old farm buildings. It was just like being in the countryside of southern England. The runway had been levelled by army bulldozers and, except for this and a few shell holes the area around B-5, seemed relatively untouched by war.

Under the trees the fitters and armourers were working at great speed to refuel the aircraft and check the armament… We went over to a tent and had some compo rations and tea for breakfast, it was still only 0500 hours but it seemed an age since we had left Hurn to enter this new world.

We were expecting to take off immediately to support the attack on Caen but it was not until 11.00 hours that we made our first operation from France. We attacked a strong point of dug-in anti-tank guns at a crossroads near Caen. The area was covered in cannon fire and

---

20    Denis Sweeting, *Wings of Chance*, p. 101.

rocket explosions. The usual fierce flak came at us from nearby Carpiquet. Norman called up to say he had been hit and was streaming oil from the hydraulic system and he had to make a wheels up crash landing at B-5 with no flaps or tail trim. One of the new pilots taxied into a shell hole after landing, damaging his propeller and undercarriage. Paul Ezanno, very angry at this, made some pointed comments to the unfortunate pilot.

We were all back on the ground in less than 30 minutes after take-off, it was remarkable that we had packed in so much and lost two aircraft in such a short time.

Later we went off again to attack another strong point on a crossroads north-west of Caen. No transport was visible on the roads on the German side, but in contrast trucks were pouring down the roads on our side, unharried by air attacks.[21]

As it began to rain Sweeting and his fellow pilots were released at 2030 hours and sent by truck to B10 Plumetot, where they would be accommodated and reunited with their kit and tents:

When we arrived we found the pilots who had travelled over in the Dakotas putting the finishing touches to their personal trenches which they had dug out inside their tents and into which their Safari beds were fitted, some trenches were 6 feet deep. They were full of stories of nightly air raids and of the noise of our anti-aircraft barrage. Pieces of shrapnel came down and cut holes in the tents.

We looked at their trenches with amused contempt which turned to fury when we found they had done nothing to sort out our kit for us and it was all lying in a heap on the airfield. After a struggle we found our gear and erected our tents, far too tired by now to take advice on digging trenches.

The evening meal was very good and drinks in the bar were free. The airstrip was run by a Canadian Wing which was now in the process of being disbanded. They had an excellent French Canadian cook who proved that a good meal could be made from standard Air Force rations. Because of the disbandment the Canadians were giving away their bar stock and if required everybody could have a bottle of whisky a day.

Eventually we crawled into our tents, dog tired after twenty hours of activity and due to be up and away to B.5 by 05.30 hours.

No sooner had we lain on our beds than an air raid started. We could hear the German aircraft, their engine notes changing as they weaved through our anti-aircraft fire. Guns were firing all around the airstrip; in a brief lull we heard the whistling of shrapnel as it came down hitting the trees around us.

I realised that the old hands at B10 had got the right ideas with their slit trenches, but it was too late to do anything now. This new phase in our war was going to be different, we no longer would return to the peace and quiet of England at night.[22]

The basing of the 2nd TAF in France increased both the sortie rate and the availability of single-engine fighter aircraft to the front-line commanders. This meant that air superiority was more easily maintained, and the Army build up could be developed free from enemy air interference, with the notable exception of night raids. At times the Allied ground forces could become complacent about this security from enemy air attack and took it for granted. Shortly after the D-Day landings, Eisenhower apparently visited Normandy with his son John, a lieutenant in the American Army. As they observed the long convoys of nose-to-tail vehicles that had taken no

21   Denis Sweeting, *Wings of Chance*, p. 102.
22   Denis Sweeting, *Wings of Chance*, p. 102.

Hawker Typhoon pilots of 121 and 124 Wings discuss operations at B2 Bazenville.
(Crown Copyright – Air Historical Branch)

trouble to camouflage, conceal or even disperse his son remarked 'You'd never get away with this if you didn't have air supremacy.' Eisenhower's blunt reply to his young off-spring was both simple and accurate, 'Son, without air supremacy I wouldn't even be here'.[23]

Spitfires and Mustangs were used by the RAF to maintain air superiority and the Typhoon focussed on the ground attack role using its 3-inch rockets and cannon. As we have seen these rockets had already been used extensively prior to the invasion, during raids on French radar sites, anti-shipping strikes and in the Italian campaign. The beauty of the rocket was the simplicity of its design, comprising little more than a simple cast iron tube with a 60lb High-Explosive (HE) rocket head. The Typhoon could carry eight of these rockets (6 if it had a drop tank fitted for longer range work) and depending on the pilot's inclination they could be fired in one single eight rocket salvo, or in pairs. Flying Officer Pat Pattison flew with 182 Squadron in Normandy and explains how they were used:

> There was a switch in the cockpit labelled 'pairs' and 'salvo'. You selected whichever you required and pressed the 'tit' on the throttle lever, once for the whole lot to go or four times to fire the eight rockets two at a time. Our normal attack was from 8,500 feet and in either a 45 or 60 degree dive, with everything shoved forward and during the latter part of the dive you opened up with cannon if there was any ground fire, to keep the ground gunner's head down. We had the old GM2 gunsight, which was a fixed ring gunsight and we had to make certain settings on that for R/P [Rocket Projectiles]. We used the centre dot, aiming high to allow for the drop in the trajectory, with the cannon initially, and then towards the end of

---

23   John Eisenhower, *Strictly Personal* (New York: Doubleday, 1974), p. 72.

the dive you took aim with the bottom leg of the cross and used that when you were within range of the R/P.

During the firing sequence you obviously had to hold the aircraft fairly steady but then we were getting so low and in fact the pull out was very close to the ground, most of the time below 500 feet – and if you hit the target absolutely right on, say an ammunition dump, or an oil tank, which would explode, you had to break pretty sharply to avoid both the debris from the rockets and also from whatever was flung up from the explosion.[24]

The Typhoon pilot had to be flying very steadily when they fired the rockets, for even a slight skid or yaw of the aircraft at the time of launch could dramatically disrupt the rocket's trajectory. It typically took a while for the pilots to become adept at rocket firing and armament camps were held for squadrons to conduct live-firing exercises, both before and after the invasion. Many who had fired rockets on operations were chastened by their poor performance on the range, but with practise the quality of marksmanship could be improved.

David Ince had originally started the war as an Army officer in the Royal Artillery, before he successfully transferred to the RAF as a Typhoon pilot. He recalls his experience of firing rockets on the Gower Peninsular in South Wales:

The APCs [Armament Practice Camps] provided range facilities, a supply of bombs and RPs aircraft servicing and rearming. The rest was up to the squadrons. For those like myself, who had been forced to learn on the job, it was a golden opportunity.

We flew with eight practise smoke bombs or four RPs and the benefit of continuous prac-tice, with rapid feedback of results, produced a dramatic improvement. The final squadron average, 25 yards low level and 30 yards dive bombing, seemed a reasonable basis on which to go back to war. But we had certainly hoped for better than 27 yards with RP. While I discovered that individual sortie averages like 7 yards, 10 yards and 6 yards respectively were equally possible.[25]

The Rockets were simple for the armourers to fit on to the Typhoon, a simple case of aligning the saddles on each end with the rail and then sliding back and forth to check it had free move-ment. The rails only required a slight oiling now and then and the rocket needed little attention in storage, a small bag of silica gel in the back of the tail to stop the cordite deteriorating was all that was required. The final preparatory stage immediately before operations would be for the rocket to be plugged into the electrical firing system, this was done with a small two pin plug fixed by a small threaded fixing ring. When the pilot fired the rocket, the cordite would start to burn from the tail travelling along the cast iron tube towards the rocket head. On some occasions the rocket could misfire, this might mean it just dropped off the rails without getting up to speed, or in some cases the aircraft would come back with a live rocket still on the rails. In these instances, the armourers would approach the offending munition very gingerly, in case the cordite was slowly burning and had not yet reached its maximum combustible rate.[26]

The Typhoons were initially employed on standard close and general air support tasks, using the processes that had been developed in the Western Desert and further refined in Italy. The aircraft normally operated as a group of eight against pre-planned targets. Denis Sweeting

24   Norman Franks, *Typhoon Attack*, p. 88.
25   David Ince, *Brotherhood of the Skies – Wartime Experiences of a Gunner Officer and Typhoon Pilot* (London: Grub Street, 2010), p. 88.
26   Norman Franks, *Typhoon Attack*, p. 88.

Armourers fit extra 60-lb rocket-projectiles to the four normally carried on both of the wing rails of the Hawker Typhoon Mark IB. Double tiering rockets was an innovation brought in later on in the war.
(Crown Copyright – Air Historical Branch)

describes a typical operational sortie his squadron undertook, that of destroying the Headquarters of the German 84th Corps at the Chateau La Meauffe near St Lo. As his formation of Typhoons approached the target, they found the cloud base was much lower than briefed, forcing the aircraft down to 2,000 feet and making them an easier target for any light flak:

Everything appeared quiet as we sped towards the target; the CO was map reading while the rest of us kept a sharp look out for the hordes of German fighters which we expected to encounter. Nothing happened – no flak – no fighters and nothing appeared to be moving on the ground. Suddenly Dave Davies voice came on the radio, 'Baltic aircraft – target coming up eleven o'clock – echelon starboard for low level attack'. I looked down and there, about three miles away, was the large chateau surrounded by trees with a long circular drive leading to it with a spacious lawn in the middle. It made a splendid target, large enough for all of us to hit.

I veered my aircraft further away from the leader to give more room for aiming, selected the eight rockct salvo on the firing switch checking that the gun button was on 'fire'. The rest of the squadron had now spread out behind in echelon and we were all set. 'Going down Baltic Squadron', called the CO dipping his port wing to commence a shallow dive, with me about 100 yards behind. We came over the tops of the trees and I saw the flash underneath his wings as he fired his rockets and then he pulled his aircraft up and to port. I started firing my cannons and saw his rockets explode on the front of the building. Now less than 300 yards away, travelling at over 400 mph, I fired my rocket salvo and heaved the aircraft into a steep left hand climbing turn to avoid any flying debris and to follow the CO. By the time I had pulled around and could see the chateau again our fourth aircraft was just firing his rockets. They hit the drive just in front of the building which by then had flames and smoke pouring out of it. With the rest of our aircraft on their way in, more and more rockets exploded on the walls and the smoke and flames rose higher. One could not imagine that any 84 Corps staff inside could have survived.

As we circled around to reform the squadron, the CO called 'Good show Baltic Squadron'. Some flak had now started to come up from the woods as the German gunners belatedly manned their guns.[27]

The targets attacked by the Typhoons included both pre-planned ones nominated by the Army and cleared by the Air Support Cell, as well as fleeting or impromptu targets identified by the Forward and Visual Control Posts. Dennis Sweeting again describes how the system worked in North West Europe:

We now started flying the 'Cab Rank' system first devised in North Africa. We had a section of four aircraft on continuous patrol over the front lines. The section leader was provided with a large scale map of our operating sector marked off in sixteen squares and a red line weaving across known as the bomb line, behind which we were not to make any attacks. On the ground with the forward troops, there was a Visual Controller in an armoured vehicle who would pass on to us targets giving one of the squares as a reference. Each quarter of the square was called Part 1 to 4 in a clockwise direction. We were therefore given quite a close reference plus a description of the target. Sometimes to assist us further, the army would put down red marker smoke as well.

It was no easy matter to hold and examine the map in your throttle hand and search for the target at the same time. Often 88 mm guns would be firing at us before we even crossed our lines. When finished with the map, there was nowhere to put it in the cockpit, except to sit on it. As the targets were often concealed vehicles or gun positions we had to come down low to identify them. Then light flak would start up, although the target usually kept quiet until they realised we were coming at them, when they opened up with everything they had.

On one of my first Cab Ranks, we were given a target of dug-in tanks at Rocquancourt, south of Caen and just west of the road from Caen to Falaise which we had nicknamed 'Flak Alley'.

As we approached the area 88s opened up, and as I led the section down the light flak started. I heard several loud bangs on the aircraft, but the controls and the engine seemed unaffected. When pulling up after firing my rockets there was another bang in the fuselage behind me. From a safe height I watched the other three Typhoons following and satisfactory columns of smoke coming out of the trees indicating we had hit and set on fire at least three tanks. Looking at the aeroplane after landing four hits were found, none in vital places, but unpleasantly close to the cockpit.[28]

These Cab Rank operations clearly depended on the VCP and contact car's ability to direct the Typhoons to the target. Normally this presented no problems, but their positions close to the front

---

27   Denis Sweeting, *Wings of Chance*, p. 88-9.
28   Denis Sweeting, *Wings of Chance*, p. 115.

Hawker Typhoon Mark IB of 184 Squadron RAF raises clouds of dust as it takes off from B2.
(Crown Copyright – Air Historical Branch)

line meant that they could sometimes be easily knocked out, as Major General Pip Roberts, the Commander of 11th Armoured Division, recalled during Operation GOODWOOD:

> During the whole of this day frequent calls were made for direct air support, mainly for rockets. These calls were not only made but also accepted to the full, but I cannot say, because I do not know, the actual casualties, if any, inflicted on the enemy armour. There is no doubt, however, that these air attacks most definitely deterred the offensive spirit of the enemy, and it was noticeable that, as a result of these attacks, the enemy showed a great reluctance to come into the open. Personally, I do not believe that many casualties were inflicted and one of the reasons for this was that the VCP allotted to the Armoured Brigade suffered casualties from shelling, not only to the vehicles in which they were mounted but also to the personnel themselves, and consequently the VCP could not be used as such but was only able to operate as a Tentacle [i.e it could accept requests and pass information back – but could not positively direct and control aircraft overhead].[29]

Not only could the VCP or Tentacles be knocked out, the fog of war could also intervene, and control of the Typhoons could go awry. Generally, the air-ground measures in Normandy worked well, but the commander of 51st Highland Division, Major General Bullen-Smith, made his feelings about RAF accuracy clear in a letter to his higher headquarters on 14 June 1944:

> Even under existing conditions, where a bombline is given which is thought to be simple, grave errors are made by the RAF. Further, when targets are given to the RAF which are on, it is thought, easily recognisable features, similar very grave errors have been experienced.

---

29   P.B. Roberts quoted in *Staff College Battlefield Tour 1954 Course* (Shrivenham: Joint Services Command and Staff College Archives).

An example of this happened yesterday evening. I asked for an air attack to be made on the village of DEMOUVILLE 1067. The nearest troops of mine to this village were at TOUFFREVILLE 1368. The target lay on the main rd CAEN –TROARN, yet, for over an hour, beginning at the time selected by me and accepted by the Air for the attack on DEMOUVILLE, my troops in the wood at 1370, and Airborne Troops further North, were bombed, shot at by rockets, and machine-gunned by Typhoons. As soon as the attack began yellow smoke was put up. Yellow triangles were laid and vehicles and ambulances were pulled into the open, yet the aircraft persisted in their attack.[30]

On a more positive note the RAF's air support in Normandy was usually very effectively combined with artillery fire from the Army. Artillery was an important capability to the British in Normandy, indeed to say it was well resourced would be an understatement. Eighteen percent of the men in 21st Army Group were gunners (as opposed to 15 percent infantry for instance) and if one considers those non-gunners providing logistical or other support to the artillery then this figure rises to about a third of the Army Group's total strength. Therefore, the role of the Air OP was as important as ever and in Normandy they were equipped with the new Auster MK IV aeroplane, which provided greater visibility and stability for the Royal Artillery pilot. The Auster squadrons, though theoretically part of 2nd TAF, were permanently allocated to the Army based on one squadron of 16 aircraft for each Corps, the RAF exercising little say in their operational use. The Auster's ability to land almost anywhere meant that once again siting an Advanced Landing Ground for an Air OP was simply a process of finding a suitably large field. Captain Ian Neilson, 652 Squadron, landed on D-Day and describes the process:

I set out on my James 125cc two stroke motorcycle in the usual cloud of blue smoke to reconnoitre the three possible Advanced Landing Grounds (ALGs) which we had selected in advance from the vertical air photographic cover. I went up the road to the south through St Aubin D'Arquenay and found the first area – off to the east of the road leading down to the River Orne and the 'Pegasus' Bridge. It was littered with wrecked gliders, parachutes and anti-landing poles. It soon became obvious that even if we cleared suitable lanes for our aircraft, the whole place was in full view of the opposition to the east across the Orne valley. There was also very little tree cover and that was on the west side near St Aubin… I went off in a north-westerly direction towards field No. 2… The second field was alongside and to the north of the lateral road running eastwards from Douvre. In addition to a number of large trees on its eastern side, it also turned out to be a minefield.

Having rapidly decided that this was not acceptable, I went south–westwards toward Perier and the village and farm of Plumetot. Our third choice was a large area – in fact, three fields to the east of the farm and its orchards, with large trees on the south. Apart from various obstacles such as anti-landing poles, electric pylons, a large concrete water tank and quite a lot of wire fences, it seemed acceptable. The surface was smooth and there were no dead animals. There was good cover for many vehicles. Having returned to collect the ground party, it now being breakfast time on D plus 1, we demolished all that was required at Plumetot and that evening were 'operational'. A radio message to Captain Linton at 3 Div enabled him to get a message through to the Sqn who were by now at Selsey Bill. At 0815 hrs on D plus 2 the first five of 652 Sqn's 16 Auster IV aircraft arrived to be followed during the next few days by the remainder.[31]

---

30   TNA WO 171/1527, War Diary of 51st Highland Division, Air Support –14 June 1944.
31   Royal Artillery Museum Archives, MD 2878, Paper by Captain Ian Neilson, Normandy 1944 – The Role of the Air Observation Post.

The Austers followed their standard practise of flying at very low heights over friendly forces; they were in fact forbidden to fly within 2,000 yards of a known enemy position or above 600 feet. But this modest height coupled with the agility of their aircraft still allowed them to focus deep into the enemy's rear. One Auster observer described the technique used:

> The aeroplane skimmed the trees and the guns fired. As they did so the pilot pulled up into a steep climb, arriving at the top of it as the shells fell on their distant target. A few seconds of steady flight to observe and transmit the next fire order, and a swift swoop down to tree-top level whilst the guns were re-layed and fired. Here was a sector where leisurely flying at 1,000 feet was 'not on'.[32]

To improve the aircraft's survivability a protection plan was frequently created, giving each Air OP flight a 'refuge' strip close to its allotted zone with a troop of 40 mm Bofors light anti-aircraft guns, local warning radar and ground observers to support it.[33] In many cases the Air OP aircraft were most vulnerable when at their Advanced Landing Grounds, which in Normandy were inevitably very close to the enemy front line and well within artillery range. As a result, many squadrons took the precaution of borrowing a bull-dozer to excavate pits down which the aircraft were run. The pits would be deep enough for the wings to be almost at ground level, which helped to minimise damage from shell splinters during enemy artillery fire. Captain Ian Neilson describes the pattern of life for the Air Ops:

> In Normandy our sorties were usually of about 20-30 minutes duration depending upon the fire task and the amount of enemy fighter interference. We were enormously impressed by the weight of fire and accuracy of the bombarding ships of the Navy. Our radio links with the Bombardment Liaison Officers on board the bombarding ships and with all the Field and Medium Regiments worked well – in spite of having to twiddle knobs: there were in those days no automatic crystal controls and push buttons. In addition to the three 25-pounder Field Regiments of 3 Div, we had the Medium Regiments of 5 AGRA and the Naval Guns of HMS *Rodney*, *Warspite*, *Belfast*, *Diadem*, *Mauritius* and the 15-inch guns of the Monitor HMS *Roberts*.
>
>   The height of our sorties depended on the nature of the target, the time of day and likelihood of FW 190 interference. We carried out much counter-battery registration and harassing fire – as well as full Regimental; (Mike) and Divisional (Uncle) targets- even the very occasional Corps (Victor) target. One had always to be careful to avoid our own shells and on one occasion I observed a large shell – clearly a 5.5 inch – passing onwards and upwards beneath my left wing.'[34]

During the period from 8–30 June, 652 Air OP Squadron flew 856 sorties and conducted 458 shoots. The Air OPs helped the Army's artillery play a dominate role in the close battle, which in turn freed the RAF for strikes well behind the front lines.

As well as attacking deliberate targets the RAF's fighter bombers were also free to conduct armed reconnaissance and strike targets of opportunity. These missions were important not just

---

32   H.J. Parham & E.M.G. Belfield, *Unarmed into Battle*, p. 77.

33   N W Routledge, *History of the Royal Regiment of Artillery – Anti Aircraft Artillery* (London: Brasseys, 1995), p. 317

34   Royal Artillery Museum Archives, MD 2878, Paper by Captain Ian Neilson, Normandy 1944 – The Role of the Air Observation Post.

for the destruction they caused, but also because they forced the Germans off the roads in daylight and generally hampered their movement. David Ince describes one such armed reconnaissance in the area of the Falaise Pocket:

> The two Typhoons taxied out to meet at the runway threshold, clattered on to the PSP tracking and took off in a gathering storm of dust.
>
> We turned east, crossing the twin waterways of the River Orne and the Caen Canal, catching a glimpse of Lisieux Abbey in the distance – brilliant white, almost luminous. A dramatic outline far removed from the ugly scenes of devastation which lay ahead. For the enemy had been forced to move in daylight and was paying the price.
>
> The roads leading across the open plain were littered and blocked with wrecked and burning transport. Columns of smoke hung in the summer sky. In the midst of all this carnage more vehicles, of every sort and description, motorised and horsedrawn, continued to straggle out from the hilly countryside to the south east. These were the survivors who had fought their way out of the trap at Falaise, only to face annihilation from the air on their final dash to the Seine.
>
> But before we turned our attention to the roads there was something else, the wingco's voice sounded in my ears: 'Bigshot going down now – enemy gun position'
>
> As I followed, searching the ground ahead, bare earth showed faintly through camouflage netting, revealing the tell-tale outlines of newly dug weapon pits close to the bottom of a reverse slope. 88s probably, part of some hastily assembled battle group, ready to fight it out to the bitter end defending the flanks of the retreat. A dangerous trap set to catch the advancing Canadians as they topped the crest ahead. But lack of time had prevented adequate concealment and, in revealing their position, the Huns had given us an opportunity to hit them first.
>
> Cannon smoke trailed back suddenly from the wingco's Typhoon and his first burst ripped viciously through one of the crudely camouflaged emplacements.
>
> No time to take in more as I opened fire on another, seeing the flash of exploding shells in its shadowy depths, followed by a burst of flame. Back on the stick, and a gun barrel, long as a telegraph pole, centred in my gunsight. The cannons thumped again. A fleeting impression of crouching, stumbling figures engulfed in a carpet of firecrackers – then up and away.
>
> As we swung hard to port the flak came up, late and inaccurate. Moments later we caught a half track, accompanied by a large lorry, skulking along the edge of a wood and both erupted in flames. There seemed to be ambulances everywhere threading carefully amongst the wreckage on the roads. All were plastered with huge red crosses. Difficult to believe that every one was genuine. But we left them alone. There were plenty of other targets. I spotted two Tiger tanks tucked under cover and went after them. The wingco stood off; probably to watch my shooting! I was hitting them OK – one pass at the cooling louvres, and the second at the tracks. But my shells were bouncing off. My four cannons were like peashooters against their armour.[35]

Armed reconnaissance played a critical part in the overall interdiction effort, by sealing off the frontline and preventing the Germans from either reinforcing the front, or fleeing from the advancing Allied armies that by mid-August 1944 were beginning to break out of the bridgehead. If the RAF aircraft spotted a larger convoy that warranted a greater attack, then additional Typhoons could also be dispatched. Desmond Scott, who commanded a Typhoon wing throughout the Normandy battle, describes his efforts to speed up the response time for these larger targets:

---

35   David Ince, *Brotherhood of the Skies*, p. 83.

When we arrived in Normandy we worked mainly to a pattern set by 84 Group Operations Control. Early morning reconnaissance patrols sighting enemy road convoys would report to group operations, who would dictate to me the number of squadrons I should dispatch. This system backfired once or twice, and so I decided to do away with the middle man – Group HQ. When the reconnaissance squadron took off at first light the others would stand by on cockpit readiness to scramble off at a moment's notice. When the reconnaissance squadron sighted a road convoy it radioed immediately to our own operations room stating the nature of their find and the size of the required reinforcements – one, two or even three squadrons. One squadron would attack the column and remain until the next arrived. This method kept the convoy stationary, its drivers and tank crews hiding in the ditches or other handy cover. This meant that no convoy could disperse into the orchards and woods that covered large areas of Normandy. From the first sighting, Typhoons would

A Visual Control Post (VCP) operating from a Humber scout car in 83 Group's sector of operations in Normandy. (Crown Copyright – Air Historical Branch)

attack continuously until the whole column was aflame from end to end. The old system allowed a break in our attention, and by the time the next squadron arrived the enemy would be dispersed out of sight in the woods.

It was a very successful departure from orthodoxy, and was able to stand us in good stead at various times later in the campaign, particularly when Group HQ were changing their position while trying to keep up in the advance.[36]

As the allies advanced into France, the German railway system would also become an important target for fighter bombers in these interdiction operations. Strafing trains with cannon and machine guns was found to be more accurate and effective than using rockets and the pilots learnt to 'walk' the rounds along the carriages and engine. Pilots had to be careful though as, depending on what they were carrying, some locomotive's wagons might explode under attack, in addition many German trains included at least one flak position and sometimes as many as three; one behind the locomotive, one in the middle of the train and a third at the end. When attacking such well-protected targets, the fighter bombers would fly in line astern, 150 yards apart, and parallel to the train. At the right

---

36   Desmond Scott, *Typhoon Pilot*, p. 120.

moment they would turn 90 degrees, the leader striking the locomotive and the second, third and fourth aircraft individually attacking the three flak positions. Pierre Clostermann transferred from Typhoons to Tempest aircraft in late 1944, the latter aircraft being increasingly used on armed reconnaissance and interdiction tasks as the war progressed. His account is from the winter of 1944/45:

> In the grey dawn a column of smoke began to rise amongst the long wisps of mist over the monotonous snow-covered plain. Then another a little further along the black line which meandered through the immaculate whiteness of the country-side.
>
> 'Train, 2 o'clock, Talbot Leader!'
>
> The four Tempests slid down to 3,000 feet in the frozen air and their polished wings caught the first gleams of a dingy dawn. We obliqued towards the second train and instinctively four gloved hands, benumbed by the cold, were already pushing the prop lever to fine pitch. We could make out the locomotive and the flak truck in front of it and the interminable mixed train dragging painfully behind.
>
> Without dropping our auxiliary tanks, we went into a shallow dive at full throttle…350…380…420…450 m.p.h. The blood throbbed in my parched throat – still that old fear of flak. Only about a mile or two now. I began to set my aim for about 20 yards in front of the locomotive.
>
> Now! I leant forward, tensed. Only 800 yards. The first burst of tracer – the staccato flashes of the quadruple 20 mm flak mounting – the locomotive's wheels skidding with all brakes jammed on – 500 yards. I was skimming over the snow-covered furrowed fields. Rooks flew off in swarms. My cannon roared – the engine driver jumped out of his cabin and rolled into the ditch. My shells exploded on the embankment and perforated the black shape that loomed in my sights.
>
> Then the funnel vomited a hot blast of flame and cinders, enveloped in the steam escaping from the punctured pipes. A slight backward pressure on the stick to clear the telegraph wires, a quick dive through the smoke, then once again, the sky in my windshield, covered with oily soot. Pulling hard on the stick I broke in zigzags. Live coals seemed to fly round my plane, 'Le Grand Charles', but whether they were flak or ricochets from my No.2, I couldn't say. The usual fiery white puffs began to hang in the air. A glance backwards. The locomotive had disappeared, shrouded in soot and spurting steam. People were scrambling out of doors and tearing down the embankment like agitated ants.
>
> Red 3 and Red 2 caught up with me, while Red 4 was still disentangling himself from the very dense flak spouting from the three flak trucks. I made my section do a wide climbing turn and we set course for the second train. It had certainly been warned by radio. It had come to a standstill and the smoke now rose vertically from it. I waggled my wings, unable to make up my mind. No point in attacking this one, as the flak crews must be expecting us all set.
>
> 'Hallo, Talbot, no use, chaps, they've got the gen. Break away to starboard, one, eight, zero!'
>
> Christ! Red 4 has gone crazy! 'Talbot Red 4, don't attack!'
>
> The Tempest kept on down just the same, pointing at the locomotive.
>
> 'Come back. Break, you fool!'
>
> The flak opened up, and I could see the trails of smoke from Red 4's wings as he fired. Then an almost imperceptible explosion along the fuselage, the Tempest slowly turned over, still keeping on its course. Almost on its back now, it just missed one of the trucks and crashed by the line. I could have sworn I heard the explosion. The inevitable mushroom of heavy black smoke, shot with burning petrol vapour immediately rose from the scattered debris.[37]

---

37   Pierre Clostermann, *The Big Show*, p. 191.

A Hawker Typhoon Mark IB of 439 Squadron RCAF taxies through water at B78 Eindhoven, Holland, while leaving its dispersal loaded with two 1,000-lb bombs for an attack on a rail target behind the German lines. (Crown Copyright – Air Historical Branch)

Still from film shot by a Hawker Typhoon of 181 Squadron RAF while attacking trucks in railways sidings at Nordhorn, Germany, showing a salvo of 60-lb rocket projectiles heading for the target, which has already been hit. (Crown Copyright – Air Historical Branch)

Attacks by fighter bombers were rarely one-sided affairs, in fact the Germans progressively equipped their front-line forces with prodigious quantities of flak, which presented an enduring major threat in every Typhoon operation. Small calibre German AA fire (e.g. 12.7mm) was effective up to 3,000 feet, this was complemented by the automatic 20mm/40mm fire which was effective up 6,000 feet and usually set to burst at a pre-determined height. This gave novice pilots the false impression that they were safe once they had flown through it, an entirely erroneous view as the cannon shells would detonate on impact and still inflict tremendous damage if they hit an aircraft. This medium level AA fire was probably the most lethal to the fighter bombers.

The Typhoons would therefore normally cruise at about 7–8,000 feet, above the height of the 20 and 40mm cannon fire. They could still be engaged by the larger calibre 88mm flak, but this was generally inaccurate against the fast-moving Typhoons. Flying Officer J.G. Simpson of 193 Squadron gave his view on the flak:

> The thing that worried most of us quite a bit was the fact that the Germans would put up a carpet of 20 and 40mm stuff. Little white puffs you could get out and walk on. Round about 3-4,000 feet this was and one had to dive through it. You didn't think of the shells that were coming up and had not yet exploded, unless they hit you! It seemed much safer to go through the white puffs rather than fly around and try to screw your courage to dive down through it. I think on the low level shows you never saw the flak that hit you, and I personally felt very much afraid of flak on a low-level operation. After an attack and you begin to pull up you are a better target for the light flak and there's no doubt that the German gunners were a pretty brave lot.[38]

The German gunners were not only brave but also highly skilled and canny. Charles Demoulin was a highly experienced Belgian Typhoon pilot with 609 Squadron and by the Autumn of 1944 had become attuned to the German flak-gunner's tactics and tricks, as well as being able to identify the carefully camouflaged Germans:

> My No.2 today is Flt Sgt Teather, newly arrived in the squadron, and I want to give him some experience with an op near our own lines. It is with a tinge of regret that I left Mouzon on the ground, but each pilot has to take his share of the work. Before take off, I explained clearly to Teather that I wanted him to stick with me like a shadow. Even so, I feel sure that when the flak opens up, he will be surprised at his baptism of fire.
>
> The Controller has given me the supposed location of the German tanks. A glance at the map on my left knee, followed by a long look at the ground below my wing, and I find the cross roads that serves as the pinpoint. I look at it carefully, but find no trace of the enemy. Not far away there is a little wood, still with leaves at this time of the year, and something tells me that it's not a healthy spot. Behind, the village of Saint Laureins looks deserted, with a little road leading to Saint Margriete, near the Belgian border. You would think we were in the waiting room of Paradise, there are so many saints around. But, here comes the yellow smoke to mark the front line; once past that little coloured cloud, we may shoot at anything that moves. But nothing moves.
>
> 'Hello Control, Red One here. I have had a good look at A3 F7 but I can't see any jokers. Please confirm your instructions.'
>
> 'Hello Red One, Control calling. I confirm A3 F7 – probably behind the farm courtyard. Out'
>
> If I can't see anything then it's because they are well camouflaged, so the only thing to do is go down and see what happens – but keeping ready to fire instantly.
>
> 'Digit Red and Blue Sections, I am going down alone. Wait till they open fire then give them hell.'
>
> Now, down we go at full throttle and take a good look while my five Typhoons orbit up top.
>
> The wing goes down, the engine roars and the ground comes up at full speed while the red dot sits over the suspicious orchard: 400, 425, 440 mph and at 500 feet the merry-go-round begins. A curtain of fire is thrown at me from the orchard, and from the little wood.

---

38   Norman Franks, *Typhoon Attack*, p. 204.

German mobile quadruple 40mm flak gun pictured in Normandy, 1944. (Bundesarchiv)

At the same moment, I fire my cannon and let my rockets go, aiming at the dark patches I can now see under the fruit trees. I spray them all the way down, then steep turn away near the ground, keeping well clear of the little wood.

Great! Everything going to plan! Those sods were playing dead until the last moment – but now some of them will be dead for quite a while. As I climb up for another attack, my friends dive, one after the other, on the orchard. All but Teather. He hesitates a moment then goes for the wood.

There's no time to warn him by radio; his plane is already a ball of fire, and he hits the ground near the road. An explosion, then the horrid black smoke billows up. That's all that's left of a young sprog meeting battle for the first time. Bad luck maybe. But why go straight for the lion's mouth? I had warned him about the wood. But inexperienced, he probably thought of only avoiding the flak coming from the orchard and so he fell into the trap.[39]

The casualty rate in the Typhoons inevitably rose during these operations. Between 6 June and 1 September 1944, a shocking 56 percent of the Typhoon force engaged would be killed in action. This high rate was partly because when flying at such low altitudes there was little time for the pilot to bale-out if his aircraft was damaged badly. In addition, as the aircraft was often hit when diving at the target any damage to control surfaces would quite often prevent the pilot from pulling out of the dive altogether. Flying Officer H.G. Pattison of 182 Squadron recalls one such occasion:

In these attacks we went in individually; we didn't go on in pairs or as a four. Once the target was sighted and confirmed then we went down at intervals – 1, 2, 3, 4, and once the

---

39   Charles Demoulin, *Firebirds! Flying the Typhoon in Action* (Shrewsbury: Airlife Publishing Ltd, 1987), p. 165.

bloke ahead had broken away, you were concentrating on aiming then didn't see anything of them. It was a question of getting away from the target area and eventually, if you were lucky, joining with the rest to go home.

On the break I felt about five strikes underneath me; not surprising as there was intense heavy and light flak in the target area. Breaking left had put me on the safety course from the target and my immediate reaction was to check the instruments. To my surprise, the oil pressure was falling rapidly, and within five seconds, stopped at zero coincidentally with the propeller coming literally to a shuddering halt as the engine seized. The whole airframe shook but did not fall apart. Then came decision time. To pull up from the deck and bale out or to continue as far as possible with excess speed and hope to force land behind our lines. I quickly opted for the latter course and kept going. On the way I switched off the fuel and all electrics, then tightened my straps.

Speed was obviously decaying fairly rapidly and at, I suppose, 250 mph I decided to pull up and look for somewhere to put down as all I could see were trees. My lucky star must have been shining brightly as, at about 200 mph, I saw a large clear space ahead. This turned out to be a ploughed field or, at least, it was very rough. Speed dropping to 150 mph I jettisoned the hood, selected flaps down and started pumping like hell. Fortunately they went down and I was committed.

The available space did not look too generous so I had to force the aircraft onto the ground at, I guess, somewhere between 120 and 140 mph – rather fast! After two or three ricochets it stayed down and we ground to a halt with clods of earth flying everywhere including into the cockpit. Sudden silence while I disembarked and crawled under a wing tip – fortunately there was no fire – then the silence became very noisy. German tanks to the east, British tanks and artillery to the west and me in the middle being fired on by both sides. Needless to say I was somewhat concerned as to what might happen being in such an exposed position. After 30-45 minutes of enormous twitch, the firing stopped and a Canadian Army Captain drove out in a jeep and picked me up. I was debriefed at his HQ and a kindly gentleman instructed a soldier to furnish me with a tumbler of Scotch. It was quite full and only a little was lost due to a trembling hand on its way to my lips.[40]

Although the Typhoons suffered losses, this was dwarfed by the level of destruction they visited on the Germans. *Wehrmacht* soft skinned vehicles, as well as the large quantities of horse-drawn transport they still used, were especially vulnerable. Usually such destruction was dispersed over a wide area, but the German attempts to evade the Allied armies by fleeing through the neck of the Falaise pocket in mid-August 1944, meant that the *Jagd-bombers,* or *'Jabos'*, as the Germans called them, were presented with a concentration of targets unmatched in the campaign. Immediately after the battle David Ince, together with a small party of fellow pilots, travelled to the Falaise pocket and was able to observe at first hand the destruction they had caused:

Our truck jolted and rumbled on down the winding roads to the south and east of Falaise. The sickly sweet odour grew steadily worse, until it dominated the senses, and there was no escaping its dreadful embrace. Surrounding us on every side was the reality of what had been happening, down there in the Bocage, inside the ring of steel which had closed and tightened around the German armies in Normandy. It was like a vision of the apocalypse.

From Trun to Vimoutiers ran the awful highways of death where the retreating columns had been cornered, and systematically destroyed, as they tried to escape. Stalled nose to tail

---

40   Norman Franks, *Typhoon Attack*, p. 145.

they had been devastated by nonstop air attack, on roads swept by torrents of artillery and mortar fire, until hardly a living creature remained.

We climbed down from the truck and walked among them in a valley still as the grave itself, where no birds sang and nothing moved except the flies and maggots. They lay where they had fallen, amongst the debris of their broken weapons and ruined vehicles. Some were hideously torn and disfigured, or charred and blackened until their shrunken corpses were hardly recognisable as those of human beings.

Others lay seemingly untouched, calm and peaceful, handsome in death, their sightless eyes staring forever into space. The horses were the saddest sight of all. Unable to escape they had been mown down where they stood. Their bodies swollen and distended, their noble heads grimacing in rigor mortis, pitiful beyond words.

The scale and horror of it all was almost too much to take, and it was a thoughtful little party which returned to St Croix Sur Mer that night.[41]

Official studies were made into the level of destruction meted out by the Allied air forces in the Falaise Pocket. A joint RAF and Army Operational Research Section study concluded that though massive damage had been inflicted on soft skinned vehicles, little had been done to German armour; in fact only ten out of 301 tanks and three out of 87 armoured troop carriers were destroyed.[42] This contrasted dramatically with pilot's claims but was not altogether surprising. Tests had already shown that a German tank could only be knocked out by a direct hit from a Typhoon rocket and as we have seen that was very hard to achieve, even in the benign conditions of an armament practice camp. What was perhaps more surprising was that during Typhoon attacks many German tanks had been abandoned by their crews, despite it theoretically being one of the safest places to be during a fighter bomber strike. As one British intelligence summary revealed:

Interrogation of prisoners has shown without question that German tank crews are extremely frightened of attacks by RP… Crews are very aware that if an RP does hit a tank, their chances of survival is small. It is admitted that the chances of a direct hit are slight; nevertheless, this would hardly be appreciated by a crew whose first thought would be of the disastrous results if a hit is obtained.[43]

Furthermore, experienced tank crews told their interrogators that when attacked from the air they remained in their tanks, which usually suffered no more than superficial damage (from cannon strikes or bomb near misses). Yet these same tank crews also said they had great difficulty in preventing the inexperienced men from baling out when Allied aircraft attacked.[44]

This Operational Research work highlighted the importance of morale amongst fighting men and how air attacks and air power can undermine it catastrophically. At Falaise the sheer volume of fire raining down on withdrawing German formations, armoured or otherwise, was often enough to cause the collapse of otherwise determined soldiers. In addition, many of the AFV or tank crews found they could no longer operate their vehicles even if they wished to, this was because either soft skinned vehicles had been wrecked around them and blocked them in, or the supporting fuel

---

41    David Ince, *Brotherhood of the Skies*, p. 84.
42    Ian Gooderson, *Air Power at the Battlefront*, p. 115.
43    TNA AIR 37/415 Headquarters RAF No.38 Group, Tactical Bulletin No.45, *Tactical Employment of RP Aircraft*, October 1944
44    ORS 2nd TAF/No.2 ORS Joint Report No.3, *Rocket Typhoons in Close Support of Military Operations*, in *Operational Research in North West Europe* (Quoted from Ian Gooderson's *Air Power at the Battlefront*, p. 116.)

A road near Chambois, south-east of Trun, Normandy, filled with wrecked vehicles and the bodies of retreating German soldiers following an attack by Hawker Typhoons of 83 Group. (Crown Copyright – Air Historical Branch)

bowsers had been destroyed along with their fuel. These air attacks also had a positive effect on British morale. The sight and sound of the RAF striking the Germans before their own ground attacks went in, as well as the actual destruction inflicted on the enemy clearly buoyed up British assaulting troops. This was an important additional benefit that generals appreciated, particularly when they requested the use of heavy bombers in close support.

The capabilities of Bomber Command and the American Eighth Air Force in unlocking stalemates on the battlefield were too potent to be ignored. During the North-West European campaign heavy bombers were used on numerous ground support tasks including the assaults on Caen (Operation CHARNWOOD), Le Havre (Op ASTONIA), Boulogne (Op WELLHIT), Goch/Kleve (Op VERITABLE) and Wesel (Op WIDGEON). At Caen the Army was concerned that the RAF might drop their bombs short and hit their own troops, so the target area was moved further from the British frontline with the result that the RAF largely missed the enemy's main defensive positions. Instead the raid created obstacles of rubble that hampered the following British assault. RAF heavy bombers were used more successfully in disrupting the move into battle of II SS Panzer Corps during Operation EPSOM. The strike by two hundred RAF heavy bombers dropped over 1,000 tons of bombs onto German concentration areas in Villers Bocage, creating chaos and confusion as well as inflicting significant damage on the Panzer Divisions.

Operation GOODWOOD is perhaps the best-known occasion when Montgomery called upon the Air Force to help his assault against the Germans facing him. The object of GOODWOOD was to break out of the southern flank of the Orne Bridgehead and occupy high ground south and south-west of Caen, which could then be used to initiate an armoured thrust towards Falaise. This plan fitted into Montgomery's larger strategy of attracting German armour to his side of the beach

An Avro Lancaster of 514 Squadron RAF flying over cloud cover during a daylight attack on fortified villages east of Caen as part of Operation GOODWOOD. (Crown Copyright – Air Historical Branch)

head, thus creating the best possible chance for the Americans to break out against the weaker opposition that faced them.

The GOODWOOD attack was to be launched down a long narrow corridor and the Army requested Air support in supressing the opposition on the British flanks, neutralising the enemy opposition directly in front of the assaulting VIII Corps and striking enemy gun positions out of range of the British artillery. The Air Force commanders accepted the Army's request not simply because they wished the Army to break out, but also because they recognised that the area south and south east of Caen was perfect real estate upon which to build their airfields. This issue had been a cause of considerable frustration between the air force and ground commanders over the preceding month. Indeed, under Montgomery's original plan the air force had expected such areas to have been captured early in the invasion, Caen after all had been expected to fall on D-day itself. This lack of progress on the ground was brushed aside by Montgomery, who maintained that his plan to draw the majority of Germans onto his side of the bridgehead so that the Americans could break out in the west was working. Indeed it was, but the congested bridgehead meant that there was not enough space for 84 Group's airfields to be built and many RAF squadrons remained based in the UK unable to generate the sortie rates they wished.

The GOODWOOD air support plan was much more detailed and complex than previous occasions and included 1,512 heavy bombers and 343 medium bombers.[45] The main features of the plan were heavy bombing on the flanks of the advance (Areas H and A) by 463 Bomber Command aircraft using a massive weight of bombs (mainly 1,000lb General Purpose (GP) and 500lb GP),

---

45    See Figure 3a and 3b on page 189.

for in these areas cratering was acceptable. Bomber Command would also attack Area M but with less destructive munitions as cratering was not tolerable. In the middle of the corridor of advance (Areas C, D, E, F and G) the American Eighth and Ninth Air Force would attack gun batteries and other enemy positions. Cratering was not acceptable here, so these aircraft used 500lb GP and 250lb fragmentation bombs.

The GOODWOOD targets were to be marked by Mosquitoes from the Pathfinders dropping red target markers from 22,000 to 30,000 feet guided by Oboe, these could be corrected where necessary by yellow markers dropped from the Master Bomber or his deputy. The Bomber Command aircraft flew in one gaggling stream between 5,000 to 10,000 feet and each aircraft bombed individually and at their own discretion against their allotted targets. The Americans flew in much neater formations and bombed as boxes of eighteen aircraft on the leader's command. The British bombing was far more accurate than the Americans, though Bomber Command did have the advantage of operating during the best part of the day, before the smoke and haze got going. Some American bomb-aimers delayed their release because of a concern to avoid friendly forces becoming casualties and many bombs fell beyond the target areas – some by as much as four miles. More accurate bombing of the corridor might have helped GOODWOOD, but Dempsey's basic concept of using heavy bombing in support of the offensive in this sector was potentially flawed as the area was too large and the German defences too dispersed.

Keith Jones served as the second-in-command of a Northamptonshire Yeomanry tank squadron, which was spearheading the GOODWOOD assault as part of the 11th Armoured Division. Deployed near the start line in his Cromwell tank, he remembered the bombing well:

> About 5 a.m the Pathfinders were heard. I shifted my position for the hundredth time, hoisted myself upright to park on the cupola rim. The sticky warmth of the tank interior contrasted with the cleanliness of the pre-dawn air. If I shivered now, the exchange was still welcome.
>
> As the multiples of four engines came closer, other tank hatches clanked open, crews stirred. Harry dived under the rear end with his screened cooker to prepare the morning ambrosia. Soon we were sipping at it from our seats in the pit stalls.
>
> While dark remained, the flak bursts scintillated viciously, as they must have for countless night bomber incursions over Europe, all round the barely visible droning black cargo-heavy fuselages. Flares launched to illuminate ground targets seemed only to confuse the sky picture seen from below. At an early stage we could occasionally glimpse festoons of tinsel foil twisting down to disrupt defensive detection systems.
>
> As the sky lightened, we began to identify individual aircraft, to witness the pulling power in each of four Rolls-Royce engines, knowing that just one such engine powered a Spitfire or our Cromwell tank.
>
> Some flashes where bombs landed preceded by several seconds the muffled sounds of detonation. There was no telling whether the immense destruction was on target; all we knew was that nothing landed anywhere near us.
>
> The operation continued inexorably as the time it takes for a thousand bombers to have their turn over a limited target area. From where we were, only one Lancaster appeared to be hit. It moved out of formation with a black smoke trail, flames spreading to furnace intensity. What could survive in that heat? Then parachutes appeared near the wake of the stricken craft – two, three, four...then no more, although the crew was eight?
>
> One chute was itself on fire. The plane went into a dive. We thought we heard the whining crescendo of it above all the other noises. The frame burst vividly into the ground well behind enemy lines. In the packed bridgehead, tank crews trying intensely to keep track of the baled-out airmen were already identifying with the same desperate act by which, from a few feet above ground, many of them would soon be escaping their own blazing vehicles.

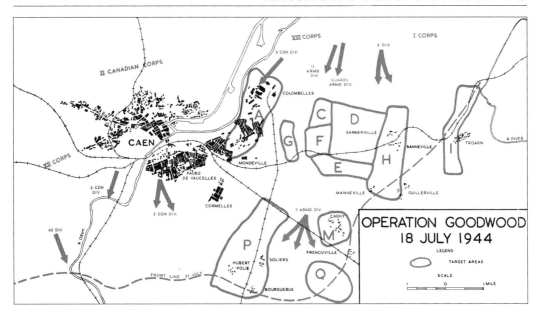

| Target | | Time | No. of Aircraft Attacking | Height in feet | Short tons of HE | No. of Markers | Mean Tonnage per acre |
|---|---|---|---|---|---|---|---|
| **Bomber Command** | | | | | | | |
| A | Colombelles | 0536/0604 | 233 | 6,500/9,500 | 1,306 | 56 | |
| | Mondeville | 0559/0617 | 230 | 6,500/10,000 | 1,228 | 48 | 1.4 |
| H | Sannerville | 0541/0557 | 234 | 5,000/9,000 | 1,217 | 56 | |
| | Manneville | 0559/0617 | 229 | 6,500/10,000 | 1,261 | 39 | 2.1 |
| M | Cagny | 0615/0625 | 102 | 6,000/10,000 | 608 | 52 | 0.7 |
| **Eighth USAAF** | | | | | | | |
| I | Troarn | 0730/0930 | | | 353 | - | 0.08 |
| P | Soliers | 0900/0930 | 571 | 14,000/18,000 | 640 | - | 0.09 |
| Q | Frenouville | 0900/0930 | | | 333 | - | 0.23 |
| **Ninth USAAF** | | | | | | | |
| C,D, E, F, G | | | 318 | 10,800/13,000 | 621 | - | |
| Totals | | | 1,917 | | 7,567 | 251 | |

Figures 3a and b 'Scale of Effort by RAF and American Bombers During Operation GOODWOOD 18 July 1944'

When the RAF completed, the USAAF began, in semi-daylight, gunning up the trail the tank must follow, to the hills of the Bourgebus ridge, aiming to treat the fortified villages in our path to the non-cratering effect of high fragmentation bombing. We watched their lower-altitude tails clearing our bereted heads and dusting away south and slightly west to annihilate opposition until all we had to do was drive. Would it be like that?

As the last of the Havocs and Marauders skated into the distance, the artillery programme took over, most guns firing from the far side of the River Orne.[46]

---

46   Keith Jones, *Sixty-Four Days of a Normandy Summer* (London: Robert Hale Ltd, 1990), pp. 79-81.

An Avro Lancaster leaves the target area (top right), as smoke from exploding bombs smothers the village of Cagny, south-east of Caen, in support Operation GOODWOOD, on the morning of 18 July 1944.
(Crown Copyright – Air Historical Branch)

From a German perspective the impacts of the heavy bombs could be horrendous. Werner Kortenhause was a member of the 21st Panzer Division opposing the British in the GOODWOOD sector, he watched the Allied bombardment with morbid fascination:

> We saw little dots detach themselves from the planes. Then began the most terrifying hours of our lives. It was a bomb carpet, regularly ploughing up the ground. Among the thunder of the explosions we could hear the wounded scream and the insane howling of men who had been driven mad.[47]

Some four months after the event, RAF Bomber Command's Bombing Analysis Unit travelled to the site of a German heavy tank company in Guillerville within area H. They observed 15 destroyed tanks, as well as numerous buildings and soft skinned vehicles that had also been wrecked. Their initial approach was to judge the proximity of the tanks to the 73 craters of various sizes in the village and try to work out what was the minimum distance at which a detonating bomb would destroy a tank. As they examined the site further, they concluded that the destruction was less

---

47  Richard Hargreaves, *The Germans in Normandy* (Barnsley: Pen and Sword, 2006), p. 141.

about minimal distances from the bombs, but more to do with the cumulative impact of many bombs, within a confined space, in a very short period of time:

> It is commonly assumed that tanks are in general immune to anything except direct hits or very near misses by bombs… At first glance, therefore, the result of this attack would suggest that a heavy tank is vulnerable to any 500 or 1000 lb. bomb which falls up to about 12 yards from it. This figure seems excessive, and should be accepted with reserve until experimental evidence is obtained for single bomb hits up to this distance. If such evidence substantiates the general conclusion which emerges from the present analysis, then it becomes simple enough to understand the fate of the 15 tanks which are the subject of the present report. If, on the other hand, experiment suggests that the band of vulnerability is significantly less than 11 yards, then an explanation would have to be sought in the fact that the tanks were subjected not to a number of hits well separated in time, but to a very large number occurring within a very short interval. When one remembers that the tank formation was blanketed by about 145 bombs averaging in weight about 700 lb., and with an average charge/weight ratio of 40%, one can obtain some impression of the physical conditions which existed at the time of the attack. For example, approximately one ton of earth is thrown up per lb. of charge. This means that some 40,000 tons of debris were set in motion in the area of the tanks during the period of the attack. The violent impulses to which the vehicles were subjected by debris, by multiple ground shocks and blast waves would perhaps be sufficient to account for their destruction without assuming that a heavy German tank is vulnerable to a single 500 lb. or 1000 lb. bomb falling up to 11 yards from it.[48]

Not all bombing by the RAF heavy bombers was accurate and sadly short bombing by Allied bombers over their own troops was not unheard of. In some cases it was a case of mistaking the target or poor navigation, but in others there was also a tendency for the bombing to creep back. The consequences of heavy bomber loads falling on friendly forces prior to an assault could be disastrous. One occasion when RAF bombers caused heavy casualties by short bombing was during a mission to support II Canadian Corps during Operation TRACTABLE on 14 August. On this occasion visibility was good with a slight wind blowing from the north. As scheduled the 811 aircraft dispatched by Bomber Command began arriving over the target area at 1400. The aim points had been correctly and accurately marked by the pathfinders and all six targets were struck, a total of 3,723 tons being dropped by the aircraft. However, 77 aircraft (44 of which ironically belonged to 6 Group RCAF) mistakenly dropped their bombs 4-6 miles north of the target. Bombardier J. G. Perry who served with a 51st Highland Division artillery regiment recalls the experience:

> We were in open country about 5 miles south of CAEN on a beautiful sunny afternoon. The time was 2 p.m.. We knew that a big attack was going in, in the area of, or towards the direction of Falaise, to be preceded by a very large force of Lancasters (some said 1,000) & which we were to support by artillery fire simultaneously.
>
> The first few squadrons passed over flying very straight on a south-easterly direction, evidently loaded with bombs. Their main objective was a wood about 4 miles south of us which Jerry was reported to be occupying in force & bombing was thought to be the only thing to move him.

---

48   TNA AIR 24/1467 Bombing Analysis Unit Report No.22 'Ground Survey of the Results of an Attack by Heavy bombers on a German Tank Concentration'.

I was off duty at the time & had just finished a letter to my wife. There was then a gap in between the squadrons overhead when apparently from nowhere a stick of bombs fell approximately two fields to the north of our position. The weather had been dry for some days and they obviously hit something very vulnerable as the area for perhaps a mile square was obliterated with smoke and dust.[49]

The next wave of Lancasters compounded the error and dropped several 1,000lb bombs in a field where Polish tank squadrons, AA guns, Canadian reserves and British and Canadian artillery were situated. Bombardier Perry and his comrades sensibly took cover:

I was in a fairly shallow slit trench face downwards (about 2½ feet deep). It wasn't my own slit trench which was about 150 yards away. The bombing continued after that as wave after wave came over and released their loads. All Hell was let loose and the earth jumped up and down as each stick of bombs crept near to where I was. All sorts of thoughts kept flashing in my mind as I lay there, my loved ones, home everything that was dear to me and finally as I was gradually getting buried alive a prayer.

A split second afterwards I had a feeling of peaceful satisfaction that I had said the prayer. A stick of bombs came whistling down much nearer than any before and I felt instinctively that I was to get it, this was it. I remembered counting the bombs as they fell in quick succession each one nearer than the last. One 2-3-4-5-6 after that I couldn't even think because 2 noises like thunder which deafened me literally lifted me out of the trench, dropped me back in and plastered earth and debris on top of me. My brain had almost ceased to function but subconsciously I had the governing feeling that I had on one or two previous occasions when I had thought it was all over and that was I must not Panic.

I began to pull my knees up towards my stomach. At first I realised that if I didn't make a tremendous effort in a second or so I would suffocate. My knees moved and I got a bit of leverage & heaved for all I was worth (mentally thanking God that I had a strong leg, back and stomach muscles). Finally when I was beginning to feel that all was over I saw a small shaft of daylight under my eyes. I took a deep breath then I rested for a second – another deep breath and then a heave for all I was worth.

The patch of daylight widened but I couldn't get any further with the heaving. I supported what I had already moved as best I could and I was able to think more clearly again. I began to dig upwards with my fingers towards the light and eventually got my head out – another short rest and then one shoulder and then the other. After that it was comparatively easy. I lay panting on God's good earth. Then I realised that another squadron was coming over. I nearly panicked then, but almost immediately came the thought – I mustn't panic. I dragged myself to my feet and forced myself to walk to my own slit trench. I got there before the next lot came. My own trench was comparatively heaven and inhabited by a Canadian. I dived in and we huddled together sideways until the bombing stopped.[50]

Bombardier Perry was lucky to have only suffered minor injuries. In the Bomber Command strike there were significant friendly force casualties, including 112 killed, 376 wounded and 142 posted as missing. A subsequent inquiry attributed the failure to several reasons, firstly that RAF heavy bomber crews were more used to night navigation and striking targets marked by pathfinders with illuminating pyrotechnics. The inquiry observed that they were simply not

---

49   Imperial War Museum 86/47/1, Private Papers of Bombardier J.G. Perry
50   Imperial War Museum 86/47/1, Private Papers of Bombardier J.G. Perry

practiced in observing the ground below their aircraft and comparing it to the map. There were also operational factors too, the RAF had suggested that as the prevailing wind was blowing from the north it would be better to bomb south to north. That method would prevent any markers being obscured by the dust and smoke that would be carried on the wind. This was opposed by the Army as it did not fit in to the Canadian attack which was rolling from north to south and the RAF relented. The third cause was that the bombers of 4 and 6 Group incorrectly bombed the area around St Aignan. This prompted the troops on the ground to put out yellow flares, smoke and Celanese strips, which was a standard response if ground troops were either being struck by RAF aircraft – or felt that they might be. Inexcusably this practice was not communicated to the RAF heavy bomber crews, who mistook these recognition strips for the yellow target markers that the Master Bomber was instructing them to bomb at the time. Worse still the original target markers were becoming obscured by the dust and smoke that had begun to blow over them from the north. Finally, a number of Air OP Auster aircraft were in the air at the time and in a brave attempt to stop the bombing fired red flares to warn off the bombers, these in turn looked like the cascading pyrotechnics sometimes used by Bomber Command.

These incidents are typical of the sorts of events that arise under what is often termed the 'friction of war', they also illustrate the particular care needed in joint operations. What was inexcusable on some of the aircrew's part was the ease with which they had abandoned their timed run-in from the coast, which they were given clear instructions to follow and which would have clearly shown that they were still some distance from their target. Unsurprisingly several crews were formally disciplined following this incident.

Of course, most aircrews were conscientious and despite the personal risks involved, did their utmost to bomb accurately. Flight Lieutenant Campbell Muirhead, a Lancaster bomb aimer, describes a mission in support of OP CHARNWOOD on 7 July:

> Another daylight op. We were told that very accurate bombing was essential – 'bring the things back if you can't be sure of your aiming point.' This because we were bombing only 1½ miles ahead of our troops (Canadians, evidently). My sighting was not right so I didn't press the tit. I told Vernon [Flying Officer Vernon the pilot] to go round a second time. God, the language which came over that intercom! Interspersed with references not only to my complete inadequacy as a bomb aimer, but also to my parentage. Can't exactly blame them – there we were, the only Lancaster left over Caen and what flak there was beginning to concentrate on us. But there was no way I was going to drop 13,000lbs of high explosive when there was the slightest possibility of the dreadful stuff killing or wounding our own troops: would have taken the load back to Wickenby first. However, I got a perfect sighting on that second run (despite what was still being said over the intercom) and placed my bombs exactly where I wanted them.
>
> Despite that second time round, on the way back we caught up with the stragglers ('B' for Baker being brand new and with that extra few knots more than most). Flying almost level with another Lanc, who was limping. Just crossing the French Coast when up came quite a scything of flak. It got him (not by the Grace of God, us). He started diving straight down. We counted four parachutes opening, praying for more but to no avail. The Lanc struck the water burst into a terrific sheet of flame. We all fell silent until over base, everybody thinking of the three men inside.'[51]

---

51   Campbell Muirhead, *The Diary of a Bomb Aimer* (Tunbridge Wells: Spellmount Ltd, 1987), p. 89.

Hawker Typhoon pilots of No. 181 Squadron RAF leave the briefing tent at B2-Bazenville, Normandy.
(Crown Copyright – Air Historical Branch)

Whether fighter bomber or heavy bomber, close air support or interdiction, it was the combination of all these aspects of Allied air power that was so effective. The cumulative impact of the Allied air power in the west, when used against the German land forces was summarised very effectively in a letter to Hitler by the German commander in the West, *Generalfeldmarschall* Von Kluge. Written shortly after GOODWOOD his sentiments would undoubtedly be echoed by other German Army commanders till the end of the war:

> My conference with the commanders of the units at Caen, forced me to the conclusion that in our present position – considering the material at our disposal – there is absolutely no way in which we could do battle with the all-powerful enemy air forces, to counter their present destructive activities, without being forced to surrender territory. Entire armoured formations allocated for counter-attacks have been caught in the heaviest air raids – the only way the panzers could be dragged out of the churned-up ground after them was to pull them out with armoured recovery vehicles.
>
> The psychological effect on the fighting troops, the infantry especially, of such a mass of bombs raining down with all the force of nature is something which must be given particularly serious consideration. It is not in the least important whether such a carpet of bombs is dropped on good or bad troops. They are more or less annihilated by it, and above all their equipment is beyond repair. It only needs this to happen a few times and the power of resistance of these troops is put to the severest test. It becomes paralysed, dies: what is left is not equal to the demands of the situation. Consequently the troops have the impression that they

are battling against an enemy who carries all before him. This must make itself felt to an increasing extent… In spite of all endeavours, the moment is fast approaching when this over-taxed front line is bound to break up. And when the enemy once reaches the open country a properly coordinated command will be almost impossible, because of the insufficient mobility of our troops. I consider it is my duty as the responsible commander on this front to bring these developments to your notice in good time, my Fuhrer.[52]

Hitler failed to heed Von Kluge's warning and after the German counter-attack at Mortain failed, Von Kluge committed suicide. Allied air support to the Army in both the Western Desert and North-West Europe had proven to be a decisive factor in defeating the Italians and Germans. It was also a cornerstone of the British and Australian approach to warfare in the Far East and combatting the Japanese.

---

52   Air Publication 3235, *Air Support*, p. 157.

# 9

# 'Strength through Unity'[1]
# Air Support in Burma

The Allies took many of the air support lessons from the European and Mediterranean theatres of operation and adapted them for operations against the Japanese in Burma and wider Asia. However, Burma always suffered from being one of the lowest priority campaigns, making do with aircraft that were significantly older than the types operated in Europe and suffering from a tenuous supply chain. Despite these equipment handicaps, its tactical approach was modern and had been carefully tailored for operations against the Japanese in the jungles and mountains of Burma and Assam.

One of the biggest differences between the European theatre and that of the Far East was the vast distances the Army and Air Force had to operate over. Burma for instance is very large, if it was placed on a map of Europe, the extreme north of the country would be in the middle of the North Sea, Mandalay approximately where Paris is, Rangoon where the Pyrenees run into the Mediterranean and Moulmein around Marseilles.[2] Victoria Point, the southern end of the long finger that parallels the Malayan border, would be three quarters of the way across the Mediterranean. Burma is surrounded on three sides by jungle-clad mountain ranges and four large rivers flow north to south across the country and into the Bay of Bengal. These rivers include the Irrawaddy river which, together with its major tributary the Chindwin, flows from the Himalayan mountains, and further to their east the Sittang and Salween rivers. All these waterways, as well as the numerous tributaries that flowed into them, presented major obstacles to movement and were also used by the Japanese as communication routes, upon which large river steamers plied. Central Burma itself was dominated by valleys which opened out into thickly wooded plains, whereas the south of the country had a scattering of low hills.

Between the Sittang and Irrawaddy rivers lie a set of jungle hills known as the Pegu Yomas. A further set of mountains, known as the Arakan Yomas, separate Burma from the coastal Arakan region. The flat river valleys are intersected by numerous streams known as *Chaungs,* which in dry weather are generally traversable, though these regularly overflow in the monsoon season causing the neighbouring paddy fields to become impassable. The cool weather in Burma lasts from mid-October to March, but the temperature rises swiftly in April and May making life unbearable. In mid-May the monsoon season usually begins and lasts until mid-September, it encompasses the whole of Burma and much of Assam, sparing only the dry zone around Mandalay and Meiktila. During this period the rivers and valleys flood, the earth tracks turn into a morass of mud, and thick clouds and thunderstorms make flying particularly hazardous. It was in this inhospitable

---

1    Motto of No.1 Squadron Indian Air Force, this squadron was equipped with Hurricane fighter bombers and fought during the Burma campaign, playing a notable ground support role during the Battle of Imphal.
2    See Map 10 for details of Burma.

and undeveloped environment that Lieutenant General Slim's Fourteenth Army, supported by the RAF's Third Tactical Air Force (3rd TAF), operated.[3]

By the middle of 1942 the British had completed their fighting withdrawal from Burma, successfully escaping over the frontier into eastern India from where they faced the Japanese in three vaguely defined fronts. These were all situated in the lower ground between the mountain ranges that ran north to south in Burma, at the southern ends of these basins ran roads and rivers from which the Japanese armies at the front could be easily supplied. The first front was the Arakan, a coastal front which potentially allowed resupply by sea. The central front was to the north of this and just south of the Imphal plain and the third and final front was in the malaria-ridden valleys to the north of Mandalay. The Japanese had most of Burma's lines of communication behind them, which connected them to the major port of Rangoon as well as their secure bases in Thailand. The construction of the Burma railway by Allied prisoners had made this latter link to Bangkok much more assured and the Japanese forces were therefore in a geographically strong position. In stark contrast the British forward positions were at the edge of a wilderness of jungle-clad and undeveloped mountains, with only poor lines of communication leading back to their major bases in India. Defending India and eventually kicking the Japanese out of Burma was therefore going to be a very difficult proposition.

The British utilised all aspects of air support during their campaign in the Far East. Close air support made a big difference to the decisive defensive battles of the Arakan in 1943 and Imphal/Kohima in 1944 and prevented surrounded British forces from being overrun on numerous occasions. When the British Fourteenth Army subsequently took the offensive in the latter part of 1944 and 1945, close air support was an essential element in neutralising stubborn Japanese resistance. Interdiction operations were also important throughout the campaign as the Japanese lines of communication in Burma were limited and river, rail and road traffic could be effectively disrupted by RAF aircraft. Given the great distances in the Burma theatre twin engine fighter bombers were normally required for air interdiction and these were also supplemented by the Liberator bombers which would strike deep into Burma and Thailand and became particularly adept at knocking down bridges including those that carried the Burma railway. There were some strategically important targets within the Burmese theatre, including Rangoon and its oil refineries, as well as the Japanese logistic hubs in Thailand. These were frequently struck by RAF and USAAF bombers flying from India – Wellingtons at first and then Liberators as the war progressed.

To begin with, the RAF flew mainly from airfields in India and were able to seize air superiority partly through the deployment of modern fighters, such as the Spitfire, to the Far East, as well as the Japanese requirement to withdraw their aircraft in order to defend against the American advances across the Pacific towards Japan itself. By 1944, the Japanese in Burma possessed about 220 aircraft in ten air regiments under the 5th Air Division, which they had concentrated away from the front line in airfields around Rangoon and Moulmein. During the Imphal offensive from March to July 1944 the Japanese re-deployed these aircraft to forward airfields in central Burma, which allowed the Allies to inflict a devastating series of blows upon them from which they would never recover. By mid-July 1944 only 49 Japanese aircraft were left in Burma.[4]

As the Allied air force strength continued to grow, their air superiority looked more and more assured. By the time the Fourteenth Army began its advance across the Chindwin in early

---

3    See Annex H for the Order of Battle of Air Command, South East Asia, 1 July 1944 – including 3rd Tactical Air Force.

4    Julian Thompson, *The Imperial War Museum Book of the War in Burma 1942-1945* (London: Pan MacMillan, 2003), p. 355.

Squadron Leader J.A. Bushbridge, the commanding officer of 34 Squadron RAF, briefs his pilots at Palel, Burma, before taking off on another sortie. (Crown Copyright – Air Historical Branch)

Consolidated Liberator B Mark VIs of 356 Squadron RAF heading for their base at Salbani, India, after bombing Japanese positions on Ramree Island. (Crown Copyright – Air Historical Branch)

December 1944 it had 827 combat aircraft and 500 transport machines.[5] These were able to operate from numerous well-positioned airfields, many of which had been part of the mammoth building programme undertaken by British and American engineers, who had constructed a total of 285 airfields by the end of the 1943 monsoon. Although a tremendous achievement, some mistakes were made in this large undertaking, on occasions local contractors had mixed too much sand with the cement requiring the re-laying of some airfields (including that at Imphal) and in some areas not enough account had been taken of the local hot-spots of Malaria. One airfield had been built in the Lushai hills and seemed perfect in many ways, except that there was a 100 percent incidence of cerebral malaria in the local vicinity. At this point in the war Burma was receiving neither enough mepracrine to be used as a prophylactic against Malaria, nor sufficient DDT to eradicate the mosquitoes. The airfield was therefore never properly used.[6]

Britain and her Allies needed to settle the command and control arrangements for the air forces in the region. Consequently, Air Command South East Asia was formed in India in November 1943 to support Mountbatten's South East Asia Command, with a subordinate Eastern Air Command, under the American Air Force Officer Major General George Stratemeyer, responsible for the Burmese theatre. Eastern Air Command included a Strategic Air Force for long range and strategic bombing operations, a Photographic Reconnaissance force, a rapidly growing Troop Carrier Command and the Third Tactical Air Force, which supported the Fourteenth Army. The entirety of Eastern Air Command was a mixed force of British and American aircraft and personnel, it offers one of the war's strongest examples of inter-allied cooperation.

Close air support was critical to the land campaign, but Burma's low priority meant that aging Hurricanes, normally MK IIs with 20mm Cannon, were still being used in 1944 and 1945 for the important close air support role. They were eventually replaced by the excellent P-47 Thunderbolt – the only theatre in which the RAF flew this American fighter bomber. Providing close air support was a challenging role in Burma, not least because of the infamous Japanese bunkers. These fortifications were in widespread use and usually consisted of a deep rectangular trench, roofed with not less than four feet of teak logs and above that four feet of earth. They usually contained twelve soldiers, with firing slits so narrow that they were very hard to detect and were often impervious to artillery shell fire.[7] The RAF dropped 250lb bombs from as low as 50 feet on these bunkers, the bombs were normally fitted with 11-second delay fuses so that they would dig themselves deep into the ground before exploding, it also allowed time for the aircraft to get clear.

Japanese transportation and troop movements were also routinely attacked, though they were often difficult to detect and identify in the dense jungle. Squadron Leader C.P.N. Newman was OC of 34 Squadron and recalled the close air support operations around Imphal in June 1944:

> Once you'd learnt to fly over these areas you knew where you were. If the Japs were attacking in a certain place you knew that they had to come up that ridge, or that road. It was really a trick that you learnt. Then you would study say, an aerial picture and say, yes, that's 200 yards up here on the right hand side and away we'd go.
>
> The success we had according to reports afterwards was very gratifying in that you didn't see vast numbers of lorries, trains, tanks, bunkers or dug-outs being blown up, and yet we'd heard afterwards that the whole of the routes were littered with burnt out trucks, or the army said a position had been knocked out.

5    Julian Thompson, *The Imperial War Museum Book of the War in Burma 1942-1945*, p. 356.
6    Air Ministry, *Wings of The Phoenix*, (London: HMSO, 1949), p. 51.
7    Air Ministry, *Wings of The Phoenix*, p. 51.

A Hawker Hurricane Mark IIC of 221 Group RAF, loaded with two 250-lb GP bombs, taxying before taking off on a sortie at Palel, Burma. (Crown Copyright – Air Historical Branch)

As soon as we'd start our dive onto a target one would open up and spray around with cannon. Once we'd dropped our bombs we'd come around for another run-in, just using cannon. We saw very little, there were no hordes of enemy troops rushing down the roads in mobs of 3,000 etc. If we saw anything, two seconds later they'd be in the jungle! Even if we caught a convoy say, by the time we'd circled it would be difficult to see where they'd gone.

We usually flew in sixes or eights, sometimes a pair, or all twelve. It wasn't easy country and when attacking bridges along little narrow streams and the bridge is only really a few planks, you just couldn't get more aircraft in... We often dropped delayed action bombs on the last sortie of the day and hoped someone would go over them in the middle of the night or something. But usually just short delay fuses for normal jobs such as bunkers etc, just so we could get clear.[8]

Flight Lieutenant E.M. Frost was a pilot in 113 Squadron and recalled the Hurricanes suitability for these missions:

The Hurricanes were ideal for the job and could take punishment from AA and on a couple of occasions survived contact with shattered tree trunks when the pilots got a bit carried away in pressing home strafing runs. It was ideal for the terrain, manoeuvrable, a good bomb load plus cannon. Weather conditions often affected operations and many strikes were aborted owing to intense storms and thick cloud. We had trouble along the Manipur River Valley where you could get boxed-in with cloud. Fortunately our formations and the fact that the Hurri had a tight turning circle enabled us to get out of some sticky spots. You could bet on cloud and rain on most days although there was always one or two gaps through the hills when returning from the Chindwin River area.

...The squadron was given a wide range of targets all of which were directly related to army actions. When the Japs were in the valley we struck as many villages on the plain along the

8    Norman Franks, *The Air Battle of Imphal* (London: William Kimber, 1985), p. 184.

western side – these were usually straightforward and easily identified. Bunker positions on hills were usually easily located but some jungle spots were obscure.

A strange bond was formed with those we supported in our bombing and strafing strikes as evidenced by a number of congratulatory messages from 17th Division. The troops had confidence in our ability and we didn't let them down. While Buck was away on leave and I was acting CO, I had the privilege to accept a Jap officer's sword from Lieutenant Colonel Misra of 5/6th Rajputana Rifles for the squadron's support on Love Tree Hill [sic, possibly Lone Tree Hill], a particularly tough bunker position.[9]

One unique feature of the Burma campaign was that the jungle, together with the geographically dispersed nature of the fighting, meant the frontline airfields were often under grave threat from Japanese ground attack. This danger was particularly acute during the fighting at Imphal in 1944, when the Japanese were often near the airfields. There were six airfields in the Imphal valley in total, including the all-weather strips at Imphal and Palel, as well as the four *Kutchi* strips at Kangla, Tulihal, Wangjing and Sapam, which could not be operated in the Monsoon rains. The jungle around Imphal offered enough cover for Japanese infantry to approach to within a hundred yards of the fighter aircraft parked at their night time dispersals.[10] The Army and newly formed Royal Air Force Regiment assisted in the defence of much of the airfields, but guard duties also fell on the ground crew and sometimes even the pilots.

Flight Lieutenant Parry recalls that at Kangla they used to joke with new arrivals that the Japanese were 'so close we share our orderly officer with them'.[11] As the fighting around Imphal intensified the airfield defences became increasingly sophisticated. So called 'boxes' were constructed usually on one of the slight rises or 'pimples' that scattered the valley floor. Trenches were dug and the Hurricanes pulled in to slight incisions made in the 'pimple'. Each section of pilots, armourers, fitters, riggers, electricians, wireless technicians and maintenance crews were responsible for their own dug outs with strict instructions to observe both the black out and a strict silence. Usually only 25 percent of squadron men were on guard duty each night, but listening to the gruesome, taunting screams of the Japanese 'jitter-parties' undoubtedly took resilience. This was especially the case as no British or Indian servicemen was under any illusion as to what would happen to them if captured by the Japanese. Henry Kirk of 2944 Field Squadron, RAF Regiment, vividly remembers being bluntly briefed by their Intelligence Officer that: 'If the Japanese break in here remember you have nowhere to go, drop a hand grenade and take them with you, do not get taken prisoner, we know they will use you for bayonet practise.'[12] For the ground crew who had to provide security for these airfields it was an unfamiliar and tense experience. Leading Aircraftman (LAC) Rae recalls the threat from both ground and air attack:

Manning the box at Tulihal was a bit nerve-wracking. We were under an Army liaison officer, Major Jollins, and I did not enjoy the two nights of being his runner during genuine 'flaps', since I was sure I would be shot by one of our own men when delivering messages to our dug outs. The Major was equally nervous and practically begged me not to put the magazine in my Sten gun unless I actually saw Japanese faces! Major Jollins paraded us each night, permitting us to see a map with green arrows – for the Japs – closing in on Imphal from several directions

9    Norman Franks, *The Air Battle of Imphal*, p. 186.
10   See Map 11 for details of Imphal and Kohima.
11   Julian Thompson, *The Imperial War Museum Book of the War in Burma 1942-1945*, p. 356.
12   Nigel Warwick, *Constant Vigilance – The RAF Regiment in the Burma Campaign* (Barnsley: Pen and Sword, 2007), p. 65.

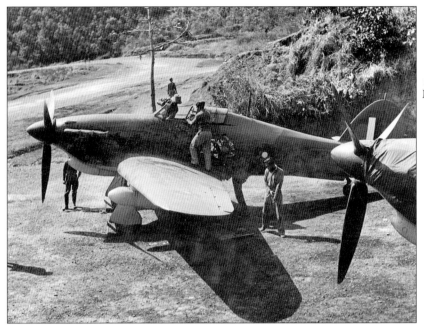

Hawker Hurricane Mark IIBs of 1 Squadron IAF undergoing maintenance in a revetment at Imphal Main, India. (Crown Copyright – Air Historical Branch)

A flying controller signals by Aldis lamp from the two-story log and corrugated iron control tower at Imphal. (Crown Copyright – Air Historical Branch)

and getting nearer every night. He apologised for not being able to reveal red arrows to show British dispositions.

Our squadron MO, Doc Sides from Dublin, had his hut sited halfway between the dispersal and the domestic compound, with its slit trenches. He used to aver that when the three air raid warning shots sounded on the Bofors gun, he would reach out for his steel helmet on the first shot, and by the time the other two had sounded and the helmet was on, the entire squadron, always led by a certain Flight Sergeant, would have disappeared past his window, making for the compound! Being the enemy's probable target improved one's sprinting power no end.[13]

Flight Sergeant C.M.G. Watson was a pilot with 615 Squadron and recalled the danger posed by Japanese artillery and mortar fire:

> We were very much out on a limb at Palel, being at the extremity of the Imphal Valley. There was a squadron at either end of the strip and we kept our aircraft in boxes – aircraft pens surrounded by high earth walls. Sometimes the Japs had field artillery overlooking the end of the strip and would lay down a barrage as we were taking off. In these conditions we staggered the take offs but I don't believe anyone was ever hit, though there some narrow escapes.[14]

The outer defences of the airfields were the responsibility of the Army, though they were supported by small numbers of the RAF Regiment who would provide a more active close defence of the airfields than the ground crew were trained to do, this included ambushes as well as night reconnaissance and fighting patrols. Elements of the RAF Regiment had already seen action in the Mediterranean, but the vulnerability of frontline airfields gave their role added prominence throughout the Burma campaign. Corporal Colin Kirby describes the patrols undertaken by the RAF Regiment during the thirteen-week siege of Imphal:

> With the dark hours there was a stillness contrasting with the heat and noise of the day. We had to stand-to facing the hills from where the Japs may appear as the light faded quickly, Brownings lowered and turned in the same direction. Later some men were stood down to get some sleep, some still on guard, others on patrol. The Corporals had to lead a patrol of six men toward the hills for two hours, so we never had much sleep. The belief was the Japs would send out small suicide parties to raid the strip and do any other damage they could. As they were fanatical and did not seem to mind dying for their Emperor, it was a daunting prospect making contact with them. We would walk quietly for a mile or so and then start to crawl over the rough ground. We halted from time to time for a breather, listening for any suspicious sounds. Muttered conversations, then I would spread them out in a diagonal line maybe 20 yards apart, with myself in 'point' position. Then every man was alone with his thoughts but I hoped still alert. I would decide if it was time to move back to the camp. We approached cautiously until near enough to make contact with the relief patrol. The men would dive for their sleeping space and I would report to the Flight Commander who had his own tent…[15]

By the end of April 1944, the number of men in a patrol had been reduced to allow others to get more rest, but there was still little respite for those who led these missions, including JNCOs like Corporal Kirby:

---

13   Norman Franks, *The Air Battle of Imphal*, pp. 135-6.
14   Norman Franks, *The Air Battle of Imphal*, p. 134.
15   Nigel Warwick, *Constant Vigilance – The RAF Regiment in The Burma Campaign*, pp. 55-6.

That night I took out four men on patrol. It was the middle of the night. We had heard of the daring Jap raiding parties who ventured on to the plain to inflict what damage they could... I led them out some way; before us open ground. It was very dark. By now we were finding moving over the ground more difficult; 100 yards began to seem like a mile. I dropped two after we had gone some distance, and then after a little more distance covered, the other two. I pressed on alone for a little longer, keeping what I hoped was straight line. I stopped with my back resting against a small tree, Sten gun on lap. The only sound was an occasional hyena with its mournful cry. I felt very much alone. I heard a noise to my front and moved into a crouch position and cocked the Sten. I told myself it was my imagination or perhaps a hyena or wild dog? It was there again! I gulped and pointed the gun ahead and let off a few rounds, turned and hurried back. I bumped into one of the others his mate had already moved back to the first two. I collected them and we approached the camp cautiously. 'Corporal Kirby's patrol returning!' I shouted. Everybody was already on stand to peering anxiously into the night.[16]

The efforts of the ground crew, RAF Regiment and most importantly the Fourteenth Army itself, succeeded in keeping Imphal open. In turn the RAF Hurricanes were able to provide close air support to the defending infantrymen, as Flight Lieutenant Parry recalled:

I was on one daytime sortie which was so close to the strip that our ground crew were able to watch the whole operation, lasting twenty minutes, from take off to landing.

I did a lot of strafing at Kohima, which was the only bit of Burma that looked like a First World War battlefield from the air, with masses of shell holes, no trees, and artillery rounds and mortar bombs going off as we flew in. I was a bit worried I would get hit by our own artillery and mortars.

At Imphal, for example at the battle of Bishenpur, one could see the Japs from the air sometimes, especially tanks out in the open. We worked a 'cab rank' system of two aircraft permanently airborne during the day, which was called in on targets when identified by an RAF liaison officer with the forward troops. We were quite effective against tanks because they would have to close down. We carried mixed belts of ammo: ball, incendiary, high explosive, semi-armour piercing and armour piercing. Armour piercing and incendiary was good against tanks. Our warrant officer armourer used to provide the right mix for whatever targets were about that day. When tanks appeared, we were supposed to call in tank-busting Hurricanes MK IIDs with two 40mm guns. But we used to go for the tanks anyway hoping to hit fuel tanks and disable tracks.[17]

As well as the Hurricane, the RAF and Indian Air Force also operated six squadrons of the American built Vultee Vengeance dive bombers. The RAF had been opposed to procuring dive-bombers as a matter of principle and the Vengeance had not been declared fit for service in either Europe or North Africa because of its vulnerability to AA fire, but it was successfully used in the Far East, including Burma and the South-West Pacific. The Vengeance operated with distinction during the Arakan campaign in 1943, at the siege of Imphal-Kohima and in support of the Chindits second operation in 1944, after which the aircraft was taken out of service. Arthur Gill was a squadron leader in 84 Squadron and recalls their missions:

---

16   Nigel Warwick, *Constant Vigilance – The RAF Regiment in The Burma Campaign*, pp. 55-6.
17   Julian Thompson, *The Imperial War Museum Book of the War in Burma 1942-1945*, p. 368.

From their hillside post, LACs A. Nickson and F. Yewbrey of the RAF Regiment point out Japanese positions in the Imphal Valley to their commanding officer, Squadron Leader T.F. Ryalls.
(Crown Copyright – Air Historical Branch)

I think what worried me was that many times they told me that the enemy were within one hundred yards of our front-line troops. That is very close for bombing, even dive-bombing. The only way then that you could accept a target like that was by bombing parallel to our lines. We'd say, 'Well show me exactly where the front line is and confirm that we have not got any troops further east than that point.' They would do so and we would find and identify the target and the British troops, and then we would bomb parallel to them, so that any over-shoots from drift – and this was usually longitudinal, you would very seldom get a lateral drift – would fall clear of our own boys but still among the Japanese. Dive-bombing, of course, was the natural method for this sort of thing. In fact I remember that on one target we had a signal that said, 'Japanese commander in north-east room of house', which amused us and seemed a trifle optimistic, but it serves to show what the Army ultimately came to expect of dive bombers by then.[18]

One aircraft that was slow enough to see through the jungle canopy and identify targets was the Auster with which the Air Observation Posts (Air OPs) were equipped. As we have seen

18    Peter C Smith, *Jungle Dive Bombers at War* (London: John Murray, 1987), p. 74.

the Army's Air OP flights had been developed in Tunisia and then successfully used in Italy and North-West Europe primarily in registering and controlling artillery fire. In the European Theatre, the proliferation of German AA weapons meant that Air OPs were normally limited to flying on the Allied side of the frontline, climbing to height and having a quick glance at the enemy target. In Burma the air situation meant that Air OPs were less vulnerable flying across the front line and their slow speed allowed the pilots to observe activity beneath the jungle canopy, often identifying Japanese ground defences in some detail. Ted Malen-Jones was a pilot with 656 Squadron and recalled conducting a detailed reconnaissance of Japanese positions near the town of Monywa, along the Chindwin river. Malen-Jones had been sent to investigate after the leading units of 32 Brigade had encountered formidable defence positions on the immediate approaches to the town:

> I went up at first light the following morning in order to assess the situation and try to establish the likely extent of the prepared positions. The Brigade Commander, Brigadier Mackenzie, had asked that I pay special attention to the area either side of the road and railway… I made several runs along the whole length of the chaung from the river to a point about one and a half miles to the north-east… At first I could not see a great deal more than I had done the night before, but, as I became more confident and moved in closer, there was little doubt that along the whole length of the east bank of this little chaung the Japs had constructed various types of defence positions. Some of them, particularly those covering the road, had a wide field of fire, while others among the trees, seemed to be sited for reasons that could only be understood at ground level. I realised that it would be useful to the infantry if I could prepare a sketch, but I needed to have a closer look.
>
> I returned to the airstrip to think it through and to prepare a map on which I could plot the exact positions. I divided the area of defences into two sectors roughly 800 yards either side of the road. Having discussed the plan with the Battery Commander I took off and registered the central point of each sector. We then put down five rounds gunfire on the eastern sector using smoke. This made an effective 'carpet' for me to fly over at treetop height and to inspect the defences on the other side. It was necessary to make a number of runs over the area as the layout of bunkers and foxholes gradually became apparent.[19]

Malen-Jones transferred these new positions on to his sketch pad and returned to the operations room to report the results. There, he briefed the Commander Royal Artillery (CRA) as well as the Brigade and Divisional Commander. These senior officers were impressed with what he was able to report and directed Malen-Jones to make a further sortie after the artillery had put down smoke on the western sector once more.

> Back in the air for the next trip, I found it comparatively easy to identify the system. Some of the bunkers seemed to be interconnected and entrances to them from the rear were easy to spot, usually having large timber lintels with well worn pathways leading into them. The smoke had been drifting nicely towards the town and enabled me to fly well over and behind the system. I was confident that I now had a good idea of the intentions behind the layout of the bunkers and had already decided that I wanted to have a further look at the first sector, particularly down by the river. It also occurred to me that, if I was to be a target from the ground, this would already have happened and it was quite likely that the Japs did not fire at me for

---

19    E.W. Malen-Jones, *Fire by Order – Recollections of Service with 656 Air Observation Post Squadron in Burma* (Barnsley: Pen and Sword, 2012), p. 106

fear of giving their positions away to our forward troops. They might also have linked the smoke with an imminent attack rather than a screen for my Auster.[20]

Malen-Jones was able to fly well into the town without attracting fire from the ground and after successfully completing his sortie landed his Auster and returned to the headquarters, where he marked the Japanese positions on a blackboard. He recalled leaving the Divisional and Brigade Commanders, as well as the Air Liaison Officer and CRA, on their knees around his blackboard discussing their options. Two days later, after an air strike and artillery barrage, 32 Brigade captured the town of Monywa.

As in Europe, the Allied control of the air compelled the Japanese Army to restrict their movement to the hours of darkness. In order to interdict this Japanese transport, the Allied air forces also had to operate night sorties, as Flight Lieutenant Parry illustrates:

RAAF Vultee Vengeance on a jungle airstrip.
(State Library of Victoria, Melbourne, Australia)

Night operations were very fruitful, even when we didn't destroy trucks, because the presence of aircraft slowed down the progress of the Japanese road convoys. When we came overhead they would usually park. Furthermore, once you spotted a road convoy and reported its location, the chaps going out at dawn would be able to work out where it had laid up for the day – they hardly ever risked moving at day.

On one occasion, I was out on an intruder raid armed with bombs, and saw a large Jap convoy on a road crossing an open plain – a good place to attack. I dropped one bomb on the road ahead of the convoy, hoping this would be difficult to get round, and another behind them. I kept a patrol over the area, until another intruder pilot arrived. It was Squadron Leader Arjun Singh the CO of Number 1 Indian Squadron. I told him where I was, and he

---

20   E.W. Malen-Jones, *Fire by Order – Recollections of Service with 656 Air Observation Post Squadron in Burma*, p. 106.

took over the standing patrol until dawn, when more aircraft appeared and dealt with the convoy. Some Japs got away but most were caught.

The Japs were very good at camouflage. About an hour before dawn they would pull off the road under the trees on the sides. If there was insufficient cover, they would cover their vehicles with branches cut from further in. After a while we realised that the vegetation by the road was light coloured because of the covering of dust, whereas the branches brought from some way in was dark green. So we flew along the road looking for what looked like new growth, standing out fresh green against the khaki-coloured vegetation.

The Japs also took advantage of areas used by our Army during the retreat of 1942, where we had set up refuelling points at intervals along the main road. Here vehicles had collected and been struck by the Japanese air force, or perhaps had been immobilised and abandoned. From time to time the Japs artfully parked some of their own vehicles among these trucks during the day. So we learned the pattern of the layout of these parks, and were able to spot when new trucks had been popped in. It used to annoy new pilots when they excitedly reported a concentration of vehicles, only to be told, 'don't bother with those, they are our own left behind in 1942.' Then perhaps a couple of days later, we would attack one or two of these parks where we had spotted some additional trucks, and the new pilots couldn't work out how we knew.

Sometimes smoke coming from cooking fires would betray the position of a parked up Jap convoy. Even so, it could be frustrating, because although you could make out the vehicles from dead overhead, when you come in on an attack heading from say half a mile out, at an angle of dive, the trees covered the target and it was hard to spot exactly where they were. Just occasionally you would catch them in the open daylight. Once I saw a Jap staff car on a winding road in the mountains. I strafed it, and saw it go over the edge down the hillside. I assume all the occupants were killed. On another occasion my flight was returning from a 'Rhubarb', when we spotted a truck on a bare hillside. Only my tail-end-charlie had any ammo left and he asked permission to break off and attack. I said 'yes', so in he went. I don't know whether he hit the truck or not, but the whole hillside behind it went up in an enormous ball of flame. I assume the truck was refuelling and he hit a fuel dump.[21]

Another important part of sealing off the battlefield from re-supply and reinforcement was the destruction of Japanese bridges. The Vengeances felt they had skill and accuracy in this regard, though weather could be a frustrating factor as Squadron Leader Arthur Gill recounts:

We did bomb the Ya-Na'n bridge several times. Of course they would rebuild it again. In a case like that we would send over only about six to eight aircraft to destroy a bridge, didn't need more than that. Vital roads as well. Intelligence sources would come back that the Japanese have now occupied such-and-such and they would tell us where they were actually operating. Not jungle targets at this stage of the war so much, this is on the Imphal plain, all paddy fields and marshland very, very wet country.

When the monsoons came we found that 12 aircraft would take off, fly all the way to the target and couldn't find it because it would be completely covered with cloud, 'weathered out'. So I said to the AOC, Air Marshal Vincent, could I have a Spitfire, then I, or one of my Flight Commanders, could fly over to the target area and if it was clear, signal back in plain language to come and get them. I said it would save thousands of wasted flying hours. We flog all the way out and all the way back wasting engine hours and fuel. He said 'That sounds all

---

21   Julian Thompson, *The Imperial War Museum Book of the War in Burma 1942-1945*, pp.366-8.

right' and gave me this Spit and we called it 'The Looker'. On one occasion I flew out to the target and ran into these two Japanese fighters and I shot one down. I got a pat on the back with one hand and a good ticking off with the other as they didn't know I was out there. They threatened to take my Spit away if I did it again.[22]

The Vengeances would normally carry two 500lb and two 250lb bombs to the target. Arthur Gill continues:

On some such specialised strikes we had all bombs fused with 11-second delay. In fact on the Ya-Na'an bridge which we bombed several times, we would not only drop 11-second delay bombs which would blow the bridge up after we had flown away from it, but we would also drop 12-hour, 24-hour and 36-hour delay bombs. So that as they came back and repaired it and said that was a good job, Boom! But of course it would worry them once this had happened because they couldn't see where the bombs had dropped into the water and so on and would not know when the next one was due to go off.

With the monsoons the cloud stretched from 30,000ft down to ground-level and so finding a target was a problem. But as the cloud lifted in between storms one could often get to the target, but at a lower level, say at 5,000ft instead of our normal 12,000ft or 13,000ft. So we devised this system of nipping in and out of the cloud, but you hadn't got enough height to peel off and dive vertically because you'd kill yourself. So what we did was introduce this shallow dive technique of running up alongside the target and doing a gentle turn-off, keeping the target in sight all the way, and diving down at only 45 degrees.

This could never be as accurate as proper dive-bombing which, despite what the 'experts' have since kept on repeating, we always carried out at between 85-90 degrees. So it would not be as accurate as that but you had to adjust for conditions and gauge it.[23]

One type of target that was perhaps unique to the Burmese theatre were the Japanese river steamers. The Japanese use of the rivers as lines of communication was widespread at the beginning of the campaign, but it did not take the British long to begin to attack them and make their use of the waterways impossible.

Squadron Leader 'Bush' Cotton describes attacking these enemy vessels:

On the morning of 25 February, I took off with six Hurricanes to carry out an offensive patrol over the Moulmein-Martaban area. As usual, Sergeant Wheatley was my number two. We had come to know the Moulmein estuary well over the past few weeks, and hoped to find some shipping we could beat up. We cruised at about 5,000 feet, with the formation stepped up into the sun, undulating slightly, in loose line abreast, etched against the pale-blue horizon; the sun sparkled on the dark cobalt waters of the Gulf of Martaban as we left the coast and headed for the estuary…

As we approached Martaban, then occupied by the Japanese, situated on the north bank where the estuary broadens into the gulf, we spotted a large river boat, with one smokestack forward, steaming on a course to the west of the Sittang river. We were in a perfect position for strafing. I closed my hood, and turned on the gun button and the reflector sight. I went into a shallow dive, increasing speed; I told the others on the R/T to follow in line astern. I went in to the attack.

---

22   Peter Smith, *Jungle Dive Bombers at War*, pp. 85-6.
23   Peter Smith, *Jungle Dive Bombers at War*, pp. 85-6.

Hawker Hurricane Tac R Mark IIC of 28 Squadron RAF, is prepared for an armed reconnaissance sortie at Sadaung, Burma. (Crown Copyright – Air Historical Branch)

As I descended, a cannon, mounted on the top awning just forward of the funnel on the top deck, winked at me. Waiting until I was in range, I opened up on the cannon, whose crew promptly collapsed, one falling over the side. I kept my finger on the button and raked the boat from stem to stern. Pulling out of my dive, I swept over the boat at about 10 feet and saw at a glance that the boat was full of Japanese troops in full war-gear. I watched Sergeant Wheatley going in as I circled up and around. The boat appeared to burst into a white sheet of flame from the funnel to the stern.

The other chaps went in, and smoke started to billow up, casting a long shadow on the glassy waters beneath. As I went in for the second time, figures appeared like fleas, disturbed by powder, jumping from a dog's fur. Some disappeared beneath the water, others popped up to be extinguished by the spray kicked up by eight guns delivering 160 bullets a second from each aeroplane.

My imagination told me they were not my guns and the dots on the water were not human beings, but like the puppet figures of a miniature rifle range at the circus, whizzing round on an axis when hit.

When we had no ammunition left, I called the boys together and we made off home as fast as possible at sea level, leaving the boat still burning, but afloat and not moving.[24]

Whilst the operational tactics and weaponry used in Burma may have been recognisable to pilots in Europe and the Middle East, the weather in Burma was uniquely and notoriously bad. The monsoon

---

24    M.C. Cotton, *Hurricanes Over Burma* (London: Grub Street, 1995), p. 264.

weather not only hampered and disrupted air operations, it was frequently downright lethal as Cotton relates:

The Monsoon conditions were badly hampering our activities at this time. The problem of flying fighters in monsoon weather was one that had not been experienced by many squadrons, because in the 1942 monsoon season the RAF was in retreat, or back in India along with the Army, and had very few aeroplanes anyway. We wondered if, at the height of the monsoon period in 1943, we would be stood down for any length of time, but orders from above were that 'the RAF will maintain maximum effort during the Monsoon period'.

On one occasion during this monsoon period, a Spitfire fighter squadron was returning from Imphal after being posted away from that area for a rest period. Its twelve aircraft flew into a monsoon cloud, where six

Japanese river craft under air attack between Kyaukpadaung and Muale in Burma. (Crown Copyright – Air Historical Branch)

pilots were killed and eight aircraft destroyed, owing to the enormous forces in the cloud which prevented the machines from maintaining their stability and either crashing into the ground or one another.

Today no aircraft flying in these areas, on military or commercial flights, would do so without a radar set which could pick up this turbulence ahead of the flight path and avoid it, but in our time there was no such thing. It was always a gamble on entering cloud, that one might strike an active cumulo-nimbus embedded in the mass, and that could spell disaster. The prevailing winds are to the north-east in the Bay of Bengal in the monsoon season (summer months), and these pick up a tremendous amount of moisture and form themselves into huge cumulonimbus clouds. Sometimes the base of these clouds is solid rain, about 200 to 300 feet above the ground, before the cloud-base proper begins. From then on the cloud could extend up to heights exceeding 30,000 feet. The bottom of these clouds could be from 1 to 10 miles in diameter. In very bad weather, the huge clouds, together with layers of less turbulent cloud, practically touch one another, and consequently one could have an almost incessant wall of rain between oneself and one's destination.

In our day, there were two ways of operating aircraft in monsoonal weather. One way was to fly in the rain under cloud base, a few feet above the ground. This was all right if one was flying alone, or with a single section of four machines, because they could formate together on the one level. With a whole squadron it required the other two sections to tuck under and behind the leader's section in line astern and, with only 200 feet to play with, the leader had a job to maintain height without wiping the lower section off on the ground. More often than not, any aircraft with exposed fabric on the control surfaces could have this beaten off in the rain, and this constituted a danger if allowed to persist.

The other way was to try and pick out the smallest cumulonimbus clouds and fly a variable course between them. This might be at any height from 5,000 to 30,000 feet, but the trouble with that system was that, even if we were flying a squadron of twelve aircraft, sometimes we had to fly in cloud. We would not know what we were heading into and might fly into the middle of a particularly bad one. When that happened, the only hope of survival was to turn over and bale out... Naturally, on some days the monsoon was less severe than on others, but one could safely say that there was no day which one could count on to be totally free of danger during the monsoon weather. The only good thing about this sort of weather was that the Japanese were more sensible than we were and did not fly during most of it, and were therefore no real threat to us in the air while we went about our other tasks.[25]

Squadron Leader Andrew Millar led 20 Squadron during the latter part of 1943 and into 1944 and was with the Hurricane-equipped squadron when it moved to Chiringa airfield, situated just north of Cox's Bazar on the coast. He describes how easy it was to be caught out by the monsoon weather:

The first day of June produced a beautiful morning with not a cloud in the sky. I decided we would make the most of it and arranged for a flight of aircraft to carry out a strike near Akyab. Strictly speaking a Met forecast had to be obtained before a sortie, but communications were not good and I did not feel like wasting time waiting for a weather prediction when the weather was so obviously perfect.

We took off and headed south. Roger Cobley, Eddie Fockler and an Australian called Jenkins were among the pilots, but I cannot remember the others. As we flew on, I could see a few cumulus clouds forming ahead of us and as the cloud base was near the ground I decided to hop over them. I started to climb, gradually at first and then more steeply as I found that the cloud tops were piling up and increasing height more quickly than we were. Westwards out at sea, the sky was still clear, so I turned to starboard and with seven other Hurricanes continued to climb, hoping to go around the storm that was building up so rapidly over the land.

Within a few minutes it was clear that we would not only have to abandon the sortie but that we were going to have difficulty in getting down safely. We reduced height to sea level in the pocket of clear sky in which we were flying. To the north the weather had clamped down and there was no chance of getting back to Chiringa. We flew round a storm at sea and then headed towards the coast. We found ourselves near 'Hove' with a curtain of black cloud down to sea level enclosing us in a clear area about a mile across. I switched on my R/T and carefully made my voice sound relaxed so as not to cause any panic among the others. 'Puffball' was our call sign. 'Hello, Puffball formation,' I called 'Puffball leader calling. I am going to fly north through the cloud, to see what conditions are like further up the coast. Wait here until I let you know.'

---

25    M.C. Cotton, *Hurricanes Over Burma*, p. 180.

I entered cloud at a low height. My climb and descent instrument showed that I was losing height and I pulled back on the control column, just as breaking waves became visible beneath the edge of my mainplane. After that I concentrated hard on keeping the machine straight and level and was relieved to come out from the storm into some relatively clear weather around Cox's Bazar. Quickly I called up the others and told them the situation and then went into land with a feeling of great relief.

The others came in one by one. The clear patch had already disappeared before the last plane was down. This was flown by Jenkins the Australian, who had recently joined the Squadron and was not very experienced. However, he brought his aircraft in very steadily in the heavy rain and made a safe landing. Not all the aircraft had arrived. Roger Cobley's Hurricane was missing, We discovered later that he had made a precautionary landing on the sand with his undercarriage up, near 'Hove'. Later, Wing Commander Chater, whose wing we were in at Chiringa, wanted me to bounce Roger for writing off a Hurricane, but there seemed ample justification for his action and I refused.

When I landed at Cox's Bazar, the AOC's de Havilland Rapide was picketed down by the runway and the AOC was standing nearby. My heart sank as I was well aware that I had not asked for a route forecast before the sortie, but as I approached him, his first words were to criticise the Met Office who had told him that the weather was going to be perfect, so that he too had been lucky to make it to Cox's Bazar.[26]

The monsoon was a miserable time in Burma for ground crew and aircrew alike, particularly for those at the austere airfields and landing grounds near the frontline. Despite their cotton trousers and thin green battle dress, the pilots were normally bathed in sweat at the end of their sorties, when they would retire to the 'box' – the only area of the airfield that was properly defended. Supper in the muddy fronted 'mess' would invariably be bully beef and was eaten on wooden benches and trestle tables under a leaky roof. The pilots would then head to their hut or tent and perhaps read a letter or book under a hurricane lamp that attracted swarms of night insects. With little to do most pilots would try and go to sleep at an early hour. The humidity of the jungle was also oppressive, turning everything green and mouldy, even the pilot's blankets were damp and mildewed. The official history of the air war in Burma captures the dispiriting nature of the monsoon weather and climate well:

> The weather was now at its worst and, at the front the cloud ceiling was sometimes down to 100 feet, below which Spitfires and Thunderbolts were doing their dangerous work, while back at their bases the airfields were whipped into mud by the storms, making yet more difficult the work of the maintenance crews. For many of these airmen, who never had the glory and excitement of operations, this was the fourth monsoon of the Burma War, and they found that being accustomed to it did not make it any better. Sometimes it was so hot that they could not touch the aircraft without suffering burns, and sometimes it was so wet that they could sail to work in a dinghy.
>
> The varieties of bane and bother which the Burma monsoon could bring to the airmen truly seemed endless. The heat caused engines to lose power because of the increase of intake temperatures, distorted the 'Perspex Panelling', cooked ammunition till it exploded spontaneously, varied the tyre pressures throughout the day, rendered any exposed petrol highly dangerous and, because of abnormal expansion, made riveting uncertain. In its effect on the men it brought exhaustion to many and death to some.

---

26   Andrew Millar, *The Flying Hours* (Fighting High Ltd, 2015), p. 133.

Ground crew of an RAF Spitfire squadron which has just moved to a new airfield in Central Burma, struggle to erect their mobile workshop in the strong winds, immediately prior to a monsoon. (Crown Copyright – Air Historical Branch)

A light anti-aircraft gun crew of the RAF Regiment at an airfield on the coast of Bengal, India, wave to a Hawker Hurricane on its return from a sortie over the Arakan, Burma. (Crown Copyright – Air Historical Branch)

In the dry spells dust, a commodity which was indeed not peculiar to the monsoon, required the fitting of special filters to engines. Every open bearing had to be constantly polished and any fluid left in cans became almost solid with dust unless sealed. Whatever the precautions taken, the dust got into engines and generators, as well as into food, ears and eyes, so that the men cursed the dust and ached for the rain that would lay it, forgetting that the rain brought its own miseries.

Humidity and the rain corroded metals probably no faster in India and Burma than anywhere else, but there was very much more of it. Portable shelters were at one time introduced to place over aircraft noses while engine repairs or changes were being effected. They were found, however to be impracticable because the sudden winds whipped them away. When bamboo mess-bashas and even aircraft were flung on their backs by the cyclonic winds that sprang up immediately before the onset of the monsoon, there was little liking on the airfields for portable shelters.

Vermin, and particularly white ants, added their portion to the airmen's burden. Sometimes because of the heat, and sometimes because of white ants, wooden aircraft such as Mosquitoes were known to break up in mid-air until new dopes were found to prevent it. Occasionally, when new types of aircraft were brought to Burma, the changes of temperature and the vibration of flight powdered the glue; whole wings developed a flutter and then snapped off. Sometimes there was no remedy for these troubles and all aircraft of certain types had to be grounded, but most often the engineers found the cure.

One nuisance which they could not counter was the tendency of insects, rodents and birds, from scorpions to tree-rats, to make their homes inside the cowlings, causing varying degrees of dismay and discomfort to the men who found them and not always improving the functioning of the engines.

It may be thought that since the monsoon comes each year men could prepare for these phenomena, but that is a false view. Each monsoon brought something new and, moreover, it would not have been possible to work at all if everything had been picketed down and sheltered against the worst violence. A cloud of blossom would suddenly rise from a tree and climb a thousand yards into the air, as at the airfield at Sinthe, and this would be the first sign of a frightful storm. Or a Liberator, properly picketed down, would be thrown over a Bengal base like a butterfly. Unprecedented precautions would have to be taken immediately.[27]

The distances within the Burma theatre were so great that if the important tasks of general support or interdiction tasks were to be undertaken successfully, then the RAF would need to strike targets much deeper into enemy territory. Consequently, the Beaufighter was given a new lease of life over Burma. Its speed and robustness enhanced its survivability, and its four 20-mm cannon and rockets could tackle a wide variety of targets. The Japanese quickly learnt to fear and respect the Beaufighter, giving it the name 'whispering death' because of the surprisingly quiet approach it was able to achieve when flying low level. Brian Hartness recalls flying the various types of Beaufighters over Burma, including the Mk VI, which was in service until the summer of 1944:

Of all the Marks of Beaufighter which saw operational service – and I flew them all – the Mark VI was undoubtedly the best. She had none of the odd tricks of the Merlin engine Mk II, and none of the performance spoiling appendages of the Mk X. I think I preferred the fore and aft instability of the straight tail plane Mk VI which could be pulled round in a steep turn rather tighter than a Mk VI with the dihedral tailplane, though the latter was more stable in

27    Air Ministry, *Wings of the Phoenix*, p. 140.

level flight. The service ceiling for the Mk VI is quoted as 16,000 feet or so, but I took one to over 20,000 feet on several occasions. The best feature was her low-level maximum speed. Most of these (Mk VIs) could exceed 270 knots which meant we could outdistance an Oscar 'on the deck'.

Our CO, Harry Daish, with me as a passenger, ran away from a Hurricane at Amarda Road. Harry had persuaded the Hurricane pilot to do this test and we landed highly elated. There was one Mk VI on 27 Squadron towards the end of my tour that could outfly the lot, JL 567, 'K', which was a real lady. She could be trimmed 'hands off', and at normal cruising power was 20 knots faster than any of them, while at full power she exceeded 300 knots. She was allotted to me as 'my' aircraft and I kept very quiet about her when I discovered this remarkable performance – in case some 'senior' officer took her off me.[28]

The Beaufighter's main role was to roam deep into enemy held territory looking for likely targets. By this stage of the war the only significant air threat was the Nakajima Ki-43, though even these had been largely driven out of the forward airstrips by the end of 1943. The Ki-43's light armament and marginal speed advantage meant that most pilots did not unduly worry about them, instead they joked that they were more concerned about the American P-38 Lightning pilot's apparently poor aircraft recognition and who occasionally misidentified the Beaufighter as a Japanese aircraft.[29]

As the Japanese transport system was progressively forced to operate during darkness, many Beaufighter operations were launched at night and the two weeks either side of the full moon were when Beaufighter crews were most active. In addition, daylight strikes against trains, vehicles and airfields were usually mounted at first and last light, which also necessitated either a long outbound or return night-flight at low-altitudes. Any ground attack undertaken during particularly dark nights, either under a veiled moon, or during the monsoon, was a dangerous undertaking though most pilots still felt more comfortable and protected by the night-time skies.

Many Beaufighter sorties were mounted against targets of opportunity in a specific area, with a secondary target area designated in case the first could not be struck because of low clouds or other reasons. Initially operations were conducted by sections of two aircraft, but as the war progressed more and more sorties were flown by single aircraft. On some occasions flights of four aircraft would fly together to an initial point or RV and then split up and patrol in different directions. Operations involving more than four Beaufighters were rare and usually reserved for major targets such as airfields or marine shipping. There were also some unusual operations conducted by the Beaufighters in Burma, including low-level night attacks against searchlights at Rangoon to assist the Liberators' bombing missions and night-time intruder operations around major Japanese airfields, such as Meiktila.

During low-level patrols, Beaufighter pilots would intermittently pull up sharply from tree-top heights to an altitude of a couple of hundred feet to observe ahead and to aid map-reading navigation, then dive back to the deck again. On finding a target, such as a locomotive, boat or motor transport, the pilot would climb steeply, manoeuvring his aircraft for a good line of attack and then dive while firing cannons or rockets. He would then pull out in a steep turn to observe damage, take evasive action or prepare for another attack. Taking a second pass at targets was common in Burma, which was in stark contrast to practices in Europe where heavy German AA fire usually prevented repeat attacks.

28   Chaz Bowyer, *Beaufighter*, p. 158.
29   Atholl Sutherland Brown, *Silently into the Midst of Things* (Sussex: Book Guild Ltd, 2001), p. 55.

Ground crew pull the chocks away from a Bristol Beaufighter Mark VIF of 27 Squadron RAF. The aircraft is piloted by Flying Officer D.J. Innes who is preparing to take off at Agartala, India. (Crown Copyright – Air Historical Branch)

Low-level aerial photograph taken by an attacking Bristol Beaufighter Mark VIF of 27 Squadron RAF. It shows Japanese goods wagons under fire on the railway line between Monywa and Sagaing in central Burma. (Crown Copyright – Air Historical Branch)

The way the attack was made varied, depending upon the type of target, though most pilots followed standard patterns based on wider experience and knowledge. Locomotives were generally attacked in dives up to 30 degrees from the quarter until large quantities of steam began to be emitted from the engine indicating that the boiler was blown, or the fire box was destroyed. The Beaufighter would then strafe the carriages and box cars with 20 mm cannon fire at its leisure. Pilots would often attack railway stations and make as many as four passes against these facilities, even though the smallest of railway stations was protected by AA guns and the larger ones on the main lines to Rangoon or Bangkok were often heavily defended.

To protect their transport from air attack the Japanese began to build bamboo shelters for locomotives and covered these in earth. These sometimes forced Beaufighters to attack along the railway line, which increased the hazard from flak and made their cannon attacks less effective. When motor transport was exposed out on the open plains it was easy to spot and attack, but most Japanese vehicles were encountered in forested hilly terrain, or at night. As the Hurricanes and Thunderbolts had found, speed was then essential as the vehicles would extinguish their masked headlights and get off the road and into tree cover quickly. In those circumstances Beaufighter attacks were therefore made immediately at whatever angle was possible. Oil production and storage facilities were popular targets and also protected by light and heavy AA fire, which meant that they could only practically be struck at night and in one swift pass. Pipelines were more lightly defended and easier game, it was also found that they were most vulnerable and best attacked where they crossed small gullies. Japanese airfields were always well defended and therefore usually attacked at dawn with four to six aircraft, the Beaufighter crews found that the airfield's warning systems were usually good enough for them to have scrambled a few aircraft just before the Beaufighter's launched their attack.

The Japanese efforts to camouflage vehicles and equipment steadily improved throughout the war, transport was always well covered with foliage and nets and branches would even be used to hide river steamers when moored alongside the bank. Unsurprisingly, the Japanese soldier was normally brave under attack manning his AA guns with determination and courage and more than one Beaufighter is also thought to have been downed by the small arms fire of ordinary Japanese soldiers.[30] Dennis Spencer was a navigator on Beaufighters and recalls a long interdiction sortie he undertook with his pilot Geoff Vardigans:

> We turned and flew northwards up the Irrawaddy towards a similar railhead, on the opposite bank, about three miles away. There was nothing to be seen here either and, as briefed, we followed this branch line for 18 miles to where it joined the main Rangoon to Prome railway at a town called Letpadan. We had planned to follow this line northwards, almost to Prome, before breaking off and heading back over the mountains. Letpadan was a town a bit smaller than Henzada and there had been no information about ack-ack batteries on our 'flack' [sic] map. Nevertheless, it was big enough to almost certainly have some Japanese troops garrisoned there and had we flown across it we would certainly have encountered machine gun fire. Instead we skirted round it to the south and east, taking a good look before swinging back to join the railway again, just north of the town.
>
> At this point, an oil pipeline, which ran beside the railway, was clearly visible. This prompted Geoff to ask me if I knew the current state of the pipeline, that is whether it was carrying oil or not, according to our latest intelligence. This pipeline ran all the way to Prome and then followed the Irrawaddy river round to the oilfields at Yenangyaung and Chauk. These oilfields were still producing some oil at this time and, as I understood it, the Allied policy was not to do any more structural damage to production plant, which presumably they hoped

---

30   Atholl Sutherland Brown, *Silently into the Midst of Things*, pp. 55-7.

to recapture before long, but rather to constantly attack and breach or set fire to the pipeline. Of course the Japanese were continually repairing it, but at least it made it very difficult for them to transport oil down to Rangoon in any quantity. However the pipeline had not been mentioned at our briefing so I could only say to Geoff that I was not sure.

'Shall we give it a burst anyway then?' said Geoff

The terrain was flat scrubland, with a few wooded areas. There were no villages or dwellings in sight and this seemed to be a good place to make an attack where there would not be any opposition.

'Yes' I replied, little knowing that the very timing of my remark almost signed my own death warrant. Geoff banked to the right, climbing up three or four hundred feet, then turned left and made a shallow dive towards the pipeline. I had swivelled my seat so that I was facing forwards, as I usually did when we made such an attack. This was because while we were diving I could see along the top of the fuselage and make an independent observation as to where the cannon shells struck and what damage was done. He gave a short burst with the four 20mm cannons. These fired mixed armour-piercing, high explosive and incendiary rounds at a rate of about 10 a second, with devastating results. I saw smoke and debris fly up and flashes from the incendiaries, but as we flattened out, I lost sight of the target before I could see whether there was any leakage of oil or real fire.

As we flashed over the railway, Geoff started to climb and turn to the right, intending to double back so that we could take a good look and assess the damage. I remember scribbling 0717 hours, the time of the attack, on my pad... and then it happened. Over the intercom I heard Geoff mutter 'Christ!' Simultaneously, there was a tremendous bang. The whole aircraft shuddered and seemed to move sideways, just as if we had collided with something. It banked violently to the left, diving towards the ground, while a strong smell of petrol fumes wafted down the fuselage.

This was it, one of the worst 'what if' scenarios was actually happening. I was convinced that Geoff had been killed, or seriously injured, and that I was sitting helplessly in a pilotless Beaufighter diving into the ground. Damage must have caused a massive leakage of petrol, so however we hit the ground we would explode in a ball of fire. There would be no escape! Events in my life really did rush through my mind with incredible speed, together with all sorts of reasons why I was too young to die. Simultaneously, I had the weirdest sensation that the real me was sitting on my shoulder, relatively unperturbed and ready to 'bale out' of my body. At this moment I noticed a cloud of red soil dust swirl up from the wing tip, which must have been only a few inches from the ground. Then, as though to prolong the agony, the plane seemed to level up.

'Are you O.K. Denny?' said Geoff. Never in our many hours of flying together, before or since, had I been so relieved to hear his voice.

'Yes!' I shouted, 'but climb! I can smell petrol and we may have to bale out.'

But Geoff, who had the advantage of knowing what had happened, and that the plane was still under his control, kept his cool. 'I'll climb in a minute,' he said, 'but we'd better get out of range first. Are you sure it's petrol you can smell?'

Even as he spoke, I realised that, in the heat of the moment, I had jumped to the conclusion that the vapour was petrol – but it was not.

'No,' I replied. 'It must be hydraulic fluid.'

Geoff was relieved to hear this because, although it might mean that we would have trouble with the flaps or undercarriage later, we were not in immediate danger, and he could continue low flying. It was only when I then asked him what he meant by 'getting out of range' that he realised I did not know what had happened.[31]

---

31   Dennis Spencer, *Looking Backwards over Burma* (Bognor Regis: Woodfield Publishing Ltd, 2009), pp. 124-30.

Geoff Vardigans explained that he thought the Beaufighter had been fired upon by a well-camouflaged AA battery that had only been spotted at the last moment. It seemed as if a cannon shell had hit the Beaufighter but had fortunately not exploded. Vardigans streaked away from the target at low-level, abandoning the mission and setting a westerly course for the coast and a transit back across the sea to the nearest Allied airfield at Feni. Despite efforts to lower the undercarriage it was apparent that the hydraulics were seriously damaged:

> As we were on the downwind leg, he suddenly said to me 'Do you want to bale out Denny? If you do, its OK with me.'
> This took me completely by surprise, as I had not even considered the possibility…
> 'No why?' I replied. 'You are not worried about making this landing are you?'
> He then said that he thought he could handle it alright but was just wanting to give me the option because, although he knew the correct drill for making a crash landing, he had never actually done one before. Certainly crash landings were fairly commonplace in the wartime RAF but, like Geoff, most pilots attempting one would be doing it for the first time. It was a matter of putting theory into practice – with only one chance of getting it right. However, I had faith in Geoff and there was no way that I would bale out and leave him to it. By the time we completed our circuit and he started his approach it was 0955 hours and I noted that we had been airborne for five hours and ten minutes.
> As we neared the ground I was conscious that our speed was appreciably faster than normal because we had no flaps. Indeed just before we touched down the ground seemed to be whizzing past below, but perhaps this was also partly because I was about four feet nearer to it than during a normal landing. Everything now depended on Geoff. I felt helpless, knowing that I had no control over what would happen in the next few seconds.
> I felt a slight bump as the tailwheel, which was a fixed one, touched first and then the front made contact, with hardly a bounce, as the whole aircraft slithered along the flat, grassy ground. Of course, I was jolted and bumped about a bit and there was much noise and juddering as the propeller blades were bent and forced to a halt. This would all have been a bit frightening had I not experienced the crash at Crosby-on-Eden the previous February. That had been much worse. By the time we slithered to a standstill, a few seconds later, Geoff had switched off the ignition and fuel valves. We both jumped out. It was a textbook 'belly flop' to use the RAF jargon. How wonderful it felt to have both feet firmly on the ground. We stood there, jubilant that we had done it and were safe.[32]

Atholl Sutherland Brown was a pilot in 177 Squadron and also recalled the dangers of Japanese ground fire during a sortie on the 27 September 1944:

> We were briefed for an offensive patrol by ourselves along two branch railways in central Burma that met the main line at Thazi junction. I was wrenched out of a sound sleep at about four in the morning. I quickly evacuated my bowels, a fairly automatic reaction; donned my light drill flying suit, tied my money belt full of silver Rupees around my waist, put my Kukri (Gurkha) long curved knife on my belt, checked for my goulee (ball) chit and silk escape map and grabbed my leather helmet which I had for months laid aside in favour of earphones. The chit, money and map were aids for escape if you survived a crash landing in Burma; no one thought seriously about parachuting out of a Beau, flying like we did along the deck. We were picked up by a 3/4 ton truck for a cool, jolting ride to the hard standing of our Beau,

32   Dennis Spencer, *Looking Backwards over Burma*, pp. 124-30.

'E' (NV 260). I drank a sickly sweet cup of tea in a dirty mug given to me by a cheerful erk (mechanic) and took part in some light banter; strapped on my parachute and climbed the ladder behind the cockpit and swung like Tarzan into my seat. This was formed of a deflated dinghy attached to the chute in which the gas bottle invariably cut into one's ass. When Alf [W/O AJ Aldham] was ready I fired up the engines, did the cockpit check which was 'A' OK, waved away the chocks and quickly taxied to the end of the strip. After the vital action check was completed we were charging down the runway, tail up in the darkness, lifted the wheels and climbed away.

Our route took us close to Mt Victoria (10,018 feet) so we climbed over it and let down towards the Irrawaddy as dawn cracked in the east. We passed close to the twelfth century temple city of Pagan, seeing the multitude of domed and pyramidal spires over the plain as silhouettes. Further on in increasing light the cone of Mt Popa was black against the brilliant dawn. It was a beautiful clear morning as we picked up the railway before Meiktila. This was a little dodgy as this town was the site of the largest group of airfields from which most of the Japanese sorties were flown. We skirted the airfields picked the railway again and followed it to Thazi Junction and then up the branch line climbing into the Shan plateau toward Taung-gyi. Although the weather was perfect in the plain, the plateau was enveloped in solid cloud so we went to our second target which was to stooge around Meiktila and Thazi before following the main line south. We caught two lorries climbing up the mountain road and set them alight, then a bowser (gasoline truck) and a staff car near Meiktila and did the same to them. We exhausted our ammunition (250 rounds per cannon) soon after we headed south and so I said to Alf 'I'm turning on to 270 (west), give me a corrected course for base.' Alf said, 'I think you should go farther south, Skipper.' By then I had turned and was speeding over the scattered acacias and continued stubbornly. Alf was right: within seconds I flashed over an empty revetment (blast shelter) and saw a minor grass airstrip ahead which was well south of the main group. At the same time light flak started coming up at us so I began jinking among the trees, throwing maps and loose gear flying around the cockpit. We were hit by numerous bullets and exploding shells. One blew up Alf's radio in his face and another caused black oil to pour out of the engine nascelle. Thinking it was engine oil I had to start climbing to give us a chance of getting home on one engine. As soon as I did black explosive puffs of heavy flak started bursting around us. The oil plume had stopped quickly and I realised it was hydraulic not engine oil so I dived to the deck again and flew an erratic course out of the area.

There were either no Oscars at Meiktila, or they didn't find us for we continued with our battered craft over the mountains to Chiringa. It was difficult to assess the damage in the air; we had no radio and no hydraulics but both of us were unscathed. I made a pass down the runway to indicate I had no landing gear or flaps, came around again and approached as slowly as I could while still trying to grease her onto the grass. It went not too badly except we struck a plank roadway which caused more damage than necessary. My head crashed into the gunsight but it only hurt and did not break the skin. Thank goodness for the fluke of switching back to a helmet. We had thirty-seven bullet and shell holes in 'E' but she lived to fly again.

At the debriefing I was given hell by Willy for not avoiding the roadway, I gave myself hell for not paying more attention to Alf, but mostly I was thankful we survived. This became more poignant that same day as two of my better friends and basha neighbours, did not return from their sortie, F/O Mac Mackay and F/O A.J. Ede.[33]

---

33   Atholl Sutherland Brown, *Silently into the Midst of Things*, p. 150.

In the early part of 1945, the Fourteenth Army began to advance deeper into Burma and its ultimate objective of Rangoon, as it did so it was accompanied by the supporting squadrons of the RAF's Third Tactical Air Force. In many cases the fire support the air force provided during the advance was essential in helping the British capture heavily fortified Japanese positions. The descriptions of close air support in this book have tended to focus on the perspectives of the airmen. In contrast, the following account below is from the assaulting infantry's perspective and captures an occasion in late January 1945, after the 19th Indian Division crossed the River Irrawaddy in two brigade assaults at Thabbeikkyin and Kyaukmyaung. The division's remaining third brigade, the 98th Indian Infantry Brigade, was tasked to destroy a strong Japanese unit in the village of Kabwet – halfway between the two bridgeheads on the East side of the river. The 2nd Battalion, The Royal Berkshire Regiment was given the mission and after the initial attack on 21 January had stalled, recognised the requirement for strong fire support if their mission was to be successful. It is typical of many occasions in the campaign, when the infantry worked with the air force to overcome Japanese resistance, such joint operations required the closest level of coordination between the services.

Major John Hill was the officer commanding B Company and remembers how Lieutenant Colonel Finch, the commanding officer of the battalion approached the problem:

> Harold Finch now decided that any attempt to take the enemy position must be preceded by far heavier fire support. From 23 to 27 January, preparations to launch a full-scale battalion attack were put in hand, supported by bombing from the air, while the enemy were contained and harassed by day and night. During this preparation period, the company continued improving the position, patrolling day and night, manning observation posts and improving our superiority over the enemy by allowing him no peace and harassing any movement on the hills to our front with rifles, light machine-guns and medium machine-guns... The commander of the Royal Artillery brought a medium-gun troop up to us on the 24th and fired at point-blank range over open sights at many actual and imaginary bunkers on the hill. There were many direct hits, as we later discovered. They also achieved the object of clearing the undergrowth from the hillside which, of course, the daily airstrike did extremely well, too. As a result, we obtained better and better observation, day by day, of the enemy positions.
>
> Aircraft came in at about midday on 24, 25, 26 and 27 January, bombing and strafing the hill opposite us. The usual form was, for the whole company, less a small protection party, to withdraw 1,000 yards under artillery, mortar and light machine-gun fire. The mortars put down smoke at five minutes before the set time and the aircraft had a target pin-pointed by smoke for them as they came over. The first waves were B-25 Mitchells and then Hurribombers, bombing and strafing. We all came back and reoccupied the position when the bombing had finished. This plan worked well and the aircraft seldom missed the right target. Immediately the air strike finished, we would fire with light machine-guns, medium machine-guns and mortars, while a patrol crept up to see whether the Japanese were still there. They always were. The difficult part was withdrawing the company daily without the enemy knowing what was going on [this was presumably because of the safety distances required by the bombardment]. We did this in various ways: sometimes under cover of smoke, sometimes by fire, sometimes by moving nearly everyone early on, before daylight, behind our hill. We had, of course, to lay on an immediate counter-attack plan to retake our own position in case the Japanese managed to get up before we could get back.[34]

---

34   John Hill, *China Dragons* (London: Blandford, 1991), pp. 86-8.

As the day of the attack approached, the battalion tried to synchronise the supporting fires of the RAF with the Army's indirect fire assets, such as artillery, mortars and Vickers medium machine guns. It was essential that the Japanese were suppressed for as long as possible and remained cowering in their trenches until the assaulting infantry of B Company and D Company were almost on top of them. Major John Hill explains the final assault on Kabwet and how important air support was in his rifle company's, as well as the battalion's, overall success:

The 29th dawned and the plan, for what was hoped would finish Japanese resistance, was based on a Zero Hour (H Hour) of 12 noon. The fire plan included: four squadrons of B-25 bombers, based at Calcutta, dropping 1,000-and 500-lb bombs from H minus 25 minutes to H minus 10 minutes; then one squadron of Hurribombers from H minus 10 to H Hour, completing their bombing runs by strafing the enemy position.

I thought that this huge weight of fire-power on enemy in open country, even if dug in, must kill them and so demoralise them that we would have a simple task. It had not occurred to me that there would be much of a fire-fight. I was even looking forward to taking prisoners. How I was mistaken!

Our friends from the 115th Field Regiment, the Sikh machine-gunners, and our own 3-inch mortar and small arms were to give covering fire over our heads from H minus 10 to H Hour. During this time the battalion was to move to a start-line about 50 to 100 yards short of the enemy-held hill, very close up, B Company on the right, D Company on the left. The Hurribombers would make dummy runs on the enemy position after H Hour to keep the Japanese heads down and the artillery and mortars would lift their fire, being controlled by wireless, 100 yards at a time. H Hour would be signalled by firing red Very lights. If ever synchronization of watches was important, this was one such occasion. Split-second timing was needed to co-ordinate the arrival of bomber aircraft from India, while gunners and mortars, 1,000 and more yards to our rear, fired over our heads along with Vickers machine-guns and other small arms. Meanwhile, we were to move forward and cross the start-line. All conforming to H Hour. Any unsynchronised watch would spell disaster and loss of life. Huge columns of smoke and dust signalled the results of the bombing from the B25s, which arrived on time, as we moved forward from our assembly area to the start-line, everyone with their bayonets fixed.

All went according to plan and we found ourselves 50 yards from the enemy position. We had been briefed thoroughly and in front of us lay a bare brown hill with enormous craters 20 feet across and a few tangled bushes and trees. We were lying down, waiting for the red signal, with the noise of aircraft and the continued rattattatting of the Vickers guns overhead. The time was about 11.52 and I looked for a few seconds at the aircraft as they swept in, spitting viciously at and beyond the hill. To my horror as I looked at one, just overhead, a bomb detached itself and came straight on at us. I shouted 'Down' – we were already quite flat! The next minute it hit the ground with a dull thud and nothing happened! I breathed again. The bomb was obviously not fused…

I glanced around at our men as we lay on the bare, dusty earth. Just ahead of me there was a bren-gunner and his No. 2 from 4 Platoon and to their right Sgt Davies of 6 Platoon, with another two riflemen hugging the ground. Cradling their rifles in the crooks of their arms, out of the dust, they were ready to go. Our two signallers lay just behind me and some ten yards behind them Ian Wallace, our FOO with his small group of gunners. Beyond them, I could see our mortar sergeant and some more men of Company HQ, all lying expectantly while the barrage of gunfire and the crumps of our mortars continued with unabated ferocity…

Suddenly the noise of the Vickers swung to our left flank, no more sharp flat cracks immediately overhead. We rushed madly up the hill, gaining courage with every yard, on the right someone firing. The right platoon going slowly, the left platoon going well and now half-way up the hill; the right platoon going again, more firing, a man hit – there *are* Japanese. Damn, I thought, having hoped they would all be killed or give in. Another hit to my right, the right platoon held up, a Japanese light machine-gun and grenades. The little B-----. Someone firing back. The platoon sergeant of 6 Platoon, Davies, with blood on his shoulder and holding it. Suddenly finding myself looking at a Japanese just about to fire at me, ten yards off! Instinct – fire back: one dead Japanese soldier. Still on again, another Japanese, a grenade out and into his hole, explosion and groans, on again, bayonet – and now the platoons are moving again. In with the bayonet, shouting, and sticking a third Japanese in the chest. More shooting and no more Japanese to be seen. Those chaps in 6 Platoon were very sticky and ought to have done better. On my left, 4 Platoon, with no casualties, on the position, but two dead Japanese. On my right, 6 Platoon, with three casualties, on the position and about eight dead Japanese. We were there! …We were right to take this hill. We now dominated the whole enemy position down to the river.[35]

The use of such fire support from the air in deliberate set piece battles to overcome Japanese strongpoints was to be a distinctive feature in the British Army's advance south. It was increasingly delivered by RAF P-47 Thunderbolts which had now arrived in theatre and were replacing the older Hurricanes in many RAF squadrons in Burma. A total of 830 Thunderbolts were brought into RAF service during the war and they served exclusively in the South East Asian Command rather than in Europe. It was not just the aircraft that were changing during these final stages of the campaign, by 1945 a new weapon in the form of Napalm was also being widely employed by 3rd TAF in Burma.

The new Napalm bombs consisted of a jellified petrol, which was made by adding aluminium naphthenate to the fuel (hence the name Nap-alm). The Napalm was normally carried in a belly tank on the aircraft to which an igniting fuse was attached and the bomb dropped just short of the objective area from an altitude of 75 to 100 feet. This caused the tank to break up and the Napalm to ignite, creating a sheet of intense flame that covered a wide area. RAF Pilots found that Napalm was good as a general incendiary against dug-in positions, supply dumps, buildings and motor transport. Its ability to cling to objects and penetrate openings made it a particularly lethal weapon.

In order to keep up with the Army's advance, the squadrons from 3rd TAF frequently leap-frogged from airfield to airfield while also maintaining continuous air support to the Army. Many of these advances forward were accomplished by air transport, as Millar of 20 Squadron describes:

Soon we were on the move again, this time to Monywa, a place we had attacked not long before. We were getting accustomed to squadron transfers, which were now done almost entirely by air. Earlier we had had an advance party, air party, ground party and rear party. At Thazi we had still had an advance party, which had included 'laskars', the Pathan camp followers who had dug latrines prior to our arrival. Dingle Bell had been on the ground party moving to Thazi, and had called in at Khampat – where I had crashed the Hurricane – but he was unable to salvage much from his location. Now, with air lifts, we were adapting to a new pattern of squadron move. The whole squadron would be lined up on either side of the airstrip in various sections, consisting of both personnel and equipment. At the expected time, Dakotas would arrive, take on a load and depart for the new airfield. On this occasion, Warrant Officer Watson, who was an ex-bookie, had a blackboard showing the time that the

---

35   John Hill, *China Dragons*, pp. 86-8.

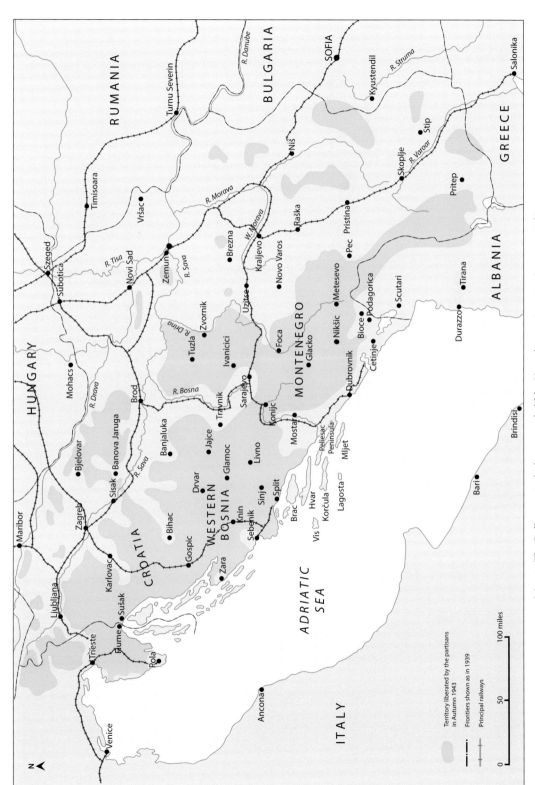

Map 1  The Balkans – including areas held by Yugoslav partisans in Autumn 1943.

i

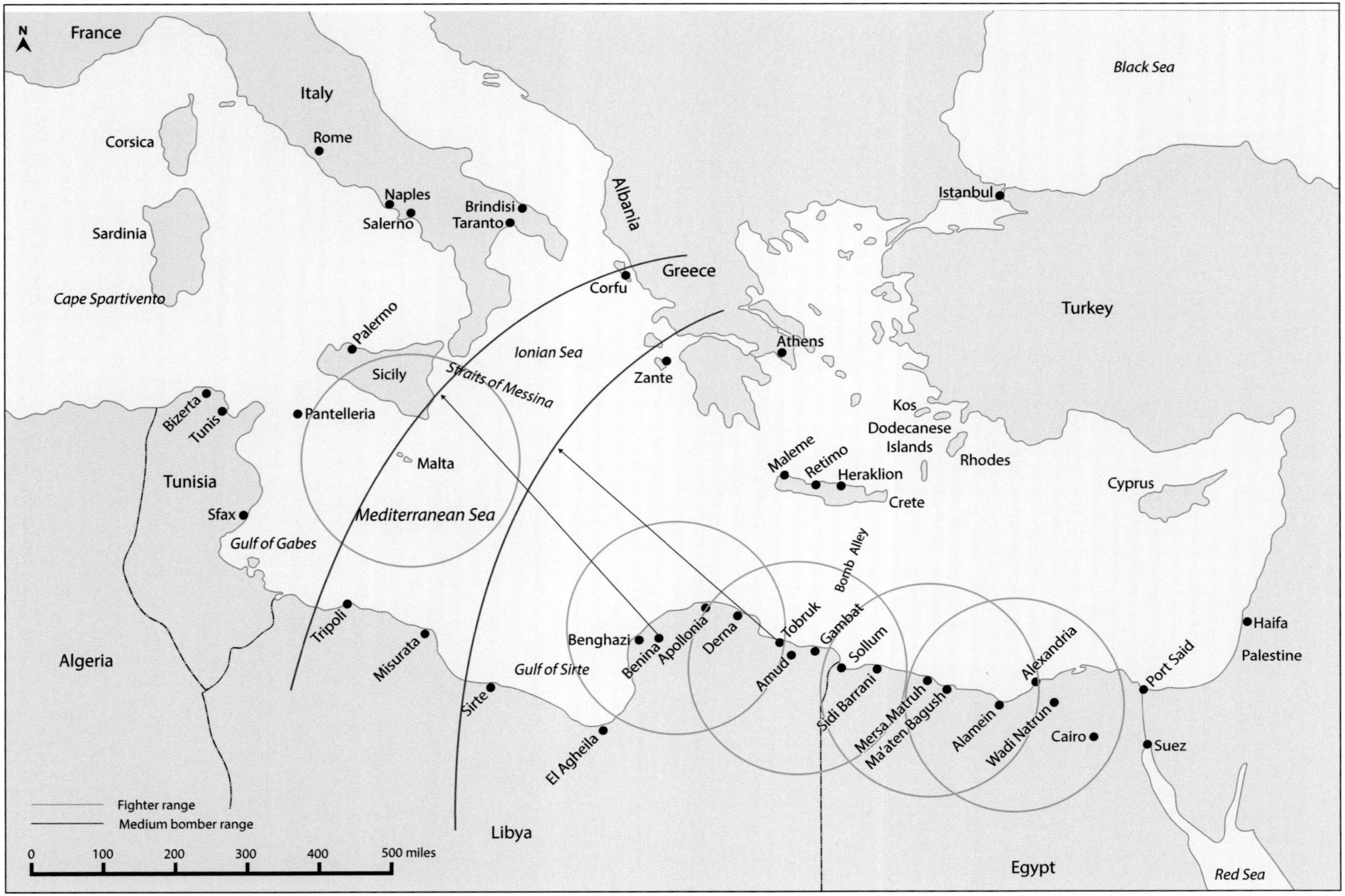

Map 2 Allied air power in the Eastern Mediterranean.

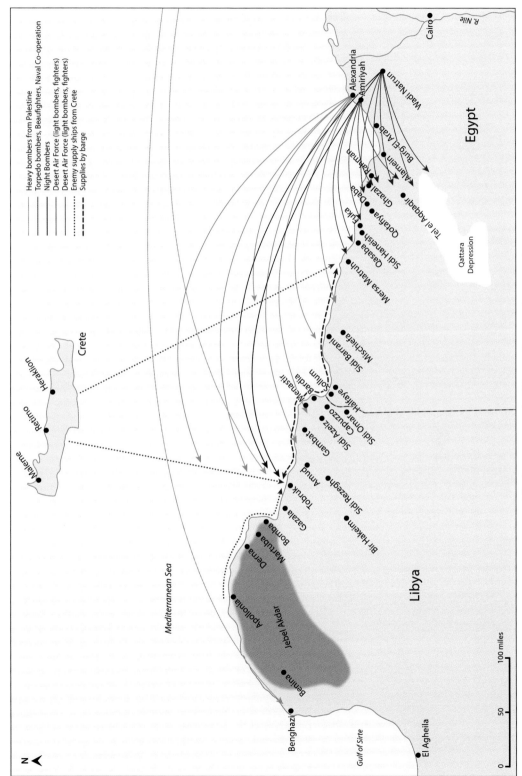

Map 3 Allied air power in the Western Desert – August 1942.

Legend:
- Heavy bombers from Palestine
- Torpedo bombers, Beaufighters, Naval Co-operation
- Night Bombers
- Desert Air Force (light bombers, fighters)
- Desert Air Force (light bombers, fighters)
- Enemy supply ships from Crete
- Supplies by barge

iii

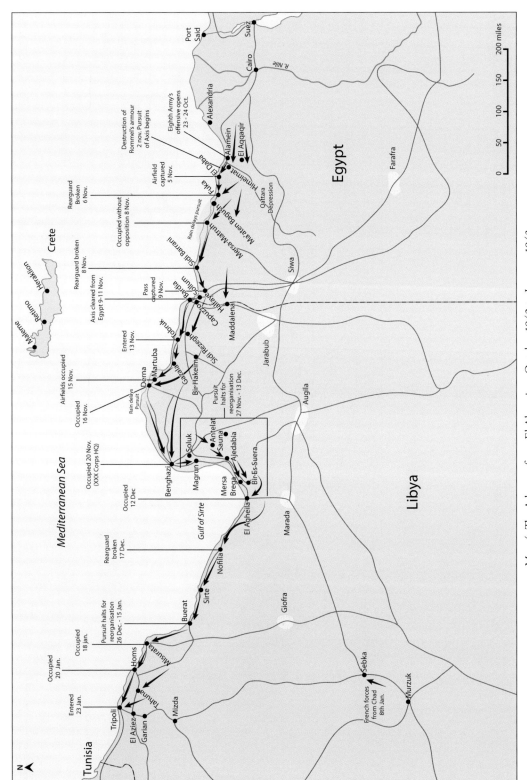

Map 4 The Advance from El Alamein – October 1942 to January 1943.

iv

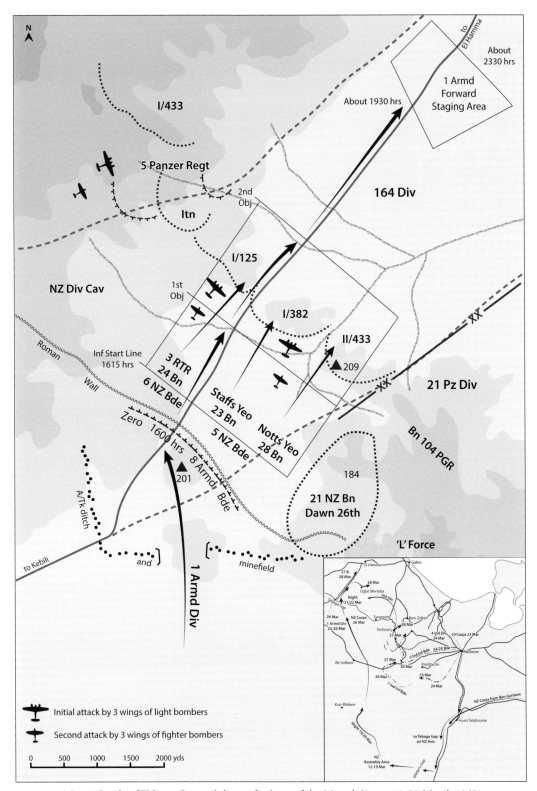

Map 5 Battle of Tebaga Gap and the outflanking of the Mareth Line – 19-28 March 1943.

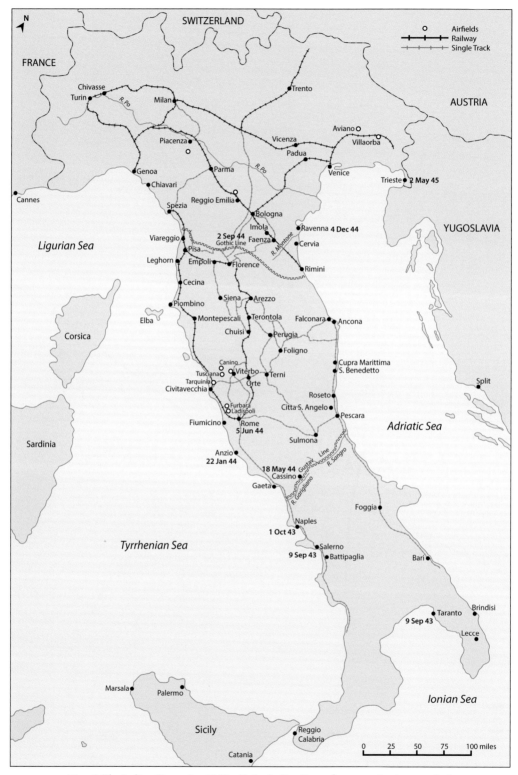

Map 6  The Italian Campaign 1943–45. Including lines of communication attacked
as part of Operation STRANGLE.

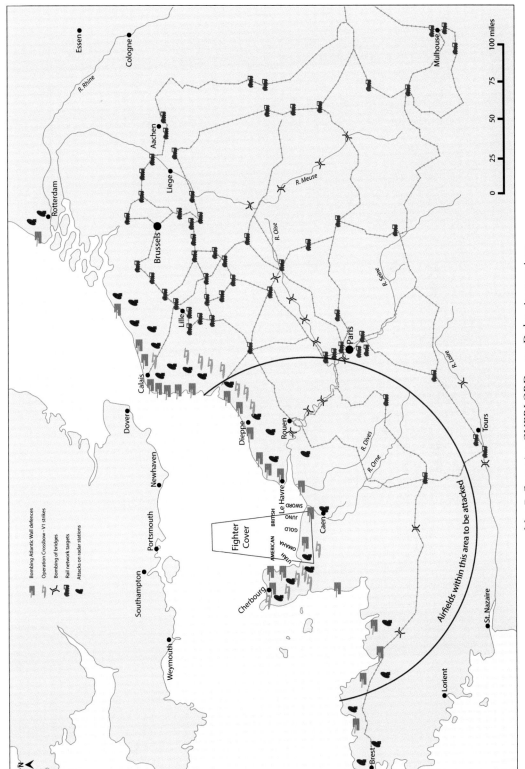

Map 7  Operation OVERLORD – pre-D-day air operations.

vii

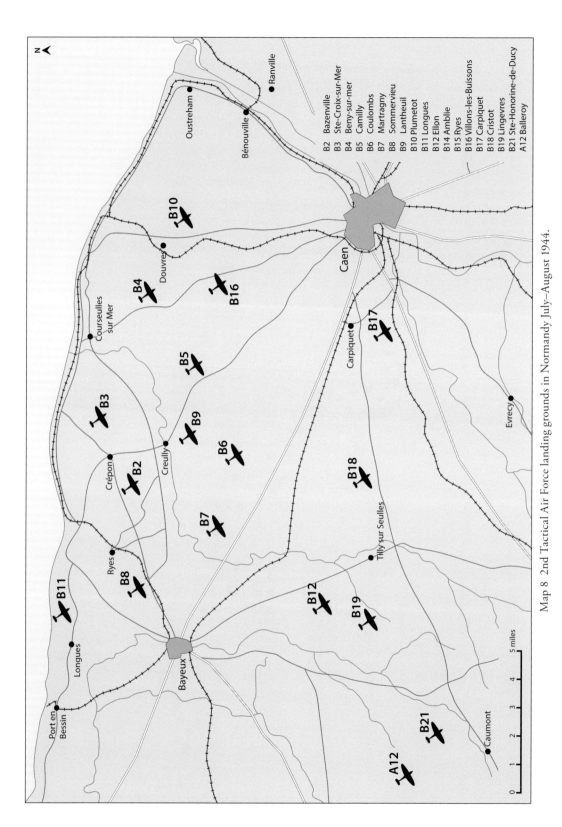

Map 8  2nd Tactical Air Force landing grounds in Normandy July–August 1944.

B2   Bazenville
B3   Ste-Croix-sur-Mer
B4   Beny-sur-mer
B5   Camilly
B6   Coulombs
B7   Marttragny
B8   Sommervieu
B9   Lantheuil
B10  Plumetot
B11  Longues
B12  Ellon
B14  Amblie
B15  Ryes
B16  Villons-les-Buissons
B17  Carpiquet
B18  Cristot
B19  Lingevres
B21  Ste-Honorine-de-Ducy
A12  Balleroy

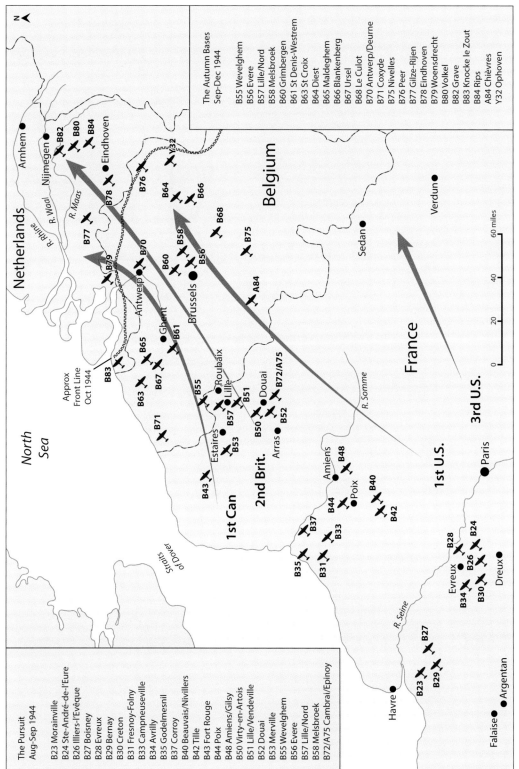

Map 9  2nd Tactical Air Force landing grounds in North West Europe – Autumn/Winter 1944.

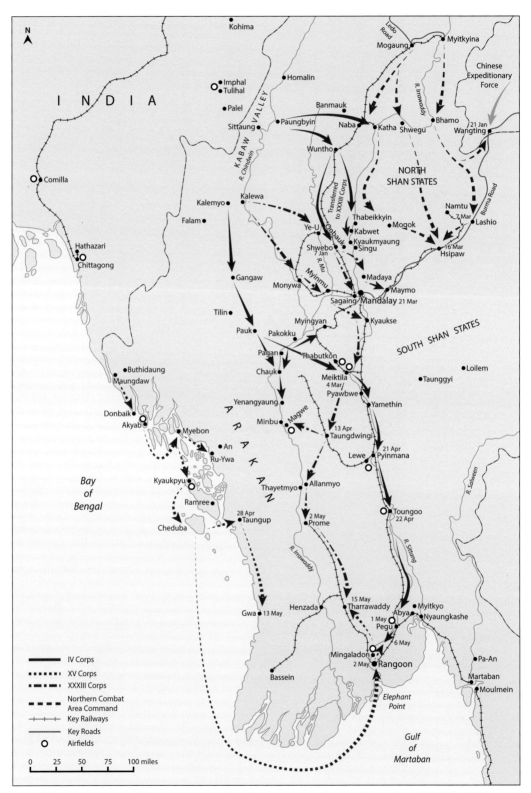

Map 10  Overview of Burma – showing British reconquest of Burma, November 1944–May 1945.

x

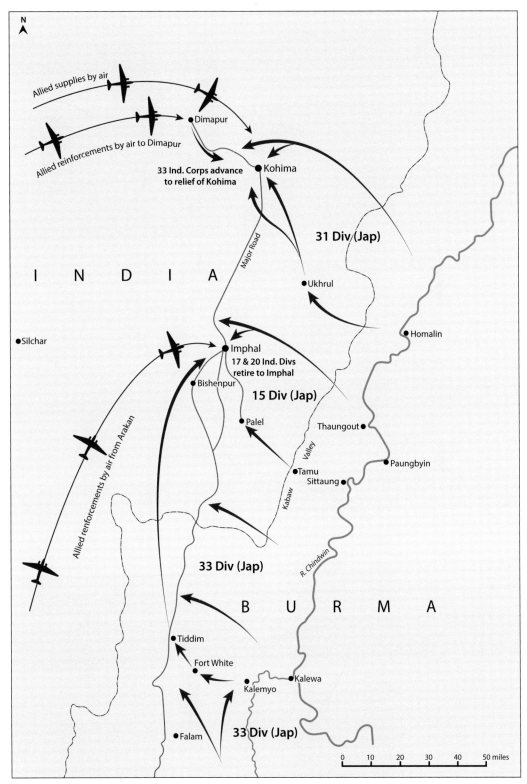

Map 11  Japanese Attacks on Imphal and Kohima and Allied air reinforcements – March–April 1944.

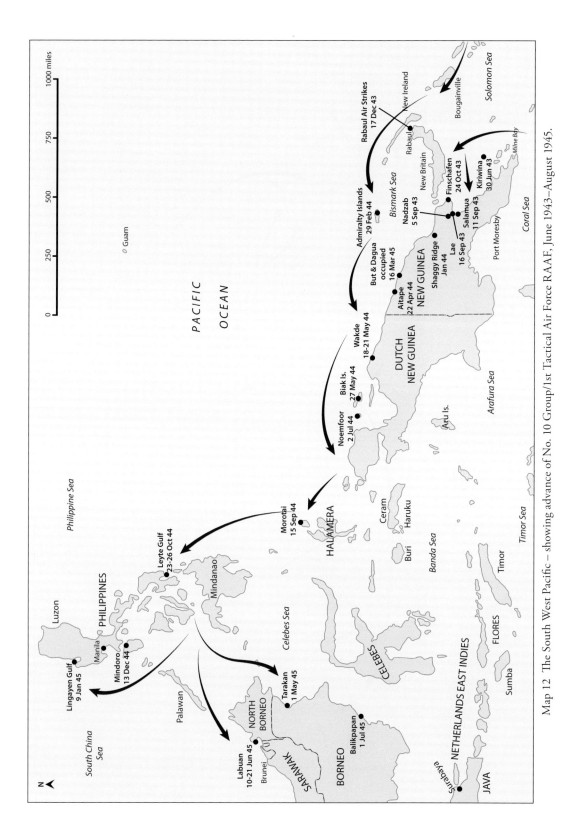

Map 12  The South West Pacific – showing advance of No. 10 Group/1st Tactical Air Force RAAF, June 1943–August 1945.

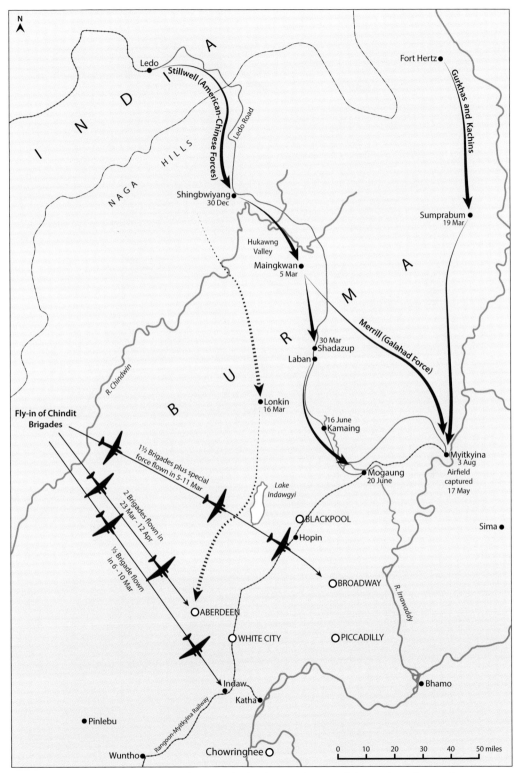

Map 13  Air Supply operations for Second Chindit Expedition and the northern front in Burma, December 1943–August 1944.

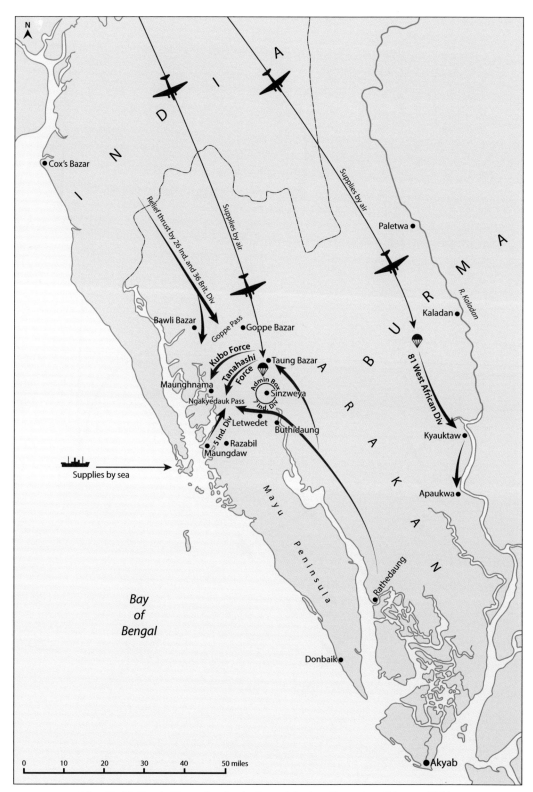

Map 14 Air Supply Operations in the Second Arakan Campaign, February 1944.

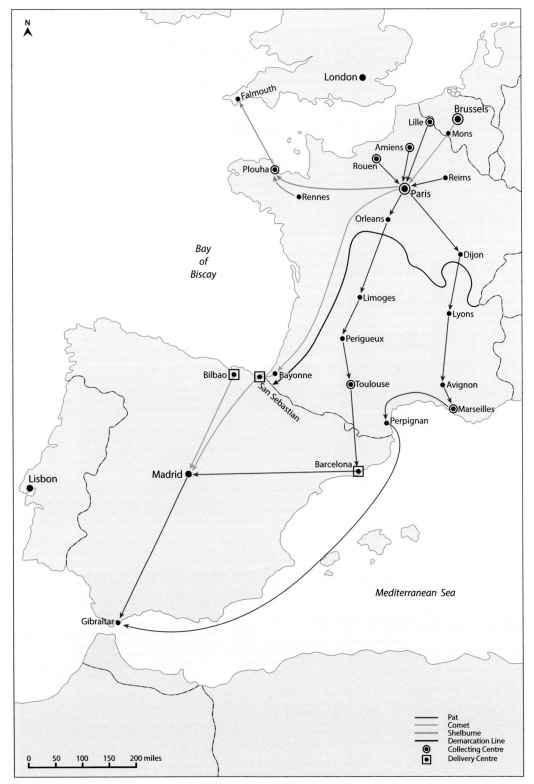

Map 15  Main evasion routes from occupied Europe 1940-44.

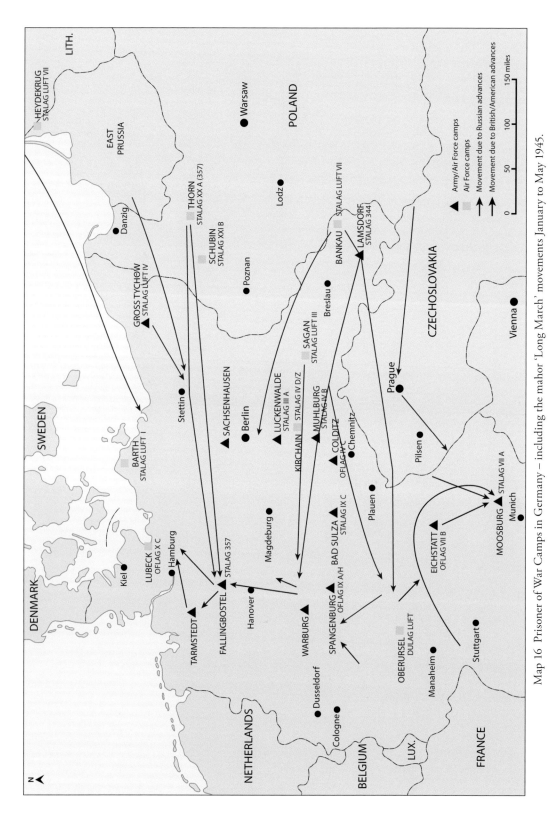

Map 16 Prisoner of War Camps in Germany – including the mahor 'Long March' movements January to May 1945.

Thunderbolt Mark II of 30 Squadron RAF, taking off from Chittagong, India, for a sortie over the Arakan front. (Crown Copyright – Air Historical Branch)

A flight of 30 Squadron Republic Thunderbolt II fighters taxies for take-off from Cox's Bazar, India, on 5 November 1944. The Hurricanes parked alongside the taxiway probably belong to either 28 or 176 Squadron. (Crown Copyright – Air Historical Branch)

first Dakota was due to touch down and was taking bets on the minutes before and after this time, as to when the plane would actually land! I provided fighter cover for a C-46, which was leaving for Monywa at the same time as I did, in a Hurricane IID. I do not think I would have been every effective, but it may have reassured the transport pilot and I would have done my best if the need had arisen.[36]

---

36    Andrew Millar, *The Flying Hours* (Hitchin: Fighting High Ltd, 2015), p. 157.

This air movement was not limited to just the RAF elements of the Allied advance on Rangoon. Almost the whole of the Fourteenth Army's leading elements were now being supplied and maintained by Air Transport, on occasions significant combat elements would also be carried forward to secured airfields in order to maintain the momentum of the advance. Without this logistical support from the air it is almost impossible to conceive how Burma could have been re-taken from the North. The use of air transport to support the Fourteenth's Army's land campaign will be picked up later in Chapter 14.

Flying Officer J Brindley of York, a pilot serving in a Bristol Beaufighter squadron, sitting at the controls of his aircraft before taking off from an airfield in Central Burma. (Crown Copyright – Air Historical Branch)

# 10

# 'No Turning Around'[1] Royal Australian Air Force Air Support to the Campaign in the South-West Pacific

Burma was not the only campaign in the Far East where Commonwealth air power made a significant contribution to victory. The Royal Australian Air Force's actions in the South-West Pacific were also an important element in the war against the Japanese, yet they are part of a campaign that has been largely bypassed by historians. It was a theatre where the RAAF missions formed part of the much larger American Fifth Air Force effort, and where the Australians were sometimes treated in an arbitrary and dismissive manner by the Americans who directed operations. Despite this background, the Australians played an important role in the South-West Pacific and deserve credit for stopping the Japanese in their tracks in New Guinea and then helping to turn the tide against them. This action allowed General MacArthur, the Supreme Commander of the South-West Pacific Area, to concentrate his forces in one central drive through the Philippines to Japan itself.[2] To MacArthur's west, Admiral Nimitz, the Commander-in-Chief of the Pacific Ocean Areas, was also advancing across a string of Pacific islands presenting the Japanese with a two-pronged threat they were unable to block.

An important moment in the campaign in the South-West Pacific, came when the Americans in Guadalcanal combined with the Australians to neutralise and isolate Rabaul and break the Bismark Islands barrier (July 1942 to May 1944). The elimination of Rabaul was a strategic defeat for the Japanese, not simply because they lost an important offensive capability, but also because of the large wastage in aircraft and ships they had incurred in trying to retain it. It marked the point that Japanese military power increasingly withered, while that of America and its allies grew exponentially. The final phase of the Allied offensive saw the Australians play a predominantly flank protection role, assisting in the neutralisation of Dutch New Guinea, Halmahera and Celebes, as well as launching an amphibious invasion of Borneo just as the war came to an end.

The South-West Pacific campaign was different to other Commonwealth air operations for several reasons. First, while many RAAF airmen and squadrons served in the Mediterranean, North-West European and Burma campaigns, they did so largely as part of the RAF and under its central direction. In the South-West Pacific campaign the RAAF acted independently and though treated as a junior partner to the American Fifth Air Force, they nevertheless built up their own

---

1    Motto of 31 Squadron Royal Australian Air Force. This Squadron was formed in August 1942 and equipped with Beaufighters. It conducted long range fighter and ground attack missions against Japanese targets in Portuguese East Timor and the Netherlands East Indies as part of 1st Tactical Air Force (RAAF).

2    See Map 12 for overview of South-West Pacific and details of the Australian advance from Papua New Guinea to Borneo.

Flying Officer E.B. Tainton of 76 Fighter Squadron, RAAF, taxies his P-40 Kittyhawk from the runway through palm trees towards the dispersal area. (Australian War Memorial)

Fellow pilots of 76 Squadron RAAF, lend a hand to push Squadron Leader Truscott's plane back into the dispersal bay, as he steps out of the cockpit. (Australian War Memorial)

operational groups and established their own Tactical Air Force (First Australian Tactical Air Force). Second, this was a campaign where maritime capability was as pre-dominant as air and land power in defeating the enemy. Typical operations saw Japanese island garrisons seized through amphibious assaults, after which the newly captured ground was used as an area from which air power could be projected and a further amphibious manoeuvre prepared and executed.[3] On New Guinea itself the sea was often used as a way of bypassing Japanese positions altogether; this was accomplished with amphibious hooks that turned the enemy's maritime flanks and avoided logistically difficult and costly overland offensives.

However, before any Allied advance could be considered the Japanese offensive needed to be stopped in its tracks. In New Guinea this was achieved on the Kokoda trail and at Milne Bay by a combination of stubborn defence on the ground by the Australian Army and an increasingly assertive RAAF. Critical to this combined success was the build-up of Port Moresby and Milne Bay as operational bases, with the construction of airfields an early priority for the RAAF. Air Commodore Bill Garing was sent to Milne Bay as the Commander of the RAAF and recalls selecting and building the site:

> The criteria in the case of Milne Bay was, (a) level ground, (b) clear approaches. And the only way you could get level ground and a bit above the level of the sea was by cutting down the coconut trees. And remember that we had to pay ten pounds each for everyone we cut down. Oh yes, ten pounds. And that was paid, I think, to Burns Philp. Well, that had to be done and they cleared them and got it out of the way and put the strip down. It was most difficult to get strips in Milne Bay because every night it rained six inches of rain and whilst I was there during the battle every night it rained and every night the Japanese sent a destroyer in and shelled the place. So it was all very exciting I suppose… it was a good long strip; it served its purpose very well indeed. In fact, it was a war winner. So did the other one, the second strip we chose which was on slightly higher ground and on even drier ground.[4]

The Australians were to build three landing strips in all at Milne Bay, which were occupied by the Kittyhawk-equipped 75 and 76 Squadrons in August 1942. These airfields were defended by an Australian Army militia brigade and the veteran 18th Brigade, which had fought at Tobruk. On 25 August, a sizable Japanese amphibious force, backed up by aircraft operating from New Guinea airfields and Japanese warships providing naval gunfire support, landed six miles east of Milne Bay. As the Japanese advanced on the base they found they were immediately opposed by stubborn Australian infantry, supported by the RAAF Kittyhawks providing close air support.

The major type of attack launched by the RAAF Kittyhawks against the Japanese at this early stage were strafing attacks, where they used their 6 x .50 Calibre machine guns against the Japanese landing barges coming ashore, as well as on the Japanese infantry in the jungle. The weight of fire put down by the Kittyhawks was punishing. During the first 24 hours each aircraft in 75 Squadron is estimated to have fired somewhere between 1,400 to 1,500 rounds of ammunition during each attacking sortie, with the squadron conducting a total of 26 sorties throughout the day. No.76 Squadron is also judged to have fired around 35,000 rounds that day.[5] The Australian Army and RAAF coordination remained close throughout this important defensive battle. Army liaison officers would brief the pilots before each sortie and to aid target marking and friendly force

3    George Odgers, *Air War against Japan 1943-45* (Canberra: Australian War Memorial, 1957), p. 498.
4    AWM SO1664: Sound recording interview with Bill Garing.
5    Mark Johnston, *Whispering Death*, p. 211.

recognition the Australian infantry would fire flares at the target, which indicated both their own position and in what direction they needed the supporting fire. Pilot Officer Nat Gould was flying Kittyhawks with 75 Squadron during the battle and describes the technique in a little more detail:

> The army, of course, were well and truly in combat with the Japanese and we were out to give them close air support. And, again, it was a fairly simple way of indicating targets because the jungle was immensely thick there – terribly thick – and there was no front-line as such. You didn't know where your fellows and the other side were. In fact, it was very blurred. So what the army would do is signal their front position with a Very light through the jungle canopy and it would go something like this: a green Very pistol cartridge would come up and then a white one for every 100 yards or so from that light towards the direction the lights were going which they'd want us to strafe. It was their way of indicating a target – there was no other way you could do it because the jungle was just impenetrable, it was just so thick.
>
> So we'd take off and in the Kittyhawk we had six .5s – six-guns with .5 ammo in – and we'd take off, fly back, wait for the green light to come up, try to mark it in the featureless jungle where it did come up –- that was a difficult thing to keep your eye on some spots – say it was that tall coconut tree or something – and then count the whites and come in over your own people so you wouldn't strafe them and shoot into the trees. You couldn't see anything, except you shoot into the trees and you'd empty your guns into that and you'd only be airborne for about ten minutes. You'd take off, pull round – because the Japs were right at the end of the strip practically – and then come back and land. And you'd always take off over their area, so you'd crouch down in the cockpit under your armour-plating and get out over the water and pull your wheels and flaps up, come back and strafe and then you'd come back to land over them, flat out, wheels and flaps down, no pretty landing, just push the aeroplane onto the ground, hold it there till you're well and truly on the ground, then pull your throttle off and then they'd rearm you and you'd go and do it again. And you might do half a dozen of these, at ten minutes a flight.[6]

The Kittyhawks were used for targets even as small as snipers who were usually located high up in palm trees. Although the pilots could rarely observe the results of their sorties, they were reassured by the Australian ground troops that during their attacks 'palm fronds, bullets and dead Japanese snipers were pouring down with the rain'.[7]

The Australian Kittyhawks are estimated to have fired 100,000 rounds over the period 26–28 August – the peak of the Battle for Milne Bay. This large volume meant that the rifling on many of the barrels on the Kittyhawk's machine guns was worn through and 300 barrels were estimated to need replacing at the end of the battle. Nat Gould recalled his armourer giving him a graphic demonstration of the state of his Kittyhawk's guns:

> I can remember the armourer saying to me, 'Have a look at this' and he had one of my gun barrels out and he took out a brand new .5 round and he just dropped it straight through – there was no rifling left in the gun at all. In fact, when you fired your gun you usually had a bit of tracer at the end to let you know you're getting to the end of your run and you could see the tracer coming out, spiralling like a great big barrel in front of you, which meant your rifling had gone.[8]

---

6    AWM S00578: Sound recording interview with Nat Gould.
7    Douglas Gillison, *Royal Australian Air Force 1939-42* (Canberra: Australian War Memorial, 1962), p. 613.
8    AWM SOO578: Sound recording interview with Nat Gould.

No. 80 Squadron RAAF P-40 Kittyhawk arriving back from a strike, with bomb racks empty.
(State Library of Victoria, Melbourne, Australia)

It was not just serviceability of weapons that was proving taxing for the ground crews. Keeping the Kittyhawks flying in forward landing grounds such as Milne Bay was also very difficult, though the aircraft was turning out to be surprisingly resilient in what was an unusually austere environment. Bruce Brown describes the runway at Milne Bay:

> Well, the first airstrip at Milne Bay was probably the worst airstrip I've ever operated off in my life and ever likely to. Initially, when we first landed there, it wasn't so bad because it hadn't had any traffic on it really and it was newly laid and consisted of steel interlocking matting as I term it [Pierced Steel Planks or 'Marsden Matting' as it was sometimes called by the RAAF]. So, consequently, the wet season was on as I mentioned earlier and with all the traffic then that started to take place at Milne Bay, even with the Hudsons then joining in later on and the Beauforts carrying torpedoes, the steel matting started to sink into the mud. So we had a greasy surface to operate off and it was so muddy that eventually we had to land without flaps... because the ribs at the back of the flaps were broken due to the mud hitting the flaps and forcing it back.[9]

It says a lot about the Kittyhawk's rugged nature that it was still able to operate in such conditions. Tyres were regularly being worn out on the rough steel and the usual practise after each Kittyhawk sortie was for the ground crew to throw buckets of water over the aircraft, before checking for damage from the mud thrown up by the aircraft's undercarriage. Despite these efforts it was still judged that the aircraft's speed was reduced by 'at least 20 miles an hour', thanks to the accumulated mud that was stuck to the wings and other parts of the Kittyhawk's airframe.[10]

9   AWM SOO583: Sound recording interview with Bruce Brown
10   Mark Johnston, *Whispering Death*, pp. 219 and 222.

Sanitary conditions were also poor at the Milne Bay landing ground and more than one third of 76 Squadron were reporting sick by the end of the first month of the deployment, the majority with malaria. This disease was prevalent throughout the Australian area of operations in the South-West Pacific and would only be mastered through better preventive measures including mosquito nets, covering exposed skin at night and spraying DDT sometimes from aircraft, particularly as the war progressed. The persistent illnesses, unhygienic and dreary environment had a debilitating effect on the pilots as Nat Gould recounts:

> It was very primitive, I remember that. It was in the middle of a big coconut planation. The strip was literally just carved through the coconut trees and there were dispersal bays for the aircraft just off this pierced-steel planking and stuff I was talking about. And, rain, my goodness me, I don't think it ever stopped raining. It was awful.
>
> Our living conditions: we had the typical army tents – I think we had four to a tent. I can remember it very clearly – mud up to your ankles. We put these sort of duck-boards in to give you some sort of a dry area. We had stretchers and mosquito nets, and the mosquitoes there were enormous. They were very malarial type mosquitoes, and I gather even worse than that you get dengue and black water and stuff up there. In fact, I got malaria – I think most of us had it at one stage. The food was awful; absolutely awful after the things we'd been used to in civilised messes and pubs in England. It really was dreadful. Half the time you couldn't even get a cup of tea, it was, you know, just so wet and what have you.
>
> And, I know, I don't want to sound heroic or anything, but I know I had malaria and dysentery at the same time and it's very unpleasant going off at both ends. And I can remember being quite ill and the squadron doctor… Bill Deane-Butcher, would come in and look at you and say, 'Don't you get out of that bed' and as he walked out of the tent the squadron commander would come in and say, 'Right, get airborne' and so you'd have to go and fly. And, it sounds a bit squalid but I know I'd be sitting up at 20,000 feet in a Kittyhawk on patrol of some sort with diarrhoea, you'd just be… you'd feel it all going down the back of your legs and there's nothing you could do about it for the next hour. You just had to sit in it. So it was pretty unpleasant.[11]

The Australian position at Milne Bay was very precarious for a period. So worried were local RAAF commanders that the Japanese would be able to infiltrate at night and destroy the aircraft on the ground, that on the night of 26 August 1942 the squadrons flew their aircraft back to Port Moresby. This was bound to have a negative effect on the Australian troop's morale and Bill Garing described how this influenced the way this difficult decision was made and subsequently communicated:

> Neither then, nor now after I've reached nearly eighty years of age, would I ever agree to the air force receiving commands from another service whilst there was a senior officer present. And there is no way in which General Clowes [Commander of Milne Force – the Australian Army troops at Milne Bay] being what he was would have given direct orders. He's attributed to in one or two cases I understand. Now the one in particular I will illustrate is the night that he decided that he probably couldn't hold the second strip and that the Japanese might break through. Now the situation was that I was not going to leave my aeroplanes sitting on the ground to get shot up by some infantryman – no way. So what did I do? I ordered them up to Port Moresby and General Kenney [The American Fifth Air Force Commander under whom

11   AWM SOO578: Sound recording interview with Nat Gould.

the RAAF were operating] was well aware of this, because the signal went ahead of them and he agreed wholeheartedly to the whole thing. Now they stayed up there only overnight… and the next morning at daylight they took off and came back. But during that late afternoon, as they went off, all of the troops around the place saw these aircraft take off and there was no aeroplanes left on the airfield, or few anyway. But, you can imagine, they thought, 'Good God, the Japs are going to win. We're a goner'.

Now… General Clowes lent me a little armoured personnel carrier with a driver and I went right round all of our [RAAF] troops… in the area of Milne Bay and spoke to them personally and said, 'Look, we've sent the fighters off for safety's sake. The army's not sure that they can hold the Japanese tonight but they are going to need every one of you to assist them and therefore none of you will go to sleep tonight. You'll just stay awake and you'll stay armed and you'll stay ready and you'll keep your ears open and the moment you see a Japanese you get stuck into 'em because your life now depends upon that. The fighters will be back tomorrow morning', and with those words the boys were very happy and when they came back in the morning you can imagine their super elation. In other words, they weren't given a story…

But that's how critical it was and you recall that in the set-up at Turnbull strip there was a sergeant – Australian army with a machine gun post there – and he was building it up just at the edge of the strip on the opposite side from where the Japanese would come up the coast and swing around. The first thing he saw was a Japanese scout appear on the edge of the runway and he turned the gun and pressed the trigger but he hadn't cocked it and he hadn't put the ammunition in properly and he had to quietly do that – and just as well he didn't press the trigger because in a few moments, out walked about twenty-odd Japanese, roughly a platoon of them. Now, if he'd fired the gun, they would have gone round and encircled him and so on and that might have been another turning point in the battle. As it happened he had his machine gun all set up and going when these appeared and he waited for the appropriate time and he let 'em have it. Well he shot a lot of them and they backed off. That's the furthest point they got towards the Australian army.[12]

The threat from the Japanese to the RAAF pilots and aircraft was not solely confined to a ground assault on the airfield. Japanese small arms or AA fire could also be hazardous to the attacking Kittyhawks. On other occasions experienced airmen like Squadron Leader Peter Turnbull, the commander of 76 Squadron, could get themselves in trouble through executing dangerous and complicated manoeuvres too close to the ground. Colin Lindeman was one of the 76 Squadron pilots and describes Turnbull's death:

It was during the early stages of the Japanese invasion of Milne Bay and Peter had sighted, from the air…a Japanese tank moving along the northern shore and he was strafing it. From my subsequent observations, I think that what happened to Peter is that he pressed his attack a little bit too keenly with the result that he got very, very close to the coconut trees, through which the road ran, and I think he probably had a high-speed stall. Because subsequently, when the army people got in touch with the Squadron to say that they'd found an aircraft crashed in the coconut trees on the north side, we thought it would have to be Peter's aircraft. Our medical officer, Norman Newman, and I went out…to the site and to find and bury Peter, well, we went out along the northern shore by…I think canoe with one of the army fellas and landed at a little perimeter held by the army. Incidentally, when I got ashore, the first bloke to welcome us was a school mate who I hadn't seen for probably…ten years – Captain

---

12   AWM SOO586: Sound recording interview with Bill Garing.

Colin Kirk. But we recognised one another straightaway. Anyhow, he led us to the site of the crashed aircraft and my firm observation and opinion is that Peter must have got into a high speed stall because the aircraft was on its back; there was no evidence of enemy fire, but the… airscrew was damaged and the cockpit-canopy had been sheered off, or shorn off, and Peter, of course, was decapitated. My principal object of going out, of course, was to destroy what was secret equipment in the Kittyhawk then, the IFF wireless…which I did. And then we got Peter out of the cockpit and buried him. It was a very sad occasion, but we also subsequently learned that that night, this little perimeter that was held by Colin Kirk and his platoon, was overrun by the Japanese and all of them were killed.[13]

On the 6 September 1942, the Kittyhawks at Milne Bay were reinforced by the Beaufighters of 30 Squadron. The first batch of Beaufighters flown by the RAAF were those that had been built in Britain, but in due course the Australian Commonwealth Air Corporation (CAC) also began to build the aircraft in Australia. This development was a natural progression from the CAC's earlier work in building the Beaufort bomber, which possessed 75 percent commonality in parts and processes with the Beaufighter. This included the wings and undercarriage, though the Hercules engines on the Australian Beaufighters were imported direct from the Bristol Company's factory in Britain.

A total of 365 Beaufighters were constructed in Australia during the war and the CAC was able to produce one aircraft a day at the peak of Beaufighter production, the first of which began to arrive with Australian front line units in May 1944.[14] The Beaufighter's powerful forward armament of 4 x 20mm cannons mounted in the fuselage, with a further 6 x .303 machine guns in the wings, made it deadly at strafing Japanese soldiers in the jungle. The aircrew usually used a mixture of 50 percent high-explosive incendiary rounds and 50 percent standard ball ammunition in the 20mm cannons, while four of the .303 machine guns were loaded with armour piercing rounds and the remaining two had incendiary rounds. Some Beaufighter pilots also fired .303 tracer rounds, though many found it distracting and did not like warning the enemy that they were being attacked and from which direction.

While it was in service with the RAAF in the South-West Pacific, the Beaufighter yet again confirmed its reliability as a rugged aircraft. The only disadvantage with the Beaufighter was the terrific torque of its powerful engines on take-off, for the unwary this created a dangerous swing that could be hard to control and was particularly dangerous on some of the more narrow and rudimentary landing grounds carved out of the jungle. The Beaufighter's long range meant that it could perform important strikes deep in the enemy's rear, this included enemy airfields where its attacks were an important element in securing air superiority over the Japanese. Squadron Leader Brian 'Blackjack' Walker was the commander of 30 Squadron at the time and describes why the Beaufighter was chosen for the deployment to New Guinea and Milne Bay:

The Beaufighter was chosen because it was a rugged aeroplane with awesome fire power…with four cannon and six machine guns we thought it would make an excellent ground strafer and that is exactly what it did, because if you hit anything with a Beaufighter it was hit and it was hit for good. The worst place to be was in front of an angry Beaufighter, because you are likely to get a dose of lead poisoning and the result was that there were many [Japanese] aeroplanes

---

13   AWM SOO548: Sound recording interview with Colin Lindeman.
14   Brian Weston, *The Australian Aviation Industry* (Royal Australian Air Force, Air Power Development Centre, 2008), p. 13.

RAAF Beaufighter operating in Tawitawi in the Phillipines. (State Library of Victoria, Melbourne, Australia)

Preparing the 500 lb bombs to load onto Beaufighter (State Library of Victoria, Melbourne, Australia)

sitting as burnt out wrecks in New Guinea as a result of the efforts of the Beaufighter. That was the reason it was chosen and that was the reason it was used.

In fact, I understand that the nips didn't like it very much but they used to call it 'whispering death' because not only was it a rugged aeroplane but it had two sleeve valve engines which made it very, very quiet. It had fairly enormous horsepower and the result was that we would find a target and belt it before the nips even knew we were there. Of course we would take advantage of all the natural cover we could get from terrain as well, but that does not take anything away from the Beaufighter's quiet approach. It was a very, very satisfactory aeroplane.[15]

By 31 August 1942, the Australian Army at Milne Bay was counter-attacking the Japanese and by 5 September the Japanese commander had ordered a withdrawal to Buna in New Guinea. Many of these soldiers were subsequently intercepted and routed by the Australians. General Rowell the experienced Australian commander of the New Guinea Force commented that the 'decisive factor' was 'probably the actions of 75 and 76 Squadron RAAF.' Major General Clowes his subordinate at Milne Bay went further and stated that the Kittyhawk squadrons 'incessant attack over three successive days proved the decisive factor.'[16] The action at Milne Bay was important not just for local tactical reasons, it also marked the first occasion that any Allied troops had stood against a Japanese offensive and won. This success was used as an example to motivate other Allied troops outside the South-West Pacific area of operations, including Slim's Fourteenth Army in Burma. Equally important, the victory at Milne Bay allowed the Australians and Americans to begin to take the offensive against the Japanese in New Guinea.

The campaign in the Pacific has sometimes been caricatured as a battle for airfields. One where offensives were launched under an umbrella of air superiority, which then required the advancing ground forces to capture, secure and sometimes even construct airfields, from which the air force could subsequently operate from. It is therefore not surprising that the Allies took to the offensive in New Guinea by the capture of a clearing at Wanigela, mid-way between Milne Bay and the Japanese held base at Buna on the coast, where they subsequently flew in thousands of troops by Dakota and advanced towards the Japanese. These advancing forces were supplied by American transport aircraft which even brought in 25-pounder artillery pieces to the new airstrips constructed at Popondetta and Dobodura, just 15 km from the enemy's defences. Australian Wirraway aircraft soon began operating from Dobodura, routinely dropping their load of 2 x 250lb bombs as well as being used as Air OPs to spot for the artillery. The slow speed of the Wirraway was an advantage in this role, as was their ability to carry an observer as a second crew member. Spotting Japanese positions required the aircraft to fly extremely low and the circling aircraft was reportedly a great morale boost to the Allied ground troops. Surprisingly, the enemy often ignored the Wirraway's presence altogether, a habit which irritated and frustrated the Australian aircrew. One pilot commented 'Sometimes the little swine wouldn't even look up, let alone take cover, I used to get incensed and more than once I went down and shot them up.'[17]

The RAAF also assisted the land battle through air interdiction missions that cut the Japanese lines of communication to the front line and sealed off the battlefield. The maritime nature of the South-West Pacific theatre meant that ships were primarily used by the Japanese for re-supply and reinforcement. During the Battle of the Bismarck Sea on 3 March 1943, the growing Allied

---

15   *Whispering Death: Beaufighter, the Forgotten Warhorse*, 2007 documentary, Enhance TV.

16   David Wilson, *The Decisive Factor: 75 and 76 Squadrons – Port Moresby and Milne Bay 1942* (Brunswick: Banner Books, 1991), p. 190.

17   Mark Johnston, *Whispering Death*, p. 241.

Two images of a strafing attack carried out by American Mitchells and RAAF Beaufighters on the Japanese held Madang Landing Ground, Papua New Guinea. The Japanese aeroplanes on the ground have burst into flames when hit. (State Library of Victoria, Melbourne, Australia)

air superiority and offensive strike capability demonstrated to the Japanese that such methods of supply were no longer practical. The Japanese convoy that was sailing to Lae on that day was interdicted by a strong force of RAAF Beaufort's dropping torpedoes; American B-25s conducting low-level bombing; B-17 Flying Fortresses undertaking high level bombing; RAAF Kittyhawks giving air cover and Australian Beaufighters supressing the ship's AA defences. 'Black Jack' Walker recalled this decisive action:

People don't realise now but I can assure you that it was known…there was a convoy going in to reinforce Lae and I think it was one of the last big Japanese pushes in that area. They had missed out on Moresby and so they were determined to try and hold on to Lae. Eventually there came the great day and the battle was on. There was a slight difference of opinion but I always thought we only had eighty-eight aeroplanes but my friend, Air Commodore Garing, tells me we had ninety-one…I think in all there were at least twenty-two ships in this convoy… On that day and the day following, the Beaufighters went in first and they took on the ack ack and, of course, the Japanese ships split up as soon as they could see aeroplanes coming in to attack which is what you would normally do; they'd start turning.

Of course, we were instructed to hit or to strafe the ship from stem to stern in which case you would probably get the bridge and if you killed or accounted for one or two people on the bridge, that meant the ship would be without proper control. I think that's exactly what happened. Because come that fateful day my observer was in no condition to fly and I saw these twelve aeroplanes take off and it was more than I could stand, I admit. I thought, I can't let those characters go out alone. So I tore around the camp and I found some poor little green observer who had just come up from down south and I don't think he'd ever flown a mission and I said, 'Get into that aeroplane.' We flew over and the only people that I could see that I could join, because my own Beaufighters had gone on ahead, were a bunch of Lightnings, so I joined up with them.

As we were getting near the rendezvous point – the Americans… they'd never heard of radio silence, and they were chattering away to themselves and they said, 'Listen, Black Jack, you better get that Beaufighter out of the way, it will be no bloody good in a dogfight'. I think they could see that there were some Zeros approaching. So I decided it was time to get out, too. Anyhow, the Beaufighters went in and I was observing it from the side and all these ships – honestly, I've never seen anything like it. B25s going in at zero feet. In fact I could see a Beaufighter and a B25 were both going in at the same time and I thought, get out one of you. Anyhow, the B25 bloke saw the Beaufighter going in so he peeled away and turned around and came in again and the Beau went in and that was that. That ship was hit, and I think it must have been an ammunition ship or something like that because a circle appeared above it and then my attention was distracted for a moment and I looked back to where this ship was and… there was nothing there. It had disappeared. It must have blown up. Twenty-two ships were eventually cleaned up by between eight-eight and ninety-one aeroplanes, so don't tell me that air power is not effective.

That attempt by our Japanese friends to reinforce Lae was definitely put on ice… Bill Garing was responsible because he had had maritime experience and this was a maritime exercise in some ways. It was he who instructed us how to go in and hit the ships from stem to stern and aim for the bridge and I think that that was partially responsible for the success… of that battle, because there was no doubt about its success. I have heard from subsequent reading that…there were Japanese destroyers standing by overnight and they did rescue an

awful lot of the personnel and either got them into Lae where they would not be very effective,
I should think, or back to Rabaul from where they had assembled.[18]

The Battle of the Bismarck Sea marked a turning point in the conflict in the South-West Pacific.
From now on the Japanese were unable to routinely resupply, reinforce or retreat from their
garrisons in the region. Over time their isolated troops would progressively become starved of
resources and incapable of any meaningful offensive action. These lonely Japanese outposts would
be bypassed by the main body of MacArthur's offensive operation as it drove through New Guinea
and the Philippines directly towards Japan.

The American and Australian success in late 1942 and early 1943, together with the prospects
of yet more advances, led the Australians to judge that they needed more mobility in their air
organisation. They required a new RAAF formation that could move forward in 400 or 500-mile
bounds, establish a base from which they could attack and defeat the enemy, before advancing
again and fighting once more. This RAAF formation would have to be agile enough to keep up
with the American advance up the New Guinea coast towards the Philippines, which MacArthur
hoped to reach by late 1944. MacArthur had made it clear that his advance would be swift and
that he intended to bypass some of the enemy garrisons, rather than engage them all individually
which ran the risk of slowing his campaign down.

Up to that point the RAAF structures in the South-West Pacific had been adaptations of the
area force concept used for the defence of mainland Australia. These types of headquarters and
formations were simply not designed for expeditionary operations, therefore the RAAF formed
10 Group under Group Captain Scherger in September 1943. No.10 Group was designed with
'compactness, high mobility and clean-cut channels of command from top to bottom'.[19] Initially
the new formation's combat power was based around an attack wing of Vengeance dive-bombers
(77 Wing), as well as a fighter wing of Kittyhawks (78 Wing).[20] The group was also supported by
operational base units, medical units and repair and salvage teams, though many other services
had been dispensed with to avoid a cumbersome support structure. The commander of the forward
echelon justified the spartan nature of support services within 10 Group with the comment that:
'this was the last chance to keep the RAAF always up with the advance towards Japan.'[21]

No.10 Group continued to grow during the campaign and eventually evolved into the First
Australian Tactical Air Force (1st TAF) on 25 October 1944. By that stage it included four wings,
three of which were fighter wings (78 and 81 Wings with Kittyhawks and 80 Wing with Spitfires)
and the fourth was an attack wing (77 Wing) containing three squadrons of Beaufighters. 1st
TAF had also absorbed two mobile airfield construction wings which played a critical role in
constructing the airfields required in the Australian advance.

Initially the campaign in New Guinea and the South-West Pacific had required a large number
of single engine fighters to combat Japanese fighter aircraft and these RAAF fighter squadrons were
fully employed in their air superiority role. At Milne Bay too, the Kittyhawks, when conducting
close air support, had generally strafed the Japanese with their machine guns rather than drop
bombs. However, by the Autumn of 1943 the number of Japanese fighter aircraft encountered
by the RAAF was dropping. Some Australian pilots became frustrated with the lack of air-to-air
fighting and some members of 76 Squadron, who had seen service in the Middle East, requested
that racks for carrying bombs were fitted to their aircraft. This suggestion was carried out by 10

18    AWM SO1645: Sound recording interview with Brian Walker.
19    George Odgers, *Air War against Japan 1943-45* (Canberra: Australian War Memorial, 1957), p. 182.
20    An order of battle for this group is enclosed at Annex I.
21    George Odgers, *Air War against Japan 1943-45*, p. 183.

P-40 Kittyhawk crew from 80 Squadron RAAF sign off duty after returning from a mission.
(State Library of Victoria, Melbourne, Australia)

Group's armament team and the Kittyhawk pilots were trained in the technique of dive bombing, though some were apparently initially dubious of the wisdom of carrying heavy bomb loads over water, as well as the increased risks on take-off. Indeed, the rough and ready nature of many of the landing grounds at New Guinea meant that occasionally bombs did break loose during take-off and it was not uncommon for them to be seen skidding across the runway.[22]

One of the earliest Kittyhawk fighter bomber ground strikes was made in the autumn of 1943 by 76 Squadron, who were then based on the island of Kiriwana. Their target was Gasmata airfield in New Britain, and the sortie was part of the offensive to break the Bismarck barrier. On 21 September 1943, twelve aircraft of 76 Squadron were despatched, each carrying a single 500lb bomb. They bombed from 2,000 feet yet only four bombs hit the target.[23] It was a small and unspectacular beginning, but the scale soon ramped up. On 6 December another strike was launched further along the New Britain coast at Arawe, this was in preparation for the landing there by the American 112th Cavalry Regiment. A total of sixty-three Kittyhawks from Nos. 75, 76, 77 and 78 Squadrons attacked the Gasmata bomb dumps, diving down from 13,000 to 3,000 feet before dropping their bombs. The assault landing itself was also preceded by a strike from thirty-four Australian Kittyhawks, who dropped bombs in sections of four aircraft from 1,000

---

22  George Odgers, *Air War against Japan 1943-45*, p. 82.
23  George Odgers, *Air War against Japan 1943-45*, p. 83.

A Kittyhawk aircraft of 76 Squadron RAAF undergoing maintenance by members of 12 Repair and Salvage Unit RAAF on the island of Kiriwina – 31 January 1944. (Australian War Memorial)

feet, before circling back to conduct strafing attacks with their .50 calibre machine guns at tree top height.[24]

In early 1944, the Kittyhawk's role as a fighter bomber was complemented by the Vengeance dive-bombers which operated with 12, 21, 23 and 24 Squadron of 77 Wing. The Vengeance again proved that it was an ideal aircraft for delivering precise strikes against enemy positions. For example, 24 Squadron was based on the recently captured airfield of Nadzab in New Guinea, from where they supported 7th Australian Division's operations to capture 'Shaggy Ridge' in the Finisterre range of mountains to the north. As part of this battle, Brigadier Chilton's 18th Brigade was tasked to capture the ridge including features known as Protheroe I, Protheroe II and McCaughey's knoll. The RAAF supported 18th Brigade's attack in six separate strikes between 17 and 22 January 1944.

These six strikes against Shaggy Ridge were undertaken by a mixed force of No.4 Squadron CAC Boomerang aircraft, Vengeances from 24 Squadron and Kittyhawks from 78 Squadron. The strikes were led in by the Boomerangs, which though designed initially as a fighter had proved more suitable as a light ground-attack aircraft. In these operation's the Boomerang's agility and the ease with which it could be flown meant that it could get close to ground targets and avoid the enemy's fire as well as rough terrain. The Boomerang was well armoured and featured a wood and aluminium frame that could withstand significant battle damage. Flying in pairs the Boomerangs

---

24   George Odgers, *Air War against Japan 1943-45*, p. 126.

would indicate the target to larger aircraft by either diving down and firing tracer at it or dropping a 20lb smoke bomb. The twelve or so Vengeances would then drop their own ordnance on the targets, a successful attack meant that as many as twenty-two 1,000lb bombs (about nine tons of high explosive) would hit the target in quick succession, these strikes were then usually followed up by the Vengeances quickly strafing the Japanese position. In all of these operations the Kittyhawks typically flew above the Vengeances at 4,000 feet and acted as top cover. Though once the Vengeances had attacked, they usually dived down themselves to drop their own bombs and conduct strafing attacks.

During the Battle of Shaggy Ridge the accuracy of the Australian strikes varied. The Japanese would sometimes anticipate the bombing attack and fire their own smoke shells to distract the attackers. On other occasions clouds and rain squalls blotted out the target, though this was sometimes only temporary, and patience and persistence were often rewarded. On 20 January for instance, Squadron Leader Honey led his twelve Vengeances in an orbit over the target for twenty minutes before the clouds parted sufficiently for him to observe the smoke shells, as well as the target, and deliver his ordnance. Fourteen out of the twenty-two bombs dropped by the Vengeance's struck the target accurately. By 23 January the Australian 7th Division had captured McCaughey's Knoll and the fight for Shaggy Ridge had been won.[25]

The Australians operated the Kittyhawk throughout the South-West Pacific Campaign and it proved to be a good aircraft that served them well. It was just as well, as neither the British, nor the Americans, were prepared to furnish them with anything more modern. Consequently, the Kittyhawk remained the mainstay of Australian close air support and its tough and rugged nature meant it was able to operate on many austere airfields in New Guinea and the Netherlands East Indies. This was a great advantage as many landing grounds in the South-West Pacific were so rudimentary that aircraft like the Spitfire and P-38 Lightning simply could not cope with the conditions. As one example of this widely accepted benefit, General MacArthur substituted the P-38 equipped American 49th Group with the Australian No. 78 Wing primarily because of his 'desire to place in the Aitape and Hollandia areas [of New Guinea] the maximum number of P-40 (Kittyhawk) aircraft, which are more adapted to operate with minimum facilities.'[26] It was not just the aircraft's ability to land and operate in rough terrain that was important in this theatre, the competition between Australians and Americans for space on the congested airfields meant that it was important for the RAAF to generate as much operational output from their squadrons as possible. Group Captain Scherger, the commander of 10 Group RAAF at the time, describes the pressures:

> On the rather inflexible 'planned flying, planned maintenance' adapted from the R.A.F. by our technical people, it was estimated that only 600 hours per month per squadron could be flown in the fighter wing – whereas we were being called on to fly up to 1,500 hours per month per squadron. It was remarkable at the time that the maintenance men we had were quite capable of dealing with the extra maintenance, but the provision of spares, particularly of spare engines, and the number of pilots allotted to each squadron was nowhere near adequate for this amount of flying.
>
> After considerable interchange of signals with R.A.A.F Headquarters, the Deputy Chief of the Air Staff personally visited the Group (Air Commodore McCauley arrived at Nadzab on 4th March) and was convinced by General Whitehead that either our units flew the hours required of them or they would not be given aerodrome space in the forward areas. As a result

---

25    George Odgers, *Air War against Japan 1943-45*, p. 186.
26    George Odgers, *Air War against Japan 1943-45*, p. 206.

RAAF fitters servicing a Vultee Vengeance. (State Library of Victoria, Melbourne, Australia)

24 Squadron RAAF Vultee Vengeances aircraft on their way back to base after a strike.
(State Library of Victoria, Melbourne, Australia)

of this visit, the number of pilots per squadron was increased to thirty and the number of aircraft to twenty-four, with a further thirty-six in immediate reserve at a repair and service unit. It was gratifying to find later that the steps taken by Air Force Headquarters to build these units to a level where they were capable of rates of effort comparable with those of the Americans, resulted, later in the year, in the squadrons of No. 78 Wing consistently outflying similar American units.[27]

It was during this period that the Vengeance dive bomber was abruptly withdrawn from front line service in March 1944, primarily at the direction of the Americans who favoured giving other aircraft room at these congested airfields. This was not without reason, the Vengeance lacked the range of other strike aircraft such as the P-38 Lightning, or Beaufighter and it was unable to carry a greater weight of bombs than the Kittyhawk, which of course needed no escorts and could also operate as an air superiority fighter. The Vengeances were also getting old, serviceability issues were apparent and in the hot conditions the aircraft needed the full length of the 6,000 feet runway at Nadzab to get airborne. A final factor was that the United States Army Air Force had never been persuaded by dive-bombing and although an American aircraft, the Vengeance was not brought into service with them. Dive bombing was largely a United States Navy endeavour and there was an element of United States Army Air Force prejudice against dive bombing operations and aircraft. This measure was a considerable blow for the Australians who had bought a total of 400 Vengeance aircraft, yet in the end only obtained six weeks' worth of combat service out of them.

On a more positive note, many of the Australian crews of the Vengeance aircraft were subsequently converted onto B-24 Liberators, and the addition of this superb long-range bomber to the RAAF inventory added considerable prestige and capability to the service. No.77 Wing's departing Vengeance squadrons were also immediately back-filled by a squadron each of Bostons, Beauforts and Beaufighters. The mix of three aircraft types in this wing initially caused significant administrative headaches for 10 Group, until they were eventually consolidated into just three Beaufighter squadrons.

The Bostons were another example of the Australians receiving second-hand aircraft, though more successfully in this instance. This particular batch of Bostons had originally been ordered by the French at the very beginning of the war. On the surrender of France in 1940 the planned delivery was quickly transferred by the Americans to the Netherland East Indies, but when that colony fell in 1942, the Australians took them on. As we have already seen the Boston was a capable bomber in Europe and the Middle East, but its introduction into service in the South-West Pacific was initially fraught with problems.

The Bostons of 22 Squadron were deployed to Ward's airfield at Port Moresby in October 1942 and soon began to conduct bombing missions. They found however that in their first few bombing sorties the aircraft just seemed to blow up in mid-air, at first it was thought that flak was the culprit, but it was subsequently discovered that the 20lb fragmentation bombs being used were so light and temperamental that the aircraft's slipstream caused them to strike each other and detonate prematurely.[28] The bombs were quickly withdrawn from service and replaced with larger American designed parachute fragmentation bombs (para-frag) and parachute demolition bombs (para-demo). These bombs could still be dropped at low level with an instantaneous detonation fuse but were fitted with small silk parachutes that deployed when the bomb was released from the aircraft, slowing down its descent and preventing the attacking aircraft being hit by the bomb's blast. The 100lb para-frag bombs were relatively small and had just one parachute – the 250lb

---

27   George Odgers, *Air War against Japan 1943-45*, p. 194.
28   Mark Johnston, *Whispering Death*, p. 325.

RAAF road graders preparing a strip for Auster aircraft after they were unloaded from LSTs which brought 10,000 tons of strip building equipment to Tarakan. Indonesia. (State Library of Victoria, Melbourne, Australia)

bombs – two parachutes and a 500lb bomb carried four parachutes. They were found to be highly effective in attacks on airfields and Japanese anti-aircraft positions.[29]

As well as new aircraft and a sensible command and control structure, 10 Group was also adapted into a more mobile force for the next offensive stage of the war. This included the incorporation of two airfield construction wings (61 and 62 Wings) who ensured the group could keep up with MacArthur's advance. These wings consisted of two airfield construction squadrons each, whose role was to advance with the forward troops and begin the task of building the necessary airfields and landing grounds that the attack and fighter wings would subsequently occupy. The airfield construction troop's role often meant they had to disembark with the forward echelons of amphibious assault troops, so that they could start their task as quickly as possible. As one example, on 20 April 1944 Wing Commander Gale together with Squadron Leader Jamieson, a civil engineer, landed at Aitape at 0700, just fifteen minutes after the first wave of assault troops. Shortly after Gale's party arrived a small detachment of No. 13 Survey and Design Unit landed and then, thirty minutes later, the headquarters of No. 62 Wing, the main party of 13 Survey and Design Unit and No. 7 Mobile Works Squadron.[30]

By midday on 20 April, the soldiers of the American 41st Infantry Division had occupied the airstrip at Tadji and Gale's engineers were surveying and pegging out the landing ground. Gale

---

29    George Odgers, *Air War against Japan 1943-45*, p. 370.
30    George Odgers, *Air War against Japan 1943-45*, pp. 210-1.

determined that the abandoned airfield was too overgrown with Kunai grass, only roughly graded and not long enough for fighter operations. The engineers of 7 Squadron therefore set about grading and extending the runway. The rain interfered with their construction by making the top-soil difficult to work with and there was also light enemy small arms fire hampering activity, though without causing any Australian casualties. The following day further RAAF reinforcements arrived including 5 and 6 Work squadrons, 10 Works Supply Unit and 4 Maintenance Unit. The ground parties of 75, 78 and 80 squadrons also arrived as did elements of 10 Group's headquarters.

These extra engineers set to work immediately, though there was still sporadic sniper fire sweeping the area. Despite the hard work of these new reinforcements the airfield was still not ready by the end of this second day. The engineers therefore continued to work during the night and laid a Pierced Steel Planked runway 100 feet wide and 3,900 feet long. After a total of 41-hours-worth of work the landing ground at Aitape/Tadji was completed by 0800 hours the next day (22 April). The first Australian Kittyhawks from 78 Squadron landed at the airfield that afternoon.[31]

As the Australians leap-frogged from one location to another on the flank of MacArthur's American advance, 10 Group and their engineers followed in their immediate wake and repeated this pattern of construction at numerous other locations across the South-West Pacific. The creation of the Australian Airfields at Aitape (April 1944), Noemfoor (July 1944), Morotai (September 1944), Mindoro (December 1944), Balif (January 1945), Tarakan (May 1945) and Balikpapan (July 1945) act as a trace for the major Australian advances and there were many other minor landing grounds also constructed. Squadron Leader Overend was an officer in 61 Airfield Construction Wing and recalls the assault on Mindoro on the 15 December and his own squadron's arrival:

> Up at 4 a.m. to general quarters. Coffee and roll for breakfast. Naval guns are in action as an enemy transport is picked up by escort. It is hit within three minutes and a large fire starts, lasting some hours. Then there is dead silence. Orders were received late last night for 3 Airfield Construction Squadron to go in on the first wave. After dawn, Mindoro is dead ahead and naval bombardment commences. Ships are forming into beach lines and into waves. Enemy aircraft appear low down and are held off by anti-aircraft fire. Beach markers are visible. San Jose is prominent, red roof and black stack on the sugar mill. The beach has a grass verge and the infantry are landing ankle deep. Eight LST's [Landing Ship Tank] are moving into the shore at White Beach. Infantry are moving inland slowly across the grass flats. On the last lap as we go in, six [enemy] aircraft appear directly overhead. Five are shot down by anti-aircraft fire but a sixth successfully suicide-dived into the rear LST. A second LST is also hit. Even after being shot down while in a suicide dive the pilot attempts to complete his mission. We make a dry landing on a good beach. Survivors from damaged LST's are being brought ashore. The R.A.A.F. is being unloaded first.[32]

The Australian engineers on Mindoro laboured all day to get their equipment off the LSTs, suffering casualties from a Japanese suicide aircraft that crashed into the open doors of an LST. With the added assistance of an American Engineer Battalion they finished the airfield on 19 December 1944.

Inevitably all the airfields constructed by the engineers were different to one degree or another, this usually depended on the local geography, geology and resources dedicated to the task. Colin

31  George Odgers, *Air War against Japan 1943-45*, p. 211.
32  George Odgers, *Air War against Japan 1943-45*, p. 377.

A Mobile Works Squadron bulldozer hauling machinery ashore at Balikpapan for work to begin on repairing the captured Seppinggar airstrip. (State Library of Victoria, Melbourne, Australia)

Lindeman of 76 Squadron recalls the different landing strips he operated on throughout the campaign, as well as their various strengths and weaknesses:

> I think Tadji had the worst conditions because we moved the squadron in there only one or two days after our troops had landed there. The American Navy had softened up the area with shelling from their ships but, nevertheless, the Japanese were just outside the perimeter and were sniping quite happily when we were taking off and landing. And the strip was pretty new; again, a metal strip. It was extremely crowded because Australian Beauforts were there and I think Beaufighters, although I could be incorrect there. Anyhow, the conditions on the little strip were very, very crowded and that made things a little bit dicey, particularly if everyone wanted to come in and land at the same time.
>
> Well, there were quite a few casualties [from snipers close to the airfield] and quite a few of the aircraft on the ground were hit. But…it wasn't all that bad. We used to go out and strafe the perimeter on the request of the army people. From memory, I think it was all American army there. I don't think there were any Australian army fellas there at that stage which, you know, in fact, didn't fill us with the same confidence had they been Australians.
>
> Nadzab was a huge base really. I don't know how many landing strips were there but it could accommodate the American A-20s and the Bostons and either two or three Kittyhawk squadrons. The strip was very good on the low-lying kunai parts just to the west of Lae. Hollandia was even bigger; our strip wasn't all that hot but there were I think three strips there too and there was a fair amount of traffic there too – air traffic – because that was where General MacArthur had his headquarters at that stage. Generally speaking the strips at, or the

Corporal Clarke and Corporal W.H. Radke shown loading the guns of an RAAF single-seater fighter aircraft.
(State Library of Victoria, Melbourne, Australia)

one at Noemfoor was built by Australian airfield engineers and it was a beauty. The surface
was like glass. Biak was quite good too. But… I think the diciest one was Tadji because of the
smallness of the strip, the proximity of the Japanese snipers and the huge volume of aircraft
operating from it.[33]

As the campaign progressed the need for the Kittyhawk to act as an air superiority fighter would
become increasingly rare. Indeed, even the new Spitfires which began arriving in the New Guinea
and Netherlands East Indies in the last year of the war were seldom employed in those roles. In the
thousands of sorties flown by the RAAF in the last nine months of the war only five contacts were
made with enemy aircraft and during this same period the three air superiority Spitfire squadrons
of 80 Wing only succeeded in shooting down three aircraft. It highlights the extent to which the
Japanese air force had been cleared from the skies and the degree to which Allied air superiority
had been achieved.

The lack of a role for some pilots partly explains a drop in morale amongst First Australian
Tactical Air Force personnel in the final stages of the Australian campaign in the South-West
Pacific. This was compounded by several other factors, firstly the environment at the airfields
carved out in the jungle was lonely and austere. At places like Morotai, far from civilisation, an
airmen would return to an isolated airfield and a canvas tent, mud and bully beef. There was also a
feeling that the Australians were being marginalised in an unimportant flank and rear area security

33   AWM SOO548: Sound recordings interview with Colin Lindeman.

role, leaving the Americans to drive up through the Philippines towards the Japanese mainland. Perhaps more importantly HQ 1st TAF interpreted this marginal role as one that required the Australian airmen to regularly and repeatedly strike small pockets of bypassed Japanese positions. Though these enemy forces were increasingly irrelevant, it was a task which nevertheless still carried considerable risk to attacking aircraft as Colin Lindeman relates:

> Well, the danger was from ground fire. I remember one particular episode. We were operating out of Tadji or Aitape, which is the same place, down towards – I forget where the target was – south. One of the last places where the army got the Japanese out of. Anyhow it was a pretty strongly held Japanese area and in strafing down there one day we encountered a hut at the foot of the promontory on which the anti-aircraft gunners were situated. And flying over this hut I could see the Japs tearing out of the hut, going to the base of the hill, and obviously they had ladders and things inside there and going out on top to man their anti-aircraft guns, which were machine guns; not heavy ack-ack. So we came back and we strafed the hut and strafed the gun's position but not very successfully I think, because I said to myself, 'Well, I'll go down the next morning and do the job properly'.
>
> So next morning we went down and sure enough, got the Japs in the hut. Some of them got out and I think that they might have been a little bit prepared for us because as we came back for a second run over the machine gun positions, I got hit with just one bullet which entered the cockpit just behind me. It penetrated the self-sealing fuel tank; it severed the hydraulic line which, as you know, would have operated the flaps and the landing gear and so on, and it also severed the rudder pedal. So, I knew I'd been hit from the jar on my feet. It wasn't long before I discovered I didn't have any rudder which meant there was a little bit of a dicey return to Tadji. It wasn't very far away, only about quarter of an hour perhaps. The aircraft flies quite easily without a rudder, with aileron control and rudder trim tab. But the lack of hydraulics was a bit worrying because it means I had to wind down my landing gear manually and then land without any rudder which was quite an interesting operation... I think it followed the normal pattern. Wheels down, airscrew in fine pitch, and mixture enrich – but winding down the undercarriage took quite a while. Then you had to pump the flaps down manually. Then I think I got out of the aircraft fairly quickly and one of the ground staff...or a fitter came up to me and said, 'Gee, Col, you're a bit lucky. Just one little bullet did all that damage'. So I was probably a little bit careless in making the attack in the same pattern for two days in a row. It's the sort of thing I learned not to do.[34]

A prevailing view began to emerge amongst some RAAF aircrew that these operations did not seem to be contributing much to the wider war effort. Kittyhawk pilot Jock Scott commented that 'all we did was to make the Japs use up their endless supply of anti-aircraft ammo and improve their shooting. They were isolated, unsupplied, ineffectual and without an effective role to play in the war. Except to shoot at stupid buggers in Kittyhawks.'[35] The pilots and some of their commanders increasingly felt that the expenditure in aircrew and aircraft was simply not worth the operational benefit of destroying these minor targets. There was also a sense that staff officers at 1st TAF were not measuring the effectiveness of these Australian operations on damage to the enemy, or the contribution that might make to the wider Allied operation, but on a much cruder calculation of hours flown and targets struck. In December 1944, the highly experienced Group Captain Wilfred 'Woof' Arthur took over command of 81 Wing at Noemfoor. He was initially enthusiastic

---

34   AWM SOO548: Sound recordings interview with Colin Lindeman.
35   Mark Johnston, *Whispering Death*, p. 396.

No. 78 Squadron RAAF P40 Kittyhawks on Morotai Island. In the foreground is P-40 A29-558, code HU-N, 'Watch my Form'. (State Library of Victoria, Melbourne, Australia)

about the missions then being flown by his unit, but gradually became unsettled by the waste and unnecessary danger the operations generated. He reduced the level of operations being conducted by his wing and drew up for his superior headquarters an operational balance sheet weighing the operational gains against the enemy, together with the wing's aircraft losses. His analysis showed that during the period October to November 1944, 81 Wing had lost 11 pilots and 15 aircraft, but in turn had only destroyed 12 barges and six motor transport vehicles.[36]

Senior staff officers initially disputed and ignored Arthur's findings, but he persisted. The matter eventually came to a head when an exasperated Arthur was able to persuade other operational RAAF commanders to tender their resignations from the service (once the operational phase they were in was completed). The RAAF was surprised and shocked into action and a commission, under Mr John Vincent Barry KC, was set up to investigate the resignations and the poor morale in 1st TAF. Despite some institutional obfuscation by the RAAF, Barry concluded that:

> From about the beginning of January 1945 there was a widespread condition of discontent and dissatisfaction within 1st T.A.F. at Morotai. The two main factors which brought about that condition were the opinions generally held about the nature of the operational activities upon which the wings were engaged and the attitude of the senior staff officers, Group Captain Simms and Group Captain Gibson. As that widespread condition developed and existed without his being aware of it the A.O.C. 1st T.A.F. failed to maintain proper control over his command.[37]

Barry's judgement added that the expenditure on the operations far exceeded the material damage inflicted on the enemy and that they were therefore wasteful. This was backed up by a study from the RAAF's Operational Research Section which also reported:

36  Mark Johnston, *Whispering Death*, p. 396.
37  George Odgers, *Air War against Japan 1943-45*, p. 446.

RAAF Pilots of a Kittyhawk squadron based at Noemfoor return from a daily strike.
(State Library of Victoria, Melbourne, Australia)

RAAF ground staff assemble Auster aircraft, for use as an artillery spotter for the Australian Army at Tarakan,
Indonesia. (State Library of Victoria, Melbourne, Australia)

The results achieved hardly appear to provide a reasonable return for the effort expended…
These operations indicate the wastefulness inherent in the tactical employment of air forces…
against small pockets of the enemy…in this theatre.[38]

The so-called 'Morotai Mutiny' highlighted the difficulty operational commanders face when measuring the effect of their activities. It takes moral courage to challenge senior orthodoxies and the incident arguably reflects credit on the individual Australian operational commanders at wing level, including Arthur, as well as the overall Australian/RAAF system that in the end backed the right, rather than most senior, judgement.

Operations against these bypassed Japanese garrisons were bound to be frustrating, but morale had fortunately returned to a more even keel by the time 1st TAF launched their final operations of the war against northern Borneo. This included two major landings at Tarakan and Balikpapan which demonstrated the increasing scale and sophistication of Australian joint operations, as well as the strong coordination between the Army, Royal Australian Navy and RAAF. The final Australian amphibious assault of the war at Balikpapan in Borneo was preceded by strikes from twenty Australian Liberator bombers of 21, 23 and 24 Squadrons, which were supplemented by attacks from Kittyhawk fighter bombers from 1st TAF. So effective was the air and naval bombardment that there was not a single Australian casualty in all seventeen assault waves. The damage inflicted by the RAAF was severe and included the destruction of oil storage tanks, refinery and cracking plants as well as 441 buildings in the southern part of the town. The Dutch complained that the bombardment was excessive and resulted in needless destruction. The Australian commanders, both Air Force and Army, remained adamant that the strikes were proportionate and justified the bombardment stating that it had to be as heavy as possible in order to reduce casualties.[39]

The Australian campaign in the South-West Pacific took many of the lessons and techniques learnt in Europe, the Middle East and Burma and applied them to their own theatre. The unique character of the South-West Pacific also required the RAAF to consider mobility, target marking and administrative matters in a manner utterly different to anywhere else. The efficiency with which they tackled these challenges is admirable, yet only marred by the frustration many of them clearly felt as the Americans relegated them to a peripheral flank protection and rear area security role in the latter stages of the campaign. Nonetheless, it remains a campaign worthy of study in what a junior air force must do to make itself operationally relevant to a larger partner.

The preceding chapters in this part of the book have all focussed on the contribution the air force made to the land campaigns through firepower and strikes. The next chapters will examine the significant contribution the air force was also able to make through the provision of air transport, for the movement of troops and airborne operations.

---

38   George Odgers, *Air War against Japan 1943-45*, p. 446.
39   George Odgers, *Air War against Japan 1943-45*, p. 484

# Part VII
# Air Transport Operations

# 11

# 'Nothing is Impossible'[1]
# Airborne Forces

In 1936, General Wavell led a small British Military Mission to Minsk, Russia where he and his team observed a series of military manoeuvres, during which the Red Army successfully demonstrated their embryonic airborne capability by dropping 1,500 parachutists. Wavell was impressed with the performance commenting 'If I had not witnessed the descents, I could not have believed such an operation possible.'[2] Despite this, his team's report concluded that though the demonstration was undoubtedly spectacular, they could see little tactical value in the use of paratroopers and no obvious military role. This view was further reinforced by the Committee of Imperial Defence in 1937 who considered the likelihood and impact of airborne raids against Britain in time of war as negligible.[3] Even intelligence reports of the Germans undertaking their own glider and parachute training, did not prompt the British to re-consider developing their own airborne force. Instead, they remained sceptical of the survivability of transport aircraft and gliders during such operations, as well as cautious of tying down large numbers of troops and aircraft in a role for which they could not see an obvious use.

On 9 April 1940, this British ambivalence was rudely shattered during the opening sequences of the Norwegian campaign, when a German airborne operation successfully captured the Norwegian airfield at Sola, near Stavanger. The Germans followed this on 10 May 1940 with an amazingly successful neutralisation of the Belgian fortress at Eben Emael – by just eighty-five glider-borne assault engineers landing on top of the fort. There were yet more airborne operations during the invasion of the Netherlands, which succeeded in capturing several bridges and airfields in advance of the German invading forces. Despite sometimes heavy German casualties during these operations, especially in the landings near the Hague, the German airborne operations were successful in capturing their objectives and in generating significant confusion and alarm behind the Allied lines. These events prompted the British to reconsider the utility of airborne forces once more and Winston Churchill characteristically lent his own impetus to the subject on 6 June 1940:

> We ought to have a corps of at least 5,000 parachute troops, including a proportion of Australians, New Zealanders and Canadians, together with some trustworthy people from Norway and France... I hear something is already being done to form such a corps but only I believe on a very small scale. Advantage must be taken of the summer to train these troops, who can none the less, play their part as shock troops in home defence. Pray let me have a note from the War Office on the subject.[4]

---

1   Motto of the Glider Pilot Regiment.
2   *By Air To Battle – The Official Account of the British Airborne Divisions* (London: HMSO, 1945), p. 8.
3   Air Publication 3231, *Airborne Forces,* (London: Air Historical Branch Air Ministry, 1951), p. 1.
4   Air Publication 3231, *Airborne Forces*, p. 2.

As a result of the Prime Minister's memo the RAF and Army set up a joint training centre at Ringway (now Manchester Airport). There, a small group began training using converted Whitley bombers from which the paratroopers simply dropped through a hole cut in the aircraft's floor. Initial progress was slow, not least because of problems with the type of parachute to be used. This was speedily resolved with the development of the 'G.Q.' model or 'X-type' parachute, it proved so suitable that it quickly became the standard parachute for British airborne forces for the remainder of the war and well into the 1960s. The X-type was a static line parachute, which meant it was attached to the aircraft and opened automatically as the soldier exited the plane. It was a major improvement because the parachute's deployment was spread smoothly through the rigging lines to the canopy and this meant that though the parachute filled more quickly with air, it was a less sudden action than in previous systems. This dramatically reduced the shock load, or 'jerk', as the canopy opened and the rigging lines suddenly became taut.[5]

As the parachute and harness were being developed, so too was the clothing the paratroopers wore, with many of the designs being copied from German equipment and thinking. This included a parachute jumping jacket which covered the paratrooper's equipment, preventing it getting snagged on rigging lines, a parachute smock made of windproof material with very large pockets and, at least initially, boots with thick rubber crepe soles. These special boots were later found to be unnecessary and ordinary hob-nailed Army leather boots were re-introduced later in the war. The paratrooper also wore a brimless steel helmet, which was more aerodynamic than the standard issue one and less likely to cause injury as he hit the ground. He also carried a parachute knife, strapped to his right leg, with which to cut himself free if necessary.

The parachute itself was housed in an inner bag divided into two compartments. This bag was then contained within a pack carried on the soldier's back and attached to his parachute harness. As the paratrooper left the aircraft, the inner-bag was pulled violently out by a static line which was attached to one end of the bag and secured by a webbing strop to a strong point in the aircraft at the other end of the line. The length of the static line was twelve feet six inches, this was long enough to ensure that the parachute would only begin to be pulled open when it was well below the aircraft. In a typical parachute aircraft, such as a Dakota, a steel cable ran along the length of the aeroplane and a 'D-ring' at the end of the webbing strop was clipped to this and moved freely with the paratroopers as they shuffled one-by-one towards the exit.[6]

Once the paratrooper exited the aircraft, he would fall for one to one and a half seconds before the strop pulled out the static line in the top half of the inner bag, and then the line itself pulled the parachute from the bottom half. The canopy of the parachute then opened with a whip-like crack, arresting the paratrooper's fall and allowing him to float towards the earth at a rate of 7-metres per second.

The X-type parachute canopy measured twenty-eight feet in diameter and was made of a mixture of silk, cotton and nylon with twenty-eight rigging lines, running from the edge of the canopy to four D-rings each of which were attached to web risers or 'lift webs' on the harness. In the middle of the canopy was a circular hole – the vent – twenty-two inches in diameter. This prevented undue strain on the canopy when it opened and stopped the parachute swaying violently from side to side as it fell. When not in use the parachute was stored in its bag and could be left there for two months before it needed inspection and re-packing once more, a process which would take about twenty-five minutes. The parachute was only used for twenty-five descents before it was declared unsafe.

The paratrooper typically jumped from a height of about 600 feet and therefore had little time to correct any problems in the air, such as twisted rigging lines, but his greatest challenge was

5   Air Publication 3231, *Airborne Forces*, p. 21.
6   *By Air To Battle – The Official Account of the British Airborne Divisions*, p. 12.

A Douglas Dakota Mark III of 575 Squadron RAF based at Broadwell, Oxfordshire, drops paratroops over an airfield during an airborne exercise. (Crown Copyright – Air Historical Branch)

always to land correctly and without injury. It was hard for the soldier to gauge the precise moment at which he would strike the earth, particularly at night, therefore paratroopers were taught to roll and flex the ankles, the knees, hips and back immediately on touching the ground. It was also imperative that the legs were kept together with the soles of the feet parallel to the ground, this meant they both hit the earth simultaneously and absorbed the impact better. Once he had landed the paratrooper would collapse his chute, operate the quick release gear to remove his harness and then set off for his rendezvous point.[7]

As well as establishing a new paratroop capability, the Army and RAF were also developing a glider-borne element to be part of the new airborne force. The advantage of using gliders was that troops could be landed together as a team and assault an objective much more quickly and effectively. The glider could also carry heavier equipment, such as anti-tank guns and jeeps, as well as important stores including ammunition. Most importantly, if the gliders were cast off a sufficient distance away, then they could make a silent approach to their specific targets, which would potentially achieve tactical surprise. It was felt, at least initially, that the nature of parachuting required individuals to volunteer and these were drawn from every regiment and corps across the British Army. The individual volunteers then became part of the new Parachute Regiment battalions making up the Parachute Brigades (e.g 2nd Battalion, The Parachute Regiment). In contrast the glider-borne troops were generated by converting existing infantry units en-masse into glider infantry battalions in an Airlanding Brigade. Consequently, these battalions all retained their original regimental titles such as 1st Battalion, The Royal Ulster Rifles, or 2nd Battalion,

---

7    *By Air to Battle – The Official Account of the British Airborne Divisions*, p. 13.

Horsa Mark I, DP726, of the airborne Forces Experimental Establishment based at Ringway, Cheshire, in flight under tow. (Crown Copyright – Air Historical Branch)

The South Staffordshire Regiment. Creating Airlanding battalions was therefore a much simpler process, even with the additional training required of infantry in the airborne forces. So successful was this approach, that a similar process was subsequently adopted for some of the parachute battalions that were formed later in the war. For instance, the 9th Battalion Parachute Regiment was raised from the 10th Battalion, The Essex Regiment, though only 200 soldiers from this battalion passed the demanding airborne selection and it still required additional volunteers from elsewhere in the Army to meet its proper war establishment of 733 men.[8]

By the end of 1940, four glider designs were being considered, these included the General Aircraft Hotspur which was an 8-seat glider for training; the Airspeed Horsa – a 25-seat glider that could be modified to carry equipment and would be the main operational aircraft; the Slingsby Hengist – a 15-seater designed as an insurance against the Horsa proving unsuitable and finally the General Aircraft Hamilcar – a large tank-carrying glider. By August 1941, the Horsa proto-type had proved satisfactory and the decision was taken to cancel the Hengist which never saw operational service. Constructing the gliders for this new force proceeded slowly, as it had taken some time to decide what types were needed and the Ministry of Aircraft Production order was initially so small that it did not warrant production of the necessary jigs on a large scale. As the glider designs were being settled a vociferous debate was also being waged between the Army and the Air Force as to who should fly these aircraft. Many in the RAF took the view that teaching soldiers to fly was impractical, Harris, who was working as Deputy Chief of the Air Staff at the time, offering the view that:

> The idea that semi-skilled, unpicked personnel (infantry corporals have, I believe even been suggested) could with a maximum of training be entrusted with the piloting of these troop carriers is fantastic. Their operation is the equivalent to forced landing the largest sized aircraft without engine aid – than which there is no higher test of piloting skill.[9]

8   Stuart Tootal, *The Manner of Men* (London: John Murray, 2014), p. 162.
9   Mike Peters and Luuk Buist, *Glider Pilots at Arnhem* (Barnsley: Pen and Sword, 2009), p. 4.

The RAF took the view that the Army's glider pilots should be trained as standard operational aircrew and after a conversion course on gliders they should be seconded to RAF units, where they would undertake normal operational flying. These glider pilots would only be returned to the glider role prior to an airborne operation. The Army did not relish this approach, not just because it looked like a back-door way of augmenting RAF pilot numbers, but also because of the seriousness with which the Army took the glider pilot's role once his flight was completed. For most normal service pilots, the successful completion of a flying sortie meant a return to an airfield and a chance to relax and rest in what was usually a safe and secure environment. In contrast, the glider pilot's sortie was a strictly one-way journey to what was likely to be a dangerous battle and he would almost certainly have to fight once on the ground. The glider pilot therefore had to be as much a soldier as an airman. The Army view prevailed with the formation of the Glider Pilot Regiment which, along with the Parachute Regiment, would form part of the new Army Air Corps. The first members joined the Glider Pilot Regiment in March 1942 and the pioneering commander of its 1st Battalion (and a future leader of the whole Regiment) was Lieutenant Colonel George Chatterton.

Chatterton judged that to be successful the glider pilots would need to have a 'dual personality'. This would need to consist of first, 'the flexibility of the pilot for his long tow to the target' and second the esprit and discipline of a soldier 'in order that he should stand up to the rigours of battle at the end of his journey'. Chatterton had personally witnessed the impressive conduct of the Grenadier Guards at Dunkirk, he therefore asked the Brigade of Guards to provide the necessary warrant officers to deliver the training and discipline for his new unit. Such an attitude was not easy for the RAF instructors to understand and they were often taken aback at the highly disciplined bearing of the newly arrived cadets, but Chatterton persisted in his approach and argued that all the RAF could see 'was the turning out of the pilot, not what he had to face on stepping from the glider.'[10] The performance of the glider pilots in battle, particularly in Sicily and at Arnhem, vindicated Chatterton's approach.

The glider pilots underwent 12 weeks training at an Elementary Flying Training School (EFTS), four weeks at Glider Training School (GTS) and then a final six weeks at a Glider Operational Training Unit (GOTU). After this they were awarded their Army Flying Badge (the same as that worn by the Royal Artillery Air OP pilots).[11] Nonetheless it was not an easy transition from soldier to pilot as Lawrence Wright, who was an RAF instructor at the Glider Training School at RAF Thame makes clear:

> Some of the soldier pilots, conditioned to obey orders, proved slow to disobey when occasion demanded; unequal to the transition from an obedient member of a squad to a responsible captain of an aircraft. Arriving home too low for the regulation left-hand circuit, but well placed for a safe right-hand one, a stickler might attempt the former, and crash according to orders. The Army tended to frown on our relatively lax discipline, but we might have aggravated this difficulty, had we tried to reduce all airmanship to a drill. A spell of flat calm, following a week of strong winds, was the undoing of several of these less adaptable types, and there was a memorable series of overshoots. These usually ended with a swing into the dispersal area; one tended to look out of one's window now and then during this epidemic, and seeing a Hotspur coming in especially high, I picked up the telephone, and had the ambulance closely following it as it charged the wooden fence above the railway cutting. Lodging in one of the stout steel supports, the glider stopped dead, except for its cockpit and

---

10    George Chatterton, *The Wings of Pegasus* (London: Macdonald, 1962), p. 28.
11    Lawrence Wright, *The Wooden Sword* (London: Elek Books Ltd, 1967), p. 59.

Stirling GT Mark IV 'W' of 196 Squadron RAF, towing an Airspeed Horsa glider for a training sortie.
(Crown Copyright – Air Historical Branch)

nose, which showered like confetti down the bank and on to the track. Rolling unhurt to the bottom, the pilot scrambled up, and emerged to meet the stretcher-bearers at the fence; the sight seemed to upset him, for he promptly passed out.[12]

In contrast, Wright also recorded an incident at the Exercise Unit which showed one of the sergeant glider pilot trainees throw aside conventional army discipline and confidently assume the authority of a captain of the aircraft, regardless of the seniority of his passengers.

> Taking a full load of army officers who had never been in a glider before, he had a General in the second pilot's seat. There was no wind, and the tug seemed unequal to its task; as the hedge approached, both tug and glider pilot were reaching for their cable releases. The General chose this moment to enquire casually
> –'Tell me, have you any means of communicating with the aeroplane if you are in trouble?'
> and got the stern reply
> –'Keep quiet, I **am** in trouble!'[13]

As the personnel for the Airborne force began to form up, the greatest challenge facing those creating the new capability was the paucity of aircraft, like the Whitley, to conduct either parachute or glider training. This was simply because in the early part of the war the RAF required these same aircraft to conduct bombing operations over Germany and could not afford to divert them to glider-tug or parachute training duties in any significant numbers. This meant that the airborne forces were not able to train the glider pilots or conduct the collective exercises that the parachute and glider-borne units required. Almost a year on from his first memo on airborne forces, a concerned Winston Churchill demanded a full display of the airborne capability and travelled up to Ringway on 26 April 1941 to observe it personally. Chatterton recalled that what the Prime Minister saw was not impressive:

---

12   Lawrence Wright, *The Wooden Sword*, pp. 66-7.
13   Lawrence Wright, *The Wooden Sword*, pp. 66-7.

It was not a very successful effort, for there was a very limited number of tug aircraft and parachute aircraft, and all that could be produced were a few Whitleys for the parachutists, about thirty in number, and nine Hectors towing nine Hotspur gliders, one of which I flew.

The parachutists dropped in a field, which did not impress Winston, owing to their small number, and the nine Hotspurs which were released at 10,000 feet came in to land in front of the gathered VIPs. The first glider overshot and nearly ran the Prime Minister down, two landed correctly, and then I followed the leader of the next three. The leader turned in to land, hit the top of the trees edging the field and took his wing off – I can still see the splinters as it cartwheeled in front of me. I landed with my heart in my mouth and only just stopped in time in front of the Prime Minister. It is the only time I have had a close up of this famous man. It is amazing to relate that no one was seriously injured that afternoon, and I understand that Winston was furious at the poverty of the numbers with which we had tried to impress him. I also believe that fireworks from Downing street gushed.[14]

Churchill's impatience would probably have been tested further by the accounts of the successful German invasion of Crete a month later, on 20 May 1941. This successful assault was spearheaded by 350 aircraft that dropped 10,000 paratroopers and also included a substantial glider force.[15] The events on Crete added further impetus to British plans, though ironically the German casualties amongst their airborne forces at Crete were so severe, that they rarely used them in their parachute or glider role for the remainder of the war (Leros being an obvious exception – though only at battalion level). Churchill's frustration is easy to understand, but the reality was that the British airborne forces would inevitably remain embryonic until the supply of heavy bomber and transport aircraft for them to train on had improved. For the airborne forces the period from 1940–43 is therefore characterised by modest efforts to train individuals and small groups, as well as the execution of several small-scale operations, such as the highly successful raid on Bruneval, northern France (27–28 February 1942). This operation, to capture a Wurzburg Radar and bring it back to the UK for technical evaluation, was carried out by Major John Frost's C Company of the 2nd Battalion, The Parachute Regiment, who were dropped from twelve Whitley bombers operating from RAF Thruxton. Though the Bruneval Raid was highly successful, others including a parachute assault to demolish an aqueduct near Monte Vulture, southern Italy (7 February 1941), as well as a glider borne assault to destroy the heavy-water plant at Vemork in Norway (19 November 1942), were costly failures. Both involved the loss of all assaulting troops to negligible effect.

Whether successful or not, these operations and raids still provided valuable experience. Moreover, the issue of how the airborne forces should develop began to become inextricably linked to the inevitable desire that sooner or later the Allies would have to open a second front with Germany. It was anticipated that this invasion would necessitate an amphibious assault landing against heavily defended beaches and in such circumstances the British believed it would be advantageous if airborne forces could be dropped behind the coastal fortifications, as part of a vertical-envelopment that would unhinge the German defences.[16] It was therefore on that basis that plans for establishing the 1st and 6th Airborne Divisions were drawn up.

This decision partly subordinated airborne operations to British amphibious operations and doctrine, which generally favoured a dawn assault on the coast to exploit surprise. The consequence of this was that the British airborne forces would need to be dropped during the preceding night, prior to the amphibious operation beginning and would have to secure their objectives during the

---

14   George Chatterton, *The Wings of Pegasus*, p. 28.
15   Stuart Tootal, *The Manner of Men*, p. 162.
16   Air Publication 3231, *Airborne Forces*, p.48.

hours of darkness. This contrasted with the German approach, which had employed their own airborne forces in daylight operations. The first two large-scale operations launched by the British, in Sicily and Normandy, both entailed night drops prior to amphibious landings, which placed a terrific demand not just on the airborne forces themselves, but also on those airmen transporting the gliders and paratroops to their landing and dropping zones in darkness.

By early 1942, the numbers of Horsas being produced was steadily increasing and greater numbers of tug aircraft also began to appear, mainly in the form of obsolete bombers such as Albemarles initially, and then Stirlings and Halifaxes subsequently. These tugs formed part of No. 38 Wing – a newly formed formation of three squadrons created on 15 January 1942 and dedicated to support airborne operations. It was co-located with the headquarters of 1st British Airborne Division to enable joint operations. The new Glider Pilot Regiment was also growing at their base in Shrewton, on Salisbury Plain, and the system of flying training was beginning to produce increasingly large numbers of glider pilots. For many of them their first encounter with a Horsa glider after having trained on the diminutive 1,661lb Hotspur left a lasting impression. For one thing the Horsa was significantly bigger, it was 7,500lbs when empty and weighed 15,500lbs fully loaded, effectively carrying almost its own weight in cargo. Its 88-foot wingspan was also much bigger than the diminutive Hotspur and meant they were sometimes larger than the converted bombers which towed them (eleven feet more than the Albemarle for instance).

The tug was attached to the glider by a Y-shaped tow-rope with two quick release points on the leading edge of the glider's wing. This helped keep the glider laterally straight, but towing a glider was not an easy task for the tug pilot who had to nurse his aircraft as it pulled the heavy glider. The easiest towing position for the tug pilot was one that kept the rope horizontal at the tug end; in the Horsa's case this meant the glider would fly about twenty feet above the tug, known as 'high-tow'. If the glider flew immediately behind the tug it would end up wallowing in the slip stream, putting strain on the rope and making the passengers sick, the constant surging would also tire out the tug pilot. A position below the slipstream known as 'low tow' was often used in poor visibility, or in cloud, because the glider pilot could see the rope more clearly. Tow speeds up to 160 mph were safe for the Horsa, though in practice these were unlikely to be reached.[17] Glider pilot Will Morrison describes the Horsa he encountered at No. 1 Heavy Glider Conversion Unit at RAF Brize Norton:

> The method of towing was by the yoke system whereby the tow rope was secured to a quick release point under each wing of the glider converging into a single tow line hooked into a secure point in the tail of the tug which like the glider had a quick release mechanism. The main object of the joint method for releasing was that once the glider had cast off the tug was able to drop its end of the rope before landing.
>
> When fully loaded, the gliders were capable of carrying 25 troops and their equipment, or alternatively, a 6-pounder anti-tank gun together with a jeep for towing plus ammunition. The Mark I Horsa was loaded through a side door on the port side just forward of the main spar. To enable heavy equipment to be loaded a system of ramps was used, and to unload in action the tail section was removed. The Mark II Horsa had the additional improvement of a hinged nose, and the tail section could be removed speedily by activating explosive bolts… To assist in landing the Horsas, they were fitted with huge flaps like barn doors which were operated by compressed air stored in bottles at 200 lbs per square inch. In addition, they were also equipped with air-controlled brakes on the main landing wheels which were very efficient. Some idea of the effective braking power of the flaps can be judged by the exercise we were taught in training whereby full flap was applied as the Horsa crossed over the perimeter fence

---

17   Lawrence Wright, *The Wooden Sword*, p. 69.

A jeep being unloaded from a Horsa glider. Photo dated 20 April 1944. (Crown Copyright – Air Historical Branch)

at 2,000 feet. One literally stood the glider on its nose, and pointed at the runway. The flaps stopped the speed building up, and the pilot just levelled out at the appropriate moment, and then made a normal landing.

The Horsa was a well-designed and strongly-built aircraft, but could be tiring to fly on long flights, especially if there was a degree of turbulence, and I have experienced this personally. But to be fair those were extreme conditions and during normal flights there was no problem, and we were well able to cope.[18]

George Chatterton describes a typical flight in a Horsa:

One afternoon I flew the first of the Horsa deliveries. It was an extraordinary experience. The procedure is for the tug and glider to move into position with the ground crew waiting by the glider. Silence is noticeable, as compared with the noise of the engines of the ordinary aircraft. The crew by the bomber signal her forward until the rope is taut along the runway, then the thumbs-up signal is given to the glider ground crew, who, in turn give it to the glider pilot in charge of the glider. He sits on the left, or port side of the glider cockpit. Interwound in the hemp rope is the intercommunication wire between the tug pilot and the glider pilot.

This intercom was the same as that used internally within the bomber, or tug, for the pilot to communicate with other members of the aircraft crew. In effect the glider crew become part of that intercommunication which allowed them to hear all that was going on including comments on course, wind speed or any new radio communications received. Once the tug pilot had satisfied

---

18    Will Morrison, *Horsa Squadron* (London: William Kimber, 1988), p. 38.

himself that the crew and glider were ready for take-off, he would gradually rev his engines. Chatterton continues:

> The tug moves slowly forward and the glider pilot holds the brakes on until the rope is fully taut, when, gradually, the glider moves forward behind the tug. It is a thrilling and strange sensation. The dust flies up from behind the tug and the speed increases – fifty miles, sixty miles, seventy-five miles an hour. The glider pilot eases back the control column, the nose wheel comes off the runway and into the air the glider jumps. The tug aircraft still rumbles along the runway and the glider at the end of the rope flies above it. The only sound is the rush of the slipstream – a clear roar of rushing air. The handling is rough, for there is no finesse in glider construction. Soon the tug leaves the ground, the runway drops below, and the whole combination is airborne. The ground below slowly recedes and both aircraft climb into the sky. It is a delightful sensation and one that can never be produced by other means.
>
> At 2,000 feet the tug levels out and flies on a course. At this height the glider pilot, who is above the tug, drops into the low-tow position below the tug. In lowering the glider he slides through the slipstream of the tug, and flies below the tug to keep the rope just above the cockpit. There are only two positions, high and low. The latter is used for bad weather flying, for by flying in the position of the 'V' of the rope, the glider can keep roughly in position. From above, it is almost impossible to keep position if in cloud or fog.
>
> At the end of the exercise the tug flies back to the airfield on receiving a radio signal from the ground that the glider may land. The glider pilot reaches forward and pulls the tow-rope release handle, the rope snapping away out of its sockets in the wings. There is a slight jolt, then a feeling of exaltation as the tug rushes away. The glider becomes incredibly smooth and a strange silence comes over the cockpit. On my first flight in a Horsa I felt that I never wanted to come down again, but just to drift up there for ever. The height indicator does not permit this; eyes must be kept on the airfield lest the glider get too far away and unable to get back to the runway.
>
> It was borne in on me, as I flew this great bird of wood and glue and bits of tin, that the training in flying a conventional aircraft was suited also to flying gliders. We never 'rumbled in' in powered aircraft, we always throttled back and ticked over into a glider landing. I found myself using the same technique for judging and assessing height as before.
>
> As the pilot turns into the final run he pulls the flap lever to half flap and with a great hiss from the air bottles, and from the wings, two flaps or air brakes come into position. The glider checks and the nose is pushed down. At the right moment the full flap is pulled on and the glider takes on an ever steeper angle. The ground rushes up, the control column is eased back and the glider lands safely and gently and runs forward only a few yards in doing so.[19]

A military glider's performance bears little resemblance to that of a civilian sports glider, which by catching thermals and wind currents can remain aloft for many hours. In contrast, a military glider will begin its descent as soon as it casts off from its tug, this makes sense as its role is simply to deliver troops and equipment to a specific Landing Zone (LZ) in a controlled manner.[20] In free flight the best glide speed was about 80 mph when loaded, with a flight path descending at the rate of 1 in 13. The Horsa was perfectly designed for tactical landings in confined spaces and could descend at the rate of 1 in 1.5, a fantastically steep rate, yet its huge flaps limited its speed to just

---

19   George Chatterton, *The Wings of Pegasus*, pp.34-5.
20   Landing Zones (LZs) are areas designated for glider landings in Airborne operations. Dropping Zones (DZs) are those identified for paratroops.

100 mph during this manoeuvre. This design meant that when the pilot was landing the glider, he would simply make one final turn into wind, point the nose at the required touch-down spot, dive down, round out, land on the undercarriage just above stalling incidence, rock on to the front wheel and apply the air brakes. For massed landings on crowded LZs the gliders might use higher speeds, which meant longer runs and enabled the first gliders to reach their appointed places at the top of the LZ, leaving the landing area behind them clear for subsequent ones. The glider wheel's air brakes were often useful in steering the aircraft on the ground and avoiding obstacles, including the other gliders that had already landed.[21]

From 1942, the increased levels of training for the airborne forces meant that the techniques of massed glider and parachute operations could begin to be improved. It was found that it was comparatively easy to arrange paratroop drops and not difficult to keep the parachutists at a reasonable level of proficiency. Indeed, large paratroop exercises were now becoming routine. The new Airborne Division was also increasingly adept at joint-planning with 38 Wing staff, including selecting the drop zones, air routes and timings to support the Army's tactical aims. During exercises the paratroop aircraft were usually given an individual time to drop their troops over the DZ, this was usually 30 seconds apart, with separation at altitudes varying from between 450 feet to 800 feet. In daylight this meant flying in line-astern but at night each aircraft had to fly individually. The requirement for aircraft to fly to precise airspeeds so that they all arrived over the DZ at the specific time required very high standards of both navigation and airmanship.[22] Proficiency in paratroop dropping by 38 Wing steadily increased and mis-drops were becoming less frequent, but whether that standard could be maintained in operational circumstances over unfamiliar countryside was still uncertain.

In contrast to parachute aircraft, the gliders were usually released from their tugs at the higher altitude of between 1,000 to 2,500 feet. The question of deciding the exact spot at which to release was a delicate one, typically a point was selected prior to take-off based on forecasted wind speed and direction. As that point was approached, the navigator of the tug would inform the glider pilot of the actual wind speed and direction who would then cast off from the tug at what he felt was the right moment. The flight to the objective took careful management when there were numerous gliders in the sky. 'Vic' formations or line astern were typically flown, but the slipstreams created by numerous aircraft could result in the rearmost aircraft being in a constant battle with the air pockets and eddies caused by the tug and glider combinations in front. The practise of 'stepping-up' was therefore usually adopted, a remedy which meant a difference in height between the first and last combinations of as much as 500 feet.

A method for speeding up the launching of large numbers of gliders into the air was also developed. The previous practise had been to fly-off gliders and tug combinations almost individually and it took valuable minutes for the tug aircraft to taxi on to the runway, the glider to then be towed on by a tractor and the tow rope connected at both ends before launching. This process could take considerable time if the exercise or operation was large, perhaps involving thirty or more gliders and tugs. During this time the first glider-tug combinations that had taken off would all have to orbit above the airfield, waiting for the last aircraft to join the formation. To improve this method, all the gliders were marshalled on to the runway before take-off and parked in a staggered line two abreast. The tugs were then fed onto the runway from alternate sides and the combinations would take off on both the left and right-hand sides of the runway. This speeded up the process, whilst reducing the effect of slipstreams. The only disadvantage of this system was that the available take-off run for the lead aircraft was reduced by as much as 300 yards (plus the

---

21   George Chatterton, *The Wings of Pegasus*, p. 69.
22   Air Publication 3231, *Airborne Forces*, p. 80.

Aircraft assembled at Tarrant Rushton, Hampshire. On the runway are General Aircraft Hamilcar heavy-lift gliders, preceded by two Airspeed Horsa troop-carrying gliders, while parked on each side of them are Handley Page Halifax glider-tugs of 298 and 644 Squadrons. These aircraft were used to reinforce the 6th Airborne Division perimeter on the afternoon of 6 June 1944. The manner in which the aircraft are laid out aids the speedy dispatch of the formation – but also takes up several hundred yards of available runway.
(Crown Copyright – Air Historical Branch)

length of the tow rope itself – another 100 yards). This became less of a problem as more powerful aircraft, such as the Stirling, were brought into service, but it was still difficult for aircraft like the Albemarle. The final difficulty the new system presented was one of wind direction, this was because the increasingly modern aerodromes had three concrete runways, which allowed take-offs in six different directions. As one of the three runways was always much longer than the other two, most pilots preferred to use this one, so long as any cross-wind did not exceed 12–15 mph. The new system of marshalling meant an assessment of wind direction and the decision on which runway was to be used, had to be made much earlier. Any substantial change required a complete re-marshalling, which was inevitably a frustrating and time-consuming business.[23]

There were also several innovations in marking LZs and DZs. Many of these were made by Major John Lander, a glider pilot, parachutist and the first commander of the Independent Parachute Company. Lander's unit consisted of 'Pathfinders' who would land by parachute shortly before the main drop, deal with any local opposition they encountered and most importantly mark the DZ/LZ with Holophane lights and radio beacons including the Rebecca-Eureka radio beacon. Major Lander was clearly an imaginative man who also developed and pioneered the use of kit bundles, which paratroopers could lower on a 20-foot piece of rope as they made their descent. These bundles meant that items of equipment up to 60lbs in weight could be carried, they even made the parachutists landing gentler – as the parachute canopy noticeably slowed, once the bundle hit the ground. Kit bundles remain in use across airborne forces around the world to this day.[24] The following chapters will cover how this new airborne weapon of war was employed and further developed in operations in North Africa, Sicily and North-West Europe.

23   Air Publication 3231, *Airborne Forces*, pp. 81-2.
24   Lawrence Wright, *The Wooden Sword*, p. 96.

# 12

# 'Prepared for all Things'[1]
# Early Airborne Operations

The 1st Parachute Brigade was the first airborne formation to operate overseas when it was deployed to Tunisia in late 1942. The Brigade had been added to the British order of battle at the last-minute after key exponents of British airborne forces had pressed for its inclusion, even though this meant the formation would have to operate without much of their enabling staff or administration and accept a great deal of improvisation. The Tunisian campaign coincided with the increasing contribution of the United States to the war, including the provision of the Dakota transport aircraft which became the workhorse of both the American and British airborne forces. Although the Dakota often operated as a tug for gliders, it was more commonly used as a paratroop aircraft where it was able to drop twenty men from a side door on its port side. It was these American Dakota[2] aircraft of the United States Army Air Force's 51st Transport Wing, rather than 38 Wing RAF, that were used in the first large-scale drop of British airborne forces on 16 November 1942. During this operation the 1st Parachute Battalion flew in 35 American Dakotas from Maison Blanche airfield in Algeria, to Souk-el-Arba in Tunisia. They were then dropped in daylight and joined up with nearby French forces at Beja, to hold the cross-roads until the First British Army linked-up with them. That operation was a success, but a similar subsequent one to raid the airfield at Oudna in Tunisia involving 2nd Parachute Battalion on 3 December, was less so. This was probably because the operation was put together very hastily, the intelligence underestimated the German response and there was no representation of airborne planners at First British Army Headquarters. This meant that when the First British Army's advance, which was to have brought relief to 2nd Parachute Battalion, was cancelled, the paratroopers were forced to execute a long and painful withdrawal back to British lines harried by German air and ground attacks along the way.[3]

This was the last airborne operation conducted by British forces in North Africa, though they continued to fight as normal infantry till the campaign's conclusion in April 1943. The Army felt that in Tunisia, airborne forces had proved both their utility and potential – all they needed now was an adequate and efficient air component with which to properly exploit it at the next opportunity. The Allies' plans to invade the island of Sicily (Operation HUSKY) appeared to offer just such an opportunity and the chance to employ the entirety of the 1st Airborne Division, including the glider borne troops of the 1st Air Landing Brigade. In common with British amphibious

---

1   Motto of 296 Squadron RAF. This squadron was initially equipped with Whitleys before converting to Albemarles in January 1943. They were flown to Algeria in June to take part in the airborne landings at Sicily before returning to the UK in October of that year and converting to Halifaxes. Subsequent operations with 38 Group included D-Day, Arnhem and the crossing of the Rhine.

2   Dakota, the name adopted for the type by the Commonwealth air forces, will be used for consistency even for American aircraft, rather than their designation – C-47 Skytrain.

3   Air Publication 3231, *Airborne Forces*, pp. 61-2.

doctrine, the beach-assault was to be undertaken at dawn, which meant that the airborne forces would need to secure their objectives prior to the assault and hence a night drop was necessary.

Operation HUSKY was scheduled for a favourable moon period in early July 1943 and incorporated both the US 82nd Airborne and British 1st Airborne Divisions. The Americans would drop to the west of the British on the night of 9/10 July and cover the landings of the American Fifth Army. The British plan would involve three successive and sequential operations to support the British Eighth Army on the south-east of the island. The first operation was on the Ponte Grande bridge south of Syracuse and was undertaken by the glider-borne troops of 1st Airlanding Brigade. The second involved the capture of the bridge and high ground west of Augusta and utilised the 2nd Parachute Brigade. The final objective of taking the Primasole bridge over the river Simeto was to be undertaken by 1st Parachute Brigade. A fourth formation, 4th Parachute Brigade, was kept in reserve.

The British paratroops would be dropped by American Dakotas, this time from both 51st and 52nd Troop Carrier Wing, Troop Carrier Command, part of the new Allied North West African Air Force. Deploying 1st Airlanding Brigade was more of a challenge, primarily because no British Horsas were immediately available in North Africa. It was solved in two ways, firstly by using American Waco CG-4 gliders, sometimes referred to as Hadrians by the British. However, the Waco was much lighter than a Horsa and could only carry 3,700lbs, the equivalent of 14 men and a small handcart. Additionally, a Waco could not be towed any faster than 150 mph or their flimsy tails might fall off. That minimum speed was easy for the Dakotas, but perilously close to the stalling speeds of 38 Wing's Albemarles and Halifaxes which had been flown out to Tunisia to act as tugs for HUSKY. It had initially been judged impossible to deploy Horsas to North Africa because they were too bulky and fragile to be shipped by sea and a 1,300-mile tow seemed an impossibly long distance. No. 38 Wing challenged that last assumption and used a Halifax to successfully complete a 1,500-mile trial endurance tow of a Horsa around the UK. Planning therefore commenced to send 36 Horsa-Halifax combinations from Portreath, Cornwall to Sale, Morrocco by the end of June (in what was known as Operation BEGGAR). There would then be a further 1,000-mile trip from Sale to Kairouan, in Tunisia, from where the airborne assault would be launched.

In the end only 30 Horsas were despatched from the UK and only 19 of these Horsas successfully completed the trip to Tunisia. The balance crashed into the sea, or various parts of North Africa. Nonetheless the surviving Horsa's contribution would be critical, for only they were able to bring into battle heavy equipment, such as 6-pounder anti-tank guns and their accompanying jeeps. Wacos could do either one or the other, but not both together, an obvious operational limitation. These anti-tank guns were a vital element in the airborne troop's ability to defend the captured bridges. A second Horsa ferry operation was undertaken in August (Operation ELABORATE) involving 23 Horsa and tug combinations, of which only 15 reached North Africa, though these arrived too late to play any role in the fighting in Sicily.

Operation LADBROKE was the codename for the initial operation by 1st Airlanding Brigade on Sicily and took place on the night of 9/10 July, it was the first massed glider operation by the Allies and remains controversial to this day. The British intended to fly 137 gliders to Sicily, 127 of these were Wacos which would land just beyond the beach and deposit two air-landing battalions (1st Borders and 2nd South Staffordshires) to subdue local opposition. The remaining 10 gliders were Horsas and would be used around the Ponte Grande bridge in a coup-de-main style operation.[4] There were many concerns about the operation prior to its launch, including the skill of the glider pilots themselves, many of whom had received little training in recent months. This

---

4   George Chatterton, *Wings of Pegasus*, pp. 68-70.

Planning and preparations January– July 1943, a jeep is loaded onto an American Waco CG-4A glider in Tunisia. (Crown Copyright – Air Historical Branch)

was tackled in two ways. First, a group of 60 glider crews were sent to North Africa in April to receive concentrated training on Wacos. On arrival in Tunisia they found the gliders had not yet arrived from the United States and when they did, three weeks later, they were found to be unassembled and in crates. With no-one else available the resourceful glider pilots constructed their own aircraft based on the instructions found in each crate. These delays reduced the time available for training, particularly for exercises at night or in similar conditions to those expected to be encountered during HUSKY. A second group of fifty glider crews had been held back in the UK for concentrated training with 38 Wing, before subsequently travelling by ship to arrive in North Africa just before the invasion. A message had been sent back from North Africa to ensure that the training these glider pilots received was concentrated on Waco and Horsa night landings in moonlit conditions. For whatever reason the message did not get through, no relevant operational training was undertaken and many of these crews could therefore not be used as first pilots.

The skill of the American Dakota crews in conducting airborne operations was also to prove deficient. Their training was hampered by the continual demands on them to conduct routine freight and transport duties in North Africa. When the American crews were released from these duties to train and prepare for the invasion, the airborne planners were told that there was concern over the wear on their aircraft's engines and limitations were therefore imposed on the number of flying hours they could devote to airborne exercises.[5]

A final problem was that the outline planning of the airborne operation had been conducted in Algiers and Egypt, far away from the airborne experts and consequently the sites selected for the

5    TNA CAB 106/687, 1 Airborne Division Report on Operation 'HUSKY', Part 1, 1943, p. 2.

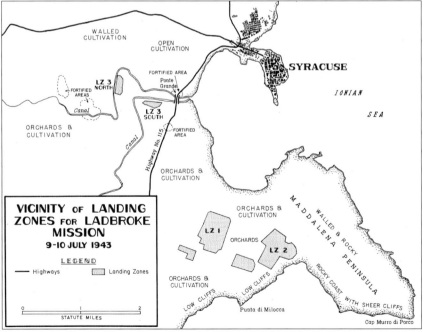

Figure 4a and 4b  Air Photograph and Map of area of glider landings during Operation LADBROKE (TNA, CAB 106/688, *1st Airborne Division Report on Operation 'HUSKY', Part 2*, 1943)

airborne landings were generally unsuitable. Lawrence Wright was one of the few RAF officers from 38 Wing involved in the operation, he was shocked when the plan was briefed to him:

> That gliders could be used in this way was contrary to all we had learned to date, and to the lessons of Crete, especially with glider pilots trained to the present low standard. About 500 of them had completed the Horsa course, but some with so few hours flying that Chatterton had to divide them into first and second pilots, none of the latter being fully experienced even by day. About 50 such crews were resuming their training in Algeria, and about 60 more were to follow, but in the past six months at home they had averaged only about 8 hours in Horsas.
>
> None had done night landings, none had flown Hadrians [Wacos], but within six weeks they must fly these some 300 miles, mostly over water, by night and land by moonlight on a defended coast. The air plan based on this army requirement, when revealed later, seemed unsound in every detail. There was no obvious rendezvous point at which to fix position before the run-in to release, such as we had long thought essential. This run-in would be down moon, the worst direction for map reading. Because the unarmed and unarmoured Dakotas must not fly over the defences, the release point must be out to sea, and could be judged only by its apparent distance from a dark and unfamiliar shore. There were to be no radio aids or lights on the landing zones; the independents would not precede the force, for fear of alerting the defences.
>
> We studied the photographs. They had been taken from a great height, with short midday shadows, and there were no really good stereo pairs of the LZs. On comparing the terrain at Syracuse allotted to gliders, with that at Augusta and Catania allotted to paratroops, I thought at first that the photographs might have been transposed by mistake. Catania was quite good glider country; Augusta very doubtful; but the chosen (and best available) area near Syracuse was appalling; a neck of land bordered by sea cliffs, rocky slopes and dense orchards; the fields were very small and separated by stone walls.[6]

It seems as if the HUSKY planning had been badly handicapped by not involving the necessary airmen early on, this was a mistake as these were the only individuals who understood the capabilities of the gliders and the way they could be landed at night. There also seems to have been a strong desire amongst some of the army commanders to employ the airborne forces and demonstrate their utility, regardless of the risk. Army experts, including Chatterton, raised concerns too as Lawrence Wright relates:

> Chatterton implied much the same. I found him upstairs…working out release heights, afraid to allow much excess in case the gliders overshot right across the peninsula, inclined to rely on the American assurances that their tug pilots could order off the gliders at the right spot for a straight glide in, landing to a set drill. He confided that Hoppy [Maj Gen Hopkinson, Commander of 1st Airborne Division], having shown him the plan and sensed his immediate doubts, had given him half an hour in which to choose between accepting it as it stood, or resigning his command.[7]

A total of 135 Waco gliders and eight Horsa gliders were to be used in this first major operation. The majority of Wacos were towed by the 108 American Dakotas, the remainder, as well as the Horsas were towed by Albemarles and Halifaxes of 38 Wing.

---

6    Lawrence Wright, *The Wooden Sword*, pp. 127-8
7    Lawrence Wright, *The Wooden Sword*, pp. 127-8.

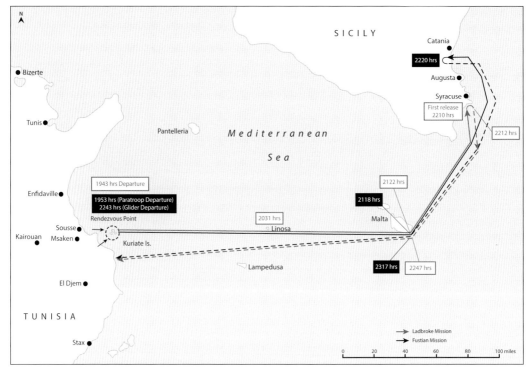

Figure 5  Air Routes to Sicily.

The aircraft would take off from six separate airfields around Kairouan in Tunisia, the first departing at 1850. They would then RV over Kurlate island before heading east to Malta, where searchlights had been lit to mark the island. A new north-easterly course and another 89 minutes of flying would take the combinations to within 3,000 yards of the coast, when the tugs would turn parallel to shore, keeping 3,000 yards off it and heading towards Cape Murro di Porco. The tugs required the gliders to release 3,000 yards out because of the enemy radar-directed anti-aircraft fire, which could potentially cause significant damage to the vulnerable Dakotas. The gliders would therefore cast-off approximately 2.5 miles from the Cape, turn, fly the remaining 3,000 yards to the coast and land at their allotted LZs at various times around 2230 hours. The approach flight was made even harder by the requirement to fly at 100 feet across the sea to avoid radar detection, only climbing to 1,500 feet when nearing the Sicilian coast.

Throughout the afternoon of 9 July, it became apparent that the winds were strengthening from the North-West which was to have a dramatic effect on the operation. For when the inexperienced American Dakota pilots approached the Sicilian coast and encountered searchlights and anti-aircraft fire for the first time, some of the pilots panicked and demanded the gliders cast off, even though some were still too far out to reach land. Some intercom links had also been broken on the long voyage, which meant that in some cases the tug released the glider with no warning – an action that was strictly against accepted practice. Staff Sergeant Mills, who piloted No. 31 glider, recounts the dramatic night:

> The North African coastline drew nearer, and in a few moments the blue ocean, turning to grey, seemed to stretch endlessly before us. I glanced at my watch and saw it was 7:15 p.m. What an impressive sight it was as the other formations converged on us, forming a gigantic armada. I felt proud to be taking part in this great invasion. A flight of Mustangs wheeled above in the sunshine to give us a feeling of security.

An Airspeed Horsa I glider waits to be towed off from the runway at Goubrine II, Tunisia, during the 1st Airborne Division landings in Sicily in July 1943. (Crown Copyright – Air Historical Branch)

Below us we observed odd ships here and there, their bows cutting large white vees in the water. I noticed that the crests of the waves were getting more pronounced, pointing to a strengthening of the wind. The sun sank rather quickly towards the sea as I handed over control to my co-pilot, and I looked round at my passengers. They seemed cheerful enough munching barley sugar, but rather quiet, I thought. I glanced at the waves again. Yes, the crests were much larger. The wind must be getting very strong, almost up to gale force. The aircraft began to toss, but Dennis showed her that he was the master. I hoped that our navigator would make allowances for drift. Just in case I had better warn him. I raised my 'mike' but to my dismay it was completely 'dead'. The nylon rope had probably stretched, snapping the intercom cable which was carried along its length. All we could do now was hope.

'I have control' I shouted, and Dennis settled back for a well-earned rest. Darkness had fallen swiftly, so that I had to line up on small pin-points of blue light arranged along the wings of the Dakota. I could still pick out the dim outline of the tug, and at intervals could see short flashes from the glowing exhausts. Then, just ahead, half a dozen powerful search-lights stabbed the night sky. Malta! We were dead on course. We approached the island low, and in the strange artificial half-light I could see the preceding combinations banking into the turn to bring them on course for Sicily.

I began my turn, and the light became steadily weaker as we left Malta behind. It was dark again, and the glider began to buck in the turbulent air. I hoped that no one would be sick, as we wanted to be in fit condition to do battle on landing. Over three hours had passed since we had left the dusty air-strip at El Djem, and I quickly calculated that we should be there in less than half an hour. Damn that intercom.

Then, without warning, the sky became alive with searchlight beams, and streams of white-hot tracer began to form strangely fascinating criss-cross patterns on the dark back-cloth of the Sicilian sky. I quickly ordered Dennis and the troops to get on their equipment in readiness for the landing, so that we could be out as soon as we touched down. I was in my gear already, having seen to that earlier while Dennis had been at the controls.

Then – tragedy! My towing rope had run into trouble and to my horror, it came tearing back towards us with its connecting tackle striking the top of the cabin with a tremendous report, but luckily not breaking the Perspex. For a moment I was stunned, and then as I pulled the cable release I quickly sized up the situation. I judged that we were roughly two miles from the dark smudge that I knew to be Sicily, so now I had to carry out an action I dreaded – ditching! And I was unable to swim!

As I gave the order to remove all equipment, remove the side exits and secure safety harness, I perceived a lone searchlight. It was particularly noticeable as it was immensely powerful and had an unusual blue beam. I turned away from it and saw that in the strong off-shore wind we were losing height rapidly. I remembered a training lecture we had back home, when we were told that if we ever had to ditch in a rough sea, the safest way was to land along the troughs and not in the wind which is the normal method. This instructor, whose name I can't recollect, probably saved the lives of us all. I sincerely thank him.

The angry sea reached up towards us, the white crests acting as a flare path. We approached closer. I held off as long as possible and, as we touched, it seemed as if a giant hand held us and tried to drag us under. I pitched forward, nearly breaking my safety harness. The sea surged in and in seconds was up to my waist. I released myself and picking up a loose object – a rifle, I think – I battered the cabin roof out. By now only my head was showing, as I somehow dragged myself clear. Next minute I was sitting on the wing, watching the cabin disappear below the waves. Only the mainplanes now showed above the water. I wondered how long they would remain like that; if they sank below the surface all we had to support us were our small, now inflated lifebelts. A quick count told me that so far, all had survived the ditching – Dennis having escaped with me and the other six through the side doors. One chap had banged his head on the way out, but fortunately this was the only casualty.

We were all alone, I judged at least a mile from shore. The sea was rough, tossing us up and down like a cork. When I look back I wonder how we managed to stay on that wing, which is not an ideal shape for sailing. We linked arms lest one of us slipped over the side. Our legs were in the water, surprisingly quite warm, while the rest of our bodies froze in the strong wind. I was fascinated by small points of light floating by on the surface of the water, later being told that this was caused by Phosphorous.

I cursed my luck. To think that out of more than a hundred and thirty gliders, I would be the only one to come a cropper in the sea. Then the powerful blue searchlight I had seen earlier changed the direction of the beam to the horizontal and began methodically to sweep the sea, to the accompaniment of glowing streams of tracer from shore-based machine guns. There must be something else to shoot at besides us, I thought.[8]

Staff Sergeant Mills and his glider load were picked up at 0330 by the *Ulster Monarch*. As dawn broke Mills went on deck to find 'to my surprise there were several gliders still floating in the bay. I hadn't been the only one after all.' Far from it, of the 143 gliders loaded in North Africa, a total of 122 arrived near Sicily, of which half were released outside the stipulated distance of 3,000 yards offshore. Only fifty-four gliders managed to reach shore against the prevailing wind (and these were scattered over 25 miles) and a total of 68 gliders had ditched in the sea. Only 16 gliders could be described as having landed close to, or near their LZs and only 13 of these without serious damage to the crew and passengers. At least a dozen gliders hit stone walls in the small

---

8   George Chatterton, *The Wings of Pegasus* (London: Macdonald, 1962), pp. 77-9.

British airborne troops wait to board an American WACO CG4A glider.
(Crown Copyright – Air Historical Branch)

and constricted fields, this crash usually broke the pilot's legs and injured the passengers.[9] Staff Sergeants 'Taff' Evans and 'Dick' Martin were in glider 88 and recalled their journey and landing:

> The tug-glider combinations were flying echelon starboard – four combinations to each echelon – and we were the end combination of our echelon. The flight to Sicily, skirting Malta was at 50–200 feet, which was rather difficult owing to the gale but which Dick and I managed well whilst the daylight lasted. It became very difficult when darkness fell and we were 'formating' on the three small lights on the tug's wings and tail. There were times when we lost sight of these in the squalls brought by the gale. As we approached Sicily, the formation rose to its operational height of 1,900 feet, thereby coming within radar range of the defence radar. This resulted in anti-aircraft gunfire. We flew steadily on for a short while until, suddenly, to our amazement and consternation, our tug aircraft turned fairly steeply to starboard and flew through the formation, weaving to port and starboard for several minutes. I had impressions of other aircraft flashing past us in the blackness and not very far away either! Dick and I were hard pressed to follow and the five or so minutes flying through the formation seemed more like five or so hours! It was an absolute miracle that the tow rope didn't snap.[10]

As his glider slowly approached the Sicilian coast and began to climb to altitude, Evans tried to calculate when would be the best time to release. At the back of his mind no doubt was the cargo he carried; a handcart of volatile PIAT anti-tank bombs, as well as members of the Border Regiment.

> I recognised that we were now approaching our target area and released the glider. We were at 1,900 feet (approx) but still over the sea, when two searchlights from the peninsula came

9    Lawrence Wright, *The Wooden Sword*, pp. 158-9.
10   K Evans, *The Eagle Magazine,* The Regimental Magazine of the Glider Pilot Regiment.

on and immediately picked us up. We were sitting ducks at that height and the light ack-ack guns fired a lot of shells at us. The balls of fire were whipping past the cockpit and I could see them going through the wings. I flung the WACO about as much as I dared; bearing in mind the load we were carrying. So dive, stall turn, dive again, steep turn etc, until I managed to shake off the searchlights. When we were free, Dick and I could see properly and we were still over the sea. However, I headed for where the land was and suddenly there was a great flash, a tremendous crash, pain and oblivion… Afterwards we discovered we had just skimmed the cliff top, passing through a high-tension electrical cable and smashing through a big stone wall. Three or four of the Border men had been injured and Sergeant Cherry put them in the shelter of part of the starboard wing. Dick had a 'greenstick' fracture of the left thigh bone, whilst my left foot was broken in half and I had injuries to my chest and throat where I had gone through the front of the glider. Dick and I were put in the port side of the wreckage. When the injured were settled, Sergeant Cherry took his half dozen fit men to try and link up with the main force of the 1st Airlanding Brigade, but after an hour or so they returned as they could not find anybody.[11]

The net result of two months intensive effort involving 150 aircrews, 150 glider pilots and 2,000 airborne troops was the delivery of just 78 personnel to Ponte Grande bridge and some isolated actions by scattered units. The small band of glider troops at the bridge held onto it until the afternoon, when casualties had reduced their ranks to just 18 survivors and their ammunition ran out. Although the Italians then captured the bridge it was very quickly re-taken by the British seaborne force before the Italians could demolish it. The total airborne casualties (killed, wounded and captured) during this first operation were 600 of which 250 were members of 1st Air Landing Brigade who had drowned in the sea.[12]

It was subsequently discovered in the post operational review that most of the gliders that had failed to reach land had not been released within gliding distance. In some cases, they had been ordered to release by the tug, in other instances the tug pilots had released the gliders themselves. This unilateral action was only carried out by the American Dakota pilots, probably as the protocol in 38 Wing was that the cable was never cast off by the tug except in dire emergencies. This practise seems to have been observed by the RAF pilots during the operation. The glider pilot's difficulties were sometimes made more challenging by the tug pilots taking evasive action, as well as switching off their subdued formation lights – without which the glider pilot struggled to keep station.

The second operation planned by the Airborne Division in Sicily, the drop of 2nd Parachute Brigade around the Augusta area, never took place as the advancing Eighth Army's swift capture of the objective made the operation redundant. The third operation, (Operation FUSTIAN) by 1st Parachute Brigade, involved a parachute drop onto four separate DZs on the night of 12/13 July. A total of 116 Parachute aircraft were involved of which eleven were British Albemarles and the remainder American-crewed Dakotas, including many of the crews who had taken part in Operation LADBROKE. There were also 19 gliders taking part, 11 Horsas and eight Wacos, which would be towed by Halifax and Albermale aircraft and use two LZs, both of which were sited near the objective of the Primosole Bridge.

The aircraft followed a similar route to that of the gliders on the previous operation. Heading across the Mediterranean from Tunisia, transiting over Malta before heading north east, to follow the eastern Sicilian coastline and make a landfall at the mouth of the River Simeto. There were

11   K Evans, *The Eagle Magazine*, The Regimental Magazine of the Glider Pilot Regiment.
12   Lawrence Wright, *The Wooden Sword*, p. 157.

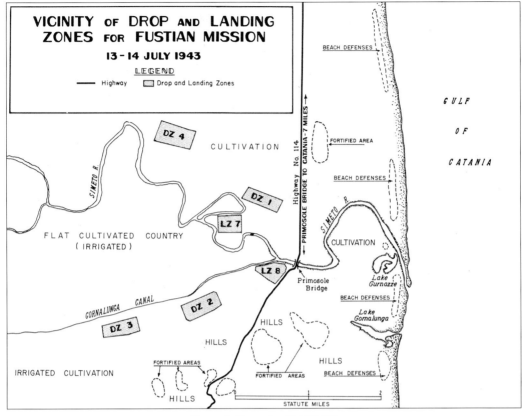

Figure 6 Operation FUSTIAN.

then three separate routes taken by the aircraft which depended on which DZ/LZ was being used. After they had dropped their paratroopers the aircraft would reverse course and fly a more southerly and easterly return leg back to North Africa.[13] The route deliberately kept the aircraft ten miles out to sea, so that they avoided over-flying the Allied invasion fleet who were notoriously wary of any aircraft and highly likely to open fire. This had been the experience of the 82nd US Airborne Division during their operation on the 9/10 July when 23 Dakotas had been reportedly shot down by the fleet. The Allied air planners were anxious to avoid a repeat of such a calamity.[14]

Lance Corporal Albert Osborne was a member of 1st Parachute Battalion's Anti-Tank Platoon and wrote to his brother about the parachute drop and action at Primosole bridge. His experience highlights that operational parachute jumping rarely goes as well as the peacetime practices.

> The morning of the job we got ready, every man fit and keen, we made up little bundles of our personal belongings and attached a little note – If I fail to return, please forward this to my mother, these were left behind in our kit bags. Time came when we had to part camp for the airfield, men that couldn't go, owing to being wounded in other actions, wished us luck.
> We got to the air-field where we met our crew, and we got the dope from the pilot just what he was going to do on the final run-in. Then we got the last boost up by our commander

---

13  TNA CAB 106/689, 1st Airborne Division Report on Operation 'HUSKY', Part 3, 1943, pp. 1-4.

14  Lawrence Wright, *The Wooden Sword*, p. 159.

('Men you know your jobs and just what you are expected to do, at all costs it will be done. Don't let anything get in your way, whatever you encounter you know just how to deal with it. The enemy have seen you in N. Africa, he knows you, he don't like you, and will do all he can to stop you, but he will not. That is all gentlemen. Good luck, God's speed and a safe return').

It was 8.00pm. and at 8.30pm. we were due to start, and scheduled to arrive in Sicily, behind enemy lines, at 10.30pm. so we all assembled and wished each other luck. The 8th Army was to relieve us after 12 hours, although we weren't worrying about that part, because we could depend on the 8th Army. Take off – we smoked and talked a lot, and after a time flying, we saw Malta, 'Not far to go lads, hook up, 40 minutes to go'.

Just as we were to approach the coast of Sicily, we got keyed up for a hot reception from enemy flak. We got it O.K. more than we expected, flashes came from all over the place, it was terrifying.

During this time our aircraft was hit, the port side engine, it choked up and stopped. From then on the aircraft was bumping, swaying, diving and climbing to dodge the flak. We were tossed from one side of the plane to the other, we knew that any second it would be time for us to jump, so we scrambled to the door the best way we could, and to look down at that sight was no joke. Then on came the Red light ('Action Station') in a second on came the Green light ('Go') and out we went. It was just like jumping into an inferno, the country side for miles was ablaze, tracer bullets were coming up at us from enemy machine guns on the ground.

Floating down by parachute, thinking any time I would be dead before I touched down it seemed weeks before I hit the deck, actually it was only a matter of seconds. It does not take long to get down from a 300 ft drop, but it was terrifying. Then I gave a sigh, a sign of relief when I hit the deck, it took me several seconds to pull myself together as I had a rough landing. I said something to myself, you can guess what it was, then I went to find my detachment, two men.

I wasn't sure of my position, but I went forward about 200 yds, took a look round but couldn't see anything, but could hear enemy voices. I didn't fancy that at all, as I had no weapons, just two hand grenades and a fighting knife, but I scrambled through the bush under cover of darkness to my original position and tried another way. Then I saw a parachute hanging over the telegraph wires, I stopped and a quivering uncertain voice came from a bush ('Who's that?'). I gave the pass word, it was one of my men, and he had a hand grenade ready to throw it at me, if I had been one of the enemy, because he was as scared as I was.

We had another look round, and we still could hear enemy voices, even more nearer and more of them, then I looked for some nice cover and said, 'Let's go', it's dangerous hanging around near parachutes, so we went to find the last man, he wasn't far away, but slightly hurt from a bad landing, although it wasn't much. We still had to get to our containers, for our weapons, because until we got our weapons, we couldn't defend ourselves. We found the container, what a sight! my heart went down in my boots as the parachute of the container failed to open and [it had] crashed to the ground, the weapons were absolutely unserviceable.

All this time we could still hear enemy voices quite near and bullets were flying all over the place, you can guess what we felt like. From the time we jumped from the plane all this happened in 15 minutes. We then made for the objective, a bridge about 1000 yds away, and on our way we came across a reserve supply of weapons, so we soon armed ourselves with one Bren gun and two rifles.[15]

---

15   Extracts of Albert Osborne's letter were included in a local newspaper article shortly after and are available at <www.pegasusarchive.org>. Corporal Albert Osborne, aged 23, was killed in action on the 21st September 1944, during the Battle of Arnhem. He is buried at the Airborne Cemetery at Oosterbeek.

Armstrong Whitworth Albemarle Mark Is of 296 Squadron RAF, lined up at Goubrine II, Tunisia, while taking part in the airborne landings on Sicily. Photograph taken from under the wing of a Waco CG-4A glider. (Crown Copyright – Air Historical Branch)

A sergeant major glider pilot of the Army Air Corps and a glider tug pilot of 296 Squadron RAF studying a map of Sicily at Goubrine II, Tunisia, in preparation for the 1st Airborne Division landings in Sicily. (Crown Copyright – Air Historical Branch)

Staff Sergeant Protheroe was flying one of the eleven Horsa gliders in the operation and was to land very close to Primosole Bridge. Protheroe was becoming quite an experienced glider-pilot at this stage having flown his Horsa from Cornwall to Morrocco, during Operation BEGGAR. His Halifax tug pilot, Flight Lieutenant Grant, was also experienced having towed a glider to the Ponte Grande bridge during Operation LADBROKE, three nights earlier. Protheroe describes the operation:

> The day came when we were briefed for the operation on the Primosole bridge. We were to carry an anti-tank gun team (this consisted of an anti-tank gun, a Jeep, and gun team with two other members of the battery) and we were to land in a field south-west of the bridge and adjacent to it. There were a number of WACO gliders taking part in the operation, and their landing zone was further west of the bridge and on the north side of the River Simeto. During the briefing I met our tug pilot Flight Lieutenant Grant who was flying a Halifax. I recognised him from the days when he gave me instruction in Hotspurs. At the briefing we were told we would approach the landing zone at about 2,000 feet from the coast south of the Simeto river....
>
> As time went on you could see the outline of land on the port side of the glider in the moonlight. In the distance we could see the lights of a town which was obviously Catania. A strange sight bearing in mind that an invasion had taken place not many miles to the south. We turned inland and soon tracers could be seen, some between us and the tug. We could hear what sounded like small arms rattling on the gun or the Jeep. There was no sign of a landing strip marked by a flare path, all I could see was fire and smoke. The tug pilot said 'Here we are' or words to that effect. I replied that I had no idea where we were. The tug pilot then came back and said that he could make another run in and this he did. On the second approach I could see the reflection of the moon in the river, and later the bend in it, and a silhouette of the superstructure of the bridge. After pull-off I approached the road south of the bridge and put on full flap so that I could land as close to the road as possible and avoid running into the river. Sergeant Kerr said, 'Don't forget the electrical pylons,' to which I replied, 'We are OK; we are almost over the road; the pylons are behind us.' No sooner was this remark made than there was a crash and sparks flew in all directions... The impact had practically destroyed the Horsa cockpit and we had been thrown from our seats and were travelling along the ground at a fair speed. I was praying that I did not contact anything before we came to a stop. As we extracted ourselves from the damaged glider a few bursts of machine gun fire came from a pillbox on the south-west corner of the bridge. We made for the bank of the Simeto to take cover until the reception was more cordial. The firing soon stopped and I realised Sergeant Kerr wasn't with us, I went back to the glider and Sergeant Kerr had injured his leg and was still there. Seeing he was as safe there as anywhere else I rejoined the gun crew.[16]

The gliders found that the German AA defences around the Primosole bridge were very alert and some aircraft were hit and crashed into various obstructions around the constricted LZs. This frequently injured the pilots and troops and also meant that the glider fuselages were sometimes so buckled and bent that the cargoes of 6-pounder anti-tank guns or jeeps could not be easily extracted. As one example, it took the crew and passengers of Glider 129 four hours to extract the gun and a further five hours to remove the jeep from the splintered and twisted fuselage of

---

16   Protheroe, *The Eagle Magazine,* The Regimental Magazine of the Glider Pilot Regiment.

the aircraft.[17] When dawn broke on 14 July, the British defenders at Primosole Bridge could only muster 120 personnel and though they were able to defend the bridge for much of the morning, they were few in number and their position became gradually untenable. The British airborne troops eventually withdrew from the bridge, but not before removing all the charges and preventing the Germans from demolishing it. Just as at Ponte Grande it was swiftly recaptured by the advancing Eighth Army within a few hours. The paratroopers would probably have had a better chance of holding on to the bridge if more of 1st Parachute Brigade had been able to reach it, but less than half of the British aircraft and less than a third of the American aircraft dropped within half a mile of the DZ. Only ten percent of the troops could be mustered at the DZ itself and only one sixth ever succeeded in joining the battle.

The reasons for such a poor showing were varied. Poor navigation undoubtedly played its part and in addition the evasive action taken by some Dakotas caused the paratroopers to stumble, tangle their static lines and sometimes prevented them from exiting the aircraft promptly over the DZ. Furthermore, 24 Dakotas responded to the flak by simply turning away from the coast and brought their sticks of parachutists all the way back to North Africa. Some did so as a result of an order from an American squadron commander not to drop. One British Albemarle also turned away, the captain of this aircraft was subsequently judged by the RAF to have failed in determination.[18]

Many airborne commanders felt that if closer liaison had occurred between them and the American Dakota crews, then they would have been able to convince them of the necessity of dropping, even against enemy opposition. Disappointingly and despite the efforts of the air planners, there were also many instances where the fleet shot at (and hit) the transiting air fleet. It is estimated that ten Dakotas were shot down by friendly naval anti-aircraft fire. The airborne operations in Sicily starkly exposed many issues including poor navigation, faulty co-ordination with naval forces, as well as dubious airborne and joint planning. These were all captured in the official report on the operation which wisely concluded:

> There is one point from this operation that surpasses all others in importance. The Air Force must be able to drop a substantial proportion of the parachute force at the right place and at the right time if such operations are going to be fully justified. The methods by which this standard is achieved form primarily an air problem. At the same time liaison between the army and air forces who actually participate in these operations can never be too close. Such contact will greatly contribute to the solving of this problem.[19]

Allied commanders might have concluded, much as Hitler had, that massed airborne operations were either unlikely to be successful or were just not worth the cost in the manpower, aircraft and material they attracted. It says much that commanders such as Eisenhower and Montgomery retained faith in the capability and continued to press the case for their use in future operations. The operations in Sicily also exposed to the airborne and air planners the difficulties they faced in executing accurate large-scale airlifts at night, including a long approach over water. There was probably not an air force in the world that was either trained or skilled enough to accomplish it at that time and Allied aircrews would need much more experience and practice in low level flying, navigation and judging distances in moonlight if they were going to be successful. Furthermore, the effect of AA fire at Sicily had been to widen the drop and make it less accurate, therefore

---

17   Mike Peters, *Glider Pilots in Sicily* (Barnsley: Pen and Sword, 2012), p. 247.
18   Lawrence Wright, *The Wooden Sword*, p. 159.
19   TNA CAB 106/689, 1st Airborne Division Report on Operation 'HUSKY', Part 3, 1943, p. 17.

considerable attention needed to be made in planning the routes to avoid these concentrations in the future. Finally, the selection of the LZs/DZs also needed much greater care in the future, to ensure they were generally larger, more easily identifiable and had fewer surrounding obstructions.

The next British operation to incorporate airborne landings was Operation OVERLORD which involved a total of three Allied airborne divisions. The planning for this operation was much better organized than HUSKY,[20] with responsibility for the airlifts placed under the Air Commander-in-Chief and an Airborne Air Planning committee was set up to coordinate the airlift within wider elements of the plan. The amphibious assault for OVERLORD was again due to take place at dawn and the airborne planners were faced with the difficulties of a night-time drop once more, with all the challenges that entailed.

Operation OVERLORD's airborne element included the American 82nd Airborne and 101st Airborne Divisions, who would parachute in to protect the American western beachhead, as well as the British 6th Airborne Division who would perform a similar role on the British eastern flank. 6th Airborne Division would achieve this mission by concurrently capturing the Breville Ridge to block a potential advance, seize bridges over the Caen Canal and River Orne (now known by their more the famous names of Pegasus and Horsa bridges), destroy a series of smaller bridges over the River Dives and neutralise the gun battery at Merville.

The British had clearly learnt lessons since Sicily, training was prolonged and included a full-dress rehearsal in England on 21 April 1944 that involved 700 British and American aircraft. The efforts to brief the aircraft crews and airborne troops on OVERLORD lasted three days, during which period the airborne troops were locked in their camps and sealed-off from the outside world. Elaborate models, air photographs and even a filmed fly-through of the approaches to the DZs and LZs (using a model and a cine camera to simulate different heights and approaches) were all available to brief crews. This clearly made a difference for critical elements of the operation including the assault on Pegasus and Horsa bridges (Operation DEADSTICK), where five of the six gliders successfully landed men of the 2nd Battalion Oxfordshire and Buckinghamshire Light Infantry in extremely small LZs, very close to their targets. Operation DEADSTICK involved 43 mission-specific dress rehearsals which was undoubtedly a major factor in its success. It was to be described by Air Chief Marshal Leigh Mallory, the overall Air Commander for D-Day, as 'One of the most outstanding flying achievements of the war.'[21]

There was also a greater number and proportion of RAF aircraft used to fly the British troops in during Operation OVERLORD. By October 1943, No. 38 Wing had become 38 Group and included 10 squadrons, four of which were equipped with the powerful Stirling which could be used as both a tug and parachute aircraft. Many of the crews of these squadrons obtained night-flying experience over France through occasional missions to the French resistance to drop supplies. Both Chatterton, now promoted to Brigadier, and Air Vice Marshal Hollinghurst (AOC 38 Group) had also successfully argued that the glider pilot battalions should be withdrawn from the structure of the two airborne divisions (1st and 6th Airborne). They were instead renamed wings and co-located with 38 Group's aircraft at their airfields, this ensured the glider pilots were constantly immersed in air matters, as well as giving them the chance to establish close working relationships with the tug pilots who would tow them on operations.

The British also formed 46 Group, which contained five squadrons of Dakotas based at airfields in Oxfordshire and Wiltshire. This formation had a total of 150 Dakota aircraft that had been

---

20  To be fair to the HUSKY planners, it was the largest amphibious and airborne invasion ever attempted at that point, they were split geographically across the Mediterranean and many key leaders were still occupied in defeating the Germans in Tunisia.

21  'Heroes of Pegasus Bridge', *The Independent*, 31 May 2009.

Oblique aerial photograph showing Douglas Dakotas of 233 Squadron RAF, lined up on the perimeter track at RAF Blakehill Farm, Wiltshire, for an exercise with the 6th Airborne Division, 20 April 1944.
(Crown Copyright – Air Historical Branch)

provided by the United States under lend-lease arrangements in January 1944. These aircrews were typically less experienced than those in 38 Group. The Dakota was a much more suitable aircraft for jumping, it held twenty paratroopers comfortably and the size of the fuselage and the wide door allowed the soldiers to easily exit it with a leg bag, or equipment such as a rifle or Bren gun carried in a felt valise. The kit bundles were used much more widely in Normandy than in Sicily and the paratroopers were consequently less dependent on containers which were dropped separately and sometimes hard to find. The ease with which a man could jump from a Dakota also ensured that after the first paratrooper exited, the others could follow him out in quick succession. Such short intervals meant a fully loaded Dakota could deploy its stick of parachutists in just thirty seconds, typically with only a fifty-metre spacing between soldiers.[22]

A combined HQ for 38 Group and 6th Airborne Division was set up at Brigmerston Farm, Milston on Salisbury Plain. There, the two organizations collectively planned the operation including the selection of three dropping zones in Normandy known as V, K and N, which would receive the parachutists of 3rd and 5th Parachute Brigades on the night of 5/6 June. The D-Day route took the Dakotas across the channel, via rendezvous (RVs) at Bognor Regis, Littlehampton and Worthing which avoided the Allied invasion fleet and potential friendly AA fire. The aircraft

---

22   Stuart Tootal, *The Manner of Men*, p. 82.

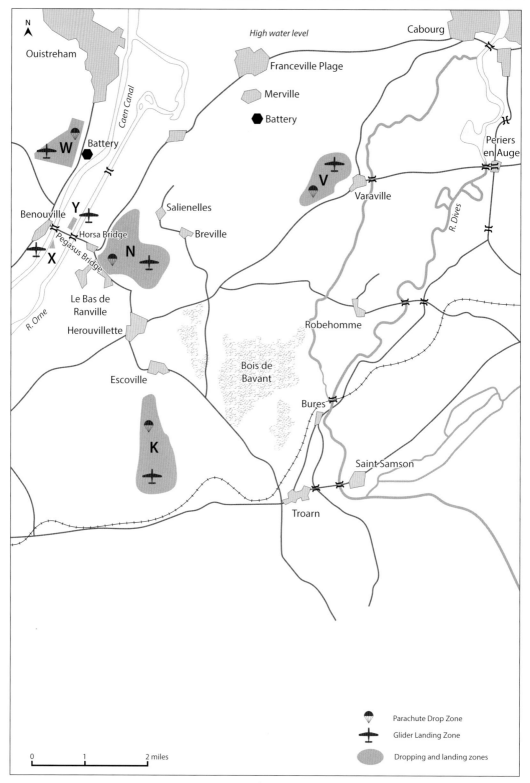

Figure 7  DZs and LZs in Normandy.

crossed the coast just east of Le Havre, making a sharp turn to starboard and running in to the DZs from the North East. There were few helpful distinctive geographical features in this last stage of the run in for the pilots to pick out and even the small ports of Cabourg and Ouistreham looked confusingly similar.

As he began his final approach to the DZ, the pilot would switch on the subdued interior lighting on the aircraft and the radio operator would unbuckle himself and exit the cockpit through the crew door into the back of the aircraft. Once there he would take up his duties as a dispatcher. The crew would be monitoring the Rebecca set to pick up the distance and bearing of the DZ and trying to visually detect and identify the Holophane lights. These were set up in the shape of a 'T' which both marked the DZ and confirmed the direction of the wind and dimensions of the drop zones. Only a few of the Holophane lights were successfully set up on the night, sometimes because of mis-drops, or on other occasions because they were sited in fields of high standing crops which meant the approaching pilots could not see them. Furthermore, at DZ V the only path-finder Eureka equipment to survive the landings intact could not be recovered and set up before the main lift arrived. Worse still the DZ K pathfinder team had been mistakenly dropped at DZ N, these soldiers failed to recognise the error and set up the Eureka set anyway. Most pilots there-fore had to fall back on maps and dead reckoning to find the DZs and this produced mixed results.

When he estimated he was five minutes out from the DZ, the pilot would switch the red light on over the parachute door, this gave warning to the paratroopers and aircrew that the drop was imminent. The radio operator was now at the back of the aircraft and standing by the exit on the port side, facing the paratroopers who were sitting along the length of the aircraft. To prevent himself from falling out, he would fix his belt-strop to a strong point near the door of the aircraft and instruct the soldiers to 'Stand Up! Hook Up! Check Equipment!'. This drill was very familiar to the parachutists. Even though they might not be able to hear the dispatcher's voice, they would struggle to their feet, clip the D-ring snap links of their static lines to the cable running the length of the aircraft and turn to face back down the aircraft towards the door at the tail. The dispatcher would order them to sound off for an equipment check and they would check their own equip-ment, of snap link, helmet, chin-strap, harness, leg-bag fastenings and then turn around to do the same checks on the man behind. The last man, who was number twenty, would then firmly slap the shoulder of the man in front shouting 'Twenty, Okay!' This was cascaded down the line, each man slapping the shoulder of the man in front until the first man in the stick shouted 'One Okay! Stick Okay!' giving the dispatcher the thumbs up. The dispatcher would then guide the number one to the door. It tended to be the case that those with heavier loads in their leg bags, such as radios etc were positioned nearer the front, as it was harder for them to move down the aircraft encumbered with parachute, felt valise and a heavy leg bag. The lead parachutist would place his left leg firmly on the edge of the door to give himself a good jump-off, whilst steadying himself by holding on to the door frame with one hand.

The pilot would be flying the Dakota at an altitude of 500 feet and would throttle back and slow down to 100 mph, this was just above the stalling speed of the aircraft. With the fuel mix set to rich, the propellers pitch re-set and flaps selected he would alter the trim of the aircraft to bring up the tail wheel, which helped prevent any parachute from getting snagged on it. This change in the aircraft's attitude would be felt by the paratroopers, who would know they were in the very last moments before the drop.

When the aircraft was over the DZ the red light would be extinguished and the green light would come on. The dispatcher would shout 'Go!' as he slapped the first man on the shoulder and helped push him out into the rushing air. Each jumping paratrooper would be immediately replaced by the man behind as they shuffled down the aircraft, the dispatcher controlling the rate of exit and steadying the flow to a regular rhythm as best he could. Refusals were less common in the Dakota than the converted bombers, perhaps because it was much easier for the dispatcher and the man behind to propel someone faltering at the last moment. Keys to a successful drop were good drills inside the aircraft, sound navigation and a steady approach by the pilot, which on D-Day often required cool nerves given the level of anti-aircraft fire around. Ronald Warren was a Dakota navigator on 575 Squadron based at RAF Broadwell and describes his sortie:

> We were detailed to take paratroops from Broadwell in Oxfordshire to a field beside the River Orne at Ranville near Caen. The first vic of three Dakotas led by Wing Commander Jefferson was due to drop at 00.57.00. The second vic led by Squadron Leader Cragg was due to drop at 00.57.20. I was the navigator of the lead aircraft of the third vic piloted by Flight Lieutenant Dixon. Our dropping time was 00.57.40.
>
> We took off in loose formation and I was busy for some time making sure that we were on the right course at the right speed to arrive at Ranville at the right time. Twenty seconds between aircraft is not a big margin so, as soon as things were running smoothly, I looked through the astro dome to see how close we were to the six aircraft in front. To my horror there was nothing there but empty black sky. What had I done wrong? Where had I boobed? I looked back and saw the lights of aircraft stretching back as far as the eye could see and probably beyond. For some reason the first two vics had not formed up. I shot back to my position and for the next hour worked like never before making sure that we were on course and time to arrive at Ranville at the correct time.
>
> We crept very slightly ahead of our time so that our ETA became 00.57.00 I should perhaps have instructed the pilot to knock two or three knots off our speed, but I figured that with nobody in front and the whole invasion behind us, early was better than late, and in any case 00.57.00 was the leaders dropping time. We arrived and Jock Young our 4th crew member took over the map reading for the last few hundred yards. Then the fun started.
>
> Gerry Brown, the wireless operator went to the rear to see the boys out. The first four left in orderly fashion, they were Military Police, but the fifth man with a mortar barrel stuffed up his jumper fell in the doorway and blocked the way for the others. By the time they got him back on his feet we were past the DZ. Gerry passed the information on but, because he forgot to release his microphone button he didn't hear Dixon say that we would go round again so I had to nip back and tell him. They all went out in good order the second time round. With all the excitement only Jock noticed that we were being fired at but nothing hit and we made our uneventful way back to base. Because of the delay we were on the end of a very long queue for landing. It was a bit of an anti-climax and I didn't mind the mild telling off I got for being 40 seconds early over the DZ.[23]

Flight Lieutenant P.M. Bristow was a Dakota pilot on 575 Squadron and recalls dropping his paratroopers that night:

> By 1800 hours all our aircraft were marshalled on the perimeter track and taxi tracks so they could file out in the correct order for take-off. I forget now how many aircraft went from Broadwell that evening but I think it was two or three squadrons. I do remember that not only was mine the last squadron to go, but as I was in 'C' Flight I was amongst the last of our squadron. It was a long wait and not without anxiety, for one had no sort of idea what reception we might meet. I do remember a strong sense of occasion and however small the part, one felt one was taking part in an historic event.

23   TNA AIR 28/115, *RAF Broadwell*.

Short Stirling Mark IVs of 196 and 299 Squadrons RAF, lining the runway at Keevil, Wiltshire, on the evening of 5 June. They are just about to emplane paratroops of the 5th Parachute Brigade Group for the invasion of Normandy. (Crown Copyright – Air Historical Branch)

The first to get airborne in the last of the daylight were all towing gliders… Aircraft carrying paratroops started their take-off about an hour later and not until it was quite dark. There should have been a full moon that night but there was 10/10ths cloud cover so the night was dark. We had normal runway lighting for take-off but no navigation lights were used and we had to observe strict radio silence. Our signal to go was a green light from the control caravan at the end of the runway and we went off at pretty long intervals of one minute and thirty seconds. There was certainly no sign of the aircraft ahead of you by the time it was your turn to go. The whole flight was scheduled; so long after take-off and turn on to such and such a course; after another interval turn to a different heading, with times to leave our coast at Littlehampton, to make landfall at Normandy and a time to drop. Streams of aircraft were going off from several other fields, many destined for the same DZ, so they all had to be interlocked. So far as I could judge the staff work must have been good.[24]

Bristow's aircraft was flying in a Vic of three and his Vic was third in the squadron. Formation flying is not a normal part of a transport pilot's expertise, but his crew had practised in the preceding months, when Bristow caught up with the aircraft in front, he found that there were now just four of them. At that point he decided he would be much more relaxed if he dropped back and flew on his own:

Bill Dyson was giving me regular fixes from his Gee box and confirmed we were on course and running on time. We had taken off at 23.30 and were due to drop at 01.10. Our stick went down within 30 seconds of the exact scheduled time.

---

24   TNA AIR 28/115 *RAF Broadwell*.

We were carrying twenty paratroopers and an Alsatian dog that had been trained to jump from the back of a lorry. On a temporary rack fitted below the belly of the aircraft we carried a number of small anti-personnel bombs. We had been briefed to drop these as we crossed the Normandy beaches so that if there were any defenders they would be encouraged to keep their heads down. There were also a couple of folding motor-cycles in cylindrical canisters. Shortly before we made landfall something exploded on the land right ahead. A vast sheet of yellow flame lit up the sky for a second or two and in that I saw a line of aeroplanes all going the same way, all at the same height, and I was part of this game of follow-my-leader. I made myself think I was all alone on a night course on Salisbury Plain, but kept very keyed up to take smart evasive action if I got close enough to anyone else to see them. I felt the slip-stream from other aeroplanes in front from time to time but once that rather shattering light had died down never actually saw another.

Bill Dyson and the Gee box brought us in for a perfect land-fall and Robbie Burns and I found we could see enough to make our way visually to the DZ. Robbie was a RAF navigator and was just ex-Ulster University, he was a bright boy. There were not always enough pilots for every crew to have a second pilot, so I was given Robbie as a map reader and that was a lucky day.

We had been told we should be crossing heavy gun emplacements and that our bombers would be dealing with them before we arrived to prevent them bombarding the Navy. Whatever had happened to them had burnt them up to such effect that we passed over a number of glowing plates of ferro-concrete. The heat must have been generated inside but here was the topside of a concrete roof glowing like a red-hot plate of steel. I have always wanted to know more about those glowing gun-pits.

Rebecca-Eureka was working by now to help lead us in. This was a short-range homing device actuated from a portable ground station. Now the illuminated direction Tee could also be seen and we were almost there. The paratroops had been standing lined up with the red light on – well back from the door opening – and at this point they got the green. Doug Strake my Canadian w/Op was acting jump-master and was able to speak to me down the intercom and he told me all was ready and well. I had started the drop at the right height, the right speed and all was as right as we could make it until I lost contact with Doug. I should wait for him to tell me it was OK to open up, but he was silent and we were steadily losing height and advancing on the Germans who were clearly belligerent as witness the flames in the sky not long before. I was sure it was one of our lot that had bought it, though I was later told that it was a Stirling. A moment later and Doug came through again to say everything had gone and I opened throttles, made a climbing turn to port and disappeared into cloud where we all felt nice and snug.

When he joined us in the cockpit Doug told us that the dog, who with its handler was the last to go, had followed all the others to the door, and as it came to its turn to follow its handler out, had decided this was not the same thing as jumping from the back of a lorry, and backed away from the door and retired to the front of the fuselage. Doug had had to unplug himself from the intercom, catch the dog and literally throw it out. Several weeks later he met one of our stick in Oxford who had been sent home wounded and he said they had eventually found the dog.[25]

Private John Russell was a member of 8th Battalion Parachute Regiment and dropped on to DZ 'K' three miles to the south of Ranville. They were the only Battalion to have a DZ for their

25   TNA AIR 28/115 *RAF Broadwell*.

5 June 1944 – Paratroops of the 5th Parachute Brigade Group have their equipment checked for the last time before boarding their aircraft at Keevil airfield, Wiltshire, ready to take part in the opening phase of the Normandy campaign, Operation TONGA. (Crown Copyright – Air Historical Branch)

exclusive use. He describes the chaos that could ensue when anti-aircraft fire played havoc with the unarmed transport aircraft:

Private Richardson was Major Hewetson's batman and was seated No.2 on the starboard side opposite the open 'door'. I believe No.4 was Private Cooper (all kit-bag men were seated near the exit.) It was dark there when we boarded and very little was spoken on the flight (by anyone!). I was No.6, C.Q.M.S. Peters (No.20) came along during the flight. Pte Donovan who was having problems with his kit-bag; I believe he was No.7 (he was slightly forward of me in the aircraft, not opposite). We approached the French coast – I could see what looked like the Le Havre peninsular and the R. Seine mouth (looking past No.4 and the 'door' opening). A bloke, perhaps No.9, suddenly asked, 'What are those flashes?' Someone answered, 'Flak.' Silence. Then came a tremendous 'crack' like a greatly magnified rifle bullet going past. (I presumed it was an 88 shell passing.) Exploding shells could be heard, but their 'Karumph's seemed some distance away – then came a much closer 'Karumph' and shortly after a terrifically loud metallic-sounding 'Bang', or 'Klang', as a fragment hit nearby. Richardson gave a short gasp. Silence. Then either No.1 Major Hewetson or No.3 came across, and with No.4 unhooked Pte Richardson.

Low voices; then the plane violently switched from side to side as the pilot took evasive action. Damn near slithered off my seat as the kit-bag lurched about. I braced feet and shoulders whilst holding my kit-bag with right hand and pulling No.4's kit-bag against the seat to control that, for No.4 was holding Richardson presumably to prevent his body going slipping towards the exit. The aircraft kept jigging about and all of us were concentrating on first staying seated. Either No.3 or No.5 muttered 'Bugger this!' and those were the only words to reach me – otherwise nobody nearby spoke. I don't recall hearing any noise from the wounded man. The plane steadied and the 'Red' came on, we stood and waited for the 'Green'. Richardson was on the floor just ahead of me it seemed. He gave a low moan or groan, then exhaled a sigh, followed by a deeper sigh, that ended in the 'death rattle' as his lungs emptied.

Then came the 'Green' and the 'wap' of the strops [these are the sounds of the static line webbing strops hitting the door opening when released from the parachute canopy]. Left palm against the door frame, I swung my leg and kit-bag out. The bag grazed the door frame and somehow my right foot twisted and jammed my left foot against the opposite door frame. Down to my knees I was out of the plane, but felt my legs and bag jammed, so as the slipstream hit me I spun round and hit the plane aft of the 'door' opening with open palms and pushed. I came free (but did I get boot assistance by No.7?). Realised that my kit-bag was fouled and tried to free the lower pin, but no luck for it was twisted over. The harness prevented my reaching far down. Bending the leg to lift the damned bag closer to my hand was very tiring. Decided the unseen dark ground was getting too close so took up a landing position and hit almost immediately. (We normally jumped from 450 to 500 feet height, so at 1 a.m. on a dark night one hadn't much time to 'muck about.') Fully expecting to feel & hear the 'Shlock!' of a dislocated ankle (at least).

I landed without mishap. Nothing untoward happened – but that rod & pin were a real problem to release. Got it free & emptied the bag. Suddenly Sgt Snow went past, saying 'Get up, Russell.' (no offer to help or enquire if O.K.!) Shouldered the gear and looked for the red and green 2-inch mortar parachute flares that marked the R.V. and should have been 'up there'. No sign but a small red and green light were 'down there' low on the horizon. Miles away! I looked up at two aircraft passing above. One was a 'Halifax', t'other was an 'Albemarle' – Not being all 'Dakotas', Russell sensed a 'balls up' had occurred!!! (Our correct D.Z. (drop zone) was Touffreville (about seven miles inland). Our objective was the Troarn (and the Bures) bridge about a mile away. My 'stick' landed near Ranville (the 5th Brigade's D.Z.) at 01.00 hrs approx. Our orders were to 'maintain the Troarn Bridge objective' if dropped in wrong area – avoid combat (unless necessary) until you reach the Troarn objective. My stick was spread out through the 12th & 13th Bns and a small group of us (under Major Hewetson) headed for Troarn about 4 miles away.) Round about, against the night sky, steams of 20mm cannon 'flak' were weaving upwards (but not in our area). Occasionally a spent bullet whistled or hissed overhead.[26]

As at Sicily the parachute drops on the night 5/6 June were again scattered. Some pilots confused the River Dives and the River Orne, with the result that many groups were dropped well to the east. As the Germans had deliberately flooded this area, some of the unfortunate paratroopers drowned struggling to extract themselves from their harnesses and kitbags. Nevertheless, there were enough paratroopers who had successfully landed for the main objectives to be seized.

The 6th Airborne Division's parachute drops included several airborne sappers who began to clear the landing zones for the sixty-eight Horsa and four Hamilcar gliders that were scheduled to land at 0320. These glider loads contained the Divisional HQ, additional Royal Engineers and the 17-pounder anti-tanks guns of 4th Anti-tank Battery, Royal Artillery. These 17-pounder anti-tank guns, which were carried in the Hamilcars, were a critical element of the division's defence against

---

26   D-Day account of Private John Russell, 8th Battalion Parachute Regiment, accessed via <https:www.pegasu-sarchive.org> 2 March 2020.

Paratroops of 5th Parachute Brigade wait in the dark before boarding their aircraft for Operation OVERLORD. (Crown Copyright – Air Historical Branch)

German armour. The OVERLORD glider landings were fortunately much more successful than at Sicily, Sergeant Eddie Raspison was the second pilot on Glider Number 30, which carried a group of Royal Engineers to help demolish anti-landing obstacles, including many wooden poles. He described the fly in:

> Norman Jenkins and I carried a load in Horsa LF 918 with 'B' Squadron, consisting of four RE [Royal Engineer] paratroopers, a jeep and trailer loaded with pole demolition charges... I understand from those aboard that there was a shortage of airborne RE gliderborne personnel skilled in the job of shearing poles at ground level. Much to their consternation, they had been detailed to go in with us and my attempt to convince them that they were far more likely to get down in one piece with us, rather than by parachuting in did nothing to alleviate their misgivings at being transported in our wooden contraption.
>
> It is of interest to note that prior to crossing the French coast our Albermale tug (how their pilot's hated their aircraft!) was hit by anti-aircraft fire and its port engine caught fire, which necessitated the feathering of the propeller. The offer to cast-off, to give the tug a chance of survival, met with the gutsy reply of 'Hang on – I'll get you there' from the skipper, Flying Officer Mike Brott, a New Zealander. He did get us there and to our gratification just made it back to the coast, crash landing in a field without any injury to the crew.
>
> Our landing approach to the narrow 'runway' where the poles had been cleared in advance, was normal until we passed over the green direction-indication lights. Then another glider passed just feet below us, going in the opposite direction! This at our height of only 150 feet, necessitated an immediate decision to turn several degrees to starboard, chancing a collision with the poles to the side of our allotted landing area. We fortunately avoided poles but were

Discarded parachutes and Airspeed Horsa gliders lie scattered over 6th Airborne Division's landing Zone 'N' between Ranville and Amfreville in Normandy, 6 June 1944. (Crown Copyright – Air Historical Branch)

brought to an abrupt stop in a small field by a haystack that hit our port wing. The load and paratroopers, the latter very thankfully, were disembarked without undue difficulty. We never did discover who went the wrong way below us or what happened to them, but did elicit the fact that we were the ones going in the proper direction.[27]

Operation OVERLORD witnessed the first use of the Hamilcar glider, the largest wooden aircraft constructed by the British during the war. Manufactured by the General Aircraft Company it had a high wing and large, powerful flaps, which were operated by servo-pneumatic means and enabled the pilot to control the angle of the glide and successfully land in confined spaces. The Hamilcar weighed 36,000lbs fully loaded; a significant weight for a tug to tow. The cargo itself could be up to 17,500lbs and included a variety of different loads such as a Tertrach Light Tank, two Bren gun universal carriers, a 25-pounder gun with tractor, a 17-pounder anti-tank gun with tractor, Bailey pontoon bridge equipment or forty-eight panniers of equipment and ammunition. After landing, the Hamilcar would sink on to its skids by releasing high-pressure oil in the undercarriage's shock absorbers and causing them to telescope in. A wide door in the nose of the aircraft would be opened and the vehicles driven out on a ramp. For rapid deployments the vehicles would start their engines in the glider while still in the air, exhaust gases being vented out through temporary extension pipes and the metal chains and anchorages, which held the vehicle in place, could be instantaneously de-coupled by pulling on a lanyard. This allowed tracked vehicles to exit in as little as 15 seconds. The interior of the Hamilcar glider resembled a wooden barn; the passengers physically separated from the crew who sat perched in a cockpit at the top of the aircraft. Sergeant Jock Simpson was one of the pilots who flew a Hamilcar into Normandy in the early hours of 6 June:

> A short time after midnight we rolled down the runway and took off, heading towards the Channel and wondering what lay in store for us. The atmosphere in the glider was electric as our passengers, the gun crew, were rather excited as they were unable to see anything and consequently, kept calling on the radio telephone until Tommy Taylorson got mad, told them to 'shut up' and said that he would keep them informed when anything transpired.
>
> As we crossed the Channel, tense but calm, we could see the white wakes of the ships of the sea-borne forces as they made their way across the water. The flight was uneventful until we approached the French coast, where we encountered medium and light anti-aircraft fire coming from Le Havre. Fortunately, we escaped being hit, but our Canadian tug pilot, Flying Officer Baird was hit by a bullet between the toes. Some strong adjectives were heard over the radio telephone, but he carried on and did not falter in his duty.
>
> We proceeded inland, until the tug pilot pointed out the cross-roads in front of us and gave instructions for us to cast off at that point and then to turn right and make a normal approach and landing. At this stage things became very serious as we realised that it was the point of no return and in all honesty, one must admit to having some degree of fear and apprehension.
>
> As we approached for the landing we could see that the area was obstructed by masses of poles standing in the ground and obviously placed there by the Germans as landing obstacles. However, we were very relieved when we realised that our wings were too high, 17 feet above the ground, to be affected, but unfortunately that was not the case for the Horsas landing in the same area, as their wings were below the height of the poles – consequently they sustained severe damage.
>
> After we rolled to a stop we got out, opened the nose door and released the valves on the landing legs, allowing the Hamilcar to settle on the skids. When the load was released the tractor pulled the gun and ammunition down the ramps. We looked around to see if any of the other Hamilcars were near, but found only the one. This glider had suffered severe damage to the undercarriage, making it impossible for the gun crew to get their equipment through the nose door. Therefore, instead of us going with our own gun, Lieutenant Taylorson and I assisted Staff Sergeant England and Sergeant Hill to cut through their fuselage at the tail end. This proved a considerable task, but with the help of other men, we managed to tow the load through the tail section as daylight was breaking.[28]

---

28   Kevin Shannon and Steven Wright, *One Night in June* (Shrewsbury: Airlife Ltd, 1994), p.120-2

The final element of the D-Day operation was known as Operation MALLARD and took place in the evening of the 6 June, after the amphibious landings had taken place earlier that day. MALLARD consisted of a flight of 256 gliders (246 of which successfully landed on their correct LZs) and delivered airborne reinforcements, equipment and supplies to the 6th Airborne Division's defensive position on the left flank of the British invasion beaches. The operation took place at dusk and initial fears that the low flying tugs and gliders would be a sitting target for enemy AA fire proved largely unfounded. At the same time as MALLARD was being executed, Dakotas of 46 Group carried out Operation ROB ROY and dropped 116 tons of supplies on to DZ N. The routes and timings of MALLARD and ROB ROY were carefully arranged with the Royal Navy and this, together with the strikingly visible black and white stripes on Allied aircraft wings, meant that the friendly fire incidents witnessed at Sicily were much reduced. Not one aircraft on Operation MALLARD was fired upon by the Navy, though some on ROB ROY were, two being so badly damaged that they were forced to turn back, and one had to ditch.[29] Simpson recalls the arrival of this last flight of gliders:

> After having a bite to eat we decided that we could best assist the expected squadron, who were to arrive later that day loaded with Tertrach tanks, by laying out a large directional arrow made up of parachutes. This took up a fair bit of time, but shortly after this we observed that the sky was filled with tugs and gliders. As Horsas and Hamilcars approached the landing zone, the Germans opened up with mortar fire, creating havoc whilst gliders were landing. After unloading, some of the Tertrach tanks made a concerted attack and disposed of the mortars.
>
> The first figure whom we recognised was Major Dickie Dale, our Squadron Commander, who nonchalantly walked across the landing zone wearing his red beret instead of his helmet, which at that time contained a large bottle of whisky. The mortars had created quite a bit of damage to the gliders, and unfortunately we found that one of our pilots had been quite seriously wounded when a mortar bomb had exploded at his feet. Sergeant Hill and I volunteered to stay with him until the medics arrived to take over. He was in extreme pain and whilst with him we administered two injections of morphine, which we were supplied with before any operation. The medics were too late as he died in our arms.
>
> After this we proceeded to join the Squadron where they had taken up position. By this time, Sergeant Hill and myself were feeling rather cold and dejected, but Major Dale seeing our plight, poured out some of his whisky for us before we moved into our defensive position. Needless to say, the whisky was gratefully received.[30]

The British OVERLORD airborne operations had been a success. They had successfully secured the eastern flank, captured the key bridges and neutralised the Merville Battery at a critical moment. The RAF's ability to deliver airborne forces accurately on DZs and LZs had greatly improved since Sicily but was still far from perfect. Only 51 out of 95 aircraft dispatched dropped the 3rd Parachute Brigade on the correct DZ, 5th Parachute Brigade fared even worse with only 16 out of 70 aircraft hitting the DZ accurately.[31] Many aircraft landed their sticks within sufficient distance for them to re-join their units subsequently, but the Parachute RVs that night were chaotic and units were often short of paratroopers. Lieutenant Colonel Otway, the CO of 9th Battalion, the Parachute Regiment probably had the worst experience and had to assault the Merville Battery

---

29   Air Historical Branch, *The Second World War 1939-1945, Airborne Forces*, p. 132.
30   Kevin Shannon and Steven Wright, *One Night in June*, pp. 120-2.
31   Air Publication 3231, *Airborne Forces*, p. 132.

A Hamilcar heavy glider clears the airfield at Tarrant Rushton, during an airborne exercise, it is towed by a Handley Page Halifax target tug of 644 Squadron RAF. (Crown Copyright – Air Historical Branch)

Short Stirlings tow Horsa gliders carrying part of 6th Airlanding Brigade, 6th Airborne Division, towards the Normandy coast on the evening of 6 June 1944. (Crown Copyright – Air Historical Branch)

with just 150 men of the 640 who had jumped.[32] His Battalion's successful attack is a lasting testament to the character of the men involved. The pre-D-Day glider landings that night were much more successful than the paratroop drops, with 52 of the 98 British gliders dispatched successfully landing on the correct LZs.

In contrast to the night drops the airborne landings at dusk on the 6 June (Operations MALLARD and ROB ROY) were highly successful and pointed to the advantages of a daylight operation. Though the danger of flak might be increased, future planners justifiably wondered whether the advantages of simpler navigation and more accurate concentration on the DZ/LZ outweighed that risk? Furthermore, now that the continent of Europe had been invaded future airborne operations were unlikely to be tied to a dawn amphibious assault. Therefore, more ambitious airborne schemes for daylight operations that would support Allied operations on the continent began to be generated by the British airborne planners.

---

32   Stuart Tootal, *The Manner of Men*, p. 118.

# 13

# 'We are Bringing Gifts'[1]
# Later Airborne Operations

The 6th Airborne Division remained committed to operations in the Orne Bridgehead until August 1944, but their sister formation, the 1st Airborne Division, was itching to get into action. To enable this all the glider pilots involved in OVERLORD were immediately sent back to the UK in preparation for the next operation, which airborne leaders hoped would happen quickly. Frustratingly for 1st Airborne Division, the summer of 1944 saw them constantly planning and preparing for a series of operations that were all cancelled at the last minute, usually because the constantly changing situation at the front made them redundant. By mid-August 1944 the German front in the West was collapsing and it began to look like the war was coming to an end, consequently the pressure amongst the airborne community for one last operation intensified.

In September 1944, HQ 21st Army Group had drafted Operation MARKET GARDEN, a plan to outflank the German Siegfried line by seizing bridges over three major rivers. These included the River Maas at Eindhoven to be taken by the American 101st Airborne, the River Waal at Nijmegen to be captured by the American 82nd Airborne and the Rhine at Arnhem to be seized by the 1st British Airborne Division (including the 1st Polish Parachute Brigade). MARKET GARDEN was very different to other airborne operations, in that this was the first sizeable Allied drop to be undertaken in daylight. This decision was based not just on the positive experiences of MALLARD and ROB ROY, where concentrated drops and landings had been successfully achieved, but also because the overwhelming Allied day-time air superiority would prevent interference from enemy fighters and permit ground-attack aircraft to suppress anti-aircraft fire. This was an important factor, as the transport aircraft would have to cover over one hundred miles of enemy territory on their transits and some of this route was near the highly effective German night fighter bases that habitually attacked Bomber Command's raids on Germany. Therefore, in contrast to the airborne operations in Normandy and Sicily, the hours of darkness gave little protection to the transports and a daylight operation was preferred.[2]

The Allied airborne planners quickly established that there was not enough air transport to lift all three Divisions in one go. The view was therefore taken that it was probably best to establish the airborne operation from the bottom up, or in the order in which they were to be relieved by the British ground force. Consequently, the 101st Airborne would fly to Eindhoven complete, the 82nd Airborne would be flown in two lifts to Nijmegen and the 1st Airborne Division would need three lifts before they were fully established at Arnhem. One significant constraint was that the air force planners took the view that to fly two sorties in one day would not be possible. This was

---

1    Motto of 620 Squadron RAF. This Squadron was equipped with Stirling bombers and provided glider tugs as well as parachute aircraft. Aircraft in the squadron were employed during Operation OVERLORD, Operation MARKET GARDEN and Operation VARSITY.

2    See Annex N Airborne Operations – Air Movement Summary (Parachute drops and Glider Landings) for further details on accuracy of drops and landings for both OVERLORD and MARKET GARDEN.

Paratroops of 3rd Platoon, 21st Independent Parachute Company, assemble at RAF Fairford,
Gloucestershire in front of Short Stirling Mark IVs of 620 Squadron RAF parked on the perimeter track.
(Crown Copyright – Air Historical Branch)

because they expected the typical Autumnal dawn fog at that time of year[3] to close airfields for the early part of the morning and the distances involved would not allow a second lift to be generated in daylight. Consequently, the lifts had to be spread over several days and many have argued, with the benefit of hindsight, that this was too long. Furthermore, the available air transport to lift the actual fighting troops could have been increased by not flying out the headquarters of Browning's 1st Allied Airborne Corps, which took up a total of 38 gliders and tugs. There was little point to Browning's HQ deploying on MARKET GARDEN, as all airborne divisions would be fighting independently of each other until they linked up with the advancing British ground forces, at which point they came under command of Horrocks' XXX Corps and not Browning.

The selection of the DZ/LZs at Arnhem also remains controversial to this day. Airborne troops invariably wish to be landed as close to their objectives as possible and for the British this was the bridge in Arnhem itself. The area immediately north of the bridge objective was heavily built-up and unsuitable as either a DZ or LZ, but there was open land to the south of the river that initially looked promising. On closer inspection it was found that the land was crisscrossed with a network of ditches, each of which was 2–3 metres wide and 1.5 metres deep. These divided the ground into plots 50–100 metres in width and 100–200 metres in length and it is scarcely surprising that the airborne planners were reluctant to utilise it, given the difficulties small fields and stone walls had caused at Sicily. Even if gliders had successfully landed there, many of their cargoes might have been stranded and unable to get over the narrow footbridges that connected the various fields. This area might have been suitable for parachutists, yet the planned air route, which avoided the AA concentrations around Rotterdam, the Dutch coast and the Hague, had the aircraft approaching

---

3    It should be noted this was well before the 1956 Clean Air Act. At the time the source of much of Britain's heating and power, both domestic and industrial, came from coal – which caused frequent fog and smog conditions, even rural areas were sometimes affected. The prediction of early morning fog on 17 September 1944 was therefore a realistic assessment and as it turned out entirely accurate.

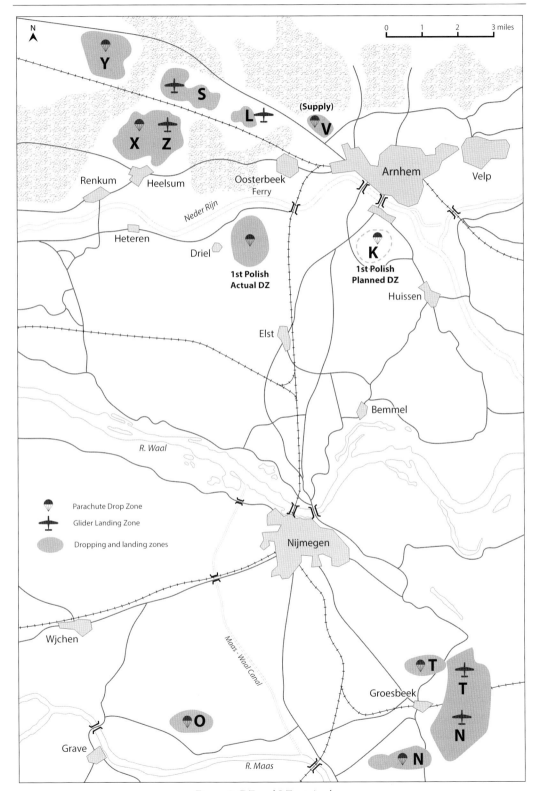

Figure 8  DZ and LZs at Arnhem.

the DZs from the south. Using this route would therefore take the aircraft over the considerable AA defences of Nijmegen, Arnhem and Deelen airfield, and the RAF objected to its use as a DZ.[4] Major General Roy Urquhart, the commander of the 1st British Airborne Division, agreed with the logic and decision at the time, but the issue has been regularly resurrected as one of the major factors in MARKET GARDEN's failure. Urquhart acknowledged subsequently that he should have taken more risk in retrospect:

> We must be prepared to take more risks during the initial stages of an airborne operation. It would have been a reasonable risk to have landed the Division much closer to the objective chosen, even in the face of some enemy flak... Initial surprise was gained, but the effect was lost because it was four hours before the troops could arrive at the bridge. A whole brigade dropped at the bridge would have made all the difference. Both the Army and RAF were over-pessimistic about the flak.[5]

Alternative DZs and LZs were found well to the west of the town, around the area of Wolfheze, which is roughly 65 feet higher than the polder land south of the town and much better drained. Some of these DZ/LZs were as close as two and a half miles from the objective, others as far away as eight miles. This would necessitate a long march by the airborne troops and tied down the entirety of 1st Air Landing Brigade in defending the DZs/LZs until the final drop on the third day.

Given the large numbers of false starts experienced over the summer, the days spent in preparation for MARKET GARDEN must have felt very familiar to the experienced glider pilots and soldiers of 1st Airborne Division. Private Alexander 'Sandy' Masterton was part of 1st Battalion, the Border Regiment's Anti-Tank Platoon and recalls loading the 6-pounder gun into a Horsa:

> As the loader I flew with the gun and jeep, which were securely held by chains and quick release shackles to metal channels bolted to the floor of the glider. The gun was hitched to the jeep ready to be towed out of the glider and the jeep was laden with stores, equipment, petrol and six pounder shells, which were strapped in boxes to the bonnet and on top of the front bumper. Had the glider been hit by small arms fire or flak, then results would have been spectacular to say the least. The gun and jeep were loaded in by ramps through the large door on the port side of the glider behind the cockpit. The jeep was loaded first, then the gun, which was man handled into place. There was very little clearance within the fuselage so the operation proved somewhat difficult. As the steering wheel of the jeep would strike against the frames of the glider, it was removed by releasing the butterfly nut that held it in place and laying it on the passenger seat. The two steel loading ramps were carried in the glider and were fixed down to prevent movement.[6]

The constant cancellation of 1st Airborne Division's operations over the summer had created an atmosphere of frustration amongst the glider pilots and RAF aircrew, together with scepticism that they would ever deploy. Flying Officer Bassarab, of the Stirling equipped 299 Squadron, recalled the final briefing before the first lift for Arnhem on Sunday 17 September 1944:

---

4    For the relevant terrain reports see TNA WO 171/393, 1st Airborne Division War Diary, September 1944, TNA Air 37/1214 Allied Airborne Operations in Holland, September-October 1944 and the Hollinghurst papers RAF museum AC 73/23/49.
5    Chester Wilmot, *The Struggle for Europe* (London: Collins, 1952), p. 272 and p. 275.
6    Stuart Eastwood, Charles Gray, & Alan Green, *When Dragons Flew*, (Great Addington: Silverlink Publishing Ltd), p. 105.

A Short Stirling Mark IV glider tug of 295 Squadron RAF starts its take-off run at Harwell, Oxfordshire, towing an Airspeed Horsa Mark I with troops of the 1st Airborne Division on board. It is heading for Landing Zone LZ 'N' at Arnhem. (Crown Copyright – Air Historical Branch)

Three times the crew and glider pilots trooped into the briefing room, observing a red tape strung out over the map of Europe indicating the routes to be flown, listening to estimation of enemy fighters and flak opposition, and complete details as to navigation, weather reports, runways, maintenance, and the job to be done on reaching the Landing Zone (LZ). Each time the operation was cancelled and the pent up anxiety and energy yet received another set back. The normal reaction was to have a few (pints) and retire early for yet another day.

Finally on Saturday…the camp was sealed, everyone concerned proceeded to the briefing room at 1400 hrs and Group Captain Troop gave the fourth preview of the Airborne operation in hand.

Details for further operations were carefully arranged, the Navigators again made their flight plans, checked courses and distances, made notes of Radar aids to be given and re-checked with other Navigators. The Bomb Aimers drew in tracks, noted flak positions and all prominent features. The pilots checked their petrol loads, carefully gone over by their Squadron Commanding Officer. The ground crews worked feverishly on all aircraft checking every last detail and the Radar chaps checked all sets giving a final OK. Lastly the gunners changed their ammunition so that it would include daylight tracer and tested their guns for harmonization and firepower. The glider pilots had a separate brief as to the detail of the jobs they were to do, now the preliminaries were over the stage was set.[7]

Staff Sergeant Wally Holcroft of F Squadron, Glider Pilot Regiment was at Blakehill Farm and recalled surprise at the operation being 'on':

We were told to parade in the RAF briefing room at 0830 hrs on Sunday morning… When we arrived we found everything in readiness, tables were laid out to accommodate each glider

---

7    R.N. Bassarab, 299 Squadron RAF, by permission of *The Eagle* magazine.

crew and his respective tug crew. The first words of the briefing officer were 'The Ops are on'. I looked at Norman Hartford my co-pilot, he grinned. We were scheduled to take off at 10 am. After receiving the latest weather reports and other relevant information, Hartford and I decided to walk down to our glider and give it a final check. Before we left the briefing room we had another look at the maps and pictures of the landing zone. I got it firmly fixed in my mind.

Hartford and I were lucky, we were taking in our glider twenty-eight men of the Border Regiment. Some of the fellows were taking Jeeps and guns. That would mean they would have to spend time on arrival taking the tail off the glider, to unload the stuff. Taking the tail off a big Horsa is bad enough when you have time to do it. Working under fire would certainly not help matters. Mick (Hall) too, had passengers, and I found he was next in the train to me. As we were taking troops of the same regiment it looked as though we could stick together after landing. That was what we wanted; we made a little pact to keep with each other throughout the operation.

When we reached the glider I found the troops all ready to emplane. The Officer in charge of them introduced himself to me and I to him. I asked him how the men were feeling. He said they were all as 'keen as mustard'. I had a chat with one or two of them and told them that I would certainly get them to Holland OK and in return I was expecting them to take good care of me on the ground. They said it would be a piece of cake, once they got to Holland. It was good to see such excellent spirits.

The whole of one end of the runway was crammed with gliders and tug aircraft. There was to be another 'lift' the following morning by another flight which had joined us from another station because their place was not large enough to deal with them all. It all looked very impressive that September morning, all lined up and ready for heaven knows what.

I walked around from one glider to the other chatting with the various pilots. I had a parting with Mick. We wished each other the best of luck on the journey. At ten minutes to ten I climbed aboard my glider; the troops were already seated inside. I quickly checked their straps and gave them one or two final instructions as to positions they should take up in case of a forced landing on the sea.

Making myself comfortable in my seat I checked over the controls with Hartford. Hartford had been my co-pilot for six months and we had got organised together perfectly. He was a splendid chap and very easy to get along with. I asked him what he thought about everything. He was quite confident we should make the trip OK.

Promptly at ten o' clock the Tow Master waved the first glider away. I was about twelfth down the line. In less than six minutes from the first glider taking off, I saw my tug taxiing slowly on to the runway in front of me. I gave the OK for take off over the intercom, and the rope stretching between us began to tighten. Then we began to move, slowly at first then with ever increasing speed. It is always a tense moment or two during take off with a full load of passengers, as everything depends on the aircraft being correctly trimmed. I watched the airspeed indicator creep round to eighty miles per hour and at that speed pulled back gently on the control column and the glider lifted off the ground. A second later the Dakota in front of me became airborne too, our first worries were over.[8]

The airborne landings on 17 September were some of the most successful of the war. Most of the British gliders and sticks landing accurately and un-hindered, mainly because of the large size of the DZs and LZs, the natural advantage a day-light drop conferred and a virtually impenetrable fighter escort. This allowed the troops to assemble quickly and move off to their objectives faster

---

8    Imperial War Museum 13198, W Holcroft, *No Medals for Lt Pickwoad*, (Unpublished memoir), 1945, p. 8.

than at OVERLORD. The daylight visibility did of course mean that the pilots were much more aware of how crowded the skies were around the landing and drop zones. Sergeant Brian Tomblin, was with Lieutenant Alec Johnston at the controls of an E Squadron Horsa, loaded with infantrymen of 7th Battalion, King's Own Scottish Borderers and recalls the demanding final approach to the LZ:

> We were not the only plane in the air; in fact it began to look a bit chaotic. There were gliders, tugs with ropes dangling, all heading to do their 'own thing.' Our landing zone was now fully clear to us, we applied half-flap and the glider responded by dipping its nose. Full-flap was put on, and our angle of descent steepened to that typical Horsa attitude and we headed towards a ground haze of smoke and fire from buildings burning in the district. The 'Red Devils' were once again landing in enemy territory.
>
> We sank fast towards the treetops – 'Hell, we are going to hit them, can't put the flaps up again, No – it's OK' – we skimmed over the trees of the Oosterbeek woods and the ground rushed up to us steeply. Hard back on the stick, and we shot along the ground to the surface. Brakes on hard 'Mind that horse charging about scared out of its wits.' To stop and get out quickly was our object. The brakes hissed quietly, we careered across the field, and the wheels sank into the soft sandy soil as we slowed jerkily to a halt. For a fleeting second we sat there in this smallish field tucked away in the woods – we were once again smugly satisfied that we had brought the old girl and its passengers to the right place at the right time. Our first relief was that we hadn't struck any mines placed there. The crackle of small arms brought us out of our momentary pause, we switched the flaps up out of habit, and then took part in the feverish activity to get out as we were a sitting target for any nasty Germans in the area.
>
> The strange eeriness of that Dutch Sunday morning was then broken by the skirl of bagpipes playing 'Blue Bonnets' and our Scottish borderers headed off in that direction for their rendezvous. Alec and I checked our operational kit, and did our quick change from pilots to soldiers. In the air above us, in chain after chain, tugs and gliders stretched back almost 20 miles, still protected by Allied fighters. Air traffic was so dense that the pilots likened it to Piccadilly Circus. Incredibly, despite Royal Air Force predictions of intense anti-aircraft fire, this immense glider cavalcade encountered little resistance. The pre-assault bombing had been more effective in the Arnhem area than at Eindhoven and not a single tug or glider was shot down in making their approach.
>
> Our tugs flew off, with ropes waggling behind, to be dropped at the pilot's whim on anything that might resemble the enemy. One Horsa found the tree tops coming through the floor of the glider as they ran out of height, and the floor was ripped to pieces forcing the glider down on its nose … remarkably no one was hurt.
>
> Two gliders raced across our landing field and went straight into trees, ripping their wings off as they did so. An 8-ton Hamilcar touched down on the soft soil, its nose dug into the earth and the weight and speed drove the glider into the ground to lift its tail high, and flip the Hamilcar over on its back. With the pilots sitting in the 'hump' on the top of the Hamilcar it was useless to attempt to dig them out.[9]

In contrast to OVERLORD, where glider pilots were evacuated swiftly, those involved in MARKET GARDEN were given instructions to rendezvous with their wing HQs immediately after landing. As the battle developed, they were given different tasks to help defend the

---

9   Mike Peters and Luuk Buist, *Glider Pilots at Arnhem* (Barnsley: Pen and Sword, Barnsley, 2009), pp. 84-5. Correspondence between Sgt B Tomblin and Luuk Buist 1991.

Airspeed Horsas are hooked up to their tow ropes on the east-west runway at Fairford, Gloucestershire for their flight to Arnhem on 17 September 1944. The Horsas parked on the left were used for the second lift to Arnhem on 18 September. (Crown Copyright – Air Historical Branch)

1st Airborne Division's defensive perimeter at Oosterbeek, just west of Arnhem. Elements of No. 1 Wing, Glider Pilot Regiment were used as the divisional reserve and helped defend the Royal Artillery's light gun positions, whereas the pilots from No. 2 Wing were employed as a front-line infantry regiment within 1st Air Landing Brigade. The character and leadership qualities of the glider pilots, all of whom were either SNCOs or officers, meant that they played an important role in the coming battle and their casualties were correspondingly high as a result.[10]

The planned deployment of 1st Airborne Division, in three successive lifts over three days, gave the Germans ample opportunity to organise their defences and attack the second and third lifts that took place on 18 and 19 September. The parachute drops and glider landings on those days suffered much heavier opposition as Sergeant Ron Driver, flying a Horsa containing soldiers of the Polish Parachute Brigade, from Keevil could testify:

> We became aware of some black puffballs of flak straight ahead. As we got nearer this increased in density until when we were only about, I suppose, a mile away... I remember saying to Bert 'The tug's heading straight for it, surely he's not going to go into that?' but he ploughed remorselessly on.
>
> We concluded that we had arrived; I took over the controls from Bert while he concentrated on looking for our landing site. In next to no time we had entered the box barrage. After a while, probably only seconds, there was a tremendous bang near us, it seemed the glider was pushed sideways, for a split second the controls went 'sloppy', no feel at all.
>
> Then Bert yelled above the din 'OK Ron I've got it', seconds later he yelled, 'release!' I pulled the cable release and Bert immediately banked to port and put the glider into a steep dive.
>
> The landing zone was straight ahead and we were doing a fair lick of speed. Bert called for flap and we started to reduce speed, he took it down and I thought we are going to make a

---

10   Mike Peters and Luuk Buist, *Glider Pilots at Arnhem*, p. 295.

perfect landing. The ground ahead was fairly smooth, looked as though it had had some crop on it that had been recently lifted and we touched down.

Immediately the cockpit canopy was showered with soil, grass, stones etc and we were thrown violently about. We eventually came to rest and the dust outside started to settle. We undid our safety belts and got out of the door that the Poles had opened. We looked up at the barrage and the combinations still coming in.

I remember saying to Bert 'Christ have we come through that lot.' We just stood there then moved away from the glider still looking at the sky and the planes still arriving and those that were hit diving down with smoke trailing.

I remember one Horsa that came down towards the west of us. It ended up in a kind of flat spin, hit the ground with a hell of a whack and seemed to fall to pieces. I had been conscious of things buzzing by my ears and I shouted to Bert 'there's a lot of June bugs about', he replied, 'What the hell are they?' I replied 'they are flying beetles, if they hit you in the face they will give you a nasty smack'. No sooner had I said it, about fifty yards or so away a fountain of earth appeared and the horrible truth dawned. I screamed at Bert, 'they are not beetles but bullets'!

We looked at each other, and then both crawled back to the glider. The reason why we had slewed round on landing was that we had lost a landing wheel, I expect, by the explosion near to us in the air, it had taken off a couple of feet of the wing tip too. The undercarriage was still intact and it was this that had dug into the soft ground.'[11]

Even after the 1st Airborne Division was established at Arnhem, it still had to be re-supplied by air until the advancing ground troops of Second British Army linked up. This became an increasingly hazardous task for the Dakotas, Stirlings, Halifaxes and Albemarles of 46 and 38 Group. The Germans were quick to identify the DZs being used for re-supply and were able to engage the Allied transport fleets with both fighters and concentrated AA fire. Flying Officer Jim Marshall of 620 Squadron flew on one of the earlier supply-dropping missions and noted that even by that stage the opposition was already beginning to become very severe:

Our next lift took place on the 19th September. We carried twenty-four containers on the bomb-racks and had four panniers for pushing out of the hatch. Soldiers of the Royal Army Service Corps were on board to assist with the dispatching of the panniers. This lift did not go as smoothly as our first. We were in a long line of Stirlings in pairs following each other, but we didn't see the fighter support this time and quite a bit of flak was coming up en-route. The streams of aircraft started to merge and we would see Stirlings all over the sky. The odd aircraft would be hit and we would see it go down and cartwheel on the ground or crash in a mushroom cloud. Each time this happened the pairs seemed to ease away from each other so that by looking you could see where the trouble was and avoid flying over that spot. We now had several separate lines of aircraft. At the DZ it was amazing, as I seemed to spend my time dodging panniers and containers being dropped from aircraft which were higher than the briefed dropping height. The flak from the ground was bad but the chances of being hit by a pannier full of landmines seemed greater. I certainly breathed a sigh of relief when our load had gone and we were able to swing away from the area.[12]

The worst day for re-supply was 21 September, when a supply mission was intercepted by the *Luftwaffe*. During this operation 23 aircraft were shot down and 61 sustained damage, within

11    Mike Peters and Luuk Buist, *Glider Pilots at Arnhem*, p. 181
12    Dennis Williams, *Stirlings in Action with Airborne Forces* (Barnsley: Pen and Sword, 2008), p. 158.

Men of a Royal Army Service Corps despatch unit prepare to drop panniers from a Douglas Dakota during an airborne exercise. (Crown Copyright – Air Historical Branch)

190 Squadron only three of the 10 aircraft dispatched succeeded in returning to their base at RAF Fairford. These high losses were partly because the fighters, which were supposed to have been escorting the transport aircraft, had been grounded by bad weather. Jim Marshall's next sortie was on this day and he described the heavy opposition now being encountered:

Our next flight to Arnhem was on 21 September. As the Fairford aircraft were starting to taxi out, the armourers reported a short circuit in my bomb racks, so I was held up. I still hoped to catch up with the stream but the CO drove onto the runway ahead and stopped me from rolling. It had been decided that I would rendezvous with a Dakota squadron over Eindhoven, where we would have the cover of a Thunderbolt fighter wing for our run in to Arnhem. During the trip to Eindhoven everything seemed normal and I circled there awaiting the Daks; they arrived but there were no fighters. So I took up a position ahead of them and started my run-in. Our DZ was on the front lawn of a large house which apparently was about all we still held. On the way in, one did not require a bomb aimer to map read as the trail of burning Stirlings and Dakotas pointed the way. The DZ seemed to be surrounded with the German tanks using their 88s as anti-aircraft guns. They were hitting us, and I even saw German soldiers behind trees with their Schmeissers and they too were hitting us. Looking back I could see the Daks taking an awful pasting and one, which was on fire, held course until its crew had pushed out their panniers over the DZ and then it crashed in flames. Another Dak looped the loop before going nose first into the roof of a house.

With all the [Allied] fighter strength available on the continent, I think that somebody had their finger in, for we did not see any friendly fighters and it appeared that the main stream, which I had been delayed from joining, had run into fighters from Deelen, a German base just north of Arnhem and so close that they could almost shoot us down as they did circuits of their own field. Fortunately, they were all refuelling when we came in. There were some shell holes in our aircraft and I think they later counted two hundred bullet holes, but the four engines kept turning as we raced home… One dispatcher had a bleeding knee where some shrapnel had scraped it and that was the total of our casualties.

On our return to Fairford we were told to taxi the aircraft to the dump. I think it was 'Archie' Andrews, an American in RCAF, who landed at the same time as I did – a body could stand upright in the holes in his tail. However, things were not good at base; in the Officers' Mess the girls were all in tears and they even gave me a hug as I walked in. I lived on a site that was towards the gate – one of the aircrew officers' sites – I was alone, there was nobody left on the site. I walked around the different Nissen huts hoping to find someone, but no. The following night we were the only operational crew assigned and my crew hardly talked to me. I think they thought I had volunteered.[13]

Flight Lieutenant Edwards of 271 Squadron was flying a Stirling on 21 September and describes encountering the German fighter aircraft that engaged the air transport fleet approaching Arnhem:

We had successfully dropped our panniers on the DZ area and turned for home climbing to 7000ft and the first indication I had that anything was wrong was when I saw about six fighters, which I could not identify as allied, on my port side. Before I could make sure of their identity we were attacked from behind, strikes being obtained on the fuselage and wings; tracer also appeared bursting ahead of the aircraft and under the impression that it might be flak I took suitable evasive action. After a moment, however, I saw, out of the corner of my eye, what was unmistakably a Fw 190 commencing an attack from the port side. His cannon fire was passing across ahead of the aircraft as I pulled back the stick and kicked hard on left rudder and avoided attack and dived for cloud. I then warned the crew of the presence of fighters and the W/Op Sgt Randall took up station in the astrodome. We reached cloud before a further attack materialised but this cover did not last long and as soon as we broke from cloud another attack came from astern resulting in several strikes.

The next few minutes were spent in dodging in and out of what cloud cover was available and during this time we were subjected to three more attacks all of which registered hits on our aircraft. The navigator gave me a course to steer but the compass just then was so badly upset that I was unable to follow the course given and the frantic dodging about in the past few minutes made it impossible for my co-pilot to give me a pinpoint. The Fw 190 was obviously taking his own time in making his attacks and was always above and astern so that it was extremely difficult for the W/Op in the astrodome to anticipate the exact moment of attack. I had full revs and throttle up to now and had found in my preliminary dive for cloud that the elevator trim was u/s [unserviceable]. During the sixth and last attack I lost aileron control and so gave the order to bale out. The co-pilot and navigator jumped at that time and I was under the impression that the rest of the crew and despatchers had also gone but later I found that this was not the case.

After barely a minute I looked round and saw three despatchers sitting by our cabin door and asked why they hadn't jumped and one of them said they could not, so I concluded they must have been wounded, and I then decided to stay in the aircraft and crash land, but almost immediately both propellers went into 'fully fine' and I throttled back in preparation for crashing. We were then approximately at 6000ft when the a/c [aircraft] went into a steep dive

13   Dennis Williams, *Stirlings in Action with Airborne Forces*, p. 168.

I found that I had regained partial aileron control and at about 1000 ft from the ground I held off to reduce speed. We were passing over a village with numerous haystacks and I shouted 'standby for crash landing' although I am pretty sure no one heard me. I selected 'flaps down' but whether I got my flaps down I shall never know. I remember frantically trying to strap myself in with one hand but found this impossible. At about 50 ft up I opened the pilots escape hatch and the draught caused a great rush of flame from the back of the cabin. A despatcher came lurching forward crying 'Christ the flame is coming right in'. This was the first idea I had that the aircraft was on fire (I learned later that fire had been raging for some minutes) and the cabin was now well alight, so I stood up and put my head out through the escape hatch and rested it on my forearm, my other hand still being on the control column. I looked along the port wing and had a glimpse of it being smashed against some small trees and then the aircraft hit the ground.

With the impact I was thrown half out of the hatch and was enveloped by a sheet of flame. I hung on because I feared being thrown completely out in the path of the aircraft which was still sliding along the ground. Suddenly the nose dipped and the tail was almost vertical and as it fell back I was flung out backwards on to the top of the aircraft whence I fell to the ground in front of the starboard engine. I picked myself up and ran away from the machine which was now a mass of flame. The aircraft had crashed in a small clearing surrounded by trees and as I ran towards these I saw the FW doing a steep turn at about 1000 ft directly above. I also realised now that the W/Op and one despatcher had crashed with me and had got clear of the aircraft and sensing that the FW might attack us again I warned the other two to take cover in the trees. I barely had time to get to the trees myself when the FW returned and commenced to strafe us.[14]

Edward's and his companions survived the attentions of the Focke-Wulf pilot and were able to make contact with friendly Dutch civilians, who escorted them to the 101st Airborne Division at Grave. By 27 September he had been evacuated to Down Ampney airfield and subsequently received the Distinguished Flying Cross for his courage and conduct. The members of Edward's crew who had parachuted out of the crippled Stirling were picked up by German forces and placed in captivity. The losses of RAF transport aircraft in 38 Group and 46 Group over the MARKET-GARDEN period were stark and unprecedented, a total of 46 Stirlings lost in 38 Group and 27 Dakotas in 46 Group. Frustratingly, most of the supplies were never retrieved by the British because the DZs had all been captured by the Germans. British radio communications were so bad during MARKET GARDEN that the requests to alter DZs were never received at the air bases in the UK.

Throughout the battle of Arnhem the glider pilots had played an important role in every facet of the battle, underlining the value of their training as infantrymen as well as pilots. Their final task during the battle was to act as guides for the survivors of the 1st Airborne Division and mark the withdrawal route for the division as it was evacuated across the River Rhine on the night of 25 September. This was a highly responsible role which they accomplished with great skill and it further demonstrates the continued faith the senior airborne commanders had in the Glider Pilot Regiment's officers and men. That MARKET GARDEN was an overall failure is beyond doubt, but despite the planning mistakes and strong German reaction a small element of the 1st Airborne Division (Lieutenant Colonel Frost's 2nd Battalion, the Parachute Regiment) did successfully hold the northern end of Arnhem bridge for a total of 96 hours, 48 more than the plan had stipulated.

---

14    Airborne Assault Museum 1302, Statement from Flight Lieutenant Edwards on experience of Operation MARKET GARDEN.

Their action was described by the American commander of the 82nd Airborne Division, General Jim Gavin, as 'the outstanding independent parachute battalion action of the war'.[15]

The operation ultimately failed because of the delay in linking-up with the advancing ground elements of Second British Army. This delay arose for many reasons, but the failure of the 82nd Airborne Division to quickly capture the key objective of the Nijmegen Bridge until 20 September is undoubtedly a major one. Major General James Gavin's plan mistakenly prioritised taking the Groesbeek heights over seizing the Nijmegen bridge and he did not have enough troops to accomplish both objectives simultaneously. Gavin's shortage of troops might have been less pronounced if he was able to utilize his glider pilots in the same manner as the British. This would have required them to have received a similar level of infantry combat training as their British counterparts and been imbued with the same fighting ethos. Instead, American glider pilots had no responsibilities after landing their gliders and were, as one observer put it, 'strolling around like tourists with Leicas. Not trained even to use a rifle, they could not even take over guard duties and so release as many combat troops as possible to sway the outcome of the battle'[16] Gavin had reached the same conclusion whilst MARKET GARDEN was still being fought, writing on 25 September to Major General Paul Williams, the commander of IX Troop Carrier Command, under whose command the American glider pilots lay:

> In looking back over the past week's operations, one of the outstanding things, in my opinion, and one thing in most urgent need of correction, is the method of handling our glider pilots. I do not believe there is anyone in the combat area more eager and anxious to do the correct thing and yet so completely, individually and collectively, incapable of doing it, than glider pilots.
>
> Despite their individual willingness to help, I feel that they were definitely a liability to me. Many of them arrived without blankets, some without rations and water, and a few improperly armed and equipped. They lacked organization of their own because, they stated, of frequent transfer from one Troop Carrier Command unit to another. Despite the instructions that were issued to them to move via command channels to Division Headquarters, they frequently became involved in small unit actions to the extent that satisfied their passing curiosity, or simply left to visit nearby towns… At this time glider pilots without unit assignment and improperly trained, aimlessly wander about, causing confusion and generally get in the way and have to be taken care of.[17]

This American approach clearly compares unfavourably to the capabilities of the British glider pilots and the significant responsibilities placed upon them during the actual fighting.

The lessons of MARKET GARDEN, OVERLORD and HUSKY were all factored into the planning of the final airborne operation in Europe, Operation VARSITY, which supported the British crossing of the Rhine on 24 March 1945. In contrast to the rushed planning for MARKET GARDEN, the airborne staff officers had ample time to study and deliberate on all aspects of the airborne plan. Operation VARSITY was also the largest airborne lift in history, involving 16,000 men from the British 6th Airborne and American 17th Airborne Divisions. These were both simultaneously and successfully dropped in one lift, landing just a short distance in front of the advancing Second British Army, and only after it was clear that the river crossing of the Rhine, between Rees and Wesel, had been a success. This single lift was made possible by an increase in

---

15   Lawrence Wright, *The Wooden Sword*, p. 236.
16   Lawrence Wright, *The Wooden Sword*, p. 236.
17   Gerard Devlin, *Silent Wings* (Chatham: Mackays of Chatham Ltd, Kent, 1985), p. 279.

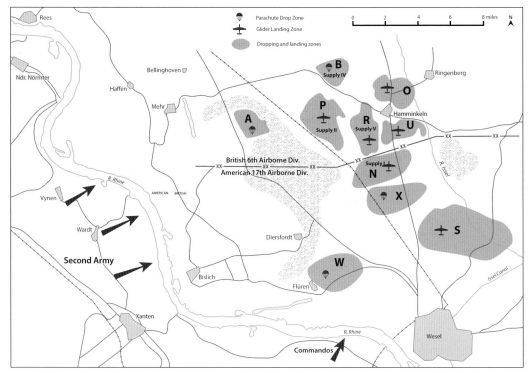

Figure 9  DZs and LZs used during Operation VARSITY.

the numbers of RAF aircraft in 38 and 46 Group to 440 machines, 60 more aircraft than were available at the time of Operation MARKET GARDEN. Furthermore, the re-supply drop for VARSITY was conducted just six hours after the first landings and the operation was declared a success at 1500 hours the same day. The operation's quick success has meant it is almost seen as an airborne anti-climax after MARKET GARDEN, but it was not without problems.

During the fly-in to the Rhine LZs, a total of 35 gliders did not reach their release points, mainly because of broken tow ropes and slip stream problems, these were predictable problems in a long transit flight from East Anglia and were not unexpected. More concerning for the pilots of both gliders and aircraft was the large smokescreen that had been established by the Second British Army to cover their own river crossing. This screen was very visible to the pilots as they approached the Rhine, for it was 50 miles wide and having been maintained over a period of nine days, very thick. Unsurprisingly several of the LZs east of the Rhine were obscured by both the screen, as well as the smoke and dust generated by the 4,000-gun artillery barrage supporting the assault river crossing, all of which compounded the glider and tug pilot's difficulties. In many cases the glider pilots involved in VARSITY were not nearly as well trained as those that had operated in Normandy and the Netherlands. The casualties amongst the glider pilots at Arnhem were so heavy that many new replacements had been quickly brought in to bolster the numbers. These included significant numbers of inexperienced RAF aircrew drawn from the reserve pool, who were given a crash course on gliders and some basic infantry training. In contrast, the RAF tug pilots were increasingly competent, Squadron Leader T.C. Musgrave commanded 296 (Airborne Forces) Squadron and in a post war report described Operation VARSITY from his unit's perspective:

> This report deals only with the part played by 296 and 297 Sqns, each supplying thirty Halifax/Horsa combinations, and operating from RAF station EARLS COLNE, ESSEX.

These two squadrons were the first Airborne Forces squadrons to be formed, and were associated with the airborne operations in SICILY, NORMANDY and ARNHEM, apart from Special Operations Executive and Special Air Service experience. Due to the shielding of personnel by the Air Council, the knowledge of airborne technique was not dispersed by normal RAF 'operational tour' postings and consequently the standard of efficiency had reached its peak by March 1945. It will be exceedingly difficult to attain this standard at an early stage in any future war due to the limitations of aircraft availability for airborne exercises, and the dispersion of personnel with the necessary knowledge at low level…

Of the sixty Horsas to be delivered [by the two squadrons], fifty-nine released at the correct point, and the remaining one suffered a broken tow rope and landed behind our own lines. The failure was due to slipstream from preceding aircraft, and the remnants of the rope still attached to the Halifax were brought back for examination in accordance with the briefing.

To revert to take-off, sixty combinations took off in fifty-six minutes, of which thirty had been pre-marshalled using 500 yards of our 2,000 yard runway. There was a tendency to overload Horsa gliders by soldiers, not unnaturally, adding extra ammunition. This practice will not occur in future. The organization necessary to ensure the successful take-off of such large numbers of combinations is too long to be discussed here, but suffice it to say that the direction of take-off decided by the weather decision on D-1 was most fortunately the right one. Moving one hundred and twenty airframes when aircrew should be resting is not a good start for an operation and wind forecasts so far in advance are not always accurate.

The form up was fairly good, but with the usual tendency to straggle at the back. Course was set on time, in excellent weather with no cloud, and very good visibility. On joining the main stream behind some hundred Stirlings, it was observed that they were also strung out, intermingling their station serials. Aircraft varied in height by some thousands of feet in an effort to avoid slipstream but a fair effort was made to close up and release at the right height at the target.

The route was simple, with simple navigational aids. When crossing the Channel, DUNKIRK was clearly visible due to the enormous visibility. Since airborne forces flying East could have only one significance for the enemy, it is apparent that if the enemy forces at Dunkirk had made the right signal and it had reached the right person, it might have had a most unpleasant effect.[18]

Visibility was good up to the Rhine, but the East bank was fairly thick with a grey/white smoke streaked with black in places. This was, as nearly as I can remember, at 1033 hours, as my serial was three minutes early. The head of the stream had been eight minutes early, and it was almost impossible to lose these three minutes without some form of dog leg. The effect of this early arrival on the gunner's fire plan has been discussed elsewhere. The cause was partially a tail wind, and partially a slight miscalculation of airspeed in the planning stage.

The visibility at 2,500 feet over the LZ was excellent, with the smoke cloud well below. Flak was moderate, although my third aircraft was shot down in flames immediately after he had released his glider at the correct place. It was my impression that flak was being directed at the gliders, going in to land through the fog of war, and not at the aircraft to the same extent. This was confirmed by the casualty percentages. Out of four hundred and forty aircraft at 2,500 feet, seven were lost, but the glider pilots suffered 29% losses.[19]

---

18   The isolated German garrison at Dunkirk was still holding out, even at this late stage of the war. It finally surrendered to the Czech Brigade that had been besieging it on 9 May 1945.

19   British Army of the Rhine, *Operation VARSITY – Directing Staff Edition,* (Germany: HQ BAOR, 1947), p. 49.

The task for the novice glider pilots was made even more complicated by the nature of the LZs themselves. Perhaps in response to the difficulties at Arnhem, the commander of the glider pilots, Brigadier Chatterton, decided to land the gliders in relatively small tactical groups, as close as possible to the objectives of the glider troops they were carrying. This contrasted with the success of the MARKET and MALLARD glider landings which had used a small number of larger and more easily visible LZs. During Operation VARSITY the pilots found that after reaching their release point and casting off, they had to descend through the thick dust and smoke, and quickly try and identify their assigned landing zone, sometimes having to circle to locate it. This frequently led to them being heavily engaged by German AA guns. The fire from these was heavier than expected because Operation CARPET, the Second British Army plan to shell selected German flak positions for the 30 minutes immediately prior to 'P-Hour',[20] had been cut short by eight minutes due to the early arrival of the airborne fleet.[21]

The cohesion of the landings quickly fell apart and many of the Horsa and Hamilcar gliders became widely scattered, even those that had landed successfully soon found themselves being accurately engaged by German fire on the ground. Lieutenant D.S.M. Turner was a Horsa pilot during Operation VARSITY and carried soldiers from 1st Battalion, the Royal Ulster Rifles. He describes the fly in:

> Prior to the operation, the Glider Pilot Regiment had been concentrating more on individual spot landings as opposed to the mass landing technique used on concentrated LZs on previous operations. This was done with a view to a tactical landing in the future. The Regiment was briefed to land 6 Airlanding Brigade on LZs near HAMMINKELN and to land 2 OXF BUCKS and 1 RUR coup-de-main parties on the bridges over the ISSEL.
>
> All the squadrons involved attended the Battalion's briefings, the individual squadron briefings and finally the air briefing by the RAF.
>
> Several units of the Regiment were attached to 46 Group and were moved to East Anglia into the 38 Group RAF area. This was to concentrate the force and save time 'forming-up' in the air as well as to save flying time.
>
> On the morning of 24 March the visibility was good and all the combinations were airborne except for one which was unable to take off owing to the tug undercarriage collapsing. The stream formed up over HAWKINGE and flew from there to WAVRE and thence in a double stream at 2,500 fleet to the target area. No fighter opposition was met en-route. A small percentage of gliders released prematurely owing to slipstream trouble, but most of them staggered a few hundred feet either above or below the briefed height of 2,500 feet in order to try and avoid slipstreams.
>
> On running up to the RHINE, one could see that the general area was enveloped in a thick haze. Three check points were marked on our maps; points A, B and C all five minutes flying apart, check point C being the release point. A predetermined release point is not strictly adhered to but acts as a guide to the Glider pilot.
>
> We were flying at roughly 2,900 feet (to avoid slipstream) and point A was easily seen; from there on, nothing could be distinguished on the ground. The flak was extremely heavy and concentrated and flying in position behind the tug became harder as the surrounding air was more than a little bumpy. As we could not see our own LZ or anybody else's we remained on tow.

---

20   P-Hour: the time the first parachutist exits the first aircraft of the airborne armada.

21   British Army of the Rhine, *Operation VARSITY – Directing Staff Edition*, p. 47.

Hamilcar gliders lined up at Woodbridge in Suffolk, the evening before Operation VARSITY.
(Crown Copyright – Air Historical Branch)

Suddenly we saw the autobahn below us, and as a result of careful study previously of air photographs, we knew where we were.

We released and did a tight 270 degree turn to port and saw the church spire of HAMMINKELN in front of us.

Owing to the immediate vicinity being rather crowded with gliders we applied full flap, which results in a very steep dive and went down on the LZ as briefed. The five members of 1 RUR were none the worse after their unorthodox approach and proceeded to unload the jeep and trailer containing the petrol and ammunition. Suddenly there was a loud hissing and one of the main wheels was hit. This stopped the unloading temporarily and we returned the fire. At this period we saw a Horsa in flames and when about 50 feet from the ground the starboard main plane was blown off. The glider landed a little roughly, but the occupants were unhurt except for a few minor bruises. The episode says a lot for the strength of construction of and manoeuvrability of the Horsa glider.

The load was removed from the glider via the nose and a quick survey made of the glider, which was found to have been holed considerably. We were not aware of any personal attention in the air except for a continuous bumping underneath. After some opposition we reported to the 1 RUR RV.[22]

The losses amongst the glider-borne force were high, 27 percent of the glider pilots became casualties, and 40 percent of the soldiers in 6th Air Landing Brigade, most of these occurring during the actual landing. As one example 2nd Battalion, the Oxfordshire and Buckinghamshire Light Infantry is reported to have lost half their strength in a period of about twenty minutes.[23] Many

---

22   British Army of the Rhine, *Operation VARSITY – Directing Staff Edition*, p. 75.
23   TNA WO 171/4320, *6th Air Landing Brigade Headquarters War Diary, 24 March 1944*.

of the cargoes and equipment in the gliders were either destroyed or damaged beyond repair, and the brigade was only able to recover 29 percent of their 75mm Howitzers, half their 25-pounders, 56 percent of their 17-pounder anti-tank guns, 29 percent of their 6-pounder anti-tank guns, 46 percent of their jeeps, 44 percent of their carriers and half their light tanks.[24] Lieutenant Colonel Paul Gleadell was the commanding officer of 12th Battalion, the Devonshire Regiment and remembers the flight towards his landing zone:

> A final handshake with the AOC of the Station and then we closed the doors. Everyone strapped themselves in and put their cigarettes out. We were fortunate in having a Squadron Commander of Glider Pilots and his RAF Sergeant co-pilot with whom we had flown on a recent Exercise. My Jeep and trailer were lashed amidships; I had the first seat on the starboard side and then came my batman, and one of the Regimental Police. Opposite us were the IO and a Private of the Intelligence Section. 'Tail-end Charlies' were my Signaller and Jeep Driver. Our glider chalk number – 188.
>
> Promptly at 0630 hours our Tug started up and we taxied forward behind one of the A Coy gliders to the head of the main runway. A pause, and then off we went – slowly at first and then quickly gathering speed, we bumped along the runway, until the gentle sway of the glider and the cessation of thuds indicated we were airborne. Everyone shouted the customary 'Airborne' and then settled down to face the long journey. We had not been off the ground a few seconds before the pilot turned round and drew my attention to the leading glider, its tow rope broken, circling down to find a spot for an emergency landing. Flying at 2,000 feet, the crossing was comparatively smooth, except for the usual air-pockets. Standing in the pilot's cockpit and looking out along the tow rope over the Halifax, one could see the long procession stretching out into the horizon. Once BRUSSELS was reached, and the stream of American aircraft joined in at 6,000 feet the air seemed to be filled by the massive armada. Darting in and out of the vast convoy were the Allied fighters, keen eyed to mark any threat of enemy interference from the air.
>
> Visibility was excellent on the way and the landmarks easy to pick up. Occasionally, one detected a lone glider circling down and one hoped that their forced landing would be a good one. The noise of air rushing through the glider made conversation difficult; unless one stood in the cockpit, there was little one could see through the small portholes on either side of the fuselage; the hours, therefore, slipped tediously by.
>
> At 1000 hours we cheered up as the tea-container was passed round, after which we strapped in. As we approached the REICHSWALD, scene of the recent fighting, visibility lessened. At last, the long winding silver riband of the RHINE hove into view – but beyond one could see nothing. In fact, once over the river visibility was scarcely a furlong, as the whole of the LZ was covered with a thick pall of smoke, dust and ground mist. That we were over the area was apparent from the flak, and with a sudden wrench we cast-off and drifted downwards. At first all was quiet, in marked contrast with the last four hours on tow. Then, as we came close to the ground the sounds of battle could be distinctly heard.
>
> The heavy flak and, more particularly, the light flak, and the small arms fire was still active, and the glider shuddered as a shell burst nearby. The Pilot signalled that he was going to try a landing, but the restricted view made him level up again with a sudden jerk. A burst, and then another, of bullets pierced the glider hull; the first struck the Jeep, fortunately missing the petrol tank, and the second wounded one of the soldiers in the back. Again the Pilot tried a landing, and again he levelled up, losing height all the while. A few seconds – they seemed

---

24   Terence Otway, *Airborne Forces*, p. 318.

hours – later, he turned round and said – 'I can't see a darned thing, but I'll do the best I can for you.' There was a crash, the floor boards were torn open and we found our feet being dragged along the ground for a few yards; at the same time the wounded man was hurled forward against the cockpit. With a jolt we came to rest, and according to our prearranged deplaning plan, the door was slid open and one of the men dashed out, Bren in hand, to take up a covering position. We had no idea where we were, except that we had stopped inches short of a particularly deep bomb crater.

Bullets appeared to be coming from three directions, and a 20 mm opened up from the autobahn, 120 yards away. There was a rush of air as a great Hamilcar Glider slid over our heads and crashed in the smoke a few hundred yards beyond. We were overjoyed to be hailed, suddenly in English. It was a platoon of 2 OXF BUCKS and they were firing in our direction. There was no chance of extracting my Jeep and so between us we carried our one casualty towards our friends. We then realised that they were on the banks of the ISSEL astride the railway bridge, and that we had landed between them and the enemy from RINGENBERG. Some Germans came out from a nearby copse, and were rounded up. I was naturally anxious to get to HAMMINKELN as soon as possible, so we left the casualty with that Coy HQ of 2 OXF BUCKS and made our way South along the railway track. The sound of shellfire and machine guns, coming from all sides, was deafening, and every now and again we came on a glider blazing furiously, one or two with their crews trapped within and little one could do to extricate them. One glider, or what was left of it, had wrapped itself round a massive tree. The whole situation seemed chaotic, and I wondered if we should ever get it unravelled. Every farm house appeared to contain a defended post and isolated battles were being fought out all over the LZ and beyond.[25]

During the days preceding the river crossing the RAF had been striking a variety of German targets around the area. These operations included armed reconnaissance and interdiction missions, as well as pre-planned targets designed to disrupt communications and generally help isolate the battle area. For Operation VARSITY, a number of Typhoon squadrons were also selected for an anti-flak role in support of the airborne landings. Aircraft were armed with either 4 x 60lb HE rockets and 4 x 60lb fragmentation rockets, or alternatively a number of (anti-personnel) 'Cluster' bombs, including a proportion of air-burst bombs for better anti-personnel effect. The squadrons were briefed to fly in sections of four aircraft at ten-minute intervals, the first section was scheduled to begin its strikes half an hour before the first wave of transport machines was due.

Squadron Leader Bob Spurdle was a New Zealander whose remarkable wartime career included action in the Battle of Britain (on Spitfires), the South Pacific (on Corsairs) and in North-West Europe (on Spitfires and Tempests). In March 1945 he was posted to 1st Allied Airborne Corps to assist in air ground support, an initiative that stemmed from Operation MARKET GARDEN where poor communications had resulted in hardly any close air support being provided to 1st Airborne Division in Arnhem. To ensure air strikes could be called upon rapidly during Operation VARSITY, it was decided that an RAF Air Ground support team would be included within the force, Spurdle was to lead this four-man RAF team and recalls the fly in and the heavy anti-aircraft fire:

It took us two hours and forty minutes to cross the Channel, drone over the flooded Dutch fields and be cast adrift. Two hours and forty minutes of thinking, worrying, nail biting doubts, regrets and promises to be a better man in the future. If there was to be a future!

25   British Army of the Rhine, *Operation VARSITY – Directing Staff Edition*, p. 72

Operation VARSITY, Handley Page Halifaxes and Short Stirlings tow Airspeed Horsa gliders over the French countryside shortly after crossing the English Channel, en route to the landing zones east of the River Rhine. (Crown Copyright – Air Historical Branch)

The whole glider vibrated, occasionally lurching violently when caught in the Stirling's slip-stream. Creaks and groans of straining woodwork, the clinking of chain ends. It was bitterly cold: Dowlin and I sagged in our hard seats. It was too tiring to shout above the sound of rushing air. At the rear of the Horsa, behind the jeep and trailer, were Simpson and Holmes. After about an hour I heard crackings and splintering from the back. Good God, the bloody thing's falling apart! But it was only the two airmen hacking peep-holes in the plywood fuse-lage with their knives, to see what was going on outside.

They tell me some of the men slept quite soundly on the long flight, but for me the experi-ence was too intense, too bizarre.

We were nearing the drop zone. I could see our Stirling tug slowly weaving as if checking its position. Others tended to drift across our path into some sort of approach pattern. Down below, by peering over the two pilot's shoulders, I saw gun flashes, sometimes rocket-firing Typhoons dived past and through the armada stream to engage German flak emplacements.

They'd slide down in speeding curves, straighten up and then rockets streaked away, trailing grey gases, to burst in clouds of earth and smoke.

A thin brown haze smothered the whole area below; above, a brilliant blue sky. Hundreds, uncountable aircraft, Stirlings, Dakotas, Horsas, Wacos, Albemarles, Hamilcars, all in a huge multi-tiered-unending stream. Fighters weaved above and on either side. We were in the vanguard group of the glider train, following immediately behind the paratroopers and combat infantry gliders.

Just in front of us a Stirling was hit by flak. A flash, a puff of smoke, then it staggered down to port, falling from the sky. Its glider slipped its towing-cable and veered sharply away to starboard; then the huge bomber ponderously reared up, up, up, to fall over backwards as we curved out of its path. A few parachutes and it was gone out of sight behind us. To our left a glider's tail plane broke off and the crippled machine was hastily cast adrift by its tug, the nylon rope whipping back in the slipstream. The fuselage and wings started to turn end over end at an astonishing speed of rotation; pieces broke off. The tail unit went. First soldiers, then a jeep, tumbled from the wreck. The men looked like puppets jerked by a madman – arms flailing – to fall thousands of feet to the waiting earth.

I'd seen enough and, with thoughts in turmoil, clambered back to my seat. Now the sounds of battle were continuous – above the muted roar of motors and the hissing slipstream I could hear all manner of thuds and bangs. The thin plywood skin of the glider seemed to quiver with the din. Every now and again there would be a sharp whacking sound as the glider was hit by shrapnel or from flak bursting close by; the air was tainted with the smell of high explosives. I took off my tin hat and tried to squat on it. I guess I was trying to protect my genitals – an instinctive male reaction. Again I ventured a look ahead just in time to see our tow rope snake off and be towed away by our tug. I bet they were pleased to get shot of us. The glider crew were nattering away, the co-pilot gesticulating towards some feature below. 'I see it! Yes! That's it!' shouted the glider's captain, who promptly dropped his map and took over the controls. I clambered right forward and, clutching the pilots' seat frame, stared out at the fantastic sight.

Parachutes hung festooned from trees or lay spread over green fields like fallen washing. Already a few gliders were on the ground and more and more were diving steeply at incredible angles to level off and plough across the rough fields. Wreckage, more and more, was scattered by the planes hitting the German poles erected to deny safe landings.

'Hold on!' shouted the co-pilot, and I clutched harder as full flap was applied. The Horsa heaved up, then dropped, nosing over into a heart-stopping swoop towards the deck. The lift spoilers whistled in the slipstream, tracer shells arced overhead. More and more bangs and thuds with the whole scene wreathed in smoke; men running or lying still on the fields.

Mortar bursts, black and ugly with cores of dull red flame, flickered at random across the earth, more running figures, dead animals, trees, ponds, a farmhouse and then – Crash! – and we were down.

Lurching and rumbling the big glider rocketed and heaved noisily over grassy farmland towards a belt of trees. Both pilots were swearing and cursing as they strained on rudder pedals to steer it clear of obstructions. Hanging on grimly I stared, fascinated, as bushes, fences and gates slid past. A loud bang! and the nosewheel burst through the flooring – the glider skidded crazily on, lurching and bucketing in clouds of sods and dust. A last crunch and we were there.[26]

---

26   Bob Spurdle, *The Blue Arena* (Manchester: Crecy, 1986), pp. 184-6.

The true extent of the glider landing problems were mitigated by a mis-drop of paratroopers from 17th Airborne Division on some of the British LZs, as well as the actions of the parachute brigades, who suffered fewer casualties. This was despite many of the DZs also being sited close to, or in some cases on their objectives. Lieutenant Colonel Richard Pine-Coffin was the commanding officer of 7th Battalion, the Parachute Regiment, part of 5th Parachute Brigade and landed at DZ 'B' near the town of Hamminkeln, he recalled the new approaches that his battalion had taken to suppress any enemy they might find on, or very near, their DZ:

> My Battalion was ordered to establish itself at this end of the DZ and to take on all opposition which might interfere with the other two battalions, which were to capture the bridge. In short 7 Para Bn came down looking for a fight, which is not a bad role for any battalion.
>
> The enemy in this area would be automatically taken on during the forming-up process and it was hoped that the sight of the massed drop would so lower his morale that this would not be too difficult. We all hoped very hard that this would be so because a parachute battalion is very vulnerable indeed until it has formed up. In fact it doesn't exist at all; it is just a collection of individuals, or at best small bodies of men, moving in the general direction of the RV. To land on top of, or even within small arms range of, an enemy position had long been a parachutist's nightmare, but on this occasion we did it and got away with it too.
>
> The drop was at 1010hrs and was from rather higher than we like for an operational drop; it must have been from nearly 1,000ft. This would normally have been an advantage, as it seems that the longer one is in the air the better the chance of spotting a landmark as you come down. But in this case everyone was pretty anxious to get down quickly because it was far from healthy in the air. The German flak gunners weren't getting much success in shooting down the Dakotas so a lot of them switched and burst their shells amongst the parachutists instead; this was most unpleasant and we suffered a number of casualties before we even reached the ground. There was mortar bombing and shelling on the ground but it was a great relief to get there just the same.[27]

Lieutenant Colonel Pine-Coffin relates that his 7th Parachute Battalion tried out several new techniques during Operation VARSITY, these included several to do with the drop itself and subsequent forming up:

> The first one [technique] was in the actual allocation of aircraft to companies. Originally the aircraft used to fly-in singly in line astern and each would drop its parachutists as it passed over the DZ. This was quite effective but it took a comparatively long time to get the whole force on the ground. The Americans had a quicker way which was very suitable for a daylight drops. They flew their planes over the DZ in a tight formation and all the parachutists jumped from the aircraft at the same time with the result that practically the whole force was in the air together and a great deal of time was saved. Viewed from the ground it was most spectacular as the air seemed completely filled with parachutists and it had many advantages from the airborne point of view too. The snag lay in the muddle you got on the ground. There was a most appalling mix-up of units and sub-units all over the DZ and our experiment was aimed at lessening this problem.
>
> The normal method of allocating aircraft for these saturation drops, as they were called, was to give the first nine aircraft to one company, the next to another and so on. This was very

27  British Army of the Rhine, *Operation VARSITY – Directing Staff Edition*, p. 66.

neat on paper and it looked good in the air too because the formation was made up of waves of nine aircraft; on the ground it was a complete muddle however.

We found out this weakness on a practice jump shortly before the operation: on this exercise we couldn't go to our RV at all because the enemy was holding it so we had the job of trying to work out the muddle before attacking them. It was an almost impossible job so we put on our thinking caps and next time we allotted all the aircraft down one flank of the formation to one company and all down the other flank to another. Bn HQ and the third rifle company were put in the middle but their aircraft also ran from front to rear of the formation rather than across it. The result was that although everyone was still pretty muddled up on the ground the bulk of those in any one area were from the same company. It worked extremely well and was particularly useful for A Coy who, for some odd reason were nearly all dropped well beyond the DZ. When he saw what had happened the Coy Commander collected together everyone who was near him and brought them in as a formed body. A Coy was late getting to its positions and this had repercussions… but it was able to keep together.

The suddenness of the drop had the desired effect and we found the Germans slow to react. The battalion was in this position for five hours and during that time there was no really serious attack put in on us. There were various attacks on the B Coy position by parties of about a platoon strong or slightly more, and at one time C Coy on the Left… took on about a company that was working round their flank. It was the A Coy position that came in for the worst time. You remember A Coy came in rather late and when they arrived they found that their area was a very nasty spot. Their casualties were high and so were those of the mortars and MMG [Medium Machine Gun] men who were with them.

It is difficult to generalise about the opposition because it was so varied. Some Germans fought extremely hard and others seemed to regard the war as lost and fight accordingly. Some of the German Paratroops who had fought so well on the other side of the RHINE, were in this area and we expected a harder tussle than they gave us. At the risk of creating a wrong impression about the opposition, I would like to tell you the story of one of my NCOs who was dropped in the country beyond the DZ. As this man was coming down he could see someone on the ground just about where he expected to land, and as he got lower he could see it was a German paratrooper armed with a Schmeisser. There was really nothing he could do about it and so he cursed his luck and landed in a heap, as one does, at the German's feet. He told me afterwards that he shut his eyes and waited for the burst from the Schmeisser but it was so long in coming that he opened them again to see what the hitch was. He found that the German was busy collapsing his chute for him and when he had done this he helped him out of the harness, unpacked his Bren Gun from the kit bag and then surrendered to him. When he had got over the shock of all this the NCO noticed that about twenty more Germans had arrived and they all surrendered to him too. At the same time within a mile of all this, other parties of Germans were putting up desperate fights.

The casualties of 7 Para Bn had been high and were chiefly caused by the flak while we were in the air and the shelling and mortaring of the positions during the day. Once the drop is over it is better to get as far away from the DZ as you can because it soon becomes the target for every gun and mortar that can be scraped up but, in our case, the job was on the DZ and we had to stay put and take whatever was sent over. The total casualties were 92 out of just over 500 dropped – that is just under 20%.[28]

---

28   British Army of the Rhine, *Operation VARSITY – Directing Staff Edition*, p. 66.

Operation VARSITY acted as the finale for airborne operations in Europe. The size and scale of Allied air transport had now grown and matured to the extent that two divisions could be flown in just a single lift. VARSITY was undoubtedly a success, but it still highlighted the inherent risks of airborne operations, even when time and resources were available for detailed planning. Meanwhile in the Far East, air transport was being used in a highly imaginative manner to assist the mobility and manoeuvre of General Slim's Fourteenth Army. The jungle terrain and poor road and rail communications in Burma meant that it was an operational theatre that was particularly suited to light infantry operations, as well as the use of aircraft to move Army formations from one area of the front to another.

# 14

# 'The Friendly Firm'[1]
# The Use of Air Transport in the Far East

Air transport was used by the British for many purposes besides airborne operations. For much of the time it was as an unremarkable method of moving small numbers of personnel quickly around a theatre, but occasionally its use had a more direct operational impact. That was certainly the case during Rashid Ali's rebellion against the British in Iraq in April 1941. This growing crisis in Iraq prompted the British to fly troops from the 1st Battalion, the King's Own Royal Regiment from Karachi in India, to Shaibah airbase near Basra. These forces were flown in Valentias, Atalantas and Douglas DC-2s, in an airlift that began on 17 April and which by the end of the month had successfully transported 300 soldiers from Basra to the besieged RAF base at Habbaniyah near Baghdad. There they came under the command of the RAF defending the base and played an important part in the British victory there.

British ambitions to use air transport operationally also increased as the size of the Allied air transport fleet grew. The use of Dakotas to rapidly reinforce Kos island with the Durham Light Infantry in 1943 was one instance and in June 1944 an entire infantry division, 52nd Lowland Division, was converted into an air-portable formation. Though this Division was never used in that role, but instead fought gallantly as a standard ground formation in the latter part of the North-West European campaign.

Air casualty evacuation had been an enduring element of the RAF's air transport role throughout the Second World War and by the summer of 1944 it was being routinely used in Normandy to quickly evacuate casualties to base hospitals in England. Casualty evacuation by air began from the Normandy bridgehead on 13 June, a week earlier than had been anticipated in planning. It was initially a little ad hoc but by 18 June it had been placed under the command of HQ 11 Line of Communication Area and became much better organised. A Medical Air Liaison Officer was appointed to 83 Group RAF and 81 Base General Hospital was made the collecting centre and focal point for those nominated to be evacuated by air. A single airfield was also identified (B14 near Amblie) as the sole point of air evacuation and an RAF casualty evacuation unit was established at the airfield. The capacity of this medical unit was modest and on several occasions a field dressing station or even a casualty clearing station was established nearby to help hold and treat casualties prior to their journey. During the month of June 1944, a total of 3,176 casualties (of whom 2,113 were stretcher cases) were evacuated by air from Normandy back to the UK.[2]

---

1   Nickname given to 194 Squadron RAF. This was a Dakota equipped squadron, one of many that provided air transport to the Chindits and Fourteenth Army.
2   F.A.E. Crew, *Army Medical Services, Campaigns, Volume IV North West Europe* (London: HMSO, 1962), pp. 190-1.

The arrival and reception of casualties by air into the UK was organised and controlled by an air evacuation headquarters, formed from HQ Salisbury Plain District, and based at Stratton St Margaret. It had representatives from all three services, the wartime Emergency Medical Services (EMS) and the Canadian Army. All transport aircraft were to fly into airfields situated in the Swindon area (Blakehill Farm, Down Ampney and Broadwell). Occasionally the airfield at Watchfield was also used to preserve the security of airborne operations mounted from the previous three airfields. The RAF established a casualty evacuation centre of 200 beds at each airfield with facilities for urgent surgery and resuscitation, and the nearby EMS hospitals of Stratton St Margaret and Oxford were also available for urgent cases. For the remainder of the casualties an ambulance train would take them from a newly constructed railway siding near Shrivenham to the various home base hospitals.[3] An important aspect of this air casualty evacuation operation was the use of nursing orderlies from the WAAF. There were an estimated 200 nurses involved, who formed part of 46 Group's Air Ambulance Unit, christened the 'Flying Nightingales' they provided essential nursing care on the flights back to the UK. LAC(W) Edna Birkbeck recalls the flights and patients:

> Some of the wounded were very badly injured but you couldn't let it get to you. Despite the severity of their injuries, and, on one occasion, having to crash land after engine failure, none of my patients ever died on any of my flights. They always wanted tea, those that could drink. We'd carry an industrial sized urn and they'd always want to know when we were over the coast. I'd tell them when we were over the coast. I'd tell them and say it won't be long before you're home, and they'd cheer.[4]

The WAAF nursing orderlies were trained at an air ambulance course at RAF Hendon which taught them the use of oxygen, how to administer injections and colostomies, as well as dealing with certain types of injuries including fractures and burns. For their air duties they were classified as aircrew, receiving an extra eight pence a day flying pay. Most nurses received positive support when performing their duties, though an occasionally odd reception was sometime encountered. LAC (W) Roberts describes her initial reception:

> The pilot of the Dakota in which I did my training flights was Scottish, Warrant Officer Jock McCannell. After the first few trips I had the feeling he didn't want me there and eventually I asked why. He said it was nothing personal, that he'd come from a fishing family and fishermen would never put out to sea with a woman aboard as it was bad luck. During that first week in June us women were grounded, while all the planes took part in the landings. Jock's was one the few that didn't return and I thought of the women in the boat.[5]

It was however in Burma that the use of air transport was incorporated into a land campaign in a larger and more fundamental manner. The potential for using air transport as an integral element of Fourteenth Army's campaign had first occurred to General Slim during his retreat from Burma in 1942. At that time the RAF's modest air transport element had played a small but important part in evacuating elements of his army, as well as the civilian population, to India. For

---

3    F.A.E. Crew, *Army Medical Services, Campaigns, Volume IV North West Europe*, pp. 67-70.
4    <rafblakehillfarm.co.uk> accessed on 3 April 2019, quotes by kind permission of Vincent Povey and Kara Holliday.
5    <rafblakehillfarm.co.uk> accessed on 3 April 2019, quotes by kind permission of Vincent Povey and Kara Holliday.

the remainder of 1942, as well as for much of 1943, the strong Japanese air force in Burma made any British use of transport aircraft in frontline areas a highly dangerous affair. However, by late 1943 the British had wrested control of the air from the Japanese and the use of air transport to move ground forces around or conduct re-supply became both a practical proposition, as well as a significant operational advantage in a country where the lines of communication were sparse and tortuous.

The Chindit campaign of 1943 was an important part of this development and provided an opportunity for experimentation that altered British perceptions on how a jungle campaign might be waged. Prior to the first Chindit operations, the British Army could be accused of being overly tied to their road lines of communication. The Japanese were acutely aware of this and understood that sometimes all they needed to do to force the British to abandon a defensive position, was conduct an out-flanking march through the jungle and put in a roadblock behind the British. Under these circumstances the British would predictably turn back to deal with the problem, often weakening their original position or withdrawing from it altogether. The commander of the Chindits, Brigadier Orde Wingate, advocated a different approach, arguing that in an age of air transport most of what the lorries brought up by road, could just as easily be carried by aircraft. These supplies could be delivered directly to the soldiers, either by dropping the cargo by parachute or by landing on rudimentary airstrips cut out of the jungle. Wireless communications and efficient liaison with the RAF were essential requirements to make this system work, but it had the potential to free the Army from being excessively tied to road transportation and logistics.

The Chindits also believed that air power could partially replace the artillery which could not be taken with them on their long-range penetrations into the jungle. As artillery ammunition is normally the logistician's biggest headache, this helped reduce their administrative tail markedly.[6] To support Wingate's first 1943 expedition, which aimed to penetrate beyond the Chindwin and Irrawaddy rivers, the RAF allocated 31 and 194 Squadrons. These two squadrons initially consisted of little more than three Dakotas and three Hudsons at any one time – which is hardly a vast air armada.[7] The squadrons were given the use of Agartala as an operational base, the RAF's best airfield in the region.

Wingate's Chindits were formed around the 77th Brigade, whose 3,000 men were divided into seven columns, each equipped with mortars, machine guns and a five-man RAF section. A squadron leader, who was always a pilot, led this small RAF team in arranging the necessary supply drops and air strikes for the Chindits. The RAF section communicated back to its air headquarters through the 1082/83 RAF radio set, a piece of equipment that was so bulky it required three mules to carry its parts when broken down. The first Chindit columns set off from India by foot on 6 February 1943 and four months later 2,182 survivors marched back, each Chindit having walked at least 1,000 miles over the harshest terrain in the world. In support of them the RAF had flown 178 sorties and dropped 300 tons of supplies, usually on large paddy fields or the occasional jungle clearing, the technique continuously improving as experience grew. The air transport support provided to the Chindits included an emergency drop of dinghies, to help one party cross a swiftly moving river and the landing of a Dakota in a jungle clearing to evacuate 17 sick and wounded men back to India. Only eight air strikes were called for during the operation, but the expedition was successful in penetrating beyond the Irrawaddy, cutting the main north-south railway and causing destruction and confusion behind Japanese lines. Most importantly from an air perspective it proved that British forces could, in certain circumstances, be sustained through air supply alone.

---

6    Louis Allen, *Burma, The Longest War 1941-45* (London: Phoenix Press, 1984), p.120.

7    Henry Probert, *The Forgotten Air Force* (London: Brassey's, 1985), p.136.

A casualty being loaded into a Vultee Stinson Sentinel Mark II of 194 Squadron RAF for evacuation from a forward air strip in Burma. (Crown Copyright – Air Historical Branch)

Having established the concept, Wingate received a greater degree of senior support for his second Chindit expedition in January 1944.[8] This included the allocation of an American 'Air Commando' to the Chindits, this formation was a self-contained mini air force that consisted of 35 Dakotas, 50 Mustangs, 30 Mitchells, 100 Waco gliders, ten experimental helicopters and 100 L1 and L5 light aircraft. This now meant that Wingate's Chindits no longer had to face an exhausting march in to and out of Burma, but could instead be flown over the Japanese front line directly to a series of strongholds, usually based around an airstrip, from which they could then attack the Japanese rear areas.[9] These strongholds would be established by an advance party that would fly in Waco gliders and use bulldozers to construct an airstrip. Three landing grounds were selected – 'Piccadilly', 'Broadway' and 'Chowringhee', though Piccadilly was discarded when photo-reconnaissance detected it was blocked by tree trunks.[10]

Operation THURSDAY commenced on 5 March 1944. Sixty-one gliders took off that night destined for Broadway, of which 35 successfully reached the landing zone, including two containing a bulldozer which began to clear an airstrip for the aircraft about to arrive the following day. On 6 March, shortly after dusk, 64 Dakotas landed, followed by 100 more each night for the next few days. The fly in to Chowringhee began in a similar manner on 6 March, when over 9,000 men and 1,400 mules were flown in, as well as artillery and anti-aircraft guns. Pilot Officer Joe Simpson was an RAF pilot with 194 Squadron on Dakotas and remembers his trip to Broadway:

---

8   See Map 13 for details of the Second Chindit Expedition.

9   Terence O'Brien, *Out of the Blue – a Pilot with the Chindits* (London: Arrow Books, 1984), pp. 47-9.

10  Controversially Wingate had not actually ordered any photo reconnaissance of the landing grounds – in the mistaken belief it would compromise the site. The photographs were taken by an American pilot who had disobeyed orders.

We were last in [to Broadway] because it wasn't until long after the first plane had landed that they sent in this signal saying they wanted water. So, I was the reserve airplane and told to take in water and they gave me a small bowser full of water and several fifty-gallon drums of water, and I was delighted to have my first operational flight in command. I landed at Broadway, long after everyone else, and a Chindit bristling with guns and knives opened the door and said 'What have you got?' and I said 'I have got your water', very pleased with myself. 'Water! What the hell have you brought water for? What we want is men and ammunition' so I said 'I am terribly sorry, I have only got water'.

He said 'You had better get out of here quickly, because dawn is not far away and you have got to be off the strip', I said 'well you get this water off, because I can't take off with it on'. So we rolled out the fifty gallon drums on to the airfield and then tried to get the bowser out, but there was no way we could get it through the door man-handling it. We turned on the tap, to try and get rid of as much of it as we could, left the tap on and he shouted 'Off you go! Off you go!' So I eventually got him to get some men to man-handle it to the front of the airplane where my crew lashed it down and we tried to get off.

Now I was completely disorientated by the kerfuffle and the early morning mist that had come down. I suddenly spotted two lights, which must be the runway lights, so I lined up with those and I said well we will have to open up on this throttle before we let go. I had just about got full power, about to let go and a man rushed in front of with a torch waving at me and I shut down the engine and throttled back and he said 'these are the last two lights on the runway you are facing the wrong way'. I wished I could meet that man again, because my goodness me he saved me from an awful catastrophe. We turned round and took off and again in the confusion I had forgotten that immediately after take-off I had to make a fifteen degree turn to the right and this I did not do. The first I knew I could hear the trees battering the bottom of the aeroplane and that brought it all back to me in a flash. So I did a stall turn steeply to the right and pulled it up and again the Dakota was marvellous, it answered the call and when I got back to base the fitter and engineer said 'where have you been sir?' as the engine cowlings were full of twigs and leaves, but that was no problem with the Dakota, it could take any amount of abuse like that.[11]

The Chindits established further strongholds later in the operation, including 'Aberdeen', 'White City' and 'Blackpool' all of which contained rudimentary landing grounds for the Dakotas to fly into. In addition to the transportation of men and supplies the Chindits also needed to have their pack animals brought in by Dakota, though this was not necessarily without problems as Joe Simpson relates:

The problem with mules was that they are mulish and difficult to handle. What they [the RAF] did is fixed up stalls made out of bamboo in the aircraft and you somehow got the mules on board and then lashed them in to position. They would cram in up to six mules in there, they occasionally caused a lot of trouble, one broke loose in the airplane and the captain was most upset to find troops shooting inside his air plane trying to kill this mule with bullets flying all over the place. Anyway they managed to shoot it and that was alright...

We were at this strip waiting to take off and Wingate with his posse of redtabs [Officers of the rank of Colonel and above] was inspecting the operation and troops were having particu-lar trouble with one mule, which just did not want to walk up the ramp and they were cursing and swearing and General Wingate, a very religious man, he went and tore them off a strip

---

11   IWM Sound Archives, Catalogue Number 12736, Joe Geoffrey Simpson interview.

A Douglas Dakota of 177 Wing RAF, ploughs its way through the monsoon water on arrival at a forward airfield in the Arakan, Burma. (Crown Copyright – Air Historical Branch)

for using that sort of language and he said it was quite unnecessary. 'I shall show you how to do it'.

He took the mule's halter and led it around the aeroplane, chatting amicably to him all the time and telling him what a good fellow he was, and all this sort of thing and up the ramp. Still the mule refused to go and dug its fore-feet in and so he turned it round and walked it round the aeroplane, and I think he did this three times and still the mule wouldn't board.

He turned round and said to his retinue 'get here, get behind this thing' and all these red tabs, who weren't used to this sort of work, were all heaving and pushing. And then he could see the crew of Sergeant Heck laughing away, the Captain was Sergeant Wally Kimble a Rhodesian and he was laughing. And Wingate said 'come on you three help as well' and Sergeant Kimble said 'No Sir, I am supposed to fly that aeroplane and if I get kicked in the leg that aircraft does not go.' They never got the mule on board.[12]

There were probably few planes that could cope with these conditions as well as the robust and dependable Dakota. Simpson relates how much he approved of the aircraft and the advantages it possessed:

If you ever want to give me a Christmas present, give me a Dakota, it is the most wonderful aeroplane, I have told my kids save your pocket money and buy me a Dakota. It really was a dream of an aeroplane… I flew ten years in Dakotas because I flew it in the RAF and in civil aviation and I never had any problems. It was easy to do the simple things, take-off and landings, but you had to be very careful to do good runs in all conditions but, I suppose like all aeroplanes once you mastered it, it became very flexible.

You see we were landing on these jungle strips…they give you a minimum of 900 yards that was cleared, but they often did not clear all the trees at either end and you therefore had to clear the trees and there was your 900 yards. We learnt to be able to do very, very short

---

12   IWM Sound Archives, Catalogue Number 12736, Joe Geoffrey Simpson interview.

landings. In the Dakota it stalled with a load on at about 60–65 knots and if you brought it in one percent above the stall she was perfectly manoeuvrable and once you cut the power she stopped.[13]

The Dakota needed to be very robust, given the state of some of the airstrips and the quality of airmanship amongst the air transport crews also needed to be high. Simpson talks through some of the difficulties transport pilots faced when flying in support of the Chindits:

> Well, all the strips had problems... Most of them had hills on one end or the other, like Broadway, where take off involved a fifteen degree turn to the right, Aberdeen if you overshot, you had to make a thirty degree turn to port and fly up the valley. It did not normally affect you if your landing was alright at Aberdeen, because we landed one way and took off the other, so that you were using the good approach end for both take-off and landing. White City was a very short strip, Chowringhee was very small and they were only used for a very short time. Aberdeen was in use for a long, long time and was a very good strip. Good approaches, apart from that disadvantage if you overshot. We had one chap with whom I did a lot of my early flying, a New Zealander called Ray Milsop, and for some reason or other he overshot at Aberdeen and went straight on and hit the hill instead of going up the valley.
> When the Chindits were surrounded they built a strip called Blackpool, which was near the Indawgi lake, we had to get them out and rearm them and it was all done in a great hurry. We went over there and I could see lots of people touching down and not having enough runway and they were opening up and going round again. I said I am not going to do that, no way, because of the difficulties of starting off with a heavy load on and trying to pick up speed and inevitably there were hills around. I said I am going to get down on the end of the runway. So we were dragging it in at about 68 knots with a load on and quite safe and just as we got to the end of the runway there was a damn great tree they had left standing, we had to get over that and I plonked it down and there was a tremendous crack and the undercarriage on the port side collapsed and immediately the airplane burst into flames. So there we were belting down the runway and I was holding it up on the one wheel we had left and we just swung off to the left but clear of the runway. After the war I met the chap who was in charge of building the strip at Blackpool, he told me that they did not clear the very end of the runway because the bulldozer had broken down and they had left a mound of earth at the very end of the runway, where they did not think anyone would touch down. That is what I hit, because you could not see it.[14]

The air support given to the Chindits was not simply confined to flying them into the strongholds. Once the columns marched into the jungle it would be up to the RAF to keep them supplied, typically for weeks at a time. Squadron Leader Terence O'Brien was the RAF section leader attached to a Ghurkha column in the Chindits and describes the selection and setting up of a drop zone:

> This drop was in a Taungya [a clearing to plant food crops] beside a village, the perfect combination, for the help the villagers gave could make a dramatic difference in recovery. The Kachins were always eager to help, not only because they are hospitable by custom – and nature also, it seemed to us – but also because they always received some of the parachutes in return and these were prized rewards; they wove their own cloth, usually in the sloped-line

13   IWM Sound Archives, Catalogue Number 12736, Joe Geoffrey Simpson interview.
14   IWM Sound Archives, Catalogue Number 12736, Joe Geoffrey Simpson interview.

patterns you associate with Aztec designs, but much preferred manufactured cottons and these became unobtainable after the Japanese invasion.

Strangely enough we never had a free-fall – mule fodder, say – or a streamed parachute ever hit a house on a village drop. About a quarter of our drop might be free fall, and about ten-percent of parachutes failed, so the drop site could be a dangerous place; on moonless nights even a parachuted load could be a deadly missile, unseen, unheard, in its rapid descent. We had no fatalities, our worst casualties were broken limbs, but I know at least four deaths in other columns. The free drops were in double bags, the outer one being bigger than the actual container; the inner one would usually burst on impact, spilling the contents into the bigger bag, but it was extremely rare for that second one to fail – I saw a load of boots once ripped open by a jagged stump. We operated the Aldis, the most reliable method of contacting the pilots, so had to be out in the open.[15]

The RAF section leaders with the Chindit columns were supposed to follow a well-articulated set of rules for air drops. These included setting up an L-shaped set of fires 100 yards apart from each other, with the RAF officer standing at the base of the 'L', 50 yards from the last fire. The whole 'L' had to be no larger than 500 yards by 200 yards. There was also a host of other, sometimes impractical, rules to follow. These included that the DZ should be on the summit of a cleared ridge, with nothing higher than 100 feet within five miles, that the drops should preferably take place in moonlight and that fires should be lit 15 minutes before the estimated time of arrival (ETA) of the aircraft. The procedure also dictated that the ground party should wait for the aircraft to signal first and that the RAF officer should reply from the base of the L. The last aircraft to drop would signal 'FIN', to indicate the drop was complete. Terence O'Brien remembers that these rules were very rarely observed:

We set our fires within any cleared ground we could find, hillside or valley, even as short as 200 yards – better a drop in which you collect only 20% rather than reject a site and starve. We took the drop any hour of the night, moon or no moon, never lit the fires until we actually heard the aircraft (firewood usually too precious), and the faintest engine sound sent us flashing the Aldis continuously and often firing off a green Verey light to ensure attention. I signalled from a protective point which could be anywhere on the site at all, never bothered to put out an arrow if we changed sites (as if 5 miles made any difference to a pilot!) and never ever gave the homing signal… We never missed an aircraft that was sent to us.

All experienced collectors took up protected positions when free-falling loads were being dropped. With a tree trunk between you and the plane you could feel fairly secure; when parachutes were coming down however you had to be out in the open to mark them on your chart, so you had no protection from streamers. The proportion of such failures was disgraceful; almost certainly the responsibility lay with the packers at base and the types of parachutes used, not with the despatchers.[16]

The parachutes that failed to open may have been the so-called 'Parajutes'. This was a necessary improvisation by the British in Burma, that arose from a lack of silk, or other materials with which to make parachutes. Forced to adapt General Slim had approached the Indian Jute industry who produced a rudimentary design that partially solved the problem, though it always had a much

---

15   Terence O' Brien, *Out of the Blue – A Pilot with the Chindits*, p. 130.
16   Terence O'Brien, *Out of the Blue – an RAF pilot with the Chindits*, pp. 131-3.

A RAF wireless unit attached to a British Army column operating in North Burma arranges for food and supplies to be dropped. (Crown Copyright – Air Historical Branch)

higher failure rate than either a silk or cotton parachute. Unsurprisingly, the use of Parajutes was limited to less valuable or fragile loads and never to drop personnel.[17] O'Brien continues:

> In a three aircraft drop we have had as many as six streamers, which is an appalling record. The load could be over sixty pounds, a solid block of K rations [American individual ration packs], steel petrol containers, a box of ammunition, deadly missiles which could be fatal in a direct hit. Though the army officers gave them unstinted praise, the standard of the pilots varied. You tried to give the pilot a clear run-line and a left hand circuit that would keep him safe at 250 feet but it was not always possible; sometimes there would be only a short run at a safe height, sometimes a right hand circuit would be needed to keep low. In such cases many pilots simply stayed very high and carried out their normal drill. This was the worst fault, dropping at excess height. Drift could be disastrous, for if a chute missed you on a ridge you had no chance of finding it five thousand feet down in a nearby valley. Not once did I see a pilot start with a single parachute marker, a simple technique in which all of them should have been trained because it was the only way to ensure accuracy: you drop the marker on estimated windspeed-direction, aligning engine-nacelle say on some ground feature as drop checkpoint, bank sharply to note actual landing spot, then adjust on your checkpoint accordingly for subsequent runs. Most pilots charged straight in and flung out half a dozen parachutes from directly overhead, irrespective of wind direction. Some adjusted after faulty runs,

17   William Slim, *Defeat into Victory* (London: Cassell and Co, 1956), p. 225.

A Dakota drops supplies by parachute to troops of the Fourteenth Army deployed south of the Irrawaddy river.
(Crown Copyright – Air Historical Branch)

some did not. The pilots, both American and British, were like any other group of men – some were conscientious, some were not.[18]

Finding the column's DZs at night was a difficult task for the RAF pilots and given Chindit dependency on their air lifeline, one that was taken very seriously, certainly by the RAF leadership. Joe Simpson recalls the importance the CO of 194 Squadron, Wing Commander Pearson attached to these missions:

> He tried to institute a relationship between a particular column which you were supplying and 194 Squadron, so that you could say you know these people although you had never actually met them, but had supplied them here and there and it worked very well indeed. The Army played their part very well, when you got a particularly good drop they would send you back a 'Strawberry' as opposed to a 'Raspberry' and he [The CO] always insisted that the crews were told they got a 'Strawberry' and in my logbook you will see several times I got a 'strawberry'. Which meant all my load was delivered on to target… Our biggest problem out there was weather, flying through the monsoon, with no aids at all and very poor maps was very hard work. Particularly for someone like myself who was very inexperienced…that's your dropping zone and you had to find your own way there in whatever the weather.
>   We developed a very good technique, we always took as much fuel as we could on board, because the Dakota was a very willing work horse, overload it and it would still perform very well… When you got to your dropping zone and it was covered by fog or cloud or whatever you just pushed off and waited for an hour and came back in. Very seldom did you do an aborted sortie. I got some in my book and we often found out that the aborted sortie was because the Army had to move on and there was no personnel to man the dropping zone. Having found the dropping zone, which was very difficult, if you did not get the signal lights you would go back home. But it did not happen very often…
>   …We did not know what radar was out there and it was just a matter of trial and error. The maps were very inadequate you would go to a place and you would fly above and let down. You would try going in on the tree tops and you would go up a valley and find that the valley was closed by a cloud at the other end and you would circle up and come out again. Our navigators were absolutely superb and modified the existing maps so they could tell where you were.[19]

By the time of Slim's Second Arakan offensive in January 1944, the RAF/Chindit techniques used in the first 1943 expedition had filtered out to the wider Fourteenth Army. Flight Lieutenant John Braithwaite was a Dakota pilot with 62 Squadron, based at Komilla and recalls supporting 81st West African Division as they advanced down the Kaladan valley.[20] The drops he made were usually on to ad-hoc DZs, with codenames such as 'Popinjay' and his aircraft was usually escorted by five or so Hurricanes for protection against any Japanese fighters. He describes this period of operations and how the drops were made:

> The West Africans were moving down the river valleys in the Arakan and had to be supplied wholly by air, there was no other way of doing it…the things like rice and sugar and clothes, the soft stuff, was dropped at ground level in double sacks and the more vulnerable heavier

---

18   Terence O'Brien, *Out of the Blue – an RAF pilot with the Chindits*, pp. 131-3.
19   Imperial War Museum, Sound Archives, Catalogue Number 12376, interview with Joe Geoffrey Simpson.
20   See Map 14 for Air Supply in the Arakan campaign.

stuff, like ammunition, rum and that sort of stuff were dropped by parachutes. The parachutes were connected by static wire to the aircraft and you pushed the parcel out and it opened its own parachute, they were dropped at about 300 feet. The people on the ground would mark a dropping zone with white crosses in the river valley, generally a sand bank, and we would go down to ground level and drop between those markers. Very often it meant descending six or seven thousand feet because of the mountains down into the river valley and then climbing out again and quite often it took ten or a dozen trips to get rid of the cargo because dropping zones were so short. We had two launchers in the back and a series of lights and as we came up to the dropping zone we put a green light on and they would kick the stuff out and we would put a red light on at the end of the dropping zone and they would stop and we would climb up and go round again until completed. We carried three and a half tonnes of supplies and we were doing sometimes two trips a day, in extreme cases three trips a day. There were occasional interferences, occasionally ground fire, but not a great deal, the main hazard was the operation itself and the terrain.[21]

Routinely supplying divisions was one thing, but in February 1944 the Japanese cut off 7th Indian Division and part of the XV Corps administrative area who were operating in the Arakan. The battle, which came to be known as the Battle of the Admin Box, witnessed the first occasion when an entire British division, with all its vehicles, equipment and personnel, was cut off from its ground line of communication, but because it was supplied entirely by air throughout the battle, held its positions and successfully fought the Japanese off. Simpson describes these operations:

We would be given a load and a dropping zone and we would go down there and drop the load…the load would be anything from food and ammunition to barbed wire – anything they wanted down there. The Royal Indian Army Service Corps would load up the aeroplanes and we would drop whatever we were told, the loading procedures were haphazard in the extreme, we would be told we had 6,000lbs of stuff but you couldn't check it. I remember one occasion we were taking sugar and the sugar had been outside in the rain all night so heaven knows what it weighed, but its dry weight was 6,000lb and it had soaked up all that rain and was much heavier.

In the Arakan in particular, we were flying right over the Jap lines so we got a lot of trouble from small arms fire, and they were very good with their small arms fire. But you just had to ignore it and get on with it… Joe Curtiss, was a Canadian, and the trip after I flew with him, he had one engine put out by ground fire and he had to come back on one engine. Everybody was hit a little bit, but usually nothing very serious. We lost one or two aircraft down there, but they just did not return, and it is very difficult when you are down there flying low and suddenly an aircraft just goes into the ground. You don't know why? May have been misjudgement or small arms fire, there was no court of enquiry, just the request for a replacement aircraft and crew.[22]

As a result of the air supply operations 7th Indian Division were able to defend their positions and hold on, but it should be remembered that this lifeline only existed because of the air superiority achieved by the RAF. During the first 13 days of the operation, three squadrons of Spitfires destroyed 65 Japanese fighters. Had these Spitfires not been available it is hard to believe that the air supply operation could have been conducted at all. Even so, on 8 February 1944 the Japanese

---

21   IWM Sound Archives, Catalogue Number 12288, John Cecil Braithwaite interview.
22   IWM Sound Archives, Catalogue Number 12736, Joe Geoffrey Simpson interview.

A Dakota of 177 Wing climbs away from a dropping zone near Sinzweya, Burma. It has dropped supplies
by parachute to elements of the 7th Indian Division surrounded by the Japanese in the Kalapanzin valley
during the Second Arakan campaign. Collapsed parachute canopies can be seen lying in the dry riverbed.
(Crown Copyright – Air Historical Branch)

air opposition was sufficiently intense to cause some of the supply aircraft to turn back. On that
occasion it was only the leadership and personal example of the American Dakota transport
commander, Brigadier General Old who, flying an aircraft himself, led the air fleet in and ensured
that the supply drop took place.[23]

The Allied air re-supply operation provided everything the beleaguered forces in the Admin
Box needed. This included rations, ammunition, petrol, medical supplies and even socks, razors
and toothpaste. The only item that apparently could not be provided was a replacement hat for the
divisional commander, Major General Messervy, whose head was apparently an unusually large
size. Norman Bowdler was a trooper with the 25th Dragoons and remembers the aerial re-supply
to his armoured unit while it was besieged in the Admin Box well:

> I suppose it was about a week after we were first surrounded that the first air drop came and
> that was a big relief to see these Dakota aircraft. They flew up the valley quite low, they were
> being fired at all the time by the Japs on top of the hills and you could actually see the blokes
> pushing the loads out of the door… sugar and flour and rice and that sort of things came
> down in hessian sacks and they were very, very strong because I suppose they dropped them
> from a height of 500 feet and with its forward speed as well it would hit the deck and bounce
> and roll… I saw a guy get killed by a sack of sugar, got hit in the back and crushed. He was
> running at the time trying to get out of the way poor devil, it was nobody's fault just an acci-
> dent and these guys I did admire them up there…without them we would not have survived.

---

23   Louis Allen, *Burma the Longest War*, p. 178 and p. 187.

Members of the crew of a transport aircraft prepare to drop supplies over an airfield on the Arakan front.
(Crown Copyright – Air Historical Branch)

Once they got going it was a daily occurrence and it was an amazing sight to see these lumbering great things flying up the valley, 500 feet off the deck being fired at by these Japs on top of the hills. To see 40-gallon drums of aviation fuel, coming down on the end of a parachute, was a sight to behold. And also ammunition. Our 75mm ammunition used to come down in a tri-pack, there would be three 75mm shells in a triangular wooden case and they would come down on a parachute. There were times in the early stages when the Japs spotted this and took up positions near the foot of the hills and the moment the drops hit the deck, they were out there trying to grab this stuff for themselves. It ended up with us having to fight them to get our grub, so that meant another battle... You'd see stuff go astray and think oh Christ we can't get that, it would mean having to go through Jap lines to go and get it, but that was unusual, it did happen – but it was unusual.[24]

The RAF transport squadrons and Slim's Fourteenth Army were pioneers not just in aerial re-supply, but also in the movement of large numbers of troops by air. In March 1944 General Slim recognised the vital need to bring in reinforcements to the Kohima and Imphal positions, which were facing a Japanese major offensive. He appealed to Mountbatten, the Supreme Allied Commander Far East, to lobby the American chiefs of staff to reinforce his small RAF transport force with additional Dakotas. Mountbatten got the point and signalled the Americans, stating that unless he heard to the contrary, he was transferring thirty American Dakotas from the China ferry route[25]

24  IWM Sound Archives, Catalogue number 22342, Norman Bowdler interview.
25  The China ferry route was used to fly supplies from India to Chiang Kai Shek's Chinese Nationalist forces – the route took the transport aircraft over the Himalayas and was known as flying 'the hump'.

and would use them to move the 5th Indian Division from the Arakan front to Imphal.[26] The chiefs of staff backed Mountbatten's actions, beginning a movement that was to prove decisive to the outcome of the Imphal battle. Slim himself described it:

RAAF dropping supplies by parachute over Burma, 1944.
(Courtesy of State Library of Victoria, Melbourne Victoria)

> The fly in of the 5th Indian Division began on the 17 March. By the 20th its first brigade, 123, had deplaned in Imphal. On the 24th, Divisional Headquarters was complete and by the 27th the divisional troops and a second Brigade, 9, were also in. Their transport was limited to mules and jeeps, but the officers and men, fresh from their Arakan triumphs were in fine form.[27]

Simpson, together with other pilots from 194 Squadron played an important part in the air transportation of 5th Indian Division and he recalled the mixture of loads he had to carry during this busy period:

After the Arakan they moved them all up to the siege of Imphal, we moved divisions and brigades including their 25 pounders, an important move because Imphal was cut off. The first time I took a 25 pounder on board, it was dismantled and stripped down and lashed down and I said 'Where is the breech?' The breech is a massive thing about 250lbs and they said 'Oh we put that right in the rear in the toilet.' So that was right aft of the Centre of Gravity, and we made them take it out and put it right forward due to the balance of the aircraft. The Dakota is a very flexible aircraft you could have the Centre of Gravity within 54 inches, which is a lot, but 250lbs stuck right down in the tail of the aircraft would have been a bit too much for it... It [the 5th Indian Division] was impressive because these chaps had had some six years overseas experience. They had been through East Africa, had been through the desert, they had been overseas for

---

26   See Map 11 for Imphal and Kohima area.
27   William Slim, *Defeat into Victory* (London: Cassel and Co Ltd, 1956), p. 306.

a long time. They had been in the Arakan, in the Admin box, which was a terrible place for them and we were going to pick them up and fly them up to Imphal, which was starting to be besieged. As long as they had a cup of char and a cigarette they didn't mind, they just carried on they never complained about anything seriously. Wonderful spirit they had these troops, marvellous discipline.[28]

With the enemy pressing in on Imphal and Kohima, there were now 130 RAF and American Dakotas available to the British for air transport, with a further 20 C-46 Commando aircraft also on loan. This was still not enough to meet the logistic demands of the forces at Imphal, which became entirely cut off from 29 March 1944. From that moment on the allies had to sustain, entirely by air, the four divisions around Imphal, as well as 221 Group with its local airfields. This totalled 150,000 Army and 6,000 RAF personnel altogether. Another appeal from Mountbatten for a further 70 Dakotas, prompted the Combined Chiefs to divert 64 American and 25 RAF Dakotas from the Mediterranean to Burma. In a land/air conference at Comilla on 17/18 April 1944, it was judged that the garrison would need 540 tons of supplies per day, which initially seemed workable, but then the demands of the Chindits as well as the West Africans in the Kaladan valley had to be factored in as well. Worse still, a period of unexpectedly bad weather resulted in a dangerous backlog of supplies accumulating.[29]

To mitigate this the daily rations issued to the troops was decreased and 50,000 men, including two field hospitals, were evacuated by air from Imphal to India to reduce the logistic demands of the garrison. Simultaneously a forward staging depot and airfield was established at Kumbhirgam, 50 miles from Imphal, which reduced the requirement for Dakotas to carry their loads all the way back to base if bad weather prevented them from flying over the mountains to Imphal. These measures reduced the daily demand to just 412 tons which, with the extra Dakotas, the Allies were just about able to meet until the siege was lifted on 12 June 1944. This air transport achievement was both impressive and unprecedented: 120,000 Allied troops had been wholly supplied by air for three months, a new division had been flown in and 50,000 personnel as well as 10,000 sick and wounded had been evacuated. Figure 10 below shows just what a close-run affair it had been:

| Period | Target | | Attainment | | Shortages on Target | | Average daily delivery |
|---|---|---|---|---|---|---|---|
| | Stocks | Reinforcements | Stocks | Reinforcements | Stocks | Reinforcements | |
| 18-30 April | 3,180 | 3,250 | 1,926 | 1,479 | 1,254 | 1,771 | 148 |
| May | 13,423 | 7,750 | 6,040 | 5,011 | 7,383 | 2,739 | 194.8 |
| June | 10,890 | 7,500 | 10,858 | 6,071 | 32 | 1,429 | 362 |
| Total | 27,493 | 18,500 | 18,824 | 12,561 | 8,669 | 5,939 | – |

Figures for reinforcements in numbers of troops.
Woodburn Kirby, *The War Against Japan, Volume 3* (London: HMSO, 1961) Appendix 26.

Figure 10  Deliveries in tons to IV Corps on the Imphal Plain during Operation 'STAMINA', 18 April to 30 June.

The RAF's ability to supply the garrison by air, was limited by the lack of air strips at some small and isolated strongholds including Kohima, supplies therefore had to be dropped on those

---

28    IWM Sound Archives, Catalogue Number 12376, Joe Geoffrey Simpson interview.
29    Henry Probert, *Forgotten Air Force* (London: Brasseys, 1995), p. 185.

Troops of 5th Indian Division loading a jeep into a Douglas Dakota Mark III of 194 Squadron RAF, during the reinforcement of the Imphal Garrison. (Crown Copyright – Air Historical Branch)

positions. This included howitzer ammunition directly onto the gun positions and sometimes even water in car inner-tubes. The close confines of the Kohima perimeter meant that some of the supplies dropped inevitably fell into enemy hands.[30] Arthur Campbell served with 4th Battalion, the Royal West Kents at Kohima and explains how these drops could be desperately frustrating, despite the courage and best efforts of the RAF and American crews:

At 1425 we dashed out into the small clearing and laid down the yellow strips in the shape of a 'T', our code letter. As we expected, no sooner were the strips laid than the snipers started searching for us. Peter and I each armed ourselves with a Very pistol, he with red cartridges, me with green. The red lights would tell the pilot not to drop, the green ones to go ahead.

Exactly at 14:30, the first batch of planes, three Dakotas, came into view. They circled round for a while and I fired one green light to tell them to start dropping. Apparently the pilots did not see it, because the three planes continued circling. After a while I saw them coming in for the first run, and they passed clean over us without dropping their loads.

I shouted, 'By God, Peter, they're dropping in the wrong place!' As they passed over the Fort the bundles came out of the tails of the planes, the parachutes opened and the loads descended slowly into the Japanese lines. Frantically the signaller repeated his tuning and netting calls while Peter blazed off his red signal lights one after the other, but the planes continued on the same circuit. In the space of twenty minutes they dropped all their loads on the Fort, while we were powerless to stop them.

Many of the hungry men on the perimeter, men dried up with thirst, men without grenades, without mortar bombs for support, men who had seen no mail for ten days, were watching. Many men in the dressing station who knew that only water and drugs and medical

30   Henry Probert, *Forgotten Air Force*, p. 187.

equipment, provided they came today, would save their lives were watching. They knew what it meant for the Japs to receive our stores; it meant that the mortar ammunition and grenades would be fired against them; it meant that there would be no drugs to take away pain or save wounds from rotting. But they watched the whole heart-breaking performance while the planes moved not a yard this way or that from their chosen course. They went on dropping until they were empty, then flew away.

Peter and I waited for the next batch, not long in coming, and this time they picked us up and the drop was accurate. The pilots had a difficult run in because of the ridges and the hills surrounding the D.Z., but they took every conceivable risk to skim over the tree tops and so put the stuff down into our tiny clearing. These three planes circled only twice, then came straight in on their run after I had given them the green light. The first plane belched out the four panniers; the parachutes opened and down they came, swinging gently, right on to the D.Z. Other loads followed from the two planes behind... One of the boxes had rolled quite close, and I noticed Peter was already looking at it with strange expression. The markings on the box were quite clear: 'AMN HOW 3.7 INCH'. We had only two 3.7-inch [Howitzer] guns in the place and we were unable to use them.[31]

Arthur Campbell realised that the loads had got mixed up between their own DZ and the one at Jotsoma. It meant that they would not get the water, ammunition, grenades and mortar bombs they had asked for:

Meanwhile the planes droned on overhead, dropping the rest of their loads with perfect accuracy, all packed with useless stuff. Soon they went away and a third batch of only two planes approached. These found us at once, and started dropping as soon as I gave them the signal. On the second time round, after dropping only four of his panniers, a pilot took one risk too many. As he came in on his run, he skimmed too low over Jail Hill, his wing tip catching an upstanding tree and slewing round the machine. At once it went out of control, tearing a great path through the forest, burning and withering the foliage, leaving a brown track of tangled tree trunks and shrivelled brushwood, a scar on the hillside that was to mock us in days to come. We could hear the sounds of tearing metal and smashing wood as it ripped through the jungle; then we heard the explosion and saw the flames and smoke shoot skyward. The one plane remaining finished its drop and went away.

Peter and I gathered the men waiting to clear the D.Z. and set them to work. Two or three bundles were caught in the trees and the men climbed up and cut them down, leaving the parachutes festooned. Others were lying out in the clearing, exposed to the snipers, so that six men had to dash out, grab the bundle and drag it under cover before removing the parachute harness and straps. After an hour and a half we had twenty panniers collected...

We found that we had received in all three-quarters of the medical stores we had asked for, but no water, no mortar ammunition, no grenades. Peter and I reported the result to John Laverty. He reached for the microphone and called Brigade. He was furious.[32]

The demands on the transport aircraft were immense. Initially they operated from Comilla and Agartala airfields which, whilst close to the air supply depots, were frustratingly at the end of a very long, land line-of-communication from Calcutta. Chittagong, Feni and Sylhet airfields were also brought into service and a joint planning staff established to make the best of the scarce air assets.

---

31   Arthur Campbell, *The Siege – A Story from Kohima* (London: George Allen and Unwin Ltd, 1956), p. 177.
32   Arthur Campbell, *The Siege – A Story from Kohima* (London: George Allen and Unwin Ltd, 1956), p. 177.

This meant a wide variety of missions for the Dakota pilots. They could start their day at Agartala and drop supplies to the West Africans in the Kaladan valley, before returning to Chittagong to pick up supplies and fly them to Imphal, from where they might then evacuate casualties to a base hospital. Alternatively, a Dakota might start at Sylhet with a mission to land supplies to the Chindits, then collect passengers from a jungle airstrip before flying to Imphal to bring out surplus personnel. It required a highly efficient ground set up and an aircrew prepared to fly themselves to the point of exhaustion.[33] Despite all the vagaries of the Burmese weather, the rate of aborted sorties for May 1944, the worst month, was only six percent.[34]

The defensive success at Imphal in the summer of 1944 allowed Fourteenth Army to regain the initiative and begin their own offensive against the Japanese. In this final year of the campaign, the use of air transportation in providing mobility to the Army was fundamental to the land campaign's success. That the potential of air transport was incorporated so effectively is partly to do with the sterling efforts and flexibility of the RAF's air transport force in theatre, but also the increasingly 'air minded' nature of Fourteenth Army, including their commander General Slim:

> We very soon realised that if we were going to make the best use of this great new weapon of air supply we must, with our limited resources in aircraft, provide a simple, flexible organization of control and operation, that would suit any normal formation without elaborate preparation. We approached the problem from the starting-point that transportation by air was no more extraordinary than movement by road, rail or boat; it was merely one method of moving things and men. There is indeed only one test of air mindedness, and that is not whether you can fly an aeroplane, but whether you regard it as a vehicle. If you do you are airminded; if you regard it as anything else – a weapon, a sporting adjunct, or a bag of tricks – you can be an Air Marshal, but you are not airminded.[35]

As Slim planned his advance onto the central plain of Burma[36] he foresaw the need for two of his divisions, the 5th and 17th Indian Divisions, to change from being formations transported purely by road, to divisions where two of the three brigades would be completely mechanised and the remaining brigade entirely air-portable. In this air-portable brigade no vehicle would be larger than a jeep and even the 25-pounder artillery would be fitted with a shorter jury axle, that would allow it to be loaded onto a Dakota. The scales of equipment, supplies and ammunition for these brigades were also reduced and a greater reliance placed on rapid replenishment from the air.

To make this system work a new Combined Army Air Transport Organisation (CAATO) was established, which worked with the Anglo-American Combat Cargo Task Force (CCTF), to ensure that the air supply to Fourteenth Army was as effective as possible. Communication links from the front-line Army formations to the air supply bases and depots were also improved using 'Beach Groups'. These units were normally used for controlling beach landings, but as the amphibious operations within the Burmese theatre had been reduced in scale, they were re-roled as forward airfield maintenance organisations. Though these new organisations were outside the immediate command and control of Fourteenth Army, they were found to operate very effectively during the British final offensive in Burma, which began with the crossing of the Chindwin River in December 1944.[37]

---

33　See Annexes O-P for further details on air supply during the Imphal battle.
34　Henry Probert, *Forgotten Air Force*, p. 185.
35　William Slim, *Defeat into Victory*, p. 165.
36　See Map 10 for reconquest of Burma.
37　William Slim, *Defeat into Victory*, p. 386.

The Army's dependency on air supply, as well as Burma's battlefield geography, necessitated frequent alteration of British operational plans. The air bases supporting Fourteenth Army's advance were already 250 miles away at the beginning of the offensive, a distance judged as the limit of economical air supply. If the British plans to exploit south of Mandalay were successful, then more and more numbers of aircraft would be needed to achieve the same level of re-supply to the advancing troops. The only answer was to build new air bases closer to the front line, but such construction work would be very hard to achieve along the axis of Fourteenth Army's advance, which was itself at the end of very poor land lines of communication. This problem was overcome in January and February 1945, when the British launched a series of small amphibious assaults on the Japanese-held islands of Ramree, Akyab and Cheduba. These islands all possessed excellent airfields which could be used as logistic hubs and were within the important 250-mile radius of the planned advances.[38]

The new airfields were linked to new forward landing grounds brought into use in central and southern Burma as the British advance continued. These included those constructed by the Japanese, as well as the pre-war airfields abandoned by the Allies during their withdrawal in 1942. Most of the these were fair-weather strips and on many airfields, the Japanese had been able to carry out denial measures, which necessitated considerable repair work by Army engineers. The engineers also constructed many new airstrips at suitable places on the axis of the advance of the formations concerned; these were initially no more than earthen runways some 2,000 yards in length and 50 yards wide. So quickly were they built that they were often in operation within just three days of work beginning on them.

As the 1945 advance progressed the airfields in use formed several distinct geographical groups. These included the five airfields in the Kalemyo area, five in the Shwebo area, five in the Monywa area, eight around Mandalay, five in the vicinity of Pakokku and four around Meiktila. The exception to this clustering was in areas where the construction of airfields was unusually difficult, such as in the Myittha valley. The RAF's transport squadrons used some 50 forward airfields during 'EXTENDED CAPITAL' as this operational period became known. This large number of airfields also excludes the many short strips built by troops for light aircraft and these proved invaluable for the evacuation of casualties, as well as for liaison and communication purposes. The RAF tried to ensure that transport aircraft had exclusive use of these airfields, so that the steady flow of air supply was not interrupted, though on occasions the tactical squadrons of 221 Group and 224 Group, which were both providing air support for Fourteenth Army, would also make use of them.[39]

The airheads established in the forward area meant that the transport aircraft could land with their loads, but supply-dropping was sometimes used when operationally necessary, the disadvantage being that less tonnage could be carried if the supplies had to be packed in bundles and easily moved to the door. An airhead included all installations, depots and dumps established in an area controlled by the forward airfield maintenance organization in charge of it. Corps and divisional forward maintenance areas were established at or near the airheads, for handling their daily maintenance and holding reserve stocks. A rear airfield maintenance organization was established at each base airfield and was responsible for loading the aircraft with supplies and stores, these were delivered from stocks obtained from nearby supply depots or those held at the airfield. Each rear airfield maintenance organisation was controlled by CAATO, to which all demands were made by Army formations within the tonnages allotted to them by Fourteenth Army. A forward airfield maintenance organisation, comprising a headquarters and two control

38   William Slim, *Defeat into Victory*, p. 165.
39   See Annex Q and R for further details of air supply provided over this period.

Surrounded by an assortment of baggage, tents, boxes and chickens, personnel of an RAF Spitfire squadron which is moving to another airfield in Central Burma, watch as a Douglas Dakota Mark III of 117 Squadron takes off. (Crown Copyright – Air Historical Branch)

centres, was allotted to Fourteenth Army headquarters and to each corps. These units controlled the reception of stores, supplies and reinforcements into the forward airheads, as well as the distribution to their allotted formations. From mid-January 1945, 130 tons was fixed as the daily allotment for the maintenance of each division and for corps troops. This total was made up as follows: supplies and rations 52 tons, petrol, oil and lubricants (POL) 33 tons, ammunition 21 tons, ordnance stores 14 tons, engineer stores 3 tons and miscellaneous supplies 7 tons. Each tank brigade was allotted 70 tons a day.

This aerial re-supply was essential in enabling the Fourteenth Army to achieve a stunning series of advances through a combination of motorised and air-portable forces. The Battle for Meiktila was one such occasion, where motorised brigades of 17th Division captured the airfield at Thabutkon, just to the north of the town on 26 February 1945. The 99th Brigade was flown in to secure it properly, allowing fuel and other combat supplies for the motorised brigades to be air-lifted in and Meiktila to be attacked from three sides. As the Japanese counter-attacked the town, a second air-portable brigade (the 9th Brigade from 5th Indian Division, based 700 miles away at Jorhat) was also flown in on 15 March and reinforced the defenders and their air-bridgehead.[40] Fifty-four Dakota sorties were undertaken on the first day of this move, flying in brigade HQ and 3rd/2nd Punjab Regiment. The formation needed 142 aircraft sorties before they were complete at Meiktila. The 9th Brigade received only twenty-two casualties during their fly in,[41] though at times the airfield at Meiktila came under serious enemy attack which made re-supply to this frontline position a very tricky proposition. Brian Stanbridge of 31 Squadron recalls taking supplies in:

40   Louis Allen, *The Longest War*, pp. 438-52.
41   Louis Allen, *The Longest War*, p. 447.

Men of 2958 LAA Squadron RAF Regiment loading a 20mm Hispano anti-aircraft gun by hand on to a Dakota at an airfield in Burma, 1945. (Crown Copyright – Air Historical Branch)

> The strip was taken over every night by the Japanese and retaken every morning by our troops. It was under constant mortar fire which caused the loss of several aircraft while unloading. Our turn rounds were the quickest ever. We could never be sure who was in control of the landing field so each morning we would look carefully at the troops on the side of the strip during the landing run.[42]

The advance from Meiktila began in early April 1945. It was essentially a race to reach Rangoon before the monsoon set in at the end of May and turned the roads to mud, as well as disrupting flying. This was a race in which air supply was once more a critical factor, though efforts to maintain the pace meant that delivery methods became more and more ad hoc. Flight Lieutenant Dix a navigator with 267 Squadron recalls:

> In some sectors the Army was advancing so rapidly that the actual front-line position could only be guessed. We would be briefed to fly as far south as we thought safe along the road and railway towards Rangoon and drop our load to any allied army unit we could identify. We would see a small group of tents or Jeeps at the side of the road, and wait in a small circuit for them to identify themselves if we had any doubts whether they were ours or theirs. We would drop some of the load, then fly south to find more campsites. It was obvious that this kind of free roaming drop could not have been carried out if the Japanese had had any heavy guns to fire at us.[43]

---

42  Henry Probert, *The Forgotten Air Force*, p. 265.
43  Henry Probert, *The Forgotten Air Force*, p. 271.

The demands on both aircrew and the despatchers were heavy. Norman Finchett was an air gunner flying Dakotas but was routinely used to despatch loads too. He gives a good example of the duties involved after he joined 194 Squadron, operating out of Imphal in January 1945:

> The first day of flying [with 194 Squadron] was unique because it was the first time I was ever sick in an aircraft… We had a call and went up to the assembly point, near the cookhouse, and breakfast was being cooked and rather stupidly I decided to have some breakfast. I later found out that no one had breakfast before they flew on their first mission, but I had bacon and tinned tomatoes. I remember it well, and my first flight was what we called a 'free drop' where we had bags of rice on board the aircraft… The boys in the crew that I had joined told me what would happen and how we would sort of stack these bags of rice in the door. Walking up and down a Dakota aircraft dragging sacks of rice ten yards or so really upset my stomach and by the time we had done the first drop I was being sick in the Elsan [chemical lavatory] in the back. So, after that I never had breakfast first thing in the morning…
>
> We used to do about four flights a day and take off between five and six in the morning. The actual flying time to where the forward areas were was roughly about an hour and a half from Imphal by aircraft, so in three hours we were back in the airbase itself and used to have breakfast then… At the Imphal air strip the Indian Army Service Corps would load the aircraft for us with whatever supplies we were taking forward. We never knew where we were going until we got to the airfield itself and then found out. If we were doing a landing some-where, it was just a case of take-off set your course where you were going, do your landing and the army used to come on board and help us drag the stuff off into lorries. But of course, if you were doing what we called 'free drops', or supply drops the actual movement of the cargo to the doorway had to be done by the aircrew itself, because we had no extra bodies in Burma to assist us in doing this. The other thing was that in Europe the Dakota was fitted with roller tracks to help bring the stuff down the aircraft to the door. But in Burma we had the earlier type of Dakota that never had these fitted, so we had to drag everything up and down, includ-ing drums of petrol or oil or other types of equipment, to the door.[44]

Though the air supply for Fourteenth Army's advance worked highly efficiently throughout this critical period of his campaign, Slim could not relax for a second. For he operated under the constant threat that his air transport, much of which was American, might be taken away from him. On several occasions throughout his campaign in Burma, large numbers of aircraft were taken off him with either little or no notice and the Army and RAF staff officers would be forced to quickly recalculate their plans. The most serious occasion during the final advance was on 10 December 1944, just as the offensive was beginning. General Slim recounts his surprise at the time:

> I was awakened in my headquarters at Imphal by the roar of engines as a large number of aircraft took off in quick succession and passed overhead. I knew loaded aircraft were due to leave for 33 Corps later in the morning, but I was surprised at this early start. I sent somebody to discover what it was all about. To my consternation, I learnt that, without warning, three squadrons of American Dakotas (seventy-five aircraft), allotted to Fourteenth Army mainte-nance, had been suddenly ordered to China… The supplies in the aircraft already loaded for Fourteenth Army, were dumped on the Imphal strip and the machines took off. The noise of

---

44   IWM Sound Recording, Catalogue Number 31067, Norman Finchett interview.

their engines was the first intimation anyone in Fourteenth Army had of the administrative crisis now bursting upon us.[45]

Fourteenth Army and its supporting RAF staff had to drastically readjust their planning, which involved de-scoping and reducing the air supply allotment for XV Corps. Further threats to withdraw aircraft to China also occurred in March 1945, at what was a critical moment in the Meiktila battle. On that occasion Mountbatten had managed to persuade the Americans to delay their withdrawal of aircraft until the capture of Rangoon. This last stage of the campaign turned into a race against the weather, as the monsoons in Burma were expected to begin on 15 May and indeed there were heavy pre-monsoon storms both on 29 April and between 3-11 May, which caused some early flooding of airfields and roads. Since airfields could not be used, resort had to made to supply dropping direct to army formations and units, which reduced the tonnage below the estimate.[46] In the end there was just enough air transport available to maintain the advance at the necessary rate, but one can't help sympathise with those conducting the land campaign who ought to have been spared all this extra anxiety.[47] Figure 11 below shows how close the margins were.

| Month in 1945 | 14th Army's estimated daily requirements | ALFSEAs forecast of daily air deliveries at 250 miles radius[48] | Actual Average Daily Deliveries | | | |
|---|---|---|---|---|---|---|
| | | | Air | Road | Inland Water Transport | Total |
| March | 2,428 | 1,860 | 1,682 | 175 | 190 | 2,047 |
| April | 2,700 | 1,921 | 1,789 | 3 | 458 | 2,250 |
| 1-15 May | 2,830 | 2,075 | 1,605 | - | 660 | 2,265 |

Figure 11   14th Army's Estimate of the Supply Position from March to May 1945, and Actual Deliveries in Tons per Day.

General Slim was nevertheless proud that the fabric of his campaign in Burma incorporated both land and air operations. That obviously included close air support and air interdiction, but it was perhaps the large-scale use of air transport that was the most novel and distinctive aspect of Burmese air operations. As Slim puts it:

It was one of our contributions towards a new kind of warfare and I think it fair to say that, to a large extent, we discovered by trial and error the methods of air supply that later passed into general use. We were the first to maintain large formations in action by air supply and move standard divisions long distances about the fighting front by air.[49]

Slim also argued that there were several fallacies and misconceptions about air transport:

---

45   William Slim, *Defeat into Victory*, p. 397.
46   See Annex S for further details of air supply during Operation EXTENDED CAPITAL.
47   Henry Probert, *Forgotten Air Force*, p. 249.
48   Estimate made on the 25 February 1945
49   William Slim, *Defeat into Victory*, p. 546.

The first was to overlook the fact that our pattern of operations depended, almost entirely, on a very large measure of air supremacy. Until a degree of air superiority amounting to at least locally to dominance had been secured neither air supply, movement, nor tactical support could be carried on with the certainty and regularity our operations demanded… A second fallacy was that air supply is entirely a matter to be arranged by the air forces; that the only thing required are the aircraft and the men to fly and maintain them. The organization of air supply is as much a job for the army as for the air force. It is as important as flying the aircraft that the immensely varied stores, properly packed, should arrive at the right airstrips at the right time; that they should be sent to the right units, and that on arrival, unloading, distribution, and delivery should be swift and unerring… Among the most strategically dangerous ideas that half-baked thinking on air supply provoked, was that, even if surrounded, positions could be held for months provided they might be maintained from the air. In fact, troops thus cut off even if fed and maintained, eventually lose heart, and air supply is so easily interrupted; the weather or a few well sited anti-aircraft weapons can easily put a stop to it. Air supply is only half the answer. The other half is an adequate relieving force which, however good the prospect of air supply, must appear in a reasonable time and which the beleaguered garrison must know will appear.[50]

---

50  William Slim, *Defeat into Victory*, p. 546.

# Part VIII

# Clipped Wings

Given the many types of missions and roles the air forces of the British Commonwealth undertook, it is scarcely surprising that many of them became casualties of one sort or another. This final part of the book studies what efforts the British took to recover and treat these casualties and if beyond rescue, what their experience was like at the hands of their captors.

# 15

# The Guinea Pigs

Operational flying was arguably one of the most dangerous duties in the Second World War. Pilot error, aircraft faults, enemy action and just bad luck were all directly responsible for aircrew deaths and injuries. In other instances, enemy fire might cause damage to the aircraft, yet the pilot and his crew might still be able to maintain some form of control of the machine and successfully battle to return the aircraft home. For the pilot of a single seat aircraft the decision to abandon his machine could be quickly made without reference to anyone else; his decision was typically based on his chances of being rescued if he baled out, whether the aircraft would disintegrate on landing, and if wounded, whether he was strong enough to fly the aircraft for the remainder of the journey. The captains of larger aircraft might order the crew to bale out depending on where they were and if over occupied enemy territory what the risk of capture was, or if over the sea, the chances of being rescued. Frequently, the captain would put his faith in the crew's ability to fight and save their aircraft and the efforts some crew members went to in this regard are quite extraordinary. The Victoria Cross citation for New Zealander, Sergeant James Ward offers an impressive example:

> The KING has been graciously pleased to confer the VICTORIA CROSS on the undermentioned non-commissioned officer in recognition of most conspicuous bravery:-
> NZ401793 Sergeant Pilot James Allen Ward

On the night of 7 July 1941, Sergeant Ward was second pilot of a Wellington bomber returning from an attack on Munster. While flying over the Zuider Zee at 13,000 feet his aircraft was attacked from beneath by a German Bf 110, which secured hits with cannon-shell and incendiary bullets. The rear gunner was wounded in the foot but delivered a burst of fire sending the enemy fighter down, apparently out of control. Fire then broke out in the Wellington's near-starboard engine and, fed by petrol from a split pipe, quickly gained an alarming hold and threatened to spread to the entire wing. The crew forced a hole in the fuselage and made strenuous efforts to reduce the fire with extinguishers, and even coffee from their flasks, without success. They were then warned to be ready to abandon the aircraft. As a last resort Sergeant Ward volunteered to make an attempt to smother the fire with an engine cover which happened to be in use as a cushion. At first he proposed discarding his parachute to reduce wind resistance, but was finally persuaded to take it. A rope from the aircraft dingy was tied to him, though this was of little help and might have become a danger had he been blown off the aircraft.

   With the help of his navigator he then climbed through the narrow astrodome and put on his parachute. The bomber was flying at a reduced speed but the wind pressure must have been sufficient to render the operation one of extreme difficulty. Breaking the fabric to make hand and foot holds where necessary and also taking advantage of existing holes in the fabric, Sergeant Ward succeeded in descending three feet to the wing and proceeding another three feet to a position behind the engine, despite the slipstream from the airscrew which nearly blew him off the wing. Lying in this precarious position he smothered the fire in the wing fabric and tried to push the engine cover into the hole in the wing and on the leaking pipe from which the fire came. As soon as he had removed his hand, however, a terrific wind blew the cover out and when he tried again it was lost. Tired as he was, he was able, with the navigator's assistance, to make a successful but perilous journey back into the aircraft. There was now no danger of fire spreading from the petrol pipe as there was no fabric left near it and in due course it burned itself out. When the aircraft was nearly home, some petrol which had collected in the wing blazed up furiously but died down quite suddenly. A safe landing was made despite the damage sustained to the aircraft. The flight home had been made possible by the gallantry of Sergeant Ward in extinguishing the fire on the wing in circumstances of the greatest difficulty and at the risk of his life.[1]

The recommendation for a VC was a matter of some debate amongst RAF senior officers, some of whom questioned whether his actions had an element of self-preservation. Churchill, in what may be an apocryphal story, was perhaps more appreciative of the Sergeant's actions. He summoned Ward to 10 Downing Street where the shy New Zealander was apparently nervous of the Prime Minister and found it difficult to answer his questions. Sensing Ward's embarrassment, Churchill said 'You must feel very humble and awkward in my presence?' Ward hesitantly replied 'Yes, Sir.' To which Churchill responded, 'Then you can imagine how humble and awkward I feel in yours.'[2]

Fire was often the greatest cause of injuries to aircrew in damaged aircraft. The fuel stored in the aircraft tanks, as well as the oxygen cylinders, ammunition and other pyrotechnics often combined to make a lethal cocktail of fuel and accelerants. If a fire started in the aircraft the pilot could do little more than close the throttle, feather the prop, turn off the fuel supply and ignition, before then selecting the Graviner extinguishing system which blasted inert gases at the engine. The crew would then resort to the rudimentary portable fire extinguishers they had to hand to extinguish the flames. Larger aircraft were in some ways better off, as they usually possessed Lanser self-sealing fuel tanks. This design covered the aircraft's metal fuel tanks with chemically treated rubber linings that would absorb the shock wave of any projectile that hit it. This would reduce the velocity of the bullets to the extent that they would hopefully not ignite the contents of the tank, in addition when the tank was penetrated the Lanser's rubber material would swell and stretch, to close and seal any bullet holes or ruptures. Effective though they undoubtedly were, the self-sealing tanks all added extra weight to the original aircraft design. This was not normally a problem for bombers, where the sealant systems around the fuel tanks in the aircraft wings added a mere 100 pounds to what were already large and heavy aircraft. However, it was more problematic for lighter single-engine fighters where any extra weight drastically altered the aircraft's performance. For that reason, the RAF's primary fighter aircraft were not initially fitted with self-sealing Lanser wraps.

Fire also posed a greater risk to the pilots of fighter aircraft because of where the fuel was stored on their machines. The Spitfire and Hurricanes were both designed to be fast aircraft, which necessitated highly streamlined aerodynamic designs with wheels retracting into the wings, in which guns and magazines were also usually housed. This left little space in the wings for fuel. The Hurricane had only half its fuel tanks in the wing, the remainder was in the fuselage and the Spitfire had no fuel tanks in the wings at all. In addition, the size and position of the aircraft's wing span and chord[3] often necessitated a heavy front load to obtain the optimum centre of gravity. This was resolved by placing the fuel tanks for both the Hurricane and Spitfire behind the engine and

1    Supplement to the London Gazette, 5 August 1941.
2    C Fadiman, *The Little Brown Book of Anecdotes* (London: Little Brown Book, 1985), p. 122.
3    The chord of a wing is determined by measuring the distance between the leading and trailing edges in the direction of the airflow.

A Handley Page Halifax, B.I L9506/TL-X of 35 Squadron, that had crash-landed at Bircham Newton during the night of 15/16 June 1941. The aircraft had left its base at Linton-on-Ouse to strike Hannover but was attacked by a German fighter during the mission. All of the crew survived. (Air Historical Branch)

in front of the pilot's cockpit. As an example, the fuel load in the (pre-1942) Spitfire's nose, directly in front of the pilot, consisted of 48 gallons of fuel in the upper tank, 37 gallons in the lower tank together with two smaller tanks of oil (5.8 gallons) and glycol (18 gallons). In the Hurricane the reserve tank of 28 gallons, together with an oil tank (7 gallons) and a glycol tank (18 gallons) were placed directly in front of the pilot and there were also two wing tanks of 25 gallons located either side of him.[4]

Though the Hurricane carried some fuel in the wings, the design potentially posed a greater danger to its pilots than the Spitfire. This was because the area where the wing met the body of the aircraft, known as the wing root, was not closed by either armour plate or any sealing material. The result was that there was a direct channel between the fuel tank and the cockpit and if a fire broke out in a wing fuel tank, a natural draught could blow the blazing fuel directly onto the pilot, especially if the guns had been fired and the linen patches covering the gun ports were blown off.[5] The horror of fire entering the cockpit of a small single seat fighter needs little embellishment and blazes could quickly reach furnace-like temperatures. Such was the heat that pilots often described the colourless flames that would quickly crumble and melt the dashboard, or how the temperatures were so high that the paint on the fuel tank would flake off in front of their eyes.

Pilot Officer Geoffrey Page was a Hurricane pilot at the start of the war and became one of the RAF's earliest burns casualties. He recalls how he was shot down during an attack on a formation of Dornier 215s:

> The distance between the German leaders and my solitary Hurricane was down to three hundred yards. Strikes from my Brownings began to flash around the port engine of the Dorniers.
>
> The mass of fire from the bomber formation closed in as I fired desperately in a race to destroy before being destroyed.

---

4   E.R. Mayhew, *The Guinea Pig Club* (London: Greenhill Books, 2010), p. 27.
5   E.R. Mayhew, *The Guinea Pig Club*, p. 49.

Squadron Leader Geoffrey Page studies a map with a group a 132 Squadron pilots who took part in the first Spitfire operation into Germany on 26 April 1944. They flew over territory between Aix-la-Chapelle and Cologne – a round-trip of some 800 miles. Page, who was badly burned during the Battle of Britain, is second left and with him are: Pilot Officer Bob Harden RNZAF (extreme right, holding map) and Flying Officers D.J. Watkins, R.O. Webster and J.E. Ford. The aircraft is Page's personal Spitfire IX, MK144/FF-O. (Air Historical Branch)

The first bang came as a shock. For an instant I couldn't believe I'd been hit. Two more bangs followed in quick succession, and as if by magic a gaping hole suddenly appeared in my starboard wing.

Surprise quickly changed to fear, and as the instinct of self-preservation began to take over, the gas tank behind the engine blew up, and my cockpit became an inferno. Fear became blind terror, then agonised horror as the bare skin of my hands gripping the throttle and control column shrivelled up like burnt parchment under the intensity of the blast furnace temperature. Screaming at the top of my voice I threw my head back to keep it away from the searing flames. Instinctively the tortured right hand groped for the release pin securing the restraining Sutton harness.

'Dear God, save me…save me, dear God…' I cried imploringly. Then as suddenly as terror had overtaken me, it vanished with the knowledge that death was no longer to be feared. My fingers kept up their blind and bloody mechanical groping. Some large mechanical dark object disappeared between my legs and cool, relieving fresh air suddenly flowed across my burning face. I tumbled. Sky, sea, sky, over and over as a clearing brain issued instructions to outflung limbs. 'Pull the ripcord – right hand to the ripcord." Watering eyes focused on an arm flung out in space with some strange meaty object attached to its end.

More tumbling – more sky and sea and sky, but with a blue clad arm forming a focal point in the foreground. 'Pull the ripcord, hand' and brain again commanded. Slowly but obediently the elbow bent and the hand came across the body to rest on the chromium ring but bounced away quickly with the agony of contact.

More tumbling but at a slower rate now. The weight of the head was beginning to tell. Realizing that pain or no pain the ripcord had to be pulled, the brain overcame the reaction of raw nerve endings and forced the mutilated fingers to grasp the ring and pull firmly.

It acted immediately. With a jerk the silken canopy opened… It was then that I noticed the smell. The odour of my burnt flesh was so loathsome that I wanted to vomit. But there was too much to attend to even for that small luxury. Self preservation was my first concern, and my chance for it looked slim. The coastline at Margate was just discernible six to ten miles away. Ten thousand feet below me lay the deserted sea. Not a ship or a seagull crossed its blank, grey surface.[6]

As Page descended under his parachute, the shock of his severe injuries started to take hold and he began to shiver and feel very cold. Much of his clothing from his thighs downwards had been blown off by the exploding gas tank and he had also lost a shoe. As he struck the sea Page knew he had to discard his parachute, this required him to undo the four metal harnesses clasped by the metal release box which lay over his stomach. This was normally a simple act of turning the circular metal disc on the box 90 degrees and then banging it to release the harnesses. In his burnt state, it was torture:

I plunged feet first into the water. Despite the beauties of the summer and the wealth of warm days that had occurred the sea felt icy cold to my badly shocked body. Kicking madly, I came to the surface to find my arms entangled with the multiple shrouds holding me in an octopus-like grip. The battle with the metal disc still had to be won, or else the water-logged parachute would eventually drag me down to a watery grave. Spluttering with mouthfuls of salt water I struggled grimly with the vital release mechanism. Pieces of flesh flaked off and blood poured from the raw tissues.

Desperation, egged on by near panic, forced the decision, and with a sob of relief I found that the disc had surrendered the battle. Kicking away blindly at the tentacles that still entwined arms and legs, I fought free and swam fiercely away from the nightmare surroundings of the parachute. Wild fear died away and the simple rules of procedure for continued existence exerted themselves again.

'Get rid of the chute, and then inflate your Mae West,' said the book of rules, and 'float about until rescued'.

'That's all very well' I thought, 'but unless I get near the coast under my own steam, there's not much chance of being picked up.' With that I trod water and extricated the long rubber tube with which to blow up the jacket. Unscrewing the valves between my teeth, I searched my panting lungs for extra air. The only result after several minutes of exertion was a feeling of dizziness and a string of bubbles from the bottom of the jacket. The fire had burnt a large hole through the rubber bladder.[7]

Page reconciled himself to having to swim for shore, an agonizing process as the helmet cut into the raw surface of his chin, the buckle and leather having been fused into one solid mass that prevented him from removing it. Page was astonishingly lucky and was picked up by a passing merchant ship which let down a dinghy. As the small boat circled without attempting to pick him up a seaman's voice called out. 'What are you? A Jerry or one of ours?' Page furious with the chain of events shouted: 'You stupid pair of fucking bastards, pull me out!' He was brought ashore and

---

6   Geoffrey Page, *Shot Down in Flames* (London: Grub Street, 2011), pp. 86-8.

7   Geoffrey Page, *Shot Down in Flames*, pp. 90-1.

Firemen spray foam over the wreckage of a burning De Havilland Mosquito at Predannack, Cornwall, after it caught fire over the airfield and crashed from 200 feet following a practice flight. Wing Commander J.A. Mackie, the Commanding Officer of 157 Squadron RAF, together with a Czech RAF doctor and a member of the crash crew, made a frantic attempt to rescue the pilot and observer of the burning Mosquito. The observer Flying Officer Scobie survived, though badly injured, but the pilot, Flying Officer J L Clifton was killed.
(Air Historical Branch)

taken to a general hospital for surgery, where the doctors, for understandable reasons, refused his request for a mirror to see his face. Yet as the anaesthetist searched for a vein to inject him, Page not wishing to see the needle enter the skin looked upwards and away and caught 'sight of myself in the reflector mirrors of the overhanging light. My last conscious memory was of seeing the hideous mass of swollen, burnt flesh that had once been a face.'[8]

Only a few years earlier, severe burns victims would have had only a very slim chance of survival, even if they had reached a hospital in a timely manner. Up until the very end of the 1930s most severe burns casualties had died almost straight away. Shock had been the primary cause of these deaths, which meant that the casualty had lost dramatic quantities of bodily fluid at the site of the burns and that the body had tried to compensate for this loss by shifting fluid from one vital organ to another. Starved of the liquids and proteins they needed, the organs would shut down one by one, starting with the kidneys, then the liver and the brain last of all. This lethal fluid shift was not properly understood by the medical community until the late 1930s and it was still the case as late as 1937, that half of the patients admitted with serious burns to the Royal Glasgow Infirmary for example died within 24 hours. Within three days, three-quarters of the patients were dead. In

8    Geoffrey Page, *Shot Down in Flames*, p. 97.

most cases, patients with serious burns were simply given large doses of morphine to ease the pain in what was expected to be their final hours.[9]

To counter the effects of fluid shift, doctors had begun to administer saline in the 1920s. However, they were worried about side effects and the amounts they gave were initially too small to make a substantial difference, they therefore initially achieved little more than extending life for a few days or more. Nevertheless, these experiments had at least established a precedent and in the 1930s doctors began to explore the full ranges of plasma and saline transfusion therapies, that not only replaced fluid but also contained protein too. Transfusions began to be given more regularly, as well as in larger amounts, which meant that serious burns patients began to survive their injuries in much greater numbers. It was one of the most important clinical breakthroughs of the last century and transfusion dramatically helped many servicemen in the Second World War, including substantial numbers of RAF aircrew. Of course, these improved survival rates resulted in significant numbers of burns victims that now required longer term treatment, to help them recover from their injuries and try to regain some quality of life. This posed an entirely new challenge for both the medical profession and the RAF.

As so few people had previously survived severe burns, the existing treatments of damaged tissue and skin were for minor rather than major burns. Tannafax, a gel of tannic acid, was the coagulant treatment in general use within the RAF at the outbreak of the war, it came as a tube of jelly and was found in every Hospital, ambulance and medical officer's bag. Tannafax was painted on the burns and formed a scab-like chemical dressing under which the wound was protected. When the new tissue had grown underneath the coagulant was removed just like a scab. Coagulants might have been suitable for small and minor burns, but by the beginning of the war there was concern amongst some surgeons that for severe burns they were downright dangerous.

Archibald McIndoe was one such individual, he was civilian consultant surgeon in plastic surgery to the RAF and as war broke out became responsible for the increasing numbers of RAF burns casualties. From a cottage hospital in East Grinstead, McIndoe developed a special centre for the treatment of burns casualties, in 1939 this only amounted to 42 RAF aircrew with serious or severe burns, but by 1940 that number had risen to 378, the vast majority of whom were in Fighter Command.[10] McIndoe noted that the typical injuries these fighter aircrew suffered were the so-called 'Airman's Burn', which was characterised by deep scorching burns on the face and hands. These were categorised as 'whole thickness burns' which destroyed sebaceous glands, hair follicles, sweat glands and nerve endings.

An RAF Medical Staff Memorandum touched on these injuries:

> This is a burn of almost unvarying characteristics due to the sudden exposure of unprotected parts of the body to intense, dry heat or flame, as though the entire patient were thrust into a furnace for a few minutes and then withdrawn. The distribution is characteristic:-
>
> (i) Both wrists and hands, particularly the backs, the fingers, often the entire surface of the hands. If gloves have been worn, only the wrists are involved. Holes in glove fingers have been responsible for severe localised burns…
>
> (ii) The face in the 'helmet' area. When goggles are pushed back, the forehead, eyebrows and eyelids are severely burned. Usually the eyelids near the lash edges escape. The eyes themselves are not often burned. The oxygen mask may protect the face but the cheeks, nose and ears are often involved.

---

9    E.R. Mayhew, *The Guinea Pig Club*, pp. 33-5.
10   E R Mayhew, *The Guinea Pig Club*, p. 45.

A Canadian flight sergeant is strapped into his Spitfire at a base in southern England, 1942. (Air Historical Branch)

(iii) The neck between chin and collar, extending on both sides to the mastoid area [temporal bone behind the ear].

(iv) The anterior and inner surfaces of the thighs if the trousers are thin. The lower legs between the trousers and boot tops if flying boots are not properly adjusted…

Deep searing burns, usually of 'third degree', involve areas of tremendous functional importance – the hands and eyelids in particular.[11]

McIndoe found that coagulation treatments on these 'high functional areas', particularly the hands and eyes, were causing terrible problems. For instance, when the Tannafax gel was painted round the fingers it dried into a stiff unyielding casing which hampered circulation and swelling. This often led to infection and necrosis (gangrene) and caused the pilot terrible pain and sometimes loss of his fingers. Terrible scarring would also occur, which not only made a very poor surface for subsequent skin grafting, but also pulled the fingers back into a kind of frozen claw. Geoffrey Page recalls the tannic acid treatment used on him:

Then for the first time I noticed the hands themselves. From the wrist joints to the finger tips they were blacker than any negro's hand, but smaller in size than I had ever remembered them to be. I shared the V.A.D's [Voluntary Aid Detachment nurse] expression of horror… 'That stuff's only Tannic acid. It's not the colour of your skin.'[12]

---

11   TNA AIR20/6452: Plastic Surgery Within The RAF, pp.1-2.
12   Geoffrey Page, *Shot Down in Flames*, pp. 104.

As time went on Tannafax turned Page's hands into the notorious 'Tannic acid gauntlets', these were so firmly stuck on that they could only be removed under anaesthetic. Page recalls looking at the results after a painful operation that had removed them:

> I looked down at the two unbandaged objects lying propped on a sterile pillow. The pink-ness of the tissue paper thin skin covering my hands made me think of newborn babies… However the joy of seeing my hands unencumbered by the crippling effects of the Tannic acid more than made up for the physical discomfort. The joy was short lived. Day by day my strength increased and with it the condition of my hands deteriorated. Fraction by fraction the tendons contracted bending the fingers downwards until finally the tips were in contact with the palms. Added to this the delicate skin toughened by degrees until it had the texture of a rhinocerous hide, at the same time webbing my fingers together until they were indistin-guishable as separate units.[13]

The problems with Tannafax necessitated a new approach and McIndoe advocated an entirely different form of treatment for both immediate first aid and longer-term wound care. His new treatment was very labour intensive and consisted of applying loose weave dressings, normally Tulle grass impregnated with soft paraffin, halibut oil and balsam of Peru to the trauma site. This mixture was kept in a metal tin and gently warmed to make the dressings pliable. The dressings kept the wound clean, dry and intact and were flexible enough to be used in jointed areas such as feet, hands and eyes. They were easy to remove to clean the wound, or to inspect for any signs of infection, which would then be treated by antiseptics, including sulphanamide powder which was gently blown on to the wound through a straw.

This new treatment regime was established by McIndoe in Ward III of the cottage hospital at East Grinstead. There were many other new innovations instituted there as well, for instance layered linen was used rather than woollen blankets to prevent infection, the beds were specially designed so that headrests could be removed, and dressings re-applied with the minimum of discomfort. Anaesthetists adapted the patients gas masks to account for different facial injuries and specially selected chefs were brought in to ensure the patients' diet was a suitable one for those struggling with face and jaw injuries. More unusually a large barrel of weak beer was placed in the middle of Ward III, as McIndoe understood that keeping patients hydrated was important, and that the young aircrew were far more likely to drink pints of beer than they ever would water. The hospital atmosphere was jocular and relaxed, the medical staff often joining in the antics of the wounded aircrew. This included John Hunter, East Grinsted's talented chief anaesthetist, who had a standing agreement that he would buy a patient a drink if he had made him sick after surgery.[14]

The labour-intensive nature of the treatments also meant that a greater proportion of nursing staff were male orderlies. Strength was particularly necessary in the second stage of burns treatment, which included frequent saline baths where dressings, or clothing still attached to the patient, had to be gently removed and the wound kept flexible by moving joints under water. These baths were also important in promoting granulation, the creation of a suitable grafting surface. The order-lies had to be strong, but also gentle enough to lift patients out with great care. Unsurprisingly their devoted attention to their patients meant that a powerful bond was established between the nurses and the vulnerable aircrew. Leo Tremblay, who was wounded during a night training flight, recalled one of the staff:

---

13   Geoffrey Page, *Shot Down in Flames*, pp. 104-5.
14   E.R. Mayhew, *The Guinea Pig Club*, p. 78.

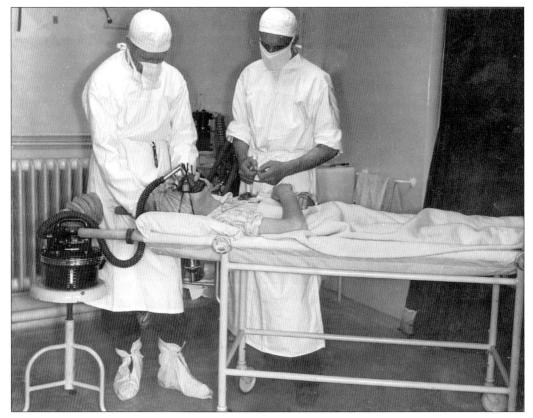

A member of the RAAF undergoes surgery for burns treatment. (Courtesy RAAF museum)

I remember particularly one of the orderlies whose name was Johnny Ingram. Johnny treated me with respect and an uncommon devotion. When my health condition improved and I was able to go out of the hospital, Johnny would take me out in a wheelchair into East Grinstead to the Whitehall Restaurant… We would have a few (sometimes more than a few) beers and excellent food…you see after 57 years, these are people I should never forget.[15]

McIndoe was wise enough to address not just the clinical aspects of his patients' treatment, but also the psychological aspects of their recovery. Paramount in this was the relationship between the surgeon and the burnt aircrew, where the shared object was to produce 'a face which does not excite pity or horror. By doing so we can restore a lost soul to normal living.'[16] To do this McIndoe treated his patients as stakeholders in the treatment they would receive. He described the importance of this approach in his own words after the war:

Depending on the nature of the burn, a plan is proposed at the very outset and carefully explained to the patient. It will consist of the requisite number of operations, together with time intervals between each session during which educational or training opportunities are

15   E R Mayhew, *The Guinea Pig Club*, p. 65.
16   McIndoe lecture to the Royal College of Surgeons, 1958, quoted from E.R. Mayhew, *The Reconstruction of Warriors* (London: Greenhill, 2004), p. 76.

instituted. The progressive effect of each operation is explained to the patient and an assessment made of just how much improvement he can expect from it immediately and remotely. As far as possible the plan is rigidly adhered to by the surgeon. Thus the patient can himself plan his life between operations and a degree of confidence and trust is thus built up between surgeon and patient which I consider absolutely essential for a successful outcome both physically and psychical [sic]. His co-operation is essential; therefore he should understand clearly what is being done, how it is to be done, and how long it will take…

At all times it must be borne in mind that it is one thing to cure the patient of his disfigurement and deformity, it is another to carry through such an arduous programme and end up with a normal human being. Throughout the surgical period and for long after it the patient will lean heavily on the surgeon for mental support, for hope and encouragement…If [the relationship] deteriorates, trust and confidence will disappear and the progression which should characterise the particular plan will also disappear.[17]

The patient normally received considerable mental support and solace from his fellow ward members. This was given added momentum in June 1941, when some of the East Grinstead patients founded the Guinea Pig Club. Membership was strictly limited to those burns victims who had been under surgery, as well as the staff who treated them – including McIndoe himself. The club described itself: 'as the most exclusive Club in the world, but the entrance fee is something most men would not care to pay and the conditions of membership are arduous in the extreme.'[18] The Guinea Pig club was a formal expression of the self-supporting camaraderie and humour amongst the patient community of Ward III. Sergeant Harold Taubman, a bomb aimer on Lancasters with 460 Squadron RAAF, remembered waking up on his first day at East Grinstead:

In the next bed is Paul Hart: 'All right Aussie' he says, 'Have a cigar' he says. Some bloke in a wheelchair, his leg in plaster, chases a nurse along the ward shouting 'Taxi, taxi!'; There is a lovely sound as Tim Walshe opens and pours a bottle of beer…then, the daily saline bath, and the bathroom boys, Johnnie and Eddie and their ceremonial shaving off of my bomber command moustache and its posting back to Australia…visits to London, the Players Theatre and Whitehall nights…aah, good things happen to Guinea Pigs.[19]

The Guinea Pig Club grew to 649 personnel in total and flourished well after the war, with many re-unions taking place at East Grinstead. These were normally very boozy events and usually included frequent renderings of the Guinea Pig Anthem:

We are McIndoe's army,
We are his Guinea Pigs.
With dermatomes and pedicles,
Glass eyes, false teeth and wigs.
And when we get our discharge
We'll shout with all our might:
'Per ardua ad astra,' We'd rather drink than fight.

---

17 McIndoe lecture to the Royal College of Surgeons, 1958, quoted from E.R. Mayhew, *The Reconstruction of Warriors*, p. 76.

18 McIndoe lecture to the Royal College of Surgeons, 1958, quoted from E.R. Mayhew, *The Reconstruction of Warriors*, p. 78.

19 Harold Taubman, *How I became a Guinea Pig*, *The Guinea Pig Magazine*, Winter 1965, p. 12.

John Hunter runs the gas works,
Ross Tilley wields a knife.
And if they are not careful
They'll have your flaming life.
So, Guinea Pigs, stand steady
For all your surgeons' calls;
And if their hands aren't steady
They'll whip off both your balls.

We've had some mad Australians,
Some French, some Czechs, some Poles.
We've even had some Yankees,
God bless their precious souls.
While as for the Canadians –
Ah! That's a different thing,
They couldn't stand our accent
And built a separate Wing.

As well as a notorious social occasion, the Guinea Pig annual reunion was deliberately used by McIndoe and his team to ascertain how their patients were getting on, both physically and psychologically, and whether further treatment was required. Most importantly the club provided a self-supporting pastoral network that helped individuals who might be struggling, which in time came to include burns casualties from more recent conflicts. The support they gave to the 47 severely burned men, mostly Welsh Guardsmen, who became casualties when the Royal Fleet Auxiliary *Sir Galahad* was struck by Argentinian jets during the 1982 Falklands War, was a powerful example.

McIndoe's support for the Guinea Pigs did not end at the East Grinstead hospital gates. Part of the patient recovery process also included visiting the local amenities in the periods between surgery. Though this could be a nervous moment as Harold Taubman recalled:

> Those first sorties into the world outside the hospital were painful, especially for the youngest amongst us. Without hands, for instance, it was impossible to do anything without assistance. It was embarrassing to have someone pouring beer down your throat, wiping your mouth, blowing your nose, handling your money. It was even more embarrassing to have to make for the gentlemen's cloakroom in pairs. Naturally no young man experienced such a loss of his independence without resenting it strongly, for it made him as helpless as a small child and robbed him of all his dignity.[20]

McIndoe did much to bring town and hospital closer together, dignitaries were invited to the hospital and lectures, seminars and concerts arranged. To East Grinstead's credit the population intuitively understood the important rehabilitation role they also had to play and regularly invited patients into their houses and to dances. Several places became sanctuaries for the Guinea Pigs, the Whitehall Restaurant in particular became a home from home after the young female staff there resolved to 'look them full in the eyes and just see them, and treat them as if we don't see it. We'll look at them and not look away from them and speak to them. And that's what we did …and we got so used to it we never took any notice after that.'[21] The locals who frequented the

---

20   Bill Simpson, *The Way of Recovery* (London: Hamish Hamilton, 1944), p. 65.
21   E.R. Mayhew, *The Reconstruction of Warriors*, p. 156.

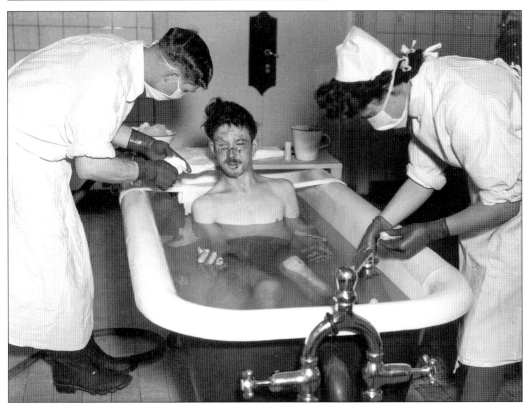

A member of the RAAF who is suffering from burns is immersed in a saline bath, an important method in the treatment and recovery of burns casualties. (Courtesy RAAF museum)

Whitehall also made a determined effort, Stella Clapton recalled her husband telling her sternly as they were about to enter the Whitehall for the first time, 'Don't you bat an eyelid when you go in, not an eyelid.'[22] The owners of the complex in which the Whitehall stood also opened the cinema, with reserved seats for the Guinea Pigs and gave them standing invitations to dances at the Rainbow Ballroom. East Grinstead became an important initial step between the hospital and full public life for the Guinea Pigs, it was a controlled environment in which the town had accepted McIndoe's challenge to be a part of the patient's recovery. Not for nothing did it become famous as 'The Town that did not Stare'. A term it is rightly still proud of today.

Though the initial Guinea Pigs were mainly fighter pilots, a growing number of casualties began to originate from Bomber Command as the war progressed. Many of these were aircrew extracted from burning aircraft that had been downed near their bases in Lincolnshire, Yorkshire and Nottinghamshire. Mrs Amelia Broadberry was a farmer's wife at Roe Wood Farm, Winkburn in Nottinghamshire. On 21 June 1941, a Polish 301 Squadron Wellington bomber was returning from a raid on Bremen when the propeller of their starboard engine fell off; the dramatic increase in revolutions caused the engine to overheat and burst into flames. As the Wellington was too low for the crew to bale out, the only solution was a quick forced landing. Unfortunately, the aircraft struck some trees as it neared the ground and crashed near Roe Wood Farm, bursting into flames as it did so. Mrs Broadberry describes what happened next:

---

22   E.R. Mayhew, *The Reconstruction of Warriors*, p. 157.

The farm where we live is a bit isolated; there are just my husband and myself, two young sons and a daughter. Early one morning, about half-past three, quite dark, we heard an aeroplane very low. It's engine was faltering and all at once it stopped and a second or two afterwards we heard a heavy thud which seemed to shake the whole house. It sounded very close, though actually it was about 250 yards away. 'That's a plane down,' said my husband. It was a fine clear night, and we could see a little flicker of flame, which looked like an ordinary kitchen fire, on our barley field where the plane had crashed.

I sent my youngest son, Tom – he's thirteen – across to the village telephone, while my husband and our eldest lad, George, went to get spades from the out-houses to put the fire out. I followed them, and we ran across the two fields between us and the plane. Just as we got near we heard foreign voices. There was an alert on at the time and we thought they were Jerries who had made a crash-landing. My husband whispered to us to keep down. The ammunition started going off and we thought it was the Jerries firing. As I've said, ours is a very isolated place and we wondered if it wouldn't be better to make our way back to the house and wait for daylight. Then we heard someone moaning in pain. The flames were getting bigger now and my husband said: 'Jerry or no Jerry, we can't see him burnt to death, we must get him out.' He started to get up and I grabbed his ankle. 'You lie still,' he said, 'George and I'll see what we can do.' Anyway, all three of us crept down the hedge until we got to the flames. The flames were big now and there was a series of loud explosions as the petrol tank burst. I thought they were bombs. We started to get the men out. While we were doing so, we saw two more men of the crew near the plane. The blaze was very bright. My husband was up with his spade and challenged them. One of them called back. 'We're with you,' he shouted. 'We are Poles.' He pointed to his shoulder badge with 'Poland' on it. Both of them were dazed.

The man who had answered took me round to the other side of the plane, where he knew another man was trapped, and we got him out. He was still unconscious. George and my husband also got a man out. The noise of the flames and the bullets exploding was terrible. They said there was a fifth man underneath the fuselage. He must have jumped just before the 'plane crashed. We couldn't find him. He must have been killed at once.

The tail of the machine had broken off. We never saw this part until the flames shot up. It must have turned over and over; and was some yards away from the rest of the plane. The rear gunner was trapped by his legs, but as his part of the machine wasn't actually on fire we left it until we'd got the more dangerous ones out. It took us about fifteen minutes and then my husband and George went to free this last man while I ran back to-the house for our little first-aid outfit, and got my daughter to boil some kettles. I've been trained as a nurse and I bandaged the men's wounds, while my husband and George rigged up the tail fin of the plane as a screen from the flames, and started chopping the man free with a couple of axes they'd brought.

The fire was terrible now and bullets flying about like mad. The tracer bullets showed us where they were going and it was a nasty corner. The Poles were very badly injured. They must have been very fit to stand the loss of blood they did. They tried to help us but were naturally dazed and couldn't do much. The plane was melting and the melted aluminium formed into pools on the ground just like water. My husband and George worked on with their axes – it took them an hour and a half to get their man free. Bullet-proof glass and flexible aluminium is difficult stuff to chop. Besides they were frightened of hitting the man. The airman was conscious only now and then, again he must have been in great pain. Anyway, they got him out.

It was all a bit of bad luck. The plane had been damaged in a raid over Germany and was gliding down to make a landing when it just failed to clear the outside trees of a wood.

A Handley Page Halifax heavy bomber in flames after crash-landing on its return to base on 18 February 1944. The bomber had been on a raid over Germany. (Air Historical Branch)

> Another three or four feet and they'd have cleared them and probably made a good landing in the barley field. It was a great pity; they were splendid lads, those Poles.[23]

Mr Harry Broadberry and Mrs Amelia Broadberry were both awarded the British Empire Medal for their bravery, they were the first married pair to both receive this decoration simultaneously.

To cater for the increased numbers of burns casualties from Bomber Command, McIndoe established burns units in RAF hospitals at Cosford, Rauceby, Ely and Halton. These hospitals served the increasing number of Bomber Command casualties as the War developed.

McIndoe recognised the patients needed a strong sense of pride to help them recover, but most convalescing service patients were required to wear a drab functional uniform called hospital blues. McIndoe felt it made them look like convicts and instead he invited them to wear whatever they wished: a suit, or jacket and trousers, or RAF uniform, most patients chose the latter. The Air Ministry played a commendable role in supporting these initiatives and successfully fought a running battle with the Treasury to prevent the aircrew from being medically discharged whilst undergoing treatment and instead kept them within the service. This was initially for a maximum period of two and a half years but in 1947 it was extended indefinitely.[24] The RAF sensibly avoided the temptation to hide away these disfigured aircrew, instead the Guinea Pigs became a strong plank of RAF publicity and were invited to tour factories and give talks as heroic examples of the finest elements of the RAF. This all aided the patient's longer-term recovery and rehabilitation.

The story of the Guinea Pigs and their treatment is an inspiring one, yet as Geoffrey Page's account illustrates such treatment was only available if the casualty was successfully recovered to an RAF hospital. Page was astonishingly lucky to have been plucked from the sea by a merchant vessel, for at that stage of the War the British Air Sea Rescue service was still relatively immature.

23   Polish Air Force, *Destiny Can Wait – The Polish Air Force in the Second World War*, pp. 126-7.
24   E R Mayhew, *The Guinea Pig Club*, p. 178

# 16

# 'The Goldfish Club'
# Shot Down and in the Drink

In 1938 the AOC Bomber Command, recognising that his crews' future operational role would entail long flights across the North Sea to Germany, expressed concern over the rescue facilities available to the bomber crews who might have to ditch in the sea. His perspective was a sound one, as rescuing airmen was important from both a humanitarian and morale perspective as well as in maintaining combat effectiveness through the re-introduction into front line service of personnel who had been rescued. As a result, the Air Ministry directed that the pre-war fleet of just 16 rescue motor launches, ten of which were based in the UK and a further six overseas (Malta, Aden, Basra, Ceylon, Penang, Hong Kong) should be expanded by a further 15 High Speed Launches to be run by the RAF Marine Craft section.

Despite this modest improvement the Battle of Britain demonstrated that the RAF still needed to do much more in developing a responsive and comprehensive air-sea rescue capability. During the last 21 days of July 1940, a total of 220 RAF aircrew were posted as killed or missing, of which a large proportion of the 'missing' were lost over the sea. Consequently, Air Vice-Marshal Keith Park, who was commanding 11 Group at the time, established a coordinated local rescue service that employed Army Cooperation Command Lysander aircraft to spot the ditched airmen and the RAF's Air Sea Rescue launches and Royal Navy light craft to rescue them. This practice was formalised by the Air Ministry in August 1940 and in due course a Directorate for Air Sea Rescue services was established in 1941 within Coastal Command. This new directorate had the responsibility not only to provide the necessary craft and equipment, but also to coordinate air-sea rescue operations for aircraft and their crews. It was also in charge of developing new rescue equipment (including dinghies, air-dropped equipment, location devices etc) and for training the aircrews in their use. In the first four months of the new organisation's operations the percentage of crews recovered rose significantly, from 20 percent to almost 35 percent.

The system for close range rescues seemed to be working well and involved cooperation between RAF Air Sea Rescue, the Royal Navy, the Observer Corps, HM Coastguard, the Royal National Lifeboat Institute, and Trinity House. Yet it was apparent that search and rescue for longer-range recoveries was more problematic. These difficulties were for several reasons, firstly the RAF's High Speed Launch was designed to get to a casualty as quickly as possible and was therefore very fast. To achieve this speed the launch's overall sea-worthiness had been compromised and as a result they struggled in heavy seas and bad weather. To solve this, the Royal Navy provided Rescue Marine Launches, a design based on the successful Fairmile B Motor Gun Boat, which were bigger than the RAF High Speed Launch and able to cope with the poorer weather frequently encountered in places such as the North Sea. Secondly, it was judged that a dedicated aircraft with a greater range than the Lysander was needed to assist in the longer-range rescues. Operational aircraft had undertaken this work up till then, but time was always required to load them with the necessary rescue stores and the pilots, inexperienced in air-sea rescue, found it difficult to co-operate with surface craft and coordinate searches. The need for dedicated aircraft, with specially trained crew and a longer range was an obvious requirement and the Air Ministry agreed to allocate two squadrons of

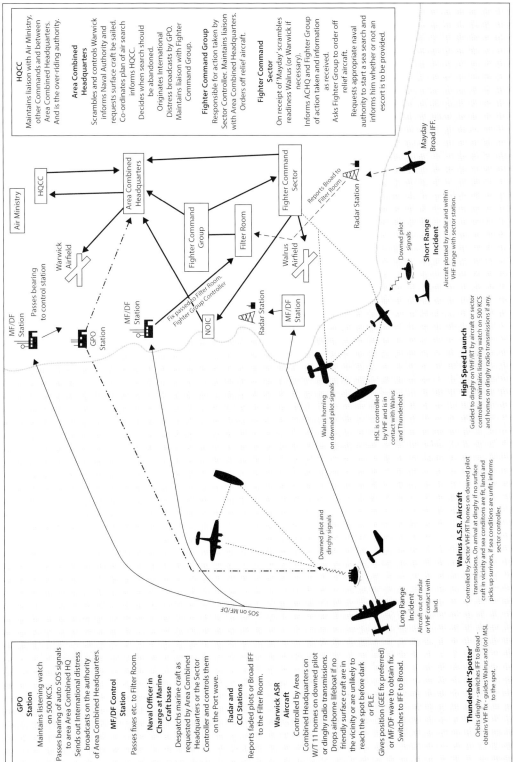

Figure 12  Air Sea Rescue Organisation and Chain of Communication.

Hudson aircraft equipped with ASV radar.[1] This approach was also copied in the Mediterranean, as well as in India and the Far East, though the greater distances involved in these latter theatres typically necessitated the use of the Catalina and Sunderland aircraft for longer-range search and rescue.

The most important contribution that the new directorate made was arguably in the area of training and education. Each RAF station was directed to appoint an Air Sea Rescue Officer and it was his role to ensure that all training was up to date and competently carried out by crews. The directorate's training provided useful advice to crews on the actions required if their aircraft was to ditch, turning the whole process into a drill with a specific task allocated to each individual member.

A Lockheed Hudson Mark III air-sea rescue aircraft of 520 Squadron RAF flies over High Speed Launch No.181 of 71 Air Sea Rescue Marine Craft Unit while returning to Gibraltar. (Crown Copyright – Air Historical Branch)

As an example, in a large aircraft like a Lancaster the first action was for the pilot to inform the crew they were going to ditch, this prompted the crew to take up their crash positions. The bomb aimer, rear turret and mid-upper gunner would leave their locations, check the front parachute hatch was properly closed and open the mid and rear ditching hatches. The wireless operator would signal course, height, air-speed, position and time as well as their estimated point of ditching.[2] It was important that this was done quickly and before altitude was lost, as this would increase the chance of the signal being received. The wireless operator would also switch the IFF to transmit a continuous distress signal and in the last moments of ditching clamp down the radio transmitter on permanent send, so that any receiving stations could get a fix on where the aircraft had ditched, or where the signal was last received. As he approached the sea, the pilot shouted 'Ditching Stations', closed the fuel jettison cocks and switched on the navigation and landing lights if it was at night. He would then try and land the aircraft into wind unless the sea was rough in which case he might try and land

1    Graham Pitchfork, *Shot Down and in The Drink* (Kew: National Archives, 2005), pp.1-12.
2    Air Publication 3232 *Air Sea Rescue* (London: Air Historical Branch, Air Ministry, 1952), Appendix 7.

between the wave troughs. Just before striking the sea the pilot called 'Brace for ditching' and disconnected his intercom lead, as would all other crew. Once the aircraft had successfully ditched and settled on the sea, the crew would leave through their dedicated exits. The pilot going through cockpit roof hatch, the engineer, navigator, wireless operator and bomb aimer through the middle exit and the two gunners via the rear exit. As they left the aircraft, the two gunners activated the dinghy release mechanisms, releasing the life rafts which were then grabbed and secured by the engineer and navigator. The bomb aimer and wireless operator picked up packs containing emergency rations, fresh water and the dinghy radio. Earlier in the war pigeons in containers had been carried, though this was discontinued after many of them were either drowned in their cages, or had become so wet they could not fly. On the night of 15/16 September 1944, Flight Lieutenant Vic Motherwell RCAF was the pilot of a Halifax that had to ditch after bombing Kiel. His rear gunner, Joe Hickson RCAF relates the story:

> We must have been hit by flak, for as we pulled away I could hear Vic talking to the engineer Jack Porter that all was not well. It appeared that we were losing fuel and hydraulic fluid so we could not raise our bomb doors, but I was feeling safer now that we had left the target area and had once again been cloaked in darkness. But we were losing altitude and falling way behind the rest of the force. Soon we were down to 1,000 feet and Jack was wondering if we had enough fuel to get us over the North Sea. It was even discussed if we should try for France, but that was ruled out as no airfield was available for a bomber to land on, especially at night, and in our shape we would surely crash. We decided to chance it to England.
>
> It wasn't long before Jack reported our gas was going fast as we had to use extra gas to keep us in the air, with our bomb doors, wheels and flaps hanging down. Our wireless operator was sending out SOS on emergency procedure as I continued to watch out for night-fighters, knowing that ditching in the North Sea had become a reality.
>
> We were about three quarters across the North Sea when Jack said we had only 15 minutes of fuel left. Shortly after that, the Skipper told me to get out of the turret and with the others, take up position, then clamped the key down. I then heard the skipper say, 'We are going in!' and turned on the landing lights. 'Where is the water,' he asked, 'we are at 200 feet and no water?' But then: 'I see the water – hold on – this is it!'
>
> I felt the plane hit the water just lightly, then hard, and at the same time the round bomb-inspection door popped open between my legs. Water shot up like a fire hose, then a big wave of water came over my head – then it was pitch dark. When finally I was able to get up, the water was up to my chest. I saw our mid-upper just going up the ladder through the top hatch, so gave him a push and scrambled up after him, pulling the dinghy release handle as I went (as it was my designated responsibility), and it came loose. I knew then that the dinghy must be inflating and as I came out the hatch I could see in the dim, early morning light, the Halifax floating perfectly, with the wings awash and the props bent back.
>
> The dinghy was floating just off the edge of the wing with the rest of the crew already in it. I jumped down on the wing, grabbed the dinghy with my hands, and my toes anchored in the compartment from which the dinghy had emerged. The strong winds and high waves were trying to pull the dinghy away and seeing the Skipper making his way across the fuselage, I called out to him that I couldn't hold the dinghy for long. One of the boys told me not to worry, they'd grab the tailplane. I pulled myself into the dinghy, which did drift to the tail, and the skipper walked the rest of the way down the fuselage, climbed in all nice and dry! We drifted away, all pretty cramped and sitting on each other's legs as the wireless operator cut the line, freeing us from the Halifax, which was still afloat despite what we had been told – that it would sink in a couple minutes. It was now well over 10 minutes since coming down and it was still there.

Aerial photograph taken during the rescue of the crew of an American Liberator by an RAF Thornycroft High Speed Launch (HSL 2641). The rescue occurred the day after the Liberator had been shot down by Junkers Ju 88s. (Crown Copyright – Air Historical Branch)

Our navigator, Ian McGowan, had then to admit that he had lost all his gear when the wave of water swept through the machine, so we had no Verey pistol or flares. Still we were all safe and well, but then within minutes we were all being sick over the side of the dinghy – except our wireless operator, who hailed from Saskatchewan – the only real 'landlubber' amongst us![3]

Hickson's crew were lucky that their Halifax had made a gentle landing on the water, in other cases striking the sea could be catastrophic. Arthur Eyton-Jones was a 226 Squadron bomb aimer on a Mitchell Mk. II, an aircraft that was not quite as large as a Halifax, or Lancaster and had a crew of five, rather than seven. On 30 July 1943, his Mitchell aircraft was attacked over the North Sea by Me 210s and 410s, this set the aircraft on fire about 150 miles from the English coast. Eyton-Jones describes the subsequent events:

Through the blisters on either side of my compartment I could see that the wing tanks were also alight and sheets of flame, twice the length of the Mitchell, were streaming back from them. The sound of the engines died away as Dick throttled back and I could see the surface of the sea coming closer and closer as we sank down towards it. Suddenly a horrible ripping sound could be heard from the bottom of the fuselage as we touched the water, then I remember looking down at my feet in amazement as the bottom hatch, which opened outwards,

3   Norman Franks, *Another Kind of Courage – Stories of the UK based Walrus Air-Sea Rescue Squadrons* (Yeovil: Patrick Stephens Ltd, 1994), pp. 194-6.

burst in towards me and next second I was under water. There was no sensation of water pouring in: one moment I was standing braced with my back against the armoured door, the next I was completely under water. My mind told me that the only way out of the compartment was to unlatch the armoured door and climb up into the co-pilots seat, above which there was an emergency exit in the roof. I could feel that the Mitchell was sinking to the bottom of the sea. I could not see anything but groped around for the catch: instead I grasped the limp hand of Dick, which must have been hanging down by his seat. I felt very calm, although later the state of my hands belied this, and even felt surprised that I did not feel short of breath in any way. The door would not budge and it dawned on me that now I must die – there was no other way out of that trap.

Having accepted this fact I felt that it would be better to get it over with and deliberately opened my mouth to gulp in water. Suddenly I felt a sort of underwater explosion and sensed myself going up instead of down, only to feel caught and dragged down again. I turned the quick release knob on my parachute harness and gave it a bang. The harness fell away and I felt myself going up again. My head broke water; the sea was as smooth as a millpond, not a wave, not a ripple, the sun shone and there in front of my eyes not six feet away, was my service hat floating on the surface. I immediately struck out for it, picked it up and then looked around me. There was oil on the water but no trace of poor old 'Q' for Queenie, only an upturned dinghy with two people swimming frantically towards it. I joined them and after some little difficulty we righted it and climbed aboard, feeling very conscious all the time of the amount of sea under our feet.[4]

We shall pick up Eyton-Jones' story and rescue later in this chapter. Given its specific role Coastal Command understandably took survival at sea very seriously, regularly publishing useful items on the subject in the *Coastal Command Review*. Its July 1944 edition for instance, included an article on survival at sea which had been accumulated from hard won experience. The authors caveated all the advice with the phrase 'if possible' – recognising that in many circumstances the actions they recommended would simply not be practical:

Assuming that the crew have properly adjusted their life-jackets and taken up ditching stations, the following points are most important:

Do not remove any clothing. Heavy clothing in the water does impede swimming and it does make it harder to climb out of the water into the dinghy, but it does not sink you. It becomes saturated with water and therefore about as heavy as water. Its buoyancy is about neutral although it takes some time to expel all the air so that at first, heavy clothing actually buoys you up. In the dinghy the advantages of having all the clothing you can, even if it is wet, to serve as protection against the cold are so great that you should wear as much as possible and discard none.

If you can, take into the dinghy one or more parachutes and any spare clothing. Since this is additional to all the rest of the emergency equipment, it will often be impossible, but they are very useful if available.

Do not get into the water from the aircraft unless you must. That may sound foolish, but before now people have dived in to rescue some quite unimportant piece of equipment. When the emergency arises you should instinctively avoid going in if it can be helped. It makes a tremendous difference if you can avoid getting wet through at the start. If you must go in, slide or jump in as gently as possible, hold your nose and close your mouth tight. Diving

---

4    Arthur Eyton-Jones, *Day Bomber* (Stroud: Sutton Publishing, 1998), p. 82.

boldly into a rough sea with a Mae West on is unpleasant and makes your chances of swal-
lowing sea water much greater. Sea water in the stomach increases seasickness very markedly.

If you are in the sea do not swim aimlessly. You may become exhausted very quickly in
these conditions and then there will be no more swimming. Float long enough to make sure
of an objective and then go for it. Wearing a Mae West in rough water you will get along best
on your back.

If you have an injured man in the water, it is difficult to get him into the dinghy by pulling
first his head, then his body and finally his legs aboard. As he comes in, he tends to push you
away from the buoyancy chamber against which you are kneeling, so that both you and the
dinghy are unbalanced. Float him horizontally against the dinghy first and then roll him, first
on to the top of the buoyancy chamber and then on board.[5]

By the middle of the war the British had developed a series of different dinghies for the aircrew,
these included small ones designed for individual aircraft pilots, as well as bigger ones for entire
crews. For larger aircraft the 'H' type dinghy was often used, it was circular in shape and installed
in a stowage compartment on the top of the aircraft's wing. When the aircraft ditched and sea
water met an electric switch, a $CO_2$ bottle was activated and the dinghy was automatically inflated
and released, remaining tethered to the aircraft by a small rope. There were smaller variants of the
'H' type that followed the same circular design, including the 'M' type for three-man crews and
the 'L' type for two people. The 'H' type was eventually replaced by the 'Q' type dinghy, which
had a more rectangular 16-foot boat-shaped design and included a mast with a sail, as well as a kite
from which the aerial for the dinghy radio could be flown. By the end of 1943 'Q' type dinghies
were being used in all larger aircraft.[6]

The RAF also improved the contents of the dinghy, including the crew's survival packs. These now
contained a floating torch and knife, telescopic mast, flag and sail, paddles, baler, wooden stoppers,
dinghy cover, fluorescene (a chemical dye that helped aircraft spot the dinghy) and a waterproof
Verey pistol with cartridges. Survival rations were also provided which included chocolate, Horlicks
tablets and drinking water. Important though these dinghy provisions were, getting into the dinghy
in the first place sometimes remained a considerable challenge, as Flight Lieutenant Richard Rivaz
recounts when his Whitley aircraft crashed into the sea on 1 March 1941:

> There was a terrific crash, and the lights went out. We were hurled forward and drenched
> with icy water…and completely blinded by the darkness which was intensified by the sudden
> change from the light. We struggled to our feet with the water above our knees and the waves
> crashing against us through the doorway.
>
> I groped for the dinghy and hurled it through the opening. I was holding on to the rip cord
> and could feel the dinghy inflate…and I was surprised at the speed with which it did so. I
> heard someone shout – 'Quickly, sir'…and felt the drag of the dinghy against the rope in my
> hand as I hauled it to towards the aircraft…
>
> The rope suddenly became slack. It had broken! I hurled myself into the sea and felt the
> dinghy with my hands. I did not notice the cold. The dinghy was being hurled and tossed
> about like a cork…and I, too, with it as I was washed across it…
>
> Arthur and Martin were there, too; I think I pulled them on top …but Bill was still in the
> water, and I had hold of him by the arm. God! What a weight he was! I was kneeling and

---

5    Coastal Command Review, July 1944 – quoted from Graham Pitchfork, *Shot Down and in the Drink*, pp.
     18-9.
6    Graham Pitchfork, *Shot Down and in the Drink*, pp. 25-7.

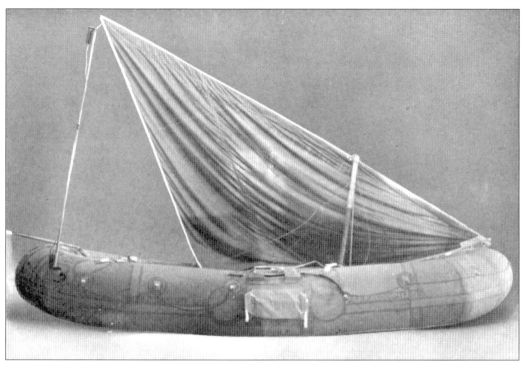

'Q' type crew dinghy. (Crown Copyright – Air Historical Branch)

hauling on Bill as hard as I could and, shouting to the others to help: Arthur half gasped and shouted back that he could not, as I was kneeling on top of him. So I was!… Poor old Arthur. He struggled from underneath me and got a hold on Bill, who was a dead weight and nearly drowned. Martin had hold of his other arm, and I had hold of his clothing round his shoulders. He was kicking with his legs and imploring us to pull him with us…

We had to get him aboard: that was all I could say or think. We must not lose him…we could not leave him. He was a living body: we were alive…and he must live too! The waves were breaking over us furiously, and we were being hurled about unmercifully …but still we kept our grip on Bill, and still we hauled. I was using all my strength and was hopelessly out of breath. Several times we had him nearly with us, and each time a wave hit us and we fell sprawling and almost into the sea…but still we kept our hold. Arthur, Martin and I on the dinghy, and Bill in the water…and Bill was drowning and we were getting weaker. Oh God… give us strength!

The waves had washed us on board…so why should they not do the same for Bill… We began to wait for the waves, and when Bill was lifted so we pulled…and at last Bill – and after how long I have no idea – we had him with us! Bill lay gasping and grinning on the dinghy with us!

There were four of us huddled together and hurled about…but there should have been five. I think Arthur was the first to voice our thoughts…but up to now all our energies had been on Bill: we had him in our hands, and by our efforts we saved him. But Clive was not with us.[7]

---

7   Squadron Leader Clive Forigny a Flight Commander in 102 Squadron and pilot of the Whitley. In Flt Lt Rivaz's original book which was written in wartime he refers to Forigny as 'A----'. In the text above I have included his actual forename.

We could now see better, and we saw him. He was fifty yards away, standing on the fuse-lage of his sinking aeroplane…the aeroplane in which he had saved us…and we could not save him. There he was alone and waiting. We saw him when we rose with the waves …and lost him when he went down with them. All the time we were getting farther away…and all the time his aeroplane was sinking…

What could we do? The answer was, nothing…absolutely nothing! We could only watch …and thank God for our own lives: we had no paddles and no one could swim in a sea with waves higher than a house. We did not know if Clive had seen us. We shouted …but our shout was blown back at, and behind, us.

We watched Clive. We watched him disappear with his aeroplane…and were silent…[8]

Squadron Leader Clive Florigny was never seen again, but Rivaz and the remainder of the crew were more fortunate and were spotted by a Blenheim that directed a trawler to them. Rivaz survived the war, but tragically on 13 October 1945, the B-24 Liberator in which he was a passenger caught fire on take-off from Brussels, killing all on board.

At the beginning of the war fighter pilots were only issued a Mae West and had no dinghy to rely on at all. In contrast, the RAF had noticed and admired the *Luftwaffe* fighter pilot's one-man dinghy that was carried on the pilot's back and inflated with a small CO2 bottle. The British copied the design and christened it the 'K' type, making it available for both fighter pilots and the crews of larger aircraft, where it supplemented the bigger dinghies.[9] Fighter pilots were well aware that the forward centre of gravity on their aircraft meant it would usually plunge nose down the moment it hit the sea and they would therefore need to make a very quick exit. The prospect of floating in a tiny 'K' dinghy was also nothing to look forward to. Flight Lieutenant Tadeusz Turek was a Polish Typhoon pilot in 609 Squadron, he was flying in a fighter sweep over France, in September 1943, when he encountered a large German Army camp bristling with anti-aircraft guns:

I could see some soldiers zeroing those guns on me, others running to their positions – some machine guns ready to fire, they wanted me to be nearer. I was not in the best position to make an attack so promptly shot into the clouds, acutely aware that some flak must have been following me there. The comfort of invisibility gives a sense of security – blessed are the clouds. However, I decided to increase my height and alter course, when suddenly there was a hell of an explosion around me. Dark smoke and the smell of gunpowder in the cockpit. Those guns had got me – by radar – which was some salvo!

I glanced at my wings, which looked like sieves, especially the left one. Looking at my hands and body, I could see no sign of blood but surely I must have been hit? I checked my legs, but to my surprise I was absolutely untouched. My relief was shortlived, for the engine then gave a cough. I looked at the instruments – the oil temperature was up but the pressure down. The cooling system temperature was rising and the engine coughed again. The picture was getting worse and I could feel some hot oil on my face. On the outside of the cockpit I saw smoke; then the engine stopped.

I now had the decision to bale out or ditch. I was now out of the clouds and I could see Smith to my left about 400 yards away, but was too low to bale out. I called Smith who told me I was on fire, so I asked him to watch my ditching as I headed down, smoke and oil impairing my view.

8    R C Rivaz, *Tail Gunner* (Endeavour Press, 2017), pp. 41-2.
9    Air Publication 3232 *Air Sea Rescue*, pp. 6 and 35.

A pilot in a dinghy waves a flag to an Air Sea Rescue Supermarine Walrus amphibious aircraft circling overhead during a training exercise. (Crown Copyright – Air Historical Branch)

The ASR Walrus has landed and is now motoring up to the pilot and his dinghy.
(Crown Copyright – Air Historical Branch)

I could, however, see how rough the sea was – it was almost white everywhere. To land with, or against the waves meant instant submersion and death. The only answer was to land on the crest of a wave and hope for a cushioning effect when it sank into a trough. I aligned the aircraft and saw below me the speeding waves coming closer with every second. There was a sudden and great impact, like hitting a wall. I saw in that moment the ASI reading 150 mph. I hit my head and in that instant all I could see was a red glow of flames – everywhere.

I was knocked out on hitting the sea because someone had removed the head cushion from the armour plate. It did hinder baling out, true, but in a crash-landing it could save life. It caused me some loss of memory.

When I came to, I was up to my neck in water. The front of the Typhoon had vanished and I could not move – I was totally paralysed and could feel nothing. I was going to drown. The oncoming waves were about to bury me. Then a moment of sheer genius. I was due to get married in three weeks and that thought was enough. 'Lad, if you don't get out, you'll never get married.'

My fingers grabbed the release harness and I was free. I wasted no time in paddling, and looking back, I saw the tail of my Typhoon just vanishing. Blowing up my Mae West, I then had to release my parachute which was holding my bottom up and head down. This was easier said than done. On the ground it was easy, just turn the release and hit it, but in the water – how? I had already consumed a lot of water; it was time to stop this slow drowning. I took a deep breath, bent double under the water and pressed the release with both hands. Success but then – NO! – the strap from my Mae West to the dinghy snapped. Deep breath and I dived for the parachute, to which was attached my dinghy. I grabbed it and it came to the surface, unclipped the dinghy and the parachute, then sank out of sight.

Meticulously, as at the drill in the swimming baths, I removed the dinghy from its cover, spread it out, and gently, a little at a time, I filled it with gas from the bottle. Job done, I pulled myself, as per instruction, from the narrow end up to the top. Then I was sitting comfortably but still in water. Then I felt sick, and was sick. I tried to do it overboard, but, proverbially, the wind blows into one's face. I was now getting rid of all the sea water I had swallowed, and my previous meals, in reverse order. I was sick, on and off, for two hours.[10]

Climbing into a single seat dinghy in the Channel must have been a lonely and uncomfortable experience, those in the tropics may have been warmer but the diminutive size of the dinghy brought other concerns. Flying Officer Dave Bockus RCAF was flying his Spitfire Mk.VIII on an armed reconnaissance over Burma on 11 January 1945 when his engine failed. Rather than be caught by the Japanese on land, he headed out to sea and after a long glide ditched his aircraft into the Bay of Bengal. Bockus also only just managed to get out of his cockpit in time and then set about climbing into his dinghy:

Many a pilot has drowned because he released the compressed air into the dinghy too quickly, as a twist could form and blow a hole in the dinghy. It is not so easy to think about these things when dangling in the water and thinking about sharks. Those dinghies are difficult to get into. Once in, I started paddling out to sea. Another sinking feeling when I realised that the covering Spits were looking too far North. You realise what a tiny speck you are on a large ocean.[11]

10   Norman Franks, *Another Kind of Courage – Stories of the UK based Walrus Air-Sea Rescue Squadrons*, pp. 143-4.

11   Arthur Banks, *Wings of the Dawning – The Battle for the Indian Ocean* (Malvern: HMR Ltd, 1993), p.53.

In these instances, the pilot's or aircraft crew's chances of survival would depend upon how quickly they could be rescued. Until that moment arrived, they would have to survive in one of the harshest environments in the world. Coastal Command's advice from the July 1944 edition of *Coastal Command Review* adds further details to the challenges aircrew, in all types of dinghy, had to contend with:

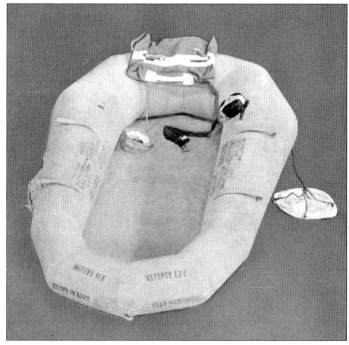

'K' Type fighter pilot dinghy. (Crown Copyright – Air Historical Branch)

> Having got away in the dinghy there are three things you should do at once. It is very important to have these fixed firmly in mind so that you do them instinctively. They may seem very difficult at the time and the immediate results will certainly not seem worthwhile, but the effect of neglecting them is very great later on. They are:

1. Bale the dinghy – probably the most important single means of preventing the effects of exposure.
2. Fix the weather apron.
3. Make arrangements to collect rainwater.

Quite often men are picked up after many hours in a waterlogged dinghy and they say they were 'all in' and could not bale it out. It is easy to understand how they felt and to sympathise, but if some instinctive urge to carry out a routine could have made them bale, they would have been in a much better condition.

It is much the same with the weather apron. You are very cold, you fix it and probably do not seem much warmer. It is a nuisance and prevents moving around. It does not seem to help, but 12-18-24 hours later you will be in far better shape if you have used it.

Rain may fall in the first hour. You may be in the dinghy a long time therefore you cannot waste any rain. Arrange to be able to use the apron to collect it so that it runs down into a depression. Have something ready to store it in and use a sponge to transfer it from the apron to the container. Wash the salt off the apron with the first few drops of water and collect the rest.

Next sit on something if you can. If you sit on the dinghy floor only a layer of fabric intervenes between your nether regions and the cold Atlantic. This is very depressing. It is not safe to sit on the buoyancy chamber, so try to sit on an emergency container, a bit of crumpled up clothing, a parachute or part of it. It helps a lot.

Then assess your crew. You want to know who will be your right-hand man on whom you can rely in 6-10 days time if you should still be there. All the evidence suggests that in survival at sea, mental make-up is much more important than physical strength. If two men are of equal character, the physically fit would do better. On the other hand a quiet determined individual, particularly if he is well-educated, will generally survive well even if he is of poor physique. A very fit, strong man, noisy and demonstrative and perhaps a bit empty-headed, will often succumb quite easily.

Then establish a routine, giving everyone some duties to do. Dinghy and lifeboat crews who lie in the bottom and do nothing rarely survive long exposure. Those who keep active and attentive do much better. If you have an injured man do not, out of kindness, excuse him all duties and leave him to lie idle. Try to find some job in the routine he can do and get him to do it. It is really kinder and helping him more.

If you are in good order, you should try to arrange some sleep rota. Often there is no room for this, but sometimes there is unfortunately not a full crew in the dinghy. Sleep in short watches of about two hours, and detail someone to watch over the sleeper so that he can relax without the fear of falling over the side. If you are really exhausted do not sleep, but try to stay awake. To help you, energy tablets are provided in the emergency flying rations and they have full directions on the box.

Now you can give some attention to the refinements of protecting yourself against exposure. If you have ditched at night, do not strip off your wet clothing in order to dry it until the day is a few hours old. You lose more heat by exposure than you gain from the small amount of drying. When you do take things off dry at high noon, do it in layers. If you have a relatively windproof garment, dry one layer from underneath it first, then replace it and dry another layer from underneath, retaining the windbreaker meanwhile. Finally, when you have two (or more) layers of dryish clothing available to wear, remove and dry the wind-breaker.

Keep moving if possible. If you cannot move your limbs because of lack of space, tense and relax muscles without moving limbs.

Keep your flying boots on, provided they do not feel tight. They help to keep your feet warm. When the boots feel tight, however, it means that the feet are swelling and then boots hamper the circulation and do more harm than good. Remove them and never replace them. Wrap your feet up loosely and keep them as dry as you can. Parachute silk is good if you have any. If your feet are numb and swollen do not rub them…

Without any water at all a man can survive four to six days. In exceptional cases you may last longer but this cannot be expected. The position seems to be that the body requires a minimum of 18 oz water per day to keep it in good order for long periods when resting. If about this amount cannot be obtained, it does not matter very much how much less is taken.

It is undoubtedly possible to ration water too strictly. There are many examples of men being picked up in very poor condition with considerable supplies of water available. They had instituted a very severe rationing scheme and might actually have died of thirst with water in hand. Again, the chances of rainwater within a few days are quite good in northern latitude, and it is a mistaken policy to allow yourself to get into a very bad condition and then to obtain rain water, only to find that you have gone too far to benefit much from it. Again, in air sea rescue the majority of contacts and rescues are made in the first five days. After that the rescue becomes more difficult, so that it is important that the dinghy crew should be as fit as possible during the time when rescue prospects are best and their cooperation is more fruitful…

At sea food is not nearly so important as water. Man can survive quite long periods without food. A tin of emergency flying rations contains about as much nourishment as a man normally eats in a day, so that the ration question is not very important. The emergency rations should be used in accordance with a strict routine so that they break up the day and help to keep your spirits up. The Horlicks tablet are sometimes criticised on the ground that they increase thirst. This may be true in normal circumstances, but when you are really short

High Speed Launch HSL 156 of 28 Air Sea Rescue Unit, based at Newhaven, Sussex, rescuing a downed American pilot from his dinghy in the English Channel. The figure in the duffle-coat is the Master of HSL 156, Flying Officer G Lockwood. (Crown Copyright – Air Historical Branch)

of water all dry foods tend to promote thirst and subtle differences disappear. The Horlicks tablet have an advantage (apart from their concentrated nourishment) in that they are not excessively palatable to most people and therefore they are fairly easy to ration.[12]

Reading the advice above, it might seem that to stand a good chance of survival the crews needed only to prepare well and have the right mental attitude. In reality, being adrift on a dinghy in the North Sea or Atlantic was one of the most appalling experiences imaginable. Sergeant Brian Walley

---

12  Coastal Command Review, July 1944 – quoted from Pitchfork, Graham, *Shot Down and in the Drink*, 2005, pp. 19-21.

was the second pilot on a 51 Squadron Whitley that had been bombing Berlin on 7 November 1941. His aircraft was hit in the port engine by German flak and after jettisoning their bombs, the Whitley ditched in the North Sea, where Walley managed to half-clamber, half-swim from the cockpit onto the fuselage:

My bootless left leg dragged limply behind me as I crawled along the top of the rapidly submerging fuselage, whimpering like a whipped schoolboy in utter shock. In that moment I grew up from a nineteen-year-old teenager to manhood. I pulled myself together and tumbled towards the dinghy, one moment 10 feet below, then way above my head. I was the last man out. The other four, already in the dinghy pulled me aboard.

We were not yet free. The umbilical cord still tethered us to the plane. The Skipper, knife in hand went back into the sinking wreck to cut us free. The tension snapped. His head bobbed up a metre away. As we hauled him back up into the dinghy I saw the plane's landing lights shining a good twenty feet below us in the sea. Another wave rolled by and they were gone. The sheer desolation was terrifying. Just a few thou' [thousandths of an inch] of rubberised fabric between us and such a watery grave.

We spent the next few minutes retrieving all sorts of gear, tied on with string and festooned around the dinghy. We found an air pump and repair kit, a couple of hand paddles (not much use 100 miles from land), a bottle of fresh water, two distress flares, a pocket knife and a pack of emergency rations.

Rations? Where was the duffle bag? In the flurry it had been left behind. Hot coffee later could well have saved lives. However we each carried a small pack filled with Horlicks tablets and chocolate, so we were not entirely destitute.

About this time we began to lose interest in food. Our Skipper, who must have had a bellyful of sea water was the first to lose his pre-flight supper. It was catching, for without exception we all followed suit spasmodically for the next hour or so until we just had nothing left to throw up.

My left leg ached abominably. The kneecap was broken and both thighs severely lacerated, leaving a trickle of blood to stain the water we were sitting in as it slopped around the bottom of the dinghy. I took off my remaining boot and used it as a baler. None of the others had a scratch.

Many is the time I have watched the dawn break, but never have I experienced such a sense of desolation as those first few grey streaks heralding the morning of the 8 November. In a very humble voice, our Skipper suggested we pray to God for succour. We did so most fervently, each quietly in his own way. Afterwards, feeling much better, we nibbled a bit of chocolate to keep our spirits up.

The dinghy, not surprising after all the battering, had sprung a leak. Not to worry we had the pump to keep it topped up. That was until about 10 a.m. If anything the storm had strengthened with the dawn. We would rise slowly up the face of the twenty foot waves, hang for a moment on the crest, then literally shoot down into the trough. A gust of wind more spiteful than the rest simply picked us up from one such crest and dumped us all lock stock and barrel into that raging sea.

I never saw the rear gunner or the wireless operator again. They just vanished beneath those great, grey, ugly breakers. The plight of we, the remaining three, was not much better. Weighed down with waterlogged flying gear, and suffering from the previous night's sea-sickness, not one of us could muster enough strength to clamber back. Our prospects were grim indeed. I'd had enough and had the crazy idea that I could swim home. After about 20 yards, my mother, acutely aware of the crisis, called across the miles for me to turn back. Her prayers were answered for, as I turned, the navigator rolled back into the dinghy. How he managed it after so many unsuccessful attempts I will never know. Suffice it was he who was there to help the Skipper on board then came my turn.

Yet another shock awaited us. All our meagre supplies had been lost in the capsize, except one of the flares still tied to the thwarts. We were reliant on air to keep us afloat. The loss of the pump had to be replaced by lung power. We took it in turns to blow and managed to hold our own.

Night came all too soon, the prospect of rescue disappearing with daylight. Once again, we put our trust in God and journeyed on through the storm which showed little sign of abating. We were in dire straits, sitting in about six inches of cold water, with flecks of ice on our clothing, tired out, hungry and facing a doubtful future.

That night we lost the navigator. He had scared us half to death by standing up. Another capsize would have been fatal in our weakened state. We got him settled down. He drifted off and died in his sleep, simply frozen to death.

It must have been in the small hours of the morning of 9 November when we heard the plane. We shouted and waved but never saw it, only heard it disappearing into the night. Afterwards we remembered the distress flare and could have wept at our stupidity.

Came dawn of the second day. Both of us were in bad shape now. Whenever I called up enough energy I had a blow into the inlet valve to try to keep us afloat. The time lag between blows lengthened as my energies dwindled, but the storm was at last blowing itself out and we were shipping less water.

The Skipper died that afternoon, leaving me all alone. I began to doubt my sense. I thought I could see land but when I looked again – nothing. It was only later that I realised we must have been blown over 100 miles south of where we had ditched and we were slowly drifting along the Friesian Islands.

The night could not long be put off. All pain had left my numbed body. I was settling down to a sleep that could only have one ending, knowing full well that I could not last another night, when out of the blue a Heinkel 59 seaplane roared overhead. I stared down the barrel of the front machine gun trained on me. I distinctly remember screaming out, 'No! No!! No!!!', fully expecting the burst that would put me out of my misery.

It didn't happen. I waved weakly as the pilot banked and came round to alight about 50 yards away. One of the crew climbed down onto the port float and tossed me a rope which I secured to the thwarts. They hauled me on board, followed by the bodies of my crew and finally the dinghy. I was stripped of all my freezing sodden clothes and wrapped in warm blankets. A couple of swigs from a bottle of schnapps and I went out like a light, only to come to as the plane landed at its base on the island of Norderney, where I was stretchered ashore and put straight into hospital.

That night, five kindly German doctors patched up my wounds, splinted my broken knee-cap and somehow kept me alive. In the morning, Hauptmann Karl Born, the Squadron Kommandant, commiserated with me. His words, 'For you the war is over', were to haunt me for over fifty years until I returned to Germany in 1995 when I met him once more and said 'Thank you' for my rescue. While there I was able to pay homage to my two less fortunate crew members, who now lie side by side in the War Cemetery at Sage, near Oldenburg in northern Germany.[13]

In such circumstances it is obvious that timely rescue was critical if the crew were to survive such harsh conditions. At the beginning of the war the RAF had used Lysanders to spot where crew may have ditched, these aircraft were also adapted to drop a container with extra dinghies, food, water and distress signals, as well as smoke bombs to mark the position. Finding the ditched crew in the

---

13   Brian Walley, *Silk and Barbed Wire* (Warwick, Western Australia: Sage Pages, 2000), pp. 83-6.

Crew members of a Vickers Wellington Mark III of the Sea Rescue Flight, based at Egypt, they are manning their stations in the beam gun positions of the aircraft during a search. (Crown Copyright – Air Historical Branch)

first place required the Lysander pilot to exercise fine judgement at what height to patrol in his search pattern. Too high and he might miss what was often a tiny object in a large sea, potentially just the head and shoulders of a pilot floating in his Mae West, particularly before the 'K' type dinghy was issued. If he flew too low, then the horizon was inevitably limited, and the aircraft's maximum area of coverage reduced. If a fighter had ditched, his fellow fighter pilots would sometimes circle round the spot, though this was clearly a very dangerous expedient in moments of combat and could not be maintained indefinitely. As the war progressed the Lysander was replaced with the Supermarine Walrus amphibian, an aircraft which could carry more equipment to drop to the pilot, had a greater endurance and could also land on the ocean. As the Allies gained air superiority, Walrus aircraft were able to regularly patrol over areas of the sea, from where they could respond more quickly to downed aircraft. It was a Walrus that was responsible for the rescue of the Polish Typhoon pilot Tadeusz Turek, who we had left as he climbed into his 'K' dinghy off the coast of France:

> I had ditched at 14:47 by my watch, which had stopped on hitting the water. Then I heard some engines – the boys were searching for me. I saw Spitfires and then Typhoons. Smith had stayed with me till I ditched and must have taken good bearings, but the main difficulty was that I was just a speck in a mountainous sea of waves the height of a house – 30 feet! Many times I vanished under those masses of water, to appear a few seconds later. The Spitfires found me and then lost me. It happened more than once but then one of them dropped a smoke float. To my horror, I saw his aim was so accurate that I was going to be hit by it. I

paddled furiously and the missile missed me by two feet! I still had to paddle away for it was oozing heat as well as smoke and likely to damage my dinghy.

Later a Walrus appeared and from the side cabin an arm dropped a Mae West. I paddled to it. Inside was a note which informed me that two Navy trawlers had got half-full of water and had to return to port. Landing a Walrus was impossible, so they'll try again tomorrow. The ending read: 'Stick it out pal!' Tomorrow looked a hell of a way away to me. My two Typhoons stayed with me till dusk and an Albacore till nightfall. All the rescue aircraft managed to fly close to me and give me a cheery wave, and I waved back, grateful for their concern – I was not alone.

In the night the weather improved and eventually all the clouds disappeared, so I began to navigate by the stars. There was a strong wind blowing from the west and I realised I was drifting – and fast – to the east. I estimated I was twenty miles from the French coast, so at this rate I could find myself very close to the enemy. I hated the thought of being a prisoner. Twice I had escaped from them and I was not willing to do it a third time, for this time the chances of escape were slim. I started to paddle west and continued throughout the night… Sometime about midnight a German Me 110 flew almost over me, dropping flares, continuing on a course south to north, dropping more flares from time to time. Later I heard the noise of engines, but on the sea. For some time I thought it could be our Navy and I was almost ready to fire a flare, but realised they would have to cross the German mines first. But in that direction, and at night, they had to be Germans. After a time the ship came closer, and I saw that the ship was switching a reflector on and off in an easterly direction. Although low in the sea, I realised I had to lay down in the dinghy to reduce the visible height. When the ship came closer, I could distinguish its shape and estimated that it was sailing on the west side of me. I was definitely in the path of the searchlight, and could even hear the voices of the crew. They were damn close. I laid very flat but managed to turn my head to see the sweep of the light. It stopped about 10 metres before me and started about the same distance after me. What luck!

The morning found me observing the French coast, on which I could see some single trees, I was so close. Shortly afterwards, some aircraft appeared some way off to the west, searching for me in the usual pattern. I tried to fire my flare but nothing happened, so in disgust I threw it into the sea where it instantly exploded. They had not seen me; then two Typhoons joined in and I again tried to help with flares, and this time they worked and I was spotted. I began to wonder about the rescue Walrus as I was so close to the coast, but it came and produced a landing east to west that made me wonder if there would be more of us in the drink! At that moment I saw a large column of water rising beside me. We were being fired on by coastal batteries – then another column. The Walrus then taxied up to me and a hand with a long stick and a hook on it was passed to me. I grabbed it and soon found myself sliding into the fuselage through the rear hatch. At that instant I saw another column of water. I turned to the Warrant Officer and asked if he saw it? He said no, but I was sure he had. Then just as I was rescued, I saw the Typhoons diving for the batteries and heard some rapid cannon fire. The Germans didn't fire at us again. Once in the aircraft I needed to take off my trousers since they were absolutely glued with the yellow dye [Fluoroscene], and then I watched a pile of sandwiches appear from a cupboard – it must have been over a foot tall! It was then that I noticed there were two men up in front. They tried to take off but after a few attempts I was relieved to see that the pilot abandoned the take off and decided to taxi back home. I returned to my sandwiches, but realizing they were for all of us, offered some to the crew up front. They nodded politely but refused. They were seasick.[14]

---

14   Norman Franks, *Another Kind of Courage*, pp. 144-5.

An RAF serviceman tries out an Airborne Lifeboat. (Crown Copyright – Air Historical Branch)

Dragging a pilot into a Walrus was not as easy as it sounds. The seaplane could be quite easily caught by the wind and blown across the sea, it therefore had to motor right up to the pilot, the navigator at the front using a boat hook to attach a rope to the dinghy. With this rope attached and the aircraft still underway, the dinghy would then slide back to the rear hatch, where the machine gun turret used to be. From this position the pilot was dragged into the Walrus and the dinghy sunk or recovered to prevent future false sightings and alarms. It could be a rough and ready process; some pilots were missed completely yet held on to the rope for dear life and were dragged unceremoniously through the water. They usually figured out that if they let go the aircraft would come around again. Lieutenant Beatie was an American who had served in the RAF's Eagle Squadron, he transferred back to the USAAF in September 1942 and was flying with 336th Fighter Squadron when his P-47 Thunderbolt had to ditch. He recalls his own pick up by a Walrus:

They had to make a couple of passes to set that old seaplane down and they couldn't dare stop it, for it would surely flounder. So they made two passes at me in the water, and on the second one a fellow leaned far out of the rear hatch and grabbed my hair and jerked me over and into the cabin – I was black and blue for days. I was in the water a minute or so less than an hour and the first thing the fellow did was offer me a cigarette. I took it but my mouth wouldn't close on it as I inhaled.[15]

Walrus pilots were a courageous bunch and soon gained a reputation for putting themselves and their aircraft in harm's way to rescue aircrew. On 31 October 1942 a Westland Whirlwind fighter, piloted by Flight Lieutenant John Van Shiek, was hit over Etaples during a low-level Rhubarb. His dinghy was spotted by Spitfires of 91 Squadron and a Walrus piloted by Pilot Officer Tod Hilton, with Sergeant Dizzy Seales as gunner, was dispatched. Seales describes the operation:

We took off from Shoreham, flew along to Hawkinge, refuelled and were briefed again before flying out, covered by Spitfires of 91 Squadron. After we spotted the man in the water we landed, but there was quite a bit of wear because of the swell, and so on. Tod taxied round – we were quite a way from him – and that's when I saw the mines floating about. We managed to get near him and eventually roped him in, got him on board and that's when the real trouble started.

We began taxying down a lane of mines, got our speed up and then, right at the end of the lane, there was a single mine which he hadn't seen before, sort of sealing off the lane! We were now under fire from the shore, not only light gunfire but from shore batteries as well. What would have happened if they'd hit one of the mines, I shudder to think. Seeing that mine was when the panic started! Tod was yelling back at me to come forward and then we both grabbed hold of the controls, yanked back as hard as we could, feet on the dashboard stuff, and then the suction of the hull suddenly broke and we got off. We didn't hold the height but fortunately we cleared the mine and dropped down the other side – we did bounce once or twice – and we damaged a float. In fact, when we were coming in to land at Hawkinge, it was only then that we realised the float was full of water because the wing dipped as we lost speed – talk about landing on a wing and a prayer! We both stayed the night at Hawkinge and the following day, Tod wasn't in a fit state to fly – there had been a bit of a celebration during the evening – so I caught a train up to London and then another down to Shoreham.[16]

The Walrus was a small aircraft and could not carry the larger eight-man bomber crews, though that still did not stop them coming to their aid. We left Sergeant Joe Hickson and the Halifax crew from 420 (RCAF) Squadron being violently ill on the North Sea, Hickson takes up his story once more:

We had ditched at 4:10 a.m. and we knew that by 9 a.m. or so the ASR boys would be looking for us. We sat up to look for planes but within minutes we would be doubled up and sick again even though we had nothing left to throw up. About 10 a.m. we heard some planes and spotted them far off to the north, but we could not attract their attention and we knew that within an hour the search would be called off, as we had been on ASR missions before and knew the routine. At about 5:30 p.m., the Skipper roused us all and we started to talk to each other. I was warm enough but wet from the chest down and we all had our legs cramped

15   Norman Franks, *Another Kind of Courage*, p. 64.
16   Norman Franks, *Another Kind of Courage*, pp. 47-9.

up. Later we put up the sail thinking we better head for Holland, but within a short time we spotted three Halifaxes in the distance, low over the water, but they soon turned for England and we settled down on our journey to Holland. Suddenly, three Halifaxes were heading straight for us, bomb doors open, and out fell three smoke bombs which looked at first as if they would hit us. We could see plainly the squadron code letters – they were from 420 Squadron! One 'Hally' climbed while the other two circled over us, and they dropped two containers which inflated when they hit the water, giving us two more life rafts and some supplies. We managed to retrieve one but the second floated away. We divided ourselves between the two dinghies and then three Avro Lancasters arrived, then a Warwick, and later still, a Hudson which had an airborne lifeboat slung beneath it.

It was now getting dusk, but then on the horizon a Walrus seaplane appeared, circled once, then came down to land in the rough sea and disappeared. I felt sure we would then have to rescue him but up he popped on top of another wave then disappeared again below the waves. In this way he slowly made his way to us and upon reaching us we were lifted out of the dinghy by a strong-armed airman into the nose of the Walrus. I was second to be lifted and followed the mid-upper to the tail of the machine. The others all followed, the Skipper being the last, in true Navy tradition.

With the Walrus crew of two and eight of us, it made it impossible for a take-off. I could feel the plane moving through the water, but it was dark now and closing my eyes I was soon asleep, but not soundly. We must have been taxying about an hour when the motor of the Walrus revved, then shut down abruptly – with the plane hitting something with a shuddering bang. I could not imagine what we'd hit; I thought at first it had been a mine. The motor revved again for about a minute, then again shut down and another bang. This happened a couple of more times, then I looked out of the hatch and found there was an MTB and we had bumped into the back of it, and then a couple of sailors grabbed our arms and hauled us on board.

We were put into bunks and given a glass of rum although I didn't want mine, but a sailor gladly drank it for me. In a few moments we were on our way again, towing the Walrus behind us. Getting out of my wet clothes, I put on a pair of navy blue overalls and in the bunk I closed my eyes.

It only seemed like a few seconds when a flash lit up the sky outside the cabin. A sailor came in and said a German E-boat had just shot off a star-flare, lighting up the whole sky. They cut the Walrus loose and the MTB opened up, full throttle. Did we ever move then! I guess the Germans had come out to see what all the commotion had been about off the Dutch coast. We got to the port of Great Yarmouth at 2 a.m. on 17 September and eventually got back to our base that afternoon, only to find our beds stripped, our gear stowed away and a new crew had moved in. We quickly soon sorted that lot out, remade the beds and got our belongings back. We learned later that the Navy had gone back out and retrieved the Walrus – the Germans had not found it. Our Skipper was recommended for a DFC for ditching a disabled aircraft successfully, thus saving the lives of his crew. The wireless operator was recommended for the DFM for staying at his set and sending the SOS until the last minute. We were all given 10 days' survivors' leave, starting the 21st.[17]

While a Walrus could undertake close and medium range search and rescues and pick-up smaller crews, it was clear a solution still needed to be found for recovering larger crews at longer ranges. In addition, the bomber offensive was highlighting that there would be increasing numbers of

---

17  Norman Franks, *Another Kind of Courage*, pp.196-7.

An airborne lifeboat is parachuted by a Lockheed Hudson of 279 Squadron RAF to the crew of a USAAF Boeing B-17, who had difficulty in getting into their dinghy after making a forced landing in the North Sea. (Crown Copyright – Air Historical Branch)

bomber crews forced to bale out too far for marine craft to reach them easily, or for fighter cover to be given. So far, all the dinghies that had been developed by the RAF were simply temporary expedients, designed to keep the crew out of the water until a rescue craft arrived. The arrival of the Hudson and Vickers Warwick at Air Sea Rescue units meant that much larger loads could potentially be carried and the idea of a boat that could be dropped by parachute and then motored back to friendly shores developed. This became known as the Airborne Lifeboat.

Designed by the Cowes based naval architect and yachtsman Uffa Fox, this 32-foot wooden boat was fitted with sails, oars and two 3 KW motors and could carry up to eight men. It even came with a rudimentary instruction booklet on how to sail, for those aircrew who might be unfamiliar with the skill. The craft was flown by aircraft to the site of the ditched aircrew and dropped by parachute from about 700 feet. As the parachute deployed two buoyancy chambers situated at the bow and stern of the craft inflated to ensure the lifeboat could not capsize. When the lifeboat struck the sea, an automatic mechanism fired two rockets to port and starboard, deploying 200 feet of buoyant rope either side to help downed aircrew retrieve the lifeboat and climb aboard. The introduction of the Airborne Lifeboat was problematic as it was originally designed for the Warwick, but when that aircraft's introduction into service was delayed it had to be hastily re-configured for use with the Hudson. Nevertheless 24 Airborne Lifeboats were brought into service.

The reader will recall Arthur Eyton-Jones and his two crew mates from earlier in this chapter. They had ditched their Mitchell bomber in the North Sea, after which they had spent an uncomfortable night in their dinghy. The next day brought good news as they saw four Beaufighters escorting two Hudsons, one of which had an Airborne Lifeboat underneath. Eyton-Jones takes up the story:

The Hudson pilot was obviously taking no chances. First he dropped a smoke float alongside us to show him the wind direction. Then he made several dummy runs before finally dropping the boat from a height of 700 feet. Three large parachutes deployed simultaneously to hold the boat up and as it swung down towards us there was a loud crack and a rocket line fired from the bows with a drogue attached to keep the boat's head to wind. The boat landed bow first with a slight splash some one hundred yards to one side and slightly downwind to us; the parachutes collapsed and were automatically blown clear; at the same time two more rockets fired and threw out long lengths of floating line, one on either side, so that we could pull ourselves in to the boat as we drifted down towards it. Self-righting chambers fore and aft then blew themselves up! It was a most impressive performance.[18]

With the Beaufighters thundering overhead, to encourage them into the lifeboat, the surviving crew had just started to get settled into their craft when they were startled by the sound of cannon fire. Taking courage to look over the side of their diminutive lifeboat they found it was the Beaufighters shooting up the old rubber dinghies to prevent future false alarms. Once the overhead aircraft had seen them safely into the boat, the Hudson sent a message by Aldis lamp telling them to steer 247 degrees magnetic. Eyton-Jones continues with a short description of the airborne lifeboat:

To begin with, it was not a boat in the true sense. It consisted of a series of watertight compartments which gave it buoyancy, each compartment being fitted with a removable lid secured by wing-nuts. At each end was an inflated rubber canopy which acted both as a shelter and a means of turning the vessel upright if a wave should turn it over. The wooden deck sloped slightly inwards towards a slot which ran right through the bottom of the boat so that it was self-draining; any water that was shipped simply ran out through the centre slot. The sides between each self-righting canopy were lined with rubber foam which had spaces for the oars to be used. Two engines were fitted side by side amidships, each in a separate compartment with their propellers protruding directly underneath them.[19]

Initially Eyton-Jones and his team were overjoyed with their new craft, but a string of bad luck brought near disaster upon them. They failed to get the aerial attached to the top of the mast, struggled to fit the rudder properly, the engines drowned in sea water and as the seas and wind picked up, the tiller broke off in Eyton-Jones' hand. Fortunately, he was a good seaman and used the mast and sails as a drogue to keep the boat's head into wind, though after a while the line to the drogue snapped and the small boat began to founder, turning the night into a terrible ordeal for the survivors. As the storm abated the next day the three men found themselves huddled on the port side of the boat, now the only part above water, with no engines, rudder, mast or sails and all their loose gear swept overboard. Eyton-Jones recognised that they needed to restore buoyancy and the only way to do that was to pump out the starboard hatches, but that was by no means a simple task:

To do that the hatch covers would have to be above the surface of the sea and the only way to achieve that would be to let some come into the port-hatches, which would mean losing even more of our precious buoyancy and might make us founder. There was nothing else for it so gingerly we let water into the port-hatches and the port side of the boat sank lower and the starboard side came up a little. We then stuffed clothing into the spaces for the oars on the sides of the boat and into the sluice in the centre, because by now we were so low in the water

---

18   Arthur Eyton-Jones, *Day Bomber*, pp. 85-94.
19   Arthur Eyton-Jones, *Day Bomber*, pp. 85-94.

that the sea was coming IN through this sluice instead of OUT. There followed about six hours of back-breaking work as we literally baled out for our lives. Luckily the sea was by now only slightly choppy but even so it was most disheartening to see a small wave gleefully slop back over the side as much water as we had just flung out. Slowly, ever so slowly, we gained, and at long last the hatch covers were above water. We could open the flooded hatches and start pumping out. Once this was done the boat rose rapidly in the water so that we could throw all the sodden clothing overboard and open the sluice in the centre.[20]

With buoyancy restored, the crew spent another uncomfortable night on the airborne lifeboat until the next day they were rescued, a moment of great excitement for the crew:

On Tuesday 3 August three Mitchells sighted us and remained circling for two hours until relieved by a Hudson which was later joined by another Mitchell. Mitchells and Beaufighters then came along and flew over us and went back in a stream over the horizon, returning to repeat the performance all over again. Obviously they were guiding surface vessels to us, and sure enough at 1445 hours two vessels appeared over the horizon steaming straight for us. From our position in the water we thought that they were destroyers but in fact they turned out to be RMLs (Royal Naval Marine Launches). The nearest launch came alongside with a scrambling net over the side. Sitting in the stern, I was nearest the net and although I was well aware that the Captain should be the last to leave the ship, I felt that this was no time to stand on ceremony and was helped up the net by many willing hands. In no time we were all aboard and looked after as only the Navy know how.

The rescued aircrew were dressed in bright yellow survival suits and given jerseys and fresh socks. The cook prepared bacon and eggs, but for the airmen the greatest joy was to be put to bed under warm blankets and dry clean sheets. As Eyton-Jones described, 'To be warm and dry was a luxury that cannot be described. Truly we take the important things in life for granted.'[21]

To be picked up by surface craft was a common way to retrieve aircrew, the Royal Navy Fairmile launches being used for longer distances and the RAF High Speed Launches (HSL) for those closer to shore. Frequently these vessels would be pre-positioned in places, such as the Dogger Bank in the North Sea, ready to respond quickly to stricken aircraft. On other occasions they would be concentrated to support an expected battle. As an example several RAF High Speed Launches were used during the Dieppe raid and they were amongst the last British craft to withdraw from that mission. The HSLs would often come under attack by German aircraft, therefore their original yellow decks were painted over with grey paint and they were also armed with Vickers K gun turrets and a 20mm Oerlikon cannon, though sometimes given instructions not to fire unless they were attacked themselves. These RAF rescue craft were small and lacked the seaworthiness of the Royal Navy launches, as a result there were frequent occasions when they were unable to put to sea. Keith Beken was the captain of an Air Sea Rescue launch, HSL 198, and described the rescue of Peter Horsley, a 21 Squadron Mosquito pilot, shot down on a raid over Normandy on 23 June 1944 (the day of the notorious 'Great Storm' that also disrupted the build-up of the OVERLORD landings and damaged the Mulberry harbours):

One day the nav tower flashed a message, proceed to position 55 miles, 185 degrees NE Nav. Setting course on our compass with our electric log at zero compensating for the westerly tide

20   Arthur Eyton-Jones, *Day Bomber*, pp. 85-94.
21   Arthur Eyton-Jones, *Day Bomber*, pp. 85-94.

at one and a half knots we adjusted our speed to 27 knots and set off in company with another RAF launch. Arriving at the estimated position both boats then started the usual square search going in opposite directions. The weather was very rough and getting worse. After four hours of searching and daylight vanishing we suddenly had a radio message 'return to base because of gale conditions' we were naturally furious for whilst it was no weather for us to be out in it was considerably worse for the dinghy we were searching for.

The next day we were weather bound in harbour and had to content ourselves with working out the estimated position we thought the dinghy must have arrived at with the east and west tides and the westerly gale. Next day the gale was abating so HSL 192 and my 198 set off again to the new estimated position of the dinghy we had plotted on our charts. After four hours we had spotted the dinghy, he was a Mosquito pilot and his navigator had been lost, he was being pulled up on a scrambling net as we kept an eye out on the enemy coast at Cherbourg which was about eight miles away and also keeping an eye out for enemy fighters. Three shells landed – one to port, one to starboard and one astern, nice grouping. We made off fast in a zig-zag course endeavouring to make smoke to cover our exit. The pilot was taken to Seaview and placed in the naval sick bay, where he gently recovered from three days in gale force conditions in a rubber dinghy.[22]

There is an interesting sequel to this story. About fifteen years after the rescue, HRH, the Duke of Edinburgh visited the Island Sailing Club at Cowes, together with his equerry Wing Commander Peter Horsley. While they were dining in the club's restaurant Wing Commander Horsley noticed that Keith Beken, now a renowned maritime photographer, was wearing an Air Sea Rescue tie, he by chance was wearing a Goldfish Club tie, a tie only available to pilots who had survived ditching in the sea. Together they realised that Horsley was the pilot rescued by HSL 198 and a lively re-union then took place.[23]

HSLs did not just operate in the Channel, they also performed sterling work in many overseas locations, not least of which was Malta. Francis Shute was appointed as a coxswain onto HSL 100 based at Sliema, Malta in July 1942, a period when the battle for air superiority over the island was at its most intense. The coxswain of an HSL was normally a sergeant and Shute describes the responsibilities included in the position:

The discipline of the crew, maintenance of the vessel, steering and general seamanship with some navigation, that was the skipper's primary responsibility. Now the skipper, until certainly 1941, could only be appointed a skipper in the RAF if he held a Master Mariner's certificate, but by 1942 there was a shortage of skippers and by late 1942, early 1943, Coxswains were then being commissioned as skippers. Providing they could come up to the required standards of navigation.

The skipper on [HSL] 100, my first one was Peter Tilbury. Now in pre-war times he was the skipper of a whale catcher, so he was a seaman, a bit of hare 'em scare 'em lad and came from a tough school. Later on Joe Hawtin took over as Skipper and Joe had, I think I am right in saying, a Master Mariner's Foreign Going Certificate.

Now in 1942, because the siege [of Malta] was still on and we were absolutely scarce on everything, rations, ammunition, fuel, the launch could not go to sea unless there was a very good chance of being of service. So you would only put to sea when an aircraft, perhaps coming home, had spotted someone in the drink, or an aircraft radioed in that he was crashing

22   IWM Sound Archives, Catalogue Number 13935, Peter Horsley interview.
23   Obituary *The Independent* 17 February 2007.

'Whaleback' High Speed Launches, HSLs 122 and 142, at sea off Dover, Kent.
(Crown Copyright – Air Historical Branch)

and ditching and they had some idea roughly where he might be and then we would be sent out. Now that is in contrast to what would happen a year or so later when with ample fuel, we would go out to a rendezvous position and hang around for a day when there were bombing raids on. So that any one coming home who had to ditch we were on the spot waiting for them or not so far away from them…

They [the rescues] were all very much of the same pattern. You would get a call out, you may get a position because perhaps an incoming aircraft had spotted someone in the drink. Or they picked up a radio signal from someone about to ditch, now if it was a fighter, they would put him on RDF and the best they could tell us was that he was last heard of on a bearing 037 from St Elmo so we could only go out on that. If an aircraft had reported seeing somebody in the drink and they had managed to get a cross fix on him with two RDF fixes or the aircraft had given him an accurate position, then we had a position to aim for. Now bear in mind that even a slight sea, that means a wave of just two or three feet high, it is very difficult to see a dinghy. Especially if it is a fighter pilot who has just baled out and is just in a Mae West…he may be down in the dip of a wave. We have picked people up who said you passed ten yards from me half an hour ago, but he was in one hollow and we were in the next and hadn't seen him. If it was a positive position by a double RDF fix, then you would get to it find nothing and start a square search. Square search means this, that you would take the visibility of the day – and if you said that was 300 yards and allowing now for the sea conditions which brought visibility water to water down to one hundred yards. Then from the point you start your square search you go hundred yards East, hundred yards North, hundred yards West and so on gradually opening your leg out so you are only two hundred yards now away from your original line. You now have to multiply your legs by another hundred yards visibility on your second leg and keep searching getting wider and wider hoping to find something.

If it was night-time in some respects you had a better chance, in that you would frequently stop switch off every appliance on the boat as well as engines and have every member on deck listening. Now aircrew were taught that if they heard the engines cut, they should blow the whistles on their Mae Wests like hell because we would hear it and take a bearing.

They weren't all successful, sometimes you did not find anybody. There was one occasion when we had been given what appeared to be a fairly positive position, we got to it, started the search, we hadn't gone very far in the square search, stopped everything because down in the water we could see a patch of white. The only thing it could be was a parachute and the pilot had sunk below the surface, parachute as well. We tried putting a hook over and everything, but we couldn't reach the parachute and that was the end of that…[24]

Malta's HSLs did not just rescue fighter pilots. As the war progressed and the island took on a more offensive role, a requirement to rescue crews from larger aircraft also emerged. Shute recalls rescuing the crew of a Liberator, off Malta, later in the war:

It was a mile off Benoza Point, we got to it and it was still floating and your first duty when you got to a job like that, was that with everyman you pulled aboard you would say to him 'How many on board?' Because you never knew just how many were in that aircraft, some went off with other people in them. We got the answer 'Nine'. Now we got six on board and by this time HSL 128 came out, so we left and left her to get the other three, but the people that we had picked up had already said that one of their crew was trapped in the fuselage. Now I had already used the bow of my boat, with full engine power, to try and roll the wreckage of the aircraft over, to get this fella out but without success. Though HSL 128 had cutting gear, and though they tried, they were too late and the aircraft went down and the man was lost, but between us we saved eight.[25]

British aircraft could of course be downed in distances far exceeding the range of either Walruses or Fairmile launches. The war Coastal Command waged was so far from land that downed aircraft could usually only expect help from passing Royal Navy or merchant ships, or perhaps even one of their own larger aircraft, such as a Sunderland or Catalina. Rescuing crews from the depths of the Atlantic could be a formidable proposition.

On 28 May 1943, Bill Dods was flying his Sunderland from 461 Squadron and identified a dinghy containing six men from a Whitley bomber that had ditched. He requested permission to land from his HQ at Plymouth which was given. Initially he had planned to land across the swell, but as he descended he noted the sea did not look as benign as he had hoped so he climbed once more determined to land along the swell and crosswind. Disaster struck as he touched down and an unexpected cross swell threw the Sunderland into the air, where with little speed it stalled and with great violence and noise crashed into a large wave and was completely submerged. The bows were smashed to fragments and the front of the machine from the cockpit forward was torn away, with it went Bill Dods and his co-pilot Raleigh Gipps who were sucked into the sea.

The aircraft began to sink like a stone, so the remainder of the crew climbed through an escape hatch onto the main plane and managed to retrieve one of the dinghies. Once in the dinghy they sighted Gipps some distance away and Wallace Mackie, the wireless operator, dived in to the sea and swam to him, finding him barely conscious with serious internal and external injuries. It took

---

24   IWM Sound Archives, Catalogue Number, 17277, Francis Shute interview.
25   IWM Sound Archives, Catalogue Number, 17277, Francis Shute interview.

Flying Officer G Lockwood, Master of High Speed Launch HSL 156 of 28 Air Sea Rescue Unit,
based at Newhaven, Sussex, speaking to base while in the lookout cockpit of his vessel.
(Crown Copyright – Air Historical Branch)

Mackie 30 minutes to successfully recover Gipps, an act for which he was awarded the British
Empire Medal. Bill Dods was sadly never seen again. The surviving members of the Sunderland
crew joined up with the survivors of the Whitley and together they spent the night in the Atlantic
hoping for better luck on the following day.

Gordon Singleton took off in another Sunderland from 461 Squadron at 0340 on 29 May and
was briefed to look out for the dinghies. The previous night a Wellington had seen distress flares
from the dinghies, but visibility had closed in and it had lost sight of them, nonetheless Singleton
and his crew at least had a point in the wide ocean to aim for.

As the Sunderland entered the Bay of Biscay the clouds descended and merged with a rising
sea mist to create one dirty grey blanket, dramatically reducing visibility in the process. Having
to rely purely on dead reckoning, Singleton's Sunderland arrived three hours after take-off at the
area the Wellington had last seen the dinghies. There by an extraordinary piece of luck, as well as
impressive navigation, they saw the survivors in their dinghies – just five hundred yards off the
starboard bow. Singleton dropped a smoke marker and pulled his aircraft round in a steep low
turn, wary of going too far away or else he might lose them entirely in the fog. Singleton also knew
he would have to land almost immediately and therefore could not afford to waste time jettisoning
his depth charges or trying to gain height for a conventional approach. Determined to take the
risk Singleton approached the eight-foot swell in very poor visibility, brushing from crest to crest
with the nose up and he managed to stall and land the aircraft neatly into a trough. His crew
then prepared the aircraft for taxiing in the open sea and approached the dinghies, the crew soon
climbing aboard under the shelter of the Sunderland's starboard wing. The seriously ill Gipps was
quickly carried to the wardroom.

Singleton understood that with the twenty-seven men he had on board, the eight depth charges and fifteen hundred gallons of fuel there was no way the Sunderland could take-off in the seas it was facing. Singleton had to accept the fact that only a change in the weather, or the arrival of a friendly ship could help them. A signal was transmitted to the nearest friendly ship, a Free French Destroyer *La Combattante*, asking for it to rendezvous with them, similarly a passing Sunderland picked up their Aldis lamp signal requesting they contact the same ship and guide it to them. All the while the Sunderland sat on the ocean and as visibility improved, Singleton became more and more aware of what a sitting duck the Sunderland was for any patrolling enemy aircraft.

*La Combattante* met up with them later that afternoon and took off the survivors including Gipps, as well as some of Singleton's crew.

The crew of an Armstrong-Whitworth Whitley of Coastal Command, which had come down in the Atlantic, being rescued by a Short Sunderland of 10 Squadron RAAF. (Crown Copyright – Air Historical Branch)

The sea was still too rough for the Sunderland to take-off, so they were taken in tow by the destroyer, a difficult manoeuvre given the Sunderland's natural tendency to swing into wind, a drogue was therefore deployed from the aircraft and that helped to an extent. The destroyer set off initially at ten knots, but water poured in through the open turret on the nose of the Sunderland which was impossible to close, as that would have fouled the towing rope. Before long the crew were baling like crazy. The destroyer reduced speed to five knots but even that was not enough to prevent the water from streaming in. The drogue was then torn from its moorings and Singleton had to use his starboard engine to keep the Sunderland's nose aligned with the destroyer's course. The revving of the starboard engine soon caused it to over-heat and the engineer demanded it was shut down. Singleton did so, but found the aircraft immediately swung hard to starboard, the tow rope slackened and then suddenly tightened with a jolt ripping off the bollard at the front of the Sunderland. 'That's that!' Singleton reportedly said.

Singleton was faced with the stark choice of having to either abandon his aircraft and take passage home in the destroyer or attempt to take off in the seven-foot swell, with all the risk that entailed. He opted for the latter course and ran out the depth charges to jettison them (a crew member of *La Combattante* had already taken the fuses out – known as de-lousing), the crew closed the bulkheads and hatches, shut the front turret and took up their crash positions. Singleton decided his take-off run would be into the swell, though that was seventy degrees out from the wind direction which would make the take-off even harder. He had no real alternative, for an attempt to take off into wind and along the swell would have been suicide. Singleton could also only use three of his engines, had he used all four then the Sunderland would have turned into wind. The take-off began with the Sunderland's bows hitting the swell and Singleton doing his best to maintain heading, each crash into the waves felt like it would break up the aircraft and rivers of sea water ran across the cockpit windows. Singleton could barely see out and had to try to steer the aircraft on instruments alone, his take-off is estimated to have taken three miles, during which period Singleton was as blind as a bat and the throttles of the three engines were right up against the gate. Slowly the Sunderland's speed picked up and at sixty miles an hour Singleton began to get some semblance of rudder control and was therefore able to open-up the throttle on the fourth engine. The Sunderland now began to crash from the top of one wave to another and then, suddenly and without warning, he was able to catch it from stalling back into the sea and it staggered into the sky.

The crew were initially stunned into silence after such an alarming take-off, but soon began to leave their crash positions. It was George Viner who went down to his position in the galley to find the door would not open easily. After a good hard shove, he found that a large hole, seven-foot long and four-foot wide, had been torn out of the hull by the waves. When Singleton was shown it, his comment was simply 'That's a bit awkward George'. There was now no hope of landing in the water, for the Sunderland would easily break up and sink like a stone with such damage to its hull. Instead Singleton opted to land at Angle aerodrome, a large flat airfield on St Anne's Head peninsula, near their home base of Milford Haven. A landing on land had never been done by a Sunderland before and the expectation was that it was impossible. Nonetheless, permission was given to land by the airfield commander, who had also thoughtfully positioned ambulances and fire tenders nearby and the Sunderland's crew jettisoned all weight in a hope to lessen the stress on the keel and took up their positions once more. Singleton brought the Sunderland in on the grass airfield, the twenty-six tons of aircraft hitting the ground with a bump and then its step[26], tearing through the earth like a plough. The aircraft slid on for a further hundred and fifty yards and slowly began to turn to port, knocking off the float on that side and then coming to rest with the wing tip buckled to the ground. The crew exited quickly after this magnificent landing.[27]

Air Sea Rescue was also important in the Indian and Pacific Oceans indeed many British and Australian pilots would desperately try to nurse crippled aircraft back over the sea, specifically to avoid baling out over land and capture by the Japanese. The vast distances involved in the Pacific campaign meant that only long-range aircraft such as Catalinas were useful in picking pilots up from the sea. Other long-range aircraft, including Liberators also assisted by detecting survivors in the water and dropping supplies to them whenever possible. In early April 1945, a convoy of Japanese ships, including the cruiser *Isuzu,* was sent to evacuate the Japanese garrison on Timor. This convoy was spotted by Mosquito PR aircraft and shadowed by Catalinas. On 6 April it was attacked firstly by RAAF Mitchells from 2 and 18 Squadrons, followed twenty minutes later by nine Australian Liberators, from 21 and 24 Squadrons, who bombed from 12,000 feet. The Liberators in this second wave soon came under attack from Japanese fighters, as well as the ship's

---

26   A longitudinal line along the aircraft fuselage which allows the aircraft to plane at speed and take off.

27   Ivan Southall, *They Shall Not Pass Unseen* (London: Angus and Robertson, 1956), pp. 64-72. A dramatic video of Singleton's landing at Angle airfield can be viewed at <https://youtu.be/0ZfVEoZmt-c> accessed 12 March 2017

A Short Sunderland Mk.III of 10 Squadron RAAF on the water after alighting to rescue three survivors from a Vickers Wellington of 172 Squadron, clinging to a one-man dinghy (seen at right). The Wellington had been shot down in the Bay of Biscay while attacking a German submarine on 26 August 1944. Although it was generally forbidden for flying boats to alight on the open sea in rescue attempts, the pilot of the Sunderland, Flight Lieutenant W.B. Tilley, decided the survivors could no longer wait for surface craft to arrive, and touched down to pick them up for a safe return to Mount Batten, Devon. A fourth member of the Wellington crew, Flying Officer R.B. Gray RCAF, refused to risk the lives of the other survivors by overloading the dinghy, although he was seriously injured. He succumbed during their 15-hour ordeal at sea and was awarded a posthumous George Cross. (Crown Copyright – Air Historical Branch)

The same Sunderland of 10 Squadron RAAF 'unsticks' after picking up the three survivors from the 172 Squadron Wellington, shot down in the Bay of Biscay, 27 August 1944. (Crown Copyright – Air Historical Branch)

anti-aircraft weapons. One of the Liberators was flown by Flight Lieutenant McDonald and was attacked by two Japanese fighters, who closed to within 50 feet of the aircraft before breaking away underneath. Cannon shells burst under the flight deck of the Liberator, near the nose wheel and a fire broke out which spread very quickly and forced McDonald to order his crew to bale out. Another Liberator, flown by Flight Lieutenant Ford, was also shot down by Japanese fighters at this point too.[28] A few days after this action, Warrant Officer Keith Shilling, who was in McDonald's aircraft, wrote an account of the events beginning just before McDonald gave the order to jump:

The fire drove the engineer into the bomb bays. I did not see him again. The captain (McDonald) ordered the crew to bale out. The second pilot escaped through the bomb bays. I followed thirty seconds later. About two minutes later another member jumped. He did not appear to have a parachute. I went out of the bomb bays head first, counted six and pulled the release cord. It took me about twelve minutes to come down during which time I counted six members parachuting from Flight Lieutenant Ford's Liberator. An additional member appeared to drop without a parachute. McDonald's aircraft disintegrated about 3,000 feet above the sea. It did not explode. Ford's Liberator exploded on impact with the water. Enemy fighters did not attack parachutists. My legs were entangled in the shroud lines and I had to cut away the lines with a bowie knife. Although I had seen someone land about 50 yards away heavy seas prevented my seeing him. The seas were running at about four and a half feet. I never saw any member of my crew again.

About fifteen to thirty minutes later the enemy cruiser came within 100–200 yards of me. She was heavily laden with troops. Equipment under tarpaulins was clearly visible on the decks. A machine-gun opened fire at the position I had been making for. I deflated my 'Mae West' and sank. At this time the bullets hit the water within six feet of me. The cruiser then passed on. Some fifteen minutes later an escort vessel of about 1,000–2,000 tons passed within a hundred yards of me. This vessel was also laden with troops and equipment. It continued on for five minutes, turned and came directly towards me, passing close enough for the bow wave to throw me sideways. I could hear voices from the deck. No attempt was made to pick me up or shoot me. Some minutes later, a Zero passed overhead low and appeared to be looking for survivors. I deflated my 'Mae West' again and sank to avoid detection.

About ten minutes later seven Liberators circled low and after some five minutes dropped me a dinghy which landed fifty yards away. Twenty minutes later a Catalina (of No. 112 Air-Sea Rescue Flight, captained by Flight Lieutenant Bulman) arrived and taxied close enough to pick me up. Sergeant Sayer from Flight Lieutenant Ford's crew was aboard, having been picked up earlier. I was exhausted and cold. I had swallowed a lot of salt water. We taxied around and picked up Warrant Officer Vickers, also from Flight Lieutenant Ford's crew. The Catalina took off, landing again about thirty minutes later to pick up another survivor, whom I believe to be Flight Sergeant Faichnie. He was completely exhausted and was being pulled in over the gun blisters when the Catalina was attacked by a Zero from 12 o'clock.

The Catalina caught fire immediately and sank three minutes later. I had undressed, as ordered, and was going to bed in a bunk in the waist. I had been called forward for the landing and was in the navigator's position when the attack was made. The order was given to bale out and I made my way aft. On the way a fuel line burst above me, pouring blazing fuel on to my back. This was extinguished by Sergeant Sayer who smothered the flames with a sleeping bag. I escaped out of the port blister, naked and with no Mae West. I do not remember much for a few minutes and when I regained my faculties I was being kept afloat by two members of the

---

28   George Odgers, *Air War Against Japan 1943-45*, pp. 407-8

Catalina crew, Flight Lieutenant Bulman and Flight Sergeant Scholes. These two men had to let me go after fifteen minutes owing to their Mae Wests coming undone. Flying Officer Becke helped me for the next forty-five minutes. Through the fortitude of these men I was saved from drowning. A few minutes after the Catalina was hit, the air-sea rescue Liberator (Flight Lieutenant Byfield) dropped two large dinghies and one supply canister. After an hour's struggling we reached one of the dinghies. Another Catalina (Flight Lieutenant Corrie) was directed to us by the Liberator. It landed after half an hour's battle with heavy seas and wind. We were eventually picked up. One dinghy was cut in half by the port wing float. As the last survivor clambered aboard (nine men were rescued, six from Bulman's Catalina and three from the Liberators) an Irving fighter [Nakajima J1N1 twin engine reconnaissance aircraft flown by the Japanese Navy] was sighted making for us. The enemy made his first attack as we were taking off and scored hits. Our return fire did no visible damage. A running fight ensued for about twenty minutes. The attacks ceased and we headed for Darwin, reaching there about 2230.[29]

The *Isuzu* had suffered some damage from the Australian attack, including direct hits from bombs dropped, but the speed of the convoy had not been reduced and it continued on its way. However, Warrant Officer Shilling may have taken some comfort that one of the smaller Japanese vessels was sunk by a submarine that night and *Isuzu* subsequently suffered the same fate the next day.

Fleet Air Arm pilots habitually flew over the sea as part of their duties and the practicalities of rescuing ditched pilots was often very difficult. This steadily improved throughout the war, to include using the ubiquitous Walrus amphibian which could not only land on the sea to pick up a ditched pilot, but also directly return him to his ship by lowering the aircraft's wheels and hook and landing on the carrier itself. A Walrus was frequently stood by for air sea rescue duties during major Fleet Air Arm operations and sometimes even a submarine would be earmarked for air sea rescue support which could prove invaluable.

South African Lieutenant Commander Freddie Nottingham was leading 854 Naval Air Squadron in an attack on the Sakishima Gunto islands on 27 March 1945 and piloting one of the 24 Avenger dive-bombers involved in the raid. Nottingham's aircraft was struck in the wing by anti-aircraft fire, and the wing torn away. He was successfully able to bale out, but the other two crew members were trapped and crashed with the aircraft into the sea. Though Nottingham found himself in the sea with just a lifejacket, he had at least been observed by a fellow Avenger pilot who transmitted his position to the Royal Navy Task Force. Its commander, Admiral Vian, despatched the destroyer HMS *Undine* which failed to find Nottingham, but did pick up an American fighter pilot who had been shot down fifty miles to the north off Okinawa, three days earlier. As HMS *Undine* departed an American submarine on air sea rescue duties, USS *Kingfish,* came up on the British inter-ship radio frequency to report that she had been monitoring the traffic, was near the reported area and would surface to search for Nottingham. HMS *Illustrious* launched four Corsair fighters to provide cover and assist in the search. However, after three hours and with dusk approaching these aircraft were running out of fuel and the leader radioed *Kingfish* that they would have to return to their carrier. The captain of *Kingfish* persuaded them to stay on task for just another fifteen minutes and as the aircraft fanned out for one last sweep, the pilots and the submarine lookouts all saw a red distress flare in the gathering dusk. The submarine steamed towards Nottingham and once alongside, two sailors jumped into the water and hauled him out. The American crew were quick to report over the radio 'The pilot's name is Nottingham, I repeat Nottingham' to the evident relief of his Fleet Air Arm comrades.[30]

---

29   George Odgers, *Air War Against Japan 1943-45*, p. 409.

30   David Hobbs, *The British Pacific Fleet*, (Barnse;y, Seaforth Publishing, 2011), pp. 454-456.

The crew of a disabled Catalina aircraft of 42 Squadron RAAF in their dinghies, preparing to move across to the Catalina aircraft of 43 Squadron which came to rescue them from the Pacific.
(State Library of Victoria, Melbourne, Australia)

Any British or Commonwealth pilot whose operational flying took them out to sea understood their work was inherently hazardous. The knowledge that there was an ever-increasing air sea rescue capability that would do all in its power to recover them from the sea must have given them hope in dire circumstances. Wherever Allied crewmen may have ditched, whether it was in the North Sea or the Pacific, those who survived were able to join the Goldfish Club from which this chapter takes its name. It was (and remains) an association of airmen who have been saved from the sea by lifejackets, dinghies, airborne lifeboats or other buoyancy aids. It was formed in November 1942 by C.A. Robertson, Chief Draughtsman of P.B. Cow and Co, one of the largest manufacturers of air-sea rescue equipment. The Club's badge is a winged goldfish flying over water. By the end of the Second World War the Club had over 9,000 members from all branches of the Allied services, a testament to the efficacy of the equipment and the tenacity of both survivors and their rescuers.[31]

---

31   <www.thegoldfishclub.co.uk> accessed on the 12 March 2017.

# 17

# 'The Late Arrivals Club'
# Shot down and on the Run

The British not only established an effective method of retrieving downed airmen from the sea during the war, they also devoted considerable energy to retrieving airmen who had baled out over occupied territory and needed assistance to evade capture and reach Allied or neutral territory. Escape and evasion was not a new phenomenon in warfare, but the German occupation of much of western Europe meant the chances of successfully evading increased substantially, as this sizable area contained a large population, some of whom were willing to help RAF aircrew. Some of these civilians provided just a little food and shelter, but a small and important minority were members of resistance groups who helped set up and run escape lines for Allied aircrew.

It is important not to under-estimate the scale of this enterprise. During the war almost 8,000 Allied service personnel evaded German capture and successfully reached Allied lines or neutral territory, the vast majority of these evaders were aircrew. This huge achievement was not without cost and roughly five hundred French, Belgian and Dutch civilians were either arrested and shot, or died in concentration camps. As we shall see, it was much easier to escape from western Europe than it was from other theatres of war, most noticeably the Far East.[1]

To help Allied prisoners escape and evade, a new organisation known as MI9 was set up at Wilton Park under Brigadier Norman Crockatt. MI9 helped prisoners escape in several ways. First, through the provision of training to all three services, which was initially done by MI9 officers directly lecturing aircrew. However, as the RAF expanded dramatically this proved to be unsustainable and a new approach was adopted that enrolled RAF intelligence officers, from squadrons, OTUs and RAF stations onto a central course run by MI9. This was known initially as the 'Special Intelligence Course' and then subsequently from November 1943 as the 'B' course. This gave RAF intelligence officers a strong background in escape and evasion techniques, as well as the necessary training to work as instructors on MI9 subjects. The first of these courses commenced on 5 January 1942 and covered topics ranging from immediate action on baling out, resistance to interrogation techniques, and how to travel through occupied countries inconspicuously. The work of the RAF intelligence officers was supplemented by lectures from MI9 personnel, talks from aircrew who had successfully evaded capture, as well as up to date bulletins containing the latest information on conditions in occupied Europe.[2]

The aircrew training highlighted several points, including the difference between an 'evader' and an 'escaper'. This was important as under international law an individual who was an evader and reaches a neutral country, such as Spain or Switzerland, is supposed to be interned. However, if he had been previously captured by the enemy, no matter how briefly, he is categorised as an escaper and can be repatriated to his own country. Therefore, evading aircrew were instructed to

---

1    Graham Pitchfork, *Shot Down and on the Run* (Kew: National Archives, 2003), p. 4.
2    Graham Pitchfork, *Shot Down and on the Run*, pp. 17-20.

Crews of 199 Squadron are briefed in the station operations room at Lakenheath, Suffolk, prior to a bombing sortie in March 1944. (Crown Copyright – Air Historical Branch)

always fabricate a story in which they had been briefly held by the enemy, before subsequently escaping.

If the aircrew had crashed in their aircraft, then they were instructed to destroy all secret documents and equipment before heading away from the machine. Those that had baled out in daylight were advised to delay opening their parachute for as long as was safely possible, as this reduced the chance that they were seen and gave enemy forces less time to reach the area where they landed. It was then very important to cover and hide the parachute, for if the parachute was discovered then the enemy's search of the local area would be intensified.

The crews of large aircraft were advised to separate into small parties once the navigator had given the crews their approximate position. Whether evading as individuals or as groups, all aircrew were advised to get away from the scene as quickly as possible, using hedges, ditches or woods as cover and avoiding roads at all costs. They should then hide up for a few days until the area had calmed down and the initial search had been called off. During this period the evaders should survive on the rations in the escape kit provided.

The escape kit had been designed with great care by MI9. It was made of a pair of acetate plastic boxes that fitted inside each other and contained concentrated food in the form of chocolate, Horlicks malted milk tablets, together with some Benzadrine for energy. There were also water purifying tablets, a rubber water bottle, a magnetised razor blade, needle and thread, as well as a fishing line. The RAF evader might have sewn button compasses and silk maps into their clothes and would also have been issued with £12 in the currency of all the countries they were overflying prior to the flight. He would also carry two passport-type photographs to help in forging identity cards. Specific instructions were given on what these photos should look like, including directions that members of the crew did not all wear the same borrowed jacket and tie and were all clean shaven.[3]

During this initial period on the run, the evader would adapt his clothing to make it look less military, this would include removing badges of rank and insignia as well as cutting the tops off his flying boots. These had been cleverly designed to look like an ordinary pair of civilian shoes once the upper-part was removed.[4] The proudly worn RAF service moustache was also removed. It was important that the evader understood the geography of the area and its general pattern of life, as this would help him blend in. For instance, if he was in a rural locality, he might steal a farm implement and attempt to look like a labourer going from one field to the next. Additionally, behaviour such as drinking water from streams out of tins needed to be done very discretely, it was clearly vital for survival, but no ordinary person going about their legitimate business would have any reason to take such action.

Evaders who had landed in an occupied country often judged that their best course of action was to approach a civilian for help. This was not to be undertaken lightly, especially given the risks that any civilian would run in assisting an Allied airman. The evader was advised that the best method was to contact an isolated building, perhaps a farmhouse, and ideally one that had no visible telephone wires running to it. The evader had to be cautious, preferably lying-up during the day to observe the property and then approaching at dusk or in the dark, so that if rejected they could quietly slip into the night. Those evaders who had ended up near a built-up area, were advised to head for a café in the poorer quarter, or to approach a priest.[5]

Australian Wilf Hodgson was a bomb aimer on a Halifax with 90 Squadron. He and his crew had already flown on 29 operational sorties and had just one more to do before completing their tour. Their final flight on 9 May 1944 was to drop supplies to the resistance fighting in southern France, however soon after they crossed the Normandy coast they were engaged by a German anti-aircraft battery and brought down. Wilf picks up the story:

> Our contingency plan for the event of a crash in enemy territory was to divide into three groups, each having someone with training in navigation. The navigator Phil Green, the wireless operator Roy Pask, and the flight engineer Charlie Potten, were in one group. The pilot Dave Chapple, and the gunner Ken Gandy, formed another team, and myself and Jock Cochrane, the mid upper gunner, formed the third. One of the essentials for successful evasion was to vacate the crash site quickly and put as much distance as possible from the crash before daylight. This would then ensure that the Germans would have a much larger area to search and put the odds of not being captured in our favour. The wings of our aircraft were burning and it seemed likely that the odd 1,500 gallons of petrol would go up at any time. Without further ado we wished each other a pleasant journey and the groups took off in three directions. Just three minutes had elapsed from the time we had been fired on. It would take some 35 years before we assembled in a group again.
>
> I helped Jock remove some of his bulky flying clothing and retrieved my escape kit, got maps and compasses from the kit, and we set off in a south easterly direction. In the kit there were several types of tablet including concentrated food and benzedrine tablets which were supposed to enable us to maintain a high level of energy output for several hours. I gave some to Jock and swallowed a couple myself, which seemed to have the desired effect. This was done in the dark, and it was not until next day that I discovered that we had consumed half of

3    Graham Pitchfork, *Shot Down and on the Run*, pp. 27-8.
4    Air Publication 3396, *Escape from Germany*, (London: The Air Historical Branch, Air Ministry, 1951), p. 25.
5    Graham Pitchfork, *Shot Down and on the Run*, p. 22.

our supply of water purification tablets. For several hours we clambered over thorny hedges, tramped through wet fields and skirted farms. We avoided walking on roads, and in this part of Normandy the fields were small and surrounded by thick thorny hedgerows which were extremely unpleasant to cross.

After several strenuous hours of walking, and with daylight approaching, we decided to lie low in a field, so we picked a spot away from the road in a small hollow under a hedge. Just after sunrise we attracted the attention of a herd of cows which grouped themselves around us, no doubt intrigued by the novelty of having two ex-Bomber Command crew in their patch. Soon a Frenchwoman, wearing a shawl and carrying a milk bucket, approached the herd of cows. When she saw us she dropped the bucket in fright and was about to take off. In my best schoolboy French, I explained to her that 'Nous sommes Anglais aviateurs'. She nodded and said 'Parachute?' At that time, I was in a less than normally presentable state, as my face was covered in dried blood from a cut on my forehead which had been bleeding profusely and my clothes had several rips sustained whilst traversing the numerous hedgerows. She was naturally very apprehensive, but fortunately seemed to grasp the situation.

Shortly afterwards she went back to the farmhouse and later reappeared accompanied by an old lady and a small boy. This lady could speak English, so we explained our problems to her. She arranged for a basket of food and hot coffee to be brought to us. The basket also contained a bottle of cognac which Jock put to good use later to wash the cuts on my forehead and I can still feel the sting of the cognac which has a bite about ten times as powerful as iodine.

I was stiff and sore all over and could hardly move a limb, so I lay in the grass and slept in the sun all day. Late in the afternoon, a little Frenchman carrying a pitchfork came along and told us to wait while he went to the farmhouse. He returned carrying a basket of boiled eggs, bread and butter, meat and coffee. He told us that we were near Domfront, and that Germans were garrisoned at Mayenne, about 20 miles further on. When it got dark we started walking, keeping off the roads and crossing the fields, steering with a small compass from my escape kit.[6]

On many occasions the most the evader could expect from contact with locals was food, shelter, and perhaps some civilian clothes to help their disguise. They were then sent on their way again. This was tough on the evader who might have many days of weary cross-country travelling, with only the distant hope of getting near to a border, but the German reprisals on the locals who helped downed airmen were draconian and this often dissuaded the local population from getting too involved. Some crewmen were lucky and succeeded in contacting one of the resistance organisations. This was normally marked by a series of difficult questions for the evaders, as the resistance were always wary of the Germans planting fake aircrew as a means of entrapment. Flight Lieutenant Leslie Baveystock had been shot down during a bombing raid on Cologne, he and a fellow crewman had entered a house belonging to the Nijskens family, near the town of Bree in Belgium. Mr and Mrs Nijskens were worried about sheltering them, because they did not trust the young boy that looked after their herd of cows. Nevertheless, they gave him some wooden clogs and an old raincoat and helped Baveystock dye his trousers. Most importantly they put his small group in touch with a member of the resistance who would transport them further south. So began Baveystock's journey on the 'Comet Line' which stretched from the Netherlands to the Pyrenees and, using a series of guides, passed aircrew from one stop on the line to another. It was often a fraught business as some parts of the journey were undertaken in plain public view. Baveystock, having been passed from Liege to Brussels, recalls the journey through Paris under the protection

---

6    Brian Walley, *Silk and Barbed Wire* (Warwick, Western Australia: Sage Pages, 2000), p. 272.

of Andree de Jongh, better known as 'Dedee', a brave young woman who was largely responsible for the creation of the Comet Line:

> Bob and I were now following this new Dedee, down into the Metro itself. She obtained the tickets for the three of us and we stood waiting silently for the train, which soon appeared. Inside we sat down some ten seats away from her. To our amusement, we found ourselves directly opposite two Luftwaffe girls who looked very smart and attractive indeed in their grey uniforms and forage caps, worn jauntily over their blonde hair. They took no notice of me but were obviously interested in Bob. As I have mentioned earlier, he was young and good-looking, with a fresh, boyish complexion and hair as fair as that of the two girls who now eyed him with approval. Among the typical French people in our compartment he stood out like a sore thumb and must have convinced them that he too was a German. I looked around at Bob and was half amused and half annoyed to see that he was enjoying himself tremendously, smiling away at the two girls and doing his best to get off with them. I could see the funny side of it, but was scared stiff in case they tried to get into conversation with him. I do not think that Dedee de Jongh had seen what had been going on, and I am sure that at the time Bob did not realise how stupid he was to risk larking about in this way. However, it did not last very long, as a couple of stations further along the line Dedee rose from her seat and we followed her from the train after the exchange of more smiles between Bob and the Luftwaffe blondes.
>
> From the station we found ourselves in the suburbs of the city, but I had no idea where. A short walk and we arrived at some flats where a girlfriend of Dedee lived on the first floor (the house was No. 10 Rue Oudinot, near the Rue de Babylone). This girl was a little older than Dedee, but I did not discover her name. We all had breakfast together and then the girls left us alone for the day. They took our identity cards and papers, and told us we could rest or read but were on no account to leave the flat or answer the door. Having shown us the bathroom and provided us with a razor, they departed, telling us that they must now obtain new identities and papers for us.
>
> After a clean-up, Bob and I stretched ourselves out on a couple of beds. Of course, sleep would not come, as we were still too excited after all that had happened to us. So we just lazed about and chatted. About 5 p.m., Dedee returned with a tall good-looking girl whose name I afterwards found to be Elvire Morelle. She walked with a slight limp that I took to be some sort of deformity from childhood, but years later I was to find that this was not the case. She had fallen earlier in the year while crossing the Pyrenees with a party of escapees, and had broken her leg. She had been left in the snow while help was sought, and later had been carried out on the back of their guide. By the time proper attention had been given to her, things had gone wrong, with the result that she was left with a limp. But a far worse fate lay ahead of her in the months and years ahead. Thank God we do not know the future.
>
> The two girls returned full of enthusiasm, complete with our new identity cards and papers for the next section of our journey to freedom. Eagerly, I examined my new identity card and was surprised to see that my photo from the previous card had been cleverly removed and now lay in a French cover, overprinted with an embossed German seal. I cannot remember the name they had chosen for Bob, but my name was now Jean Thomas. Anyone who understands a little French knows that Jean is pronounced more like John, and John Thomas was a name no Englishman could ever forget! They had also obtained permits for us to travel though a restricted zone, together with a letter from the Mayor of Bayonne stating that we were natives of that city and were required for urgent work.
>
> Now for the first time we learnt that we would be going down the west coast of France, over the western end of the Pyrenees, and that we would be going that very night. Our train journey would take us down through Bordeaux to St Jean de Luz. First, we would meet some

Aircrew of 83 Squadron pack their rations on the lawn in front of the hangars at Scampton, Lincolnshire, before boarding their Avro Lancasters for a night raid on Bremen. (Crown Copyright – Air Historical Branch)

other friends and have dinner with them in the city. Following the two girls, again we set off via the Metro. Paris was so full of people of all races that in the event, we did not follow the girls, but walked openly with them. They took us to a smart restaurant in the heart of the city where we met two well-dressed and charming men. Their names I was unaware of, but I have since learnt that one them was Robert Azle. We all sat together at a table in the centre of the restaurant, which, although it was still early in the evening, was almost full of people, among whom were several German Officers.[7]

MI9 had a particularly secretive branch known as IS 9 (D) which helped run escape lines like Comet. When the bulk of MI9 decamped to Wilton Park, this section had remained in Whitehall near MI6, with whom they worked intimately.

The impetus to set up these escape lines had been generated by Wing Commander Basil Embry's successful escape after being shot down near Dunkirk. Embry's solo travel across France to Spain, highlighted to the RAF chain of command the huge potential value in establishing escape lines that could help recover valuable aircrew and return them to battle. MI9 therefore began to establish several escape lines through France, Belgium and the Netherlands. Key to the running of a number of these was Captain Jimmy Langley, who had been severely wounded and captured at Dunkirk and then subsequently escaped via Marseille. Also actively involved later was Major Airey Neave, who had been captured at Calais, but subsequently successfully escaped from Colditz.[8]

---

7    Leslie Baveystock, *Wavetops at my Wingtips* (Shrewsbury: Airlife Ltd, 2001), pp. 99-100.
8    Airey Neave later became a successful MP and mentor to Margaret Thatcher. He was murdered by the Irish National Liberation Army on 30 March 1979.

It was however Donald Darling, an MI6 officer based in Spain, who together with a Seaforth Highlander, Ian Garrow, established the first significant escape line, known as the 'Pat Line'.[9] By 1941, the method of evasion was following a familiar pattern. Having been downed over Europe the airmen would hopefully be picked up by an organization that moved them through a series of safe houses to one of the collecting points established at the Hague, Amsterdam, Liege, Brussels, Paris or Marseille. They would then be supplied with papers and civilian clothes, before being escorted by a series of couriers to the Pyrenees and the border with neutral Spain.

Spain was a hard country to escape to. Not only were the Pyrenees a treacherous mountain range to cross, but they were also well patrolled and guarded by the Germans, who had established a wide 'Forbidden Zone' to the north of the border. In addition, the Spanish border guards would usually hand over any evaders they caught back to the Germans, or if the evaders were picked up well inside Spain but before they had reached the British legation in Barcelona, then the Spaniards would intern them in their own notorious Miranda de Ebro concentration camp near Vittoria. Many internees languished in the poor conditions at Miranda de Ebro for months at a time, waiting for their name to appear on the lists of those about to be released as a result of diplomatic pressure. The escape lines were all given codenames. The Pat and Comet Lines were the largest and most successful systems, but smaller lines also existed including the Marie-Claire Line which also passed evaders across the Spanish frontier.

Flight Lieutenant George Duffee was shot down over the Netherlands on what was his first ever mission, a sortie to Mulheim on a 78 Squadron Halifax flying from Breighton, Yorkshire. He eventually found his way onto the Comet Line travelling through Paris to the Spanish border where, after a brush with an overly curious stranger, he and a fellow evader spotted the local guide who would take them over the border:

> We saw the guide pedalling slowly back in the opposite direction searching for us. Edward called to him quietly from the roadside. The guide stopped and then came over to us. 'I thought you two had been caught' he said. We described our little experience to him and enquired of the other two. They had been hidden in an inn (the Larre restaurant in Anglet) about three miles further on where we were all to spend the night and in the early morning to cycle to St Jean de Luz. We found them at the inn, fed and refreshed and in a merry mood. They were overjoyed to see us and congratulated us on our good luck.
>
> Before it was light next morning we were up and away along a quiet narrow road through St Jean de Luz to Ciboure arriving there to the safety of a friendly house before the town had awakened. From the window we could see the sea and the coastal defences and many German soldiers. At the house we met yet another pilot, a South African (James Allison) who had made a forced landing in Northern France, only three weeks previously.
>
> It was not safe to have so many of us staying there so that night we were to cross the Pyrenees, with an expert guide who was to call for us as soon as it was dark. Most of that day we spent resting for we were tired after our cycle ride and wanted to store energy for the night's walk. The mountain guide (Florentino) came and brought with him several pairs of canvas shoes that would make little noise whilst we were walking. He asked us to empty our pockets of any French money that we might have, for if we were caught in Spain we could be legally charged with currency smuggling and it would be difficult for the British Consul to get us out of prison. All was ready and collecting in the doorway we bade our hostess (Catalina Aguirre) goodbye and our previous guide (Jean-Francois Nothomb) who had travelled with us from Bordeaux, came with us to visit the British authorities in San Sebastian.

---

9    See Map 15 for details of major French escape lines.

The night was dark and there was drizzle in the air. It became difficult to see the man in front of me. There were seven of us and we held hands, helping each other up the slopes of the foothills. For hours we struggled upwards, along narrow paths, known only to a few, across fast flowing streams that soaked us to the skin. Little was said as we struggled onwards hour after hour. The drizzle ceased, the clouds rolled away and we were able to see the majestic silhouette of the mountains against the starry sky. There were both German and Spanish patrols in the mountains and it was common knowledge that if one was caught by the Spanish guards, even though on the Spanish side of the frontier, one would be handed back to the Germans. Up and up treading in the footstep of the man in front, not knowing what was on either side, except the all-embracing darkness. A stream we had to cross, which was normally shallow and sluggish had swollen to a fast-flowing river (the Bidassoa) much too dangerous to walk across. There was nothing for it but to use the bridge which was guarded.

A light was showing in the hut at the end of the narrow suspension bridge spanning the river. At intervals of two minutes we crept silently across, very slowly so as not to start the bridge swaying. Those were anxious moments waiting until it was my turn to cross over. All were safely over and we proceeded on our way. Another heavy downpour of rain, again soaking our clothes which had dried through our exertions. At one point we seemed almost to climb vertically and only managed to keep going by clutching small bushes that cut our hands and scratched our legs and faces. Soon we were half-walking, half-stumbling downwards and suddenly below us, miles below it seemed, shone the lights of Spain, that meant to us Freedom! A few more minutes and we had crossed from the territory of France into the territory of Spain. But we were not safe yet. There would be Spanish guards to dodge and already it was getting light.

Our troubles were by no means over for the Spaniards had a nasty habit of clamping people into filthy, lice-ridden jails, there to rot until the formalities had been completed. We most certainly did not look like Spaniards, being predominantly fair. We supped and break-fasted in a house shown to us by our guide, washed our tortured feet and surveyed our many scratches. The Canadian pilot's feet were blistered and bleeding but he assured us it was worth it. The crossing had taken fourteen hours of continuous walking.

The British Consulate in San Sebastian had been forewarned of our arrival and arranged for an embassy car to take us direct to Madrid driving through the night. This proved to be the most dangerous part of our long journey for the Spanish driver lolled sleepily over the steering wheel and it was only by our constant prodding and unmelodious singing that we managed to keep his eyes from closing. As it was we narrowly missed several trees and quite a few cows in the road.

In Madrid there was a regular community of aviators who had either evaded or had escaped from prisoner-of-war camps. Our stay in the luxury of Madrid was however short and after a day we were driven down to the port of Seville in the south west part of Spain.

We were to pose as the drunken members of the crew of a Dutch ship bound for Gibraltar. The seaman who was to show us the way, we met in a disreputable bar, sipping whisky. Judging by the brightness of his eyes and the unsteadiness of his voice, he seemed to have carried the pose to extremes. We followed his example, imitating his roll and joining in singing lusty sea-shanties, passing; along the quayside, up the gangplank, past the Spanish dock police and onto the ship. Before being allowed to leave port the ship was subjected to a thorough search, but by then we were safely hidden in the hold. Food was plentiful, books were available and though we were on the ship for four days before it sailed the time passed fairly quickly. Course was set southwards and in a day we had sailed through the Straits of Gibraltar, could see 'The Rock' and knew that at last we were safe.[10]

Duffee arrived home on 12 October 1943, he had been away for nearly four months. He learnt that five members of his crew had been killed and two had been taken prisoner, after a short spell of leave he was asked to tour RAF stations to talk to aircrews about escape and evasion, and the members of the Resistance within occupied Europe waiting to help them.

Not all escape lines went overland, for a period in 1944 MI9 established the Shelburne Line which took evaders from Paris to Plouha, Brittany, where they would be picked up by a Royal Navy Motor Gun Boat and taken back across the channel to Dartmouth. Ron Daniel was the pilot of a 35 Squadron Halifax and had flown 24 Pathfinder missions. His 11 November 1943 trip to Cannes looked tame compared to earlier sorties, but it was on this mission that his aircraft was shot down by a Ju 88 night-fighter. He was transported via Paris and Rouen (where he feared he was almost turned in to the Germans) and eventually ended up in Morlaix where he finishes the story:

> That night we arrived at the small village of Plouha on the French coast. We were divided into groups and interrogated by Underground agents. In the early hours before dawn we formed into single file to await our guide. She came quietly out of the night this angel of the minefields. Her name was Marie-Therese la Calvez, she was 17, she was the Underground's minefield map maker. Later she was to be decorated by the British with the George Medal, and the French and Belgian Croix de Guerre and Medaille Militaire. But this night, long ago in 1944, she was to take us to freedom.
>
> We crept through the field of death and heard the breakers hissing and rolling on the sands below. German searchlights occasionally played over us and we stood still, not daring even to breath.
>
> 'Come' she would say, and the long line would move slowly forward again. Over and across the fine trip wires she weaved. A muttered gasp in the night, a quick halt, then forward again to the sea and that wonderful something in the blackness to take us home. Was this then the final goodbye to all those brave people of the Underground who had risked their lives, the lives of their families merely to keep fighting the Nazis and send strangers like me back to try again?
>
> Marie-Therese stopped suddenly and put her hand to her lips. In the brush beside us came a steady click, clicking of an Aldis lamp. Somebody was signalling something in the darkness of the surf. We scrambled down to the cliff face and trudged in the sand towards a shadow gradually growing larger.
>
> Our party of escapees numbered about 60 and this surprised me. In the darkness, I had not realised how much our group had swollen. A number of them had been wounded and their nerves were still at breaking point. With whispered consultations we held a few of them back as they tried to race across the sand at the four small rowing boats coming in. The men scrambled into the boats, while at the same time cases of sub-machine guns were unloaded for the Underground.
>
> Marie-Therese strapped a case on her slender shoulders and began her long climb back through the minefield. She waved, smiled, and was gone. I never saw her again. It was 3.45 a.m. when we boarded the rescue vessel, a specially designed craft capable of a good 40 knots. The Navy, thoughtful hosts, had put on an extra ration of 'Nelson's Blood' [rum] and we suddenly felt free again. Ahead was England. Then we heard the drone of fighter engines

---

10   http://www.conscript-heroes.com/escapelines/EEIE-Articles/Art-27-George-Duffee.htm accessed 27 Feb 2021

and we waited. From the dawn clouds roared two Spitfires – our escort, 'just in case'. Finally, we were home, at Portsmouth, and the long interrogations began. It was 21 March 1944, and I settled down to catch up on lost leave. It was not the last time I saw Paris. After the war, as a special aide to British Intelligence I returned in 1945 to seek out those who had helped me and to thank them. Madame Henri had died at Ravensbruck, and little Marie-Therese of the minefields was in England. The lights were on again in gay Paree, the war was already an unpleasant memory. In the happy little sidewalk cafes, it was hard to believe there had been a war.[11]

Successful escape and evasion attempts were made from many European countries, not just the Netherlands, Belgium and France. Escapes were made from Norway or Denmark into neutral Sweden (and then often by BOAC Mosquito back to the UK), as well as from Greece by schooner to Cyprus, or the Levant. In Italy, many aircrew were successful in crossing the frontline, particularly in the period immediately following the Italian surrender in 1943. The most difficult countries in which to evade were of course Germany and Austria, where the lack of a friendly civilian population made success so much harder.

MI9 set up operations in other theatres too. In Cairo a sophisticated operation was established which worked broadly on the same lines as MI9 in the UK and provided escape and evasion advice relevant to those operating over the Western Desert. Aircrew were reminded of the importance of their escape kit and in selecting the right footwear – emphasised by the helpful phrase – 'Always fly in the boots you intend to walk home in'. If they were shot down behind enemy lines, they were advised to travel during the cool of night and try and find some shelter during the day, whether that was a cave, derelict transport or a simple hole in the ground with camel thorn or other abandoned material pulled over for shade. They were given very clear instructions never to head south into the desert, for that only led to a slow death through thirst and starvation. Instead, they were advised to head for the coastal strip where the Arabs tended to live, though at all costs avoiding the coastal road and the towns of Bardia, Sollum, Mersa Matruh and Sidi Barrani, where there was usually a strong military presence. Unlike in Europe aircrew were provided with 'blood chits', these were written in Arabic and promised any of the local Arabs a financial reward if they looked after the airmen and escorted them to friendly lines.[12]

These blood chits were important, because by 1942 MI9 had established a network of agents amongst the local Libyan Senussi Arabs who were tasked to assist Allied evaders. It is a testament to the Senussi that despite the Italian reprisals against them they remained consistently supportive of the Allied cause and helped many aircrew escape, even in the summer of 1942 when British fortunes were at their lowest. Sometimes the Senussi's assistance involved transportation to specific rendezvous' set up by MI9, where they were then handed over to Long Range Desert Group or SAS patrols and transported back to Allied lines. On other occasions the Arabs simply followed the laws of desert hospitality and gave food, water and shelter to those passing through their area. Squadron Leader Derek Frecker and his navigator, Pilot Officer Tom Armstrong, took off from Berca airfield, Benghazi on 6 December 1942 in a Beaufighter. They were on an armed reconnaissance mission but had an extra passenger in the form of Sergeant Paddy Clarke, who was one of the ground crew and had come along for a ride. Frecker's aircraft was hit by flak whilst attacking lorries near Wadi Tamet. With damaged instruments, two hits on the starboard engine, oil pouring from the oil cooler and a shattered windscreen, Frecker turned the aircraft away from the coastal road and managed to crash land in the desert.

---

11   Edited by Brian Walley, *Silk and Barbed Wire*, p.200.
12   Graham Pitchfork, *Shot Down and on the Run*, p. 155-6.

Pilot Officer Tom Armstrong (left) and Flight Lieutenant Derek Frecker (right) looking remarkably cheerful next to their Beaufighter VI C of 252 Squadron in which they have just crashed behind enemy lines. The photograph was taken by Sergeant Paddy Clark, a member of the Squadron's ground crew, who had come along for the ride. (Courtesy of Andrew Deacon and WW2 Aircrew Remembered)

The group then set off on foot walking back towards the Allied lines, though Tom Armstrong's diary highlights the arduous nature of the travel:

> **1st Day: Sunday 6 December:** With a tank of water and remains of kit in nav. bag slung between the three of us – rather heavy on shoulders. Sgt Clarke's heels (or lack of same in stockings) giving trouble. Many rests.
> **18.15:** 'Decided to have dinner and sleep (?). Dined off one tin of bully and biscuits. Wrapped the chute silk around our bodies and lay on maps and charts – but were frozen.
> **2nd Day: Monday 7 December 01.00:** Decided it was too cold to stay still so draped ourselves with water bottles, ration bags etc and set off. Found it easier to stay on course by stars, than in daytime. Everybody pretty tired – many stops until we got cold and then walked on until we warmed up again.[13]

By the fifth day, the party had nearly exhausted their water and food but had at last reached the coastal road, which they celebrated by opening a tin of asparagus they had with them. They spent the next day hiding from military traffic and a nearby party of eighty Italian soldiers. As they were now down to just their emergency tins of water, they decided to approach a nearby party of Arabs:

> We are very miserable at daybreak. See Bedouin boy and have words with him but he does not seem to understand and is rather frightened – he runs away. Two men come near with two children. They are quite friendly when we explain who we are and what we want and

---

13   Diary of Tom Armstrong quoted from <https://theescapeline.blogspot.com> accessed 12 March 2018.

promise to look after us. They take us over the escarpment, light a fire, dry our clothes, get us as much water as we want…and make us some wizard coffee and produce dates to eat. We spend some uncomfortable moments when some neighbouring Arabs visit the gathering, but have to suffer the indignity of pretending we are Germans until they leave… We move on to another place where they dress us as Arabs in blanket like affairs – must be about four times the size of an Army blanket. Next, food is produced. German herrings in tomato sauce…hot macaroni (Italian) and tomatoes (English) while we doze for a while… One of the Bedouins has produced some soap, scented too, so we are looking forward to having a wash later. They even produced china saucers with floral design and spoons and forks. After dark they took us very cautiously to an Arab tent. Here we got more coffee, goat's milk, eggs and more macaroni etc… We seem to have struck lucky meeting this Arab – he is the Sheik of a Senussi village – about twenty tents. His name is Ali Ben Athman.[14]

The party then spent several days being hidden by the Senussi, who were clearly running considerable risks in sheltering the airmen as Armstrong continues:

**12th Day Thursday 17 December**: had a bad night last night. Many bites and much scratching. Woke up at 05.50 to find it teeming with rain and the tent full of goats.

**10.00**: Two German armoured cars came to the village. Great panic – hid under boxes and huge piles of rugs – very uncomfortable – nearly smothered us…as soon as the armoured cars had gone they took us about three miles outside the village and hid us behind some bushes…we heard the armoured cars patrolling around us all day. One came very close, about 200 yards, we could hear them talking.[15]

Having kept them sheltered and hidden for almost a week the Senussi then guided the downed airmen to a British armoured car patrol which took them back behind the British lines. Frecker and his crew had successfully evaded the Germans and Italians for fifteen days and like other successful evaders would have been enrolled into the 'Late Arrivals Club'. This unique society was set up in 1941, following a newspaper story of a Hurricane pilot who had made his way back to Allied lines after being shot down. Other aircrew recounted similar experiences and suggested an informal club be set up. Squadron Leader George Houghton, the journalist who had written the original article, designed a badge in the form of a winged boot and a certificate with the details of the individual and the date of the evasion.[16] The certificate highlighted the spirit of the organisation and evasion in general with their unofficial motto, written in capitals at the bottom of the certificate:

'IT IS NEVER TOO LATE TO COME BACK'[17]

Elsewhere, other Allied aircrew were finding that evading capture in the Far East was markedly different from either Europe or the Western Desert.

---

14    Diary of Tom Armstrong quoted from <https://theescapeline.blogspot.com> accessed 12 March 2018.

15    Diary of Tom Armstrong quoted from <https://theescapeline.blogspot.com> accessed 12 March 2018.

16    This was not the only club an evader could join. Canadian Parachute maker Leslie Irvin had founded the 'Caterpillar Club' prior to the war, membership was restricted to those who had used a parachute to bale out of a disabled aircraft. The club's motto 'Life depends on a silken thread' was very apt. The Second World War greatly swelled the club's membership to 34,000, each of whom was awarded the gold caterpillar badge by Irvin.

17    Graham Pitchfork, *Shot Down and on the Run*, p. 177.

A Vengeance Dive Bomber is forced to land in Kunai grass on Papua New Guinea, following a raid on Japanese positions at Alexishafen on the north coast of New Guinea. The pilot of the aircraft, Flying Officer Pike of Adelaide, South Australia, signals a circling aircraft, while his fellow crew member Flight Sergeant Morgan stands by. Both men successfully made it to Allied lines. (State Library of Victoria, Melbourne, Australia)

MI9 in the Far East operated under the name E Group and had similar duties to its Middle Eastern and European counterparts. The training of aircrew to evade in the jungle was probably the most important aspect of the group's work and a series of pamphlets and booklets were produced, under innocuous titles such as *Under the Greenwood Tree* and *The Jungle Hiker*. These all gave helpful guidance on surviving and evading in the jungle. Squadron Leader C.V. Beadon was a former bomber pilot working in the Air Training Branch in New Delhi in March 1943 and played a prominent role in developing the survival aids necessary for the jungle, which given the harsh environment needed to be significantly more comprehensive than those used in Europe. The survival kit included a canvas water carrier, known as a Chargal, a machete or Kukri, leech sticks, and survival rations. A money belt with 100 rupees (about £9) together with blood chits was also given to the aircrew. Survival training was taken seriously by the RAF, with schools established in Ceylon and Assam through which a total of 2,000 personnel passed.

Carrying this kit was clearly an important problem, to which Beadon concentrated much thought. He was aware that the hot climate meant that most pilots would fly in just shorts and a shirt with light suede or desert boots. This provided little protection in case of fire and also prevented the pilots from carrying the survival kit on their person, a considerable weakness as they would probably not have either the time, or presence of mind, to grab the kit as they were baling out of their aircraft. To solve this, he developed a set of overalls that were light and comfortable enough to be worn when flying yet had a multitude of pockets in which the various survival implements could be stored. Most ingenious of all was the satchel on the pilot's back. During the flight this was attached to the suit and left empty, but if the airmen had to bail out then it could be used as a handy haversack to carry the survival aids. These overalls became known as the 'Beadon suit' and the crew pictured on page 198 can be seen wearing them.[18]

---

18   Graham Pitchfork, *Shot Down and on the Run*, pp. 222-31.

One disadvantage with evading in the Far East, was that any white man passing through the area always attracted attention and would frequently be reported to the Japanese. Fortunately, the Japanese usually took some time to react to such reports, so if the evader kept moving and altered his course occasionally, he could often avoid capture. The local inhabitants were also sometimes of assistance. If a small gift was given and respect shown for local customs, then an evader was likely to be treated kindly, though experience in Burma showed that the hill tribes including Chins, Nagas and Karens were much more likely to give assistance than those on the plains. As one might imagine Japanese reprisals against any local suspected of helping were swift and cruel. Further afield in the Pacific the local population in Papua New Guinea were usually cooperative, though there was always the risk of betrayal by an individual who may have been bribed or coerced by the Japanese.

Getting back to Allied lines was always the trickiest problem. For those aircrew who may have come down in the coastal Arakan region of Burma, then the efficient Air Sea Rescue service might help extract them. For those further inland help might be provided by the agents, villagers and guides run forward of the British frontline by MI9, with specific instructions to bring evaders safely back. MI9 also had contact with clandestine groups deep in Burma and other areas of the Far East, these would be notified of any downed pilot and would try and move to assist them. Unfortunately, the scarcity of these groups and the vast distances involved meant that they were usually unlikely to be of much help. The challenges of walking out of the jungle were enough to put off the most determined of evaders, yet there were still successes.

In January 1945, Squadron Leader Bob Johnson was based with 28 Squadron, a Hurricane unit in the Kabaw valley, Burma. At the time the British Forces had just crossed the Chindwin River and were steadily advancing south. One early morning, Johnson was briefed to do a reconnaissance of Japanese lines of communication over which troops and supplies were being transported. A short distance south of Pagan, his Hurricane was struck by two large anti-aircraft shells, one of which made a large hole in the aircraft immediately between his legs and sprayed him with Glycol. Johnson continues his story:

> I was now west of the Irrawaddy and approaching the Yaw Chaung. It looked too rough for a forced landing so I decided to bale out. I told Douglas by radio of my intention and just before I pulled the wireless plug, I heard him say 'good luck old chap'. I was losing height, but stayed with it until I was passing over a village on the west bank of the Yaw Chaung. At that point I was very low so jettisoned the canopy and tried to climb out. I had difficulty standing up so jettisoned the escape panel on the starboard side and rolled out. I saw the tail plane pass in front of my face then pulled the ripcord.
>
> It seemed only a second or so until I landed with a jar and tumbled sideways. I was on top of a ridge with a deep gully to the north. My pistol was missing, probably caught on the aircraft as I rolled out. I snapped off my escape kit from under the parachute seat cushion and ran to the west along the ridge. Within a few minutes I heard voices so I went into the gulley. The wireless cord was a bother so I yanked the earphones from my helmet and stuffed mask, cord and phones into a hole in the ground. I ran west along the gulley. About 5 minutes later I heard a lot of yelling then saw people about 500 yards away running toward me along the ridge on the north side of the gully. There were others on the south ridge ahead of me. I climbed the north ridge and slid down a steep slope, the only cover was low scrub bush. By chance I slid into a shallow depression in the hillside eighteen inches or so deep and the bush was more dense at this location. I burrowed in pulling the foliage over me then remained motionless. The voices were suddenly loud and very close.
>
> I carefully slid my knife out but otherwise did not move. People came so close I thought they would hear my heart pounding but I was not discovered. At one point I looked up the

hill and saw a Japanese soldier with a rifle on top of the ridge. The talking and shouting would sometimes be close to me and sometimes at a distance and there was also the barking of dogs. I decided to stay under cover until dark and during the long wait I debated with myself the pros and cons of surrendering or fighting if I should be discovered. I decided that if there was only one I would try to silence him quickly but otherwise I'd surrender and hope for the best. It was an immense relief when darkness came and all was quiet.

I waited another hour or so before leaving my hiding place then climbed to the ridge and followed it west. I moved very cautiously stopping to listen at frequent intervals, and then the ridge levelled out. I continued west until I was getting close to a village. I gave the village a wide berth and was then in rough undulating terrain with thin bush. Walking was difficult and tiring. With the first glimmer of light in the sky I found a hiding place among roots of an old dead tree. It had been washed out some and was almost like a cave. After prodding around for snakes I crawled in and contemplated the events of the night and previous day.[19]

Johnson had landed with a compass and maps and so was reasonably confident of being able to navigate through the jungle. He decided on a route, aiming to strike the Yaw Chaung where it was joined by the Kin Chaung about 16 to 18 miles west of his present position. The map indicated there was a track that more or less followed the river, if he took this he would then be heading almost due north and could follow the mountains until he got into the Gangaw valley. That was the area that he knew British forces had been advancing towards when he had left and he estimated It might take 24 to 30 days to reach Gangaw.

By rationing himself to six Horlicks tablets per day, Johnson believed he had enough to last 38 days and he would nibble sparingly on the chocolate until it was gone. The immediate problem was water as the map indicated he would be in dry, barren and rough country to begin with, but there were some small *chaungs* marked where he might find water. Johnson remembered that a fellow flight commander from 28 Squadron, Ken MacVicar, had crashed behind Japanese lines and made his way back just two weeks before. As MacVicar had landed close to a village he had been obliged to make contact, the villagers professed to be friendly but within a half hour Japanese troops appeared and MacVicar was very fortunate to escape capture. Unsurprisingly Johnson decided to avoid contact with the Burmese if possible, travelling by night and hiding by the day. Travel by night would be slower but he concluded safety and conservation of energy were far more important. Johnson studied the map carefully committing to memory the rise and fall of the country and where the *chaungs* were. He then set off after dark on what would be an arduous trek.

As Johnson's journey continued over the next week, he found that the streams marked in his map were dry and despite digging beneath them, he was unable to find water. He began to become dehydrated and delirious and made several mistakes, including temporarily losing his kit. A lack of water was becoming critical and it was only on the seventh night that he eventually found a watering hole used by Buffalo. Foul though the water was, it was enough to quench his thirst and re-fill his Chargal.

Johnson spent the next few weeks following the same nightly pattern of trekking through the jungle, hoping to find further sources of water and eating his rations sparingly. Although clearly becoming more familiar with the jungle, Johnson still had a few alarming encounters: including a cobra that slithered across his legs whilst he was dozing, aggressive packs of monkeys and some very large spiders whose webs he would frequently blunder into at night. Nevertheless, he remained confident of where he was on his route and continued to avoid villages wherever possible, though

---

19   Squadron Leader Bob Johnson's account from <https://www.burmastar.org.uk/stories/escape-burma> Accessed 1 December 2018.

A Hawker Hurricane IIC of 42 Squadron based at Kangla, Burma, piloted by Flying Officer 'Chowringhee' Campbell, diving to attack a bridge near a Burmese settlement on the Tidrim Road, sometime in May 1944. The bombs of the previous aircraft can be seen exploding on the target. (Crown Copyright – Air Historical Branch)

on the odd occasions he blundered into them he always found the natives very hostile. As Johnson got nearer the front-line, he spotted signs of Allied activity including a Dakota dropping supplies to forward troops. He became increasingly cautious as he realised that he was now getting very close to his goal, anxious not to waste the effort he had put in so far.

All at once I was aware of voices in the bush on the east side of the track. I crept closer and concluded the language was not like any I had heard used by natives. Keeping close to the bush I crept along the track and saw the glow of some fires through the bush. Very shortly I came to a stream and was looking for a shallow place to cross when I heard a rattle of stones on the other side of the stream. I ran behind a clump of thorn bushes and crouched on one knee with my knife in my hand. I remained motionless for quite a time when suddenly there was a splash and clatter of stones. A figure, with rifle and bayonet extended rounded the thorn bush. I dived at him and we both sprawled on the ground. I lunged with my knife hitting him on the back but there was no penetration. He started to roll over. My right hand, which had been my support as I lunged, happened to be on a fair-sized rock. I swung the rock in an overhead motion and hit him in the face just as he rolled. There was no sound from him and he did not move. I got to my feet, splashed across the stream and went as fast as I could along the track. After about two hundred yards the track went across some open ground. I hurried on and was on the upgrade of a slight rise when a Japanese soldier appeared walking toward me. He was very close when I saw him and I instinctively felt that to run would be fatal. I slouched by him and as soon as I reached some bush I took cover. Almost immediately about 20 or more Japanese came along all carrying packs and rifles. There was also a couple of bullock carts. I remained in the bush at the side of the track and very shortly a large number of Japanese passed by, perhaps a hundred or more. I moved away from the track into the hills and pondered as to what my next move should be. Just at daylight I crept back down to the track and saw another small group of Japanese pass by. I went back into the hills and found cover for the day.

There had been some gunfire during the night but due to the dense growth I could not pinpoint it. It was now quite light and from my position on a ridge I could see the 2 knolls so decided I'd go in that direction. I went down the hill, passed close to some huts and saw 2 natives. They in, turn saw me but I just kept on going. I hiked across the valley to the closest knoll and climbed to it's top. I thought this would be a good vantage point from which to spot the drop zone if the DC3's [Dakotas] came back. I took my chargal from my belt and leaned down to rest it against a large tree. At that moment. I heard movement and at once saw 3 Indian soldiers coming over the crest of the hill. It flashed through my mind that I was safe at last and started to raise my hands. The soldier nearest to me had an automatic weapon at about his hip level and just as I raised my hands he pulled the trigger. There was the swish of bullets around me before I dived behind the tree. I yelled in English 'Do not fire, I'm a British officer'. There were another couple of bursts which thudded into the tree and threw up dirt from the ground. I yelled again, this time in Urdu. No answer and no sound. I pulled out my handkerchief, waved it around the tree and shouted again. Still no sound. I thought they might be circling around the knoll so I jumped up, scrambled down the hill and across the valley to the closest hill and bush. I ran along a ridge for a short distance then hid under some dead, fallen trees. All was quiet the remainder of the day. I thought the Indian soldiers must be part of a long-range patrol which could be well in advance of the main forces.[20]

Johnson, beginning to despair of being able to reach and cross the front line successfully, resolved to make one final effort. He took his final Benzedrine tablets and contacted some local natives, offering them money to take him across the line, he insisted they set off immediately and made sure they all saw his hand resting carefully on his knife. Fortunately for Johnson this set of natives proved friendly:

We walked down the valley through sparse bush for several miles and suddenly came to a stream. About 100 feet ahead of me a group of Indian soldiers were washing themselves in the stream and a soldier with a rifle was standing guard on the bank. We walked up to him and I said 'Commanding Officer kidhur hai' He looked at me and casually said 'Udhur hai Sahib' and nodded to his left. He sloped arms and off we went natives included. Within half a minute we walked into a shallow ravine where the officers of the 4th/14th Punjabi Regiment were having their evening meal. After explanations and introductions I gave the natives metal rupees from my money belt before they departed. I ate more food and was sorry for having done so.[21]

---

20    Squadron Leader Bob Johnson's account from <https://www.burmastar.org.uk/stories/escape-burma> Accessed 1 December 2018.

21    Squadron Leader Bob Johnson's account from <https://www.burmastar.org.uk/stories/escape-burma> Accessed 1 December 2018.

Johnson had successfully survived in the jungle and evaded the Japanese for some 23 days, a remarkable achievement.

For those who had failed to evade after being downed, capture by the enemy forces must have been a depressing blow. The next chapter will examine the experience of aircrew and ground personnel in captivity, some of whom were forced to show a level of bravery and endurance that equaled anything displayed in combat.

# 18

# Behind the Wire,
# The Prisoner of War Experience

In Germany treatment of POWs was tough, largely benign, and with some notable exceptions in line with the law of armed conflict. For aircrew unfortunate enough to be shot down and captured in either the occupied territories, or Germany itself, initial capture would normally mean temporary incarceration in the local police station – which was often the easiest period in which to escape. The news of the capture would attract considerable interest and local dignitaries frequently came to see the prisoners. Food and drink were often brought out and the local policemen would sometimes join in too, perhaps becoming overly-relaxed and off guard in the process. The local village gaols that were initially used were also not very secure, with only rusty bars or just a few strands of barbed wire covering the window. In 1943 alone, more airmen managed to return home by escaping from such places, or on their way to another facility, than from permanent POW camps during the whole war. Two anonymous aircrew, who subsequently succeeded in reaching England, recorded how they achieved their liberty at this early stage:

> A German Corporal called out an escort of two men, youths of about 17 or 18 years of age. We had to follow these; they were very casual and kept their rifles slung; we walked for about ten minutes. There was a ditch on one side. My companion asked them for a light so the guard gave it to him, he hit out at him, and I knocked the other one over. There was very little scuffling. We pushed them into a ditch, which was very swampy, and ran for the woods. We did not know whether we had knocked them unconscious or whether they were more seriously injured.[1]

Though this early period was the best time to escape, for many British airmen either a clear opportunity failed to present itself, or the initial shock of capture was simply too great for them to take action. Sergeant Dan London was a mid-upper gunner on a Halifax and was shot down on the night of 27 March 1944 on a mission to Berlin. He was quickly captured in a rural area not far from Hamburg and gives a good description of how bewildering the first stages of captivity could be:

> My captors were elderly men who looked like farm workers and two Mr Plods. Some were armed with shotguns, others with hefty staves. I was taken to a farm house in a small village some 30 minutes from where I was captured. The house was cold, but looked lived in. I saw myself in a mirror on the sideboard – my hair was standing on end, I was filthy and had streaks of blood all over my face. I had a gash on my forehead and had wiped the blood around. When a middle-aged woman brought me a cup of water, she looked in horror as I looked such a mess. In a short while a car drew up outside and three Luftwaffe officers came into the house

---

1    Air Publication 3396, *Escape from Germany*, (London: The Air Historical Branch, Air Ministry, 1951), p. 10.

and indicated that I should go with them. All three had pistols in their hands, so I got wearily to my feet and followed them. We travelled in the car for some time, two of the officers in the front, and the third in the back with me, still holding his pistol until we eventually arrived at a Luftwaffe station. I was taken to the guard room and was turned over to the biggest German I had ever seen. He stood head and shoulders above me, fully uniformed, tin hat and armed to the hilt. The Feldwebel waved his gun under my nose and indicated that I was to undress. My uniform was taken away. And I was made to stand with my feet apart and my hands above my head, so that the Feldwebel could make a personal search of me.

Eventually, my uniform was returned to me and I was taken to another room where three German officers were seated on one side of a table. Standing on the other side were Alan, Gerry, Murray and a short time later George and Scotty were marched in. The officers each selected one of us to question about our aircraft, squadron etc., which we, of course refused as we were required only to give our name, rank & number. Two of the officers accepted this but the third who was more senior gave us a blasting, starting with 'Fur sie, der Krieg is aus' (for you the war is over) and then in his very bad English lectured us on the futility of fighting the Germans, when we all should be fighting the Reds. He forcefully told us of the dangers of trying to escape and explained that we should be kept at the camp overnight and then taken to a POW camp.

George asked for news of Pat, and was told by the senior officer, in a tone completely different from his bullying tactics, that our pilot was dead, his charred body still in the pilot's seat.

Then we were taken out singly – two guards per man – and locked up for the night. Early next morning after a meal of black bread, margarine and foul-tasting acorn coffee, I met up with the other members of the crew in the courtyard, except George who, as the only officer, was segregated from us. We were bundled into the back of a small covered lorry, guarded by armed soldiers, and driven into Hamburg to catch a train to Frankfurt-am-Main, about 250 miles south of Hamburg. When we were led into Hamburg railway station, I was amazed to see that the high-domed glass roof seemed almost intact. However, the town itself must have been knocked about a bit, for the locals were very hostile and I was glad that we were surrounded by guards. When the locals realised who we were they surged forward shaking their fists, spitting and throwing rubbish at us. They retreated when the guards pointed their rifles at them.

The train was soon on its way, and as I looked at the others, I thought that we were a terrible advert for the mighty RAF. Our uniforms were crumpled and filthy, we badly needed a shave, and being unable to wash for two days we were beginning to pong. After an uneventful journey we finally arrived at Frankfurt, tired out, dirty and very hungry. We were still dazed from our sudden change in fortune.[2]

Captured aircrew were normally transported to *Dulag Luft*, near Frankfurt. This was the *Luftwaffe's* main interrogation centre and ran to a completely different set of rules to ordinary prison camps.[3] On arrival the prisoners were put into solitary confinement where they remained for periods varying from a day to a month. If the Germans suspected that they had information which might be of value, they were subjected to additional pressure and sometimes starved for 24 hours. Occasionally they were forbidden to wash, though this was apparently something most prisoners found relatively easy to bear. The most severe form of pressure was the overheating of the prison cells, which produced an extreme thirst and after 24 hours was enough to make most

---

2    Brian Walley, *Silk and Barbed Wire* (Warwick, Western Australia: Sage Publishing Ltd, 2000), pp. 158-9.
3    See Map 15 for *Dulag Luft* and other major POW camps occupied by aircrew.

British Prisoners peel potatoes at Stalag XVIII A, Wolfsberg, Austria. (Bundesarchiv)

men angry – though still unlikely to divulge information. In their subsequent studies of German intelligence records, the Air Ministry was able to tell that a few men had talked more freely than they ought to, though the Germans had not obtained a great deal of valuable information. British prisoners who were rude or particularly obstinate were sometimes subjected to additional harsh treatments.

When the interrogation was completed the prisoners were sent from their solitary confinement cells to the communal compound, where they remained for a period that lasted from a few days to up to three months. This flow seemed to depend upon the rate at which aircraft were being shot down and prisoners captured. The communal compound was like many other prison compounds, with a series of wooden barracks surrounded by barbed wire outer perimeter defences. There were however a few differences.

The supplies of Red Cross parcels were greater at *Dulag Luft* than at other camps and relatively large dinners of sometimes four to five courses were held to prevent stockpiles being hoarded. In addition, the huts normally consisted of just two-man rooms, as opposed to the 12-man rooms for officers in normal camps and the 100–120 men barrack blocks for NCOs. In the early years, parole was given to go to church, and wine and spirits from captured French stocks could also be obtained for special occasions. These conditions had probably been instituted to make the prisoners relax, undermine their ambitions to escape and talk a little too freely, but as the war progressed such privileges dried up. Some British took advantage of this 'generosity' and used it to prepare their escapes, so that by the end of the summer of 1941, not only had nineteen British prisoners escaped from the camp, but five others had escaped from hospitals to which they had made special trips and a number had also escaped from the trains taking them from *Dulag Luft* to new permanent POW camps.[4]

---

4   Air Publication 3396, *Escape from Germany*, p. 99.

Wilf Hodgson was a bomb aimer with 90 Squadron and had been shot down in Normandy, he had successfully evaded his pursuers for three weeks, but was eventually captured in western France attempting to cross the border to Spain. After brief spells in a series of French prisons he was taken to *Dulag Luft*. Hodgson describes a process many other aircrew captured by the Germans would have found familiar:

> When we arrived at Dulag Luft we were separated and placed in single cells, once again in solitary confinement. Next morning I had a visit from a Luftwaffe officer who sympathised with me for having been shot down. On the whole he was quite a pleasant fellow and said he was concerned that my family would not know my fate. He handed me what he said was a Red Cross form which he would send to the Red Cross in Geneva. They, in turn, would advise my family in Australia. He asked me to complete it and he would return to pick it up. I read the form. Many questions related to matters regarding my squadron, such as location, strength, technical details, type of operations and other information that would have been of great value to the Luftwaffe. Our operation involved dropping supplies to the French Resistance and I was unsure if the Germans would regard this as a legitimate military operation. No doubt they had examined our crashed aircraft in France and were aware of the type of operation. I didn't want to be connected with it.
>
> As instructed by our Intelligence Branch, in the numerous escape lectures we had been subjected to on the squadron, I completed my name, rank and service number and left the rest blank. When the 'friendly' Luftwaffe Officer returned, he took the 'Red Cross' form and read it. He became quite 'unfriendly' when he saw I had not completed it and threatened to send me back to the Gestapo in France. He explained that the information was required to establish my identity as an Allied airman before I could 'enjoy the benefits of a POW camp' as he put it. As proof of my identity I produced my identification tags and drew his attention to the RAAF uniform I was wearing, minus wings and sergeant stripes removed after I was shot down. He wouldn't accept this, saying I could have picked them up in the French woods. I said that it was not very likely and after much shouting he stormed off.[5]

By noon the next day the interrogators had decided that Hodgson was not likely to talk and together with 40–50 other airmen, he was transferred to Wetzlar prison camp.

At the beginning of the war many captured airmen were placed in old fashioned prisons which were often the hardest to escape from. Schloss Spangenberg in central Germany, for instance, was a forbidding castle that stood on top of a conical hill and was surrounded by a wide, dry moat. The moat was flagged with stone, covered by searchlights and the sheer far wall was 25 feet high and patrolled by guards. In addition, the hill on which the castle sat was made of solid rock, making tunnelling impossible. Spangenberg (*Oflag* IXA) was an ideal prison and had been used as such since the 17th Century – the carved inscriptions of former inmates were still visible on the walls. Incredibly difficult to escape from, the only successful attempts had been by walking through the front gate.[6] Fortunately for most escapees, these older prisons were only used for the first 18 months of the war or, like Colditz, for prisoners who were identified as habitual escapees.

The growing number of British aircrew shot down over Germany, meant that from the spring of 1942 new camps were opened and the RAF prisoners began to be separated from Army and Royal Navy counterparts and accommodated in hutted camps of their own. The *Stalag Luft* III camp at Sagan, Silesia was typical of these new purposely designed camps, and was ideal from the captor's

---

5    Brian Walley, *Silk and Barbed Wire*, p. 278.
6    Air Publication 3396, *Escape from Germany*, p. 10.

point of view. Its construction consisted of a rectangular clearing cut out of the pine forest that measured about a mile by two miles and stretched from the town of Sagan to the Czechoslovakian border. Within this area three compounds, two for prisoners and one for the German guards, had been initially built, though the camp was subsequently enlarged, and four more compounds were added later, one of which was in more open country three miles away.

All the prisoner's compounds were surrounded by two barbed wire fences, ten feet high and between six and seven feet apart. In the centre of the prisoners' compounds were the wooden huts in which the prisoners lived, these were neatly arranged in rows, with each hut designed to hold a hundred men, although they often contained double that number. Four or five huts stood a little apart and were used as the kitchens, latrines and washhouses. Around the perimeter of all the huts was an open space, never less than forty yards wide, and beyond that the wire. When the first prisoners arrived at the newly built camps, they found that the stumps of the trees which had been cut down were still in the ground and it was left to the prisoners to remove them. Once this was done the ground surface was either dust or mud according to the weather. The camp had a reportedly dreary aspect, surrounded entirely by fir trees, with no worthwhile view except at the northern end of the camp, where the roofs of the town of Sagan were just about visible.

The Germans had been careful in designing the defences of the camp. Between the double wire of the perimeter-fence loose coils of barbed wire were strung out thickly on the ground, so that it was impossible to walk across the intervening space. Dominating the fence, at intervals of about a hundred yards, stood watch towers in which a machine gun covered the interior of the camp. Immediately inside the wire was an area of dead ground, six to 15 yards wide and bounded by a low guard rail. If any prisoner crossed it, he could be shot without warning. At night, boundary lights lit both the perimeter and the internal camp and from each guard tower searchlights swept the compounds. To detect any attempt at tunnelling, microphones were planted at intervals of 20 yards in the ground outside the wire, these were then connected to a listening post within the German compound.[7]

Members of the *Luftwaffe* manned the prison defences and their quality varied according to whether they were reservists, or front-line troops sent back from the Russian front for a rest. As the war went on the number of guards increased, though at no time was there less than one guard to four prisoners. The guards were universally known as 'goons', which was initially explained to the Germans to be a semi-affectionate term like 'Jerry' or 'Tommy', though the reality was it stemmed from a sub-human character in a *Daily Mirror* cartoon. When the Germans eventually discovered this fact, they were apparently not very amused. The duties of the guards were to man the towers, to guard the gates, to patrol the wire and to escort any vehicles and personnel going in and out of the prison compounds.

At Sagan there were 70 guard towers in all, known as 'goon towers', each of which was manned by one sentry who had a fixed machine gun, a rifle and an automatic weapon, in case a prisoner got into an area which was not covered by the machine gun. The patrols on the ground normally carried rifles, except when an escape had taken place, when they would carry automatic weapons. To ensure they were alert a typical guard shift would last just two hours and security was further enhanced by additional guards patrolling inside the compounds with Alsatian dogs. The German camp headquarters consisted of an administrative staff as well as a special security unit whose role was detecting and preventing escapes, this security unit was divided into sections of one officer and six or more NCOs for each prison compound and these personnel were known to the prisoners as 'ferrets'. The ferrets were hand-picked and many of them had been guarding aircrew POWs since the beginning of the war. Armed with torches and extra-long screwdrivers, they patrolled the

---

7   Air Publication 3396, *Escape from Germany*, p. 11.

A German watchtower at *Stalag* 383 Hohenfels. (Bundesarchiv)

compounds in pairs from dawn till dusk, probing anywhere and everywhere for any signs of prisoners preparing for escape. They would enter rooms unannounced, listen at windows, hide under floors or inside roofs and search, or arrest, anyone they pleased.[8] Karl Pilz, known as 'Charlie' was a particularly dangerous ferret at Sagan as one of the prisoners recalled:

> Charlie was the most interesting. Tall, dark-haired; with a sallow complexion and lugubrious expression; he had once reputedly been a Social Democrat and suffered nine months' solitary confinement in the early days of the Nazi regime. Thereafter he had sold his soul and become not merely a Nazi but a determined enemy of Britain. 'Charlie' had been with Air Force prisoners from the time that the special Air Force camp was opened at Barth in 1940 and stayed with them until the Russians relieved the camp at Luekenwalde, near Berlin. Owing to the fact that he had not served at the front he did not rise above the rank of Corporal and this was a constant grievance; but whether from fear or conviction, his allegiance to the Fuhrer remained unshaken.
>
> 'Charlie' was a curious mixture of humanity and unscrupulousness. He had a genuine understanding of what a prisoner's life was like and frequently overlooked small irregularities which it was his duty to report. Often he would collect cigarette-lighters which had been confiscated and give them back to prisoners, or procure extra supplies of timber when they wanted furniture or some domestic gadget. He had some sense of sportsmanship and appreciated that escape was a game with rules. Tunnels in particular he regarded with the eye of an expert; if they were the effort of new recruits, he would pour scorn on them and ask why they were wasting their time; on the other hand a good tunnel aroused his admiration and he would take endless photographs for his escape museum.

---

8    Air Publication 3396, *Escape from Germany*, p. 12.

Nevertheless, 'Charlie' was a most dangerous opponent. He spent so much of his time in the camp that he seemed to know by instinct when anything was afoot. He had an uncanny knack of finding entrances to tunnels when all his subordinates had looked for them in vain, and he was untiring in his efforts. Frequently when off duty he would take the Alsatian puppies which were being trained as police dogs for walks round the camp in order to get a fresh view of it from the outside. At his suggestion special camouflaged hiding places were constructed in the woods from which he and others used to watch the camp from a distance through field glasses and more than once he spotted unusual activities in this way. Sometimes, in order to avoid the check kept by prisoners on those who entered the gate, he would climb the wire in some far corner in the hope of arriving in the camp before anyone became aware of his presence.

His morale was remarkable, before the invasion of Europe he was always contemptuously confident that the Allied troops would never succeed in breaking through the Atlantic Wall. Afterwards, although far too clever not to realise that the success of the invasion meant the end of Germany, he would never give way to admit the possibility of defeat.

The seamy side of Charlie's character appeared in his dealings with his fellow Germans. At all times during his career with prisoners Charlie had accepted food and cigarettes from them as gifts, but whenever he thought it would pay he never hesitated to lay traps for his own subordinates and report them for exactly the same practices. The other 'ferrets' were fully aware of this and after they received cigarettes or coffee used to bury them in the prisoner's compound and retrieve them when on night duty. After one escape, when the Gestapo were putting pressure on the German security staff, Charlie deliberately spied on certain German guards and denounced them. One was sentenced to three years imprisonment as a result and another is alleged to have been shot. Many Germans swore to get their revenge for this and all were delighted when Charlie's frequent demands for promotion were turned down.[9]

As a counter to this German security regime the British prisoners established their own system under a POW security officer. This consisted of a series of sentries who would keep a look out at the entrance points to the compound, logging and tracking Germans as they came in and out. There was normally one window in a hut with a good view and so called 'duty pilots' were placed at these key points, working in pairs, one to watch and one to act as a runner. They would be relieved every hour, though sometimes Germans still managed to slip through and cause momentary panic. The Germans understood they were being monitored on an organised basis, but there was little they could do about it. Indeed, some guards would even reportedly walk straight up to the 'duty pilots' window overlooking the compound entrance and 'book themselves in'. Part of the POW security system also included 'stooges' who would be guarding a point of particular sensitivity, perhaps a tunnelling operation, or prisoners listening to a wireless set. The stooge would stay in position for several hours and if a German came in sight, he would signal to other prisoners who might stop work on a tunnel for instance. These early warning and signals systems were often quite subtle when the Germans were not suspecting an escape, but in the later stages when the tunnel might be near completion stooges would be placed all-round the camp and sometimes used as part of a deception plan to distract the Germans from focussing on the sensitive area.[10]

The British security team's responsibilities also included safeguarding and hiding sensitive articles for escaping such as tools, maps, passes and civilian clothing. The prisoners were ingenious in creating false bottoms in boxes, drawers and floors, as well as burying articles, and though the

---

9   Air Publication 3396, *Escape from Germany*, pp. 28-9.

10   Air Publication 3396, *Escape from Germany*, (London: The Air Historical Branch, Air Ministry, 1951), p. 84.

British prisoners play a game of cricket at *Stalag* 383, Hohenfels. (Bundesarchiv)

Germans regularly searched compounds, they only ever succeeded in uncovering a fraction of the concealed contraband.

The final role of the British security team was to hide the escape of a prisoner for as long as possible. This usually involved trying to fool the roll call, the traditional way the Germans would try to discover if an inmate was absent. Roll calls were usually held twice a day at fixed hours, though after mass escapes they were more frequent. Hiding the fact that a prisoner had escaped was important in giving him extra time to get away and the efforts the security team made included dummy patients in the sick bay, whose limbs could be made to move under the blankets by bits of string pulled from the next-door room. In addition, the POW in charge of the parade could sometimes persuade the German officers and NCOs that they had miscounted by a bit of fast talking.

At each camp the British prisoners established an 'Escape Committee', which coordinated and authorised any escapes. This may seem like an irksome form of bureaucracy, but it was important that prisoner conditions were not disproportionately reduced by escapee actions, and that a larger planned escape was not compromised by a smaller attempt that benefitted only a few people. As an example, in one camp a prisoner who had been given special treatment in a nearby hospital (a privilege that had been dearly won), saw a nurse's cap and coat hanging up and on the spur of the moment decided he would simply walk out. As he was wearing a prominent moustache and flying boots, he was easily and quickly caught and more frustratingly the hospital treatment for the sick was restricted by the Germans once more. In another instance the Senior Escaping Officer had organised working parties for officers which would allow better opportunities for escape, however one individual, without announcing his intentions or undertaking any preparation, simply walked off alone, he was unsurprisingly caught within 48 hours.[11] The Escape Committee understood the importance of deception as well as security; if there was a large project, such as a big tunnel, then they deliberately contrived diversions in the form of smaller escape attempts that would attract the German's attention. The Germans were often suspicious if all was too quiet. The Escape

11    Air Publication 3396, *Escape from Germany*, p. 16.

Committee would also coordinate and prioritise the work of some of the key supporting activities for escapes, this included the work of the forgers, those converting uniforms, the map makers, and the POW intelligence staff.

The Escape Committee's POW intelligence staff had to establish important information about the outside world: Where was the nearest train station? What time did the trains leave? What did the local *Ausweis*, or pass look like? What was the normal pattern of life in the nearby towns? Where could an escapee wait in a town for several hours without attracting attention?

Despite frequently good disguises, escapees would often betray their identity by unintentionally acting out of the ordinary. For instance, local passengers could sit in station waiting rooms, sometimes even sleep in them if they had a railway ticket, but without one they would be arrested. It was common to stay in a hotel for up to three days but after that period the German police would make routine enquiries. The Intelligence staff gathered this information through several methods; German newspapers, German civilians, new prisoners or even those that had escaped, been captured and returned to the camp. Through these sources they were able to form an accurate appraisal of the pattern of life outside the compound. The intelligence section would also have a number of 'contacts' to answer these questions. These were prisoners with a good understanding of German, who could cultivate friendly German guards or civilians and elicit information from them. Sometimes they might even bribe them for materials, including wireless parts, cameras, maps, railway guides or anything else that might be helpful. The contacts work meant many hours of boring conversations listening to a guard's family history or sympathizing with his petty grievances, it also meant long periods waiting for an individual German to arrive at a specific location for a fabricated 'chance encounter'. An understanding of human psychology was important, as one prisoner who worked as a contact demonstrated when he described the motivation of a junior 'ferret' named Rudi:

> My main task during the early days was to distract Rudi's attention from various activities such as tunnel digging and the dispersal of sand. Soon I discovered that my quarry was not over-fond of work and much preferred to smoke English cigarettes beneath the trees. It was from these early conversations that I discovered his father had been a cavalry officer, though now dead, and that his uncle was a well-to-do Essen business man. He informed me also that he was married and had one son and that his mother lived with his family at Essen. Gradually I gained his confidence, mainly by asking for nothing and giving cigarettes and chocolate in return. I discovered that he hated the Nazi party, having had most of his belongings stolen from him by Brownshirts when he returned from a holiday in Italy before the war. Owing to the danger of other members of the German Security Squad – and especially its head, Corporal Griese, who was nicknamed 'Rubber-neck' – we devised a system of signals and agreed never to recognise each other in public.
>
> Having received instructions to obtain various articles which were forbidden to us, eventually I began by asking for small things such as mapping nibs or ordinary ink. These were readily forthcoming and later Rudi was supplying the camp with more useful commodities such as rubber-stamp ink and pads, printing inks, stencil blocks and eventually a radio.
>
> By this time I had managed to form an estimate of Rudi's character. He was reasonably well educated, cunning enough to keep away from the front-line, astute enough to deceive his compatriots, and sly enough to deceive me if someone else should offer him a better bargain. I sensed also that the way to his heart was to show a keen interest in his family.[12]

---

12   Air Publication 3396, *Escape from Germany*, pp. 27-8.

The perimeter fence at *Stalag* 383 Hohenfels. (Bundesarchiv)

Huts and internal fence at *Stalag* XVIIB Gneixendorf. (Bundesarchiv)

There were many different escape attempts made by British POW, but by far the most common approach was tunnelling. This was one of the safest methods of escape because while the tunnel was being built no one was in danger of being shot and when it was finally completed there was a good chance of crawling away unobserved. Except for the experts, who designed the entrance and tunnel itself, tunnelling also had the advantage of demanding less skill from personnel than other methods of escape. Most of the tunnel operations became a drill, which needed perseverance and stamina and by working in teams tunnellers built up an esprit de corps which was very important in prison life. Although tunnelling was initially exciting, the discomfort of the work, the time spent keeping watch in cold and draughty corners and the irregular hours soon wore down enthusiasm. Only one in 35 tunnels constructed was ever successful, and even on these successful occasions only a small proportion of tunnellers ever managed to make a complete get away.[13]

At *Stalag Luft* I, near Barth in western Pomerania, two officers started a tunnel in September 1941 that ran from an incinerator, close to the perimeter fence, to a sports field beyond. At 10:30 a.m. every day there was a football match and prisoners would climb onto the roof of the incinerator and gather round to get a good view and provide cover for the digging. This was done using a table knife and a board which carried the sand to the incinerator where it was mixed in with the rubbish. The tunnel was 25 feet long, had no shoring or reinforcement timbers and had taken four days of labour to complete, though this work had been spread over three weeks because of the frequent German searches. Six men hoped to use the tunnel, and it was decided to wait for an air raid when the camp lights would be extinguished and the chances of escape improved. Flight Lieutenant J.T.L. Shore, the only man to successfully escape from the tunnel, continues the story:

> On 5 October all preparations had been completed and we started nightly watches in order to take advantage of the first air raid warning. At l0.30 p.m. On 19 October I heard aircraft and the camp lights went out. I went and warned one of the party of five which was to follow me, then started crawling through my trapdoor in the hut. Unfortunately, I was wearing my greatcoat, which got caught when I was half-way through the trapdoor, and a German guard came along and almost stepped on me. He did not notice me, but walked on for about twenty feet and then stood still, watching something in one of the barrack rooms. Then the guard at the gate flashed his torch and the guard who was standing near me walked over to him. I walked after this guard, making my footsteps coincide with his, until I reached the barrack in which the man who had dug the tunnel with me lived, and called him.
>
> He came out just behind me, and I went across to the incinerator, thinking he would follow me. I got into the incinerator and banged the door at regular intervals to attract my friend's attention, but he did not appear. Then I went through the tunnel, which was partly waterlogged and pushed up the trapdoor at the other end. Looking back into the camp I saw a German guard talking to someone through the window of my hut.
>
> I got out of the tunnel and went across the football field to a ditch which had been dug by the Germans and crawled under the bottom strand of wire. As I made my way across the field I remembered that I had told my friend that I would wait half an hour for him in the wood. While waiting and watching the camp I saw two lights, and, fearing recapture, went on. After squeezing lemon over my boots and clothing to destroy the scent, as I knew that the Germans employed dogs, I set off down the main Barth-Planitz road.[14]

---

13   Air Publication 3396, *Escape from Germany*, p. 13.
14   Air Publication 3396, *Escape from Germany*, p. 107.

Shore walked solely by night and by the morning of the second day he had reached the port of Sassnitz, on the Baltic. Twice he boarded trains which he hoped were being taken on to the ferry, only to find them moving off in the wrong direction, he also tried, unsuccessfully, to board a Swedish ship but then his luck changed:

> On the way back towards the harbour I saw two Pullman coaches and got into one of them and had another drink and a wash in the lavatory. I was feeling rather despondent, and got into a second-class carriage and went to sleep, not much caring if I was discovered. I woke up about 3 a.m. and left the carriage, as it occurred to me that there might be a ferry at about 4:30 in the morning as well as in the afternoon. I scrambled into a tarpaulin-covered truck-filled with piping and from there saw the funnels of the ferry. A line of trucks was being taken on to the ferry, and I jumped off my truck, ran across the intervening fifty yards, and managed to scramble on to a low truck which was passing me at right angles… The ferry sailed at about 3.30 a.m, and during the voyage the trucks were not searched. I sat in the driving cab of the lorry. When we arrived at Trelleborg a man on a bicycle noticed me sitting in the lorry, but I managed to slip out and tried to get out of the goods yard. However, I walked off in the wrong direction and was seen going through a gate by a Swedish guard, who came after me. I was arrested and taken to a small office, where I said I was an escaped prisoner of war and must speak to the British Consul. On being told that this was impossible I said I must see the police.
>
> Two policemen arrived in a car and took me to the police station. No particulars were taken and I just said 'Harry Burton' and they recognised the name of the prisoner who had escaped before me. Later that day I was taken to the railway station and sent to Stockholm. A few days later I was repatriated to the United Kingdom.[15]

The man who followed Flight Lieutenant Shore to the incinerator was caught by the guards, and as the air-raid ended soon afterwards no one else was able to use the tunnel.

Some escaping British prisoners found it was easier to go through the wire than burrow underneath it. The mere fact that a compound had a gate which opened and closed several times a day to let people, vehicles and stores back and forth was an obvious opportunity. To be successful the individual would need to hide in a vehicle or have the necessary passes, but again it was less hazardous to life, as any prisoner caught was simply sent to the camp gaol or 'cooler' to repent. In April 1941, a Fleet Air Arm officer escaped in a box in which he had made a false bottom:

> When food parcels were issued, a wooden box containing empty tins was lifted on to a light cart by our own orderlies and pushed out of the camp. One day when a friend and I were watching the cart being pushed through the gate, he remarked: 'A great pity that the box is not just a little longer, or you might be able to think of some way in which you could hide yourself in it. I myself am far too big a man.' It was an idea, though I was rather doubtful if I could fit in the box, although I was about the thinnest man in the camp.
>
> After examining the box, we decided it could be enlarged a little and a false bottom made without attracting attention. When the enlargements were complete we decided to make a test to see if I could stay inside for the two hours which would be necessary. I squeezed myself under the false bottom and found that the only way was to lie on my side with my head and neck bent in one corner and with my knees drawn up to my chin. It was going to be most

---

15   Air Publication 3396, *Escape from Germany*, p. 107.

Red Cross parcels are delivered to *Stalag* 383, Hohenfels. (Bundesarchiv)

uncomfortable because once inside I had to remain as I was, and I would just have to hope that I would not be attacked by cramp.

Everything was ready and in the last week of April I decided to do a further test to see if, under the required conditions, I could stay the course and also to see if things worked out satisfactorily when the box was unloaded. I was locked in the box and though the cramp at times was almost unbearable, I amused myself by thinking of the German NCO, standing right alongside and not suspecting I was there. One thing I had not taken into account was that the oils and juices remaining in the tins would seep through the cracks on top of me. This made things most uncomfortable, and as I did not want to emerge covered in grease, we arranged that on the day we would have plenty of absorbent paper lining the false bottom. Otherwise the test was satisfactory.

May 2nd was the day chosen, and after being pushed through the gate the box was lifted off the cart, and while the attention of the guard was distracted by the British orderlies I opened the hinged trap we had concocted, and on receipt of a pre-arranged whistle, crawled into a small wooden hut and hid under some timber until dark, then slipped out, a free man, into the woods.[16]

This escape was not discovered by the Germans for five days, an unusually long period. This was because the Senior British Officer persuaded the Germans to conduct the roll-call inside, instead of on the parade ground because of bad weather. By cutting trap doors through the ceilings of the huts a prisoner managed to be counted twice on each occasion and fooled the Germans into thinking that no one had escaped. Even when the Germans knew that a man was missing, they still had no idea how the escape was made and on being recaptured on the Danish frontier a week later the prisoner said that he had climbed the wire.

16    Air Publication 3396, *Escape from Germany*, p. 107.

Flight Sergeant Jack Beesley, a prisoner of war for just under two years, is welcomed back home on 8 May 1945 (VE Day) after being repatriated in a Lancaster of 97 Squadron. Flight Sergeant Beesley, a bomb aimer with 97 Squadron, had baled out from a Lancaster during a raid on Mannheim on 23/24 September 1943.
(Crown Copyright – Air Historical Branch)

Although there were many who attempted to escape, a great number of inmates simply settled down to life as a '*Kriegie*' (the prisoner's own nickname for themselves that was derived from the official German title for prisoner of war – *kriegsgefangener*). They then tried to make the best of life by adapting to the routine day-to-day existence prisoner life entailed. Peter Thomson was a Lancaster pilot who was elected to be the Senior British Officer in the NCO's camp at Bankau, Silesia. He describes the POW life and the arrival of a new batch of prisoners:

The camp was a new one, my POW number was 100 and we lived in what we called 'dog boxes', made of prefabricated pine, each holding four men. We were issued with two blankets and a palliasse filled with wood wool which disintegrated rapidly. There had been a crop of rye in the camp and it started to regrow. Having been brought up on a farm I knew how good the straw was – we lined the collars of our working horses with it. So, armed with a pair of scissors, I painstakingly filled my palliasse with it and consequently slept well right up until we left the camp in January 1945…

The Germans were gathering up all air crew POWs from various army camps around Germany and transferring them to camps for air crew only. We were fortunate to get a group of 98 'old kriegies' from Stalag 383. They were a great help to me, especially their leaders, Sam Archer and Ray Heard. Most importantly they brought a radio with them, so we received the special news service for POWs from the BBC. Ray Heard would take down the news short-hand. It was then typed out and read around the camp. All copies had to be returned to me for destruction. The 'ferrets' were always trying to find the 'Dickie Bird' (which they knew existed), but never did.

Our other contacts with the outside world were through the International Red Cross. We had a visit from Dr Rossel who was very helpful. Another marvellous man to visit us was Henry Sonderburg, the YMCA secretary from Stockholm. Last but not least was the protecting power represented by two charming Swiss diplomats, who listened and made notes of all our complaints, then went to see Oberst Behr and listened to his complaints about us.

We had our first camp tragedy. A young Canadian walked out of barracks during an air raid alert and was shot by one of the posterns [gate guard]. He had heard the 'All clear' from the nearby village and thought it was the camp siren. He died shortly after from the wound. Apparently, the guard came from Dortmund and his family had all been killed in one of our raids. The young Canadian was buried in Kreutzburg with full military honours. After the war I was able to give the Canadian authorities photos of the service for his family.

By now the Germans had provided us with a doctor, Captain D.G. Howatson (RAMC) to look after our physical well-being. He had been captured at Dunkirk and had been a POW far longer than any of us. His appointment as our MO was a great relief to me.

We had a large selection of musical instruments (courtesy of the Red Cross), from piano down to piano accordion, and with no end of skilled musicians had some wonderful concerts. The theatre was also very strong, with some excellent plays. Some of the female impersonators looked the real thing!! All plays had to be censored by the krauts. The boys put on a play reading of Journey's End. We had to eliminate the word 'bosche' but could refer to them as Jerry or Fritz. Needless to say the word 'bosche' slipped out and that was the end of that play.

When asked by a couple of music types if they could hold dancing classes, I approved. They next wanted to hold a ball. I had a talk with Doc Howatson and he said we should go and have a look. It was most interesting, fellas dressed up as girls, subdued lighting and soft music; the Doc said, 'I don't think we should have any more balls!!' We had a good library which was well-patronised. We had skilled book-binders to keep the books from falling apart. There was also a very good school where students were studying for almost every degree available.

The dedication of those endeavouring to pass on their knowledge was admirable. We put on an arts and crafts exhibition and I invited Oberst Behr to a preview. Most of the paintings and sketches were of Spitfires shooting down Luftwaffe planes and of RAF bombers obliterating the major cities of the Third Reich. He was not very impressed, but then, that was his problem.[17]

The importance of food to prisoners cannot be over-stated. The Geneva Convention mandated that the rations issued to POWs should be of the same quantity and quality as those issued to depot troops. Instead, those issued by the Germans were of the same standard as given to senior citizens too old to work and averaged about 1,600 calories a day, dropping down to 1,100 on occasions.[18] The poor quality food had to be supplemented by other means – on occasions this could be by growing food, but as most *Luftwaffe* camps were built on sand this was not easy. Initially private food parcels could be sent from either neutral countries, or friends in occupied ones, however at the end of 1942 this was stopped and from then onwards only the official Red Cross parcels were distributed. These arrived regularly until late in the war, when the ring began to tighten around Germany and transportation became disrupted. The winter of 1944 witnessed a lack of parcels for several months causing severe hardships.[19]

---

17    Edited by Brian Walley, *Silk and Barbed Wire*, pp. 212-7.
18    Air Publication 3396, *Escape from Germany*, p. 59.
19    Air Publication 3396, *Escape from Germany*, p. 60.

Liberated Allied prisoners of war wait at an airfield in Belgium before boarding a line of Short Stirlings
(those in the foreground belonging to 299 Squadron) for repatriation to the UK in April 1945.
(Crown Copyright – Air Historical Branch)

Red Cross parcels varied according to their countries of origin. Food which came from
Argentina was often packed in bulk, whereas those from Canada, Britain, America, Australia
and New Zealand were packaged in parcels which gave a balanced diet for one man for a week,
averaging about 1,280 calories a day. Canadian parcels contained butter, corned beef, full cream
dried milk, raisins, prunes and a particularly popular biscuit. British parcels had porridge and
useful accessories like salt and pepper. American parcels contained excellent cheese and prunes.
A thriving 'market' existed where food could be bartered not just for other rations but items of
clothing or any other possession. A points system was used which would fluctuate with demand,
porridge being popular in winter and prunes in summer for instance. A store of food was valuable
for escape, a fact which the Germans were acutely aware of, consequently tins were frequently
pierced at the point of issue to prevent hoarding. One way round this was to produce escape 'fudge'
a combination of Ovaltine, sugar, oatmeal, chocolate or cocoa, butter or margarine, dried milk or
flour and if desired raisins. The mixture was boiled, dried and cut into flat cakes which could be
stored almost indefinitely. Less useful for escape were the illegal stills set up in camps from time to
time, these normally utilised raisins or prunes as the basis of the brew and produced an apparently
ghastly drink, which nonetheless produced the desired effect, even if it made the odd unlucky
drinker temporarily blind.

Following the invasion in Normandy and the subsequent Allied breakout from the bridgehead,
the *Kriegies* attitude to their imprisonment changed and escape attempts declined in number.
Perhaps escape seemed too risky when liberty might lie around the corner? By Christmas 1944,
as Germany began to collapse, Eisenhower himself was cautioning prisoners against escaping and
it must have seemed much better to sit tight and wait for the advancing Allies to over-run the
camps. However, many of the POW camps were situated in the eastern part of the Reich and as
the Russians advanced, the Germans unexpectedly forced tens of thousands of Allied prisoners to
move westwards, possibly in the belief that they could be used as a useful future bargaining chip.
Undertaken in the depths of winter and with little preparation, these forced marches were the

toughest experience most prisoners would encounter at the hands of the Germans. Hamish Philson had been a wireless operator/air gunner on Hampdens and was imprisoned at *Stalag* VIIIB, near Lammsdorf in Silesia. He recalled this most arduous of times for the RAF POWs:

On 22 January, 1945, at about 1400 hours, without warning, an order came over the loud-speakers of this huge camp that everyone was to be ready to move out at 1600. The camp was to be evacuated. We must carry what we wanted to take with us, as we would not return. Pandemonium broke loose as we scrambled to prepare for whatever lay ahead. Men were calling for their friends in panic, lest they became separated… We were made to form a single file. We moved past a distribution point, where each man received a Red Cross food parcel. I dangled mine on my chest, with a piece of string round my neck. I had a pack on my back and two rolled blankets. No time was wasted. We marched out of the main gates on to the road heading west. A covered army truck led the way with a machine gun mounted on the back. Guards, some with dogs, marched on both sides, armed with automatic weapons and stick grenades hanging from their belts. We were divided into columns of about 1,000 men with another truck at the rear. We started at 1600 hours and marched until 0200 the next day, covering 20 miles. We rested (in a stable, for four hours, with the dung on the floor) until 0600, then marched until 1600 and covered another 20 miles: 40 miles in the first 24 hours! Of course, we could not keep up this pace. The roads were covered with deep snow. At the beginning a snowplough cleared the deepest snow, then the first 200 men trampled the thin residue into ice. All who followed slipped and slid on the treacherous surface. This resulted in nearly everyone having intense pain in the back muscles from the effort of trying to stay upright. Very soon along the wayside were scattered discarded baggage which the owners had been forced to abandon as surplus to requirements. I remember seeing a piano accordion, a trombone, kit bags galore and before long the occasional body.

One of our greatest problems was food, when we had been on the road for a week all supplies which we carried were exhausted and we were dependent entirely on what our captors could supply. Each morning they told us that we had to march to a certain place and we would receive a bread ration, Nothing more! Sometimes we were formed up 17 men abreast and as we passed a farm cart, a loaf was thrown. Divide that among you!

The problem of feeding 1,000 men on the march at a little village at the end of the day is considerable. Obviously, communications were involved and the need to phone ahead. However, disaster struck occasionally, when for one reason or another those who were leading took the wrong road and we could not find our billet for the night. No little village could supply enough for a thousand extra mouths. Then it was a case of the cupboard was bare and we had nothing to eat. Life was grim at the best of times, but this was beyond a joke.

Before long, everyone had dysentery. Anyone who attempted to leave the column was shot. I saw this happen more than once, when hungry fellows attempted to grab a few potatoes. When nature called it was too dangerous to try to hide in modesty; you crouched by the side of the road, for all to see, while keeping a weather eye open for any unfriendly guard who might come upon you with his rifle butt. Through deep snow, then through the wetness of the thaw of spring, without the opportunity to take our clothes off for over two months and counting ourselves fortunate if we found a dry piece of concrete on which to lie at the end of a day's march and without proper food, we marched the whole way from Lamsdorf to Braunschweig, a distance of about 1222 kilometres or 750 miles. The column dispersed there early in April and I found myself responsible for 24 men who could march no further, in the Inselwall Krankenrevier (hospital), formerly a girls' school. Five or six days later, the town was surrounded and an ultimatum delivered. Surrender or be shelled! The SS tried to make every-one resist, but when morning came the street outside was littered with SS insignia which they had torn from their uniforms as they fled. The American Ninth Armoured Division tanks rolled through Braunschweig in pursuit and the British supplied the occupation troops. For about a week, Harry and I served as interpreters for Captain Bretton, who had been seconded from Scotland Yard, i/c security. In the main we cooperated with German and American doctors, arranging medical supplies. This was the point at which my dear pal Harry Lawrence and I were separated, as I collapsed and the Americans diagnosed me as having severe malnutrition, gastroenteritis, dysentery and pneumonia. The Americans without fuss, were very kind and helpful. Having pumped me full of penicillin and eggnog, they flew me back in easy stages to Rheims and then over the English Channel in a DC3. I was the only 'Limey' on board, the other passengers being American. The pilot, very considerately, called me forward to see the White Cliffs of Dover. I admit, there was a lump in my throat as I thanked him.[20]

Hamish Philson was kept in hospital for a short while until he had recovered from his malnutrition, he was then able to return to his parent's home in Glasgow at 2330 hrs on 8 May 1945, the day on which the war in Europe ended.

Though conditions were sometimes very hard in German camps, they were consistently and dramatically better than those experienced by prisoners of the Japanese. The figures speak for themselves: 27 percent of all Japanese prisoners died in captivity, whereas only four percent of Germany's Allied prisoners of war died while in prison (though this latter statistic excludes Russian POWs who the Germans treated as sub-human and used for slave labour).

Germany largely followed the Hague Convention of 1907 and the Geneva Convention of 1929, which stipulated humane standards for the treatment of POWs. Japan had also signed the Geneva Convention but never ratified it, a position she clarified in Bern in 1942, stating that she would follow the Convention as far as was possible, 'with necessary changes (*mutatis mutandis*) reflecting the customs of each nation'. That small phrase opened the door to a Japanese culture that saw those who surrendered as shameful and expendable. In addition, institutional mistreatment was encouraged by deliberately stoked hatred and contempt for white races as part of a campaign against white imperialism.[21]

Japanese discipline was habitually sadistic, even within the Japanese Army it was common for NCOs to routinely strike private soldiers. Their own punishments for error were also unbelievably harsh and occasionally included capital punishment for incompetence (normally in the form of a be-heading). For those Japanese and Korean guards at the bottom of this brutal military hierarchy, the power they were able to wield over POWs was often the first real authority thrust upon them. In many cases it went to their heads unleashing what one post-war report described as 'a genuine and vicious and almost universal streak of sadism.'[22] Those Allied airmen that were captured when their aircraft were shot down over Japanese lines could expect brutally swift treatment that encompassed torture, being buried alive or beheading.

The experience of Australian pilot Bill Newton and the crew of his RAAF Boston bomber, who were shot down on 18 March 1943 off Papua New Guinea, is sadly not an isolated incident. Newton and his Wireless Air Gunner, John Lyon, were the sole survivors of the crew of five and managed to struggle ashore, both were picked up by a Japanese patrol and immediately interrogated and tortured for information. One week later, father of two John Lyon was bayoneted to death at Lae airfield in the presence of the base commander Rear Admiral Ruitaro Fujita. This

---

20    Brian Walley, *Silk and Barbed Wire*, pp. 77-9.

21    Brian MacArthur, *Surviving the Sword* (London: Abacus, 2005), p. 2.

22    Wills-Sandford, *Report on Japanese Treatment of RAF Personnel Prisoners of War in Palembang, Sumatra, from February 1942 to May 1945,* <www.COFEPOW.org.uk.> accessed 12 December 2018.

was a common type of war crime amongst the Japanese, who saw it as a useful way to 'blood' new soldiers. John Lyon's body was buried on the airfield perimeter and only discovered in 1948. Newton was transported to Salamaua for execution, an act that was recorded in a Japanese eyewitness account as follows:

> Now the time has come, and the prisoner is made to kneel on the bank of a bomb crater filled with water…the precaution is taken of surrounding him with guards with fixed bayonets, but he remains calm. He even stretches out his neck, and is very brave. When I put myself in the prisoner's place, and think that in one more minute it will be goodbye to this world, although the daily bombings have filled me with hate, ordinary human feelings make me pity him. The commander has drawn his favourite sword … He taps the prisoner's neck lightly with the back of the blade, then raises it above his head with both arms and brings it down with a swoop…in that moment I closed my eyes. SSH! …It must be the sound of blood spurting from the arteries. With a sound as though something watery had been cut, the body falls forward. It is amazing – he had killed him with one stroke. The onlookers crowd forward. The head, detached from the trunk rolls in front of it… The head is dead white, like a doll.
>
> The savageness which I felt only a little while ago is gone, and now I feel nothing but the true compassion of Japanese Bushido. A senior Corporal laughs loudly 'Well he will enter Nirvana now!' Then a superior seaman of the medical unit takes the chief medical officer's Japanese sword and, intent on paying off old scores, turns the headless body over on its back, and cuts the abdomen open with one clean stroke.[23]

The Japanese document containing the eyewitness account was obtained by the Allies when they captured Salamaua. It was published during the war, with Newton's name being removed and unsurprisingly heightened Australian and Allied bitterness towards the Japanese. Newton's headless body was subsequently recovered by the Allies from the bomb crater in which it had been abandoned by the Japanese in October 1943. In the same month Newton was awarded the VC for his actions in the 52 sorties he flew against the Japanese, 90 percent of which had been made under heavy anti-aircraft fire. He was the first and only RAAF recipient of the Victoria Cross in the war against Japan.[24]

A total of 5,102 RAF prisoners were held by the Japanese in all theatres. The majority of these were captured in the mass Allied capitulations in Singapore and the Dutch East Indies in the spring of 1942. In contrast to the European theatre these RAF POWs included a large proportion of RAF ground staff as well as aircrew. The large POW camp at Changi, in Singapore housed a total of 52,200 British and Commonwealth POWs, the vast majority of whom were Army, though there was also a small proportion of Commonwealth air force personnel too. Changi was a vast military complex built by the British before the war and included barrack blocks, offices, cookhouses, parade grounds and so forth. Though it had been badly bombed during the Malayan campaign, Changi was repaired and used as a POW camp for the remainder of the war. There were other significant-sized camps in Java, Sumatra and Rangoon, though standards varied, and all were run under harsh and primitive Japanese conditions.

The British POWs found that their new regime was characterised by poor rations. Rice would become a nauseating staple, issued in small quantities and of such poor quality it was very hard to digest, one prisoner recounting that 'it appeared on the plate as a tight ball of greyish gelatinous

---

23   National Archives of Australia A9300, Service Record of William Newton, including translation of captured document.

24   Mark Johnston, *Whispering Death*, p. 284.

Japanese POW Camp at Pakan Baroe, Sumatra. The photographer made the comment: 'Pictures cannot show the rotten conditions and the all powerful smell'. (State Library of Victoria, Melbourne, Australia)

substance, nauseous in its lack of flavour and utterly repulsive.'[25] Not only was it tasteless it was often riddled with pests too. A cooking instruction issued to prisoners in July 1942 advised them not to reject the rice simply because it contained weevils or mealworms, but put the rice on a piece of paper in a thin layer and place it under direct sunlight. Then 'both mealworms and weevils will walk out of the rice and make their way to the end of the paper and then they will take cover under the paper. Do not arrest the progress of the mealworms whilst they are walking off the paper as they will return to the rice and die (almost immediately making it most difficult to find and remove them thereafter).' Prisoners found the monotony of the rice diet very depressing, seldom would fresh vegetables be served and meat or fish was also usually absent from the prisoner's rations, or if available provided in very small quantities and frequently rotten.

The prisoners were normally captured in what they stood up in and during the next three and a half years the Japanese never issued clothing, blankets or any bedding. By the end of the war many of the prisoners were covered in little more than insanitary rags in which they shivered miserably in the colder weather. During hotter days, some took to wearing nothing more than a 'Jap Happy' a small, loose fitting triangular cloth, worn almost as a pair of underpants, with a piece of string

25   Quote by Sergeant David Griffin accessed via AWM Exhibition Stolen Years: Australian prisoners of war – Food. <https://www.awm.gov.au/visit/exhibitions/stolenyears/ww2/japan/changi/story7> accessed 27 February 2021.

to tie at the side. Socks invariably wore out and men went barefoot in their boots, before these too rotted away. Some repairs were often made with bits of rubber and so forth, but many men were simply forced to walk barefoot. A lack of mosquito nets for prisoner's beds also meant that malaria was endemic amongst the inmates.

Letters to and from home were rare or infrequent and many POWs received only one a year for the entire period of their captivity, in addition Red Cross parcels were also practically non-existent, in some cases the Japanese guards confiscating these for themselves. Religious services were often banned, and padres singled out for abuse by the Japanese, though despite this several Christian communities flourished in POW camps and many prisoners found religion a powerful source of comfort, some even getting baptised. Books in the camps were very rare and handed round many times. Cherished and valued though they undoubtedly were, they sometimes had to be ripped up to provide toilet paper when the Japanese failed to provide even that amenity.

The infrastructure in the Japanese POW camps varied, Changi undoubtedly was well provided with strong buildings, whereas those in Java and Sumatra could be much more austere, as Wing Commander W.R. Wills-Sandford makes clear when describing one of those set up near Palembang, Sumatra:

> Never before can Europeans have lived in such primitive accommodation for so long. The huts, three of which blew down in one night, were made of bamboo and attap (dried leaf of the sage palm). The earth served for a floor and hinged flaps for windows. Rooms were seldom waterproof. No lighting, piped water, tables, chairs or benches were provided. We slept on long horizontal platforms made of bamboo slats insecurely attached to vertical supports of various heights. A great concession was made to officers and senior N.C.O.s who enjoyed the luxury of huts with a veranda on one side. Cooking facilities were primitive and latrines disgusting while some semblance of a bath could only be enjoyed after walking a quarter of a mile to one of a number of muddy wells all of which dried up in the summer of 1944. This reduced the camp to occasional washing with stagnant swamp water. Filth and intense discomfort were the order of the day. Perpetual fear of a serious epidemic clouded the horizon.[26]

The Japanese neglect of their prisoners meant that disease was frequently rife in their camps and most Far East POWs suffered at one time or another from malnutrition, beri-beri, diptheria, malaria and dysentery. Aircraftman Frank Jackson was a prisoner of the Japanese at Liang camp in Ambon, Indonesia from March 1942 to August 1945. He remembered the debilitating impact dysentery had on his comrades well:

> We were barely three months at Ambon when our first death occurred, and the cause was dysentery. This disease was to be the principal factor in the many deaths to follow. We were allowed a cemetery on the hillside facing the camp. I was on a few grave-digging parties and the experience was a frustrating nightmare. We would remove an inch or so of soil and then have to hack away at the coral. Spades were useless in this procedure so we burrowed away with either chunkels [a kind of large hoe] or pickaxes (I am not too sure whether or not we had pickaxes.) I doubt that most graves were more than two and a half feet in depth. Come the monsoon rains and coffins were exposed, having been denuded of the little covering we had shovelled over them. Soil and rocks would be restored at the earliest opportunity.

---

26   Wills-Sandford, *Report on Japanese Treatment of RAF Personnel Prisoners of War in Palembang, Sumatra, from February 1942 to May 1945*, <www.COFEPOW.org.uk> accessed 12 December 2018

The only material available for the making of coffins was bamboo. Experienced woodworkers would make strips of the bamboo and then fashion utility coffins. It was dreadful but little else could be done. It was customary for friends of the deceased to form the burial party and act as bearers. Having no Padre in the camp the burial service was recited by whoever felt capable of the duty. Thankfully we had a very able bugler in Larry Hinchley of the Army, who sounded 'The Last Post' at every burial. Larry was a great stalwart who added much-needed dignity to every ceremony. At every remembrance service I have attended or witnessed on television, vivid pictures of Larry and the sad scenes on the hill return and the tears begin to swell. I understand Larry was a member of the Salvation Army and I am very happy to record he survived and lives to this day [1992] in Bristol. His emotions must be greater than my own. Because of the intense heat and prevalence of disease, burials had to take place as swiftly as possible. It often happened that a friend died and was buried before one had returned from a working party. In such cases men [who had been] left in the camp for some reason or other would assist in the committal. Most deaths occurred overnight and in these cases friends were given the opportunity of attending the funeral in the morning. It was under these circumstances that I attended the third, I think, burial to take place at Ambon. The usual guard accompanied the cortege, as did the Japanese commandant. This officer placed fruit and vegetables on the grave, giving every sign of being very respectful. We could be little other than cynical about his offering coming too late to help our comrade. As I observed his impassive face at the graveside I did not then have the satisfaction of knowing this character was to hang in Changi Prison some four years later. Deaths were to become so frequent that Japanese officers chose to forgo attending the funerals. Their absence was welcomed.[27]

Changi, as well as some of the more permanent camps in Indonesia, could hardly be described as comfortable, yet the British prisoners encountered far worse conditions when they were to be sent to work camps, as slave labour.

In order to supply their Army in Burma the Japanese decided to build a railway line from Nong Pladuk, Thailand to Moulmein, Burma. This railway would carry supplies from the ports of Bangkok and Saigon across some of the most inhospitable terrain in the world and alleviate Japanese logistical pressures. Previous British Imperial plans to build a similar railway had always been discounted, mainly because of the inhospitable terrain it would have to cross including large rivers, ravines, mountain ranges and of course the jungle itself. The Japanese intended to overcome this difficulty by using Allied POWs and local natives, as slave labour. They believed that this would allow them to complete the 258-mile railway line by December 1943.

The first Allied prisoners left Changi for Thailand on 18 June 1942, they were followed by additional groups that were sent progressively further up the line, many of whom were under the mistaken impression that conditions would be better than at Changi. In all 330,000 men laboured on the railway, including an estimated 30,141 British, 12,994 Australians, 17,985 Dutch, 686 Americans and 270,000 native workers. An estimated 6,318 British, 2,646 Australians, 2,490 Dutch and 132 Americans died during the building of the railway, through a lethal combination of overwork, atrocious diet and disease.[28] About 50 percent of the RAF personnel captured in Singapore were sent to Thailand to build the railway, others were also sent as slave labour to build airfields in Borneo or work in mines in Japan. The work on the railway was always demanding but in February 1943, the threat of Allied advances in Burma prompted the Japanese to demand a higher work rate from the prisoners. It is often referred to as the 'Speedo' period. Shifts became

---

27    Charles Rollings, *Prisoner of War* (London: Ebury Press, 2008), p. 231.
28    Brian MacArthur, *Surviving the Sword*, p.53 and 163.

Australian Prisoners of war in Changi Prison. (State Library of Victoria, Melbourne, Australia)

longer and much more demanding, Captain Richard Sharp describes the work which all prisoners, including the Air Force personnel, were subjected to:

> Here the perpetual fetch and carry of the earth and rubble filled baskets as the men dig down into the cutting and strew the waste rolling down the slope. There the constant clink of steel on stone as the pairs of hammermen (one holding, one hitting) chisel out their metre-deep holes ready to take the blast charges. And on both sides of the river, timbers are prepared for the viaduct; on this the officers' party bore the holes, and carry the huge beams to their assembly point, while on the other, Chinese coolies trim the logs with axes, bore them, and have elephants to drag them down to the water's edge, from where they are floated – so heavy that they half sink – across to the bridge side. There is no let-up in the work. To a Jap, none was working so hard that he could not work harder, and 'Speedo – hurriupoo' was their unchanging yell. Work by day, work by night. Day shifts, night shifts, no shifts at all. When they tried to bring in the shift system, 3 shifts of 8 hours was suggested, approved, and lasted 2 days. 8 hours was not enough work for a man. Then two 12-hour shifts and then the system broke down, and things became a scramble. But on 16 April, the viaduct was completed; and in the end, in the heat that poured off the rock face, the troops were set to metalling the south cutting. Starting at the foot, they picked up a stone out of heaps that had earlier been sent tumbling down, clambered the 150-ft slope, dumped their load and came down, to go round and up again in a continuous ant-like motion.[29]

29  Brian MacArthur, *Surviving the Sword*, p. 96.

POWs walking along a stretch of railway line near Pakan Baroe, Indonesia.
(State Library of Victoria, Melbourne, Australia)

Sanitary conditions in some of the camps carved out of the jungle were appalling. Toilets were little more than open pits and the water supply became infected with cholera which spread wildly, killing many and necessitating special quarantine camps to be set up. Tropical ulcers also became a prevalent and notorious killer. There were occasions when these could be successfully treated and controlled, but in the appalling conditions on the railway line, with no medical supplies, they simply grew larger and deeper until the exposed bone turned black and gangrenous. Early treatments simply consisted of using a sharpened spoon to scrape away pus and infected flesh, then covering the wound once more with a banana leaf or other improvised bandage. Some brave doctors conducted amputations under these most appalling conditions, using carpenter's saws as instruments, sometimes with successful results. These painful procedures were usually undertaken without recourse to either anaesthetic or any form of pain killer.

Japanese brutality was a constant feature of day-to-day prison life in whichever camp or country the prisoner was held in. Beatings would be handed out for minor infractions, such as failing to bow in front of guards, or failing to bow low enough. Sometimes a prisoner would be struck because the guard had not been able to make himself clear and grew frustrated. Officers, doctors and padres who attempted to protect the wider group of prisoners were often singled out for punishment. There were a variety of punishments which the Japanese administered including solitary confinement, beatings with sticks, forcing the prisoner to kneel on bamboo sticks whilst carrying a heavy weight or making him stand to attention while holding a block of wood or other heavy object over the head. It was the routine and casual manner with which these beatings were inflicted which was particularly vicious. Pilot Officer Shearn was a prisoner in Java and recalls one narrow escape:

> An order came through that that the prisoners were to surrender all articles of gold. I had some evening studs and cufflinks with gold backings. I decided to bury them so that they would not fall into the hands of the Japanese. After I had done so the Japanese issued a further order to the effect that their first order had not resulted in many gold articles being handed in and they were certain quite a lot had been retained by the prisoners. They therefore extended the time for compliance with their requirements. If an appreciable quantity of further gold articles was forthcoming all would be well and no action would be taken against those who had disobeyed the first order. If, however, there was not a satisfactory response to the second order, collective punishment would be inflicted on the whole camp. After reflection I mistakenly decided to dig up my hidden evening studs, etc, and to hand them in. Shortly after having done so, despite the indication that no further action would be taken, I found myself towards the end of a longish queue down which an infuriated Japanese was battering his way with an iron rod. I experienced that uncomfortable sensation of my heart and stomach changing places as this sadistic lunatic got nearer and nearer my place in the queue. However, to my relief, before he actually reached me he apparently became exhausted with the efforts he had been making. After taking a swipe or two at the unfortunate interpreter (I think he was E.M. MacDonald, a friend from Malaya who had taught himself Japanese), he dismissed the remaining potential victims.[30]

If the Japanese wished to find out information, about an illicit radio for instance, they would frequently resort to torture, usually administered by their counter-intelligence or security personnel, the *Kempetai*. These abuses included thumbscrews, cigarette burnings on the body (noses and ears were particularly singled out) and sticking sharpened bamboo underneath finger nails. Water

---

30   Charles Rollings, *Prisoners of War* (London: Ebury Press, 2008), p. 303.

torture was also practised, which sometimes involved placing a rice sack over a prisoner's face and pouring water from a four-gallon can. The prisoner would be compelled to swallow large quantities of water and his stomach would swell considerably, the Japanese guards would then jump on it to make the prisoner talk.

What remains the most admirable aspect of the Far East POW experience is the extent to which the men would care for each other and help those less fortunate than themselves. This assistance often came from within one of the many small bands of five or six men the prisoners formed, known as *Kongsis*. Many POWs believed they would never have survived without the support of these friends. A *Kongsis* group would share food, clothing and other luxuries, but most importantly look after the sick and injured members of the party when required, fetching food and bathing those with dysentery or other ailments. On a larger scale the dreadful appearance and condition of the Allied slave worker parties returning in December 1943 from the Burma railroad camps to Changi, was a shock to the inmates who had not left that camp. Those who had stayed at Changi went out of their way to share what little they had in tobacco, rice, salt and clothing to those who were visibly less fortunate than themselves.

Allied prisoners of war after liberation of Changi, Singapore.
(Courtesy of State Library of Victoria, Melbourne, Victoria)

Almost all the Japanese work camps included RAF personnel to one degree or another. In Indonesia RAF POWs were employed to build aerodromes, as well as a railway, and half of the RAF captured in the fall of Hong Kong were sent to Japan to work in mines.[31] The Japanese work parties sent to the Spice Islands in April 1943 had a disproportionately large number of RAF prisoners. A total of 1,600 of the 2,061 POWs taken to the island of Haruku were members of the RAF, as well as 600 of the 1,024 taken to Ambon. Haruku was to become widely regarded as one of the most horrendous POW experiences of the war.

Haruku[32] was chosen by the Japanese as the site of an airfield, from which they hoped to fly captured Flying Fortresses to attack Australia, some 600 miles to the south. The work to build the airfield was back-breaking and made additionally cruel by the scorching temperatures and the painful glare of the sun off the bright white coral, which gave the POWs photokeratitis (now more commonly known as snow-blindness). However, the biggest killer at Haruku was dysentery. Brought to the island by the prisoners themselves, the disease ran like wildfire through the unsanitary camp where there was no running water, or adequate washing facilities for the POWs to maintain even the most basic standards of hygiene. The Japanese refused to allow sea latrines to be constructed (basically toilets on a wooden pier over the sea), as they claimed the sea belonged to their Emperor and that would be a mark of disrespect. The conditions quickly became foul as RAF servicemen James Home remembered when he describes the open latrines:

> A bamboo rail was placed along the length of these trenches for the sick to hold on to but on more than one occasion a weakened man could not hang on, and would fall into those filthy trenches with their seething masses of large fat maggots. All this happened in full view of everyone else and we found it impossible to imagine anything more revolting and degrading, but it was all part of the exercise to humiliate us. In order to try and control the developing epidemic, we needed much more time and some help, yet the criminal lack of response from the Japs escaped all logic. A week or two longer [to prepare latrines] would have paid real dividends for everyone in the long term. From this time forward the Japs were totally responsible for the deaths that followed so unnecessarily on Haruku.[33]

Attempts were made to isolate the dysentery cases, the worst sufferers going into Hut One or Two, which quickly became known as the Death Huts. Dick Fowden was an RAF Medic at Haruku and administered to the sick within it, he understood the horrors of Hut One and Two more than most:

> It was mentioned that at the worst of the dysentery epidemic on Haruku 'as many as ten men died in a day'. This is an understatement. During the real 'hard time' eighteen hundred men were sick out of the two thousand on the draft, and seventeen men died, not just on one day. Seventeen died, day after day, for several days. The morgue was earth floored (the same as the huts) with a bamboo table in the middle, but the floor had to accommodate many of the dead boys. Maggots were referred to as being found in the most undesirable places. I confirm this and add that all sores were infected with maggots. Flies were laying their eggs in the corners of men's eyes, up their noses and in their open mouths. The horror of it all is beyond description. Never a week goes by without I think of the terrible conditions for those young boys to live and die in and, whilst thinking of these things, I am in my snug clean bed for which I thank God.

---

31   IWM, Catalogue number 79/4148, HMSO Command Papers, *Strength and Casualties of The Armed Forces and Auxiliary Forces of the United Kingdom 1939-1945,* July 1946.

32   See Map 12 for location.

33   Brian MacArthur, *Surviving the Sword*, p.356.

Doctors Forbes and Philps assisted the Jap doctors and Jack Plant and I assisted as orderlies, particularly in weighing the organs taken from each body. The 'slab' consisted of a sheet of corrugated iron with a half section of bamboo tied at the lower end to drain any liquids into a four-gallon petrol can. On the wards we worked twelve-hour shifts at night with usually only one person on each ward. The lighting arrangements were simply two four-hour candles to last for nearly twelve hours of darkness. There were two hundred sick men to look after on a ward at the height of the infection, so one candle had to be used at a time to assist the sick off the bamboo shelf on to a petrol can.[34]

The conditions were made more deplorable by the conduct of the Japanese and Korean guards. The camp commandant was Captain Kurashima, a lazy officer who neglected his responsibilities in camp administration and delegated the running and discipline of the work parties to the psychopathic Sergeant Gunso Mori, a thickly built SNCO who regularly struck prisoners with a cudgel of split bamboo. As Mori could not speak English, he was assisted by a Korean interpreter called Kasiyama. As the number of sick grew Mori became increasingly savage, James Home remembers his regular actions after the morning *Tenko,* or roll call, when Mori would be told that there were not enough prisoners to work on the airfield. He would line up the RAF officers alongside the men to slap them. Home describes the savagery of this:

Being 'slapped' by the Japs should not be confused with the playful slaps that may be exchanged by Westerners. It consisted of a clenched fist thrown from the thigh with maximum force ending up on the face or skull with rapid repetitive movements. Beatings came along regularly and cost very little, as cheap as a bat of an eyelid sometimes. If you were unable to take the beating, or went down purposely thinking your attacker would desist, you had made your first mistake, for then the boot would go in with obvious joy. If you could avoid flinching or showing any sign of distress you may 'save face', which, however you understand it, was their second commandment… All the sick who could stand, including those with leg ulcers, chest problems, severe neuritis, beri-beri and the many symptoms of malnutrition, were on parade. It was no use leaving anyone behind in a hut hoping to cover for them, as the guards would be flying around, joyfully looking for victims as they brandished their personal length of bamboo. Mori and Kasiyama, in their usual bawdy fashion, went viciously along the *Tenko* lines hitting over the head anyone they considered fit enough to reach the drome. Only when their quota was finally reached would they dismiss the *Tenko.*[35]

The cruelty of Mori and Kasiyima earnt them the nicknames of 'Blood' and 'Slime', after the symptoms of the dysentery that wracked the islands. For their crimes Captain Kurashima and Sergeant Mori were both executed at Singapore in 1946 and Kasiyama was given life imprisonment.

The prisoners first understood what their task on Haraku entailed when on 10 May 1943 two working parties, each of 600 men, were marched two miles from camp and halted between two hills. Private Cowling recalls that the scale of work facing the prisoners was then made apparent to them:

A nice view but where was the land that we were to make into an airstrip? You could have bowled the whole 600 over with a blade of couch grass when the guards produced 300 household hammers and chisels and ordered us to cut the tops off the hills and carry the debris into the valley. This was

34   Alfred James Fowden, quoted from *Prisoners in Java – collected articles from the Java Journal,* (Southampton: Hamwic Publishers, 2007), p. 202.

35   Brian MacArthur, *Surviving the Sword* (London: Abacus, 2005), p. 361.

A group of RAF prisoners cheer for the camera following their release from Changi Prison, Singapore, September 1945. (Crown Copyright – Air Historical Branch)

how to build an airstrip Japanese style? A truck arrived with hundreds of little baskets. These little wicker baskets were about 24 inches wide, 18 inches from back to front, and had a carrying handle on either side. Their load capacity must have been all of 25 to 30 pounds. These were unloaded and the men without hammers and chisels started carrying baskets full of our scrapings to dump in the valley. The Japanese had brought us all this way in a hell-ship to work like coolies constructing an airstrip in the most primitive manner conceivable. We were obviously an expendable commodity. Their contempt for us was plain. It was clear that they were going to get the maximum work for the minimum expenditure. I realised that my life was at stake. Our captors did not have a conscience. This was truly survival of the fittest or even more primitive straight survival for whom amongst us was fit? That night our 'meal' consisted of 20 one-pound cans of meat, a few vegetables and some rice to be shared by 2071 hungry, half-starved male adults. The rice, half cooked, measured out to half a billycan each. The hell of Haruku had started.[36]

Despite the brutality and the disease, the British POWs reinforced by Dutch prisoners who had come from the island of Amahei in October 1943, completed the runway. Ironically the airfield did not play a significant role in the war because the Allies outflanked the Japanese in the Banda Sea and bypassed that area completely. Having completed their building work on the airfield, an early batch of 550 sick and weak British and Dutch prisoners left Haruku on 25 November 1943, bound for Java on the *Suez Maru*, tragically this ship was torpedoed four days later by an American submarine, the USS *Bonefish*. All the Allied prisoners on this ship died, some machine gunned in the sea by an escorting Japanese corvette. By July and August of 1944, Haruku camp was being closed and the last

---

36    Brian MacArthur, *Surviving the Sword*, p. 359.

prisoners were waiting to be sent back to Java in one of the notorious Japanese merchantmen, now routinely called 'hellships' by the prisoners because of the shocking conditions aboard. Denis Mason, who was a member of the RAFVR, described in an official report after the war the journey he and others took from Haruku on the *Kaiysu Maru,* a 600-ton vessel, in September 1944:

> Party included myself, Flying Officer G Cranford (Cranford was almost wholly paralysed and died later on the *Maras Maru*), Capt Vander-Locke and Capt Bryan both of the N.E.I. [Netherlands East Indies] Forces, and one hundred and forty-six other ranks. The whole of this party were very sick except the two N.E.I. Forces Officers. So sick that the majority were paralysed with beri-beri. This party boarded a vessel which was a small Japanese freighter at Amboina town, situated on Ambon (or Ambonina) Island… Reaching Raha Moena on 16th September 1944 and the whole party then transhipped to a 600-ton vessel named the *Kaiysu Maru*. The senior Japanese in charge of the party was Lt [Sic Captain] Kureshema assisted by Jap Sgt Mori and Korean interpreter Kasama, with about six Korean guards. Water was issued twice a day consisting of a total of one half-pint. Food was issued twice a day of a total of 100 grammes (3½ ounces) of rice pap with nothing else. P.O.W.s had no lifebelts or other form of lifesaving equipment. The only boat the vessel carried was a small row boat capable of holding four persons, in a smooth sea. No life-rafts of any description. Firefighting equipment nil.
>
> Living conditions were rather grim on this ship. A few of the POWs just could not possibly squeeze into the area allotted in the hold so they went on deck forward. They all received a terrific bashing from Sgt Mori including Capt Vander-Locke. On boarding the *Kaiysu Maru* it was discovered that it was the same vessel that we POWs had just previously loaded in Amboina with bombs, ammunition, petrol, rice and various tinned foodstuffs. This was all stowed away in the holds and the hatch covers in position.
>
> We POWs now had accommodation on top of this hatchway and the Japs provided one small tarpaulin as sun protection. This sheet was hopelessly inadequate however, so the majority of the PWs had to just lay and roast in the sun. This state of affairs was pretty grim as for the first twenty-four hours no drink of any kind was issued. This was a steel ship reeking with petrol fumes from the cargo in the hold, also the ships position was only just south of the equator. The water position improved slightly the second day and for the twenty-four hours issue each POW was given approx one half pint.
>
> Food consisted of one meal a day of fifty grammes of rice pap. The Japanese had no excuse for this short ration as we knew that the food was in the ship's hold, also the Japs on board used to take sacks of rice and cases of dried vegetables, etc. from the hold and exchange with the natives ashore for eggs, fruit, fresh meat, etc. Jap Sgt. Mori had very little chance of carrying out his usual brutal treatment on this ship as almost the whole of the POWs were in such a shocking physical condition that they could hardly crawl let alone stand up, to be bashed about by Mori.[37]

On 20 September 1944, the ship was attacked by American Liberator aircraft. The Japanese and Korean guards immediately abandoned ship, leaving the POWs to their fate.

> I must say that the Jap ship's captain kept his head and just before he abandoned ship, he cut the rope to the stern anchor and tried to beach the vessel, but this was not successful owing to the outcrop of coral. However, I succeeded in getting all POWs successfully off the ship except for two dead, throwing each one in turn something to hang on to, such as a piece of wood or kitbag, etc. On check-up on shore, I discovered that the total loss of POW casualties

---

37    Official Report by Flying Officer Denis Mason, <www.COFEPOW.org.uk> accessed 12 December 2018.

were nine (sic) dead and several wounded. The whole rescue operation took me one to one and a half hours, and the ship eventually blew up and was a complete write off. The Japs eventually took us to Raha Moena and we stayed one night and a day at a barrack. All the POWs were naked. The Japs made no effort to supply clothing or blankets although we saw a lot of Jap forces on shore. Surely where there are forces then there are usually supplies?

Our total food for the twenty-four hours we were on shore was two balls of steamed rice each of seventy-five grammes and one sardine fish. Water supply for the same period was half a pint per PW. I appealed to Lt Kureshema and to Sgt Mori for more water and more food. Also some form of headdress, clothing and a blanket each, but nothing.

On the evening of 21 September 1944, we all boarded Jap ship *Maras Maru*, a total party of one hundred and thirty-eight POWs, Lt Kureshema, Sgt Mori, Kasama and the Korean guards. On the morning of the 21st, Capt Van del Locke was given permission to bury the dead. I regret to report being unable to bury the British dead, as I was so weak I was hardly able to walk.[38]

James Home sailed from Haruku on the *Maras Maru* and recalled finally arriving at Surabaya on 23 November 1944. The treatment and neglect of the POWs on the vessel had been shocking, many of them dying of dehydration during the voyage:

Those who survived were mere ghosts of their former selves and many were half-demented wrecks of humanity, diseased, filthy and crawling with vermin. On the given signal to offload I tried bracing myself ready to climb out of the hold and onto terra firma; knowing that some-thing most unpleasant was happening to me, I was rather apprehensive. Could I get out of the hold? Would someone offer to help Joe haul me out? – I could not afford to be left in the hold. Perhaps I had become a little panicky. I tried standing on my feet only to go crashing down in a big heap on the floor; no-one needed to tell me that I was paralysed from my waist down, a symptom of beriberi. 'For Christ's sake, Jim, what's the matter? We've got to get off this bloody ship,' said a concerned Joe, now forgetting his own troubles. 'I've had it Joe, you get out before you land in trouble.' I was concerned that he would be further punished for aiding and abetting me. I had been careless enough to become useless like those Jap animals in their fields – my future may be very short. Another semi-fit lad came across as they usually did, and together they dragged and pushed me out. It hurt like hell and each movement was agony, but I was to be forever grateful to my pals.[39]

Almost half the men (1,021 out of 2,071) who were sent to Haruku did not survive. Some died on the island, some in other camps they were sent to and yet more on the Japanese merchant ships returning them to Java. Many who did make it back to Java were too weak to survive a further year of captivity. Haruku was appalling, but should not be viewed as an isolated incident, there were indeed many similar experiences in Borneo, Japan, Malaya and other parts of Indonesia that Allied prisoners, including Commonwealth Air Force personnel, had to endure.

The experience of the Far East prisoners of war is very different to that of those captured in Europe and it must have been difficult for their comrades and family members to comprehend. What is deeply poignant is that the history of RAF and Commonwealth air force POWs in the Far East is so little understood. The story of Haruku should be much better known amongst the RAF, not just because of the high proportion of RAF POWs who worked and died on the island, but also as one of the greatest examples of courage exhibited by any British servicemen in the war.

---

38   Official Report by Flying Officer Denis Mason, <www.COFEPOW.org.uk> accessed 12 December 2018.
39   Brian MacArthur, *Surviving the Sword*, p. 373.

# Part IX

# 19

# Conclusion

The British and the Commonwealth air forces could look back on the Second World War with justifiable pride that they had made a decisive contribution to victory. At the outset such a victory had seemed far from certain, and the role the RAF and the Commonwealth air forces should play was subject to much debate. Yet the British and Allied strategy sensibly evolved as the war progressed and was shaped by pivotal events including the collapse of Britain's continental Allies, the Italian entry into the war, Germany's invasion of Russia, the Japanese offensives in the Far East, and of course America's entry into the war. These events initially posed threats and commitments that nearly overwhelmed the British Commonwealth, but they also offered the prospect of new Allies and additional ways to defeat Germany and its Axis partners. These two volumes have covered all the major air operations employed by the British in the war, across the widest geographical area. It is against this background that some of the major themes that helped and hindered the RAF and its sister Commonwealth air forces can be identified.

The RAF began the war with a series of pre-war operational concepts that were dangerously flawed. This included the view that the bomber would be able to successfully fly to the heart of enemy countries and swiftly undermine the enemy's will to fight by striking their centres of population, political life, and economic production. This was a philosophy that had originated during the 1920s and was influenced by both a revulsion to costly First World War land campaigns, as well as a desire for the RAF to be an independent air force rather than an auxiliary to the other services. Prominent air theorists and military thinkers of the day gave it the necessary intellectual substance and British political leaders, alarmed by the prospect of gas and explosives raining down on London and other cities, integrated the theory into their wider security and foreign policy approaches, including deterrence. This concept was dangerously defective, for it over-estimated the capabilities and skill of the British bomber force which could not withstand daylight fighter attack, carry the tonnage of high explosives necessary to inflict significant damage on German cities, or possess the necessary night-time navigation skills to find their way to their targets under cover of darkness. The RAF's bomber-centric approach under-estimated the will of Germany to fight and failed to recognise that a strategic air offensive was not an effective instrument or deterrent against the central element of German military power – its Army. Paradoxically, it was the British who, fearing German reciprocity against any attacks the RAF might make on German cities, were deterred from using the bombers in a strategic role for the first year of the war. Consequently, they confined their bomber missions to leaflet drops and attacks on German naval vessels outside of their harbours. This limited approach changed dramatically with the *Luftwaffe* attacks on British cities in September 1940 which prompted the British to retaliate.

An overwhelming RAF emphasis on the bomber force could have spelt disaster for Britain, but at the eleventh hour and largely at the instigations of the politicians, the RAF did begin to focus enough effort and resources to defend Britain. Under Dowding they skilfully incorporated a series of technological advances to generate the world's first integrated air defence system, which helped Britain win its first major victory of the war. Although a defensive victory, the Battle of Britain was to have longer term consequences. For the following year Germany launched an invasion on Russia and failed to subdue that foe as well – now Hitler faced the strategic nightmare of a war on

A Lancaster of 103 Squadron pauses on the flarepath at Elsham Wolds, Lincolnshire, before taking off for
a raid on Duisburg, Germany, during the Battle of the Ruhr on 26 March 1943. Three searchlights
(called 'Sandra' lights) form a cone to indicate the height of the cloud base for the departing aircraft.
(Crown Copyright – Air Historical Branch)

two fronts for the remainder of the war. The 1940 victory and emphasis on fighter defence and air
superiority did not prevent the supporters of strategic bombing from ensuring that their concepts
would remain the major plank of the RAF's approach to the war. The service's devotion to an
idea sometimes resulted in senior members of the RAF ignoring the evidence that they were not
having the impact they claimed. Indeed, it took an independently instigated study commissioned
by Churchill's scientific adviser, Lord Cherwell (the 1941 Butt report) to expose that only one in
three pilots were getting within three miles of their target and finally force the RAF to re-consider
its approach.

It was not until the middle of 1942, that the bomber fleets reached the size and capability the
pre-war advocates had dreamt of, only then was the RAF in the position to send 1,000-strong
fleets of four-engined bombers to German cities on a regular basis. But by that point the bomber
offensive was no longer perceived to be a unilateral war-winning operation, but was instead viewed
as a supporting activity that helped create the conditions for the opening of a second front in
Europe. Such an Allied opportunity was only now possible because Russia had not only survived
the initial German onslaught, but was decisively engaging the majority of the German Army on
the Eastern Front and therefore fixing the major instrument of German military power. Though
wider Allied thinking had moved on, there still remained stubborn bomber advocates like Air
Marshal Harris who refused to deviate from the pre-war mantra, arguing till very late in the war,
that with a further period of uninterrupted effort his bombers could knock Germany out of the
conflict. Harris was not alone in his views and there were sometimes occasions when the Air Staff's
judgement erred and their focus on bombers meant they were also blind to wider opportunities.

The impact the bomber offensive had on Germany's industrial production was undoubtedly
pronounced, though the comparatively late German mobilisation skews the figures somewhat and

leaves the historian surprised that their industrial production peaked in 1944. Yet, the efforts the Germans had to make in dispersing production, repairing shattered industry and maintaining productivity in the face of Bomber Command's onslaughts must be factored in to this equation. So too should the large amount of aircraft, AA guns and personnel Germany had to divert from the frontline to the defence of German cities. By the end of 1943 there were estimated to be two million Germans scattered across the Reich in anti-aircraft defence duties, of whom 900,000 were anti-aircraft gunners. This huge body of manpower was needed to man the 2,131 batteries[1] of anti-aircraft guns including many 88mm dual purpose guns.[2] The bomber offensive also forced the *Luftwaffe* to reduce its production of bomber aircraft and increase the proportion of fighters in their inventory, which altered the *Luftwaffe's* capabilities and turned it from an offensive strike instrument to a largely defensive air force. The operations of the *Luftwaffe* were also damaged by Bomber Command's missions. This included the attacks on oil refineries and plants to the extent that by the end of 1944, fuel shortages had resulted in the *Luftwaffe* only being able to operate about 50 fighters per night against Bomber Command, despite the fact that the frontline strength of night fighters was c.980 aircraft.[3] Moreover, the lack of aviation fuel during the same period had immediately been felt in reduced training for *Luftwaffe* pilots, which caused a sharp deterioration in their skill and expertise in the air.

We must also consider what was the opportunity cost to Britain in constructing this massive bomber fleet? What other war material might Britain and her allies have usefully produced in its place? Or indeed consider the wider cost of 55,573 aircrew lost in Bomber Command between 1939–45, a figure which dominates the RAF's total of 70,253 officers, NCOs and airmen killed or missing on operations. How else might these people, who represented some of the most skilled, intelligent and motivated members of the British Commonwealth, have contributed to the Allied war effort?

In contrast to weakened German industrial capacity, the British were able to steadily increase wartime production and maintain both a large first line aircraft strength, as well as the necessary quantities of reserve machines for periods of prolonged operations. This was achieved through a combination of approaches: including shadow factories established in the UK, purchasing of American machines, engines or other parts using Lend Lease arrangements, and ordering off the board so that new aircraft could be quickly brought into service. There were several British machines that were obvious failures, the Stirling, Battle and Barracuda all spring to mind as examples, but these were outweighed by some incredibly successful designs such as the Mosquito, Spitfire, Lancaster and Typhoon. The last aircraft showing how the awkward beginnings of some aircraft can be overcome with perseverance and imagination. We should particularly recall those aircraft like the Wellington, Hurricane, Sunderland and Swordfish that began and ended the war still in operational service, or machines like the Beaufighter that although eclipsed by its younger Mosquito stablemate still provided sterling service during the most difficult periods of the War. Nor should we forget the many Kittyhawks, Bostons, Liberators, Mustangs, Martlets, Corsairs and other American aircraft that were also successfully operated by the Commonwealth air forces. The plans for all these aircraft, just like the plans for manpower and training, were either laid down before the war, or at its very beginning. Taken together they meant that as the war progressed the British Commonwealth had increasing resources to channel into the many demands they faced.

---

1    1944 figure taken from Edward B Westermann, *Flak, German Anti-Aircraft Defences 1914-45* (Kansas: University Press of Kansas, 2001) Table 8.1.

2    Hilary St G Saunders, *Royal Air Force 1939-45, Volume 3* (London: HMSO, 1954), p. 386.

3    Edward B Westermann, *Flak, German Anti-Aircraft Defences 1914-45*, p. 272 and C Webster and N Frankland, *The Strategic Air Offensive Against Germany, Volume 3* (London: HMSO, 1961), p. 238.

A Supermarine Spitfire Mk Vc of 43 Squadron RAF raises the dust as it taxies to the take off point at Tusciano landing ground near Salerno, Italy. (Crown Copyright – Air Historical Branch)

One of the most famous elements of RAF wartime folklore is the 1940 letter written by Dowding to the Under Secretary of State at the Air Ministry, it bluntly warns him that Fighter Command cannot guarantee the air defence of Great Britain if further fighter squadrons are sent to France. It represents strong and clear thinking from an acknowledged air power expert, who communicated robustly and successfully to prevent the wasting of a precious military resource for political expediency. It is rightly celebrated by the RAF as an illustration of strong operational wisdom, indeed there was a copy of the letter framed outside the author's classroom at the Defence Academy to offer just that example to the staff college students. Yet, Dowding's letter should be balanced with a 1942 letter from Joubert de la Ferte, asking for just forty very long-range aircraft to help close the mid-Atlantic gap, alongside the answers from Harris and the Air Staff who utterly failed to appreciate the decisive nature of the Battle of the Atlantic, or air power's role in it. The intransigence of Bomber Command and the Air Staff in this instance almost cost Britain the war. There might also be benefit in highlighting the letters from Singapore in 1941, pleading for Spitfires or Hurricanes in anticipation of a Japanese onslaught. This letter also fell on deaf ears at a time when Fighter Command was squandering its 75 Squadrons of fighters on Circuses and Rhubarbs over northern France for negligible gain. Instead, the pilots in the Far East had to combat the Japanese Zeros in obsolete Buffalos and were inevitably shot out of the sky. Spitfires would have been equally valuable in Malta or the Western Desert in 1941, at a time when the Tomahawks and Hurricanes were struggling against the more modern Me 109 F and G. The logistical difficulties in sending these aircraft to either Malta or the Far East were undoubtedly significant, and the aircraft once sent would have been almost impossible to retrieve. Nevertheless, the Air Staff can be legitimately accused of sometimes failing to apply the correct priorities to the tasks it faced. Flexibility is rightly cited as one of the most important characteristics of air power, but it requires senior commanders to exercise imagination and a shrewd appreciation of risk if it is to manifest itself successfully at the strategic level.

It is a very rare military that accurately predicts the unique character of the war they are about to embark upon and finds that their pre-war concepts are a perfect fit. More often each side must adjust and adapt to the conflict and how to fight it, finding ways to play to their own strengths and exploit their adversary's weaknesses. Adapting to the character of the conflict required the British to introduce an effective blend of technological and tactical innovations to gain an operational advantage over the enemy. The leaders of Coastal Command showed how greater success against U-boats could be achieved by fostering a close relationship between the scientific community and operational aircrew. This allowed new technologies, such as ASV radar, to be successfully introduced and through Operational Research, new tactics to be developed, including the right way to employ its weapons. Coastal Command successfully encouraged a bottom up approach to innovation, recognising that the best ideas often originated from more junior levels. The development and introduction into service of the Leigh Light is a good example of the advantage of such an approach. Coastal Command also instituted a robust method of debriefing crews and were able to turn the handful of lessons learnt from the comparatively rare encounters with U-boats, into wider institutional knowledge through improved tactical instructions to aircrews, using mediums like the *Coastal Command Review* to do so. This contrasts with other areas, like Fighter Command, where tactical innovations were sometimes only passed around the command informally, which perhaps explains why discredited theories such as the 'Big Wing' were still being pursued by formations such as the 1st Australian Fighter Wing in Darwin as late as 1943.

It must have been hard for the wartime leaders to sift the brilliant ideas from the many erroneous ones that tend to emerge in wartime. Yet on many occasions the RAF were able to spot the talented disruptor and gave them enough authority and resources to establish their idea as an operational capability. The development of the RAF's Photographic Reconnaissance Units and Allied Central Interpretation Unit offer an excellent example of how the RAF successfully channelled the creative talents of men, like Wing Commander Sidney Cotton and Flying Officer Maurice Longbottom, to rapidly develop a prototype capability. Having established that the concept was sound, it also illustrates how adept the RAF were at scaling it up into a worldwide photographic reconnaissance organisation that contributed to just about every Allied operation and area of intelligence interest, from the strategic down to the most tactical levels. It remains curious that the popular historiography of intelligence in the Second World War does not credit air photographic reconnaissance and air photographic intelligence as much as it should. Its wider utility and vast dissemination have led many to underestimate its contribution.

The British Commonwealth's air forces were also highly effective at innovating and adapting the resources they had immediately available. Obvious examples include incorporating coast-watchers in to the RAAF early warning air defence system at Port Moresby, learning to knock V1s down by flipping them with a fighter's wing tip, adapting the Swordfish into a highly capable anti-U-Boat asset by flying them off a Merchant Aircraft Carrier, or using the Lysander to maintain contact with resistance organisations in occupied Europe. In these and many other instances, the Allies showed an imaginative approach and met a variety of unforeseen operational circumstances by improvising and adapting the tools and resources they had immediately available.

Although some held a cultural preference for independent strategic operations, it seems that the British and Commonwealth air forces were at their most effective when they were operating as an equal partner with the other services. In Coastal Command, cooperation with the Royal Navy was habitually close and supportive, the co-location of headquarters, a shared series of meetings and updates, the exchange of high-quality liaison officers all helped in generating a common understanding and approach. The Eighth Army and Desert Air Force also offer an illustration of how two services could work together and generate a unified land campaign that combined air power and ground manoeuvre. Mutual trust and confidence are such important qualities for leaders to have if inter-service cooperation is to flourish and that cannot have been easy to achieve after the disappointing campaigns in France, Greece and Crete, together with the recriminations and insults that were thrown about immediately after them. It took leadership

A Mosquito PR.IX of 544 Squadron based at Benson, Oxfordshire, pictured in late 1943. This aircraft was delivered to 540 Squadron on 4 September 1943 and passed over to 544 Squadron a month later where it was still present when they commenced day operations with the type on 15 October. By the time it was passed to 8 Operational Training Unit at Fraserburgh, the aircraft had flown 43 missions. (Crown Copyright – Air Historical Branch)

and a generosity of spirit amongst leaders like Tedder, Coningham and Broadhurst, as well as Auchinleck and Montgomery, to create the right atmosphere. By doing so they ensured that the air contribution was not something sprinkled on to the Army plan as an afterthought, but that the Army and Air Force planned the land campaign together and that the air contribution was baked in from the beginning. The transition of air-ground cooperation from the deserts to North West Europe also highlights how even an established level of mutual trust and confidence can be very easy to lose, particularly when the egos of senior officers are unleashed. Nevertheless, British air-ground tactics and techniques steadily developed as the war progressed, were copied by the Americans, and reached a dramatic conclusion during the Normandy Campaign. Later still, Slim's advance to Rangoon in 1945 demonstrated the advantages strike, air reconnaissance and air transportation can provide in difficult terrain, and the Australian First Tactical Air Force also showed how it could be successfully applied in the South-West Pacific, usually in conjunction with maritime or littoral manoeuvre.

The RAF contribution to these joint campaigns was sometimes appreciated more by the Army and Royal Navy than the Air Staff. Whether it was the Air Staff castigating Air Marshal Hill for letting General Pile have a freer hand to engage V1s, or the admonition of the Second Tactical Air Force Composite Group commanders for getting too close to their Army comrades, it seems that some very senior RAF officers were wary of too much integration. General Slim observed that the RAF did not seem to value the work Third Tactical Air Force undertook in support of his Army to the same degree as air superiority or strategic bombing roles. There certainly seems to have been a natural tendency for the Air Staff to value these 'independent' functions more than supporting the Royal Navy and Army, even if they were being treated as an equal and joint partner by the sister service.

The effectiveness of the British Commonwealth air operations and indeed the way they were able to innovate had a great deal to do with the quality of the people within the air forces, in many instances they received the very best of their societies. In leadership terms the RAF produced some of the most effective commanders in the war. Tedder stands out as the strategic leader par excellence, both for his work in the Middle East and as Eisenhower's deputy (though his 1944 period of anti-Montgomery intriguing does him little credit). Dowding and Park were assured operational leaders as they set up and operated the Fighter Command system, in Park's case he would go on to demonstrate similar skills in Malta and Burma too. The three commanders of Coastal Command, Bowhill, Joubert and Slessor, who all helped win the Battle of the Atlantic, also deserve wider recognition as do Coningham, Broadhurst and Elmhirst who laid the foundations of air-ground cooperation in the Western Desert. It would also be right to include Harris for his single-minded determination in leading his Bomber Crews through some of their hardest years of the war. Few others could have done it, though it is hard to forgive his stubborn and narrow-minded approach on many occasions.[4]

Before the war broke out, Britain correctly understood that the war with Germany was going to be a long conflict and the RAF had laid many of the necessary foundations for a ready reserve of manpower before the hostilities commenced. This included the RAuxAF, the RAFVR and the WAAF, which together provided an immediate reinforcement to the RAF's regular cohort at the beginning of the war, as well as a path for further expansion. Training the aircrew for this vastly increased air force was imaginatively tackled, indeed the ambitious British Commonwealth Air Training Plan's output of 326,552 aircrew, of whom 117,669 were pilots, illustrates the scale of the endeavour's success. Dispersing training across the Empire also meant there was important resilience in the programme when Britain became an aerial battlefield. The relative superiority of the training too was increasingly evident as the war progressed, so that by the end of 1942 British and Commonwealth pilots were receiving more hours on advanced types of aircraft than either Germany or Japan could match. It meant that there was a notable difference in both quality and quantity when the combatants met in the air.

It is evident that the RAF's operational success relied heavily on those leaders who started the war at junior rank, proved themselves to be talented and, if they survived, quickly rose through the ranks. Spitfire pilots like Johnnie Johnson and Hugh Dundas began the war as junior officers and finished it as group captains in charge of fighter wings in North-West Europe and Italy respectively. In Bomber Command Leonard Cheshire VC stands out. He too started the war as a junior officer and finished as a Group Captain, having flown 100 Bomber Command missions, including many with 617 Squadron. His VC is rare in being awarded for many operations over the course of the war, rather than just a single action. Undoubtedly a brave and talented man, Cheshire remained consistently modest and humble throughout his life, so it was entirely in character that at the investiture he insisted that he and Warrant Officer Norman Jackson (who had climbed on to the wing of a Lancaster over Germany to put a fire out) approach King George VI together. Upon reaching the King, Cheshire suggested that Jackson should receive the VC before him, stating 'that this fellow has stuck his neck out more than I did – he should get his first'.[5] There are many famous names and individuals, but so too are there many others who were also effective and inspirational to those they led but are sadly unknown to the wider public. They have received no lasting recognition, fame or formal award, just the admiring words spoken or written by those who knew them best.

---

4    See Annex T for a list of the principal air commanders during the War.

5    Tony Iveson, Brian Milton, *Lancaster: The Biography* (London: Andre Deutsch, 2009) p.230

Those they led were a diverse set of individuals with many different personalities, however amongst all the widely different human characteristics courage seems to shine through as a common strength. There is a special tone and character to the courage displayed in the air force. Sometimes it had to be exercised in a very deliberate fashion and extended over a prolonged period; those in Bomber Command demonstrated this steadfastness on an enduring basis. To go on sorties to Germany, day after day, knowing that the chances of surviving a 30-mission tour were often as low as one-in-three takes a special type of determination. Similarly, there is the fatalistic, sacrificial courage evident in the aircrew who faced the almost impossible task of operating against larger numbers of superior aircraft. Yet stoically, they went up time after time to battle against slim odds. The Buffalo and Hurricane pilots facing the Japanese in 1941 and 1942, the Hurricane pilots in Malta, or the Fleet Air Arm Fulmar pilots in the Mediterranean, all illustrate this phenomenon. Sadly, there is an absence of personal accounts and autobiographies by this latter group, probably because so few survived. The examples of courage became even more acute when the pilots must have known that their own flying skill would make little difference to their chances of survival. This must include the Typhoon or Kittyhawk pilots conducting ground support, or indeed the Stirling and Dakota aircrew who would have understood that the growing German defences around the DZs at Arnhem had quickly risen to lethal levels. Perhaps most of all it reminds us of those members of 2 Group and Coastal Command who undertook anti-shipping operations against the fiercest of opposition.

Courage was required by many of those airmen after the war too. Our society is now increasingly aware of the impact prolonged conflict can have on an individual, together with the resilience required of veterans, but in the years immediately after the war this was less talked about. Colin Lindeman was an Australian Kittyhawk pilot who fought with 75 and 76 Squadron during the campaign in the South-West Pacific. At the end of a long interview with Edward Stokes of the Australian War Memorial, Lindeman honestly captured what the aftermath of the war meant for aircrew such as himself:

> Actually, I am not ashamed to admit that the sound of an aeroplane engine upset me, if I was close to it, for a couple of years after the war…you said the war was an adventure for a lot of young people, I look at it that way too. But it's certainly left its scars and I don't think anyone that saw operational action, whether Army, Navy or Air Force, have been left without scars either physically or mentally; mentally particularly. It took me a long time to settle down and sleep at night, Div would wake me up and say, 'You're grinding your teeth' or 'You're having a nightmare', or something like that. I had a lot of nightmares…[6]

Any historian studying the RAF in the Second World War is struck by the cosmopolitan nature of the service that contained aircrew from across Britain and the Commonwealth. This Commonwealth group was of course also combined with aircrews who had escaped from occupied countries, or even travelled from neutral ones. It was therefore quite common for the crew of a large aircraft, such as a bomber, to have two or three nationalities represented in it. Single-seat fighter squadrons would often have a blend of pilots from many different countries mixed within its flights and sections. To ensure that these crews and units operated as an effective and cohesive team speaks volumes about the motivation of the individuals themselves, the quality of leadership at all levels and the sense of purpose a righteous cause infers. The skill with which Britain and the RAF welded this Allied team together should not be underestimated, I can think of no other war-fighting example where such a multi-national approach, integrated at very tactical team levels has

---

6     AWM SOO548: Sound Recordings Colin Lindeman interview.

Oblique aerial photograph taken from the observers position on a Bristol Beaufighter during an attack on an enemy convoy off Scheveningen, Holland, by 36 aircraft of the North Coates Strike Wing. Beaufighters can be seen striking the convoy's escort vessels with rocket projectiles and cannon fire. This attack was the first occasion that 60lb solid-shot rocket projectiles were used against shipping. (Crown Copyright – Air Historical Branch)

been attempted at such scale. Let alone proved so overwhelmingly successful. It would be a better story if the efforts of all those that formed the Allied team had been justly rewarded at the end of the war, yet the post-war experience of the Polish and Czech aircrew was not a happy one. By 1945 it was very apparent that Germany's occupation of Poland and Czechoslovakia was being swiftly replaced by a Soviet and Communist tyranny. The Poles, who formed the largest contingent of any occupied country to serve with the RAF, suffered further from the Labour government's approach that deliberately and determinedly tried to force the Poles to return to their country after the war. Clement Attlee's foreign secretary described the Polish military, including the air force, in Britain as 'a source of increasing political embarrassment in our relations with the Soviet Union and [Communist] Poland.' Proposing that 'everything should be done to ensure that as few Poles as possible remain in this country'. [7]

The British government banned the Polish forces in Britain from taking part in its victory parade in June 1946, and to their eternal shame invited the Soviet Union and the Polish Communist regime to send forces instead (both refused). The measure shocked many in Britain who remembered the enduring contribution Poland had made throughout the war. Winston Churchill himself profoundly regretted the exclusion of the Poles adding: 'They will be in our hearts on that day.' Air Marshal Joubert de la Ferte who had led a number of the Polish Air Force squadrons within Coastal Command commented angrily 'Have we lost all sense of decency and gratitude? Are we

---

7    Lynne Olson and Stanley Cloud, *For your Freedom and Ours* (London: Arrow Books, 2004), p. 396.

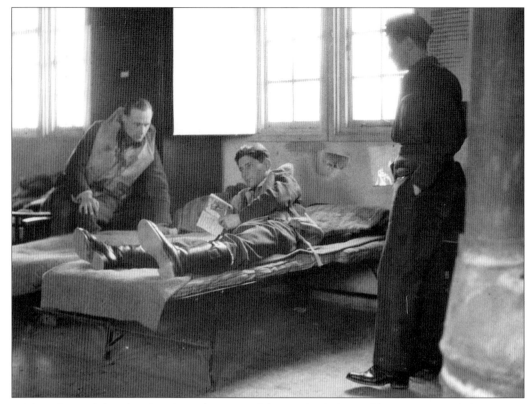

Pilots of 303 Polish Fighter Squadron relax in one of the Squadron's dispersal huts at RAF Northolt in May 1942. (Crown Copyright – Air Historical Branch)

too feeble to stand up to those who attempt to bully us?'[8] As a result of their wartime service with Britain, the Poles and Czechs who returned to their homelands would face many years of discrimination, suspicion and persecution by the Communist regimes in their own countries. Thankfully the story does not end on an entirely sour note, the magnanimity of Poland saves us from that. For once the Poles overthrew Communism and regained their freedom, some of the first acts of the new government were to bestow Polish gallantry awards on those Allied servicemen they had fought alongside during the War. This naturally included many airmen from the British and Commonwealth and perhaps demonstrates the deep and lasting bonds of friendship that had been established amongst those that had fought together for freedom.

The British and Commonwealth air forces engagement in the Second World War was truly global. The air forces had matured to the extent that speed, reach and flexibility could project air power to almost every corner of the globe. When that potential was combined with maritime and ground manoeuvre it was able to achieve a persistency and potency that was a cornerstone of the Allied way of winning. This book's original aim was to explain some of the tactics and techniques employed by the British in the war in the air, as well as highlight the challenges experienced by those who had to carry out such operations. The advantage of a two volume book also allows one to situate these activities in more than one theatre, an important aspect in demonstrating the growing maturity of operations and the different approaches that the various

8    Lynne Olson and Stanley Cloud, *For your Freedom and Ours* (London: Arrow Books, 2004), p. 398.

environments necessitated. It is right that British military history on the Second World War concentrates on Europe, which was the decisive theatre, but I also hope that this book reminds the reader of the many other campaigns across the world that Britain and its partners had to fight. It illustrates the British Commonwealth's massive contribution to victory in the Second World War and the decisive part that the RAF, Fleet Air Arm and other Commonwealth Air Forces played in that success.

# Annexes

# Annex A

# Notes for Pilots on Lysander and Hudson Pick-up Operations by Wing Commander H. B. Verity, DSO, DFC[1]

## Preparation

By far the greatest amount of work you do to carry out a successful pick-up happens before you leave the ground. These notes will give you some idea of the drill I tried to adopt and may help you to form your own technique. Never get over-confident about your navigation of Lysander ops. Each operation should be prepared with as much care as your first, however experienced you may be.

## Choosing your route

2. *Air Transport Form*. Your ATF will give the exact pinpoint of your landing ground, worked out from signals from the field and marked on a map 1 in 80,000 or 1 in 50,000. Attached will be a PRU photograph which will be helpful.

3. *Landmarks*. Having established exactly where your target is, have a look at the half million map and select a really good landmark nearby. This may be a river from which you approach the target. Check with the flak map that you will not be interfered with. Then you must work out a route, hopping from landmark to landmark, which will follow clear avenues on the flak map. Try to arrange for a really good landmark at each turning point, for example a coast or a big river. Finally, get your route approved by the Flight Commander.

## Preparation of maps

4. *Half million*. It is usual to make a half million folding route map which will take you all the way to your target and back. If your target is within 2 hours flying-range, 50 miles on each side of the track should be enough. If, on the other hand, you are going down to Lyons or Angouleme, it would be wise to have 100 miles on either side of the track. Fifty miles at each side can be turned back behind the map. When preparing this map, be careful to fold clear of important landmarks.

---

1  M R D Foot, SOE in France, (London: HMSO, 1966), Appendix D.

5. ***Quarter million maps***. Take quarter million maps of almost the whole route on short trips and of parts of the route on long trips. They are invaluable for confirming a pinpoint which is doubt-fully marked on the half million. Take a quarter million of the target area itself.

6. ***Target maps***. Target maps can be compiled with quarter million on one side and a PRU photo-graph on the other. In some cases, the 50,000 map may also be attached, but the black 80,000 is very difficult to read in the air. Do not forget that the reception committee might not be there when you first arrive. It is useful to be able to identify the field positively, even if you have to locate a barn shown on the photograph.

7. ***Diversion maps***. On every trip, however good the weather forecast, you should be prepared for a diversion when you come home. The wireless will not necessarily be working and you will feel an awful fool if you haven't the faintest idea of where to go or how to get there…

8. ***Gen cards***. Gen cards giving your flight plan data should be duplicated as a precaution against loss… Besides your navigational data, you must carry the signals and beacons for your return.

9. ***Spare maps***. Do not forget that maps sometimes get lost in the air. Not one of the maps you carry should be indispensable. You can generally find a scruffy old route map to carry with you as a spare.

10. ***Learning your route***. You can quite easily spend two hours in an armchair reading your maps before you go. It is very much easier in the air if you have done most of your map reading on the ground. The technique for pre-reading a map is something like this: first take your half million route map. Go through it systematically, following along your track. Note what landmarks you will see. Then study it to port and starboard of your track. Then study it with each of the other main types of landmark. Then re-read special parts of the route on a quarter million, and learn them up in the same way. Try to memorise the shapes of woods and the general way in which they are distributed over your map. Try to memorise any towns which you may see and the way in which other landmarks converge on them. Notice the way a coast or river runs, and the magnetic course of any given stretch.

11. ***Loading of aircraft***. Three passengers are normally the maximum carried, but four have been carried without incident in the past. As you may well imagine, that means a squash. With either three or four, it is thought impracticable for them to put on parachutes or bale out. If four passengers are carried, one goes on the floor, two on the seat, and one on the shelf. This is not recommended with heavy people.

12. ***Luggage***. Of course, the heaviest luggage should go under the seat. nearest the centre of gravity. Small, important pieces of luggage, such as sacks of money, should go on the shelf, so that they are not left in the aeroplane by mistake. Mistrust the floor under the shelf, as it is difficult for passengers to find luggage which has slipped down towards the tail.

13. ***Petrol***. The more petrol you take, the heavier your aeroplane will be for the landing and take-off; on the other hand, a very large margin of safety is recommended. You may well be kept waiting an hour or more in the target area by a reception committee that is late in turning up, or [have] to find yourself when you are lost, and you may need an hour's petrol when you get back to England to go somewhere you can land. You should have about two hours' spare petrol altogether.

14. ***Emergency kit***. If you get stuck in the mud, it is useful to have in the aeroplane some civilian, clothes. Do not put these in the passengers' compartment or they may be slung out. A good place is in the starting handle locker. You should also carry a standard escape kit, some purses of French money, a gun or two, and a thermos flask of hot coffee or what you will. A small flask of brandy or Whisky is useful if you have to swim for it, but NOT in the air. Empty your pockets of anything of interest to the Hun, but carry with you some small photographs of yourself in civilian clothes. These may be attached to false identity papers. In theory it is wise to wear clothes with no tailor's, laundry or personal marks. Change your linen before flying, as dirty shirts have a bad effect on wounds. The Lysander is a warm aeroplane, and I always wore a pair of shoes rather than flying boots. If you have to walk across the Pyrenees you might as well do it in comfort.

15. ***Conclusion***. You have a hell of a lot to do to get an operation ready. but there is quite a lot of it you can do the day before. It never matters if you prepare the op and don't do it. You may go that way some day and somebody else can always use your maps. It is most important to start an op fresh, and a good idea to have a nap or two in the afternoon or evening before you take off. Finally, you get driven to your aeroplane in a smart American car with a beautiful FANY driver, cluttered up from head to toe with equipment and arms and kit of every description, rather like the White Knight, prepared for every emergency.

## Execution

16. The notes up to this point may be called the *preparation* of a pick up operation. Now we come to the execution. The simplest form will be an imaginary night, in which I will try to visualise some of the problems which may crop up and suggest methods of thinking out the answers.

## Before take-off

17. You must make sure that the escorting officer for the agent knows the form. If he does not, you must attend to your agent yourself. Make sure that he knows how much luggage he is carrying and where it is stowed. He must know how to put on and operate parachutes, if carried, and helmets and microphones. He must try the working of the emergency warning lights. He must understand the procedure for turning about on the field. This is, briefly, for Lysanders, that one agent should stay in the aeroplane to hand out his own luggage and receive the luggage of the homecoming agent, before he himself hops out. In the rare case where the agent has night flying experience over the area in question, it may be of use to give him a map of the route. One operation failed when the pilot was very far off track and the agent, a highly experienced Air Force officer, knew perfectly well where he was but could not tell the pilot because the [intercom] was switched off.

## Running-up

18. Your running up, of course, should be thorough. Test all your cockpit lights and landing lights before taxi-ing out.

## Crossing the channel

19. One school of thought recommends crossing the Channel low down to approach the enemy coast below the [radar] screen. I am opposed to this, because of the danger of flak from the Royal Navy and from enemy convoys, besides which a heavily laden aeroplane will not climb very quickly to the height at which it is safest to cross the enemy coast...

## Crossing the enemy coast

20. It is generally safer to cross the enemy coast as high as possible up to 8,000 ft. This gives you a general view of the lie of the coast and avoids the danger of light flak and machine gun fire which you might meet lower down. On the other hand, your pinpoint at the coast is of vital importance, for by it you gauge your wind and set your course for the interior along a safe route, so it may be necessary to fly along a much lower route than 8,000 ft. to see where you are in bad weather. Don't think that you will be safe off a flak area within four miles. I have been shot at fairly accurately by low angle heavy flak three miles off Dieppe at 2,000 ft., so, until you know where you are, it is not wise to make too close an investigation of the coastline. In this case you may identify the coast by flying parallel with it some miles out to sea: Notice the course which it follows and any general changes of direction which it takes. By applying these to your map you will generally find that you must be at least on a certain length of coastline and, at best, at a definite point. When you know your position you may gaily climb above any low cloud there may be and strike into the interior on D[ead] R[eckoning].

## Map reading

21. As I indicated in the notes on the preparation of an op., most of your map reading must be done in a comfortable armchair before you take off, otherwise your maps will be of very little use to you in the air. But once in the air don't forget that map reading must never take precedence over the DR and even when you decide to follow a definite feature you must check the course of this feature with your compass. The reason for this is that you may very well find a landmark on the ground which corresponds with a point on your map, but is not, in fact, that point. I once spent a miserable two hours near Lons-le-Saunier by confusing the village of Bletterans with the village of Louhans. If you look on the map at these two villages in broad daylight you will find little similarity, but on a dark night the lie of the streams, railways and roads have some points in common. So never have faith in one pinpoint until you have checked it with a second, or even a third, nearby. This is very easy. Supposing you think you are over X town: look at your map and you will find that five miles south of it there is a large wood, for example. Fly south, and if no wood exists you will know that it is not X town and you will have to think again. If the wood is there, check the shape of it with your quarter million map and the road detail surrounding the wood and this will probably confirm that it is X town. I said that you should check the course of any feature you may be following, because it is fearfully easy to think that you are on a given railway, for instance, when in fact you are not, but railways are easily identifiable by their course.

## Map reading details

22. It may be useful if I run over the various types of landmark and try to point out their advantages and their snags.

a) *Water*

Water always shows up better than anything else, even in very poor light, if it lies between you and the source of the light. If the light is diffused by cloud, water may show up well in a large area, even beyond visibility. The best landmarks are, of course, the coast and the large rivers which should not be easily mistaken… Don't forget that seasonal fluctuations in flood and drought may alter the appearance of a river and that in some cases the land near a small stream may be flooded, giving it the appearance of a very large river. Another case where a stream may suggest a large river is when ground fog lies just along the valley, which from a distance is sometimes confusing. Lakes are rather tricky, especially if they are close to other lakes.

(b) *Forests and Woods*

Forests and woods probably show up next best to water, especially from a height or in haze. Small woods are very easily confused, but the character of their distribution over a stretch of country will help you to identify the area. Large forests, however, are very good landmarks… Woods may be particularly well identified just near the target by comparison with the target photograph.

(c) *Railways*

The next most useful type of landmark is the railway. Although a railway may not be very easily seen in itself, the lie of the track may be deduced from the contours of the land, because, of course, a railway does not tackle a very steep gradient. Sometimes a railway is given away by the glowing fire-box of an engine, by a row of blue lights (in the case of an electric railway) or by a line of smoke lying like a wisp of fog on a still night or a cluster of yellowish lights on a big junction or goods yard. As water, the railway track itself will gleam when it is between you and the moon. The great advantage of railways is that they are relatively few and far between and therefore less likely to be confused with each other. You will get to know the difference between main lines and subsidiary lines by the number of tracks and the tendency for main lines will be broad sweeps, while the subsidiary lines will follow tighter curves.

(d) *Roads*

Roads can be very confusing, because there are often many more on the ground than are marked on your map, especially a half million, and some-times a subsidiary road shows up much better than a main road. However, a route nationale, lined with poplars and driving practically straight across the country, may be very useful, and you can find your way to a town or village by the way the roads converge on it. The area north of Orleans is very open and flat and one is tempted to rely too much on roads, but they are very confusing, for the reasons given above. In general terms it is wiser to use roads as a check on other landmarks rather than as main landmarks in themselves and very often a quarter million map will be more helpful in giving the appearance of a road than a half million. If roads, railways and streams are running parallel, you should always notice in which order they lie – running from north to south or east to west. The presence of a road may be indicated from a distance by the headlights of cars moving along.

(e) *Large Towns*

Anything coming up on your track which looks like a large town or an industrial centre should be avoided on principle, in case there is flak there. This is especially true if you are not sure just where you are. This is a pity of course, because large towns are very good landmarks, but as with the coast, a town may be identified from a distance by flying round it out of range. There is very often a stream or river flowing through a town and naturally roads and railways approach it from well-defined directions. Sometimes a town – for example, Blois – is well distinguished by woods nearby. By intelligent use of these clues there should be little difficulty in guessing which town it is and then confirming it by consideration of detail. The same remarks apply to villages, but a village is not easily identified off its own bat. Neighbouring landmarks will generally identify it.

## Map reading policy

23. Map reading policy is divided into two parts, (a) anticipatory map reading and (b) finding your position when you don't know it.

### (a) *Anticipatory map reading*
Anticipatory map reading is normal when you know your position roughly and are more or less on track. In two words you look at your map first and the ground afterwards. Look ahead of your position on the map, decide what the next good landmark will be and keep your eye open until it turns up. In practice, it is as well to look out for landmarks on your track, to port of your track and to starboard of your track and wait with an open mind for any of the three to turn up. When choosing a landmark of this sort, have a look round your map to see if there is anything else at all similar with which it might be confused.

### (b) *Finding your position when you don't know it*
In this case you look at the ground first and your map afterwards. Assume that you fly on DR for a large part of your route, over fog or low cloud, and that when you reach better weather and can see the ground you have not the faintest idea where you are. On a still night your DR will prove to have been very accurate and on a windy night less accurate, but still the area in which you may be will be limited. Have faith in your DR and start using a small area of map where you should be on E[stimated] T[ime of] A[rrival]. Find on the ground a noteworthy landmark, such as a railway junction, a forest or river, and circle that until you have found it on your map. Then, as I said before, check it with a second and even a third neighbouring land-mark before you set course. If you find that you are still off track, it may be best to fly to your track at the nearest point before setting course again. If you try to be a clever boy and set a new course from your known position to your track at some distant point, you may get into trouble, but with experience you will learn how much you can trust your own arithmetic and navigational sense.

## Target area procedure

24. On approaching the target area, fish out your target map, refresh your memory of the letters and do your cockpit drill. This involves switching on the fuselage tank, putting the signalling lamp to 'Morse', pushing down your arm rests putting the mixture control back and generally waking yourself up. Don't be lured away from your navigation the siren call of stray lights. You should aim to find the field without depending on lights or to find some positive landmark within two miles of the field from which you will see the light. If you don't see the light on ETA, circle and look for it. One operation was ruined because the pilot ran straight over the field twice but did not see the light because the signal was given directly beneath him and he failed to see it because he did not circle. Once you have seen the light, identify the letter positively. If the letter is not correct, or if

there is any irregularity in the flare path, or if the field is not the one you expected, you are in NO circumstances to land. There have been cases when the Germans have tried to make a Lysander land, but where the pilot has got away with it by following this very strict rule. In one case where this rule was disobeyed, the pilot came home with thirty bullet holes in his aircraft and one in his neck, and only escaped with his life because he landed far from the flare path and took off again at once. Experience has shown that a German ambush on the field will not open fire until the aeroplane attempts to take off, having landed. Their object is to get you alive to get the gen, so don't be tricked into a sense of security if you are not shot at from the field before landing. I repeat, the entire lighting procedure must be correct before you even think of landing.

## Landing

25. You will, of course, have practised landing…until you can do it without any difficulty. On your first operation you will be struck by the similarity of the flare path to the training flare path, and until you are very experienced you take your time and make a job of it. First notice the compass bearing of the line A-B, circle steadily in such a way that you approach light A [the agent's light] from about 300 ft., so that B and C [the up-wind lights] will appear where you expect them and so that you can approach comfortably Your approach should be fairly steep to avoid any trees or other obstacles and you should not touch down before light A or after a point 50 yards from it. Notice the behaviour of your slats on the way down and don't allow your speed to drop off too much. Use your landing light for the last few seconds by all means, except on the brightest moonlit nights, but switch it off as soon as you are on the ground. Taxi back to light A and stop facing between B and C with your wing tip over light A. While taxi-ing, you will conveniently do your cockpit drill for take-off, so that you are all set when you stop. At this point you may be in rather a flap, but don't forget any letters or messages you may have been given for the agent. Watch the turn about and as soon as you hear your 'OK', off you go.

## Take off

26. Generally it is worthwhile to pull out your boost control override and climb away as speedily as you safely can.

## The homeward journey

27. Don't forget that navigation on your homeward journey is just as important as on the way out, although you can afford to be slightly less accurate as you approach the coast if you are sure you are approaching it well away from Flak. There used to be a craze for coming out over the Channel Islands, instead of Cabourg. One pilot ascribed this to the magnetic influence of his whisky flask, which he put in his flying boot but in general it was due to a feeling that you could just point your nose in the direction of home. This of course won't do, and, for the sake of your passengers you should not get shot down on the way back. So navigate all the way there and back.

## Double Lysander pick-ups

28. The difficulty with a double operation is to arrange for both aircraft to carry out their pick-up within a short time, so that the agents may leave the field before any trouble starts. Normally a limit of 20 minutes is required for the entire operation. To achieve this, pilots must meet at a rendezvous from which they can quickly get to the target, but which is out of earshot of the target, as I said in the relevant paragraph in the first half of the notes. There is always a possibility that one aircraft may not arrive. Pilots are briefed before the operation as to whether they may land if they find they are alone at the rendezvous...

## Double operation – RT procedure

29. Don't forget that the German's wireless intelligence is probably listening with some interest to your remarks. So your RT procedure should be arranged afresh before each operation and no reference should be made to place names or landing and taking-off, or to the quality of the ground, unless this information is coded. For the same reason call signs are usually changed in flight so that although you may start off at Tangmere as Jackass 34 and 35, at the target you may be Flanagan and Allan. There is no need to talk to each other en-route, except where the leader of the operation is deciding to scrub and go home...

## Treble operations

30. Treble operations are conducted in the same way as double operations, except that ten minutes should be allowed for each aircraft, so that the total time of the operation may take half an hour. As in double operations, the leader should land first to ensure that the ground is fit and secure and the others should not land until he is airborne and gives them permission.

    The first treble operation carried out took nine minutes from beginning to end, but the procedure was unorthodox. The leader landed first and took off last, acting as flying control for the other two aircraft and parking off the flare path to the left of light A, where he was turned about simultaneously with the other two. This quicker method has been abandoned because of the additional risk of having two aircraft on the ground at the same time. During double and treble operations, the aircraft waiting to land should fly within sight of the field, but some way from it, to distract the attention of any interfering people on the ground, and these aircraft may profitably organise a diversion some miles from the genuine field.

## Hudson operations

31. These are similar to Lysander pick-ups. As each crew will evolve its own technique of cockpit drill and turning about, I will not make any suggestions, except that the crew drill should be carefully thought out and practised to save time and talk during the operation. Landing a Hudson, even on a good night, is difficult on an operational flare path and pilots should not be ashamed of themselves if they muff the approach the first time and have to go round again.

## Conclusion

32. Pick-up operations have long been outstanding for the good will which exists between pilots and agents, founded during the agents' Lysander training and continued before and after pick-ups. This is most important and all pilots should realise what a tough job the agents take on and try to get to know them and give them confidence in pick-up operations. This is not easy if you don't speak French and the agent doesn't speak English, but don't be shy and do your best to get to know your trainees and passengers and to let them get to know you. Finally, remember that Lysander and Hudson operations are perfectly normal forms of war transport and don't let anyone think that they are a sort of trick-cycling spectacle, for this conception has tended in the past to cut down the number of operations attempted.

# Annex B

# Air Supply to France[1]

| Date | Successful Sorties | | | | Tonnage of Stores | | | | Agents | | | |
|---|---|---|---|---|---|---|---|---|---|---|---|---|
| | From UK | | From Med | Total | From UK | | From Med | Total | From UK | | From Med | Total |
| | RAF | USAAF | | | RAF | USAAF | | | RAF | USAAF | | |
| 1941 | 22 | – | – | 22 | 1.5 | – | – | 1.5 | 37 | – | – | 37 |
| 1942 | 93 | – | – | 93 | 23 | – | – | 23 | 155 | – | – | 155 |
| Jan–Mar 1943 | 22 | – | – | 22 | 20 | – | – | 20 | 31 | – | – | 31 |
| Apr–Jun 1943 | 165 | – | 2 | 167 | 148 | – | 1 | 149 | 41 | – | 2 | 43 |
| Jul–Sep 1943 | 327 | – | 2 | 329 | 277 | – | 1 | 278 | 92 | – | 3 | 95 |
| Oct–Dec 1943 | 101 | – | 6 | 107 | 133 | – | 6 | 139 | 50 | – | 4 | 54 |
| Jan–Mar 1944 | 557 | 52 | 150 | 759 | 693 | 73 | 172 | 938 | 88 | 6 | 20+ | 114+ |
| Apr–June 1944 | 748 | 521 | 700 | 1,969 | 1,162 | 733 | 794 | 2,689 | 88 | 76 | 96 | 260 |
| July–Sep 1944 | 1,644 | 1,366 | 1,050 | 4,030 | 3,223 | 1,925 | 1,100 | 6,248 | 258 | 263 | 474 | 995 |
| Totals | 3,679 | 1,909 | 1,910 | 7,498 | 5,681 | 2,731 | 2,074 | 10,485 | 840 | 345 | 599+ | 1,784+ |

---

1    M R D Foot, *SOE in France,* Appendix C.

# Annex C
# Standard Loads Dropped to SOE

## 1. LOAD A. 12 Containers

6 Brens plus 1,000 rounds per gun, with spares and 48 empty magazines.
36 Rifles plus 150 rounds per gun.
27 Stens plus 300 rounds per gun, 80 empty magazines and 16 loaders.
5 Pistols plus 50 rounds per gun.
40 Mills Grenades and Detonators.
12 Gammon Grenades with 18 lbs. P.E., Fuse and Adhesive Tape.
156 Field Dressings.
6,600 rounds 9 mm. Parabellum. 20 empty Sten Magazines
3,168 rounds .303 Carton. 20 empty Bren Magazines

### For 15 containers add to the above:

145 lbs. Explosive and all accessories.
6,436 rounds .303 Carton. 40 empty Bren Magazines
6,600 rounds 9 mm. Parabellum. 20 empty Sten Magazines
228 Field Dressings.

### For 18 containers add to the above:

6,436 rounds .303 Carton. 40 empty Bren Magazines
6,600 rounds 9 mm. Parabellum. 20 empty Sten Magazines
228 Field Dressings.
For 24 containers double the quantity for 12 containers.

## 2. LOAD B. 12 *Containers*

9 Rifles plus 150 rounds per gun.
11 Stens plus 300 rounds per gun, 55 empty magazines and 11 loaders.
13,200 rounds 9 mm Parabellum. 40 empty Sten Magazines.
22,176 rounds .303 Carton. 140 empty Bren Magazines.
660 Field Dressings.
145 lbs. explosives with all accessories.

**For 15 containers add to the above:**

6,436 rounds .303 Carton. 40 empty Bren Magazines.
6,600 rounds 9 mm Parabellum. 20 empty Sten Magazines.
228 Field Dressings.

**For 18 containers add to the above:**

6,436 rounds .303 Carton. 40 empty Bren Magazines.
6,600 rounds 9 mm Parabellum. 20 empty Sten Magazines.
228 Field Dressings
For 24 containers double the quantity for 12 containers.

### 3. LOAD C 12 Containers

19,800 rounds 9 mm Parabellum. 60 empty Sten Magazines.
28,512 rounds .303 Carton. 180 empty Bren Magazines.
882 Field Dressings.

**For 15 containers add to the above:**

6,600 rounds 9 mm Parabellum. 20 empty Sten Magazines.
6,436 rounds .303 Carton. 40 empty Bren Magazines.
228 Field Dressings

**For 18 containers add to the above:**

6,600 rounds 9 mm Parabellum. 20 empty Sten Magazines.
6,436 rounds .303 Carton. 40 empty Bren Magazines.
228 Field Dressings
For 24 containers double the quantity for 12 containers.

### 4. LOAD D 12 Containers

8 Brens plus 1,000 rounds per gun. 40 empty Bren Magazines.
9 Rifles plus 150 rounds per gun. 64 empty Magazines.
9,504 rounds .303 Carton,
234 Field Dressings.
145 lbs. explosive plus all accessories.
4 Bazookas plus 14 Rockets per Bazooka.
40 Bazooka Rockets.

**For 15 containers add to the above:**

3,168 rounds .303 Carton. 20 empty Bren Magazines
78 Field Dressings.
145 lbs. explosive plus all accessories
9 Rifles plus 150 rounds per gun.

**For 18 containers add to the above:**

6,436 rounds .303 Carton. 40 empty Bren Magazines
156 Field Dressings.
40 Bazooka Rockets.
For 24 containers double the quantity for 12 containers.

**Notes**

PIATS, each weapon packed with 20 bombs and ten Gammon grenades, were often sent in lieu of bazookas, and in the maquis areas the American .30 Carbines with 350 rounds per gun replaced the rifle whenever possible. The Marlin 9 mm. S.M.G. similarly often took the place of the Sten. The few empty corners in these loads might well be filled up by tricolour armbands, which were widely distributed by both SOE and SAS. They were intended to provide the 'distinctive badge or mark' required under the Hague convention to establish a combatant's right to combatant status if he fell into enemy hands. The suggestion was SOE's; it may have saved a few lives. Certainly it did a lot of good to distant Maquisards' morale, by making them feel they belonged to the Allied expeditionary forces.

# Annex D
# RAF Command Organisation

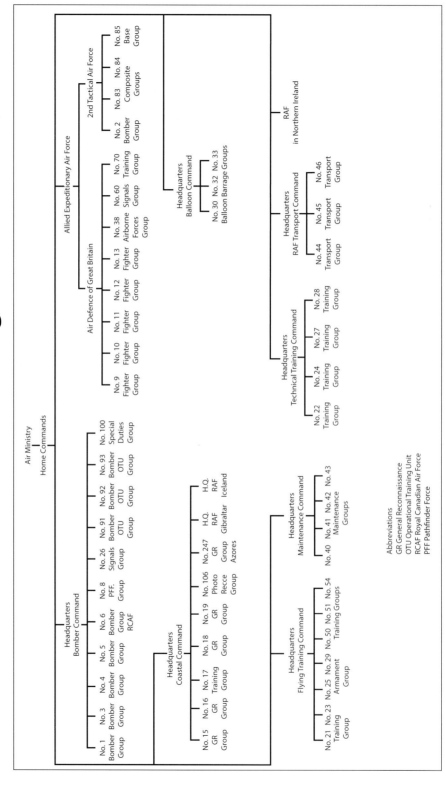

Air Ministry
Home Commands

**Headquarters Bomber Command**
- No. 1 Bomber Group
- No. 3 Bomber Group
- No. 4 Bomber Group
- No. 5 Bomber Group
- No. 6 Bomber Group RCAF
- No. 8 PFF. Group
- No. 26 Signals Group
- No. 91 Bomber OTU Group
- No. 92 Bomber OTU Group
- No. 93 Bomber OTU Group
- No. 100 Special Duties Group

**Headquarters Coastal Command**
- No. 15 GR Group
- No. 16 GR Group
- No. 17 Training Group
- No. 18 GR Group
- No. 19 GR Group
- No. 106 Photo Recce Group
- No. 247 GR Group Azores
- H.Q. RAF Gibraltar
- H.Q. RAF Iceland

**Headquarters Flying Training Command**
- No. 21 Training Group
- No. 23 GR Group
- No. 25 GR Group
- No. 29 Armament Group
- No. 50 Training Groups
- No. 51 Training Groups
- No. 54 Training Groups

**Headquarters Technical Training Command**
- No. 22 Training Group
- No. 24 Training Group
- No. 27 Training Group
- No. 28 Training Group

**Headquarters Maintenance Command**
- No. 40 Maintenance Groups
- No. 41 Maintenance Groups
- No. 42 Maintenance Groups
- No. 43 Maintenance Groups

**Allied Expeditionary Air Force**

**Air Defence of Great Britain**
- No. 9 Fighter Group
- No. 10 Fighter Group
- No. 11 Fighter Group
- No. 12 Fighter Group
- No. 13 Fighter Group
- No. 38 Airborne Forces Group
- No. 60 Signals Group
- No. 70 Training Group

**2nd Tactical Air Force**
- No. 2 Bomber Group
- No. 83 Composite Groups
- No. 84 Composite Groups
- No. 85 Base Group

**Headquarters Balloon Command**
- No. 30, No. 32, No. 33 Balloon Barrage Groups

**Headquarters RAF Transport Command**
- No. 44 Transport Group
- No. 45 Transport Group
- No. 46 Transport Group

**RAF in Northern Ireland**

Abbreviations
GR    General Reconnaissance
OTU   Operational Training Unit
RCAF  Royal Canadian Air Force
PFF   Pathfinder Force

476

# Annex E

# Order of Battle Middle East Command, 27 October, 1942[1]

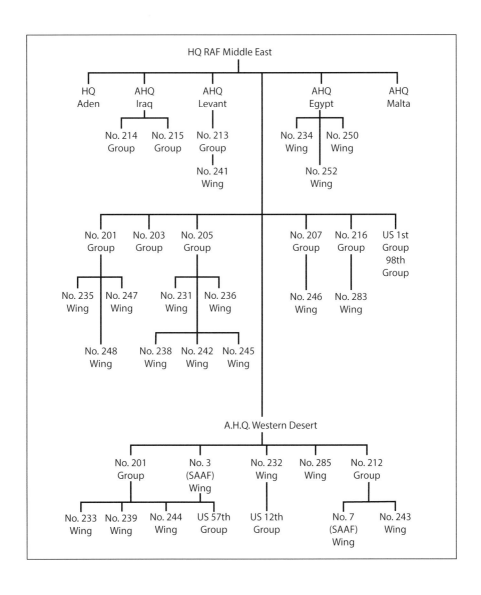

1    Denis Richards, *Royal Air Force 1939-45, Volume II*, (London: HMSO), 1954, Appendix X, p.382.

**Headquarters, Royal Air Force Middle East**

| | |
|---|---|
| 60 (SAAF) Detachment (Det) | Maryland |
| 162 Squadron | Lodestar, Wellington |
| 2 Photographic Reconnaissance Unit | Spitfire, Hurricane, Beaufighter |
| 1411 Meteorological (Met) Flight | Gladiator |

**Air Headquarters Aden**

| | |
|---|---|
| 8 Squadron | Blenheim |
| 459 Squadron RAAF (Det) | Hudson |
| Defence Flight | Hurricane |

**Air Headquarters Iraq**

| | |
|---|---|
| 237 Squadron | Hurricane |
| 244 Squadron | Blenheim, Vincent, Catalina |

**Air Headquarters Levant**

| | |
|---|---|
| 1413 Met Flight | Gladiator |
| 1438 Flight | Blenheim |
| 2 Photographic Reconnaissance Unit (Det) | Hurricane |
| 451 Squadron (RAAF) | Hurricane |

**Air Headquarters, Egypt**

**234 Wing**

| | |
|---|---|
| 889 (FAA) Squadron | Fulmar, Hurricane |

**250 Wing**

| | |
|---|---|
| 89 Squadron | Beaufighter |
| 94 Squadron | Hurricane, Spitfire |

**252 Wing**

| | |
|---|---|
| 46 Squadron | Beaufighter |
| 417 Squadron (RCAF) | Hurricane, Spitfire |

**Headquarters, Royal Air Force, Malta**

| | |
|---|---|
| 89 Squadron (Det), 227 Squadron | Beaufighter |
| 69 Squadron | Wellington, Baltimore, Spitfire |
| 126, 185, 249 Squadrons | Spitfire |
| 229 Squadron | Hurricane, Spitfire |
| 828 (FAA) Squadron | Albacore |
| 830 (FAA) Squadron | Swordfish |
| 1435 Flight | Spitfire |

**201 Group**

| | |
|---|---|
| 15 Squadron (SAAF) | Blenheim |
| 47 Squadron | Beaufort |
| 203 Squadron | Blenheim, Baltimore, Maryland |
| 230 Squadron | Sunderland, Dornier 22 |
| 252, 272 Squadrons | Beaufighter |
| 459 Squadron (RAAF) | Hudson |
| 701 Squadron (FAA) | Walrus |
| 821, 826 Squadrons (FAA) | Albacore |
| 815 Squadron (FAA) | Swordfish |

| | |
|---|---|
| 1 General Reconnaissance Unit | Wellington |
| Sea Rescue Flight | Wellington, Fairchild Ambulance |
| **235 Wing** | |
| 13 (Hellenic) Squadron, 47 Squadron (Det) | Blenheim |
| 459 Squadron (RAAF) (Det) | Hudson |
| **247 Wing** | |
| 203 Squadron (Det) | Maryland, Baltimore, Blenheim |
| 221 Squadron (Det) | Wellington |
| **248 Wing** | |
| 38, 221, 458 (RAAF) Squadrons | Wellington |
| 39 Squadron | Beaufort |
| **203 Group** | |
| 15 Squadron (SAAF) (Det) | Blenheim |
| 1412 Met Flight | Gladiator |
| **205 Group** | |
| Special Liberator Flight | Liberator |
| **231 Wing** | |
| 37, 70 Squadrons | Wellington |
| **236 Wing** | |
| 108, 148 Squadrons | Wellington |
| **238 Wing** | |
| 40, 104 Squadrons | Wellington |
| **242 Wing** | |
| 147, 160 Squadrons | Liberator |
| **245 Wing** | |
| 14 Squadron | Marauder, Boston |
| 227 Squadron (Det), 462 Squadron (RAAF) | Halifax |
| **207 Group** | |
| 16 Squadron | Wellington |
| 209, 321 Squadrons | Catalina |
| 34 Flight (SAAF) | Anson |
| 35 Flight (SAAF) | Blenheim |
| 1414 Flight | Gladiator |
| 1433 Flight | Lysander |
| **246 Wing** | |
| 41 Squadron | Hartebeest, Hurricane |
| **216 Group** | |
| 117 Squadron | Hudson |
| 173 Squadron | Various |
| 216 Squadron | Lodestar, Hudson, Bombay |
| 267 Squadron | Various |
| **283 Wing** | |
| 163 Squadron | Hudson |
| | |
| **1st Bombardment Group (Provisional)** | |
| 9 Squadron | B-17 Flying Fortress |
| Halverson Squadron | Liberator |

**US 98th Bombardment Group**

343, 344, 345, 415 Squadrons                    Liberator

**Air Headquarters, Western Desert**

1 Air Ambulance Unit                            DH 86

**3 (SAAF) Wing**

12 (SAAF), 24 (SAAF) Squadrons                  Boston

21 (SAAF) Squadron                              Baltimore

**232 Wing**

55, 223 Squadrons                               Baltimore

**US 12th Bombardment Group**

81, 82, 83, 434 Squadrons                       Mitchell

**285 Wing**

40 (SAAF), 208 Squadrons                        Hurricane

60 (SAAF) Squadron                              Baltimore

**Other Flights**

1437 Strategic Reconnaissance Flight            Baltimore

2 Photographic Reconnaissance Unit              Various

**211 Group**

6, 7 (SAAF) Squadrons                           Hurricane

**233 Wing**

2 (SAAF), 4 (SAAF), and 260 Squadrons           Kittyhawk

5 (SAAF) Squadron                               Tomahawk

**239 Wing**

3 (RAAF), 112, 250, 450 (RAAF) Squadrons        Kittyhawk

**244 Wing**

92, 145, 601 Squadrons                          Spitfire

73 Squadron                                     Hurricane

**US 57th Fighter Group**

64, 65, 66 Squadrons                            Warhawk

**212 Group**

**7 (SAAF) Wing**

80, 127, 274, 335 Squadrons                     Hurricane

**234 Wing**

1 (SAAF), 33, 213, 238 Squadrons                Hurricane

# Annex F
# Order of Battle Mediterranean Air Command, 10 July 1943[1]

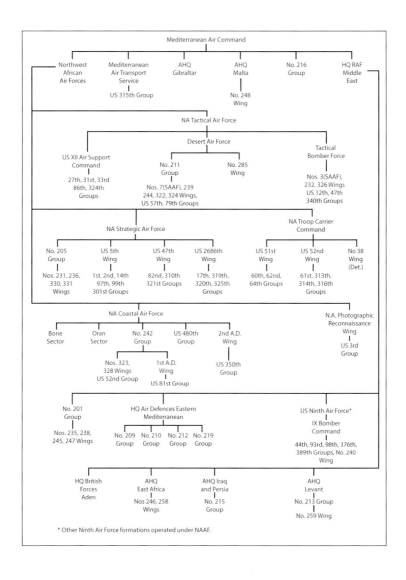

1    Denis Richards, *Royal Air Force 1939-45, Volume II,* (London: HMSO), 1954, Appendix XII, p.392.

**Mediterranean Air Transport Service**
**US 315th Troop Carrier Group**
| | |
|---|---|
| 34, 43 Squadrons | Dakota |

**216 Group**
| | |
|---|---|
| 17 (SAAF) Squadron | Junkers 52 |
| 28 (SAAF) Squadron | Anson |
| 117, 267 Squadrons | Hudson |
| 173 Squadron | Lodestar, Proctor, Hurricane |
| 216 Squadron | Dakota |
| 230 Squadron | Sunderland |

**AHQ Gibraltar**
| | |
|---|---|
| 48, 233 Squadrons | Hudson |
| 179 Squadron | Wellington |
| 202, 210 Squadrons | Catalina |
| 248 Squadron (Det) | Beaufighter |
| 544 Squadron (Det) | Spitfire |
| 813 (FAA) Squadron | Swordfish |
| 1403 Met Flight | Hampden, Gladiator |

**AHQ Malta**
| | |
|---|---|
| 23, 256 Squadrons (Det) | Mosquito |
| 40 (SAAF), 126, 185, 229, 249 Squadrons | Spitfire |
| 73 Squadron (Det) | Hurricane |
| 600 Squadron | Beaufighter (Night-Fighter) |
| 815 (FAA) Squadron (Det) | Albacore |
| 1435 Flight | Spitfire |

**248 Wing**
| | |
|---|---|
| 69 Squadron | Baltimore |
| 221 Squadron | Wellington |
| 108, 272 Squadron | Beaufighter |
| 683 Squadron | Spitfire |

**Northwest African Air Forces**
**Desert Air Force**
**285 Wing**
| | |
|---|---|
| 40 (SAAF) Squadron (Det) | Spitfire |
| 60 (SAAF) Squadron | Mosquito |
| 1437 Flight | Mustang |

**211 Group**
| | |
|---|---|
| 6 Squadron | Hurricane |

**7 (SAAF) Wing**
| | |
|---|---|
| 2 (SAAF), 4 (SAAF) Squadrons | Spitfire |
| 5 (SAAF) Squadron | Kittyhawk |

**239 Wing**
| | |
|---|---|
| 3 (RAAF), 112, 250, 260, 450 (RAAF) Sqn | Kittyhawk |

**244 Wing**
| | |
|---|---|
| 1 (SAAF), 92, 145, 417 (RCAF), 601 Sqns | Spitfire |

**322 Wing**

| | |
|---|---|
| 81, 152, 154, 232, 242 Squadrons | Spitfire |
| **324 Wing** | |
| 43, 72, 93, 111, 243 | Spitfire |
| **US 57th, 79th Fighter Groups** | |
| Six Squadrons | Warhawk |
| **US XII Air Support Command** | |
| **27th, 86th, Fighter-Bomber Groups** | |
| Six Squadrons | Mustang |
| **33rd, 324th Fighter Groups** | |
| Six Squadrons | Warhawk |
| **31st Fighter Group** | |
| Three Squadrons | Spitfire |
| 111th Tactical Reconnaissance Squadron | Mustang |
| **Tactical Bomber Force** | |
| 225 Squadron | Spitfire |
| 241 Squadron | Hurricane |
| **3 (SAAF) Wing** | |
| 12 (SAAF), 24 (SAAF) Squadrons | Boston |
| 21 (SAAF) Squadron | Baltimore |
| **232 Wing** | |
| 55, 223 Squadrons | Baltimore |
| **326 Wing** | |
| 18, 114 | Boston |
| **US 12th, 340th, Bombardment Groups** | |
| Eight Squadrons | Mitchell |
| **US 47th Bombardment Group** | |
| Four Squadrons | Boston |
| **North African Strategic Air Force** | |
| **205 Group** | |
| **231 Wing** | |
| 37, 70 Squadrons | Wellington |
| **236 Wing** | |
| 40, 104 Squadrons | Wellington |
| **330 Wing** | |
| 142, 150 Squadrons | Wellington |
| **331 Wing** | |
| 420 (RCAF), 424 (RCAF), 425 (RCAF) Squadrons | Wellington |
| **US 5th Wing** | |
| **2nd, 97th, 99th, 301st Bombardment Groups** | |
| Sixteen Squadrons | Flying Fortress |
| **1st, 14th Fighter Groups** | |
| Six Squadrons | Lightning |
| **US 47th Wing** | |
| **310th, 321st Bombardment Groups** | |
| Eight Squadrons | Mitchell |

**82nd Fighter Group**

Three Squadrons                                         Lightning

**US 286th Wing**

**17th, 319th, 320th Bombardment Groups**

Twelve Squadrons                                       Marauder

**325th Fighter Group**

Three Squadrons                                         Warhawk

**North African Coastal Air Force**

13, 614 Squadrons                                      Blenheim

36 Squadron                                            Wellington

253 Squadron                                           Hurricane

500, 608 Squadrons                                     Hudson

813 (FAA) Squadron (Det)                               Swordfish

821 (FAA ), 828 (FAA) Squadrons                        Albacore

1575 Flight                                            Halifax, Ventura

**US 480th Anti-submarine Group**

Two Squadrons                                          Liberator

**Bone Sector**

32, 87 Squadrons                                       Hurricane

219 Squadron                                           Beaufighter

**Oran Sector**

US 92nd Fighter Squadron                               Airacobra

**2nd Air Defence Wing**

153 Squadron                                           Beaufighter (Night-Fighter)

**US 350th Fighter Group**

Three Squadrons                                         Airacobra

**242 Group**

**323 Wing**

73 Squadron                                            Spitfire

255 Squadron                                           Beaufighter (Night-Fighter)

283, 284 Squadron                                      Walrus (Air Sea Rescue)

II/5, II/7 (French)                                    Kittyhawk, Spitfire

**328 Wing**

14 Squadron                                            Marauder

39, 47, 144 Squadrons                                  Beaufighter

52 Squadron                                            Baltimore

221 (Det), 458 (RAAF) Squadrons                        Wellington

**US 52nd Fighter Group**

Three Squadrons                                         Spitfire

**1st Air Defence Wing**

**US 81st Fighter Group**

Two Squadrons                                          Airacobra

**North African Troop Carrier Command**

**38 Wing**

295 (Det) Squadron                                     Halifax

296 Squadron                                           Albemarle

**US 51st Wing**

**60th, 62nd, 64th, Troop Carrier Groups**

| | |
|---|---|
| Twelve Squadrons | Dakota |

**US 52nd Wing**

**61st, 313th, 314th, 316th Troop Carrier Groups**

| | |
|---|---|
| Fifteen Squadrons | Dakota |

**North African Photographic Reconnaissance Wing**

| | |
|---|---|
| 60 (SAAF) (Det), 540 (Det) Squadrons | Mosquito |
| 682 Squadron | Spitfire |

**US 3rd Reconnaissance Group**

| | |
|---|---|
| 5th, 12th Squadrons | Lightning |
| 15th Squadron | Fortress |

**Headquarters, Royal Air Force Middle East**

| | |
|---|---|
| 148 Squadron | Liberator, Halifax |
| 162 Squadron | Wellington, Blenheim |
| 680 Squadron | Spitfire, Lightning, Hurricane |
| 1411, 1412, 1464 Met Flights | Hurricane, Gladiator |

**201 Group**

| | |
|---|---|
| 701 Squadron (FAA) | Walrus |

**235 Wing**

| | |
|---|---|
| 13 (Hellenic) Squadron | Blenheim |
| 227 Squadron (Det) | Beaufighter |
| 454 Squadron (RAAF) | Baltimore |
| 459 Squadron (RAAF) | Hudson |
| 815 Squadron (FAA) | Swordfish |

**238 Wing**

| | |
|---|---|
| 16 (SAAF) Squadron | Beaufort |
| 227 Squadron (Det) | Beaufighter |
| 815 Squadron (FAA) (Det) | Swordfish |

**245 Wing**

| | |
|---|---|
| 15 (SAAF) Squadron | Blenheim, Baltimore |
| 38 Squadron (Det) | Wellington |
| 1 General Reconnaissance Unit | Wellington |

**247 Wing**

| | |
|---|---|
| 38 Squadron | Wellington |
| 203 Squadron | Baltimore |
| 227, 252 Squadron | Beaufighter |

**Headquarters, Air Defences, Eastern Mediterranean**

**209 Group**

| | |
|---|---|
| 46 Squadron (Det) | Beaufighter |
| 127 Squadron | Hurricane, Spitfire |

**210 Group**

| | |
|---|---|
| 3 (SAAF), 33, 213, 274 Squadrons | Hurricane |
| 89 Squadrons | Beaufighter (Night-Fighter) |

**212 Group**

| | |
|---|---|
| 7 & 41 (SAAF), 94, 123, 134, 237 Sqns | Hurricane |
| 80 Squadron | Spitfire |
| 108 Squadron | Beaufighter (Night-Fighter) |

| | |
|---|---|
| 1563, 1654 Met Flights | Gladiator |
| **219 Group** | |
| 74, 238, 335, 336, 451 (RAAF) Squadrons | Hurricane |
| 46 Squadron | Beaufighter (Night-Fighter) |
| **United States Ninth Air Force** | |
| **IX Bomber Command** | |
| **44th, 93rd, 376th, 389th Bombardment Groups** | |
| Twenty Squadrons | Liberator |
| **240 Wing** | |
| 178, 462 (RAAF) Squadrons | Halifax |
| **12th, 340th Bombardment Groups** | See North African Tactical Air Force |
| **IX Fighter Command** | |
| **57th, 79th, 324th Groups** | See North African Tactical Air Force |
| **Headquarters British Forces Aden** | |
| 8 Squadron | Blenheim |
| 1566 Met Flight | Gladiator |
| Catalina Flight | Catalina |
| **Air Headquarters East Africa** | |
| 259 Squadron | Catalina |
| 262 Squadron | Catalina |
| 321 Squadron (Det) | Catalina |
| **246 Wing** | |
| 209, 265 Squadron | Catalina |
| **258 Wing** | |
| 1414 Met Flight | Lysander, Anson |
| **Air Headquarters Iraq and Persia** | |
| **215 Group** | |
| 208 Squadron (Det) | Hurricane |
| 244 Squadron | Blenheim |
| 1415 Met Flight | Gladiator |
| **Air Headquarters Levant** | |
| 208 Squadron | Hurricane |
| 1413 Met Flight | Gladiator |
| **213 Group, 259 Wing** | |
| 1565 Met Flight | Hurricane |

# Annex G

# Order of Battle Allied Expeditionary Air Force, 6 June 1944[1]

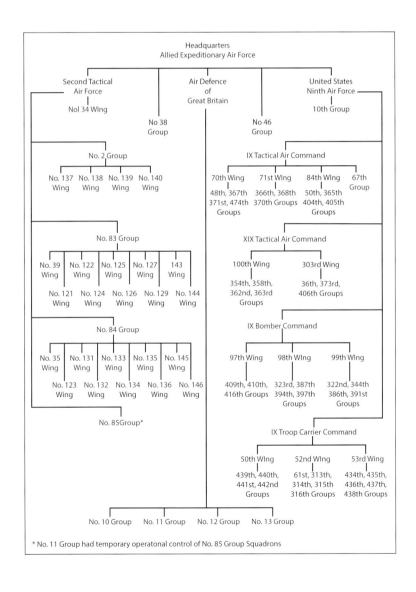

1    Denis Richards, *Royal Air Force 1939-45, Volume III*, Appendix XI, p.413.

**38 Group**

| | |
|---|---|
| 295, 296, 297, 570 Squadrons | Albermale |
| 190, 196, 299, 620 Squadrons | Stirling |
| 298, 644 Squadrons | Halifax |

**46 Group**

| | |
|---|---|
| 48, 233, 271, 512, 575 Squadrons | Dakota |

**Second Tactical Air Force**

**34 (PR) Wing**

| | |
|---|---|
| 16 Squadron | Spitfire |
| 140 Squadron | Mosquito |
| 69 Squadron | Wellington |

**Air Spotting Pool**

| | |
|---|---|
| 808, 885, 886 897 Squadrons (FAA) | Seafire |
| 26, 63 Squadrons | Spitfire |
| 1320 Flight | Typhoon |

**2 Group**

**137 Wing**

| | |
|---|---|
| 88, 342 Squadrons | Boston |
| 226 Squadron | Mitchell |

**138 Wing**

| | |
|---|---|
| 107, 305, 613 Squadrons | Mosquito |

**139 Wing**

| | |
|---|---|
| 98, 180, 320 Squadrons | Mitchell |

**140 Wing**

| | |
|---|---|
| 21, 464 (RAAF), 487 (RNZAF) Squadrons | Mosquito |

**83 Group**

**39 Reconnaissance Wing**

| | |
|---|---|
| 168, 414 (RCAF), 430 (RCAF) Squadrons | Mustang |
| 400 (RCAF) Squadrons | Spitfire |

**121 Wing**

| | |
|---|---|
| 174, 175, 245 Squadrons | Typhoon |

**122 Wing**

| | |
|---|---|
| 19, 65, 122 Squadrons | Mustang |

**124 Wing**

| | |
|---|---|
| 181, 182, 247 Squadrons | Typhoon |

**125 Wing**

| | |
|---|---|
| 132, 453 (RAAF), 602 Squadrons | Spitfire |

**126 (RCAF) Wing**

| | |
|---|---|
| 401 (RCAF), 411 (RCAF), 412 (RCAF) Squadrons | Spitfire |

**127 (RCAF) Wing**

| | |
|---|---|
| 403 (RCAF), 416 (RCAF), 421 (RCAF) Squadrons | Spitfire |

**129 Wing**

| | |
|---|---|
| 184 Squadron | Typhoon |

**143 (RCAF) Wing**

| | |
|---|---|
| 438 (RCAF), 439 (RCAF), 440 (RCAF) Squadrons | Typhoon |

**144 (RCAF) Wing**

| | |
|---|---|
| 441 (RCAF), 442 (RCAF), 443 (RCAF) Squadrons | Spitfire |

**84 Group**

**35 Reconnaissance Wing**

| | |
|---|---|
| 2, 268 Squadrons | Mustang |
| 4 Squadron | Spitfire |

**123 Wing**

| | |
|---|---|
| 198, 609 Squadrons | Typhoon |

**131 Wing**

| | |
|---|---|
| 302, 308, 317 Squadrons | Spitfire |

**132 Wing**

| | |
|---|---|
| 66, 331, 332 Squadrons | Spitfire |

**133 Wing**

| | |
|---|---|
| 129, 306, 315 Squadrons | Mustang |

**134 Wing**

| | |
|---|---|
| 310, 312, 313 Squadrons | Spitfire |

**135 Wing**

| | |
|---|---|
| 222, 349, 485 (RNZAF) Squadrons | Spitfire |

**136 Wing**

| | |
|---|---|
| 164, 183 Squadrons | Typhoon |

**145 Wing**

| | |
|---|---|
| 329, 340, 341 Squadrons | Spitfire |

**146 Wing**

| | |
|---|---|
| 193, 197, 257, 266 Squadrons | Typhoon |

**85 Group**

| | |
|---|---|
| 56, 91, 124, 322 Squadrons | Spitfire |
| 3, 486 (RNZAF) Squadrons | Tempest |
| 29, 264, 409 (RCAF), 488 (RNZAF), 604 Squadrons | Mosquito (Night-Fighter) |

**Air Defence of Great Britain**

**10 Group**

| | |
|---|---|
| 1, 41, 126, 131, 165, 610, 616 Squadrons | Spitfire |
| 263 Squadron | Typhoon |
| 151 Squadron | Mosquito (Night-Fighter) |
| 68, 406 (RCAF) Squadrons | Beaufighter (Night-Fighter) |
| 276 (Air Sea Rescue) Squadron | Spitfire, Warwick, Walrus |
| 1449 Flight | Hurricane |

**11 Group**

| | |
|---|---|
| 33, 64, 74, 80, 127, 130, 229, 234, 274 Squadrons | Spitfire |
| 303, 345, 350, 402 (RCAF), 501, 611 Squadrons | Spitfire |
| 137 Squadron | Typhoon |
| 96, 125, 219, 456 (RAAF) Squadrons | Mosquito (Night-Fighter) |
| 418 (RCAF) 605 Squadrons | Mosquito (Intruder) |
| 275, 277, 278 (Air Sea Rescue) Squadrons | Spitfire, Warwick, Walrus |

**12 Group**

| | |
|---|---|
| 316 Squadron | Mustang |
| 504 Squadron | Spitfire |
| 25, 307 Squadrons | Mosquito (Night-Fighter) |
| Fighter Interception Unit | Beaufighter, Mosquito |

**13 Group**

| | |
|---|---|
| 118 Squadron | Spitfire |
| 309 Squadron | Hurricane |

**United States Ninth Air Force**

**10th Photo Reconnaissance Group**

| | |
|---|---|
| Four Squadrons | Lightning |

**IX Tactical Air Command**

| | |
|---|---|
| 67th Tactical Reconnaissance Group | Mustang |

**70th Fighter Wing**

| | |
|---|---|
| 48th, 371st Groups – six Squadrons | Thunderbolt |
| 367th, 474th Groups – six Squadrons | Lightning |

**71st Fighter Wing**

| | |
|---|---|
| 366th, 368th Groups – six Squadrons | Thunderbolt |
| 370th Group – three Squadrons | Lightning |

**84th Fighter Wing**

| | |
|---|---|
| 50th, 365th, 404th, 405th Groups – twelve Squadrons | Thunderbolt |

**XIX Tactical Air Command**

**100th Fighter Wing**

| | |
|---|---|
| 354th, 363rd Groups – six Squadrons | Mustang |
| 358th, 362nd Groups – six Squadrons | Thunderbolt |

**303rd Fighter Wing**

| | |
|---|---|
| 36th, 373rd 406th Groups – nine Squadrons | Thunderbolt |
| Three Night-Fighter Squadrons | Havoc, Black Widow |

**IX Bomber Command**

| | |
|---|---|
| 1st Pathfinder Squadron | Marauder |

**97th Bombardment Wing (Light)**

| | |
|---|---|
| 409th, 410th, 416th Groups – twelve Squadrons | Havoc |
| 323rd, 387th, 394th, 397th Groups – sixteen Squadrons | Marauder |

**99th Bombardment Wing (Medium)**

| | |
|---|---|
| 322nd, 344th, 386th, 391st Groups – sixteen Squadrons | Marauder |

**IX Troop Carrier Command**

**Pathfinder Unit**

| | |
|---|---|
| 50th Troop Carrier Wing | Dakota |

**439th, 440th, 441st, 442nd Groups**

| | |
|---|---|
| Sixteen Squadrons | Dakota |

**52nd Troop Carrier Wing**

**61st, 313th, 314th, 315th 316th Groups**

| | |
|---|---|
| Eighteen Squadrons | Dakota |

**53rd Troop Carrier Wing**

**434th, 435th, 436th, 437th 438th Groups**

| | |
|---|---|
| Twenty Squadrons | Dakota |

# Annex H
# Air Command South-East Asia, 1 July 1944[1]

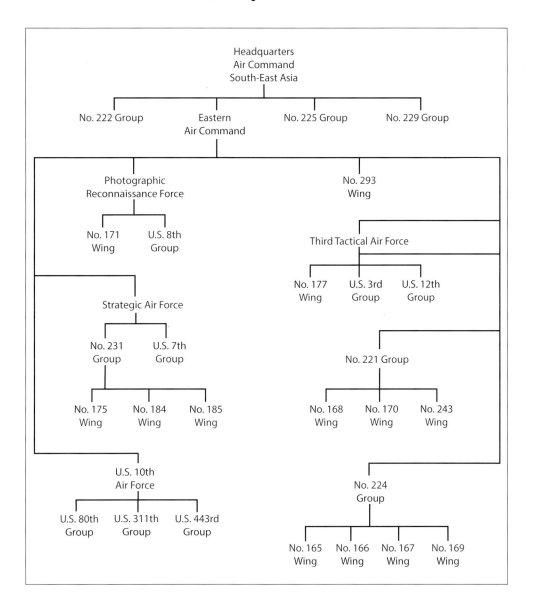

1    Denis Richards, *Royal Air Force 1939-45*, Appendix XII, p.419

**Air Command, South-East Asia**

| | |
|---|---|
| 357 (Special Duties) Squadron | Hudson, Liberator |
| 628 (Special Duties) Squadron | Catalina |

**222 Group**

| | |
|---|---|
| 17, 273 Squadron | |
| 205, 209, 259, 262, 265, 321, 413 (RCAF) Squadrons | Spitfire |
| 230 Squadron | Catalina |
| 89 Squadron | Sunderland |
| 22 Squadron | Beaufighter (Night-Fighter) |
| 160 Squadron | Beaufighter (Torpedo-Bomber) |
| 217 Squadron | Liberator |
| 135 Squadron | Beaufort |
| 23 (SAAF) Squadron | Ventura |
| 8, 244, 621 Squadrons | Wellington |

**225 Group**

| | |
|---|---|
| 5 Squadron | Hurricane |
| 27, 47 Squadrons | Beaufighter |
| 200, 354 Squadrons | Liberator |
| 203 Squadron | Wellington |
| 191, 212, 240 Squadrons | Catalina |

**229 Group**

| | |
|---|---|
| 353 Squadron | Hudson |

**Eastern Air Command**

**293 Wing**

| | |
|---|---|
| 67, 155 Squadrons | Spitfire |
| 176 Squadron | Beaufighter |

**Photographic Reconnaissance Force**

**171 Wing**

| | |
|---|---|
| 681 Squadron | Spitfire |
| 684 Squadron | Mosquito, Mitchell |

**US 8th Photo Reconnaissance Group**

| | |
|---|---|
| 9th Squadron | Lightning |
| 20th Squadron | Warhawk |
| 24th Squadron | Liberator |

**Strategic Air Force**

| | |
|---|---|
| US 490th Bombardment Squadron | Mitchell |

**US 7th Bombardment Group**

| | |
|---|---|
| Four Squadrons | Liberator |

**231 Group**

**175 Wing**

| | |
|---|---|
| 99 Squadron | Wellington |
| 292 Squadron (Air Sea Rescue) | Warwick |

**184 Wing**

| | |
|---|---|
| 355, 356 Squadrons | Liberator |

**185 Wing**

| | |
|---|---|
| 159 Squadron | Liberator |

**United States Tenth Air Force**

**80th Fighter Group**

| | |
|---|---|
| 88th, 89th, 90th Squadrons | Warhawk |

**311th Fight-Bomber Group**

| | |
|---|---|
| 528th, 529th, 530th Squadrons | Mustang |

**443rd Troop Carrier Group**

| | |
|---|---|
| 1st, 2nd, 11th, 315th Squadrons | Dakota |

**Third Tactical Air Force**

**177 Wing**

| | |
|---|---|
| 31, 62, 117, 194 Squadrons | Dakota |

**US 3rd Combat Cargo Group**

| | |
|---|---|
| 9th, 10th, 12th Squadrons | Dakota |

**US 12th Bombardment Group**

| | |
|---|---|
| 81st, 82nd, 83rd, 434th Squadrons | Mitchell |

**221 Group**

**168 Wing**

| | |
|---|---|
| 60 Squadron | Hurricane |
| 81 Squadron | Spitfire |
| 84 Squadron | Vengeance |

**170 Wing**

| | |
|---|---|
| 1 (IAF), 11, 42, 113 Squadrons | Hurricane |
| 607, 615 Squadrons | Spitfire |

**243 Wing**

| | |
|---|---|
| 28, 34 Squadrons | Hurricane |

**165 Wing**

| | |
|---|---|
| 9 (IAF) Squadrons | Hurricane |
| 152 Squadron | Spitfire |

**166 Wing**

| | |
|---|---|
| 136 Squadron | Spitfire |
| US 459th Squadron | Lightning |

**167 Wing**

| | |
|---|---|
| 4 (IAF), 6 (IAF), 20 Squadrons | Hurricane |
| 8 Squadron | Vengeance |

**169 Wing**

| | |
|---|---|
| 211 Squadron | Beaufighter |

# Annex I
# First Tactical Air Force, RAAF

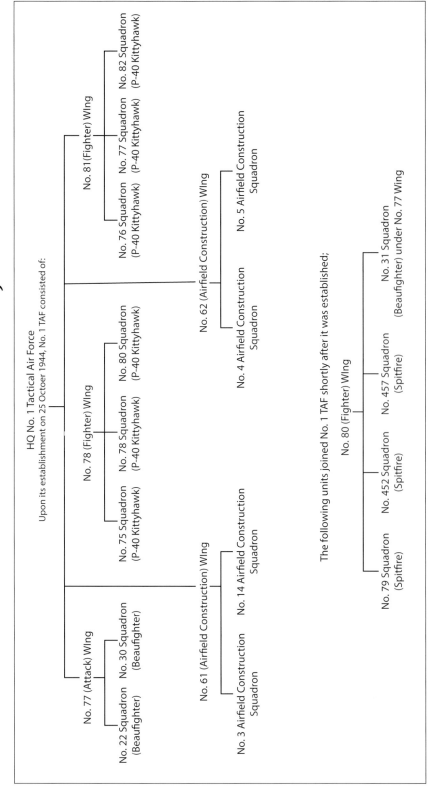

HQ No. 1 Tactical Air Force
Upon its establishment on 25 October 1944, No. 1 TAF consisted of:

No. 77 (Attack) Wing
- No. 22 Squadron (Beaufighter)
- No. 30 Squadron (Beaufighter)

No. 61 (Airfield Construction) Wing
- No. 3 Airfield Construction Squadron
- No. 14 Airfield Construction Squadron

No. 78 (Fighter) Wing
- No. 75 Squadron (P-40 Kittyhawk)
- No. 78 Squadron (P-40 Kittyhawk)
- No. 80 Squadron (P-40 Kittyhawk)

No. 62 (Airfield Construction) Wing
- No. 4 Airfield Construction Squadron
- No. 5 Airfield Construction Squadron

No. 81 (Fighter) Wing
- No. 76 Squadron (P-40 Kittyhawk)
- No. 77 Squadron (P-40 Kittyhawk)
- No. 82 Squadron (P-40 Kittyhawk)

The following units joined No. 1 TAF shortly after it was established:

No. 80 (Fighter) Wing
- No. 79 Squadron (Spitfire)
- No. 452 Squadron (Spitfire)
- No. 457 Squadron (Spitfire)
- No. 31 Squadron (Beaufighter) under No. 77 Wing

# Annex J

# Operational Aircraft of the Royal Air Force and Fleet Air Arm, 1939-1945[1]

**British Bomber Aircraft**
**1939-1941**

| Aircraft Name/Mark | Maximum Speed (i) | | Service Ceiling (ii) | Range plus Bombs (iii) | | Armament |
|---|---|---|---|---|---|---|
| | mph | at feet | feet | miles | lbs | |
| Battle I | 241 | 13,000 | 23,500 | 1,050 | 1,000 | 2 x .303 inch |
| Blenheim IV | 266 | 11,800 | 22,000 | 1,460 | 1,000 | 5 x .303 inch |
| Halifax I | 273 | 17,750 | 18,200 | 1,840 | 6,750 | 8 x .303 inch |
| | | | | Or 850 | 13,000 | |
| Hampden I | 254 | 13,800 | 19,000 | 1,885 | 2,000 | 8 x .303 inch |
| | | | | Or 1,200 | 4,000 | |
| Manchester I | 265 | 17,000 | 19,200 | 1,630 | 8,100 | 12 x .303 inch |
| | | | | Or 1,200 | 10,350 | |
| Maryland I | 278 | 11,800 | 26,000 | 1,210 | 1,500 | 8 x .303 inch |
| | | | | Or 1,080 | 2,000 | |
| Stirling I | 260 | 10,500 | 17,200 | 2,050 | 3,500 | 8 x .303 inch |
| | | | | Or 750 | 14,000 | |
| Wellington IC | 235 | 15,500 | 18,000 | 2,550 | 1,000 | 6 x .303 inch |
| | | | | Or 1,200 | 4,500 | |
| Wellington II | 247 | 17,000 | 20,000 | 2,450 | 1,250 | 6 x .303 inch |
| | | | | Or 1,400 | 4,500 | |
| Wellington IV | 229 | 13,000 | 20,000 | 2,180 | 500 | 6 x .303 inch |
| | | | | Or 980 | 4,000 | |
| Whitley V | 222 | 17,000 | 17,600 | 1,650 | 3,000 | 5 x .303 inch |
| | | | | Or 470 | 7,000 | |

---

1   Hilary Saunders and Denis Richards, *Royal Air Force 1939-45, Volumes I-III* (London: HMSO, 1954), Appendices.

**British Bomber Aircraft**
**1942-1943**

| Aircraft Name/Mark | Maximum Speed | | Service Ceiling | Range plus Bombs | | Armament |
|---|---|---|---|---|---|---|
| | mph | at feet | feet | miles | lbs | |
| Halifax II | 260 | 18,500 | 21,800 | 1,900 | 3,000 | 8 x .303 inch |
| | | | | 500 | 13,000 | |
| Halifax II-IA | 260 | 19,000 | 21,000 | 1,900 | 4,000 | 9 x .303 inch |
| | | | | 600 | 13,000 | |
| Halifax V | 260 | 18,500 | 21,000 | 1,900 | 4,500 | 9 x.303 inch |
| | | | | 650 | 13,000 | |
| Lancaster I and III | 270 | 19,000 | 22,200 | 2,350 | 5,500 | 9 x .303 inch |
| | | | | 1,000 | 14,000 | |
| Stirling III | 270 | 14,500 | 17,000 | 2,010 | 3,500 | 8 x .303 inch |
| | | | | 590 | 14,000 | |
| Wellington III | 255 | 12,500 | 19,500 | 2,200 | 1,500 | 8 x .303 inch |
| | | | | 1,540 | 4,500 | |
| Wellington X | 255 | 14,500 | 19,600 | 2,085 | 1,500 | 6 x .303 inch |
| | | | | 1,470 | 4,500 | |
| Mosquito IV | 380 | 14,000 | 33,000 | 1,620 | 2,000 | Nil |
| | | | | 1,450 | 4,000 | |
| Mosquito IX | 408 | 26,000 | 36,000 | 1,870 | 1,000 | Nil |
| | | | | 1,370 | 5,000 | |
| Baltimore III | 302 | 11,000 | 22,000 | 950 | 2,000 | 10 x.30 inch |
| | | | | | | 4 x .303 inch |
| Boston III | 304 | 13,000 | 24,250 | 1,020 | 2,000 | 8 x .303 inch |
| Mitchell II | 292 | 15,000 | 20,000 | 1,635 | 4,000 | 6 x .50 inch |
| | | | | 950 | 6,000 | |

**British Bomber Aircraft**
**1944-45**

| Aircraft Name/Mark | Maximum Speed | | Service Ceiling | Range plus Bombs | | Armament |
|---|---|---|---|---|---|---|
| | mph | at feet | feet | miles | lbs | |
| Halifax III | 280 | 13,500 | 20,000 | 1,985 | 7,000 | 9 x .303 inch |
| | | | | 1,030 | 13,000 | |
| Halifax VI | 290 | 10,500 | 20,000 | 2,160 | 7,400 | 9 x .303 inch |
| | | | | 1,260 | 13,000 | |
| Halifax VII | 280 | 13,500 | 20,000 | 2,215 | 5,250 | 9 x .303 inch |
| | | | | 985 | 13,000 | |
| Lancaster I, III and X | 280 | 11,000 | 20,000 | 2,250 | 10,000 | 8 x .303 inch |
| | | | | 1,660 | 14,000 | |
| Liberator VI | 270 | 20,000 | 27,000 | 2,290 | 4,000 | 10 x .50 inch |
| | | | | 990 | 12,800 | |
| Stirling III | 270 | 14,500 | 17,000 | 2,010 | 3,500 | 8 x .303 inch |
| | | | | 590 | 14,000 | |
| Wellington X | 255 | 14,500 | 18,250 | 1,885 | 1,500 | 6 x .303 inch |
| | | | | 1,325 | 4,500 | |
| Mosquito XVI | 408 | 26,000 | 36,000 | 1,795 | 2,000 | Nil |
| | | | | 1,370 | 5,000 | |
| Mosquito XX | 380 | 14,000 | 33,000 | 1,870 | 2,000 | Nil |
| | | | | 1,620 | 3,000 | |
| Baltimore V | 300 | 13,000 | 19,000 | 1,000 | 2,000 | 8 x .50 inch |
| | | | | | | 4 x .30 inch |
| Boston IV | 320 | 11,000 | 24,500 | 1,570 | 2,000 | 5 x .50 inch |
| | | | | 710 | 4,000 | |
| Marauder III | 305 | 15,000 | 28,000 | 1,200 | 4,000 | 11 x .50 inch |

**British Fighter and Fighter-Bomber Aircraft**
**1939-1941**

| Aircraft Name and Mark | Maximum Speed | | Service ceiling | Climb Time to Height | | Armament |
|---|---|---|---|---|---|---|
| | mph | at feet | feet | minutes | feet | |
| Beaufighter I F | 324 | 11,750 | 27,000 | 9.4 | 15,000 | 6 x .303 inch 4 x 20 mm |
| Blenheim IV F | 266 | 11,800 | 26,500 | 10 | 15,000 | 7 x .303 inch |
| Gladiator | 245 | 15,000 | 32,500 | 7 | 15,000 | 4 x .303 inch |
| Hurricane I | 316 | 17,500 | 33,200 | 6.3 | 15,000 | 8 x .303 inch |
| Hurricane II A | 342 | 22,000 | 37,000 | 8.2 | 20,000 | 8 x .303 inch |
| Hurricane II B | 342 | 22,000 | 36,500 | 8.4 | 20,000 | 12 x .303 inch |
| Hurricane II C | 339 | 22,000 | 35,600 | 9.1 | 20,000 | 4 x 20 mm |
| Spitfire I | 355 | 19,000 | 34,000 | 6.2 | 15,000 | 8 x .303 inch |
| Spitfire V | 375 | 20,250 | 38,000 | 7 | 20,000 | 2 x 20 mm 4 x .303 inch |
| Tomahawk I | 338 | 16,000 | 30,500 | 7.8 | 15,000 | 2 x .5 inch 4 x .303 inch |

**British Fighter and Fighter-Bomber Aircraft**
**1942-1943**

| Aircraft Name and Mark | Maximum Speed | | Service ceiling | Climb Time to Height | | Armament |
|---|---|---|---|---|---|---|
| | mph | at feet | feet | minutes | feet | |
| Beaufighter VI-F | 333 | 15,600 | 26,500 | 7.8 | 15,000 | 4 x 20mm 6 x .303 inch |
| Hurricane II-C | 339 | 22,000 | 35,600 | 9.1 | 20,000 | 4 x 20mm |
| Hurricane II-D | 316 | 19,000 | 33,500 | .75 | 2,000 | 2 x 40mm 2 x .303 inch |
| Kittyhawk I | 350 | 15,000 | 29,000 | 8.7 | 15,000 | 4 or 6 x .50 inch |
| Mosquito II | 370 | 14,000 | 35,000 | 7 | 15,000 | 4 x 20mm 4 x .303 inch |
| Mosquito VI | 378 | 14,000 | 32,000 | 9.5 | 15,000 | 4 x 20mm 4 x .303inch (4 x 500lb) |
| Mosquito XII (N/F) | 370 | 14,000 | 35,000 | 7 | 15,000 | 4 x 20mm |
| Mustang I | 390 | 8,000 | 32,000 | 8.1 | 15,000 | 4 x .50 inch 4 x .303 inch |
| Spitfire V-B (L/F) | 357 | 6,000 | 35,500 | 1.6 | 5,000 | 2 x 20mm 4 x .303 inch (1 x 500lb) |
| Spitfire IX | 408 | 25,000 | 43,000 | 6.7 | 20,000 | 2 x 20mm 4 x .303 inch (1 x 500/2 x 250lb bombs) |
| Typhoon I-B | 405 | 18,000 | 33,000 | 6.2 | 15,000 | 4 x 20 mm (2 x 1,000lbs or 8 x 60lb R.Ps) |

**British Fighter and Fighter-Bomber Aircraft**
**1943-1945**

| Aircraft Name and Mark | Maximum Speed | | Service ceiling | Climb Time to Height | | Armament |
|---|---|---|---|---|---|---|
| | mph | at feet | feet | mph | feet | |
| Meteor I | 445 | 30,000 | 42,000 | 15 | 30,000 | 4 x 20mm |
| Meteor III | 476 | 30,000 | 44,000 | 14 | 30,000 | 4 x 20mm |
| Mosquito XIII (N/F) | 370 | 14,000 | 33,500 | 6.75 | 15,000 | 4 x 20mm |
| Mosquito XXX (N/F) | 400 | 26,000 | 37,000 | 7.5 | 15,000 | 4 x 20mm |
| Mustang III | 442 | 24,500 | 41,500 | 10.5 | 20,000 | 4 x .50 inch (2 x 500lb bombs) |
| Spitfire IX (H/F) | 416 | 27,500 | 44,000 | 6.4 | 20,000 | 2 x 20mm and 4 x .303inch or 2 x 20mm and 2 x .50inch (1 x 500lb and 2 x 250lb bombs) |
| Spitfire IX (L/F) | 404 | 21,000 | 41,500 | 6.4 | 20,000 | 2 x 20mm and 4 x .303inch or 2 x 20mm and 2 x .50inch (1 x 500lb and 2 x 250lb bombs) |
| Spitfire XIV | 448 | 26,000 | 43,500 | 7 | 20,000 | 2 x 20mm and 4 x .303inch or 2 x 20mm and 2 x .50inch (1 x 500lb and 2 x 250lb bombs) |
| Spitfire XVI | 405 | 22,500 | 41,500 | 6.4 | 20,000 | 2 x 20mm and 4 x .303inch or 2 x 20mm and 2 x .50inch (1 x 500lb and 2 x 250lb bombs) |
| Spitfire XXI and XXII | 454 | 26,000 | 43,000 | 8 | 20,000 | 4 x 20mm (1 x 500lb and 2 x 250lb bombs) |
| Tempest V | 435 | 19,000 | 36,000 | 7.5 | 20,000 | 4 x 20mm |
| Thunderbolt I | 420 | 26,000 | 35,000 | 10.5 | 20,000 | 8 x .50inch (2 x 1,000lb) |
| Typhoon IB | 405 | 18,000 | 33,000 | 6.2 | 15,000 | 4 x 20mm (2 x 1,000lb or 8 x 60lb R.Ps) |

**British Coastal Command Aircraft**
**1939-41**

| Aircraft Name and Mark | Cruising Speed and Endurance (iv) | | Associated Bomb (or Depth Charge) load | Armament |
|---|---|---|---|---|
| | knots | hours | lbs | |
| Anson I | 103 | 5½ | 200lb | 6 x .303 inch |
| Beaufighter I C | 180 | 5 | - | 4 x .303 inch 4 x 20 mm |
| Beaufort I | 150 | 6 | 1,500 lb/1x 18-inch Torpedo | 4 x .303 |
| Blenheim IV F | 150 | 6 | - | 6 x .303 inch |
| Hudson I | 125 | 6 | 750 lb | 7 x .303 inch |
| Sunderland I | 115 | 12 | 2,000 lb | 7 x .303 inch |
| Vildebeest IV | 82 | 4.3 | 1,000lb/1 x 18-inch Torpedo | 2 x .303 inch |
| Wellington I C | 125 | 10.6 | 1,500lb | 6 x .303 inch |
| Whitley V | 110 | 9 | 1,500lb | 5 x .303 inch |

**British Coastal Command Aircraft**
**1942-43**

| Aircraft Name and Mark | Cruising Speed and Endurance (iv) | | Associated Bomb (or Depth Charge) load lbs | Armament |
|---|---|---|---|---|
| | knots | hours | | |
| Catalina I | 100 | 17.6 | 2,000 | 6 x .303 inch |
| | Or | 25 | Nil | |
| Catalina III | 100 | 14.5 | 2,000 | 5 x .303 inch |
| Fortress II | 140 | 10.7 | 1,750 | 9 x .50 inch |
| | Or | 12.9 | Nil | |
| Halifax II | 135 | 10.4 | 2,250 | 9 x .303 inch |
| | Or | 13.3 | Nil | |
| Hampden (T/B) | 120 | 7.25 | 1 x 18-inch torpedo | 6 x .303 inch |
| Hudson VI | 140 | 6.9 | 1,000 | 7 x .303 inch |
| Liberator I (VLR) | 150 | 16.1 | 2,000 | 4 x 20mm 6 x .303 inch |
| Liberator III | 145 | 11.6 | 3,000 | 6 x .50 inch |
| Liberator V | 150 | 15.3 | 1,500 | 6 x .50 inch |
| Wellington I-C | 120 | 9.3 | 2,000 | 6 x .303 inch |
| Whitley VII | 105 | 10.3 | 2,000 | 5 x.303 inch |
| Wellington VIII | 120 | 8.8 | 1,000 | 6 x .303 inch |
| Wellington XII | 140 | 8.3 | 2,400 | 7 x .303 inch |
| Sunderland II | 110 | 11.6 | 2,000 | 7 x .303 inch |
| Sunderland III | 110 | 11.9 | 2,000 | 7 x.303 inch |

**British Coastal Command Aircraft**
**1944 – 45**

| Aircraft Name and Mark | Cruising Speed and Endurance (iv) | | Associated Bomb (or Depth Charge) load llbs | Armament |
|---|---|---|---|---|
| | knots | hours | | |
| Catalina IV | 106 | 15.5 | 1, 500 | 2 x .50inch |
| Liberator III and V (VLR) | 150 | 16.1 | 2,000 | 3 x .50inch |
| Liberator VI | 138 | 10.5 | 3,500 | 6 x .50inch, 4x.303 inch |
| | Or | 12.5 | 2,000 | |
| Liberator VIII | 138 | 10.5 | 3,500 | 6 x .50inch, 4 x.303inch |
| Sunderland III and V | 110 | 13.5 | 2,000 | 7 x .303inch |
| | Or | 15 | 1,000 | |
| Warwick V | 164 | 11 | 2,000 | 3 x .50inch, 4 x .303inch |
| Wellington XIV | 140 | 10 | 1,500 | 7 x 303inch |

**Coastal Command Fighter and Strike Aircraft**
**1943-1945**

| Aircraft Name and Mark | Crusing Speed and Endurance | | Associated Bomb (or RP) load | Armament |
|---|---|---|---|---|
| | knots | hours | | |
| Beaufighter X (T/B) | 180 | 4.5 | 1 torpedo | 4 x 20mm |
| Beaufighter X (RP) | 180 | 4.5 | 8 x 25lb or 8 x 60lb RPs | 4 x 20mm |
| Beaufigher X (F/B) | 180 | 4 | 1 x 2,000lb or 2 x 500lb and 2 x 250lb | 4 x 20mm |
| Mosquito VI (F/B) | 210 | 3.5 | 4 x 250lb | 4 x 20mm, 4 x .303inch |
| Mosquito VI (F/RP) | 210 | 5 | 8 x 25lb or 8 x 60lb RPs | 4 x 20mm, 4 x .303inch |
| Halifax III | 145 | 10 | 5,500lb | 9 x .303inch |
| Wellington XIV | 140 | 9.5 | 1,700lb | 7 x .303inch |

**British Transport Aircraft**
**1939-1945**

| Aircraft Name and Mark | Still Air Range with Associated load | | Most Economical Cruising Speed in miles per hour | Maximum Speed in miles per hour | Armament |
|---|---|---|---|---|---|
| | miles | load | | | |
| Bombay | 1,500 | 10 troops | 120 at 10,000 feet | 159 at 10,000 feet | 2 x .303inch |
| | 330 | 24 troops | | | |
| Dakota C-47 | 1,910 | 26 troops with full equipment or 6,000lb freight | 160 at 10,000 feet | 220 at 10,000 feet | None |
| Commando C-46 | 1,600 | 35 troops with full equipment or 10,000lb freight | 183 at 14,000 feet | 267 at 15,000 feet | None |
| | | | 157 at 15,000 feet | | |
| Lysander | 1,410 | 500lb | 123 at 10,000 feet | 212 at 4,500 feet | 4 x .303inch |

**British Fleet Air Arm Aircraft**
**1939-1941**

| Aircraft Name and Mark | Fuel and Still Air Range at Most Economical Cruising Speed | | Most Economical Cruising Speed mph | Maximum Speed in mph | Armament |
|---|---|---|---|---|---|
| | galls | miles | | | |
| Fulmar | 155 | 820 | 170 at 10,000 feet | 253 at 10,000 feet | 8 x .303inch |
| Martlet III (Wildcat) | 136 | 1,150 | 166 at 15,000 feet | 330 at 19,500 feet | 4 or 6 x .50inch |
| Corsair | 192 | 673 | 251 at 20,000 feet | 374 at 23,000 feet | 6 x .50 inch |

| Aircraft Name and Mark | Still Air Range with Associated Bombload | | Most Economical | | |
|---|---|---|---|---|---|
| | miles | bombload | Cruising Speed mph | Maximum Speed in mph | Armament |
| Albacore | 521 | 1 Torpedo or 1,500lb | 105 at 6,000 feet | 163 at 4,800 feet | 2 x .303inch |
| Barracuda | 1,010 | 1 Torpedo Or 1,600lb | 138 at 6,000 feet | 249 at 9,000 feet | 1 x .303inch |
| Skua | 980 | 500lb | 157 at 15,000 feet | 212 at 15,000 feet | 5 x .303inch |
| Swordfish | 528 | 1 Torpedo or 1,500lb | 103 at 5,000 feet | 139 at 5,000 feet | 2 x .303inch |
| Walrus | 600 | 500lb or 2 x Depth Charges | 95 at 3,500 feet | 135 at 4,750 feet | 1 x .303inch |

i.  **MAXIMUM SPEED** was only possible for an extremely limited period. Apart from tactical manoeuvring, bomber and fighter aircraft in the main flew at speeds between 'most economical cruising' and 'maximum continuous cruising'. Varying with the different aircraft, these speeds were respectively between 55-80 percent and 80-90 percent of the maximum speed.

ii.  **SERVICE CEILING** The height at which the rate of climb has a certain defined low value (British practice 100 feet per minute). Ceilings quoted are for aircraft with full load.

iii.  **RANGE AND ASSOCIATED BOMB LOAD** The main purpose of this table is to give some idea of the relative performances of various aircraft. The figures quoted relate to aircraft flying at 'most economical cruising' speed at the specified height (i.e the speed and height at which the greatest range could be obtained). Allowance is made for take-off but not for landing, the range quoted being the maximum distance the aircraft could cover in still air 'flying to dry tanks'. Furthermore in the planning of operations a reduction range of about 25 percent had to be made for navigational errors, tactical manoeuvring, weather conditions and other factors.

iv.  **ENDURANCE** The time an aircraft can continue flying under given conditions without refuelling. This being a vital factor of Coastal Command operations an economical cruising speed, consistent with maximum safe endurance as determined under normal operational conditions is quoted.

v.  **ABBREVIATIONS** (F/B) Fighter Bomber; (F/RP) Fighter Rocket Projectile; (H/F) High Flying; (L/F) Low Flying; (N/F) Night-Fighter; (R/P) Rocket Projectiles; (T/B) Torpedo Bomber; (VLR) Very Long Range.

# Annex K

# Operational Aircraft of the German Air Force, 1939-45[1]

**German Bomber and Reconnaissance Aircraft 1939-41**

| Aircraft Name/Mark | Maximum Speed | | Service Ceiling | Range plus Bombs | | Armament |
|---|---|---|---|---|---|---|
| | mph | at feet | feet | miles | lbs | |
| Junkers Ju 87B[2] | 245 | 15,000 | 23,500 | 360 | 1,100 | 3 x 7.9mm |
| Henschel Hs 126 | 230 | 13,000 | 25,000 | 530 | 620 | 5 x 7.9mm |
| Dornier Do 17 | 255 | 15,000 | 21,000 | 1,440 | 1,100 | 7 x 7.9mm |
| | | | | Or 890 | 2,200 | 1 x 20mm |
| Heinkel He 111 | 240 | 14,000 | 26,000 | 1,510 | 2,200 | 7 x 7.9mm |
| | | | | Or 1,200 | 4,000 | 2 x 20mm |
| Junkers Ju 88 | 287 | 14,000 | 22,700 | 1,280 | 4,400 | 7 x 7.9mm |
| | | | | | | 1 x 20mm |
| Dornier Do 215 | 275 | 15,000 | 28,000 | 1,450 | 1,100 | 7 x 7.9mm |
| | | | | Or 900 | 2,200 | 1 x 20mm |
| Focke-Wulf Fw 200[3] | 240 | 13,600 | 20,500 | 2,150 | 3,600 | 3 x 13mm |
| | | | | 2700 | (Recce) | 3 x 15/20mm |

**German Bomber and Reconnaissance Aircraft 1942-43**

| Aircraft Name/Mark | Maximum Speed | | Service Ceiling | Range plus Bombs | | Armament |
|---|---|---|---|---|---|---|
| | mph | at feet | feet | miles | lbs | |
| Junkers Ju 87D | 255 | 13,500 | 18,500 | 720 | 2,200 | 4 x 7.9mm |
| Junkers Ju 88B3 | 333 | 20,000 | 25,000 | 1,280 | 2,200 | 2 x 13mm |
| | | | | | | 2 x 7.9mm |
| Junkers Ju 188 | 325 | 20,000 | 33,500 | 1,200 | 4,400 | 1 x 20mm |
| | | | | | | 2 x 13mm |
| | | | | | | 2 x 7.9mm |
| Heinkel He 111 | 240 | 14,000 | 26,000 | 1,510 | 2,200 | 7 x 7.9mm |
| | | | | | | 2 x 20mm |
| Heinkel He 177 | 305 | 20,000 | 21,000 | 2,650 | 2,200 | 5 x 13mm |
| | | | | 1,150 | 12,320 | 4 x 13/20mm |
| Focke-Wulf Fw 200 | 240 | 13,600 | 20,500 | 2,150 | 3600 | 3 x 13mm |
| | | | | 2700 | (Recce) | 3 x 15/20mm |

---

1   Hilary Saunders and Denis Richards, *Royal Air Force 1939-45, Volumes I-III* (London: HMSO, 1954), Appendices.

2   Stuka dive-bomber.

3   Known as the Condor or Kurier.

**German Bomber and Reconnaissance Aircraft**
**1943-45**

| Aircraft Name/Mark | Maximum Speed mph at feet | | Service Ceiling feet | Range plus Bombs miles lbs | | Armament |
|---|---|---|---|---|---|---|
| | mph | at feet | feet | miles | lbs | |
| Junkers Ju 88S | 370 | 26,000 | 35,000 | 700 | 1,980 | 1 x 13mm<br>1 x 7.9mm |
| Junkers Ju 188 | 325 | 20,000 | 33,500 | 1,200 | 4,400 | 1 x 20mm<br>2 x 13mm<br>2 x 7.9mm |
| Heinkel He 111 | 240 | 14,000 | 26,000 | 1,510 | 2,200 | 7 x 7.9mm<br>2 x 20mm |
| Heinkel He 177 | 305 | 20,000 | 21,000 | 2,650<br>1,150 | 2,200<br>12,320 | 5 x 13mm<br>4 x 13/20mm |
| Dornier Do 217E | 305 | 18,000 | 21,500 | 1,170 | 4,000 | 4 x 7.9mm |

**German Fighter Aircraft**
**1939-1941**

| Aircraft Name and Mark | Maximum Speed | | Service ceiling | Climb Time to Height | | Armament |
|---|---|---|---|---|---|---|
| | mph | at feet | feet | minutes | feet | |
| Messerschmitt Me 109 E | 355 | 18,000 | 35,000 | 6.2 | 16,500 | 2 x 7.9mm<br>2 x 20mm |
| Messerschmitt Me 109 F | 395 | 22,000 | 36,500 | 5.75 | 17,000 | 2 x 7.9mm<br>3 x 20mm |
| Messerschmitt Me 109 G | 400 | 22,000 | 38,500 | 6 | 19,000 | 2 x 7.9mm<br>3 x 20mm |
| Messerschmitt Me 110 D[4] A | 360 | 20,000 | 34,000 | 8.5 | 18,000 | 6 x 7.9mm<br>4 x 20mm |
| Focke-Wulf Fw 190 | 385 | 19,000 | 36,000 | 6.5 | 18,000 | 2 x 7.9mm<br>2 x 20mm |
| Junkers Ju 88 C6 | 295 | 14,000 | 24,200 | 13.8 | 16,500 | 7 x 7.9mm<br>3 x 20mm |

---

4   Marks E and F were of similar performance.

**German Fighter Aircraft**
**1942-1943**

| Aircraft Name and Mark | Maximum Speed | | Service ceiling | Climb Time to Height | | Armament |
|---|---|---|---|---|---|---|
| | mph | at feet | feet | mins | height | |
| Junkers Ju 88C5 | 347 | 20,000 | 30,200 | 10.3 | 18,500 | 6 x 7.9mm 3 x 20mm |
| Messerschmitt 109G | 400 | 22,000 | 38,500 | 6 | 19,000 | 2 x 7.9mm/13mm 3 x 20mm |
| Messerschmitt 110G | 368 | 19,000 | 34,800 | 7.3 | 18,000 | 6 x 7.9mm 4 x 20mm 1 x 37mm |
| Messerschmitt 210 | 370 | 21,000 | 29,000 | 11.8 | 19,000 | 2 x 20mm 2 x 13mm |
| Messeschmitt 410 | 395 | 22,000 | 30,000 | 11.5 | 19,000 | 2 x 20mm 2 x 13mm 2 x 7.9mm/ |
| Focke-Wolfe Fw 190A3 | 385 | 19,000 | 36,000 | 6.5 | 18,000 | 4 x 20mm 2 x 7.9mm |

**German Fighter Aircraft**
**1944-1945**

| Aircraft Name and Mark | Maximum Speed | | Service ceiling | Climb Time to Height | | Armament |
|---|---|---|---|---|---|---|
| | mph | at feet | feet | mins | feet | |
| Junkers Ju 88C5 | 347 | 20,000 | 30,200 | 10.3 | 18,500 | 6 x 7.9mm 3 x 20mm |
| Messerschmitt 109G | 400 | 22,000 | 38,500 | 6 | 19,000 | 2 x 7.9mm/13mm 3 x 20mm |
| Messerschmitt 110G | 368 | 19,000 | 34,800 | 7.3 | 18,000 | 6 x 7.9mm 4 x 20mm 1 x 37mm |
| Messerschmitt 210 | 370 | 21,000 | 29,000 | 11.8 | 19,000 | 2 x 20mm 2 x 13mm |
| Messeschmitt 410 | 395 | 22,000 | 30,000 | 11.5 | 19,000 | 2 x 20mm 2 x 13mm 2 x 7.9mm |
| Focke-Wolfe Fw 190D | 435 | 25,000 | 39,000 | 6.5 | 20,000 | 1 x 30mm 2 x 20mm 2 x 13mm |
| Messerschmitt Me 262 | 500 | 29,000 | 39,500 | 5 | 32,800 | 4 x 30mm/ 3 x 20mm or 6 x 30mm |
| Messerscmitt Me 163[5] | 560 | - | 40,000 | - | - | 2 x 30mm |
| Arado | 490 | 25,000 | 38,000 | 8 | 20,000 | 4 or 5 x 20mm |

---

5   Liquid rocket propulsion: Range 70 miles/endurance of 8.5 minutes.

# Annex L

# Operational Aircraft of the Italian Air Force, 1939-45[1]

**Italian Bomber and Reconnaissance Aircraft**
**1939-43**

| Aircraft Name/Mark | Maximum Speed | | Service Ceiling | Range plus Bombs | | Armament |
|---|---|---|---|---|---|---|
| | mph | at feet | feet | miles | lbs | |
| Savoia Marchetti Sm 79 | 255 | 13,000 | 21,500 | 1,570 | 1,100 | 3 x 12.7mm |
| | | | | 1,190 | 2,750 | 2 x 7.7mm |
| Savoia Marchetti Sm 81 | 210 | 15,000 | 24,500 | 1,030 | 2,200 | 6 x 7.7mm |
| | | | | 895 | 4,400 | |
| Savoia Marchetti Sm 82 | 205 | 7,000 | 17,000 | 2,200 | 3,200 | 1 x 12.7mm |
| | | | | | | 4 x 7.7mm |
| Cantieri Riuniti Cant Z.506 | 230 | 13,000 | 19,000 | 1,685 | 1,750 | 1 x 12.7mm |
| | | | | 1,465 | 2,640 | 3 x 7.7mm |
| Cantieri Riuniti Cant Z.1007b | 280 | 13,000 | 27,500 | 1,650 | 1,100 | 2 x 7.7mm |
| | | | | | | 2 x 12.7mm |
| Fiat B R 20 | 255 | 13,500 | 25,000 | 1,350 | 2,200 | 12 x 7.7mm |
| | | | | | | 1 x 12.7 mm |

**Italian Fighter Aircraft**
**1939-43**

| Aircraft Name and Mark | Maximum Speed | | Service ceiling | Climb Time to Height | | Armament |
|---|---|---|---|---|---|---|
| | mph | at feet | feet | minutes | feet | |
| Fiat C R 32 | 233 | 10,000 | 28,000 | 5.3 | 10,000 | 2 x 12.7mm |
| Fiat C R 42 | 270 | 13,100 | 32,000 | 5.5 | 13,000 | 2 x 12.7mm |
| Fiat G 50 | 300 | 14,500 | 32,000 | 6.4 | 15,000 | 2 x 12.7mm |
| Fiat G 55 | 380 | 20,000 | 38,000 | 5.8 | 20,000 | 2 x 12.7mm |
| | | | | | | 3 x 20mm |
| Aer Macchi C 200 | 310 | 15,000 | 32,000 | 6.25 | 15,000 | 2 x 12.7mm |
| Aer Macchi C 202 | 345 | 18,000 | 32,000 | 8.2 | 18,000 | 2 x 12.7mm |

---

1    Hilary Saunders and Denis Richards, *Royal Air Force 1939-45, Volumes I-III* (London: HMSO), 1954) various Appendices.

# Annex M

# Operational Aircraft of the Japanese Air Forces, 1942-45[1]

**Japanese Bomber and Reconnaissance Aircraft**
**1942-1943**

| Aircraft Name/Mark | Maximum Speed | | Service Ceiling | Range plus Bombs | | Armament |
|---|---|---|---|---|---|---|
| | mph | at feet | feet | miles | lbs | |
| Nakajima – Navy 96 'Nell 23' | 270 | 19,600 | 34,250 | 2,125 | 1,100 | 4 x 7.7mm<br>1 x 20mm |
| Mitsubishi – Army 97 'Sally 2' | 294 | 15,500 | 30,500 | 1,635 | 2,200 | 4 x 7.7mm<br>1 x 12.7mm<br>1 x 20mm |
| Nakajima – Army 100 'Helen 2' | 312 | 16,900 | 30,900 | 1,600 | 2,200 | 3 x 7.9mm<br>2 x 12.7mm<br>1 x 20mm |
| Nakajima – Navy 1 'Betty 22' | 283 | 13,800 | 30,500 | 3,075 | 2,200 | 4 x 7.7mm<br>4 x20mm |
| Nakajima – Navy 2 'Liz 11' | 270 | 16,100 | 29,100 | 2,990 | 7,240 | No data<br>1 x 12.7mm |
| Kawasaki – Army 99 'Lily 2' | 228 | 19,900 | 34,300 | 1,500 | 880 | 1 x 12.7mm<br>3 x 7.9mm |
| Nakajima Navy Tenzan 'Jill 12' | 327 | 15,100 | 35,400 | 1,740 | 1 x Torpedo | 2 x 7.7mm |
| Mitsubishi Navy-97 'Kate 12' | 225 | 8,000 | 27,500 | 645 | 1 x Torpedo | 4 x 7.7mm |
| Aichi Navy 99 'Val 22' | 281 | 20,300 | 33,600 | 965 | 550 | 3 x 7.7mm |

---

1 Hilary Saunders and Denis Richards, *Royal Air Force 1939-45, Volumes I-III* (London: HMSO, 1954), Appendices.

## Japanese Bomber and Reconnaissance Aircraft
## 1944-1945

| Aircraft Name/Mark | Maximum Speed | | Service Ceiling | Range plus Bombs | | Armament |
|---|---|---|---|---|---|---|
| | mph | at feet | feet | miles | lbs | |
| Mitsubishi Army 97 'Sally 2' | 294 | 15,500 | 30,500 | 1,635 | 2,200 | 4 x 7.7mm<br>1 x 12.7mm<br>1 x 20mm |
| Nakajima Army 100 'Helen 2' | 312 | 16,900 | 30,900 | 1,600 | 2,200 | 3 x 7.9mm<br>2 x 12.7mm<br>1 x 20mm |
| Nakajima Navy-1 'Betty 22' | 283 | 13,800 | 30,500 | 3,075 | 2,200 | 4 x 7.7mm<br>4 x 20mm |
| Nakajima Navy- 'Frances 11' | 367 | 17,200 | 35,500 | 2,430 | 1,875 | 2 x 20mm |
| Mitsubishi Army-4 'Peggy 1' | 346 | 18,700 | 30,100 | 1,840 | 1,875 | 4 x 12.7mm<br>1 x 20mm |
| Mitsubishi Army 100 'Dinah 3' | 420 | 10,700 | 40,600 | 1,730 | (Recce) | 1 x 7.7mm |
| Nakajima Navy Tenzan 'Jill 12' | 327 | 15,100 | 35,400 | 1,740 | 1 x 1,765<br>Torpedo | 3 x 7.7mm |
| Aichi Navy Ryusei 'Grace 11' | 350 | 19,700 | - | 1,242 | 1 x 1,765<br>Torpedo | 3 x 7.7mm |
| Aichi Navy Susei 'Judy 12' | 377 | 19,300 | 36,400 | 2,445 | 550 | 3 x 7.7mm |
| Aichi Navy Susei 'Judy 33 | 376 | 18,500 | 38,300 | 2,505 | 550 | 3 x 7.7mm |

## Japanese Fighter Aircraft
## 1942-1943

| Aircraft Name and Mark | Maximum Speed | | Service ceiling | Climb Time to Height | | Armament |
|---|---|---|---|---|---|---|
| | mph | at feet | feet | minutes | feet | |
| Nakajima Army 1 'Oscar 3' | 358 | 21,900 | 37,400 | 7.4 | 20,000 | 2 x 12.7mm |
| Kawasaki Army 3 'Tony 1' | 361 | 15,800 | 35,100 | 8.5 | 20,000 | 2 x 7.7mm |
| Nakajima Navy O 'Zeke 52' Or 'Zero' | 358 | 22,000 | 35,100 | 7.8 | 20,000 | 2 x 13.2mm<br>2 x 7.7/13.2mm |
| Kawasaki Army 2 'Nick 1' | 346 | 21,100 | 35,000 | 8 | 20,000 | 2 x 12.7mm<br>1 x 7.9mm<br>1 x 20mm |

## Japanese Fighter Aircraft
## 1944-1945

| | | | | | | |
|---|---|---|---|---|---|---|
| Mitsubishi Navy Raiden 'Jack 21' | 417 | 16,600 | 38,800 | 5.1 | 20,000 | 4 x 20mm |
| Nakajima Army-4 'Frank 1' | 427 | 20,000 | 38,800 | 5.8 | 20,000 | 2 x 12.7mm<br>2 x 20mm |
| Nakajima Navy Gekko 'Irving 11' | 333 | 19,700 | 32,740 | 12.1 | 20,000 | 5 x 20mm |
| Kawanishi Navy Shiden 'George 11' | 416 | 19,000 | 39,100 | 6.1 | 20,000 | 2 x 7.7mm<br>4 x 20mm |
| Nakajima Army-2 'Tojo 2' | 383 | 17,400 | 36,350 | 6 | 20,000 | 6 x 12.7mm<br>4 x 20mm |

# Annex N

# Airborne Operations – Air Movement Summary (Parachute drops and Glider Landings)

**Operation Tonga**
**Air Movement Summary**[1]
**5-6 June 1944**

**Parachute Sorties**
266 aircraft were detailed.
264 aircraft (99.2 percent) took off.
255 aircraft (95.8 percent) reported successful drops.
7 aircraft (2.6 percent) were missing.
4,512 troops were carried. 4,310 troops (95.5 percent) were dropped.
1,315 containers were carried. 1,214 containers (92.4 percent) were dropped.

**Glider Sorties**
98 combinations were detailed.
98 combinations took off (100 percent).
74 gliders or (75.5 percent) were successfully released.
57 gliders or (58 percent) landed on or near LZs.
22 gliders or (22.5 percent) were missing. Of 196 glider pilots 125 returned to UK, 4 were killed, 14 wounded and 53 missing.
611 troops were carried, 493 successfully released.
59 jeeps were carried, 44 successfully released.
69 motor-cycles were carried, 55 successfully released.
17 x 6-pounder guns were carried, 15 successfully released.
4 x 17-pounder guns were carried, two successfully released.
One bulldozer was successfully released.
One tank was not successfully released.

---

1    Air Publication 3231, *Airborne Forces*, p.131.

The following figures based on plots made by HQ 1st Airborne Division, give a concise, if rough picture of the accuracy of the drops. The success percentages however give no indication as to the military aspect as many of the troops, dropped outside the two-mile limit, contributed to the success of the operation. The percentages are based on all those dropped within one mile as being considered successful and those within two, miles as 50 percent successful.

## Glider Landings

|  | Landing Zone | | | | | Merville Battery | Total |
|---|---|---|---|---|---|---|---|
|  | X | Y | N | V | K | | |
| Detailed | 3 | 3 | 72 | 11 | 6 | 3 | 98 |
| On LZ | 3 | 1 | 46 | 0 | 2 | 0 | 52 |
| Within 1 Mile of LZ | 0 | 1 | 3 | 1 | 0 | 1 | 6 |
| Over 1 mile from LZ | 0 | 0 | 6 | 5 | 3 | 1 | 15 |
| Abortive | 0 | 1 | 17 | 5 | 1 | 1 | 25 |
| Percentage Success | 100 | 66 | 68 | 9 | 33 | 33 | 60 |

## 5th Parachute Brigade on 'N'

|  | 5 Bde HQ C 13 Bn | 7 Para Bn | 12 Para Bn | Total |
|---|---|---|---|---|
| Aircraft detailed |  |  |  | 131 |
| On DZ | 29 | 7 | 15 | 51 |
| Within 1 mile of DZ | 18 | 15 | 7 | 40 |
| Over 1 mile from DZ | 4 | - | - | 4 |
| Total landed |  |  |  | 95 |
| Missing and abortive |  |  |  | 36 |
| Percentage success |  |  |  | 71 |

## 3rd Parachute Brigade on 'K' and 'V'

|  | DZ 'K' 8 Para Bn | DZ V | | | |
|---|---|---|---|---|---|
|  |  | HQ Para Bn | 1 Can Para Bn | 9 Para Bn | DZ V Total |
| Detailed | 37 |  |  |  | 70 |
| On DZ | 6 | 1 | 7 | 8 | 16 |
| Within 1 mile of DZ | 2 | 1 | 5 | 8 | 14 |
| 1-2 miles of DZ | 4 | 3 | 6 | 6 | 15 |
| Over 2 miles from DZ | 21 | 1 | 16 | 0 | 17 |
| Missing | 4 |  |  |  | 8 |
| Percentage Success | 27 |  |  |  | 54 |

**Operation MARKET**
**Air Movement Summary (RAF)[2]**
**17-25 September 1944**

|  | Despatched | Successful | Unsuccessful | Casualties | Lost |
|---|---|---|---|---|---|
| **17 Sep** | | | | | |
| Pathfinders | 12 | 12 | - | - | - |
| Gliders | 358 | 319 | 39 | 6 | - |
| **18 Sep** | | | | | |
| Re-supply | 33 | 30 | 3 | 14 | - |
| Gliders | 296 | 272 | 24 | 30 | 8 |
| **19 Sep** | | | | | |
| Re-supply | 165 | 147 | 18 | 97 | 13 |
| Gliders | 44 | 30 | 14 | 9 | 11 |
| **20 Sep** | | | | | |
| Re-supply | 164 | 152 | 12 | 62 | 9 |
| **21 Sep** | | | | | |
| Re-supply | 117 | 91 | 26 | 38 | 23 |
| **22 Sep** | | | | | |
| Re-supply | 123 | 115 | 8 | 63 | 6 |
| **23 Sep** | | | | | |
| Re-supply | 21 | 21 | - | 4 | - |
| **24 Sep** | | | | | |
| Re-supply | 7 | 6 | 1 | 3 | 1 |
| **Totals** | | | | | |
| Pathfinders | 12 | 12 | - | - | - |
| Gliders | 698 | 621 | 77 | 45 | 19 |
| Re-supply | 630 | 562 | 68 | 281 | 52 |
| Overall | 1,340 | 1,195 | 145 | 326 | 71 |

**Glider Failures Not Due to Enemy action**

| Towing Failure | 28 |
|---|---|
| Tug Failure | 13 |
| Glider Failure | 5 |
| Navigation Failure | 2 |
| **Total** | **48** |

**Total British and American Aircraft and Gliders**

|  | *Despatched* | *Lost* |
|---|---|---|
| Aircraft | 12,997 | 238 |
| Gliders | 2,598 | 139 |

---

2   Air Publication 3231, Airborne Forces, p.172.

# Annex O

# Air Supply in South-East Asia February – August 1944[1]

1.  The major air transport operations carried out within the command were:
    (a) Routine supply-dropping missions to British detachments in the Chin Hills and at Fort Hertz, including the stocking of supplies at Tiddim.
    (b) The maintenance of 81st West African Division in the Kaladan Valley.
    (c) The maintenance of 7th Indian Division in Arakan between the 8th February and 6th March.
    (d) The maintenance of Special Force in Burma.
    (e) The move by air of 5th Indian Division and two-thirds of 7th Indian Division from Arakan to Imphal and Dimapur together with a proportion of their heavy equipment, including artillery.
    (f) The move by air of one brigade of 2nd British Division from Calcutta to Jorhat.
    (g) The maintenance of 17th Indian Division during its retreat along the Tiddim road.
    (h) The maintenance of IV Corps on the Imphal plain from the 18th April to 30th June, together with the evacuation of casualties and some 43,000 non-combatants from Imphal. The maintenance of part of XXXIII Corps in Assam.
    (i) The maintenance of the Americans and Chinese operating on the Northern and Yunnan fronts.
    (j) The maintenance of the Lushai Brigade.

2.  Tonnages landed, or dropped each month, excluding the maintenance of IV Corps (Operation STAMINA).

| Destination | Landed | Dropped | Total | Number of sorties |
|---|---|---|---|---|
| **Deliveries in Tons** | | | | |
| **February 1944** | | | | |
| NCAC US | 715 | 3,485 | 4,200 | 1,491 |
| Chin Hills | - | 662 | 662 | 1,520 |
| Kaladan | - | 1,074 | 1,074 | |
| Fort Hertz | 20 | 149 | 169 | |
| Special Force | - | 254 | 254 | |
| Arakan | - | 1,636 | 1,636 | |
| Total | 735 | 7,260 | 7,995 | |

---

1   Woodburn Kirby, *The War Against Japan, Volume 3,* (London: HMSO, 1961), Appendix 26.

| Destination | Landed | Dropped | Total | Number of sorties |
|---|---|---|---|---|
| **March 1944** | | | | |
| NCAC US | 910 | 3,620 | 4,530 | 1,542 |
| Chin Hills | - | 519 | 519 | 1,240 |
| Kaladan | 1 | 1,113 | 1,114 | |
| Fort Hertz | 37 | 138 | 175 | |
| Special Force | 107 | 929 | 1,036 | |
| Arakan | - | 263 | 263 | |
| Total | 1,055 | 6,582 | 7,637 | 2,782 |
| **April 1944** | | | | |
| NCAC US | 2,240 | 4,660 | 6,900 | 2,533 |
| Chin Hills | - | 1,255 | 1,255 | 1,897 |
| Kaladan | - | 1,316 | 1,316 | |
| Fort Hertz | 24 | 246 | 270 | |
| Special Force | 316 | 1,457 | 1,773 | |
| XXXIII Corps | - | 94 | 94 | |
| Total | 2,580 | 9,028 | 11,608 | 4,450 |
| **May 1944** | | | | |
| NCAC US | 1,850 | 3,350 | 5,200 | 1,868 |
| Kaladan | 34 | 1,047 | 1,081 | 1,072 |
| Fort Hertz | 10 | 139 | 149 | |
| Special Force | 50 | 929 | 979 | |
| Lushai Brigade | - | 405 | 405 | |
| XXXIII Corps | - | - | - | |
| Total | 1,944 | 6,045 | 7,989 | 2,940 |
| **June 1944** | | | | |
| NCAC US | 1,575 | 2,700 | 4,275 | 1,940 |
| Kaladan | - | 376 | 376 | 1,040 |
| Fort Hertz | 4 | 149 | 153 | |
| Special Force | 18 | 1,803 | 1,821 | |
| Lushai Brigade | - | 266 | 266 | |
| XXXIII Corps | - | 7 | 7 | |
| Total | 1,597 | 5,301 | 6,898 | 2,980 |
| **July 1944** | | | | |
| NCAC US | 5,425 | 3,575 | 9,000 | 3,898 |
| Kaladan | - | 130 | 130 | 1,682 |
| Fort Hertz | 30 | 248 | 278 | |
| Special Force | 58 | 2,132 | 2,190 | |
| Lushai Brigade | - | 387 | 387 | |
| XXXIII Corps | - | 1,235 | 1,235 | |
| Total | 5,513 | 7,707 | 13,220 | 5,580 |

| Destination | Landed | Dropped | Total | Number of sorties |
|---|---|---|---|---|
| **August 1944** | | | | |
| NCAC US | 8,100 | 4,450 | 12,550 | 5,499 |
| Kaladan | - | 58 | 58 | 1,631 |
| Fort Hertz | 23 | 175 | 198 | |
| Special Force | 35 | 478 | 513 | |
| Lushai Brigade | - | 327 | 327 | |
| XXXIII Corps | - | 1,981 | 1,981 | |
| 36th Division | 2 | 911 | 913 | |
| Myitkyina | 86 | - | 86 | |
| Total | 8,246 | 8,380 | 16,626 | 7,130 |
| Grand Total for 7 Months | **21,670** | **50,303** | **71,973** | **28,873** |

3.   Deliveries in long tons to IV Corps on the Imphal Plain during operation 'STAMINA', 18 April to 30 June:

| Period | Target | | Attainment | | Shortages on Target | | Average daily delivery |
|---|---|---|---|---|---|---|---|
| | Stocks | Reinforcements | Stocks | Reinforcements | Stocks | Reinforcements | |
| **18-30 April** | 3,180 | 3,250 | 1,926 | 1,479 | 1,254 | 1,771 | 148 |
| **May** | 13,423 | 7,750 | 6,040 | 5,011 | 7,383 | 2,739 | 194.8 |
| **June** | 10,890 | 7,500 | 10,858 | 6,071 | 32 | 1,429 | 362 |
| **Total** | 27,493 | 18,500 | 18,824 | 12,561 | 8,669 | 5,939 | - |

4.   Transport aircraft available to Fourteenth Army, February to August 1944:

| Month | Squadrons | Type of aircraft | Establishment | Total |
|---|---|---|---|---|
| **February** | RAF: 31, 62, 117, 194 | Dakota | 100 | 126 |
| | US: 1,2 | Dakota | 26 | |
| **March** | RAF: 31, 62, 117, 194 | Dakota | 100 | 152 |
| | US: 1,2, 27, 315 | Dakota | 52 | |
| **1-7 April** | RAF: 31, 62, 117, 194 | Dakota | 100 | 152 |
| | US: 1,2, 27, 315 | Dakota | 52 | |
| **18-30 April** | RAF: 31, 62, 117, 194, 216 | Dakota | 115 | 262 |
| | US: 1,2, 27, 315, 4, 16, 17, 18, 35 | Dakota | 117 | |
| | On loan from Transport Command | Commando | 30 | |
| **May** | RAF: 31, 62, 117, 194, 216 | Dakota | 115 | 232 |
| | US: 1,2, 27, 315, 4, 16, 17, 18, 35 | Dakota | 117 | |
| **1-15 June** | RAF: 31, 62, 117, 194, 216 | Dakota | 115 | 232 |
| | US: 1,2, 27, 315, 4, 16, 17, 18, 35 | Dakota | 117 | |
| **15-30 June** | RAF: 31, 62, 117, 194, | Dakota | 100 | 191 |
| | US: 1,2, 11, 315, | Dakota | 39 | |
| | US Combat Cargo Groups: 9,10, 12 | Dakota | 52 | |
| **July** | RAF: 31, 62, 117, 194, | Dakota | 100 | 191 |
| | US: 1,2, 11, 315, | Dakota | 39 | |
| | US Combat Cargo Groups: 9,10,11,12 | Dakota | 52 | |

| Month | Squadrons | Type of aircraft | Establishment | Total |
|---|---|---|---|---|
| **August** | RAF: 62, 117, 194, | Dakota | 75 | |
| | US: 1,2, 315, | Dakota | 39 | |
| | US Combat Cargo Groups: 9,10,11,12 | Dakota | 52 | 166 |
| | Non-operational: | | | |
| | RAF: 31 | Dakota | 25 | |
| | RCAF: 435, 436 | Dakota | 50 | |

5. Total Number of sorties flown:

| | | | |
|---|---|---|---|
| **Supply-dropping and landing (excluding operation STAMINA** | | 28,873 | |
| **Operation STAMINA:** | | | |
| Reinforcements | 360 | | |
| Supplies | 7,000 | 7,360 | |
| **Fly-in of troops to Central Front, March/April 1944:** | | | |
| 5th Division | 760 | | |
| 7th Division | 397 | 1,540 | |
| 2nd Division | 285 | | |
| Miscellaneous | 98 | | |
| **Total** | | **37,773** | |

6. Ground organization to handle supplies:

   (a) In February 1944 there were one British and five Indian air supply companies under command of Fourteenth Army. These were located at:

| | | |
|---|---|---|
| No.1 Company RIASC | Comilla | To supply XV Corps in Arakan |
| No. 5 Company RIASC | Chittagong | |
| No.2 Company RIASC | | |
| No.4 Company RIASC | Agartala | To supply the Chin Hills and Special Force |
| No.61 Company RASC | | |

   (b) In March Nos. 2 and 61 Companies moved to Sylhet to supply Special Force, leaving No. 4 at Agartala to supply IV Corps.

   (c) During operation STAMINA, Feni and Jorhat airfields were brought into use. These were served by No. 5 Company, leaving No. I Company at Comilla (later moved forward to Hathazari), and the existing companies were reinforced by additional sections.

   (d) During STAMINA these air supply companies had, in addition to their normal duties, to act as a link between the army and the R.A.F. station commander. This proved to be unsatisfactory. Later a Rear Airfield Maintenance Organization (R.A.M.O.), made up of a small headquarters with staff and service representatives and a variable number of service units according to the quantity and range of stores to be handled, was introduced.

7. Allocation of commodities to airfields: In order to facilitate stocking and the adjustment of priorities, and to economise in manpower and stores, the army made attempts to standardise the daily lift from individual airfields as far as was compatible with the availability of aircraft and the priority of demands from IV Corps. The air force preferred mixed commodity bases, on the grounds that aircraft stationed at a single commodity airfield would have to be

switched to another airfield if that particular commodity did not provide sufficient lift for all aircraft based there. A workable compromise was reached by the time 'Stamina' was in full swing. The final layout in use throughout June was:

## Single Commodity Airfields:

| | |
|---|---|
| Chittagong | Ammunition |
| Feni | Petrol Oil Lubricants (POL) |
| Sylhet | Supplies |

## Mixed Commodity Airfields:

| | |
|---|---|
| Agartala | Supplies, Ordnance stores, Signal stores, Mail |
| Comilla | Reinforcements, Medical, Ordnance, Ammunition |
| Jorhat | Canteen stores, Mail, Reinforcements, Ordnance stores |

# Annex P

# The Assessment by Fourteenth Army of Aircraft Required and the Airlift Available from 16 December 1944 to 15 May 1945. As calculated on 11 December 1944[1]

| Period | 14th Army Reqts2 | Available Airlift | | | Shortage in tons | Remarks |
|---|---|---|---|---|---|---|
| | | Imphal | E.Bengal | Total | | |
| 16–31 Dec | 705 | 238 | 420 | 658 | 47 | |
| 1–15 Jan | 688 | 300 | 388 | 688 | 0 | |
| 16–31 Jan | 813 | 340 | 473 | 813 | 0 | |
| 1–15 Feb | 763 | 460 | 303 | 763 | 0 | |
| 16 Feb–2 Mar | 906 | 460 | 446 | 906 | 0 | No aircraft avail for fly-in of formations (16 Feb to 17 Mar) |
| 3–17 Mar | 1,190 | 540 | 528 | 1,068 | 122 | |
| 18–31 Mar | 1,270 | 540 | 517 | 1,057 | 213 | |
| 1 Apr–15 May | 1,205 | 540 | 519 | 1,059 | 146 | |
| Thereafter | 1,200 | 400 | 300 | 700 | 500 | Approx Figures only from 15 May |

Note: The basic daily maintenance requirements within Fourteenth Army were calculated at this time to be:

| | |
|---|---|
| Infantry Division | 100 tons |
| Tank Brigade | 70 tons |
| Corps and LofC troops | 150–200 tons (depending on the number of divisions operating in forward areas) |
| RAF | 80–120 tons (depending on the number of squadrons operating in forward areas) |
| Royal Engineers (Works) | 90–120 tons |

1    Taken from Woodburn Kirby, *The War Against Japan*, Volume IV, Appendix 13.

2    Given in 'Long tons a day' These figures are requirements for maintenance. In addition, Fourteenth Army needed 5,000 sorties from the 16th February to 17th March for the fly-in of air-transported forces and, throughout the whole period, 21 sorties a day for the fly-in of reinforcements and fresh supplies (and the evacuation of casualties).

# Annex Q

# Maintenance by Air of Fourteenth Army During Phases 2 and 3 of 'EXTENDED CAPITAL', January to March 1945[1]

1.  Air bases used during 'EXTENDED CAPITAL' period January to March 1945:

    Imphal Group      Kangla, No. 2 RAMO.

                          Imphal, No. 1 RAMO.

                          Tulihal, No. 6 RAMO.

    Chittagong Group   Chittagong, No. 7 RAMO (from Agartala, opening on 2 February).

                          Hathazari, No. 5 RAMO.

                          Dohazari, No. 4 RAMO. (from Comilla, opening on 16 February).

    Comilla                 No. 3 RAMO. (This airfield was used for reinforcements only.)

| Formation | Airhead | Date Opened | Date Closed | Narrative |
|---|---|---|---|---|
| **IV Corps** | Kan | 16 Jan | 28 Feb | The Corps, consisting initially of 7th and 17th Divisions, 28 (E.A.) Brigade, the Lushai Brigade and 255 Tank Brigade moved up the Myittha valley to the Irrawaddy near Pakokku. The crossing of the Irrawaddy was forced by 7th Division, and 17th Division and 255 Tank Brigade then advanced to and captured Meiktila. The Corps was reinforced by 5th Division. |
| | Tilin | 31 Jan | 21 Feb | Maintenance of IV Corps during its advance to the Irrawaddy |
| | Sinthe | 10 Feb | 2 Apr | Maintenance of IV Corps during the crossing of the Irrawaddy at Nyaungu and during the advance on Meiktila; the subsequent maintenance of 7th Division, 5th Division and corps troops. On the 7 April Myitche passed under control of XXXIII Corps |
| | Myitche | 18 Feb | 7 Apr | |
| | Thabukton | 27 Feb | 3 Mar | Used for the fly in of 9th Brigade of 5th Division and maintenance of 17th Division and 255 Tank Brigade during the defence of Meiktila. On 21 March the airfield could no longer be used for air landing owing to enemy action. |

---

1    Taken from Woodburn Kirby, *The War Against Japan*, Volume IV, Appendix 19

| Formation | Airhead | Date Opened | Date Closed | Narrative |
|---|---|---|---|---|
| **IV Corps** | Meiktila | 4 Mar | Onwards | Used for the fly in of 9th Brigade of 5th Division and maintenance of 17th Division and 255 Tank Brigade during the Defence of Meiktila. On 21March the airfield could no longer be used for air landing owing to enemy action.<br>Airfield reopened on the 1 April and thereafter used for maintenance of IV Corps |
| **XXXIII Corps** | Taungtha | 28 Mar | Onwards | Airfield used for maintenance of 5th Division (less one brigade flown to Meiktila) and corps troops on their way to Meiktila. It was handed over to XXXIII Corps on 5 April. The Corps consisting of 20th, 2nd,, 19th Divisions, 268 Brigade and 254 Tank Brigade, advanced on a broad front from the Chindwin to the Irrawaddy and forced crossings at Myinmu, Ngazun, Kyaukmyaung and Thabeikkyin. Each formation followed a separate route, but the axes of all formations except 20th Division had converged by 18 January so that the corps (except for 20th Division) could be maintained from 18 January to 4 March from a Corps FMA formed at the Shwebo airhead |
| **HQ XXXIII Corps and Corps Troops** | Yeu | 10 Jan | 18 Jan | A corps FMA was established at Shwebo on 18 January. Reserve stocks were built up at Shwebo so that the advance could be resumed. Stocking began on 14 January at Yeu and was continued at Shwebo from 18 January. |
| | Shwebo | 18 Jan | 4 Mar | |
| | Sadaung | 11 Feb | 5 Apr | A subsidiary corps medical centre was opened at Sadaung to support 2nd Division from 12 February. The main corps medical centre at Shwebo supported 19th and 20th Divisions. |
| | Ondaw | 25 Feb | 5 Apr | The airhead at Ondaw was opened to receive stocks of POL [Petrol, Oil, Lubricants] and ammunition and engineer stores. On 4 March maintenance for the corps, less 19th Division was switched from Shwebo to Ondaw, which became the corps FMA. On the same date maintenance of 19th Division was switched from Shwebo to Singu |
| **20th Division** | Budalin | 22 Jan | 17 Feb | This airhead was used until the division crossed the Irrawaddy |
| | Allagappa | 17 Feb | 12 Mar | This airhead maintained the division in the bridgehead area south of the Irrawaddy at Myinmu |
| | Ywabo | 12 Mar | 20 Mar | |
| | Chaunggwa | 20 Mar | 26 Mar | |
| | Dwelha | 26 Mar | 9 Apr | |
| **2nd Division** | Shwebo | 18 Jan | 4 Mar | This division was maintained from the corps FMA at Shwebo and Ondaw till 12 March, by which time it had crossed the Irrawaddy and an airhead could be established south of the river. |
| | Ondaw | 4 Mar | 12 Mar | |
| | Ngazun | 12 Mar | 20 Mar | |
| | Tadau | 20 Mar | 30 Mar | On 31 March 19th Division took over Tadau airfield from 2nd Division |

| Formation | Airhead | Date Opened | Date Closed | Narrative |
|---|---|---|---|---|
| **19th Division** | Kawlin | 25 Dec | 5 Jan | |
| | Onbauk | 12 Jan | 20 Jan | |
| | Shwebo | 20 Jan | 4 Mar | Maintained from corps FMA |
| | Singu | 4 Mar | 17 Mar | |
| | Mandalay | 17 Mar | 4 Apr | |
| | Tadau | 31 Mar | 6 Apr | |

# Annex R

# Air Deliveries in Long Tons to Fourteenth Army and XV Corps January to May 1945[1]

| Air Base | Imphal Group | Agartala | Comilla | Chittagong | Akyab | Ramree | Total | Percentage of Total | |
|---|---|---|---|---|---|---|---|---|---|
| | | | | | | | | Landed | Dropped |
| **First period of four weeks (2–29 January 1945)** | | | | | | | | | |
| RAMOs | Nos. 1,2 & 6 | No.4 | No. 3 | Nos. 5 & 7 | - | - | | | |
| 14th Army | 501 | 4,678 | 772 | - | - | - | 5,951 | 100 | - |
| IV Corps | 532 | 2,765 | 3,029 | 70 | - | - | 6,396 | 64 | 36 |
| XXXIII Corps | 9,946 | 1,981 | 21 | - | - | - | 11,948 | 55 | 45 |
| RAF | 2,134 | - | - | - | - | - | 2,134 | 100 | - |
| Total | 13,113 | 9,424 | 3,822 | 70 | - | - | 26,429 | 70 | 30 |
| **Second period of four weeks (30 January–26 February 1945)** | | | | | | | | | |
| RAMOs | Nos. 1,2 & 6 | - | No. 3 | Nos. 4, 5 & 7 | - | - | | | |
| 14th Army | 451 | - | 227 | 5,117 | - | - | 5,795 | 97 | 3 |
| IV Corps | 4,038 | - | 403 | 7,425 | - | - | 11,866 | 69 | 31 |
| XXXIII Corps | 8,018 | - | 361 | 10,144 | - | - | 18,523 | 93 | 7 |
| RAF | 5,767 | - | - | - | - | - | 5,767 | 100 | - |
| Total | 18,274 | - | 991 | 22,686 | - | - | 41,951 | 87 | 13 |
| **Third period of four weeks (27 February–26 March 1945)** | | | | | | | | | |
| RAMOs | Nos. 1,2 & 6 | - | No. 3 | Nos. 4, 5 & 7 | No. 1 | - | | | |
| 14th Army | 1,567 | - | - | 8,252 | - | - | 9,819 | 97 | 3 |
| IV Corps | 3,965 | - | - | 9,915 | 1,083 | - | 14,963 | 78 | 22 |
| XXXIII Corps | 5,199 | - | - | 11,817 | - | - | 17,016 | 84 | 16 |
| RAF | 1,833 | - | - | 3,499 | - | - | 5,332 | 100 | - |
| Total | 12,564 | - | - | 33,483 | 1,083 | - | 47,130 | 87 | 13 |
| **Fourth period of four weeks (27 March–23 April 1945)** | | | | | | | | | |
| RAMOs | Nos. 2 & 6 | - | No. 3 | Nos. 4, 5 & 7 | No. 1 | No.2 | Total | | |
| 14th Army | 2,827 | - | - | 10,410 | 591 | - | 13,828 | 92 | 8 |
| IV Corps | 1,381 | - | - | 7,258 | 8,689 | - | 17,328 | 84 | 16 |
| XXXIII Corps | 2,478 | - | - | 11,371 | 643 | - | 14,692 | 87 | 13 |

---

1   Taken from Woodburn Kirby, *The War Against Japan*, Volume IV, Appendix 22.

| Air Base | Imphal Group | Agartala | Comilla | Chittagong | Akyab | Ramree | Total | Percentage of Total | |
|---|---|---|---|---|---|---|---|---|---|
| | | | | | | | | Landed | Dropped |
| RAF | 775 | - | - | 3,314 | 77 | - | 4,166 | 100 | - |
| Total | 7,461 | - | - | 32,353 | 10,200 | - | 50,014 | 88 | 12 |
| **Fifth period of four weeks (24 April–21 May 1945)** | | | | | | | | | |
| RAMOs | Nos. 6 | - | No. 3 | Nos. 2, 5 & 7 | No. 1 | No.2 | Total | | |
| 14th Army | 4,753 | - | 1,475 | 7,455 | 363 | - | 14,046 | 91 | 9 |
| IV Corps | 285 | - | - | 4,957 | 5,105 | 1,681 | 12,028 | 63 | 37 |
| XXXIII Corps | 511 | - | 5 | 9,610 | 2,142 | 528 | 12,796 | 85 | 15 |
| RAF | 354 | - | - | 5,413 | 69 | - | 5,836 | 100 | - |
| Total | 5,903 | - | 1,480 | 27,435 | 7,679 | 2,209 | 44,706 | 83 | 17 |
| **Grand Total** | | | | | | | **210,230** | **84.5** | **15.5** |

| Air Base | Chittagong Group | Akyab | Ramree | Total | Percentage of Total | |
|---|---|---|---|---|---|---|
| | | | | | Landed | Dropped |
| **First period of four weeks (2–29 January 1945)** | | | | | | |
| RAMOs | Nos. 4,5 & 7 | - | - | | | |
| XV Corps | 2,442 | - | - | 2,442 | 0.5 | 99.5 |
| **Second period of four weeks (30 January–26 February 1945)** | | | | | | |
| RAMOs | Nos. 4,5 & 7 | - | - | | | |
| XV Corps | 2,149 | - | - | 2,149 | 4 | 96 |
| **Third period of four weeks (27 February–26 March 1945)** | | | | | | |
| RAMOs | Nos. 4,5 & 7 | - | - | | | |
| XV Corps | 1,669 | - | - | 1,669 | 2.5 | 97.5 |
| **Fourth period of four weeks (27 March–23 April 1945)** | | | | | | |
| RAMOs | Nos. 4,5 & 7 | No.1 | No.2 | | | |
| XV Corps | 89 | 31 | 280 | 400 | 13 | 87 |
| **Fifth period of four weeks (24 April–31 May 1945)** | | | | | | |
| RAMOs | Nos. 4,5 & 7 | No.1 | No.2 | | | |
| XV Corps | 3 | 309 | 529 | 841 | 4 | 96 |
| **Grand Total** | | | | **7,501** | **5** | **95** |

# Annex S

# Maintenance of Fourteenth Army During Phase 4 of 'EXTENDED CAPITAL', April to May 1945[1]

1. The Fourteenth Army plan for Phase 4 of 'EXTENDED CAPITAL' – the advance on Rangoon – was that:
   (a) IV Corps, with two fully mechanised divisions (5th and 17th) and a tank brigade, with a standard division (19th) following up and securing the line of communications, was to advance as rapidly as possible from Meiktila down the main road and rail to Rangoon.
   (b) XXXIII Corps, consisting of two standard divisions (7th and 20th), 268th Brigade and a tank brigade, was to move down the Irrawaddy River towards Rangoon.
   Both corps were to be supplied mainly by air, but priority was to be given to the thrust by the motorised divisions of IV Corps, which were expected to move far more quickly than the standard divisions moving down the Irrawaddy.

## 1.  IV Corps

The most difficult problem facing the administrative staff of Fourteenth Army was how to maintain IV Corps (totalling altogether between 70,000 and 100,000 men and 8,250 vehicles) entirely by air during its advance over some 300 miles from Meiktila to Rangoon, in view of the fact that beyond Toungoo it would be outside the range of the Akyab air base and that the Ramree air base was not expected to be fully in operation until late in April.

An airlift had been allotted on the basis of 130 tons a day for each division and for corps troops, and 70 tons a day for a tank brigade, figures which could not be exceeded in any way. If for any reason air supply fell short or proved to be abortive on any single day, it could not be made up later on. The road transport at the disposal of IV Corps was two 30-cwt. and four 3-ton general purpose transport companies, and each division had one 3-ton company and one 15-cwt. company. Troops were to be maintained from forward airfields up to the maximum range of the available motor transport; outside that range, troops would have to be maintained by supply-dropping. Since this was wasteful, it was to be avoided as far as possible.

The normal sequence of events was to be:
   (a) The reconnaissance of a projected airhead by a party carried in a light aircraft, and then its construction.
   (b) The establishment of F.A.M.O. at the airhead (the size being determined by the role of the airfield).
   (c) The issue of supplies and stores to all troops within range of the available motor transport from the airhead, any surplus over daily maintenance being stocked as a reserve.

---

1    Taken from Woodburn Kirby, *The War Against Japan*, Volume IV, Appendix 23.

(d) Should the forward troops advance beyond the range of the available motor transport from the airhead, they would have to be maintained by reserves carried with them on their own transport, supplemented as necessary by supply-dropping until the next airfield on the line of advance was ready to receive transport aircraft.

(e) The opening of the next airfield.

This system was limited in its application by the following factors:

(i) Since the available air transport in S.E.A.C. was working at the highest possible rate, any maintenance lost on one day could not be made up on another.

(ii) With the exception of Meiktila and Toungoo, all the airfields which the corps could use during its advance were fair-weather and liable to become unserviceable in wet weather.

(iii) Owing to the tonnage which could be delivered daily being limited and to the short time that an airfield would be in use, it would not normally be possible to build up any appreciable reserves.

(iv) Since the available airlift was sufficient to supply only one division and a brigade by supply-dropping at any time, the rest of the corps had either to remain within the range of its motor transport from an airhead or to live on any reserves it had been able to put by.

(v) Owing to the need for changing loads and briefing pilots, a change from supply-dropping to air landing, or vice versa, could not be quickly undertaken. Changes from dropping to air landing had to be notified to C.A.A.T.O. by 4 p.m., and from air landing to dropping by noon, on the day previous to the desired delivery.

(vi) Reinforcements were held at Comilla only, and two aircraft a day were allotted to bring them forward. Since Meiktila was located beyond the maximum economic range of Dakotas operating from Comilla, the number of reinforcements which could be supplied to points farther south would be progressively reduced.

Despite its many drawbacks, the administrative plan drawn up on this basis proved in practice to be satisfactory, and supplies of ammunition and equipment for the various engagements during the advance were always adequate. To overcome delays caused by supply-dropping, forward troops had, however, often to be put on a reduced scale of rations since they had to carry the maximum number of days' subsistence in their own transport while between airheads. Towards the end of the advance heavy storms began earlier than usual in south Burma and almost all airfields south of Meiktila became unserviceable. The corps was then forced to subsist on supply-dropping at a net rate of 175 tons a day instead of the normal air-landed 460 tons a day. This meant that all troops had to be placed on half rations for some twenty-four days until the port of Rangoon could be opened for maintenance.

## 2.   XXXIII Corps

The problem of maintaining XXXIII Corps in its advance down the Irrawaddy towards Prome offered less difficulty. Up to and including Magwe, the corps was within economic range of transport aircraft operating from the Chittagong air base. An airlift of 460 tons a day, reduced to 410 tons after the 23rd April, had been allotted to the corps. The road system along the east bank of the Irrawaddy was good and there was adequate motor transport. Moreover, an Inland Water Transport (IWT) company with a lift of 140 tons a day and a radius of 50 miles was available and there was a possibility that this lift could be increased during April. Petrol could also be floated down the river in rafts made up of drums. It was planned that, until an airhead could be opened at Magwe, corps headquarters, corps troops, 268th Brigade, and 2nd Division (until it was flown out) were to be supplied by road from the Taungtha airhead, and that 7th Division was to be supplied from Myitche by road and by IWT. to Yenangyaung and beyond this point by road. Supplies for 20th Division, moving south-west from Meiktila towards Magwe and Prome, were to be flown in to a succession of airstrips in a similar manner as IV Corps. For any advance beyond Prome it would, however, be necessary for the corps to be allotted some of the airlift from the Akyab air base, since the forward troops would not only be beyond the range of motor transport from Magwe but also beyond the economic range of transport aircraft operating from the Chittagong air base.

3.  The airfields used by IV and XXXIII Corps during April and early May were:

| Formation | Airhead | Date Opened | Date Closed | Narrative |
|---|---|---|---|---|
| **IV Corps** | Meiktila | 1 Apr 45 | Remained in use throughout period | The corps consisting of 5th, 17th and 19th Divisions and 255 Tank Brigade was given the task of undertaking the advance in Phase 4 of 'Extended Capital' from Meiktila by road and rail to Rangoon. The 19th Division came under command on 5 April, and was maintained from Meiktila from 6 April. Dwehla and Kume airstrips were also used |
| | Tatkon | 20 Apr 45 | 22 Apr 45 | Maintenance of 17th Division and corps troops and topping up of 5th Division before action at Shwemyo Bluff |
| | Lewe | 23 Apr 45 | 30 Apr 45 | Maintenance of 17th Division |
| | Toungoo | 24 Apr 45 | Till end of period | Maintenance of 5th Division and corps troops, stocking of 17th Division for its advance on Pegu and maintenance of 19th Division from 26 April. |
| | Pyuntaza | 30 Apr 45 | 2 May 45 | Maintenance of 5th and 17th Divisions |
| | Payagyi | 2 May 45 | Till end of period | Maintenance of 5th Division and corps troops and topping up of 17th Division before action at Pegu |
| | Zayatkwin | 8 May 45 | 12 May 45 | Supplementary to Payagyi |
| | Rangoon (Mingaladoon) | 19 May 45 | - | |
| **XXXIII Corps** | Taungtha | 5 Apr 45 | 4 May 45 | During March it was decided that the corps, consisting of 7th and 20th Divisions, 268 Infantry Brigade and 254 Tank Brigade, would move south on the axis of the Irrawaddy. The Corps FMA was therefore moved from Ondaw to Taungtha when the airfield was over from IV Corps. Myitche, which was the airhead for 7th Division, was also taken over when the division came under command of XXXIII Corps. The airheads for the corps during its advance therefore were Taungtha and Myitche until Magwe was opened on 4 May |
| | Magwe | 4 May 45 | | |
| **20th Division** | Kume | 9 Apr 45 | 15 Apr 45 | |
| | Meiktila | 15 Apr 45 | 23 Apr 45 | |
| | Natmauk | 23 Apr 45 | 29 Apr 45 | |
| | Taungdwingyi | 29 Apr 45 | 2 May 45 | |
| | Ywataung | 2 May 45 | 5 May 45 | |
| | Prome | 5 May 45 | 23 Apr 45 | |

| Formation | Airhead | Date Opened | Date Closed | Narrative |
|---|---|---|---|---|
| **2nd Division** | Myingyan | 31 Mar 45 | 5 Apr 45 | * Closed when division flown out to India |
| | Taungtha | 5 Apr 45 | * | |
| **7th Division** | Myitche | 7 Apr 45 | 4 May | |
| | Magwe | 4 May | - | |

# Annex T

# Principal Air Commanders in the Second World War

|  | Date of Appointment |
|---|---|
| **Chiefs of Air Staff RAF** | |
| Marshal of the Royal Air Force Sir Cyril L N Newall | 1 September 1937 |
| Marshal of the Royal Air Force the Lord Portal of Hungerford | 25 October 1940 |

**HOME**

| **Bomber Command** | |
|---|---|
| Air Chief Marshal Sir Edgar Ludlow-Hewitt | 12 September 1937 |
| Air Marshal Sir Charles F A Portal | 3 April 1940 |
| Air Marshal Sir Richard E C Peirse | 5 October 1940 |
| Air Marshal Sir Arthur T Harris | 22 February 1942 |

| **Fighter Command**[1] | |
|---|---|
| Air Chief Marshal Sir Hugh C T Dowding | 14 July 1936 |
| Air Chief Marshal Sir W Sholto Douglas | 25 November 1940 |
| Air Marshal Sir Trafford Leigh-Mallory | 28 November 1942 |
| Air Marshal Roderic M Hill | 15 November 1943 |

| **Coastal Command** | |
|---|---|
| Air Chief Marshal Frederick Bowhill | 18 August 1937 |
| Air Chief Marshal Phillip B Joubert de la Ferte | 14 June 1941 |
| Air Marshal Sir John C Slessor | 5 February 1943 |
| Air Chief Marshal Sir W Sholto Douglas | 20 January 1944 |
| Air Marshal Sir Leonard H Slatter | 30 June 1945 |

| **Army Co-operation Command**[2] | |
|---|---|
| Air Marshal Sir Arthur S Barratt | 20 November 1940 |

| **Flying Training Command**[3] | |
|---|---|
| Air Chief Marshal Sir Arthur M Longmore | 1 July 1936 |
| Air Marshal L A Pattinson | 27 May 1940 |

---

1 Renamed Air Defence of Great Britain 15 November 1943 to 15 October 1944

2 Army Co-operation command existed from 10 December 1940 to 31 March 1943 when it was disbanded and most of its assets placed under Second Tactical Air Force.

3 Known as Training Command prior to 27 May 1940.

Air Marshal Sir William L Welsh                                    7 July 1941
Air Marshal Sir Philip Babington                              17 August 1942

## Maintenance Command
Air Marshal J S T Bradley                                       31 March 1938
Air Marshal D G Donald                                       12 October 1942

## Technical Training Command
Air Marshal Sir William L Welsh                                  27 May 1940
Air Marshal J T Babington                                          7 July 1941
Air Marshal Sir Arthur Barratt                                     1 June 1943

## Transport Command
Air Chief Marshal Sir Frederick W Bowhill                     25 March 1943
Air Marshal the Hon Sir Ralph A Cochrane                 15 February 1945

## RAF Ferry Command
Air Chief Marshal Sir Frederick W Bowhill                        18 July 1941

## OVERSEAS

## British Air Forces in France[4]
Air Marshal A S Barratt                                      20 November 1940

## Deputy Supreme Allied Commander Europe
Air Chief Marshal Sir Arthur Tedder                          17 January 1944

## Allied Expeditionary Air Force[5]
Air Chief Marshal Sir Trafford Leigh-Mallory               13 November 1943

## Second Tactical Air Force
Air Marshal Sir Arthur Coningham                             21 January 1944

## Mediterranean Air Command[6]
Air Chief Marshal Sir Arthur W Tedder                       17 February 1943

## Mediterranean Allied Air Forces
*Deputy Air Commander-in-Chief, MAAF and Commander-in-Chief, Royal Air Force, Mediterranean and Middle East*

---

4   The Advanced Air Striking Force and the Air Component, which were brought under Air Vice-Marshal Barratt's Command on this date, were commanded by Air Vice-Marshal P H L Playfair and Air Vice-Marshal C H B Blount respectively.
5   Headquarters Allied Expeditionary Air Force was disbanded on 15 October 1944, on absorption into SHAEF.
6   Higher operational control over Middle East Air Forces, including Malta, and over Northwest African Air Forces. Mediterranean Air Command became Mediterranean Allied Air Forces on 10 December 1943, into which formation Middle East and Northwest African Air Forces were absorbed.

| | |
|---|---|
| Air Marshal Sir John Slessor | 14 January 1944 |
| Air Marshal Sir A Guy R Garrod | 16 March 1945 |

**Royal Air Force, Middle East**

| | |
|---|---|
| Air Chief Marshal Sir William G S Mitchell | 1 April 1939 |
| Air Chief Marshal Sir Arthur Longmore | 13 May 1940 |
| Air Chief Marshal A W Tedder | 1 June 1941 |
| Air Chief Marshal Sir W Sholto Douglas | 11 January 1943 |
| Air Marshal Sir Keith Park | 14 January 1944 |
| Air Marshal Sir Charles E H Medhurst | 8 February 1945 |

**Air HQ Western Desert**

| | |
|---|---|
| Air Vice-Marshal Arthur Coningham | 21 October 1941 |
| Air Vice-Marshal Harry Broadhurst | 31 January 1943 |

**Desert Air Force**

| | |
|---|---|
| Air Vice-Marshal Broadhurst | 10 July 1943 |
| Air Vice-Marshal W F Dickson | 6 April 1944 |
| Air Vice-Marshal R M Foster | 3 December 1944 |

**Eastern Air Command, Africa**

| | |
|---|---|
| Air Marshal Sir William L Welsh | 2 November 1942 |

**Commander-in-Chief Far East**

| | |
|---|---|
| Air Chief Marshal Sir H Robert M Brooke-Popham | 18 November 1940 |

**Air Forces in India**

| | |
|---|---|
| Air Marshal Sir John F A Higgins | 6 October 1939 |
| Air Marshal Sir Patrick H L Playfair | 26 September 1940 |
| Air Chief Marshal Sir W Sholto Douglas | 11 January 1943 |

**Air Command, South-East Asia**

| | |
|---|---|
| Air Chief Marshal Sir Richard Peirse | 16 November 1943 |
| Air Marshal Sir A Guy R Garrod | 27 November 1944 |
| Air Chief Marshal Sir Keith R Park | 25 February 1945 |

**Third Tactical Air Force**

| | |
|---|---|
| Air Marshal John Baldwin | November 1943 |
| Air Marshal Sir Alec Coryton | 15 August 1944 |

**RAAF South-West Pacific**
**10 Operational Group/First Tactical Air Force RAAF**[7]

| | |
|---|---|
| Group Captain Frederick Scherger | 13 November 1943 |
| Air Commodore Harry Cobby | August 1944 |
| Air Commodore Frederick Scherger | 10 May 1944 |

---

7   No. 10 OG's name was changed to First Tactical Air Force (No. 1 TAF) on 25 October 1944.

# Bibliography & Sources

## Air Historical Branch Monographs

Air Publication AP 3396 *Escape from Germany,* issued by the Air Ministry 1951
Air Publication AP 3368 *The Origins and Development of Operational Research in the Royal Air Force,* issued by the Air Ministry 1963
Air Publication 3231 *Airborne Forces,* issued by the Air Ministry 1951
Air Publication 3232 *Air Sea Rescue,* issued by the Air Ministry 1952
Air Publication 3235 *Air Support,* issued by the Air Ministry 1955
Air Publication SD719 *Armament Volume 1 Bombs and Bombing Equipment,* issued by the Air Ministry 1952
Air Publication SD737 *Armament Volume 2 Guns, Gunsights, Turrets, Ammunition and Pyrotechnics, Bombs and Bombing Equipment,* issued by the Air Ministry 1954
Air Publication 3368 *Operational Research in the RAF,* issued by the Air Ministry 1954

## Air Historical Branch Narratives

AHB/II/116/16 Photographic Reconnaissance
AHB/II/117/1 The Bombing Offensive Against Germany
AHB/II/117/2 Air Defence of Great Britain
AHB/II/117/3 The Royal Air Force in the Maritime War
AHB/II/117/4 The Campaign in Norway
AHB/II/117/5 The Campaign in France and the Low Countries
AHB/II/117/8 Middle East Campaigns
AHB/II/117/10 The Sicilian Campaign
AHB/II/117/11 The Italian Campaign

## Imperial War Museum Documents

Bowdler, Norman, Interview with Imperial War Museum, Sound Archives, 22342
Braithwaite, John, Cecil, Interview with Imperial War Museum, Sound Archives, 12288
Finchett, Norman, Interview with Imperial War Museum, Sound Archives, 31067
Perry J G, Private Papers, Imperial War Museum Documents Collection, 86/47/1
Phillips S, Private Papers, Imperial War Museum Documents Collection, 12607 03/33/1
Holcroft, W, Private Papers, Imperial War Museum Documents Collection, 13198
Simpson, Joe Geoffrey, Interview with Imperial War Museum Sound Archives, 12376
Swanton, F A, Private Papers, Imperial War Museum Documents Collection, 2077
HMSO Command Papers, Strength and Casualties of The Armed Forces and Auxiliary Forces of the United Kingdom 1939-1945, July 1946, 79/4148

## Australian War Memorial Documents

Gibbes, Robert, Interview with Australian War Memorial, Sound Archives S00938
Garing, Bill, Interview with Australian War Memorial, Sound Archives S00586
Gould, Nat, Interview with Australian War Memorial, Sound Archives S00578
Piper, John, Interview with Australian War Memorial, Sound Archives S00577
Lindeman, Colin, Interview with Australian War Memorial, Sound Archives S00548
Walker, Brian, Interview with Australian War Memorial, Sound Archives S01645

## The National Archives (Kew)

ADM 199/1040: Commander C A de W Kitcat, Report of Proceedings, dated 5 October, 1943
AIR 20/6452: Plastic Surgery Within The RAF
AIR 20/8319: Operations: General (Code 55/1): SOE pick-up operations
AIR 20/2970: Use of Bombers in Close Support of the Army Memorandum by Group Captain Embry, A V M Slessor 17 May 1941
AIR 23/1395: Churchill quoted in letter Charles Portal to Arthur Tedder, 5 September 1941
AIR 23/1826: Desert Air Force Papers, The Employment of Fighter Bombers – Policy
AIR 23/8576: SOE pickup operations: Lysander training
AIR 24/1467: Bombing Analysis Unit Reports
AIR 28/115: RAF Broadwell
AIR 37/415: Headquarters RAF No.38 Group
AIR 37/1214: Allied Airborne Operations in Holland, September–October 1944
CAB 106/687 to 693: Sicily: report on operations of 1st Airborne Division in Operation HUSKY
HS 7/107: Burma country section history: operational photographs; Z Force organisation
WO 171/4320: 6th Air Landing Brigade War Diary
WO 171/1527: 51st Highland Division War Diary
WO 171/393: 1st Airborne Division War Diary
WO 201/335: HQ RAF Middle East, Royal Air Force Middle East Operational Plan, September 1940.

## RAF Historical Society Papers

Wood Derek (ed.), Seek and Sink: A symposium on the Battle of the Atlantic, Royal Air Force Historical Society, 1995
Wood, Derek (ed.), The RAF and the Far East War 1941–45: Bracknell Paper, Royal Air Force Historical Society, 1995
Wood, Derek (ed.), Reaping the Whirlwind: A symposium on the Strategic Bomber Offensive 1939–45 Royal Air Force Historical Society, 1993
Wood, Derek (ed.), OVERLORD: 1944 a symposium on the Normandy landings, Royal Air Force Historical Society, 1994
Probert, Henry and Cox Sebastian (eds.), The Battle Re-though: a symposium on the Battle of Britain, Royal Air Force Historical Society, 1990

## Other Archives

Royal Artillery Museum Archives, MD 2878, Paper by Captain Ian Neilson, Normandy 1944 – The Role of the Air Observation Post

Joint Services Command and Staff College Archives, Staff College Battlefield Tour 1954 Course

Airborne Assault Museum, 1302, Statement from Flight Lieutenant Edwards on experience of Operation MARKET GARDEN

National Archives of Australia, A9300, Service Record of William Newton


## Academic Publications

Weston, Brian, *A Coming of Age for Australia and its Air Force: The Air Campaign over Northern Australia 1943*, (Canberra, Australia, Air Power Development Centre), 2013

Hammond, Richard, *British Anti-Shipping Campaign in the Mediterranean*, (Air Power Review 16), 2013.


## Books

Adlam, Henry, *On and Off the Flight Deck: Reflections of a Naval Fighter Pilot in World War II,* (Barnsley: Pen and Sword, 2007).

Atkinson, Tom, *Spectacles, Testicles, Fags and Matches: The Untold Story of The RAF Servicing Commandos,* (Edinburgh: Luath Press Limited, 2004).

Alcock, Allan, *Hey Don't You Remember,* (Privately Published).

Aldridge, Arthur and Ryan, Mark, *The Last Torpedo Flyers,* (London: Simon and Schuster, 2013).

Allen, Dizzy, *Fighter Squadron 1940–1942,* (St Albans: Granada, 1982).

Allen, H R, *The Legacy of Lord Trenchard,* (London: Cassell, 1972).

Allen, Louis, *Burma, The Longest War 1941–45,* (London: Phoenix Press, 1984).

Alford, Bob, *Darwin 1942: The Japanese attack on Australia,* (Oxford: Osprey, 2017).

Anonymous, *Tattered Battlements: A Malta Diary by a Fighter Pilot,* (London: Peter Davies, 1943).

Anderson, Bruce (ed.), *Ploughshares and Propellers,* (Victoria: Heritage Collection RAAF Museum Point Cook, 2009).

Apps, Michael, *Send Her Victorious,* (London: William Kimber, 1971).

Arnett, Roger, *Drop Zone Burma: Adventures in Allied Air Supply 1943–45,* (Barnsley: Pen and Sword, 2008).

Babbington-Smith, Constance, *Evidence in Camera: Photographic Intelligence in World War Two,* (London: David Charles, 1974).

Banks, Arthur, *Wings of the Dawning: The Battle for the Indian Ocean,* (Malvern: HMR Ltd, 1993).

Barker, Ralph, *The Thousand Plan: The Story of the First Thousand Bomber Raid on Cologne,* (Shrewsbury: Airlife, 1992).

Barker, Ralph, *Strike Hard, Strike Sure,* (Barnsley: Pen and Sword, 2003).

Barnett, Corelli, *Engage the Enemy More Closely: The Royal Navy in the Second World War,* (London: Hodder and Stoughton, 1991).

Barnham, Denis, *Malta Spitfire Pilot,* (London: Grub Street, 2010).

Bartz, Karl, *Swastika in the Air,* (London: William Kimber, 1956).

Baveystock, Leslie, *Wavetops at my Wingtips,* (Shrewsbury: Airlife Publishing, 2001).

Beaumann, Katherine Bentley, *Partners in Blue: The Story of the Women's Service with the Royal Air Force,* (London: Hutchinson, 1971).

Beck, Pip, *Keeping Watch: A WAAF In Bomber Command,* (Manchester: Crecy Publishing, 2004).

Bendall, Dundas, *Sun on my Wings,* (Pembroke: Paterchurch Publications, 1989).

Bennett, Donald, *Pathfinder,* (Manchester: Crecy Publishing, 1998).

Bennett, Tom, *617 Squadron: The Dambusters at War,* (Wellingborough: Patrick Stephens, 1986).

Bird, Andrew, *A Separate Little War: The Banff Coastal Command Strike Wing Versus the Kreigsmarine and Luftwaffe: 1944–1945* (London: Grub Street, 2008).

Bishop, Patrick, *Air Force Blue: The RAF in World War Two,* (London: William Collins, 2017).

Bishop, Patrick, *Fighter Boys,* (London: Harper Perennial, 2004).

Bowman, Martin, *The Reich Intruders: Dramatic RAF medium bomber raids over Europe in World War 2,* (Yeovil: Patrick Stephens, 1997).

Bowyer, Chaz, *Wellington at War,* (London: Ian Allan Ltd, 1982).

Bowyer, Chaz, *History of the RAF,* (London: Hamlyn, 1978).

Bowyer, Chaz, *Beaufighter,* (London: William Kimber, 1987).

Bowyer, Chaz, *Guns in the Sky: The Air Gunners of World War Two,* (London: J M Dent, 1979).

Bowyer, Chaz, *Men of the Desert Air Force,* (London: William Kimber, 1984).

Bowyer, Chaz, *Coastal Command in War,* (London: Ian Allan, 1979).

Bowyer, Michael, *2 Group: A Complete History, 1936–1945,* (London: Faber and Faber, 1974).

Bowyer, Michael and Martin Sharp, *Mosquito,* (London: Faber and Faber, 1967).

Brown, Eric, *Wings on my Sleeve,* (London: Phoenix, 2006).

Braham, Bob, *Scramble,* (London: William Kimber, 1985).

Braithwaite, Denys A, *Target for Tonight: Flying Long Range Reconnaissance and PFF Missions in World War Two,* (Barnsley: Pen and Sword, 2010).

Brammer, Derek, *Thundering Through Clear Air: No 61 (Lincoln Imp) Squadron at War,* (Lincoln: Tucann Books Ltd, 1997).

Brickhill, Paul, *Escape or Die,* (London: Evans Brothers, 1952).

Brickhill, Paul, *The Dam Busters,* (London: Evans Brothers, 1952).

Brickhill, Paul, *Reach for the Sky,* (London: The Companion Book Club Ltd, 1955).

Campbell, Arthur, *The Siege: A Story from Kohima,* (London: George Allen and Unwin Ltd, 1956).

Campbell, Christy, *Target London: Under Attack from the V Weapons,* (London: Little, Brown Book Group, 2012).

Caygill, Peter, *Spitfire Mark V In Action,* (Shrewsbury: Airlife Ltd, 2001).

Caygill, Peter, *The Biggin Hill Wing 1941, From Defence to Attack,* (Barnsley: Pen and Sword, 2008).

Chappell, F R, *Wellington Wings: An RAF Intelligence Officer in the Western Desert,* (Bodmin: Crecy Books, 1992).

Charlwood, Don, *No Moon Tonight,* (Manchester: Crecy, 2012).

Cheshire, Leonard, *Bomber Pilot,* (St Albans: Mayflower, 1975).

Clark, David, *Angels Eight Normandy Air War Diary,* (Bloomington: Privately Published, 2003).

Clark, Ronald, *Rise of the Boffins,* (London: Phoenix House, 1962).

Clayton, Tim and Craig, Phil, *The End of the Beginning,* (London: Hodder and Stoughton, 2002).

Clostermann, Pierre, *The Big Show,* (London: Chatto Windus 1953).

Clutton-Brock, Oliver, *RAF Evaders,* (London: Grub Street, 2009).

Collier, Richard, *Eagle Day: The Battle of Britain,* (London: J M Dent, 1980).

Collier, Basil, *Defence of the United Kingdom,* (London: HMSO, 1957).

Cooling, Benjamin Franklin, *Air Superiority,* (Washington DC: Air Force History and Museums Program, 1994).

Cooper, Anthony, *Kokoda Air Strikes,* (Sydney: University of New South Wales, 2014).

Cooling, Benjamin Franklin, *Close Air Support,* (Washington DC: Office of Air Force History, 1990).

Conyers Nesbit, Roy, *Eyes of the RAF: A History of Photo Reconnaissance,* (Godalming: Bramley Books, 1996).

Conyers Nesbit, Roy, *Coastal Command in Action 1939–45,* (Stroud: Sutton Publishing, 1997).

Conyers Nesbit, Roy, *The Battle of the Atlantic,* (Stroud: Sutton Publishing, 2002).

Conyers Nesbit, Roy, *Woe to the Unwary: A Memoir of Low Level Bombing Operations in 1941,* (London: William Kimber, 1981).

Corbin, Jimmy, *Last of the Ten Fighter Boys,* (Stroud: History Press, 2007).

Cotton, M C, *Hurricanes Over Burma,* (London: Grub Street, 1995).

Cropper, Eric, *Back Bearings: A Navigator's Tale 1942 to 1974,* (Barnsley: Pen and Sword, 2010).

Cross, Kenneth, *Straight and Level,* (London: Grub Street, 1993).

Cull, Brian, Lander, Bruce and Weiss, Heinrich, *Twelve Days in May,* (London: Grub Street, 1995).

Cull, Brian and Sortehaug, Paul, *Hurricanes Over Singapore,* (London: Grub Street, 2004).

Cull, Brian, Lander, Bruce and Galea, Frederick, *Hurricanes over Malta,* (London: Grub Street, 2001).

Cull, Brian, Lander, Bruce and Galea, Frederick, *Spitfires over Malta,* (London: Grub Street, 2005).

Currie, Jack, *Mosquito Victory,* (London: Goodall, 1983).

Currie, Jack, *The Augsburg Raid,* (St Albans: Goodall, 1987).

Currie, Jack, *Battle under the Moon: The documented account of Mailly-le-camp,* (Manchester: Airdata publications Ltd, 1992).

Darby, Phil, *Press on Regardless,* (Privately Published, 1997).

Davidson, Basil, *Partisan Picture,* (Bedford: Bedford Books, 1946).

Davies, Norman, *Rising 44: The Battle for Warsaw,* (London: Viking, 2004).

Deakin, Frederick, *The Embattled Mountain,* (London: Hutchinson, 1972).

Delve, Ken, *Nighfighter,* (London: Cassell, 1995).

Demoulin, Charles, *Firebirds: Flying the Typhoons in Action,* (Shrewsbury: Airlife Ltd, 1987).

Deere, Alan, *Nine Lives,* (Manchester: Crecy, 2005).

De Guingand, Freddie, *Operation Victory,* (London: Hodder and Stoughton, 1947).

Devlin, Gerard M, *Silent Wings*, (Chatham, Mackays Ltd, 1985).

Douglas-Hamilton, James, *The Air Battle for Malta,* (Barnsley: Pen and Sword, 2006).

Downing, Taylor, *Spies in the Sky: The Secret Battle for Aerial Intelligence During World War Two,* (London: Little, Brown, 2011).

Duncan Smith, W G G, *Spitfire into Battle,* (London: John Murray, 2002).

Dudgeon, Tony, *Wings Over North Africa,* (Shrewsbury: Airlife, 1987).

Dundas, Hugh, *Flying Start: A Fighter Pilots War Years,* (New York: St Martin's Press, 1989).

Eadon, Stuart, *Kamikaze: The Story of the British Pacific Fleet,* (Worcester: Square One Publishing, 1991).

Edwards, Gron, *Norwegian Patrol,* (Shrewsbury: Airlife Publishing Ltd, 1985).

Edwards, Gron, *Flying to Norway Grounded in Burma: A Hudson Pilot in World War II,* (Barnsley: Pen and Sword, 2008).

Embry, Basil, *Mission Completed,* (London: Quality Book Club Ltd, 1956).

Ehlers, Robert, *The Mediterranean Air War,* (Lawrence: University Press Kansas, 2015).

Ehlers, Robert, *Targeting the Third Reich: Air Intelligence and the Allied Bombing Campaign,* (Lawrence: University Press Kansas, 2009).

Escott, Beryl, *Our Wartime Days: The WAAF in World War II,* (Stroud: Alan Sutton Publishing, 1995).

Escott, Beryl, *Women in Air Force Blue: The Story of Women in the Royal Air Force from 1918 to the Present Day,* (Yeovil: Patrick Stephens Ltd, 1989).

Evans, Bryn, *The Decisive Campaigns of the Desert Air Force 1942–45,* (Barnsley: Pen and Sword, 2014).

Evans, Bryn, *Air Battle for Burma: Allied Pilots' Fight for Supremacy,* (Barnsley: Pen and Sword, 2016).

Eyton-Jones, Arthur, *Day Bomber,* (Stroud: Sutton Publishing, 1998).

Forrester, Larry, *Fly for your Life: The Story of R R Stanford Tuck,* (Guildford: Biddles Ltd, 1973).

Foster, Ronald, *Focus on Europe: A Photo-Reconnaissance Mosquito Pilot At War, 1943–45,* (Ramsbury: Crowood Press, 2004).

Franks, Norman, *Dark Sky, Deep Water: First Hand Reflections on the Anti-U-Boat War in WW II,* (London: Grub Street, 1997).

Franks, Norman, *Another Kind of Courage,* (Yeovil: Patrick Stephens, 1994).

Franks, Norman, *Beyond Courage,* (London: Grub Street, 2003).

Franks, Norman, *Conflict Over the Bay,* (London: William Kimber, 1986).

Franks, Norman, *The Greatest Air Battle: Dieppe 19th August 1942,* (London: Grub Street, 1992).

Franks, Norman, *Hurricanes over the Arakan,* (Yeovil: Patrick Stephens Ltd, 1989).

Franks, Norman, *Typhoon Attack,* (London: William Kimber, 1984).

Franks, Norman, *The Air Battle of Imphal,* (London: William Kimber, 1985).

Franks, Norman, *Spitfires Over the Arakan.* (London: William Kimber, 1988).

Freeman, Roger, *The British Airman,* (London: Arms and Armour Press Ltd, 1989).

Garbett, Mike and Goulding, Brian, *Lancaster At War,* (London: Guild Publishing, 1984).

Gardiner, Juliet, *The Blitz: The British Under Attack,* (London: Harper Press, 2010).

Gibbs, Patrick, *Not Peace but a Sword,* (London: Grub Street, 1993).

Gibbs, Patrick, *Torpedo Leader,* (London: Grub Street, 1992).

Gibson, Guy, *Enemy Coast Ahead,* (London: Pan Books Ltd, 1955).

Gibson, T M and Harrison, M H, *Into Thin Air: A History of Aviation Medicine,* (London: Robert Hale, 1984).

Gillman, R E, *The Shiphunters,* (London: John Murray, 1976).

Gillison, Douglas, *Royal Australian Air Force 1939–42,* (Canberra, Australian War Memorial, 1962).

Gladman, Brad, *Intelligence and Anglo-American Air Support in World War Two: The Western Desert* (London: Palgrave Macmillan, 2009).

Golley, John, *The Day of the Typhoon: Flying with the RAF Tankbusters in Normandy,* (Bury St Edmunds: Wrens Park, 1986).

Gooderson, Ian, *Air Power at the Battlefront: Allied Close Air Support in Europe 1943–45,* (London: Frank Cass Ltd, 1998).

Goulter, C J M, *A Forgotten Offensive: Royal Air Force Coastal Command's Anti-Shipping Campaign, 1940–45,* (London: Frank Cass, 1995).

Green, William, *Famous Fighters of the Second World War,* (Abingdon: Purnell, 1975).

Green, William, *Famous Bombers of the Second World War,* (London: Book Club Associates, 1975).

Haarer, A E, *A Cold-Blooded Business,* (London: Staples Ltd, 1958).

Hall, Roger, *Clouds of Fear,* (London: Hodder and Stoughton, 1975).

Halley, James J, *Squadrons of the Royal Air Force,* (Tonbridge: Air-Britain (Historians) Ltd, 1988).

Hallion, Richard P, *The History of Battlefield Air Attack, 1941–45,* (Shrewsbury: Airlife Ltd, 1989).

Hamilton, Nigel, *Monty, The Making of a General 1887–1942,* (New York: McGraw Hill Ltd, 1981).

Harris, Arthur, *Bomber Offensive,* (London: Collins, 1947).

Harrison, W A, *Swordfish Special,* (London: Ian Allan, 1998).

Hastings, Max, *Bomber Command,* (London: Michael Joseph, 1980).

Hayward, Greg, *D-Day to VE-Day with the Second Tactical Air Force,* (Bloomington: Author House, 2009).

Heinemann, William, *Winged Words: Our Airmen Speak for Themselves,* (Surrey: Windmill, 1941).

Hendrie, Andrew, *The Cinderella Service: RAF Coastal Command 1939–45,* (Barnsley: Pen and Sword Aviation, 2006).

Hemingway, Kenneth, *Wings Over Burma,* (London: Quality Press Publishers, 1945).

Herrman, Hajo, *Eagle's Wings:– The Autobiography of a Luftwaffe Pilot,* (Shrewsbury: Airlife, 1991).

Herington, John, *Air War Against Germany and Italy, 1939–43,* (Canberra: Australian War Memorial, 1954).

Herington, John, *Air Power Over Europe, 1944–1945,* (Canberra: Australian War Memorial, 1963).

Hewitt, J E, *Adversity in Success,* (South Yarra: Langate Publishing, 1980).

Hinsley, F H and Stripp, Alan, *Code Breakers: The Inside Story of Bletchley Park,* (Oxford: Oxford University Press, 1993).

Hoare, John, *Tumult in the Clouds: A Story of the Fleet Air Arm,* (London: Michael Joseph, 1976).

Holland, James, *The Battle of Britain,* (London: Bantam Press, 2015).

Holmes, Ray, *Sky Spy,* (Shrewsbury: Airlife Publishing Ltd, 1989).

Horden, Dennis, *Shark Squadron Pilot,* (Bromley: Independent Books, 2002).

Houghton, G W, *They Flew Through Sand,* (South Molton: P&M Typesetting Ltd, 1991).

Howard-Williams, Jeremy, *Night Intruder: A Personal Account of the Radar War Between the Luftwaffe and RAF Nighfighter Forces,* (London: David and Charles, 1976).

Hunter, Jim, *From Coastal Command to Captivity: The Memoir of a Second World War Airman,* (Barnsley: Leo Cooper, 2003).

Ince, David, *Brotherhood of The Skies: Wartime Experiences of a Gunner Officer and Typhoon Pilot,* (London: Grub Street, 2010).

Jackson, Robert, *The Secret Squadrons: Special Duty Units of the RAF and USAAF in the Second World War,* (London: Robson Books, 1983).

James, T C G, *The Battle of Britain,* (London: Frank Cass, 2000).

Jones, Geoffrey, *Attacker: The Hudson and its Flyers,* (London: William Kimber, 1980).

Johnson, J E, *Wing Leader,* (London: Reprint Society, 1956).

Johnson, J E, *The Story of Air Fighting,* (London: Hutchinson, 1985).

Johnston, Mark, *Whispering Death: Australian Airmen in the Pacific,* (Sydney: Allen and Unwin, 2011).

Jones, R V, *Most Secret War: British Scientific Intelligence 1939–45,* (London: Hamish Hamilton, 1978).

Joubert de la Ferte, Philip, *Birds and Fishes: The Story of Coastal Command,* (London: Hutchinson, 1960).

Joubert de la Ferte, Philip, *The Forgotten Ones: The Story of the Ground Crews,* (London: Hutchinson, 1961).

Judd, Donald, *Avenger from the Sky,* (London: William Kimber, 1985).

Kelly, Terence, *Hurricane Over the Jungle,* (London: Arrow Ltd, 1990).

Kent, A, *One of The Few,* (London: William Kimber, 1971).

Kilbracken, Lord, *Bring Back My Stringbag,* (London: Peter Davies, 1979).

King, Colin M, *Song of the Beauforts,* (Tuggeranong: Australian Air Power Development Centre, 2008).

Kingcome, Brian, *A Willingness to Die: Memories of Fighter Command,* (Stroud: The History Press, 2008).

Kippenberger, Howard, *Infantry Brigadier,* (London: Oxford University Press, 1961).

Kirkness, B and Poole, M, *RAF Liberators Over Burma: Flying with 159 Squadron,* (Croydon: Fonthill Media, 2017).

Konstam, Angus, *British Aircraft Carriers 1939–45,* (Oxford: Osprey, 2010).

Lacey-Johnson, *Lionel, Point Blank and Beyond,* (Shrewsbury: Airlife, 1991).

Lamb, Charles, *War in a Stringbag,* (London: Cassell, 1987).

Leicester, L Anthony, *Flights into the Night,* (Manchester, Crecy, 2010).

Levine, Alan, *The War Against Rommel's Supply Lines 1942–1943,* (Westport: Praeger, 1999).

Levy, H, *Aerodynamics of the Aeroplane,* (London, Nelson, 1943).

Lewin, Ronald, *Ultra Goes to War,* (London: Grafton, 1988).

Lindsay, Franklin, *Beacons in the Night,* (Stanford: Stanford University Press, 1993).

Lloyd, H, *Briefed to Attack: Malta's Part in African Victory,* (London: Hodder and Stoughton, 1949).

MacArthur, Brian *Surviving the Sword: Prisoners of the Japanese 1942–45,* (London: Abacus, 2005).

Mackenzie, K W, *Hurricane Combat,* (London: Grenville Publishing Ltd, 1987).

Mackie, Mary, *Wards in the Sky: The RAF's Remarkable Nursing Service,* (Stroud: The History Press, 2014).

Maclean, Fitzroy, *Eastern Approaches,* (London: Jonathan Cape, 1949).

Marshall, Ken *The Pendulum and the Scythe,* (Walton on Thames: Air Research Publications, 1996).

Marshall, Bruce, *The White Rabbit: A British Agent's Adventures in France,* (London: Pan Books, 1955).

Maslen- Jones, *Fire By Order: Recollections of Service with 656 Air Observation Post Squadron,* (London: Leo Cooper, 1997).

Mayhew, E R, *The Guinea Pig Cub,* (London: Greenhill Books, 2010).

Mayhill, Ron, *Bombs on Target: A Compelling Eye-Witness Account of Bomber Command Operations,* (Yeovil: Patrick Stephens Ltd, 1991).

McConville, Michael, *A Small War in the Balkans,* (London: Macmillan, 1986).

McIntosh, Dave, *High Battle,* (Toronto: Canada, 1990).

McInstry, Leo, *Hurricane: Victor of The Battle of Britain,* (London: John Murray, 2010).

McInstry, Leo, *Lancaster: The Second World War's Greatest Bomber,* (London: John Murray, 2009).

McInstry, Leo, *Spitfire: Portrait of a Legend,* (London: John Murray, 2007).

McGregor, Alan Peart, *From North Africa to the Arakan,* (London: Grub Street, 2008).

McIntosh, Dave, *Mosquito Intruder,* (London: John Murray, 1980).

McKay, Sinclair, *The Secret Life of Fighter Command,* (London: Aurum Press Ltd, 2016).

Middlebrook, Martin, *Convoy: The Greatest U-boat Battle of the War,* (London: Cassell, 1976).

Middlebrook, Martin, *The Berlin Raids: RAF Bomber Command Winter 1943–44,* (London: Viking, 1988).

Middlebrook, Martin, *The Schweinfuhrt-Regensburg Mission: American Raids on 17 August 1943,* (London: Cassell, 2000).

Millar, Andrew, *The Flying Hours,* (Hitchin: Fighting High Ltd, 2015).

Miller, Russell, *Behind the Lines, The Oral History of Special Operations in World War II,* (London: Random House, 2002).

Millington, G, *The Unseen Eye,* (London: Anthony Gibbs & Phillips, 1961).

Milton, Brian, *Hurricane: The Last Witness,* (London: Carlton Publishing Group, 2011).

Moore, John, *Escort Carrier,* (London: Hutchinson, 1944).

Moore, John, *The Fleet Air Arm,* (London: Chapman and Hall, 1943).

Moore, Stephen, *The Battle for Hell's Island,* (New York: Caliber, 2015).

Morrison, Will, *Horsa Squadron,* (London: William Kimber, 1988).

Muirhead, Campbell, *The Diary of A Bomb Aimer,* (Tumbridge Wells: Spellmount Publishing Ltd, 1987).

Naydler, Merton, *Young Man You'll Never Die,* (Barnsley: Pen and Sword, 2005).

Neave, Airey, *Little Cyclone,* (London: Biteback Publishing, 2013).

Neil, T F, *Onward To Malta,* (Shrewsbury: Airlife Ltd, 1992).

Neil, Tom, *Gun Button to Fire,* (Stroud: Amberley, 2010).

Nelson, Hank, *Chased by the Sun: The Australians in Bomber Command in WWII,* (Crow's Nest, Australia: Allen and Unwin, 2006).

Nesbit, Roy, *The Strike Wings: Special Anti-Shipping Squadrons 1942–45,* (London: William Kimber, 1984).

Nesbit, Roy, *The Armed Rovers: Beauforts and Beaufighters Over the Mediterranean,* (Shrewsbury: Airlife Publishing, 1995).

Nesbit, Roy, *Woe To The Unwary: A memoir of Low Level Bombing Operations in 1941,* (London: William Kimber, 1981).

Nichol, John and Rennell, Tony, *The Last Escape: The Untold Story of Allied Prisoners of War In Germany,* (London: Penguin, 2003).

O'Brien, Terence, *Out of The Blue: A Pilot with the Chindits,* (London: Arrow, 1988).

Odgers, George, *Air War Against Japan, 1943–45,* (Canberra: Australian War Memorial, 1957).

Ogley, Bob, *Doodlebugs and Rockets,* (Westerham: Froglets, 1992).

Oliver, David, *Fighter Command,* (London: Harper Collins, 2000).

Olson, Lynne, and Cloud, Stanley, *For Your Freedom and Ours,* (London: Arrow Books, 2003).

Orange, Vincent, *Coningham: The Biography of Air Marshal Sir Arthur Coningham,* (Washington DC: Center for Air Force History, 1992).

Orange, Vincent, *Park: The Biography of Air Chief Marshal Sir Keith Park,* (London: Grub Street, 2001).

Orange, Vincent, *Dowding of Fighter Command: Victor of The Battle of Britain,* (London: Grub Street, 2008).

Ott, Frank, *Air Power at Sea in the Second World War,* (Yeovil: Fleet Air Arm Museum, 2005).

Otway, Terence, *Airborne Forces,* (London: Naval and Military Press, 2019).

Overill, Tony, *Crash Boats of Gorleston,* (Bognor Regis: Woodfield Publishing, 2005).

Overy, Richard, *The Battle of Britain: Myth and Reality,* (London: Penguin, 2010).

Overy, Richard, *The Bombing War, Europe 1939–45,* (London: Allen Lane, 2013).

Overy, Richard, *The Air War 1939–45,* (London: Europa Publications, 1980).

Owen, Roderic, *The Desert Air Force,* (London: Hutchinson, 1948).

Oxspring, Bobby, *Spitfire Command,* (London: Grafton Books, 1987).

Page, Geoffrey, *Shot Down in Flames,* (London: Grub Street, 1999).

Pape, Richard, *Boldness Be My Friend,* (London: Pan Books Ltd, 1953).

Pateman, Colin, *B-24 Bridge Busters: RAF Liberators Over Burma,* (Croydon: Fonthill, 2016).

Pateman, Colin, *RAF Special Duties,* (Croydon: Fonthill, 2015).

Peake, Dame Felicity, *Pure Chance,* (Shrewsbury: Airlife Ltd, 1993).

Pearce, Frank, *Under the Red Eagle: A Tour Overseas with No. 239 Fighter/Bomber Wing of the Desert Air Force,* (Bognor Regis: Woodfield, 2004).

Peden, Murray, *A Thousand Shall Fall: The True Story of a Canadian Bomber Pilot in World War Two,* (Toronto: Stoddart, 1997).

Pelly-Fry, *Heavenly Days: Recollections of a Contented Airman,* (Bodmin: Crecy, 1994).

Peters, Mike, *Glider Pilots in Sicily,* (Barnsley: Pen and Sword, 2012).

Peters, Mike, *Glider Pilots at Arnhem,* (Barnsley: Pen and Sword, 2014).

Pile, Frederick, *Ack-Ack: Britain's Air Defence Against Air Attack During the Second World War,* (London: George Harrap, 1949).

Pike, Richard, *Alfie's War,* (London: Grub Street, 2012).

Pitchfork, Graham, *Shot Down and in the Drink,* (Richmond: National Archives, 2005).

Pitchfork, Graham, *Shot Down and on the Run,* (Richmond: National Archives, 2003).

Playfair, I S O, *The Mediterranean and the Middle East,* (London: HMSO, 1960).

Polish Air Force, *Destiny Can Wait,* (London: Heinemann, 1949).

Poolman, Kenneth, *Allied Escort Carriers of World War Two,* (London: Blandford Press, 1988).

Poolman, Kenneth, *The Sea Hunters: Escort Carriers v U-Boats 1941–45,* (London: Arms and Armour Press, 1982).

Poolman, Kenneth, *Focke-Wulf Condor: Scourge of The Atlantic,* (London: Macdonald and Janes', 1982).

Popham, Hugh, *Sea Flight,* (London: Futura Publications, 1974).

Pottinger, Ron, *Soldier in the Cockpit, From Rifles to Typhoons in WWII,* (Mechanicsburg: PA Stackpole Books, 2007).

Powys-Lybbe, Ursua, *The Eye of Intelligence,* (London: William Kimber, 1983).

Preston-Hough, Peter, *Commanding Far Eastern Skies: A Critical Analysis of The Royal Air Force Air Superiority Campaign in India, Burma and Malaya 1941–1945,* (Solihull: Helion, 2015).

Price, Alfred, *Aircraft Versus Submarine,* (London: Janes, 1980).

Price, Alfred, *Battle of Britain 18 August 1940: The Hardest Day,* (London: Granada, 1979).

Probert, Henry, *The Forgotten Air Force: The Royal Air Force in the War Against Japan 1941–45,* (London: Brasseys, 1995).

Rae, Jack, *Kiwi Spitfire Ace,* (London: Grub Street, 2001).

Rawnsley, C F and Wright, Robert, *Night Fighter,* (Manchester: Crecy, 1998)

Rennison, John, *The Digby Diary: A History of RAF Digby,* (Stroud: Aspect Publishing, 2003).

Richards, Denis and Saunders, Hilary St George, *The Royal Air Force 1939–45: Volumes 1-3,* (London: HMSO, 1954).

Richardson, Anthony, *Wingless Victory,* (London: Pan Books Ltd, 1956).

Richey, Paul, *Fighter Pilot,* (London: Hutchinson, 1955).

Rijken, Kees, Schepers, Paul and Thorning, Arthur, *Operation Oyster: The Daring Low Level Attack on the Phillips Radio Works,* (Barnsley: Pen and Sword, 2014).

Rivaz, RC, *Tail Gunner,* (Endeavour Press, 2017).

Robertson, Terrence, *Channel Dash,* (London: Evans Brothers, 1958).

Robinson, Ken, *Dice on Regardless: The Story of An RAF Sunderland Pilot,* (London: R J Leach, 1993).

Robson, Martin, *The Hurricane Pocket Manual,* (London: Bloomsbury, 2016).

Robson, Martin, *The Spitfire Pocket Manual,* (London: Bloomsbury, 2016).

Rogers, Anthony, *185 The Malta Squadron,* (Staplehurst: Spellmount Ltd, 2005).

Rollings, Charles, *Prisoner of War: Voices from Behind the Wire in the Second World War,* (London Ebury Press, 2008).

Roskill, Stephen, *The Navy at War 1939–45,* (London: Collins, 1960).

Ross, J M S, *Royal New Zealand Air Force: New Zealand in the Second World War, 1939–45,* (Wellington: War History Branch, 1955).

Rossiter, Mike, *Ark Royal,* (London: Corgi, 2006).

Sawyer, Tom, *Only Owls and Bloody Fools Fly at Night,* (London: William Kimber, 1982).

Schofield, Ernest, *Artic Airmen: The RAF in Spitsbergen and North Russia, 1942,* (London: William Kimber, 2005).

Scott, Desmond, *Typhoon Pilot,* (London: Arrow Books, 1982).

Scott, Desmond, *One More Hour,* (London: Arrow Books, 1989).

Shores, Christopher and Thomas, Chris, *Second Tactical Air Force Volumes 1-4,* (Hersham: Midland Publishing, 2008).

Shores, Christopher, *Pictorial History of the Mediterranean Air War, Volumes 1 and 2,* (London: Ian Allan Ltd, 1973).

Shores, Christopher, *Air War for Burma,* (London: Grub Street, 2005).

Sims, Edward H, *The Fighter Pilots,* (London: Cassell, 1967).

Simpson, Andrew, *'Ops': Victory at all Costs,* (Pulborough: Tattered Flag Press, 2012).

Simpson, Bill, *The Way of Recovery*, (London: Hamish Hamilton, 1944).

Slessor, John, *The Central Blue: Recollections and Reflections by Marshal of The Royal Air Force Sir John Slessor,* (London: Cassel, 1956).

Southall, Ivan, *They Shall Not Pass Unseen,* (London: Angus and Robertson, 1956).

Spencer, Dennis, *Looking Backwards Over Burma: Wartime Recollections of a Beaufighter Navigator,* (Bognor Regis: Woodfield Publishing, 2009).

Spooner, Tony, *In Full Flight,* (Canterbury: Wingham Press, 1991).

Spooner, Tony, *Warbuton's War,* (Oxford: Isis, 2003).

Spurdle, Bob, *The Blue Arena,* (Manchester: Goodall Publishing, 2017).

Smith, David, *Britain's Military Airfields 1939–45,* (Wellingborough, Patrick Stephens, 1989).

Smith, Peter C, *Jungle Dive Bombers at War,* (London: John Murray, 1987).

Smith, Ron, *Rear Gunner Pathfinders,* (Manchester: Crecy, 1997).

Smithers, Edward, *Backroom Boys,* (London: Cassell, 2002).

Stanley, Peter, *Darwin Spitfires: The Real Battle for Australia,* (Sydney: New South Wales Press Ltd, 2011).

Stewart, Adrian, *They Flew Hurricanes,* (Barnsley: Pen and Sword, 2005).

Stevenson, Derek, *Five Crashes Later: The Story of a Fighter Pilot,* (London: William Kimber, 1988).

Streetly, Martin, *Confound and Destroy, 100 Group,* (London: Macdonalds and Janes, 1978).

Stubbington, John, *Bletchley Park Air Section Signals Intelligence Support to RAF Bomber Command,* (Alton: Minerva Associates, 2007).

Sutherland Brown, Atholl, *Silently into the Midst of Things,* (Sussex: Book Guild Ltd, 2001).

Sweeting, Dennis, *Wings of Chance,* (Singapore: Asian Business Press, 1990).

Taylor, James and Davidson, Martin, *Bomber Crew: Survivors of Bomber Command Tell Their Story,* (London: Hodder and Stoughton, 2004).

Tedder, Lord, *With Prejudice,* (London: Cassell, 1966).

Terraine, John, *The Right of the Line: The Royal Air Force in the European War 1939–1945,* (London: Hodder and Stoughton, 1985).

Terraine, John, *Business in Great Waters,* (London: Leo Cooper, 1989).

Thomas, Andrew, *Royal Navy Aces of World War 2,* (Oxford: Osprey, 2002).

Thompson, Peter, *Pacific Fury: How Australia and her Allies Defeated the Japanese,* (Sydney: William Heinemann, 2008).

Thompson, Walter, *Lancaster to Berlin,* (Manchester: Crecy, 1997).

Tootal, Stuart, *The Manner of Men,* (London: John Murray, 2014).

Townshend Bickers, Richard, *Ginger Lacey, Fighter Pilot,* (London: Robert Hale, 1962).

Tuker, Francis, *Approach to Battle,* (London: Cassell, 1963).

Van Crefeld, Martin, *Supplying War: Logistics from Wallenstein to Patton,* (New York: Cambridge University Press, 1977).

Veitch, Michael, *44 Days: 75 Squadron and the Fight for Australia,* (Sydney: Hatchette, 2016).

Verity, Hugh, *We Landed by Moonlight: Secret RAF Landings in France 1940–44,* (London: Ian Allan Ltd, 1978).

Verney, G L, *The Desert Rats,* (Tiptree: Anchor Press, 1957).

Vigors, Tim, *Lives too Short to Cry,* (London: Grub Street, 2008).

Wallace, G, *Biggin Hill,* (London: Putnam, 1957).

Wallace, Gordon, *Carrier Observer,* (Shrewsbury: Airlife, 1993).

Walley, Brian, (ed.), *Silk and Barbed Wire*, (Western Australia:(Warwick Publishing, 2000).

Warwick, Nigel W M, *Constant Vigilance: The RAF Regiment in Burma*, (Barnsley: Pen and Sword, 2007).

Webster, C and Frankland, N, *The Strategic Air Offensive Against Germany, 1939–45, Volumes 1–4*, (London: HMSO, 1961).

Weinronk, Jack, *The Vaulted Sky: A Bomber Pilot's Western Desert War Before and After*, (Braunton: Merlin Books, 1993).

Wellham, John, *With Naval Wings: The Autobiography of a Fleet Air Arm Pilot in World War II*, (Staplehurst: Spellmount Publishing, 2003).

Wellum, Geoffrey, *First Light*, (London: Penguin, 2003).

Wells, Mark K, *Courage and Air Warfare*, (London: Frank Cass, 1995).

Wemyess, D E, *Relentless Pursuit*, (London: William Kimber, 1955).

White, Graham, *Night Fighter Over Germany*, (Barnsley: Pen and Sword, 2006).

Winton, John, *Find, Fix and Strike! The Fleet Air Arm at War 1939-45*, (London: Batsford, 1985).

Williams, Dennis, *Stirlings in Action with Airborne Forces*, (Barnsley: Pen and Sword, 2008).

Wilson, David, *The Decisive Factor: 75 and 76 Squadrons – Port Moresby and Milne Bay 1942*, (Brunswick: Banner Books, 1991)

Wilson, Kevin, *Bomber Boys: The RAF Offensive of 1943*, (London: Widenfeld and Nicholson, 2005).

Wilson, Kevin, *Men of Air: The Doomed Youth Of Bomber Command*, (London: Widenfeld and Nicholson, 2007).

Wilson, Kevin, *Journey's End: Bomber Command's Battle from Arnhem to Dresden and Beyond*, (London: Widenfeld and Nicholson, 2010).

Woodhall, A B, *Soldier, Sailor & Airman Too*, (London: Grub Street, 2008).

Wood, Derek and Dempster, Derek, *The Narrow Margin: The Battle of Britain 1940*, (Washington DC: Smithsonian, 1990).

Woods, Gerard, *Wings at Sea: A Fleet Air Arm Observer's War 1940–45*, (London: Conway Maritime Press, 1985).

Wragg, David, *Carrier Combat*, (Stroud: Sutton Publishing, 1996).

Wragg, David, *Fleet Air Arm Handbook 1939–45*, (Stroud: Sutton Publishing, 2003).

Wragg, David, *Swordfish: The Story of the Taranto Raid*, (London: Cassell, 2003).

Wynn, Humphrey and Young, Susan, *Prelude to Overlord*, (Shrewsbury: Airlife Ltd, 1983).

Wynn, Humphrey, *Desert Eagles*, (Shrewsbury: Airlife Ltd, 1993).

Yates, Harry, *Luck and a Lancaster*, (Shrewsbury: Airlife Ltd, 1999).

Younghusband, Eileen, *One Woman's War*, (Cardiff: Candy-Jar books, 2011).

Zuckerman, Solly, *From Apes to Warlords*, (London: Hamish Hamilton, 1978).

# Index

## Index of People

Alexander, General Harold 121, 131, 137, 139
Arciuszkiewicz, Squadron Leader E 74
Armstrong, Pilot Officer Tom 407-409
Auchinleck, General Claude 89, 115, 121-122, 454

Babbington-Smith, Constance 48
Ball, Squadron Leader Alfred 38
Bassarab, Flying Officer R.N. 300-301
Baveystock, Flight Lieutenant Leslie 401, 403
Beadon, Squadron C.V. 410
Beatie, Lieutenant 382
Bockus, Flying Officer David 374
Bogarde, Dirk 47
Bowdler, Trooper Norma 333-334
Braithwaite, Flight Lieutenant John 331-332
Brereton, General Lewis 115, 123
Bristow, Flight Lieutenant P.M. 286-287
Broadhurst, Air Vice-Marshal Harry 131-132, 134, 136, 155, 167, 454-455
Brooke, General Sir Alan 104
Brown, Bruce 231
Bullen-Smith, Major General Charles 175

Campbell, Arthur 337-338
Chatterton, Lieutenant Colonel George 259-261, 263-265, 268, 271, 274, 282, 312
Chmiel, Flight Lieutenant 79
Churchill, Peter 59
Churchill, Winston iii, 66, 68, 95-96, 140, 142, 156, 255, 260-261, 350, 450, 457
Clark, Lieutenant Colonel G.C.165, 408
Clarke, Sergeant Paddy 407-408
Clayton, Eileen 19-21
Clostermann, Pierre 160, 180
Clowes, Major General Cyril 232-233, 236
Coningham, Air Vice-Marshal Arthur 89, 108, 110-113, 115, 122-123, 125, 127, 131, 137, 154-155, 454-455
Cotton, Squadron Leader 'Bush' 209-213
Cotton, Wing Commander Sidney 32-34, 36-37, 453
Crockatt, Brigadier Norman 398

Daniel, Ron 406
Darby, Phil 101-103
Davidson, Basil 62, 64, 69-70, 72
de Guingand, Major General Freddie132-134, 136, 155
de Jongh, Andree 'Dedee' 402
Deakin, Captain Frederick 64, 66, 70, 72
Demoulin, Charles182-183
Dix, Flight Lieutenant 342
Dods, Bill 390-391
Dowding, Air Chief Marshal Sir Hugh 33, 449, 452, 455
Duffee, Flight Lieutenant George 404, 406

Edwards, Flight Lieutenant 307-308
Eggleston, Jack 34
Eisenhower, General Dwight 47, 131, 154, 156, 170-171, 281, 431, 455
Elliott, Air Vice-Marshal William 66, 68
Elmhirst, Air Commodore Thomas 109-111, 455

Embry, Wing Commander Basil 98, 403
Evans, Staff Sergeant 'Taff' 275-276
Eyton-Jones, Arthur 368-369, 385-387
Ezanno, Paul 168, 170

Fane Peers Fane, Flight Lieutenant Alfred 44-45
Finchett, Norman 343
Foster, Ronald 42
Fowden, Dick 442-443
Frecker, Flight Lieutenant Derek 407-409
Freyberg, Lieutenant General Bernard 112, 115
Frost, Lieutenant Colonel John 261, 308
Frost, Flight Lieutenant E.M. 200

Gale, Major General Richard 53
Garing, Air Commodore Bill 229, 232-233, 238
Gavin, Major General James 309
MacArthur, General Douglas 227, 242, 247
Gibbes, Robert 105-106, 109
Gill, Squadron Leader Arthur 204, 208-209
Gillam, Group Captain D.E. 'Kill 'em'162
Gipps, Raleigh 390-392
Gleadell, Lieutenant Colonel Paul 314
Glebocki, Flight Lieutenant 80
Gould, Pilot Officer Nat 230, 232

Harris, Air Chief Marshal Arthur 'Bomber' 74, 154-155, 258, 450, 452, 455
Hartness, Brian 215
Heynsham, Wing Commander David 149
Hickson, Joe 367-368, 383
Hill, John 222-224
Hodgson, Wilf 400, 419
Holcroft, Staff Sergeant Wally 301-302
Hollinghurst, Air Vice-Marshal Leslie 282, 300
Holmes, Ray 39, 48
Hopkinson, Major General George 271
Horden, Bert 106, 115-116, 134, 136, 150-151
Horrocks, Lieutenant General Brian 133, 298
Horsley, Wing Commander Peter 387-388
Houghton, Squadron Leader George 409

Ince, David 157-158, 172, 178, 184-185
Iranek-Osmecki, Colonel Kazimierz 28, 30

James, George 113
Johnson, Squadron Leader Bob 411-412, 414
Johnston, Lieutenant Alec 303
Jones, R.V. 27, 30

Kenchington, Corporal Vic 'Taffy' 141
Kendall, Douglas 49
Kirby, Corporal Colin 203-204
Kirk, Henry 201, 234
Kitcat, Commander Arthur 140-141
Koenig, General Marie Pierre 112
Kortenhause, Werner 190

Lander, Major John 266

# Index of Places

## Index of Allied Forces

## Groups

## Wings

## Squadrons

# Index of Axis Forces

# Index of Materiel

**Other Materiel**

# General Index